OVERVIEW

Contents

4   DEBUGGING AND ERROR HANDLING, MEMORY FUNCTIONS, CONVERSION FUNCTIONS, AND DATA HANDLING   145

5   DATABASE FUNCTIONS   189

13   NET API FUNCTIONS   563

ABOUT THE AUTHORS

Fredrik Bodin, 18 years old, is reading his last year of natural science in the senior high school "Tensta Gymnasium" in Stockholm, Sweden. Despite his young age, Fredrik knows several languages, such as Visual Basic, Pascal, VRML, and OpenGL. When he was young he programmed in Basic on his Commodore 64 before he moved on to his first PC in 1990.

Paolo Bonzini is a first-year university student who lives in Italy, near Milan. His father taught him programming in Basic, and he has used it on the PC for 10 years, first in the DOS environment with QuickBasic and later under Windows with Visual Basic. He used VB to program any kind of program he could find useful: ActiveX controls, data-bases, games, and utilities. He can be reached by e-mail at `bonzini.cp@net-one.it`.

Andy Carrasco lives in Denver, Colorado with his wife Valeh, and son, Steffen. He can usually be found at his job as a Visual Basic programmer in the manufacturing industry. When not suffering over deadlines, he enjoys watching mind-numbing cartoons, writing electronic music using only his computer, and puttering around in light aircraft. He can be reached at `gabrielw@ix.netcom.com`.

Tom Honaker is a freelance Webmaster and programmer living in the Florida panhandle area. He's best described as an "old-school" computer geek because his experience reaches to the days of the Commodore PET and IBX XT. He has programmed computers and microprocessors/microcontrollers using a variety of languages since age 10, and at age 27 he is reaching into assembly and C++ programming for PC-compatibles. In his off time, which is admittedly quite rare, he dabbles in electronics, amateur radio, and other technically slanted hobbies. He can be reached at `dmaster@gnt.net` and his Web site is at `http://www.gnt.net/~dmaster/`.

Ian Ippolito lives in sunny Tampa Bay, Florida. He is a Microsoft Certified computer consultant, specializing in n-tier application development and interactive Internet site design. In his spare time, Ian developed `www.planet-source-code.com`, a huge online database of free Visual Basic code. His other hobbies include weightlifting and travelling. He can be reached at `ian@planet-source-code.com`.

Jesper Madsen is currently living and working in Switzerland as a system engineer contractor. Though originally from Denmark, he is planning to move to the United Kingdom in the near future with his Danish girlfriend. As a programmer, his versatility has enabled him to program in such different languages as VB, PowerBuilder, Perl, and VC++/C. When the weather and free time permits it, he enjoys biking and skiing in the Swiss mountains. His current e-mail is `jesper.madsen@syap.ch`.

Kamal A. Mehdi is an experienced programmer who started in the early 1980s programming on the Commodore 64 home computer but then moved to Quick Basic for DOS and later to Visual Basic for Windows. Currently, he mainly develops multimedia applications, ActiveX controls, and projects for computer control of external electronic devices, but he also works with database applications and various utilities.

Kamal is an Electrical Engineer holding a B.S. degree in Electrical and Electronic Engineering since 1983. Currently, he is carrying out a Ph.D. thesis in Electronic and Computer Engineering in the field of Intelligent Self-Testing and Repairing Memories. He has a long experience in electronic system design, LAN installation, digital video production, 3D animation, interactive multimedia presentations, Web page design, and amateur radio communications. Kamal is originally from Baghdad, Iraq but he currently lives in Thessaloniki,Greece with his wife and two children. He can be reached by email at `kamal@egnatia.ee.auth.gr` or through his Web page `http://www.geocities.com/SiliconValley/Foothills/6070/`, where you can find some cool controls, utilities, and Visual Basic projects.

Langdon Oliver is an 18-year-old freshman at Old Dominion University in Norfolk, Virginia, where he plans to major in Computer Science. He started programming at the age of 15 and is now fluent in Basic, Pascal, Perl, HTML, and knows just the basics of C/C++. His submission was written in the summer of 1996 and was used to create add-ons for America Online and other various software packages. Langdon is engaged and hopes to one day find a job programming Internet software for a small business—unless, of course, he gloriously wins the lottery. He can be contacted via email at `iangdon@more4free.com ; loliv001@odu.edu`.

Larry Serflaten enjoys life in a small community in central Minnesota. Programming simple games since 1983, he began using Visual Basic at version 3. Luckily for him, programming is still a hobby, as is creating computer art and recording MIDI music files. Larry has a technical degree in electronics and works in the plastic recycling industry, operating and maintaining production machines. He can be reached at `serflaten@usinternet.com`.

Brian Shea lives in the Seattle area with his wife Terri and their two cats. Brian works as a Windows NT Network Administrator specializing in automation and security, which comes in handy because he works for a large financial corporation. In his (somewhat elusive) free time, he enjoys reading and writing science fiction, hiking in the Pacific Northwest forests, and various sports activities when the weather permits. He can be reached at `xdos@cybrtxt.com`.

Gary Wiley, currently working as a programmer for a corporation in the Lake Erie area, has been programming in Basic for 15 years. He likes hiking and camping and in his spare time (LOL) he runs a chat room for Visual Basic programmers. He can be reached at `gwgaw@msn.com` or `gwgaw@worldnet.att.net`.

ACKNOWLEDGMENTS

First, I'd like to thank my wife for her patience and understanding while this project was coming together. She was, as always, a great help and joy to have around. Second, thanks to the authors who submitted code to make this book happen. Without your cooperation and understanding this project would still be on the drawing board. Thank you.

Of course, Chris Denny, Tony Amico, Dan Scherf, and the rest of the Macmillan staff who worked hard to bring this book together deserve a huge thank you.

—Brian Shea

TELL US WHAT YOU THINK!

As the reader of this book, *you* are our most important critic and commentator. We value your opinion and want to know what we're doing right, what we could do better, what areas you'd like to see us publish in, and any other words of wisdom you're willing to pass our way.

As the Executive Editor for the Visual Basic Programming team at Macmillan Computer Publishing, I welcome your comments. You can fax, email, or write me directly to let me know what you did or didn't like about this book—as well as what we can do to make our books stronger.

Please note that I cannot help you with technical problems related to the topic of this book, and that due to the high volume of mail I receive, I might not be able to reply to every message.

When you write, please be sure to include this book's title and author as well as your name and phone or fax number. I will carefully review your comments and share them with the author and editors who worked on the book.

Fax: 317-817-7070
Email: vb@mcp.com
Mail: Chris Denny
          Executive Editor
          Visual Basic Programming Team
          Macmillan Computer Publishing
          201 West 103rd Street
          Indianapolis, IN 46290 USA

Introduction

As a programmer grows and learns through the years of programming, he not only gains experience, he also gains a code library of routines and functions that helps him write programs. These functions are often carried with him from project to project in one form or another but might never be shared with a wide audience. This book is our effort to share some of our code and experience with a broader audience.

The code gathered here literally comes from all over the world, and was put together in an effort to reach all levels of programmer. If you are looking through some code and see things that look too easy or too hard, don't worry—there's a wide variety of samples here that you can learn from. But more than that, we have tried to make this book a source code library that you can use to enhance or build your own library. Although the functions have detailed explanations, we have made an effort to ensure that each example can be clipped and pasted right into an existing project for immediate use. Hopefully, this will help you solve some of the problems you encounter during your time coding, and let you find more time for other things (even if that is more coding <G>).

The examples listed here have icons that tell you what versions of Visual Basic each one will work with, including VBA and VBScript. The code was targeted for VB5 and 32-bit programs, but much of it is compatible with VBA, VBScript, and VB4 (16-bit or 32-bit). Check the listings for details on compatibility.

Finally, I'd like to thank you for purchasing this book, and I hope that it becomes an integral part of your code and reference library.

Chapter 1

CONTROL ENHANCEMENTS

If you've ever sat back in your chair and thought, "Boy, I wish that this control would just..." then this chapter should be helpful. Here are several ways to add functionality to the existing controls in Visual Basic. From adding formatting to a text box to working with control arrays, this chapter has some useful tips and tricks for everyone.

1.1 RESTRICT INPUT IN A MASKED TEXT BOX

by Jesper Madsen

Description

The masked text box is an ActiveX control that allows only certain valid characters to be typed in a predefined format shown in the text box.

The masked text box is useful for masking personal identification numbers, currency, phone fields, and so on. An example of a masked phone field could be "+   -(0)   -   " and with a valid character string of "0123456789", the resulting phone field could look like "+41- (0)78-9993434". It's also some very useful source code if you want to add a feature that the standard masked text boxes don't have.

To implement the ActiveX control, you simply create a new user control in VB. Add a text box called Text1 (the default name) to the user control, and then paste this code.

There are some restrictions in the code as to how the user can delete characters typed in the text box:

■ Using the backspace key—The user can delete characters only starting from the back of the last character typed in. The user can also delete all characters typed in if all the characters are selected.

■   Using the Delete key—The user can use this key to delete all characters typed in only if all the characters are selected.

These are necessary to ensure that the mask algorithm isn't broken. Certainly, the more flexible you want the editing to be for the user, the more complex and cumbersome the coding gets.

Syntax

None.

Code Listing

```
'**********************************
'**   Submitted by Jesper Madsen.  **
'**********************************


Option Explicit

Const def_LFStyle = 0 ' Default LostFocusStyle = None

Public Enum LostFocusStyles
    None
    ShowRedColor ' If the user dosn't fill the textbox, the text will turn red
    MustFill ' The user must fill the textbox, before he/she can Leave
End Enum

Private OldColor As Long
Private LFStyle As LostFocusStyles ' Current LostFocusStyle
Private sFormat As String   ' A format of your choice, Spaces in this format
                            ' indicates where the ValidChars goes
Private sValidChars As String   ' The Chars that can be entered into the format
Private TP As Integer ' Text position in the textbox

Private Sub UserControl_Initialize()
  Text1 = "" ' Clear the textbox
  LFStyle = def_LFStyle ' Set Default LostFocusStyle = None
End Sub

Private Sub UserControl_Resize()
  ' Set the size so that the textbox is as big as the UserControl
  Text1.Height = UserControl.Height
  Text1.Width = UserControl.Width
End Sub

Private Sub UserControl_ReadProperties(PropBag As PropertyBag)
  ' Read the Properties from the PropBag
  sFormat = PropBag.ReadProperty("Mask")
  sValidChars = PropBag.ReadProperty("ValidChars")
  LFStyle = PropBag.ReadProperty("LFStyle", def_LFStyle)
  Text1 = sFormat ' Show the new format in the textbox
```

```
End Sub

Private Sub UserControl_WriteProperties(PropBag As PropertyBag)
   ' Write the Properties to the PropBag
  Call PropBag.WriteProperty("Mask", sFormat)
  Call PropBag.WriteProperty("ValidChars", sValidChars)
  Call PropBag.WriteProperty("LFStyle", LFStyle, def_LFStyle)
End Sub

Public Property Get Text() As String
  Text = Text1 ' Return the text from the textbox
End Property

Public Property Get Mask() As String
  Mask = sFormat ' Return the current Mask format
End Property

Public Property Let Mask(s_Format As String)
   sFormat = s_Format ' Set new Mask format
   Text1 = s_Format    ' Show it in the textbox
   ' Notify the container that the Mask's value has been changed.
   PropertyChanged "Mask"
End Property

Public Property Get ValidChars() As String
   ValidChars = sValidChars ' Return the current Valid Chars
End Property

Public Property Let ValidChars(s_ValidChars As String)
   sValidChars = s_ValidChars ' Set the new Valid Chars
   PropertyChanged "ValidChars"
End Property

Public Property Get LostFocusStyle() As LostFocusStyles
    LostFocusStyle = LFStyle
End Property

Public Property Let LostFocusStyle(ByVal New_LFStyle As LostFocusStyles)
    LFStyle = New_LFStyle
    PropertyChanged "LFStyle"
End Property

Private Sub Text1_GotFocus()
  Dim iSpaceInStr As Integer

  If LFStyle = ShowRedColor Then Text1.ForeColor = OldColor

  ' Set cursor to the start or at the end of text in the textbox
  iSpaceInStr = InStr(Text1, " ")
  If iSpaceInStr > 0 Then
   Text1.SelStart = iSpaceInStr - 1
  Else
```

```
      Text1.SelStart = TP
   End If
End Sub

Private Sub Text1_LostFocus()
   If Len(sFormat) <> TP Then ' The textbox haven't been filled so
      Select Case LFStyle
         Case ShowRedColor
            OldColor = Text1.ForeColor ' Save the old text color
            Text1.ForeColor = vbRed ' Set the new text color to red
         Case MustFill
            Text1.SetFocus ' Keep the user focused to this textbox
      End Select
   End If
End Sub

Private Sub Text1_KeyDown(KeyCode As Integer, Shift As Integer)
   If KeyCode = vbKeyDelete Then
      ' Delete all chars in textbox if and only if all is selected
      If Text1.SelLength = Len(sFormat) Then
         Text1 = sFormat ' Set the textbox to show the "empty" format
         TP = 0 ' Reset the Text position
         Text1.SelStart = 0 ' Clear selection
      End If
      KeyCode = 0 ' Ignore delete key
   End If
End Sub

Private Sub Text1_KeyPress(KeyAscii As Integer)
 Dim S As String ' String used to temporally hold the text in text1
 Dim iSepLenS As Integer
 Dim iSepLenTP As Integer
 Dim iSepLenCP As Integer
 Dim iSpaceInStr As Integer
 Dim CP As Integer ' Cursor position in the textbox
 Dim N As Integer   ' Counter
 Dim Key As Integer ' The Key Pressed

 Key = KeyAscii ' Save pressed key
 KeyAscii = 0 ' Ignore key, I'll handle what does and dosn't go in the Textbox
 S = Text1
 CP = Text1.SelStart ' Get the cursor position
 If (Key <> vbKeyBack) Then
   If (InStr(sValidChars$, Chr(Key)) = 0) Or (TP = Len(sFormat)) And
   ➥ (TP = Text1.SelStart) Then
     Beep
     Exit Sub ' Ignore char
   End If

   TP = TP + 1 'Assume the text is getting a char longer

   ' Check for separators at the text position or at the start in text1
```

```
If Trim$(Mid$(sFormat, TP, 1)) <> "" Then
  iSpaceInStr = InStr(TP + 1, sFormat, " ")
  If iSpaceInStr > 0 Then
    iSepLenS = iSpaceInStr - TP ' Get length of separators
  Else ' There are only separators in sFormat
    Beep
    Exit Sub ' Ignore char -> sFormat = kuk-ku
  End If
  TP = TP + iSepLenS ' Add length of separators in the Start of the sFormat
  ➥ to TP if any
End If

' Check for separators one position ahead of the last char in text
If Trim$(Mid$(sFormat, TP + 1, 1)) <> "" Then
  iSpaceInStr = InStr(TP + 1, sFormat, " ")
  If iSpaceInStr > 0 Then
    iSepLenTP = iSpaceInStr - (TP + 1) ' Get length of separators
  Else ' There are only separators left in sFormat
    iSepLenTP = Len(sFormat) - TP ' Get length of separators at end of
    ➥ sFormat
  End If
' Check for separators one position ahead of the cursor position in text
ElseIf Trim$(Mid$(sFormat, CP + 1, 1)) <> "" Then
  iSpaceInStr = InStr(CP + 1, sFormat, " ")
  If iSpaceInStr > 0 Then
    iSepLenCP = iSpaceInStr - (CP + 1)
  Else ' There are only separators left in sFormat
    iSepLenCP = -1 ' Mark that overwrite isn't possible
  End If
End If

If (TP > Len(sFormat)) Then ' Overwrite char at cursor position
  TP = TP - 1 ' The text didn't get longer as we are overwriting
  If iSepLenCP = -1 Then ' Don't overwrite separators at end of sFormat
    Text1.SelStart = Len(sFormat)
    Beep
    Exit Sub ' Ignore char
  End If
  CP = CP + 1 + iSepLenCP ' If there isn't a separator, 0 (nada) will get
  ➥ added to CP
  Mid(S, CP, 1) = Chr(Key) ' Put in the char (overwriting)
  Text1 = S
  Text1.SelStart = CP ' Set new cursor position
  Exit Sub
End If

Mid(S, TP, 1) = Chr(Key) ' Put in the char

Text1 = S
TP = TP + iSepLenTP ' if there isn't a separator, 0 (nada) will get added
➥ to TP
Text1.SelStart = TP
```

```
    Else '***** Handle the backspace key *****

      If Text1.SelLength = Len(sFormat) Then ' Delete all chars in textbox
        Text1 = sFormat
        TP = 0
        Text1.SelStart = 0
        Exit Sub
      End If
      If Text1.SelLength <> 0 Then Exit Sub ' Ignore deletion if only parts of the
      ➥ text is selected
      If CP = 0 Then
        Beep ' Nothing to delete at this cursor position
        Exit Sub
      End If
      If CP <> TP Then Exit Sub ' Allow deletion from the back of the text only

      ' Check for separators at the cursor position in text
      If Trim$(Mid$(sFormat, CP, 1)) <> "" Then
        For N = CP To 1 Step -1 ' Compute the length of the separator(s)
          If Mid$(sFormat, N, 1) = " " Then Exit For
        Next N
        TP = TP - (CP - N) ' Subtract length of separators from TP
        CP = N ' Set cursor to start of separator.
      End If

      ' Only check for separators one position behind the CP in the text if there
      ➥ is any
      If CP > 1 Then
        ' Check for separator(s) one position behind the cursor position in the
        ➥ text
        If Trim$(Mid$(sFormat, CP - 1, 1)) <> "" Then
          For N = (CP - 1) To 1 Step -1 ' Compute the length of the separator(s)
            If Mid$(sFormat, N, 1) = " " Then Exit For
          Next N
          CP = N + 1 ' Set cursor to start of separator.
        End If
      End If

      Mid(S, TP, 1) = " " ' Replace char at TP with " "
      Text1 = S
      TP = CP - 1
      Text1.SelStart = TP
    End If
End Sub

Private Sub Text1_MouseDown(Button As Integer, Shift As Integer, X As Single,
➥ Y As Single)
    ' This will grey (disable) all Edit menu items in the right click popup menu
    If Button = vbRightButton Then Text1.Locked = True
End Sub
```

```
Private Sub Text1_MouseUp(Button As Integer, Shift As Integer, X As Single,
➥ Y As Single)
   ' Unlock it as the Edit menu items has been disabled
   If Button = vbRightButton Then Text1.Locked = False
End Sub
```

Analysis

The code shown here is a bit complex, so I won't go into too much detail.

The KeyPress event is the event in which it's all happening. The key thing to notice is the check for separator characters in sFormat at the text position (the last character typed) and one character ahead of that position. This enables the code to move the cursor to the end of one or more concurrent separator characters when a typed character reaches the beginning of the first separator character. If the text box is full, a check at the cursor position is done to see whether overwrite is possible and if so, where to put the character.

The possibility to overwrite characters is a feature you don't normally find in a standard masked text box. If you look in the LostFocus event for the text box, you'll see another small feature that you don't have in a standard masked text box. You're able to set the text color to red or hold the focus to the text box if the user hasn't filled out the entire mask.

If you want to find out in more detail how the code works, the easiest way is to use the debugger and follow my comments.

1.2   COPY OR MOVE COMBO LIST CONTENTS

by Lenard Dean with Brian Shea

Description

This function copies or moves the contents of one list or combo box to another. You have the option of moving or copying only one item or doing the whole list at one time.

Syntax

CopyComboList(FromCtl As Control, ToCtl As Control, Optional strMode As String)

Part	Value	Description
FromCtl		Required. The source list or combo box control.
FromCtl		Required. The source list or combo box control.

continues

Part	Value	Description
ToCtl		Required. The destination list or combo box control.
strMode		Optional. When not specified copies selected items.
	-	Same as above but moves selected items after copying.
	ALL	Copies all items.
	-ALL	Copies and removes all items after copying.

Code Listing

```
Sub CopyComboList(FromCtl As Control, ToCtl As Control,
➡Optional strMode As String)

    On Error Resume Next

    Dim intN As Integer

    Screen.MousePointer = vbHourglass

If strMode <> "" Then
    UCase strMode
End If

    With FromCtl
      If TypeName(FromCtl) = "ListBox" Then
        For intN = .ListCount - 1 To 0 Step -1
          If .Selected(intN) Or InStr(strMode, "ALL") Then
            ToCtl.AddItem .List(intN)
            ToCtl.ItemData(ToCtl.NewIndex) = .ItemData(intN)
            If InStr(strMode, "-") = 1 Then .RemoveItem (intN)
          End If
        Next
      Else
        For intN = .ListCount - 1 To 0 Step -1
          ToCtl.AddItem .List(intN)
          ToCtl.ItemData(ToCtl.NewIndex) = .ItemData(intN)
          If InStr(strMode, "-") = 1 Then .RemoveItem (intN)
        Next
      End If
    End With

    Screen.MousePointer = vbDefault
End Sub
```

Analysis

As mentioned earlier, this routine copies the contents of one list or combo box control to another. Using the strMode argument you can set whether the items of the source control will be deleted after copying or whether the entire contents will be affected. Please note that because you can't select multiple items in a combo box, all items will be processed.

Let's take a quick look at what this function does. First you declare the function and enable the error handling to continue on local errors. The mouse cursor is then changed to an hourglass, which keeps the user informed that a task is being performed. Each type of control (list or combo box) is handled separately, starting with the list box.

In each case, you walk through the items on the source control and copy them to the new control. In the case of the list box, the copy occurs only if strMode is set to ALL or the item is selected. The combo box items are all copied to the new control.

Before moving to the next item, you check to see whether the strMode string contains a - character. If it does, you remove the item copied from the source control. On the ListBox source control, this occurs only if the item was selected and strMode was set to -. It also happens if the mode is set to -ALL.

Finally, before closing, the icon is returned to the default so the user is aware that the operation has completed.

1.3 CHECK BOX OPTIONS

by Larry Serflaten

Description

In some instances, an application might use several check boxes to enable the user to set properties or attributes. Often, the user settings will be saved to disk so that they can be used again for the next session. The following procedures are designed to reduce the code necessary to handle these user settings.

A check box will normally be in one of two states, checked or unchecked. The binary nature of these controls makes it easy to represent each check box's current state using one bit of a 32-bit number. Because all the check boxes will be responding identically, creating them as a control array significantly reduces the amount of code required to handle them all.

The *CBO_Click* Procedure

The CBO_Click subroutine is called from the click event of the check box array. It has two constants that determine how the check boxes will respond. When LikeOptions is set, only one check box can be checked at a time. When AllowNone is set, the condition where no check box is checked is allowed. These two switches can be used to make the check box array respond like a group of option buttons, where only one option can be checked, and to determine whether at least one check box must be checked. To set the array to act like standard check boxes, set LikeOptions to False or 0, and set AllowNone to True or 1. To set the array to act like standard option buttons, set LikeOptions to True or 1, and set AllowNone to False or 0.

The *CBO_Set* Procedure

The CBO_Set subroutine is used to set the state of the check boxes. It is used by the CBO_Click procedure to force the check boxes to respond according to the switch settings. It should be used by the programmer to also set the check boxes to a desired state.

Procedure Parameters

Both procedures require a reference to the check box array and an index value that indicates which check boxes are being used. With the array reference as a parameter, these procedures can be used to operate on more than one array, treating each array as its own separate group. The current state of all the check boxes in the array is represented by one 32-bit number, which is stored in the Tag property of the first check box in the array. This is where you can access the number that should be saved to disk for use in the next session.

The second parameter of the two procedures is used differently in each procedure. The CBO_Click procedure expects the Index parameter supplied by Visual Basic to the click event, but the CBO_Set procedure expects the 32-bit number. To keep them separate, Index is used where the Visual Basic Index parameter is needed, and CBOIndex is used where the 32-bit number is needed. An analysis of how these parameters are used follows the code listing.

Demonstration

For a demonstration of these procedures, place an array of check boxes and a text box on a new form. To build the array, place one check box on the form and set its Index property to 0. Then use the copy and paste method to add more check boxes.

With the controls in place, add the CBO_Click and CBO_Set procedures and the following code to the form's code section. Make sure that the variable CBOBusy is declared in the form's General Declarations section.

```
Dim CBOBusy As Boolean
Private Sub Check1_Click(Index As Integer)
CBO_Click Check1, Index
Text1 = Check1(0).Tag
End Sub
```

Save the form and run the program. Note the changing value displayed in the text box as you click the check boxes. For any combination of checked boxes, Text1 will show a unique value. This is the value that should be saved to disk and used as the CBOIndex parameter in the call to CBO_Set.

Syntax

```
CBO_Click CBOArray, Index
CBO_Set CBOArray, CBOIndex
```

Part	Description
CBOArray	The name of the array.
Index	Required. The index value supplied by VB.
CBOIndex	Required. The 32-bit composite value.

Code Listing

```
Dim CBOBusy As Boolean
Public Sub CBO_Click(CBOArray, Index)
Dim CBOState&, CBOIndex&
'Switches
Const LikeOptions = 0
Const AllowNone = 1
If Index 30 Then Err.Raise 6
If CBOBusy Then Exit Sub
CBOBusy = True
'Get current Index and State
CBOIndex = 2 ^ Index
CBOState = Val(CBOArray(0).Tag)
'Adjust boxes per switches
If CBOState = CBOIndex Then
If AllowNone Then
CBO_Set CBOArray, 0
Else
CBO_Set CBOArray, CBOIndex
End If
ElseIf LikeOptions Then
CBO_Set CBOArray, CBOIndex
End If
'Set new State and assign to Tag
CBOState = Val(CBOArray(0).Tag) Or CBOIndex
If CBOArray(Index).Value = 0 Then CBOState = CBOState - CBOIndex
CBOArray(0).Tag = CBOState
CBOBusy = False
End Sub

Public Sub CBO_Set(CBOArray, CBOIndex&)
Const Log2 = 0.693147180559945
Dim Bit&
If CBOIndex &H7FFFFFFF Then Err.Raise 6
CBOBusy = True
CBOArray(0).Tag = CBOIndex
Bit = 1
On Error GoTo CBOError
```

```
Do
CBOArray(Log(Bit) / Log2).Value = Abs((CBOIndex And Bit) 0)
Bit = Bit + Bit
Loop
CBOError:
CBOBusy = False
End Sub
```

Analysis

The check box array indexing must begin with 0 and use consecutive indexes to allow the actual index of the check box to represent the bit position it is associated with in the 32-bit number. The array index value is the value Visual Basic passes to the click routine in the `Index` parameter. You generate the `CBOIndex` value by setting the associated bits in a 32-bit number. If the check box with an index of 3 is checked, then bit 3 of the `CBOIndex` is set. If check boxes 2 and 5 are checked, then bits 2 and 5 of the `CBOIndex` are set.

The relationship between `Index` and `CBOIndex` can be described as follows:

```
CBOIndex = 2 ^ Index
Index = Log(CBOIndex) / Log(2)
```

In a 32-bit number, with bits numbered 0–31, Visual Basic reserves the most significant bit to represent the sign of the number. Any attempt to use bit 31 other than as designed can result in a fatal error. Therefore, only bits 0–30 can be used to represent the state of 31 check boxes. To avoid errors, the first thing both of these procedures do is validate the `Index` and `CBOIndex` parameters. If the value of the parameter is out of range, a trappable Overflow error is raised.

Setting the Check Boxes

Initialize each check box array in the `Form_Load` event. Use a `CBOIndex` value of 0 to uncheck all the check boxes, or use any other accepted number to set one or more of the check boxes in the array. Such a number would normally be read from the Registry or the application's INI file on startup.

You set the check boxes first by setting the `CBOBusy` flag and assigning the new value to the `Tag` property of the first check box. The `CBOBusy` flag is discussed in the next section. The `Tag` property allows these procedures and the programmer to access the current state of the check boxes in the array. Each array must begin with a check box that has an index of 0; storing the current state there allows each array to have its own `CBOIndex` value.

To set the check boxes, the `CBO_Set` procedure uses a bit index to access each check box. The bit index begins with bit 0 set, and shifts that bit one position to the left to test each bit in `CBOIndex`. If a bit is set in the 32-bit number, then the corresponding check box is checked in the array. To allow for arrays of different sizes, the bit shifting will continue until it reaches a value that has no corresponding check box. Attempting to access a check box that is not available results in a trappable error, and this condition signals the end of the bit-shifting loop.

Handling the Click Events

Changing the checked state of a check box, either from code or by using the mouse, will trigger the check box's click event. Statements in the `CBO_Click` or `CBO_Set` procedures might programmatically change the state of a check box, which would normally trigger the click event. To avoid processing the click events when the array needs changing, a module-level `CBOBusy` flag is tested for and set at the start of the `CBO_Click` procedure. This ensures that the first time `CBO_Click` is called (while `CBOBusy` is `False`), click event processing is allowed to execute. However, subsequent calls to `CBO_Click` are ignored until processing is complete and `CBOBusy` is reset to `False`.

Next, the value representing the `CBOIndex` of the selected check box, as well as the `CBOIndex` value of the entire array (called `CBOState`) are assigned to variables for later use.

Only two conditions must be tested to force the array to conform to the switch settings. When only one check box is checked and the user selects that check box, `AllowNone` is used to determine whether that check box should be allowed to go into an unchecked state. Otherwise, if `LikeOptions` is set, the selected check box must be set as the only check box checked. When these conditions happen, `CBO_Set` is called to force the array to conform to the switch settings.

If `CBO_Set` is called, the `Tag` property will be set accordingly. For all other possible conditions, the `Tag` property must be set to reflect the state of the user-selected check box. This is done by updating the state variable, in case a call to `CBO_Set` has changed the state of the array, and adding or subtracting the corresponding `CBOIndex` to the current state. If the selected check box is checked, the `CBOIndex` must be added to `CBOState`. If it is unchecked, it must be subtracted. After that is figured out, the new `CBOState` is stored in the `Tag` property of the first check box in the array.

Updating the Current State

During the course of some programs, it might become necessary to change the state of the check boxes programmatically, perhaps due to user input elsewhere in the program. To change one or more without effecting the state of other check boxes in the same array, either use the `Or` operator on the `CBOIndex` value to set check boxes to checked, or use the `And Not` combination to set check boxes to unchecked. The following two procedures demonstrate both methods:

```
Private Sub CBO_Check(CBOArray, CBOIndex)
If CBOIndex &H7FFFFFFF Then Err.Raise 6
CBO_Set CBOArray, Val(CBOArray(0).Tag) Or CBOIndex
End Sub
Private Sub CBO_UnCheck(CBOArray, CBOIndex)
If CBOIndex &H7FFFFFFF Then Err.Raise 6
CBO_Set CBOArray, Val(CBOArray(0).Tag) And Not CBOIndex
End Sub
```

Using the demonstration program as a reference, the number to use for the `CBO_Index` parameter can easily be determined. If the first two check boxes are checked, the value in `Text1` will be 3. If this number is supplied to the `CBO_Uncheck` procedure, then both of these check boxes will be unchecked. If 1 or 2 is supplied, then either the first or second check box will be unchecked. In this manner, these procedures will operate on one or more check boxes, while leaving the state of the remaining check boxes unchanged.

The parameters for all the procedures previously mentioned are of the `Variant` type. This allows `CBOArray` to accept the control array object, and allows `Index` and `CBOIndex` to be an `Integer` or `Long` type, compatible with the click event `Index` from the various versions of Visual Basic.

1.4 A BETTER TIMER THAN TIMER

by Paolo Bonzini

Description

This function works exactly as the standard `Timer` function with two differences:

■   It answers the number of seconds since the system was started, not the number of seconds since midnight. This is better because it guarantees that `Timer`'s result is always increasing; after all, to get the number of seconds since midnight you can use `(Now-Int(Now))*86400`.

■   It has a better resolution. In my experiments, the tick frequency for the standard implementation of Timer is about 1 kHz. Instead, this version's resolution is, on my system, about 1.4 MHz.

Syntax

`Result = Timer`

Part	Description
Result	Required. The number returned specifying the number of seconds since the system was started.

Code Listing

```
'********************************************
'* Submitted by Paolo Bonzini
'********************************************
Private Declare Function osQueryPerformanceCounter _
    Lib "Kernel32" Alias "QueryPerformanceCounter" _
    (lpPerformanceCount As Currency) As Long
Private Declare Function osQueryPerformanceFrequency _
    Lib "Kernel32" Alias "QueryPerformanceFrequency" _
    (lpFrequency As Currency) As Long

'This version of Timer is faster (it doesn't involve
'OLE automation) and also has a better resolution
Public Function Timer() As Single
    Dim freq As Currency, count As Currency
```

```
        osQueryPerformanceFrequency freq
        osQueryPerformanceCounter count
        Timer = count / freq
End Function
```

Analysis

This is a simple wrapper around two API functions, `QueryPerformanceFrequency` and `QueryPerformanceCounter`. The former retrieves how many timer ticks are in one second, the latter retrieves how many timer ticks have elapsed since the system was started. To obtain the number of seconds, simply divide the two results.

Looking at the code you might wonder what `Currency` is—the Win32 API does not know about the `Currency` data type. The actual declarations (you can find them in WIN32API.TXT) use a structure called `LARGE_INTEGER`, which is composed of two Longs, with the least significant one first. Currencies are stored in exactly the same way, only they are divided by 10000 when calculations are performed. This, however, does not matter when you divide the two currencies: in fact, `(freq/10000) / (count/10000) = freq/count`. That's why I didn't use `LARGE_INTEGER`s.

1.5 LISTBOX BINARY SEARCH

by Paolo Bonzini

Description

These functions will find an item in a sorted ListBox or ComboBox passed to the function. You can ask for either exact matches or partial matches (for example, you can pass "Vis" and the item returned will be "Visual Basic").

The Windows API provides a simple way to do this through four messages: `LB_FINDSTRING` and `LB_FIND-STRINGEXACT` for list boxes, `CB_FINDSTRING` and `CB_FINDSTRINGEXACT` for combo boxes. However, the presented functions work for both ListBoxes and ComboBoxes (while there are separate messages for each), and provide a useful example that you can modify if you need, for example, to do fast searches in a sorted array.

It is not necessary for the control's `Sorted` property to be `True`. If you sort the items manually by inserting them in the correct positions, the functions will work too. You shouldn't take advantage of the `Sorted` property because it is available only at design time; to provide a `Sorted` property in an ActiveX control, for example, you must either use two list boxes (and waste resources) or sort the items manually. Remember, it doesn't matter what you do to keep the items in the list box sorted, but it does matter that they are sorted in *ascending* order because of the algorithm used.

Syntax

```
Index = FindExact(Control, Searched[, StartingIndex])
Index = FindPartial(Control, Searched[, StartingIndex])
```

Part	Description
Index	Required. The number returned specifying the 0-based index of the item, or –1 if none is found.
Control	Required. The object expression that specifies the control in which to search. It can be any control that has List and ListCount properties—usually a ListBox or a ComboBox. VB won't signal a compile error if an invalid control is passed.
Searched	Required. The string expression that specifies the item to match (an exact match for FindExact, a partial match for FindPartial).
StartingIndex	Optional. The 0-based index of the item from which the search is to start. If omitted, the routine starts searching at index 0; that is, it searches the whole list box.

Code Listing

```
'***********************************************
'* Submitted by Paolo Bonzini
'***********************************************
'Note - as this function uses binary search, the items in
'the control must be kept sorted
Function FindExact(Control As Control, Searched As String, _
    Optional StartingIndex As Variant)

Dim I As Long, j As Long, k As Long

FindExact = -1
I = Iif(IsMissing(StartingIndex), 0, StartingIndex)
j = Control.ListCount - 1
Do
    'not found, exit
    If I > j Then Exit Function

    k = (I + j) / 2
    'If StrComp answers -1, the middle item is less than the
    'searched one, so it must be in first half. If StrComp
    'answers 1, we are looking for an item greater than the
    'middle one, which must be in second half
    Select Case StrComp(Control.List(k), Searched)
        Case 0: Exit Do
        Case -1: I = k + 1
        Case 1: j = k - 1
    End Select
Loop

'backward sequential search that finds the first matching item
```

```
Do While k > 0
    If StrComp(Control.List(k - 1), Searched) Then
        Exit Do
    End If
    k = k - 1
Loop
FindExact = k

End Function

'Note - as this function uses binary search, the items in the
'control must be kept sorted
Function FindPartial(Control As Control, Searched As String, _
    Optional StartingIndex As Variant)
Dim I As Long, j As Long, k As Long, lun As Long

FindPartial = -1
I = Iif(IsMissing(StartingIndex), 0, StartingIndex)
j = Control.ListCount - 1
lun = Len(Searched)
Do
    'not found, exit
    If I > j Then Exit Function

    k = (I + j) / 2
    'If StrComp answers -1, the middle item is less than the
    'searched one, so it must be in first half. If StrComp
    'answers 1, we are looking for an item greater than the
    'middle one, which must be in second half
    Select Case StrComp(Left(Control.List(k), lun), Searched)
        Case 0: Exit Do
        Case -1: I = k + 1
        Case 1: j = k - 1
    End Select
Loop

'backwards sequential search that finds the first matching item
Do While k > 0
    If StrComp(Left(Control.List(k - 1), lun), Searched) Then
        Exit Do
    End If
    k = k - 1
Loop
FindPartial = k

End Function
```

Analysis

These routines are fairly simple after you grasp the algorithm they employ. A binary search requires the list to be sorted; it splits the list into two parts. If the middle item matches the argument, the search ends and the middle item's index is returned; otherwise, one of the halves is discarded and the process is repeated.

To check whether the element isn't present, just check whether the range being examined is still valid. That is, if the index of the first item exceeds the index of the last item in the range, the function is finished and exits, returning –1. This is handled by the `If I>J Then Exit Function` that appears in both functions.

When a matching item is found, the program scans backward to return the first item in the list that satisfies the match. This must be done because a binary search finds a matching item's index, but it does not guarantee that it is the first matching item in the list. For example, if you have "Visual Basic" and "Visual Basic For Applications" in your control, and you look for a partial match for "Vis," the binary search algorithm might answer the index of any of the two items: the backward search ensures that the function answers the index of "Visual Basic."

The two functions are almost identical. The only difference is that `FindExact` compares the whole contents of an item with the passed string (the `Searched` parameter), while `FindPartial` only compares the first characters of each item to the `Searched` parameter. For example, if `Searched` is three characters long, `FindPartial` compares `Searched` with the first three characters of each item.

A binary search is a fairly general algorithm. You can easily use it in many other situations with small changes to the code presented here. For example, you can use it to search an array of keywords, or you can adapt it to controls that use different properties to access the list of items.

Binary search, in fact, is the fastest algorithm to look for an item in a sorted list: it is an O(log n) algorithm, which means that it will run for a time proportional to the logarithm of the number of elements in the list. The benefits of a binary search become particularly apparent in a long list. The maximum number of iterations when searching 1,024 items is just 10, compared with an average number of 512 iterations required by a traditional sequential search. A binary search of 2,048 items requires just one more iteration, while the average length of a sequential search doubles.

1.6   SYNCHRONIZED LIST BOXES

by Gary A. Wiley

Description

This shows how to synchronize two list box controls. When one list box is scrolled, the other one will be scrolled the same. If an item is selected in one list box, the item with the same list index will be selected in the other.

In order for this to work in VB 4 32-bit and 16-bit you must add two vertical scrollbars. Place the scrollbars over the list box's scrollbars and size to cover them. Both list boxes must be the same height and have the same number of items.

Code Listing

```
Private Sub List1_KeyDown(KeyCode As Integer, Shift As Integer)
    'Delete the following line for VB5.
    VScroll1.Value = List1.TopIndex
    List2.ListIndex = List1.ListIndex
End Sub

Private Sub List1_KeyUp(KeyCode As Integer, Shift As Integer)
    'Delete the following line for VB5.
    VScroll1.Value = List1.TopIndex
    List2.ListIndex = List1.ListIndex
End Sub

Private Sub List1_MouseDown(Button As Integer, Shift As Integer,
➡ X As Single, Y As Single)
    Dim dy
    'Delete the following line if you want the list box
    'to accept right mouse button clicks
    If Button <> 1 Then Exit Sub
    List1.SetFocus
    dy = Int(Y / TextHeight("A"))
    'If cursor not on a list item quit
    If dy + List1.TopIndex > List1.ListCount - 1 Then Exit Sub
    'Select item
    List1.ListIndex = dy + List1.TopIndex
    List2.ListIndex = List1.ListIndex
End Sub

Private Sub List2_KeyDown(KeyCode As Integer, Shift As Integer)
    'Delete the following line for VB5.
    VScroll2.Value = List2.TopIndex
    List1.ListIndex = List2.ListIndex
End Sub

Private Sub List2_KeyUp(KeyCode As Integer, Shift As Integer)
    'Delete the following line for VB5.
    VScroll2.Value = List2.TopIndex
    List1.ListIndex = List2.ListIndex
End Sub

Private Sub List2_MouseDown(Button As Integer, Shift As Integer,
➡ X As Single, Y As Single)
    Dim dy
    'Delete the following line if you want the list box
    'to accept right mouse button clicks
    If Button <> 1 Then Exit Sub
    List2.SetFocus
    dy = Int(Y / TextHeight("A"))
    'If cursor not on a list item quit
    If dy + List2.TopIndex > List2.ListCount - 1 Then Exit Sub
    'Select item
```

```
        List2.ListIndex = dy + List2.TopIndex
        List1.ListIndex = List2.ListIndex
End Sub

Private Sub VScroll1_Change()
        VScroll1_Scroll
End Sub

Private Sub VScroll1_Scroll()
        'Scroll list boxes by setting their TopIndex
        'property to the scrollbar's value.
        List1.TopIndex = Int(VScroll1.Value)
        List2.TopIndex = List1.TopIndex
        VScroll2.Value = VScroll1.Value
End Sub

Private Sub VScroll2_Change()
        VScroll2_Scroll
End Sub

Private Sub VScroll2_Scroll()
        'Scroll list boxes by setting their TopIndex
        'property to the scrollbar's value.
        List1.TopIndex = Int(VScroll2.Value)
        List2.TopIndex = List1.TopIndex
        VScroll1.Value = VScroll2.Value
End Sub

Private Sub SetScrollValues()
        'variable for number of visible items
        Dim dy As Integer
        'Convert list box height to number of items
        'that can be visible. We need to subtract 60
        'from the listbox height for the border
        dy = Int((List1.Height - 60) / TextHeight("A"))
        'Show or hide the scrollbars depending on the
        'number  of items in list boxes
        If dy >= List1.ListCount Then
            VScroll1.Visible = False
            VScroll2.Visible = False
        Else
            VScroll1.Visible = True
            VScroll2.Visible = True
        End If
        'Set scrollbar values
        VScroll1.Min = 0
        'Set Max to ListCount - number of visible items
        VScroll1.Max = List1.ListCount  dy
        'Set LargeChange to 1 less than visible items
        VScroll1.LargeChange = dy  1
        'Set Vscroll2 values equal to Vscroll1
        VScroll2.Min = 0
```

```
        VScroll2.Max = VScroll1.Max
        VScroll2.LargeChange = VScroll1.LargeChange
End Sub


'Use these events for VB 5 instead of scrollbar controls and
    'remove the code for the scrollbars and the SetScrollValues
    'procedure. Also remove the first line from the KeyDown and
    'KeyUp events of both list boxes.

Private Sub List1_Scroll()
    List2.TopIndex = List1.TopIndex
End Sub

Private Sub List2_Scroll()
    List1.TopIndex = List2.TopIndex
End Sub
```

Analysis

When you are removing or adding items to one list box be sure to remove or add an item to the other one, even if you add just a blank line. The `TextHeight` method, used in the `SetScrollValues` procedure, returns the height of text in the current font of a form or PictureBox control. The font and font size should be the same for the list boxes as for the form, or PictureBox if the list boxes are in a PictureBox. See online help for more information on the `TextHeight` method. Errors will be generated if the list boxes are not the same height or don't have the same number of items.

Some special consideration must be taken for sorted list boxes. First, only one list box should have its sorted property set to `True`. Otherwise, although the list boxes will be synchronized the list items will not be synchronized. Second, always add items to the sorted list box first. Then use the `NewIndex` property of the sorted list box to add an item to the other list box at the correct position. For example, if you want to display names in one list box and phone numbers in the other, set only the name list box's `Sorted` property to `True` then add items as follows:

```
lstNames.AddItem "John Doe"
lstPhoneNumbers.AddItem "123-4567", lstNames.NewIndex.
```

Note that the scrollbar's `LargeChange` value is set to one less than the number of visible items. This allows the scrollbars to emulate the action of a list box when the user clicks the area between the scroll box and scroll arrow.

VB 5 has a list box scroll event, which VB 4 does not. To use it in VB 5 remove the scrollbars and associated code and use the list box scroll event to synchronize the list boxes when scrolling. The rest of the code is unchanged.

I have tested the code in VB 5 and VB 4 32-bit. It should work in VB 4 16-bit. Although the code works in VBA, you cannot place a scrollbar control on top of a list box control. In Windows 98, if the Animate Windows, Menus and Lists option is selected in Display Control Panel, there will be a slight lag between the scrolling of the list boxes, but the synchronization will still work.

1.7   SET A DATABASE NAME FOR CRYSTAL REPORTS

by Mike Shaffer

Description

The `SetDBNameCrystal` function enables you to quickly set the database name for a Crystal Reports template, including all subreports. This routine is for use with Crystal Reports 6 and higher. If the optional database password is included, this routine will also set the password for each database reference. This is especially useful when you have multiple people working on a project. For example, you might have someone who designs report templates and then passes them to you. This function lets you quickly set the database name for the entire template (all subreports) without needing to know each subreport name.

Syntax

`SetDBNameCrystal CrystalReport1, strDBName, strDBPass`

Part	Description
CrystalReport1	Required. The Crystal Report control.
StrDBName	Required. The database name.
StrDBPass	Optional. The database password.

Code Listing

```
'***********************************************
    '* Submitted by Mike Shaffer
    '***********************************************
Public Sub SetDBNameCrystal(Report1 as CrystalReport, dbName as String,
➥ Optional dbPass as String)
    '
  ':::::::::::::::::::::::::::::::::::::::::::::::::::::::::::::::::::::::::::::'
  ':::                                                                    :::'
  ':::     Passed a Crystal Report control, will set all database         :::'
  ':::     references (including subreports) to 'dbName'. If a password    :::'
  ':::     is included, it will also set the password property.           :::'
  ':::                                                                    :::'
  ':::::::::::::::::::::::::::::::::::::::::::::::::::::::::::::::::::::::::::::'
    '
    Dim intReportCt as Integer
    Dim intCount as integer
    Dim strRepName as string
    '
    ' Determine how many subreports there are
```

```
    intReportCt = Report1.GetNSubreports
    '
    ' If there are any, set them all to dbName/dbPass
    If intReportCt > 0 Then
        For intCount = 0 To (intReportCt - 1)
            '
            ' Get the subreport name
            strRepName = Report1.GetNthSubreportName(intCount)
            '
            ' Notify Crystal which subreport we want to change
            Report1.SubreportToChange = strRepName
            Report1.DataFiles(0) = dbName
            'Set the password if it was included
            If not IsMissing(dbPass) then
                Report1.password = dbPass
            End If
        Next
    End If
    '
    ' Now we'll set the 'main' database/password
    Report1.SubreportToChange = ""
    Report1.DataFiles(0) = dbName
    If not IsMIssing(dbPass) then
        Report1.password = dbPass
    End If
    '
End Sub
```

Analysis

This function is useful for setting the database references for a Crystal Reports 6 (or higher) template, especially given the new functionality of subreports. Notice the use of the new methods `GetNSubReports` and `GetNthSubreportName`. The first returns a count of subreports contained within the Crystal Reports template, and the second is used to obtain the name of each of them. After the name of a subreport is known, the routine sets the database name (and optionally the password).

1.8   SELECT ALL TEXT IN A TEXT BOX

by Mike Shaffer

Description

The `TextSelected` routine provides a quick and easy way to select all text within a text box. This code should be placed in the `GetFocus` routine for all text box controls. The routine simply highlights (selects) all text within the text box to facilitate easy editing of the data.

Syntax

```
TextSelected
```

Code Listing

```
'***********************************************
'* Submitted by Mike Shaffer
'***********************************************
Public Sub TextSelected()
 ':::::::::::::::::::::::::::::::::::::::::::::::::::::::::::::::::::::::::::::'
 ':::                                                                   :::'
 ':::    Selects all of the text in the current textbox                 :::'
 ':::    (call from the textbox GetFocus event)                         :::'
 ':::                                                                   :::'
 ':::::::::::::::::::::::::::::::::::::::::::::::::::::::::::::::::::::::::::::'
   '
   Dim i As Integer
   Dim oTextBox As TextBox
   '
   If TypeOf Screen.ActiveControl Is TextBox Then
      Set oTextBox = Screen.ActiveControl
      i = Len(oTextBox.Text)
      oTextBox.SelStart = 0
      oTextBox.SelLength = i
   End If
   '
End Sub
```

Analysis

This routine can enhance the user interface of your application when used consistently. The `ActiveControl` property returns the control that currently has the focus and enables this routine to be relatively generic. Notice that this same technique could be used to promote consistency in other control types; for example, auto drop-down of all combo boxes when they receive focus.

1.9   SET TAB STOPS IN A LIST BOX

by Mike Shaffer

Description

The `SetTabStops` routine sets up tab stops within a list box, enabling proper alignment of tabular data using the `TAB` character regardless of the font being used. (For example, proportionally spaced fonts, such as Arial, will create words that are a different overall width than monospaced fonts, such as Courier.) This routine forces absolute tab stops based on a measurement called *dialog base units*. Dialog base units repre-sent an average character width for the currently assigned list box font. Do not confuse this with the .Columns property of the list box, which snakes information in columns over which you have little or no control.

Syntax

```
SetTabStops listbox, intTabStops, lngTabs()
```

Part	Description
listbox	Required. The list box for which tabs will be set.
intTabStops	Required. An integer that defines how many tab stops are to be set.
lngTabs()	Required. An array of values that define where each tab stop is set.

Code Listing

```
'**********************************************
'* Submitted by Mike Shaffer
'**********************************************
Private Declare Function SendMessage Lib "USER32" Alias "SendMessageA"
➥ (ByVal hWnd As Long, _
ByVal wMsg As Long, ByVal wParam As Long, lParam As Long) As Long
Private Declare Function GetDialogBaseUnits Lib "USER32" () As Long
Const LB_SETTABSTOPS = &H192

Sub SetTabStops(lListWindowHandle As ListBox, iNoTabStops As Integer,
➥ lTabPositions() As Long)
    '
    Dim iIndex As Integer          '   Index into array of tab stops
    Dim lDialogBaseUnits As Long   '   Dialog base units
        '
    Dim iDialogUnitsX As Integer   '   Horizontal dialog base units
    '
    '    Obtain the dialog base units
    '
    lDialogBaseUnits = GetDialogBaseUnits()
    iDialogUnitsX = (lDialogBaseUnits And &HFFFF&) \ 4
    '
    '    Calculate the "required" tab positions
    '

    ReDim lTabPos(0 To iNoTabStops - 1) As Long

    For iIndex = 0 To iNoTabStops - 1
        lTabPos(iIndex) = lTabPositions(iIndex) * iDialogUnitsX * 2
    Next iIndex
    '
    '    Set the required tab positions in the list box,
```

```
'     by calling the "SendMessage" api and passing the
'     handle of the listbox and details of the number of
'     tabs and their positions.
'
Call SendMessage(lListWindowHandle.hWnd, LB_SETTABSTOPS, CLng(iNoTabStops),
➥ lTabPos(0))
'
End Sub
```

Analysis

This routine helps align tabular data within a list box.

1.10   SMART (INCREMENTAL) COMBO BOX DATA ENTRY

by Mike Shaffer

Description

The `IncrLookup` routine performs smart-key lookup for combo boxes. As the user types characters into the text area of a combo box, the list is searched for matching entries. As they are found, the entry appears in the text area. As soon as a non-matching character is encountered (that is, the user has typed a character that matches nothing in the list) the remainder of the "guess" is erased. This routine goes a long way toward increasing the user friendliness of your application, and should be used consistently.

To use this routine, simply include the following line in the `KeyPress` event for a combo box:

```
IncrLookup CKeyAscii
```

Syntax

```
IncrLookup KeyAscii
```

Part	Description
KeyAscii	Required. This is the value of the key press as returned by the combo box **KeyPress** event.

Code Listing

```
'**********************************************
'* Submitted by Mike Shaffer
'**********************************************
Declare Function SendMessage Lib "USER32" Alias "SendMessageA"
➥ (ByVal hWnd As Long, _
```

```
ByVal wMsg As Long, ByVal wParam As Long, lParam As Any) As Long
Const CB_ERR = -1
Const CB_FINDSTRING = &H14C


Sub IncrLookup(ky As Integer)
    '
    ':::::::::::::::::::::::::::::::::::::::::::::::::::::::::::::::::::::::'
    ':::                                                            :::'
    ':::     Performs incremental matching during ComboBox keyin    :::'
    ':::                                                            :::'
    ':::     To use, place this line in the combo box KeyPress event: :::'
    ':::                                                            :::'
    ':::            IncrLookup {comboname}, KeyAscii                :::'
    ':::                                                            :::'
    ':::::::::::::::::::::::::::::::::::::::::::::::::::::::::::::::::::::::'
    ':::                                                            :::'
    ':::  Passed:                                                   :::'
    ':::                                                            :::'
    ':::      ky          :=       the ascii keystroke value        :::'
    ':::                                                            :::'
    ':::::::::::::::::::::::::::::::::::::::::::::::::::::::::::::::::::::::'
    '
    Dim s As String, l As Long
    Dim c as ComboBox
    '
    If TypeOf Screen.ActiveControl is ComboBox then
        Set c = Screen.ActiveControl
        If c.Style < 2 then
            ' Build the search string
            s = Left$(c.Text, c.SelStart) & Chr$(ky)
            '
            ' Now search the combobox for the string
            l = SendMessage((c.hWnd), CB_FINDSTRING, -1, ByVal s)
            '
            ' Was the string found in the list?
            If l <> CB_ERR Then
                ' Yes, so we set the ListIndex and highlight the text
                With c
                    .ListIndex = l
                    .Text = .list(l)
                    .SelStart = Len(s)
                    .SelLength = Len(.Text)
                End With
                ky = 0
            End If
            '
        End If
    End If
End Sub
```

1.11   FIND A STRING IN A TEXT BOX

by Fredrik Bodin

Description

This is a routine that searches a text box for a string and highlights it. It works by the `InStr` command, which returns the location of the string. Then the routine makes sure the text box is in focus, moves the cursor to the position, and highlights the string.

Wildcards are not accepted, but the routine can easily be modified for accepting them using the `Like` command. If the routine can't find the string, an error message appears. This routine qualifies as a search engine in a text editor as an example.

Syntax

FindString(*Control, FindStr, StartPos*)

Part	Description
Control	Required. Specifies the name of the text box you want to search.
FindStr	Required. Specifies the string you are looking for.
StartPos	Optional. Specifies the start position in the text box. Must be larger than 0, integers only. If no position is given, it will automatically start at the beginning of the text box (for example, position=1).

Code Listing

```
Private Sub FindString (Control as Control, FindStr as String ,
➥ Optional StartPos As Integer = 1 )
Dim a as integer
a = InStr(StartPos, LCase$(Control.Text), LCase$(FindStr))
If a = 0 Then
    MsgBox "Could not find string!", 0, "Error"
        Exit Sub
Else
    Control.SetFocus
    Control.SelStart = a - 1
    Control.SelLength = Len(FindStr)
End If
End Sub
```

Analysis

This routine works by using the `InStr` command, which searches the text box, returns a location in the text box, and moves the cursor to that position. Then it highlights the string by using the `SelLength` property.

```
Control.SetFocus
Control.SelStart = a - 1
Control.SelLength = Len(FindStr)
```

`Control` can be a text box, rich text box, and other types of text boxes. You use this routine according to the following syntax:

```
Private Sub FindString (Control as Control, FindStr as String ,
➥ Optional StartPos As Integer = 1
```

This means that an example could look like this:

```
Call FindString(txtMyTextbox, "Find this")
```

What happens is that the variable `Control` is assigned `txtMyTextbox`. In other words, it tells the routine in what text box to search.

Then, you can use the `SetFocus` command by putting the `Control` variable in front of it. In this case, it means

```
Control.SetFocus    -->    txtMyTextbox.SetFocus
```

1.12   UNDO A TEXT BOX ACTION

by David J. Berube

Description

The `UndoTextBox` routine is simple; call it, and it will undo the last action in a text box. If there is no action to undo, the call does nothing.

Syntax

```
UndoTextBox
```

Code Listing

```
'Declare our API functions

Declare Function SendMessage Lib "user32" Alias "SendMessageA"
➥(ByVal hwnd As Long, ByVal wMsg As Long, ByVal wParam As Long,
➥ lParam As Any) As Long
```

```
'The Hwnd parameter refers to the Window Handle(hWnd) of the target window.
'The wMsg parameter refers to the message to be passed to the target window's
➥ queue.
'The wParam(word param) and lParam(long param) are the message-specific
➥ arguments of
'sendmessage. Depending on what you pass as wMsg, they can mean different
➥ things.



'Declare our constants
Public Const EM_UNDO = &HC7
'EM is Edit Message.
'EM_UNDO is a symbolic constant meaning "undo last action in textbox".

Sub UndoTextBox(hWnd as long)
    Sendmessage hWnd, EM_UNDO, 0 , 0
End Sub
```

Analysis

The `SendMessage` API call places the `EM_UNDO` message in the text box's queue. The `EM_UNDO` message causes the text box to undo its last action.

The `EM_UNDO` message is one of the many `EM_` messages available to VB programmers. (`EM`, by the way, means Edit Message.) Here is a partial list:

```
Public Const EM_CANUNDO = &HC6
```

This message checks whether an action is "in the buffer"; that is, whether the user has changed anything since the last undo (if there was one.)

```
Public Const EM_EMPTYUNDOBUFFER = &HCD
```

Sending this message causes Windows to forget any changes the user has made to the text box.

```
Public Const EM_GETFIRSTVISIBLELINE = &HCE
```

This message retrieves the first available line in a text box.

```
Public Const EM_GETLINE = &HC4
```

This message gets the current line in a text box.

```
Public Const EM_GETLINECOUNT = &HBA
Public Const EM_GETMODIFY = &HB8
Public Const EM_GETPASSWORDCHAR = &HD2
```

This message is used to retrieve the current "password character"; that is, the character displayed instead of the text. For example, ***** instead of the user's password.

```
Public Const EM_SETPASSWORDCHAR = &HCC
```

This message retrieves the current password character.

```
Public Const EM_SETREADONLY = &HCF
```

This message takes a parameter indicating whether it should be possible to change the text box.

1.13 PASSING CONTROLS AND CONTROL ARRAYS TO PROCEDURES

by Kamal A. Mehdi

Description

Visual Basic controls and control arrays can be passed as arguments to procedures to perform various tasks on them. This enables you to write a single generic procedure or function to access and manipulate the different properties or methods of the controls in the entire project.

The properties of the control or the control array elements passed to the procedure or function can both be read and set from within the procedure or function. Elements of control arrays can have their properties read or set for each array element separately.

The sample code listing demonstrates the method by manipulating some of the properties of the form's controls that are passed to a single generic procedure. The procedure retrieves the current property setting for some of the control's properties and displays them on the control, while some other properties are changed from within the procedure and are displayed.

Syntax

```
DoSomethingOn(MyObj)
```

Part	Description
MyObj	Required. An object reference that evaluates to a Visual Basic control or control array. The name of the control or the control array is used.

Modules and Controls Required

You will need the following modules and controls to build the sample project:

Module/Control	Description
Module1	Standard Visual Basic module (.BAS)
Form1	Standard non-MDI Visual Basic form (.FRM) with controls as shown below
Text1()	Control array of three text boxes
Label1()	Control array of three label controls
Check1()	Control array of three check boxes

Place the controls on Form1 and set all the controls' Width property to approximately 5500.

Note

You can create control arrays by inserting one control on the form and copying and pasting the control on the form using either the right mouse button or the Edit menu. When you paste the control on the form, Visual Basic will prompt you whether to create a control array or not; choose Yes.

Code Listing

```
        'Form1 code
Private Sub Form_Click()

     'Pass the Text1() control array to the procedure
     Call DoSomethingOn(Text1())

     'Pass the Label1() control array to the procedure
     Call DoSomethingOn(Label1())

     'Pass the Check1() control array to the procedure
     Call DoSomethingOn(Check1())

End Sub


     'Module1 code
Sub DoSomethingOn(MyObj As Object)

     'You might replace the following code with your own code to
     'manipulate your actual controls in your project

     'The 'On Error Resume Next' is required as not all properties
     'that will be accessed might actually be available for the object
     On Error Resume Next

     'Loop through all control-array elements of the passed object
     'and retrieve or set the values of selected properties
     For Each Control In MyObj

          'Randomly set the foreground color of the control
          Control.ForeColor = Rnd * 100000

          'Retrieve the Name, Index, and ForeColor values of the control
          'and show them to its Text (or Caption) property
          Control.Text = "Hello, " & "my name is " & Control.Name & ",
          ➥ my index is " & Control.Index & ", and my ForeColor
          ➥ is &H" & Hex(Control.ForeColor)
```

```
        Control.Caption = "Hello, " & "my name is " & Control.Name & ",
        ➡ my index is " & Control.Index & ", and my ForeColor
        ➡ is &&H" & Hex(Control.ForeColor)

        'Randomly set the value of the object (if it is a check box)
        'between 0 and 2
        Control.Value = Int((2 - 0 + 1) * Rnd + 0)

        'Toggle the visible property of the control array element if its
        ➡ Index is 2
        If Control.Index = 2 Then Control.Visible = Not (Control.Visible)
    Next

End Sub
```

Enter the preceding code in the appropriate form or module as indicated. Run the project and click the form. Every element of each control array will display its Name, Index, and its ForeColor property values in its caption. Click the form several times and notice how each control will randomly change its ForeColor property and will show its current color value. The Check1() check box elements will also change their Value property randomly. In addition, array elements of all controls having their Index property value equal to 2 will have their Visible property toggled (will show or hide) each time the form is clicked.

Analysis

Passing Visual Basic controls and control arrays to procedures is notably useful when a single generic code segment is required to perform some operations on different controls rather than writing individual code for each control. This was easily shown by using an argument of Object data type in the procedure to receive the control or the control array passed to the procedure.

From within the called procedure, the control received by the argument is manipulated in code using the Visual Basic generic Control object, which represents the class name of all Visual Basic internal controls. This is notably useful because you do not need to reference the control or the control array by its name, which makes the code truly generic.

A very significant feature of the described method is that the generic procedure to which the controls or control arrays are passed can be made public and placed in a module other than the one in which the controls are located. As shown in the code listing, the called procedure is located in a standard .BAS module while the controls are on a form. This is notably useful because it enables you to pass any control in your project to the procedure regardless of where the control is located. This means that you can call the procedure from any of your project's forms and send it the controls you like. You can even call the procedure from one form while specifying the name of a control or a control array located on another form for the procedure argument.

The sample project CTRLARAY.VBP on the CD-ROM that accompanies this book demonstrates the application of the described method.

1.14   ADDING A HELP BUTTON TO AN INPUT BOX

by Kamal A. Mehdi

Description

The Visual Basic `InputBox` function enables you to add an additional button to the input box dialog for providing help to the user. This is actually useful when you want to tell the user what text he should enter in the specific input box. For example, you might want to inform the user that he should enter only upper-case characters or numbers, or that special characters are not allowed in the input box.

If the help button is added to the input box dialog, a help file path, filename, and a specific context ID in that help file must be provided. The help context ID is a number associated with a specific topic inside the help file. Each topic in the help file has a unique context ID. The help context ID will show the specific help topic to be displayed when the user clicks the Help button or presses the F1 key.

The sample code shows how this can be done using the `InputBox` function.

Syntax

```
Contents = InputBox(Prompt, Title, Default, Xpos, Ypos,
➥HelpFileName, Context ID)
```

Part	*Description*
`Contents`	Required. A string expression that returns the contents of the input box.
`Prompt`	Required. A string expression that will be displayed as a message in the input box dialog.
`Title`	Optional. A string expression that will be displayed in the title bar of the dialog box.
`Default`	Optional. A string expression displayed in the text box as the default text.
`Xpos`	Optional. A numeric expression that specifies the horizontal position of the input box dialog.
`Ypos`	Optional. A numeric expression that specifies the vertical position of the input box dialog.
`HelpFileName`	Optional. A string expression that specifies the help file path and name to use to provide context-sensitive help for the dialog box.
`Context ID`	Optional. A numeric expression that refers to the specific help context ID of the required help topic.

For more details on these function arguments, refer to the Visual Basic help topic for the `InputBox` function.

Code Listing

```
'Form1 code
Private Sub Form_Load()

    'Center for on screen
    Me.Left = (Screen.Width - Me.Width) / 2
    Me.Top = (Screen.Height - Me.Height) / 2

End Sub

Private Sub Form_Click()

    'Declare variables
    Dim HelpFileName As String
    Dim Prompt As String
    Dim Title As String
    Dim DefaultText As String
    Dim ContextID As Integer

    'Assign the help file path/name to the 'demo.hlp' sample file
    'located in the project directory
    HelpFileName = App.Path & "\Demo.hlp"

    'Assign Prompt, Title, and DefaultText to the input box
    Prompt = "Demo"
    Title = "Input Box with help button demo"
    DefaultText = "Click Help or press F1 to view the help topic with context
    ➥ ID=10"
    ContextID = 10

    'Show the input box with help button
    X = InputBox(Prompt, Title, DefaultText, , , HelpFileName, ContextID)

End Sub
```

Enter the code in your `Form_Load` and `Form_Click` events as indicated and run the project. When you click on the form, an input box will be displayed with a Help command button appended to the normal OK and Cancel buttons that appear on the input box dialog. Click the Help command button or press F1 to show the help topic for the specific input box dialog.

The help file DEMO.HLP included with the project will open and the help topic with context ID 10 specified in the `InputBox` function will be displayed.

Analysis

Providing help with the Visual Basic `InputBox` function is fairly simple. You just need to specify the help file path and name and point to the specific help context ID in that help file. An error will be shown in a message box if the specified context ID does not exist in the help file.

Similarly, you can append a Help button to the Visual Basic message box when you call the MsgBox function to provide context-sensitive help. However, the arguments for the MsgBox function are different from those used in the InputBox function. You can find details on the MsgBox arguments in the Visual Basic MsgBox help topic.

The sample project INBOXHLP.VBP on the CD-ROM that accompanies this book demonstrates how to provide context-sensitive help with the InputBox function. A sample help file DEMO.HLP is also provided.

1.15   FIND ITEM DATA IN A COMBOBOX

by Martin Cordova

Description

This subroutine locates an item in a combo box given the ItemData value. If the ItemData exists in the combo box, that item will be selected using the ListIndex property of the combo box; otherwise the ListIndex property will not be affected.

The ItemData property in a combo box is used to store a Long value related to an item in the combo box. For example, you can add customer names and the corresponding customer IDs to a combo box by using the ItemData property. This is common practice in database applications. In this scenario, you might need to locate an item inside a combo box using the customer ID instead of the customer name. This procedure solves this problem with a single procedure call.

When you change the ListIndex property, the combo box visually reflects the change by selecting (highlighting) the corresponding item in the list. Therefore, if the value passed is not found, the combo box's current selected item (if any) will remain unaffected. If the combo box contains items with duplicated ItemData values, then only the first item found will be selected and the procedure will immediatly return to the caller. Please note that changing the ListIndex property also triggers a Click event for the combo box.

Syntax

MyComboBox, MyItemDataValue

Parameter	Description
MyComboBox	A reference to a combo box control
MyItemData	A variable of type Long that represents the ItemData value to find

Code Listing

```
Public Sub ComboFindItemData(c As ComboBox, KeyValue As Long)

    Dim i As Long

    On Error GoTo ErrorHandler

    '---search for every ItemData in the control
    For i = 0 To c.ListCount - 1
        If c.ItemData(i) = KeyValue Then
            '---found, now select this item and leave
            c.ListIndex = i
            Exit For
        End If
    Next i

    Exit Sub

ErrorHandler:

    Err.Description = "ComboFindItemData: " & Err.Description
    Err.Raise Err.Number

End Sub
```

Analysis

This routine scans the ComboBox internal array of ItemData values and compares each of these values with the KeyValue passed to the routine. If there is a match the current item is selected and the routine exits.

Note that if KeyValue is not found, the current ListIndex property will remain unchanged, and if it is found, the ListIndex property will be changed to highlight the new selected item in the combo box. This will trigger a Click event for the combo box.

This routine can be very useful in database applications that don't rely on the Visual Basic data control to perform data binding between recordset data and visual controls.

Chances are this procedure won't produce a trappable error, but to have error handling code in place is good programming practice that will protect the software from any code additions made to this procedure in the future. If an error occurs (no matter the cause), the error handler will be already there to catch it.

1.16   FIND TEXT IN A COMBOBOX

by Martin Cordova

Description

This subroutine locates an item in a combo box given a string value. If an item displayed in the combo box matches this string, then that item will be selected using the `ListIndex` property of the combo box; otherwise, the `ListIndex` property will not be affected.

By changing the `ListIndex` property, the combo box visually reflects the change by selecting (highlighting) the corresponding item in the list. Therefore, if the value passed is not found, the combo box's current selected item (if any) will remain unaffected. If the combo box contains duplicated items, then only the first item found will be selected and the procedure will immediatly return to the caller. Please note that changing the `ListIndex` property also triggers a `Click` event for the combo box.

Note that the comparison is case-sensitive, but it can be easily transformed into case-insensitive by using the internal Visual Basic `LCase()` function. For example:

```
If LCase(c.List(i)) = LCase(DisplayValue) Then...
```

Syntax

```
ComboFindByText MyComboBox, MyTextValue
```

Parameter	Description
MyComboBox	A reference to a combo box control
MyTextValue	A variable of type `String` that represents the displayed value to search for in the combo box

Code Listing

```
Public Sub ComboFindByText(c As Control, DisplayValue As String)

    Dim i As Long

    On Error GoTo ErrorHandler

    '---search for every Item in the control and compare
    For i = 0 To c.ListCount - 1
        If c.List(i) = DisplayValue Then
            '---found, now select this item and leave
            c.ListIndex = i
            Exit For
        End If
```

```
    Next i

    Exit Sub

ErrorHandler:

    Err.Description = "ComboFindByText: " & Err.Description
    Err.Raise Err.Number

End Sub
```

Analysis

This routine scans the combo box and compares each item with the `DisplayValue` passed to the routine. If there is a match, the current item is selected and the routine exits.

This procedure could also work for the ListBox control, but this version is specific to ComboBox in order to make it more efficient and robust when referencing control properties. Otherwise, the `c` parameter should be declared `As Control`, losing all the strong type checking benefits.

Chances are that this procedure won't produce a trappable error, but having error handling code in place is a good programming practice that will protect the software from any code additions made to this procedure in the future. If an error occurs (no matter the cause), the error handler will be already there to catch it.

Chapter 2

INCREASED FORM FUNCTIONALITY

In this chapter are several ways to use forms and get the most out of them. These tricks can help you present your application better through some handy form functions.

2.1   ANIMATED TEXT

by Mario Gentile

Description

This routine animates text on a screen to create a visual impact. You can add a bit of flair to your words by having them horizontally scroll on the screen.

To make a simple animated text routine, place on a form a label named Label1 and give it a width of 3045. Set the AutoSize and WordWrap properties to True. Place a command button called Command1 on the form, and place a timer control named Timer1 with the Enabled property set to False and the Interval set to 200.

Code Listing

```
'********************************
'Submitted by Mario Gentile
'********************************

    'You will need to declare these variables in "General Declarations".
    Dim Start As Integer
    Dim Scroll As String

Private Sub Command1_Click ()
    'This starts the timer event that will send the text to the label on
    ➡ your form.
    Start = 0 'Begining point.
```

```
        Timer1.Enabled = True 'Enable the timer.
        Scroll = "This is a test of the Animated Sentence." 'Text to be sent
    ➥ to your form.
End Sub

Private Sub Timer1_Timer ()
    Dim Sentence As String
        Start = Start + 1      'For every interval add 1
              If Start > Len(Scroll) Then 'Stop timer at end of text
              Timer1.Enabled = False
              End If
        Sentence = Sentence + Mid(Scroll, Start, 1) 'Add one character per
    ➥ interval.
              Label1.Caption = Label1.Caption + Sentence 'Display text
End Sub
```

Analysis

When you click the command button the timer is enabled, adding one character to the sentence variable for each interval of the event. The sentence is then sent to a label on the form, creating an animated effect. You may change the output by changing the string value of the scroll variable located in the command1 click event. You probably see the many ways you can augment this code, such as giving the user an input box to set the scroll variable. Adjust the interval of the timer event to animate the text faster or slower.

This code will work without the Timer control by using a loop statement. Note that when you use a loop statement the scroll speed will vary depending on the speed of your processor, whereas the use of the Timer control enables the user to adjust the speed options. Experiment with different settings to get the results you want. If you must have more sophisticated effects you might consider using a third-party ActiveX control such as Macromedia Flash.

2.2   GET OR SET A FORM LOCATION

VB 5

by Lenard Dean with Brian Shea

Description

The GET and SET form location functions enable you to get and set the coordinates of the form's last position in the Registry. They require the ParseStr function, which can be found in the string manipulation section, to work properly.

You should place the GET function in Form_Load or Form_Activate, and place the SET function in the Form_Deactivate, Form_QueryUnload, or Form_Unload event. This is done so that when you load the form it will remember where it was the last time it was onscreen. This is a nice touch for the user, who will appreciate the extra effort.

The function returns the form coordinates as Left,Top,Width,Height. (If you don't need the returned values, just call the function as you would a subroutine.)

Syntax

```
strCoordinateStr = FormCoords(frmWork As Form, ByVal strMode As String,
➥ Optional ByVal strSection As String) As String
```

Part	Description
strCoordinateStr	Optional. The returned string value for the last coordinates of the form. Returned in the form shown above.
frmWork	Required. The form to work on.
strMode	Required. GET or SET (or SAVE) form coordinates. Only GET is handled explicitly, so the other word can be anything you choose.
strSection	Optional. The section in the Registry to get or save settings. Defaults to Startup if not specified.

Code Listing

```
Public Function FormCoords(frmWork As Form, ByVal strMode As String, Optional
➥ ByVal strSection As String) As String

 On Error Resume Next

  strMode = UCase(strMode)
  If Len(strSection) = 0 Then strSection = "Startup"

  With frmWork
    If strMode = "GET" Then
      FormCoords = GetSetting(App.EXEName, strSection, .Name)
      If Len(FormCoords) Then
        .Left = ParseStr(FormCoords, 1, ",")
        .Top = ParseStr(FormCoords, 2, ",")
        '' Only set width and height if form is resizeable.
        If .BorderStyle = 2 Then
          .Width = ParseStr(FormCoords, 3, ",")
          .Height = ParseStr(FormCoords, 4, ",")
        End If
      End If
    Else
      SaveSetting App.EXEName, strSection, .Name, .Left & "," & .Top & "," &
      ➥ .Width & "," & .Height
    End If
  End With

End Function
```

Analysis

The GET and SET form location functions perform a simple task, but it really is a nice touch that the end user can appreciate. When your application starts up, the forms will be where the user left them last. They also will stay the same size if the form is resizable.

When the function starts, it sets the error mode and then converts the strMode parameter to uppercase for later handling. Here it also determines whether the strSection parameter was passed and sets that value if it was left blank.

Next the GET functionality is tested for and handled. This part takes advantage of the GetSetting VB call to get the Registry setting from the previous operation. If this is the first time, the function continues without noticeable error. The ParseStr function (from the string manipulation section) is then used to get the individual values from the data returned. If the form is resizable, the bottom and right properties are set to preserve the form size.

The last part of the function simply sets the Registry value for the form location by collecting the Left, Top, Width, and Height properties and sending them to the SaveSetting VB call. These setting will be saved to the section specified by the strSection parameter or to Startup.

Note

The actual Registry location of this data is HKEY_CURRENT_USER\Software\VB and VBA Program Settings. A key will be created under that hive for the application name, with a subkey named for the strSection value or the value for Startup. Each form name can have a separate value in this key, which is tracked by form name.

2.3   UNLOAD ALL FORMS

by Mike Shaffer

Description

The UnloadAllForms routine provides a quick way to ensure that all forms within an application which is about to close are unloaded and set to nothing. If you are calling this routine from within Form_Unload of the main form of your application, specify Me.Name as the parameter. This prevents the UnloadAllForms routine from trying to unload a form that is already in the process of unloading itself. Otherwise, pass " " (or nothing because the parameter is optional) to the routine.

Syntax

```
UnloadAllForms strFormName
```

Part	Description
StrFormName	Required. The form name not to unload.

Code Listing

```
'**********************************************
'* Submitted by Mike Shaffer
'**********************************************
Public Sub UnloadAllForms(Optional sFormName As String = "")
 '
 ':::::::::::::::::::::::::::::::::::::::::::::::::::::::::::::::::::::::::'
 ':::                                                               :::'
 ':::     This code unloads all forms in a program prior to exiting.  :::'
 ':::     It's necessary because VB will not do it for us, and        :::'
 ':::     we'll end up chewing mucho resources...                     :::'
 ':::                                                               :::'
 ':::::::::::::::::::::::::::::::::::::::::::::::::::::::::::::::::::::::::'
 ':::                                                               :::'
 ':::     Use:                                                       :::'
 ':::                                                               :::'
 ':::         If calling from Form_Unload of the MAIN form, use:      :::'
 ':::                                                               :::'
 ':::                     UnloadAllForms Me.Name                      :::'
 ':::                                                               :::'
 ':::                                                               :::'
 ':::         If calling from another SUB, use:                       :::'
 ':::                                                               :::'
 ':::                     UnloadAllForms ""                           :::'
 ':::                                                               :::'
 ':::::::::::::::::::::::::::::::::::::::::::::::::::::::::::::::::::::::::'
     '
    Dim Form As Form
     '
    For Each Form In Forms
       If Form.Name <> sFormName Then
          Unload Form
          Set Form = Nothing
       End If
    Next Form
     '
End Sub
```

Analysis

This routine can ensure proper program exit and unloading when used properly. It will help prevent "rogue" forms and objects from staying in memory even after your application ends. Often people forget to unload a form, thinking perhaps that using the .Hide method (or setting the .Visible property to False) is enough to get rid of a form. Others might remember to unload the form but might not realize that forgetting to set the form to nothing does not allow Windows to release the resources. This routine helps ease the task by ensuring that both tasks occur properly.

2.4   SET A TITLE IN THE TASKBAR

by Mike Shaffer

Description

The SetTitle function enables you to have forms without a caption or control box while still allowing a title in the taskbar. This is especially useful for designer forms that have custom minimize or other buttons. For example, your application might consist of a form with a custom shape that you have designed to look like a television remote control. In addition to all the neat buttons and gizmos you created on the form itself, you realize that you're going to have to set the .Caption property of the form to be blank and disable the control box and minimize/maximize buttons. However, even though you have no caption, perhaps you still want your form to show up in the taskbar as something other than a blank button (because you have no caption). This routine enables you to have a title in the taskbar (and task list) without having a visible caption on your form.

To use this routine, simply include the code line (generally in the Form_Load() subroutine) to set the title.

Syntax

```
SetTitle frm, strTitle$
```

Part	Description
frm	Can be Me or any other form name
strTitle$	The title you want to define for the form

```
SetTitle frm, Title$
```

Part	Description
frm	Required. The form for which the title is to be set.
Title$	Required. The string value for the title.

Code Listing

```
'************************************************
'* Submitted by Mike Shaffer
'************************************************
Private Declare Function SetWindowText Lib "USER32" Alias "SetWindowTextA"
➥ (ByVal hWnd As Long,_
ByVal lpString As String) As Long

Private Function SetTitle(f As Form, st As String) As Long
  '
  ':::::::::::::::::::::::::::::::::::::::::::::::::::::::::::::::::::::::::::'
  ':::                                                               :::'
  ':::    Sets the title for the taskbar (must have the ShowInTaskbar :::'
  ':::    property set to 'true').                                    :::'
  ':::                                                               :::'
  ':::::::::::::::::::::::::::::::::::::::::::::::::::::::::::::::::::::::::::'
  ':::                                                               :::'
  ':::  Passed:                                                      :::'
  ':::                                                               :::'
  ':::     f          :=     The form to set the title for           :::'
  ':::     st         :=     The title (string) to set in taskbar    :::'
  ':::                                                               :::'
  ':::::::::::::::::::::::::::::::::::::::::::::::::::::::::::::::::::::::::::'
  '
SetTitle = SetWindowText(f.hWnd, st)
  '
End Sub
```

Analysis

This routine solves the sticky problem of showing a taskbar caption for a form when the form itself does not have a caption. It can be especially useful for designer forms that have their own graphical minimize/maximize buttons, title bars, and so on. Interestingly, the `SetWindowText` API call can also be used to set the `.Title` and `.Caption` property of Visual Basic controls.

2.5 SAVE A FORM'S POSITION

by Mike Shaffer

Description

The `FormPosSave` routine saves the position of the passed form in the System Registry. The companion routine `FormPosRestore` restores that form to the saved position.

These routines are used to keep track of where users prefer to have their forms located. Saving and restoring user-preferred form locations can make your program more user friendly. To use this routine, make sure that each form within your system has a unique .Tag property. Note that the form's top and left positions are saved, as well as the form's width and height.

Typical usage might occur in the FORM_UNLOAD event and would look like this:

```
FormPosSave Me
```

Syntax

```
FormPosSave form
```

Part	Description
form	Required. A form for which you want to save position information.

Code Listing

```
'********************************************
'* Submitted by Mike Shaffer
'********************************************
Sub FormPosSave(f As Form)
  '
  '
  Dim buf As String
  '
  buf = Trim$(Str$(f.Left)) & "," & Trim$(Str$(f.Top)) & "," &
➥ Trim$(Str$(f.Width)) & "," & Trim$(Str$(f.Height))
  '
  SaveSetting App.EXEName, "FormPosition", f.Tag, buf
  '
End Sub
```

Analysis

This routine is useful to enhance the user friendliness of your application. Use it in conjunction with FormPosRestore. It works by storing a Registry entry under a key defined by the form's .Tag property. The Registry entry is a string that looks like this:

lll,ttt,www,hhh

where *lll* is the form's .Left property, *ttt* is the .Top property, *www* is the .Width property, and *hhh* is the .Height property.

2.6   RESTORE A FORM'S POSITION

by Mike Shaffer

Description

The `FormPosRestore` routine restores the position of the passed form that had previously been saved (in the System Registry) using the companion routine `FormPosSave`. (See the description of `FormPosSave`.)

Note that `FormPosRestore` will attempt to restore a form's top and left positions and the form's width and height. If the form's top or left positions are located outside the visible screen, or if no position has yet been stored, the routine will attempt to center the form within the physical screen boundaries. Note that as with the companion `FormPosSave` routine, each form must have a valid and unique `.Tag` property value.

Typical usage might occur in the `FORM_LOAD` event, and would look like this:

```
FormPosRestore Me
```

Syntax

```
FormPosRestore form
```

Part	Description
form	Required. This is a form for which you want to restore position information.

Code Listing

```
'*********************************************
'* Submitted by Mike Shaffer
'*********************************************
Sub FormPosRestore(f As Form)
    '
    Dim buf As String
    Dim x1 As Long, y1 As Long, X2 As Long, Y2 As Long
    Dim pos As Integer
    '
    buf = GetSetting(App.EXEName, "FormPosition", f.Tag, "")
    '
    ' if there is no info for this form, simply center it
    If Len(Trim$(buf)) = 0 Then
        f.Move (Screen.Width - f.Width) \ 2, (Screen.Height - f.Height) \ 2
```

```
    Else
        pos = InStr(buf, ",")
        x1 = CLng(Left$(buf, pos - 1))
        buf = Mid$(buf, pos + 1)
        '
        pos = InStr(buf, ",")
        y1 = CLng(Left$(buf, pos - 1))
        buf = Mid$(buf, pos + 1)
        '
        pos = InStr(buf, ",")
        X2 = CLng(Left$(buf, pos - 1))
        Y2 = CLng(Mid$(buf, pos + 1))
        '
        ' If the form is past screen bounds, simply attempt to center it
        If x1 > Screen.Width Or y1 > Screen.Height Then
            f.Move (Screen.Width - f.Width) \ 2, (Screen.Height - f.Height) \ 2
        Else
            f.Move x1, y1, X2, Y2
        End If
    End If
End Sub
```

Analysis

This routine is useful to enhance the user friendliness of your application. It should be used in conjunction with `FormPosSave`. Note that if `FormPosRestore` is used with a form that has settings not previously saved with `FormPosSave`, this routine will simply attempt to center the form on the screen. Additionally, this routine checks to see whether the saved settings will place the form off the screen (for example, if someone saved a form position at the extreme right and bottom of the screen while in 1024×768 resolution, and then tried to restore after switching to 640×480). If the form would appear off screen, it will instead be centered. For information on how the form information is stored in the Registry, see the `FormPosSave` routine description.

2.7   CENTER A FORM ONSCREEN

by Fredrik Bodin

Description

This procedure centers a form onscreen no matter what the current screen resolution is. If the window is larger than the screen, the borders of the window will appear outside the screen. In addition, the window can be moved a specified amount of pixels in a vertical or horizontal direction.

Syntax

```
CenterForm FormName, deltaX, deltaY
```

Part	Description
FormName	Required. The name of the centered form.
deltaX	Optional. An integer that specifies the number of additional pixels that the form should be moved in the horizontal direction. Can be negative, which would mean the form is moved slightly to the left.
deltaY	Optional. An integer that specifies the number of additional pixels that the form should be moved in the vertical direction. Can be negative, which would mean the form is moved slightly upward.

Code Listing

```
Sub CenterForm(FormName As Form, Optional deltaX As Integer = 0,
➡ Optional deltaY as Integer = 0)
    FormName.Left = (Screen.Width - FormName.Width) / 2 + deltaX
    FormName.Top = (Screen.Height - FormName.Height) / 2 + deltaY
End Sub
```

Analysis

This routine is very simple. To express the calculation in another way, this is how it works:

```
FormName.Left = Screen.Width / 2 - FormName.Width / 2 + deltaX
```

The first division calculates the center of the screen, and then subtracts the local center of the form you want to center. Then it moves the form to that location and voilá—it's centered!

When you call upon this function, you might want to make it as easy as possible for you. Then you just type

```
Call CenterForm(Me)
```

Me tells the computer that the current form should be centered.

2.8 SET A FORM ON TOP

by David J. Berube

Description

The SetFormOnTop function sets the Always On Top flag of a form so that it constantly remains above all other windows. This is commonly used to create window applications such as clocks or similar programs. The infamous "eyes" program distributed on the Internet is such an application.

Using this function in your application is simple; just call with the argument a form to set on top.

Syntax

```
SetFormOnTop Me
```

Part	Description
Me	Required. A form expression that specifies the form to be set on top.

Code Listing

```
'Declare our API functions
Declare Function SetWindowPos Lib "user32" ( _
    ByVal hwnd As Long,  _
    ByVal hWndInsertAfter As Long, _
    ByVal x As Long, ByVal y As Long, _
    ByVal cx As Long, ByVal cy As Long, _
     ByVal wFlags As Long) As Long

'Declare our constants

'SWP stands for SetWindowPos

'SWP_NoSize tells SetWindowPos to ignore the cx and cy arguments
Private Const SWP_NOSIZE = &H1

'SWP_NoMove tells SetWindowPos to ignore the x and y arguments.
Private Const SWP_NOMOVE = &H2

'HWND_TOPMOST is passed to SetWindowPos to set the target window Always
➥ On Top.
Private Const HWND_TOPMOST = -1

'HWN_NOTOPMOST is passed to SetWindowPos to remove Always on Top
Private Const HWND_NOTOPMOST = -2

'Declare our variables

Public Sub SetFormOnTop(myForm as object)

    SetWindowPos myForm.hWnd,  HWND_TOPMOST, 0, 0, 0, 0, SWP_NOMOVE
    ➥ or SWP_NOSIZE

End sub
```

Analysis

This routine uses the `SetWindowPos` API in a fairly subtle way. The `SetWindowPost(SWP)` API is normally used to resize or move windows. However, the last two arguments, `SWP_NOMOVE` or `SWP_NOSIZE`, are special flags. They tell SWP to disregard the X,Y arguments and not move the window, nor should it size it.

The ability to set a form on top is a side effect. The second parameter of `SetWindowPos`, `hWndInsertAfter`, allows you to change the Z-order, or what windows are below the window and what windows are above. By setting the second parameter to `HWND_TOPMOST` you are, in essence, saying set this window to be above all windows.

In other words, you are telling Windows "Move this form to 0,0, set its width and height to zero, and set it on top. Oh, and by the way, don't move it or size it."

2.9 MOVE A WINDOW TO THE FOREGROUND

by David J. Berube

Description

The `SetForeground` routine will set a window handle to the foreground. The window handle can belong to your application or to another application. To use it, just say `SetForeground hWnd`. Or, if you prefer to use it for an internal window, just use `SetForeground myform.hWnd`.

A window handle, or `hWnd`, is something Windows uses to track windows. Each form that you create has its own `hWnd`. `hWnds` are similar to a name. If you have a form named myForm you refer to it (in VB) as `myForm`. Likewise, if you have a form with an `hWnd` of **9981**, Windows refers to it as 9981. Of course, you must use Windows names rather than VB names.

Syntax

```
SetForeground hWnd
```

Part	Description
hWnd	Required. A long expression indicating the window handle to bring to the foreground.

Code Listing

```
'Declare our API functions

Declare Function SetForegroundWindow Lib "user32" Alias
➥"SetForegroundWindow" (ByVal hwnd As Long)  As Long
'The hwnd argument specifies the window handle(hWnd) of the target window.

Public Sub SetForeground(hWnd as long)
    SetForegroundWindow hWnd
End Sub
```

Analysis

This routine is very simple. Simply pass the hWnd parameter to the SetForegroundWindow API.

Note

Many examples of this function use the SetFocus API instead. Unfortunately, the SetFocus API does not work on many windows due to the way Windows handles the SetFocus function. The SetForegroundWindow function is considerably more general purpose. Additionally, SetFocus conflicts with the VB function of the same name.

You probably want to know how to retrieve an hWnd from a form outside your application. First, place the following code in your application:

```
Private gHW                             As Integer
Private s                               As String

Private Const WM_GETTEXT = &HD

Private Declare Function EnumWindows Lib "user32" (ByVal lpEnumFunc
➥As Long, lParam As Long) As Long
Private Declare Function GetWindowText Lib "user32" Alias
➥"GetWindowTextA" (ByVal hWnd As Long, ByVal lpString As String,
➥ ByVal cch As Long) As Long
Declare Function SendMessageByStr& Lib "user32" Alias "SendMessageA"
➥ (ByVal hWnd As Long, ByVal wMsg As Long,
➥ ByVal wParam As Long, ByVal lParam As String)

Function EFindWindowByTitle(windowtxt As String)
    s = windowtxt
    EnumWindows AddressOf EnumWindowProc, 0
    EFindWindowByTitle = gHW
    gHW = 0
End Function

Function EnumWindowProc(ByVal hWnd As Long, ByVal lParam As Long) As Long
    Dim x As String
    x = vbGetWindowText(hWnd)
    If LCase(x) Like LCase(s) Then gHW = hWnd: EnumWindowProc = False:
    ➥ Exit Function
    EnumWindowProc = True
    Exit Function
End Function

Function vbGetWindowText(ahWnd As Long) As String
    Dim c As Integer Dim t As String
    If ahWnd = 0 Then Exit Function
    t = String(256, " ")
    c = SendMessage(ahWnd, 14, 0&, 0&)
    SendMessageByStr ahWnd, 13, c + 1, t
    If InStr(t, Chr$(0)) Then
```

```
        t = Left(t, InStr(t, Chr$(0)) - 1)
    End If
    If t = "" Then c = GetWindowText(ahWnd, t, 256)
End Function
```

Now, to get a foreign application's hWnd, use the following code:

```
EFindWindowByTitle "Your application title."
```

You can use wildcards in the application title. Note, however, that it will only return the first matching hWnd. So, the following would be acceptable:

```
EFindWindowByTitle "Snork*"
```

2.10 MINIMIZE ALL FORMS

by David J. Berube

Description

The MinimizeAllForms procedure minimizes all loaded forms in your project. Visual Basic does not provide this capability natively. Using this code is simple; just place MinimizeAllForms in the appropriate line of code.

Syntax

```
MinimizeAllForms
```

Code Listing

```
Sub MinimizeAllForms()
    Dim objTemp as Object
    For Each objTemp in Forms
        objTemp.WindowState = 1
    Next
End sub
```

Analysis

This routine simply loops through every form in the Forms collection (which represents all the loaded forms in your project) and sets the WindowState property to 1. Setting the WindowState property to 1 minimizes the form. If you set the WindowState property to 0 you restore the form, while 2 maximizes the form.

It is worthwhile to note the use of the For Each capability of Visual Basic. Traditionally, this task would be written like this:

```
Sub MinimizeAllForms()
    Dim objTemp as Object
    Dim I as long
    For I = 0 to Forms.Count - 1
            Set objTemp = Forms(i)
            objTemp.WindowState = 1
    Next
End sub
```

The new version not only uses less code, but is faster as well. The For Each mechanism, is, essentially, shown above. It is simply automatic as opposed to manual.

2.11   RESIZE A FORM AND THE CONTROLS ON IT

by Kamal A. Mehdi

Description

The ResizeForm procedure is a generic procedure that will resize any Visual Basic form and all the controls on that form in only one call. The procedure will resize the form while it resizes and repositions all the controls relative to the form's origin. It will also adjust the font size of the form and all the controls so that captions of controls, text strings in text boxes and list boxes, and text that might be printed on the form or on picture boxes at runtime are shown correctly.

The ResizeForm procedure enables non-uniform resizing of the form and the controls by providing a separate argument for each X and Y resizing ratio.

One more very significant advantage of the ResizeForm procedure is that there is no need to pass any of the controls existing on the form to the procedure; it only must receive the form object itself. This is what makes the procedure really generic.

The ResizeForm procedure also provides more flexibility in the resizing process by incorporating an additional argument for choosing whether to resize both the form and the controls or resize and reposition only the form's controls.

Syntax

ResizeForm(FrmName, XRatio, YRatio, Param)

Part	Description
FrmName	Required. An object reference that evaluates to a Visual Basic form. The name of the form is used.
XRatio	Required. A numeric expression that specifies the X (horizontal) resizing ratio for the form and all the controls. Specifying the value 100 for the XRatio argument results in no sizing (the form and controls are resized to 100% of their horizontal size). Data type: Integer.

Part	Description
YRatio	Required. A numeric expression that specifies the Y (vertical) resizing ratio for the form and all the controls. Specifying the value 100 for the YRatio results in no sizing (the form and controls are resized to 100% of their vertical size). Data type: Integer.
Param	Optional. A numeric expression that specifies whether to resize the form and all its controls or the controls only. Data type: Integer.

The settings for the optional Param argument are as follows:

Value	Description
0	Both the form and its controls are resized (default).
Any other value	Only controls are resized (and repositioned).

Code Listing

```
Sub ResizeForm(FrmName As Form, XRatio As Integer, YRatio As Integer,
➡ Optional Param As Integer)

    'The 'On Error Resume Next' is needed because there might be
    'some controls on the form that may not support some of the
    'properties that will be set
    On Error Resume Next

    'Check if both XRatio and YRatio argument values are valid
    If XRatio < 1 Or YRatio < 1 Then
        MsgBox "XRatio and YRatio values must be at least 1."
        Exit Sub
    End If

    'Check if only controls are to be resized
    If Param <> 0 Then GoTo ResizeControls

    'Resize the form's Height, Width, and Font Size
    FrmName.Height = FrmName.Height * YRatio / 100
    FrmName.Width = FrmName.Width * XRatio / 100
    FrmName.Font.Size = FrmName.Font.Size * XRatio / 100

ResizeControls:
    'Loop through all the controls on the form and reposition every
    'control relative to the form origin, then resize their Width,
    'Height, and Font.Size properties
    For I = 0 To FrmName.Controls.Count - 1

        FrmName.Controls(I).Left = FrmName.Controls(I).Left * XRatio / 100
        FrmName.Controls(I).Top = FrmName.Controls(I).Top * YRatio / 100
        FrmName.Controls(I).Height = FrmName.Controls(I).Height * YRatio / 100
        FrmName.Controls(I).Width = FrmName.Controls(I).Width * XRatio / 100
```

```
            'Note: The control's font will resize only if it is a true-type font
            FrmName.Controls(I).Font.Size = FrmName.Controls(I).Font.Size *
            ➡ XRatio / 100

        Next I

End Sub
```

Analysis

The generic `ResizeForm` procedure is notably useful in cases in which different types of controls on a form are to be resized and appropriately repositioned in just one step regardless of the type of each control. It solves the problem of writing individual code to resize each control. The procedure is especially useful when the form's controls must be resized and repositioned in response to an event such as the `Form_Resize()` event or might be resized in response to changed screen resolution.

The `ResizeForm` procedure uses the `Controls` property of the form object to iterate through all the form's controls and resizes them and their font size by manipulating their `Width`, `Height`, and `Font.Size` properties, respectively. It repositions the controls by adjusting their `Top` and `Left` properties based on the specified `XRatio` and `YRatio` argument values.

The use of the `ResizeForm` procedure is simple. Just call the procedure and pass the form to be resized using its name (for example `Form1`) or the `Me` keyword along with the required horizontal and vertical resizing ratios to the appropriate procedure arguments. For example, specifying the value `50` for both the `XRatio` and `YRatio` will resize the form and all the controls to half their size. Specifying `50` for the `XRatio` and `200` for the `YRatio` will resize the form and controls to half their width and double their height. The font size for both the form and the controls is always resized according to the specified `XRatio` value. The font size will be affected only if the font is a TrueType font (such as Times New Roman).

The following example demonstrates how you can resize the form and all its controls to 50 percent of their size when the form loads:

```
Private Sub Form_Load()

    Dim X As Integer, Y As Integer
    'Call the procedure and pass the form to the 'FrmName' argument
    'Also provide the X and Y resizing ratio
    X = 50: Y = 50
    ResizeForm Me, X, Y, 0

End Sub
```

Calling the procedure without specifying the `Param` argument value or specifying the value `0` will resize both the form and all its controls. Specifying any value other than `0` will resize the controls only.

The `ResizeForm` procedure incorporates code to validate the specified values for both the `XRatio` and `YRatio` arguments where an error message is displayed if any of the values is invalid. In addition, the procedure does not produce an error if one or more controls do not support the resized properties (such as the

Hscroll Bar, Vscroll Bar, or the Image control, which do not support the Font property; or the Timer control, which does not support any of the Height, Width, and Font properties). This is really important for the ResizeForm procedure to perform correctly because many other third-party custom controls that might be used in the project might not support one or more of these properties.

The sample project RESIZFRM.VBP on the CD-ROM that accompanies this book demonstrates the use of the ResizeForm procedure.

2.12 RESIZE A FORM TO THE SIZE OF THE SCREEN

by Kamal A. Mehdi

Description

The ResizeFormToScreen procedure is a generic procedure that will resize any Visual Basic form to the size of the screen (current screen resolution) and will then resize and reposition all the controls on that form appropriately. It will also adjust the font size of the form and all the controls so that control captions, text strings in text boxes and list boxes, and text that might be printed on the form or on picture boxes at run-time are shown correctly.

The ResizeFormToScreen procedure will automatically detect the currently used screen resolution and calculate the required X and Y resizing ratios to properly resize the form and all the controls. It will function in both cases in which the current screen resolution of the system on which the application is running is higher or lower than the resolution used to design the forms and the controls.

One significant advantage of the ResizeFormToScreen procedure is that there is no need to pass any of the form's controls to the procedure; just send the form object itself to the appropriate procedure argument. This is what makes the procedure really generic.

Syntax

ResizeFormToScreen(FrmName)

Part	Description
FrmName	Required. An object that evaluates to a Visual Basic form. The name of the form is used.

Code Listing

```
Sub ResizeFormToScreen(FrmName As Form)

    'The 'On Error Resume Next' is needed because there might be
    'some controls on the form that may not support some of the
    'properties that will be set
```

```
On Error Resume Next

'If the form's window state is minimized or maximized then exit
If FrmName.WindowState <> 0 Then Exit Sub

'Calculate the X and Y resizing ratio
XRatio = Screen.Width / FrmName.Width
YRatio = Screen.Height / FrmName.Height

'Set the form's origin to 0,0
FrmName.Top = 0
FrmName.Left = 0

'Resize the form's height, width, and Font Size
FrmName.Height = FrmName.Height * YRatio
FrmName.Width = FrmName.Width * XRatio
FrmName.Font.Size = FrmName.Font.Size * XRatio


'Loop through all the controls on the form and reposition every
'control relative to the form origin, then resize their width,
'height, and Font.Size properties
For I = 0 To FrmName.Controls.Count - 1

    FrmName.Controls(I).Left = FrmName.Controls(I).Left * XRatio
    FrmName.Controls(I).Top = FrmName.Controls(I).Top * YRatio
    FrmName.Controls(I).Height = FrmName.Controls(I).Height * YRatio
    FrmName.Controls(I).Width = FrmName.Controls(I).Width * XRatio

    'Note: The control's font will resize only if it is a truetype font
    FrmName.Controls(I).Font.Size = FrmName.Controls(I).Font.Size *
    ➥XRatio

Next I

End Sub
```

Analysis

The generic `ResizeFormToScreen` procedure is significantly useful in cases in which the Visual Basic application is required to display properly on different screen resolutions other than that used in the application development.

When the procedure is called in the `Form_Load()` event, it resizes and repositions the form and all the controls on it in one step, regardless of the type of each control. This provides a solution to the problem of writing individual code to resize each of the application's forms and controls.

The `ResizeFormToScreen` procedure calculates the proper X (horizontal) and Y (vertical) resizing ratios by detecting the current screen resolution using the `Screen` object's `Width` and `Height` properties and dividing them by the form's current `Width` and `Height` property values. If the current screen resolution is higher than the resolution that was used in the application development, both the X and Y resizing ratios will be greater than 1, otherwise their values will be less than 1. If both resolutions are the same, both X and Y resizing ratios are equal to 1 and no resizing will take place (the form and controls will actually resize to 100% of their size).

The procedure uses the `Controls` property of the form object to iterate through all the form's controls and resizes them as well as their font size by manipulating their `Width`, `Height`, and `Font.Size` properties, respectively. It repositions the controls by adjusting their `Top` and `Left` properties based on the calculated X and Y resizing ratios.

The use of the `ResizeFormToScreen` procedure is simple. Just call the procedure in the `Form_Load()` event and pass the form to be resized using its name (for example, `Form1`) or the `Me` keyword as an argument.

Note that the procedure will not work if the form's `WindowState` property was set to `2-Maximized` because setting this property to `Maximized` will maximize the form in any screen resolution. As a result, the procedure will be unable to determine the appropriate resizing ratios, which are based on the current form size and screen size. Also, note that the font size of the form and each control will be resized only if the font used is a TrueType font (such as Times New Roman).

The `ResizeFormToScreen` procedure incorporates code so that no error will occur if one or more controls on the form do not support the resized properties (such as the `Hscroll Bar`, `Vscroll Bar`, or the `Image` control, which do not support the `Font` property; or the `Timer` control, which does not support any of the `Height`, `Width`, and `Font` properties). This is really important for the `ResizeFormToScreen` procedure to perform correctly because many other third-party custom controls that might be used in the project might not support one or more of these properties.

The sample project FRM2SCRN.VBP on the CD-ROM that accompanies this book demonstrates the use of the `ResizeFormToScreen` procedure.

2.13 SCROLL A LARGE PICTURE ON A FORM

by Kamal A. Mehdi

Description

This sample code demonstrates how you can implement a feature that will enable the user to scroll vertically and horizontally a picture that is larger in width and height than the form window by using the Visual Basic picture box and two scrollbar controls. The code loads an image from a picture file and automatically calculates and adjusts the scrollbar's properties at runtime to accommodate the width and height of the loaded picture.

Modules and Controls Required

You will need the following modules and controls to build the sample project:

Module/Control	Description
Form1	A standard non-MDI Visual Basic form with controls as shown
Picture1	A picture box control
Picture2	A picture box control drawn inside Picture1
HScroll1	A horizontal scrollbar control
VScroll1	A vertical scrollbar control

Place the controls anywhere on the form and enter the following code in the appropriate events of the form or controls.

Note

In order for the code to function properly, the Picture2 picture box must be drawn inside Picture1.

Code Listing

```
Private Sub Form_Activate()

    "Prompt to click on Picture2 to load the picture
    With Picture2
        .Font.Size = 14
        .CurrentX = .Width / 2 - 1500
        .CurrentY = .Height / 2
        Picture2.Print "Click me to load the picture"
    End With

End Sub

Private Sub Form_Load()

    "Initialize form position and size
    With Me
        .Left = 0
        .Top = 0
        .Width = Screen.Width
        .Height = Screen.Height
    End With

    "Initialize Picture1 position and size
    With Picture1
        .Left = 0
```

```
            .Top = 0
            .Height = Me.Height - 800
            .Width = Me.Width - 500
        End With

        "Initialize Picture2 position and size
        With Picture2
            .Left = 0
            .Top = 0
            .Height = Picture1.Height
            .Width = Picture1.Width
        End With

        "Initialize VScroll1 position and size
        With VScroll1
            .Top = 0
            .Left = Picture1.Width
            .Height = Me.Height - 500
        End With

        "Initialize HScroll1 position and size
        With HScroll1
            .Top = Picture1.Height
            .Left = 0
            .Width = Me.Width - 500
        End With

End Sub

Private Sub Form_Unload(Cancel As Integer)

    "Set the form to nothing
    Set Form1 = Nothing

End Sub

Private Sub HScroll1_Change()

    "Move Picture2 to the left the value of the HScroll change
    Picture2.Left = -HScroll1.Value

End Sub

Private Sub Picture2_Click()

    "Prompt to wait and load the picture in Picture2
    With Picture2
        .Cls
        .CurrentX = .Width / 2 - 1500
        .CurrentY = .Height / 2
        Picture2.Print "Wait, loading large JPEG picture..."
        DoEvents
```

```
        .Picture = LoadPicture(App.Path & "\win95.jpg")
    End With

    "Set the properties of VScroll1
    With VScroll1
        .Max = Picture2.Height - Picture1.Height
        .SmallChange = 100
        .LargeChange = 1000
    End With

    "Set the properties of HScroll1
    With HScroll1
        .SmallChange = 100
        .LargeChange = 1000
        .Max = Picture2.Width - Picture1.Width
    End With

End Sub

Private Sub VScroll1_Change()

    "Move Picture2 to the top the value of the VScroll change
    Picture2.Top = -VScroll1.Value

End Sub
```

Analysis

Run the project and click the picture box to load the sample image win95.jpg from the image file located under the project directory. Click the scrollbars to scroll the image within the form window.

The code demonstrates how to load a large picture file in a picture box control and enable the user to scroll the picture vertically and horizontally within the form window to view the entire picture. This functionality is important in applications such as image viewers, where different sizes of pictures that might be larger than the form window are to be displayed without shrinking the image. This also helps the developer view large pictures on systems running with small screen resolutions.

The code also enables *coarse* and *fine* scrolling of the displayed image, depending on where you click the scrollbars. (Clicking the arrows located at the scrollbar ends performs fine scrolling, whereas clicking the body of the scrollbar performs coarse scrolling.) The image's coarse and fine scrolling step size can be adjusted by modifying the `LargeChange` and `SmallChange` properties of the scrollbars in code. The `Max` property value of the scrollbars is image-size dependent, and thus is calculated at runtime after the image is loaded to accommodate the entire image size.

The code is generic because it can be used in both 16-bit and 32-bit Visual Basic versions. The exception is that the picture box control in the 16-bit version can handle only BMP image files and not JPEG image files. In addition, the code can be used to display and scroll any picture size without limitations.

The sample project SCROLPIC.VBP on the CD-ROM that accompanies this book demonstrates the presented code functionality.

GENERAL FUNCTIONS AND IMPROVEMENTS

Now that you've learned some ways to improve controls and forms, you get to the functions. This group of routines takes a look at some functions that probably should have been included in VB, but weren't. So here they are for you to use, including functions that will get the application path, system font, or delay the VB program.

3.1 A BETTER SHELL

by Paolo Bonzini

Description

This function's behavior is the same as that described in the help and manual under Shell. However, there is an error in those descriptions: Although they say that Shell can open a document by supplying its name in the first parameter, the code in the runtime library does not have this capability. The code presented here works as expected. In addition, I added a parameter that enables you to specify the initial working directory.

> **Tip**
>
> You can pass a directory name to this version of Shell. It will bring up a standard Explorer window opened on that directory.

Because this is an extended version of an existing function, I named it the same as the standard function, so I can cut and paste it in my programs without changing existing code. If you prefer to avoid namespace collisions, however, you are free to rename the function; for example, you could call it ShellEx.

Syntax

```
Result = Shell(Program[, ShowCmd[, WorkDir]])
Shell Program[, ShowCmd[, WorkDir]]
```

Part	Description
Result	Optional. The process ID of the launched process.
Program	Required. A string expression that specifies the command line of the program (or document) to be launched. If it contains no path, it is searched for in the directories specified in the PATH environment variable.
ShowCmd	Optional. An integer expression that specifies how the launched program window will appear. These have the same meaning of Shell's second parameter (for example, vbNormalFocus or vbMinimizedNoFocus).
WorkDir	Optional. A string expression specifying the initial working directory of the launched process. By default, it is the path contained in Program or (if Program contains no path) the current working directory.

Code Listing

```
'**********************************************
'* Submitted by Paolo Bonzini
'**********************************************
Private Declare Function ShellExecute Lib "shell32.dll" _
    Alias "ShellExecuteA" (ByVal hwnd As Long, _
    ByVal lpOperation As String, ByVal lpFile As String, _
    ByVal lpParameters As String, ByVal lpDirectory As String, _
    ByVal nShowCmd As Long) As Long

Function Shell(CmdLine As String, _
    Optional ShowCmd As Long = vbNormalNoFocus, _
    Optional ByVal WorkDir As String) As Long

    Dim Slash As Integer
    Dim Program As String
    Dim Parameters As String
    Dim ParamStart As Long
    Dim CWD As String

    CWD = CurDir
    If Left(CmdLine, 1) = """" Then
        ParamStart = InStr(2, CmdLine, """")
        If ParamStart = 0 Then ParamStart = Len(CmdLine) + 1

        Program = Mid(CmdLine, 2, ParamStart - 2)
        Parameters = Mid(CmdLine, ParamStart + 1)
    Else
        ParamStart = InStr(CmdLine, " ")
        If ParamStart = 0 Then ParamStart = Len(CmdLine) + 1
```

```
      Program = Left(CmdLine, ParamStart - 1)
      Parameters = Mid(CmdLine, ParamStart + 1)
End If

If WorkDir = "" Then
      For Slash = Len(Program) To 1 Step -1
            If Mid(Program, Slash, 1) = "\" Then Exit For
      Next

      If Slash = 0 Then
            WorkDir = CWD
      ElseIf Slash = 1 Then
            WorkDir = Left(Program, Slash)
      ElseIf Mid(Program, Slash - 1, 1) = ":" Then
            WorkDir = Left(Program, Slash)
      Else
            WorkDir = Left(Program, Slash - 1)
      End If
End If

Slash = InStr(Program, "\")
If Slash = 0 Then
      'No path specified. If the file is executable,
      'check in the PATH environment variable; else
      'check in the current directory. Switch to the
      'working directory and try the original Shell.
      'If it returns "Illegal function call" we are
      'opening a document, else Shell has already done
      'everything and we can exit
      On Error Resume Next
      Err.Clear
      ChDir WorkDir
      Shell = VBA.Shell(CmdLine, ShowCmd)
      ChDir CWD
      On Error GoTo 0
      If Err.Number = 0 Then
            Exit Function
      ElseIf Err.Number <> 5 Then
            Err.Raise Err.Number, Err.Source, _
                  Err.Description, Err.HelpFile, Err.HelpContext
      End If

      'It's a document, the name is relative to CWD
      If Right(CWD, 1) <> "\" Then Program = "\" & Program
      Program = CWD & Program

ElseIf Slash = 1 Then
      'Relative to the root directory; only add drive letter
      Program = Left(CWD, 2) & Program

ElseIf Mid(Program, Slash - 1, 1) <> ":" Then
      'No drive, relative to the current directory
```

```
        If Right(CWD, 1) <> "\" Then Program = "\" & Program
        Program = CWD & Program
    End If

    Shell = ShellExecute(0, vbNullString, _
        Program, LTrim(Parameters), WorkDir, ShowCmd)

    If Shell < 32 Then VBA.Shell CmdLine, ShowCmd

End Function
```

Analysis

This is a wrapper around the `ShellExecute` API function; however, as you can see from its length, it has quite a lot of things to do before transferring control to the Windows kernel. First, you must split the passed command line into the program name and parameters: the index of the first character in the parameters is stored in the `ParamStart` variable. If the program name is quoted, remove the two quotes and set `ParamStart` to the position of the second quote minus one (you must subtract one because you have removed the first quote); otherwise, you consider that the program's name ends at the first space. If there is no space, the whole first argument of `Shell` is the program name.

Then, you must find what the initial working directory is if it wasn't specified in the third parameter. To do so, look for the last slash in the program name and consider everything up to that slash to be part of the pathname. Include the slash if the program path refers to the root directory (for example, \Budget.xls or A:\Setup.Exe), or else discard it (for example, C:\My Documents\WordDoc1.doc has C:\My Documents as its path). If no slash is found, the current directory is taken to be the initial working directory.

Also, `ShellExecute` needs the complete path to the file, which Visual Basic's `Shell` function does not need. To make the enhancement of `Shell` fully functional and downward compatible, you must provide them. There are four cases:

- The path starts with a \, so it is relative to the root directory of the current drive. You simply add the drive letter and a colon at the beginning of the program.
- The first parameter has a path, but it is not relative to the root directory. It must be relative to the current directory, so put it in front of the path (if necessary, you must add a backslash, too).
- The first parameter has no path, and it is a document. Once again, it is relative to the current directory, so you can proceed as in the previous case.
- The first parameter has no path, and it is a program. You must search it through the path specified in the environment.

To distinguish between the last two cases, you call the original Visual Basic `Shell` function, which is in the VBA library. If `Shell` returns an Illegal Function Call error, the file for which you are searching is a document; if it answers any other error, you raise it again to pass it to the caller, even if it is a File Not Found error, because `Shell` has already searched the whole path. If `Shell` succeeds, the new process has been spawned and you exit, returning to the caller the process ID that `Shell` returned.

Having found the complete path you can call ShellExecute and start the process. This function automatically looks in the Registry for the program to be used when performing an operation on a document (opening it, printing it, and so on); it even tries to use dynamic data exchange (DDE) to perform these operations. Because it shields the programmer from all the intricacies of the Registry and applications associated with documents, it is the simplest way to launch a document together with the application to which it is associated.

It has a quirk, though. The ShowCmd parameter does not work when you are specifying a document. Keep in mind this "feature" of ShellExecute when you use this function.

Of the six parameters accepted by ShellExecute, the first two are the most cryptic. The first is an HWND of a window used to show error dialog boxes, which you can safely set to 0. The second is the name of the operation to be performed on the file; for example, open or print. vbNullString specifies the default operation; that is, the one that is bold in the Explorer context menu for that file. Note that this function does not bring up the Explorer's Open As dialog box if a file is not associated with an application.

A return value from ShellExecute that is less than or equal to 32 indicates an error. In this case you call the standard Shell function, which will raise the appropriate error (usually File Not Found or Illegal Function Call for files not associated with an application).

3.2   RETRIEVE SHELL OUTPUT

by Paolo Bonzini

Description

This function is similar to the standard VB Shell function, but if the spawned program is a DOS program (or a Windows console program such as the standard Microsoft linker), it will return the text printed by the program on the standard output.

If the program is a Windows program, or if it cannot be found, the function returns an empty string. This happens because in both cases, the command processor doesn't write anything on the standard output. If the program is not found, the Bad Command Or File Name message (or an analogous one) is printed on the STDERR file. STDERR output cannot be caught because it is meant to go to the screen.

There is a problem with this function. Several ill-behaved command programs print their output to STDERR instead of to STDOUT; other programs instead mix their output and use STDOUT for redirectable messages and STDERR for errors that are meant to go to the screen instead of being redirected (many compilers work this way).

In this case, there is just one solution: you must hack. In the case of a compiler, for example, it might be useful not to use this function and instead look at the listing file that it produces.

Syntax

```
Result = ShellGetText(Program[, ShowCmd])
```

Part	Description
Result	Required. A string that contains the output of the program, or an empty string if an error occurs.
Program	Required. A string expression that specifies the command line of the program to be launched. It can be any program, but it makes sense to use this function only for console programs.
ShowCmd	Optional. An integer expression that specifies how the launched program window will appear. It has the same meaning as Shell's second parameter (for example, vbNormalFocus or vbMinimizedNoFocus). The default is vbMinimizedNoFocus.

Code Listing

```
'***********************************************
'* Submitted by Paolo Bonzini
'***********************************************
Private Declare Function OpenProcess Lib "kernel32" _
    (ByVal dwDesiredAccess As Long, _
    ByVal bInheritHandle As Long, _
    ByVal dwProcessId As Long) As Long
Private Declare Function CloseHandle Lib "kernel32" _
    (ByVal hObject As Long) As Long
Private Declare Function WaitForSingleObject Lib "kernel32" _
    (ByVal hHandle As Long, ByVal dwMilliseconds As Long) _
    As Long
Private Declare Function GetTempFileName Lib "kernel32" _
    Alias "GetTempFileNameA" (ByVal lpszPath As String, _
    ByVal lpPrefixString As String, ByVal wUnique As Long, _
    ByVal lpTempFileName As String) As Long

Const SYNCHRONIZE = &H100000
Function ShellGetText(Program As String, _
    Optional showCmd As Long = vbMinimizedNoFocus) As String

    Dim sFile As String
    Dim hFile As Long
    Dim lLength As Long
    Dim pid As Long
    Dim hProcess As Long

    'Create a temporary output file's name
    sFile = Space(1024)
    lLength = GetTempFileName(Environ("TEMP"), "OUT", 0, sFile)
    sFile = Left(sFile, lLength)

    pid = Shell( _
        Environ("COMSPEC") & " /C " & Program & ">" & sFile, _
        showCmd)
```

```
    'Wait for the process' termination.
    hProcess = OpenProcess(SYNCHRONIZE, True, pid)
    WaitForSingleObject hProcess, -1
    CloseHandle hProcess

    hFile = FreeFile
    Open sFile For Binary As #hFile
    ShellGetText = Input$(LOF(hFile), hFile)
    Close #hFile

    Kill sFile

End Function
```

Analysis

First, the function calls Shell with an appropriate command line. If you try a command line like LINK > TEMP.TMP, you won't get the desired behavior. This happens because only the command interpreter (COMMAND.COM under Windows 95, CMD.EXE under NT) interprets the redirection and pipe signs; Shell (and the API functions it calls) passes them verbatim to the spawned process. This function, therefore, uses a command line similar to COMMAND.COM /C LINK > TEMP.TMP. The path to the command processor is contained in the COMSPEC environment variable, and the name of a unique temporary file is given by the Windows API function GetTempFileName.

Then, the function waits for the termination of the spawned process. This involves two API functions: WaitForSingleObject (which waits for the program's termination) and OpenProcess (which transforms the PID—process ID—answered by Shell into an HPROCESS—process handle—required by WaitForSingleObject). When WaitForSingleObject returns, the contents of the temporary file are read, the HPROCESS is closed, and the file is deleted.

The waiting part is incompatible with the Win16 API. OpenProcess, WaitForSingleObject, and CloseHandle are strictly 32-bit functions; under 16-bit Windows you must replace the call to WaitForSingleObject with a loop that checks for the result of calling GetModuleUsage (which, in turn, is a function that exists only under Win16). An example of this can be found in the Visual Basic 3 help file, or in Microsoft's MSDN and Knowledge Base.

3.3   SEND TO RECYCLE BIN

by Gary A. Wiley

Description

Visual Basic's Kill statement deletes a file with no way of restoring it. The SendToRecycleBin function deletes a file and sends it to the Recycle Bin, enabling it to be restored. It also enables you to override the Display Delete Confirmation Dialog Box setting in the Recycle Bin properties.

Windows 95, Windows 98, or Windows NT 4.0 or above and 32-bit Visual Basic are required for this function.

Syntax

ReturnValue = SendToRecycleBin (*FileName*, *Progress*, *Confirm*)

Part	Description
ReturnValue	Required. A Boolean value indicating success or failure.
FileName	Required. A string expression specifying the file and path to delete.
Progress	Required. A Boolean value that specifies whether to hide the progress dialog box. Set to **False** to hide the dialog box.
Confirm	Required. A Boolean value that specifies whether to override the Display Delete Confirmation setting. Set to **False** to override.

Code Listing

```
Option Explicit

Private Type SHFILEOPSTRUCT
    hWnd As Long
    wFunc As Long
    pFrom As String
    pTo As String
    fFlags As Integer
    fAnyOperationsAborted As Boolean
    hNameMappings As Long
    lpszProgressTitle As String
End Type

Private Declare Function SHFileOperation Lib "shell32.dll" Alias _
"SHFileOperationA" (lpFileOp As SHFILEOPSTRUCT) As Long

Private Const FO_DELETE = &H3
Private Const FOF_ALLOWUNDO = &H40
Private Const FOF_NOCONFIRMATION = &H10
Private Const FOF_SILENT = &H4

Public   Function SendToRecycleBin(ByVal FileName As String, _
  Progress As Boolean, Confirm As Boolean) As Boolean
    Dim SHFileOp As SHFILEOPSTRUCT
    Dim RetVal As Long

    With SHFileOp
        .wFunc = FO_DELETE
        .pFrom = FileName
```

```
        .fFlags = FOF_ALLOWUNDO
        If Not Progress And Confirm Then
            'Hide progress dialog box
            .fFlags = FOF_ALLOWUNDO Or FOF_SILENT
        ElseIf Not Confirm Then
            'Hide confirm delete dialog box. This also hides
            'the progress dialog box
            .fFlags = FOF_ALLOWUNDO Or FOF_NOCONFIRMATION
        Else
            .fFlags = FOF_ALLOWUNDO
        End If
    End With
    'Send the file to recycle bin
    RetVal = SHFileOperation(SHFileOp)
    'Check if operation was a success
    If RetVal > 0 Then
    'File does not exist
        SendToRecycleBin = False
    ElseIf SHFileOp.fAnyOperationsAborted Then
        'Operation aborted, file not sent to recycle bin
        SendToRecycleBin = False
    Else
        SendToRecycleBin = True
    End If
End  Function
```

Analysis

Error handling is done by the Windows file system if *FileName* doesn't exist. Program execution is not interrupted.

The SHFileOperation API returns 0 on success and nonzero otherwise. If *FileName* does not exist, the Windows file system generates file system error 1026, Cannot Delete File, and this will be the return value of the API. If the user aborts the operation by clicking No in the delete confirmation dialog box, the return value of the API will be 0. Likewise, if *FileName* is in use by Windows the operation is aborted and the return value is 0. In both cases *FileName* is not sent to the Recycle Bin. Therefore, because a return value of 0 does not necessarily mean the file was sent to the Recycle Bin you must check elsewhere to determine whether the operation was actually a success. For this you must check the value of fAnyOperationsAborted of the SHFILEOPSTRUCT structure. This will have a value of False if *FileName* was sent to the Recycle Bin or does not exist. The value is True if the operation was aborted either by the user or the file system.

FOF_SILENT hides the progress dialog box. FOF_NOCONFIRMATION overrides the Display Delete Confirmation Dialog Box setting in the Recycle Bin properties if checked and also hides the progress dialog box.

3.4   EXECUTE ANOTHER PROGRAM

by Ian Ippolito

Description

When your application requires more than the Shell command can provide, this routine can be a lifesaver. Unlike Shell, the Execute_Program routine cannot only launch an executable program (.exe), it can also launch a file that has been associated with Explorer (or Program Manager) to a parent application. For example, if it is given a text file, the routine is smart enough to launch Notepad with the text file open inside it. In contrast to Shell, this routine also enables you to specify a working directory in which to run the program—a requirement for many programs. Finally, it also handles the many errors that can occur while executing an external program, such as running out of memory or not finding a file.

Syntax

Success = Execute_Program(*ProgramFilePath*, *CommandLineParms*, *WorkingDirectory*)

Part	Description
ProgramFilePath	Required. The complete path and filename of the executable or associated file to execute.
CommandLineParms	Required. The command-line parameters to be passed to the program. Typically, associated files have no command-line parameters. Pass in an empty string ("") to specify that there are no parameters.
WorkingDirectory	Required. The working directory in which the program will run. Pass in an empty string ("") to specify that there is no working directory.
Success	Returns TRUE if the program executed successfully, otherwise returns FALSE.

Code Listing

```
Option Explicit
'Execute_Program
'Runs a program and handles all possible errors'
'(such as running out of memory, file can't be opened, etc.)'
'Also, unlike the VB Shell command, it allows you to specify'
'a 'default working directory'!
'Also, allows you to run a file that is only an association--
'example:you can run a .txt file with this function!'
'Inputs:strFilePath--program to run
'strParms--program command line parms (if any)
'strDir--default working directory'
'Returns:returns TRUE=successful FALSE=failed'
'Assumes: None '
```

```
'Side Effects: None '
'*****************************************************************
#If Win32 Then
'32 bit declare
Declare Function ShellExecute Lib "shell32.dll" _
    Alias "ShellExecuteA" (ByVal hWnd As Long, ByVal lpOperation As String,
    ➥ ByVal lpFile As String, ByVal lpParameters As String,
    ➥ ByVal lpDirectory As String, ByVal nShowCmd As Long) As Long
#Else
'16 bit declare
Declare Function ShellExecute Lib "shell.dll" _
    (ByVal hWnd As Integer, ByVal lpszOp As String, ByVal lpszFile As String,
    ➥ ByVal spszParams As String, ByVal lpszDir As String,
    ➥ByVal fsShowCmd As Integer) As Integer
#End If

const SW_SHOWNORMAL = 5

Function Execute_Program(ByVal strFilePath As String, _
    ByVal strParms As String, ByVal strDir As String) _
    As Integer

    'run program
    Dim hwndProgram As Integer
    hwndProgram = ShellExecute(0, "Open", strFilePath, strParms, strDir,
    ➥ SHOWNORMAL)

  'evaluate errors (if any)
  Select Case (hwndProgram)
    Case 0
        MsgBox "Insufficent system memory or corrupt program file.", 0,
        ➥ "Error running " & strFilePath
Case 2
        MsgBox "File not found.", 0, "Error running " & strFilePath
Case 3
        MsgBox "Invalid path.", 0, "Error running " & strFilePath
Case 5
        MsgBox "Sharing or Protection Error.", 0, "Error running "
        ➥ & strFilePath
Case 6
        MsgBox "Separate data segments are required for each task.", 0,
        ➥ "Error running " & strFilePath
Case 8
        MsgBox "Insufficient memory to run the program.", 0, "Error running "
        ➥ & strFilePath
Case 10
        MsgBox "Incorrect Windows version.", 0, "Error running " & strFilePath
Case 11
        MsgBox "Invalid program file.", 0, "Error running " & strFilePath
Case 12
        MsgBox "Program file requires a different operating system.", 0,
        ➥ "Error running " & strFilePath
```

```
Case 13
        MsgBox "Program requires MS-DOS 4.0.", 0, "Error running " & strFilePath
Case 14
        MsgBox "Unknown program file type.", 0, "Error running " & strFilePath
Case 15
        MsgBox "Windows program does not support protected memory mode.", 0,
     ➡ "Error running " & strFilePath
Case 16
        MsgBox "Invalid use of data segments when loading a second instance of
     ➡ a program.", 0, "Error running " & strFilePath
Case 19
        MsgBox "Attempt to run a compressed program file.", 0, "Error running "
     ➡ & strFilePath
Case 20
        MsgBox "Invalid dynamic link library.", 0, "Error running "
     ➡ & strFilePath
Case 21
        MsgBox "Program requires Windows 32-bit extensions.", 0,
     ➡ "Error running " & strFilePath
End Select

    if (hwndProgram<>0) then
        Execute_Program = True
    else
        Execute_Program = False
        Exit Function
    end if

End Function
```

Analysis

This routine circumnavigates the limitations of the `Shell` command by foregoing it completely and instead interfaces directly with the Windows API. The `ShellExecuteA` (32-bit) and the `ShellExecute` (16-bit) API commands are powerful enough to allow a program to access file associations and working directories with just a single command.

First, the routine passes the information it receives from the user to the appropriate `ShellExecute` API command. By using the `Alias` keyword to "rename" the 32-bit API declaration `ShellExecuteA` to be identical to the 16-bit API declaration of `ShellExecute`, the program requires only one API statement for both declarations instead of the usual two.

Notice that the last parameter passed to the `ShellExecute` API command is `SW_SHOW`. This parameter is defined above and is used to specify that the program is to be launched in the typical manner (that is, not minimized or maximized). You can customize this function by passing other values to this parameter to show the program as minimized, maximized, nonactive, and a host of other options. To do so, include the following additional declarations:

```
Public Const SW_SHOWMAXIMIZED = 3
Public Const SW_SHOWMINIMIZED = 2
```

```
Public Const SW_SHOWMINNOACTIVE = 7
Public Const SW_SHOWNA = 8
Public Const SW_SHOWNOACTIVATE = 4
Public Const SW_SHOWNORMAL = 1
```

Whenever an error is encountered, the function currently prints out a message box to inform the user. This is a very helpful feature for interactive applications, but might not be appropriate for batch or behind-the-scenes processing programs, where there is actually no user sitting in front of the PC. If you use the routine in this type of program, you might want to replace the `MsgBox` lines with a custom line to output the error to your log file.

3.5 PROVIDING AN APPLICATION WITH HELP FACILITIES

by Ian Ippolito

Description

Displaying a help file to a user is easy when you use the Visual Basic `Shell` command or the `Execute_Program` routine located elsewhere in this book. However, standard Windows applications provide an array of help options, from displaying a help file's index to displaying help on how to use help itself. How do you provide this functionality to your users?

That's where these four routines come in. Use them to display the standard help options on your application's menu:

- Contents (using `Help_Contents`)
- Search for Help On... (using `Help_Search`)
- How to Use Help (using `Help_On_Help`)
- About your application (using `Help_About`)

Syntax

```
Help_Contents HelpFileName, ParentForm
Help_Search HelpFileName, ParentForm
Help_About HelpFileName, ProgramTitle, ProgramVersion, ParentForm
Help_On_Help HelpFileName, ParentForm
```

Part	Description
HelpFileName	Required. The name of the application's help file.
ParentForm	Required. The name of the form with which the help file will be associated. When the specified form is closed, the help file will automatically close as well.
ProgramTitle	Required. The title of the program.
ProgramVersion	Required. The current version number of the program; for example, 4.14c.

Code Listing

```
Option Explicit

#If Win16 Then
    'Declares for help--about

    Declare Sub ShellAbout Lib "SHELL.DLL" _
        (ByVal hwnd%, ByVal strAppNaobjParentForm$, _
        ByVal strCopyright$, ByVal hWndIcon%)

    'declares for windows help
    Declare Function WinHelp% Lib "User" (ByVal hwnd%, _
        ByVal lpHelpFile$, ByVal wCommand%, dwData As Any)

    Declare Function WinHelpBynum% Lib "User" Alias _
        "WinHelp" (ByVal hwnd%, ByVal lpHelpFile$, _
        ByVal wCommand%, ByVal dwData&)
#Else

    Declare Function WinHelp Lib "user32" Alias "WinHelpA" _
                    (ByVal hwnd As Long, _
                     ByVal lpHelpFile As String, _
                     ByVal wCommand As Long, _
                     ByVal dwData As Any) As Long
    Declare Function WinHelpBynum Lib "user32" Alias "WinHelpA" _
                    (ByVal hwnd As Long, _
                     ByVal lpHelpFile As String, _
                     ByVal wCommand As Long, _
                     ByVal dwData As Long) As Long
    Declare Function ShellAbout Lib "shell32.dll" _
        Alias "ShellAboutA" (ByVal hwnd As Long, _
        ByVal szApp As String, ByVal szOtherStuff _
        As String, ByVal hIcon As Long) As Long

#End If

Type MULTIKEYHELP
    mkSize As Integer
    mkKeylist As String * 1
    szKeyphrase As String * 253
End Type

' Commands to pass WinHelp()
Global Const HELP_CONTEXT = &H1 ' Display topic identified _
                                    by number in Data
Global Const HELP_QUIT = &H2 ' Terminate help
Global Const HELP_INDEX = &H3 ' Display index
Global Const HELP_HELPONHELP = &H4 ' Display help on using help
Global Const HELP_SETINDEX = &H5 ' Set an alternate Index _
                                    for help file with more _
                                    than one index
Global Const HELP_KEY = &H101 ' Display topic for keyword in Data
```

```
Global Const HELP_MULTIKEY = &H201 ' Lookup keyword in _
                                     alternate table and _
                                     display topic
Global Const HELP_PARTIALKEY = &H105 'for search dialog box
Sub Help_About(ByVal strCopyright As String, _
    ByVal strProgramTitle As String, _
    ByVal strProgramVersion As String, _
    ByVal objParentForm As Form)

        ShellAbout objParentForm.hwnd, _
            strProgramTitle & " " & strProgramVersion, _
            strCopyright, objParentForm.Icon

End Sub

Sub Help_Contents(ByVal strHelpFileName As String _
    , ByVal objParentForm As Form)

Dim intReturn As Integer

        intReturn = WinHelp(objParentForm.hwnd, _
            strHelpFileName & Chr$(0), _
            HELP_INDEX, ByVal "")
End Sub
Sub Help_On_Help(ByVal objParentForm As Form)

Dim intReturn As Integer

        intReturn = WinHelp(objParentForm.hwnd, _
            "", _
            HELP_HELPONHELP, ByVal "")
End Sub

Sub Help_Search(ByVal strHelpFile As String, _
    ByVal objParentForm As Form)

    'perform a help search
Dim intReturn As Integer

    intReturn = WinHelp(objParentForm.hwnd, strHelpFile _
        & Chr$(0), HELP_PARTIALKEY, "")

End Sub
```

Analysis

The first three functions—`Help_Contents`, `Help_Search`, `Help_On_Help`—all use the `WinHelp` Windows API function to perform their main actions.

You can create your own custom routines to perform additional help functionality by duplicating this API call but supplying a different third parameter. The following is a list of the options:

■ HELP_CONTEXT: Displays the topic identified by the number in the fourth parameter.
■ HELP_QUIT: Terminates help.
■ HELP_SETINDEX: Sets an alternative index for a help file with more than one index.
■ HELP_KEY: Displays a topic matching the keyword specified in the fourth parameter.
■ HELP_MULTIKEY: Looks up the topic matching the keyword in the fourth parameter in an alternative table and displays the topic.

Additionally, the code can be modified for 32-bit programs by replacing the 16-bit API declaration with the following 32-bit API call:

```
Declare Function WinHelp Lib "user32" Alias "WinHelpA" (ByVal hwnd As Long,
➥ByVal lpHelpFile As String, ByVal wCommand As Long,
➥ByVal dwData As Long) As Long
```

3.6 TERMINATE ANOTHER PROGRAM

VB 3   VB 4₁₆

by Ian Ippolito

Description

Often, Visual Basic programs actually run other Windows applications. For example, many programs bring up information files using the Windows Notepad program. This is easy to do using the `Execute_Program` method located elsewhere in the book.

However, after a program is up and running, what do you do if you want to get rid of it? There is no built-in Visual Basic function to do this. However, it can be done quickly and easily using the following routine.

Syntax

Success = Close_External_Application(*Caption*)

Part	Description
Caption	Required. The complete caption in the window of the application that will be closed.
Success	Returns TRUE if successful, otherwise returns FALSE.

Code Listing

```
Option Explicit
Declare Function FindWindow Lib "User" (ByVal lpClassName As Any,
➥ ByVal lpWindowName As Any) As Integer
Declare Function GetWindowTask Lib "User" (ByVal hWnd As Integer) As Integer
Declare Function PostAppMessage Lib "User" (ByVal hTask As Integer,
➥ByVal wMsg As Integer, ByVal wParam As Integer, lParam As Any) As Integer
```

```
Public Const WM_QUIT = &H12
Function Close_External_Application(ByVal strCaptionTitle As String) _
    As Boolean
Dim intWindowHandle As Integer
Dim intTaskHandle As Integer
Dim intPostReturnValue As Integer
    'set defaults
    Close_External_Application = False

    'get handle of window matching caption
    intWindowHandle = FindWindow(0&, strCaptionTitle)

    If (intWindowHandle <> 0) Then
        'window found
        intTaskHandle = GetWindowTask(intWindowHandle)
        intPostReturnValue = PostAppMessage(intTaskHandle, WM_QUIT, 0, 0&)

        'set return value
        Close_External_Application = True

    End If
End Function
```

Analysis

This routine uses a series of Windows API functions to perform its work. First the FindWindow API function is called to retrieve the Windows handle of the caption passed into the program. If the window does indeed exist, this information is then used to retrieve the same window's task handle using the GetWindowTask API function. Finally, this task handle is used in the PostAppMessage API function to send the WM_QUIT message to the application, which causes it to close.

3.7 DETECT A PREVIOUS INSTANCE

by Ian Ippolito

Description

The multitasking nature of the Windows operating system is one of its primary advantages over older operating systems such as MS-DOS. By allowing users to run more than one program at once, users can make better and more efficient use of their PCs.

However, this strength can quickly turn into a disadvantage when a user attempts to run two instances of the same application on his or her system and that program hasn't been designed to handle this scenario. Often this happens unintentionally, such as when a user accidentally quadruple-clicks a program icon instead of double-clicking it. Because each instance of the program assumes that it has exclusive access to Registry and .INI settings, the result is usually a mangling or loss of those settings and an erratically behaving program. To the user, the program appears to be buggy.

To guard against this happening, a program can use the following routine to detect whether another instance of itself is already running. If this is the case, the program can then shut itself down with an appropriate warning message, avoiding embarrassing results down the road.

Note that this program does not function in the Visual Basic design-time environment. To utilize it, the program must be compiled into an executable and run.

Syntax

```
Running = Program_Is_Already_Running()
```

Part	Description
Running	Returns TRUE if the program is running, otherwise returns FALSE. If TRUE, the calling program will probably want to shut down after displaying a warning message.

Code Listing

```
Option Explicit
Function Program_Is_Already_Running() As Boolean
'determine if a previous instance of this application
    'is running using VB app object
    If (App.PrevInstance = True) Then
        Program_Is_Already_Running = True
     else
        Program_Is_Already_Running=FALSE
    End If

End Function
```

Analysis

This routine utilizes a little-used property of the Visual Basic App object (itself an obscure item) to determine whether a previous instance of the program is running.

To use this routine in your program, enter the following code as the first line in your program. This will be either the Form_Load of your startup form or in the Main() startup routine, depending on your project settings.

```
If (Program_Is_Already_Running()=TRUE) then
    MsgBox "Only one instance of this program can be running at one time",
    ➥vbOkOnly,"User Error"
    Stop
end if
```

3.8   PLACING ICONS IN THE SYSTEM TRAY

by Gary A Wiley

Description

The Windows API provides the capability to add, modify, and remove icons from the system tray available in the Windows 95 shell. This functionality can be provided using only the `Shell_NotifyIcon` function that is exported by Shell32.dll. This API function also provides the capability to specify a text string for the ToolTip that is displayed when a user pauses with the mouse pointer over the icon.

Syntax

```
Call AddIcon(frm, sTip)
Call RemoveIcon(frm)
```

Part	Description
frm	Required. The name of the form whose icon is to be placed in the tray. The Me keyword can be used.
sTip	Optional. The message to display when the cursor is over the icon. If not used, the form's caption will be used.

Code Listing

```
'Module code
Option Explicit

'Declarations and constants for placing icons in tray
Private Type NOTIFYICONDATA
    cbSize As Long
    hwnd As Long
    uId As Long
    uFlags As Long
    ucallbackMessage As Long
    hIcon As Long
    szTip As String * 64
End Type

Private TrayIcon As NOTIFYICONDATA

Public Const WM_LBUTTONDBLCLICK = &H203
Public Const WM_LBUTTONDOWN = &H201
Public Const WM_LBUTTONUP = &H202
Public Const WM_RBUTTONDBLCLK = &H206
Public Const WM_RBUTTONDOWN = &H204
```

```
Public Const WM_RBUTTONUP = &H205
Public Const WM_MOUSEMOVE = &H200
Const NIM_ADD = &H0
Const NIM_MODIFY = &H1
Const NIM_DELETE = &H2
Const NIF_MESSAGE = &H1
Const NIF_ICON = &H2
Const NIF_TIP = &H4


'API declaration to place icon in tray
Private Declare Function Shell_NotifyIcon Lib "shell32" Alias _
        "Shell_NotifyIconA" (ByVal dwMessage As Long, _
            pnid As NOTIFYICONDATA) As Boolean

Public Sub AddIcon(frm As Form, Optional sTip As String)
    'Sub to place icon in tray
    With TrayIcon
        .cbSize = Len(TrayIcon)
        .hwnd = frm.hwnd
        .uId = vbNull
        .uFlags = NIF_ICON Or NIF_TIP Or NIF_MESSAGE
        .ucallbackMessage = WM_MOUSEMOVE
        .hIcon = frm.Icon
        'set tool tip text
        If sTip = "" Then
            .szTip = frm.Caption & vbNullChar
        Else
            .szTip = sTip & vbNullChar
        End If
    End With
    'Places icon in tray
    Call Shell_NotifyIcon(NIM_ADD, TrayIcon)
    'Hide the form
    frm.Hide
End Sub

Public Sub RemoveIcon(frm As Form)
    'Sub to remove icon from tray
    With TrayIcon
        .cbSize = Len(TrayIcon)
        .hwnd = frm.hwnd
        .uId = vbNull
    End With
    'Removes icon from tray
    Call Shell_NotifyIcon(NIM_DELETE, TrayIcon)
End Sub

'Sample Form code. You will need to create a menu called mnuTray
Option Explicit

Private Sub Form_Load()
Call AddIcon(Me)
End Sub
```

```
Private Sub Form_MouseMove(Button As Integer, Shift As Integer,
➡ X As Single, Y As Single)
    Dim lMsg As Long
    lMsg = X / Screen.TwipsPerPixelX
    Select Case lMsg
            Case WM_LBUTTONDBLCLICK
                'code for left button double-click
                Me.WindowState = 0
                Me.Show
            Case WM_LBUTTONDOWN
                'code for left button down
            Case WM_LBUTTONUP
                'code for left button up
            Case WM_RBUTTONDBLCLK
                'code for right button double-clicked
            Case WM_RBUTTONDOWN
                'code for right button down
            Case WM_RBUTTONUP
                'code for right button up
                'typically show a popup menu
                'with at least one menu item
                'to exit the application!
                Me.PopupMenu mnuTray
        End Select
End Sub

Private Sub Form_QueryUnload(Cancel As Integer, UnloadMode As Integer)
    Call RemoveIcon(Me)
End Sub

Private Sub Form_Resize()
    'Use this code if the ShownInTaskbar
    'property is set to true
    If Me.WindowState = 1 Then
        Me.Hide
        Exit Sub
    End If
    'Other code for form resize event
End Sub

Private Sub mExit_Click(Index As Integer)
    Unload Me
End Sub

Private Sub mHide_Click()
    Me.WindowState = 1
End Sub

Private Sub mShow_Click(Index As Integer)
    Me.WindowState = 0
    Me.Show
End Sub
```

Analysis

Although placing icons in the tray is fairly simple, there are some special considerations if the form's ShownInTaskbar property is true. When hiding the form, set its WindowState property to 1, minimized. Then use code as shown in the form resize event to hide it. When showing the form, first set its WindowState property to 0, normal; or 2, maximized, and then use the Show method. This way you can be sure the form's resize event will always be fired when showing and hiding the form.

3.9 ANIMATED TASKBAR ICONS

by Then Nam Kheong

Description

Whenever a program is started, the taskbar will have a button with the program icon and description of the program. The icon of the taskbar button is boring, which might make your program boring too. You can make your taskbar icon alive by adding some routine at Timer1_Timer().

Syntax

None.

Code Listing

```
'***********************************************
'* Submitted by Then Nam Kheong
'***********************************************
Private Sub Timer1_Timer()
    Form1.Icon =Image1(idx).picture
    Idx = (Idx + 1) Mod 3    Animation counter. Number 3 means that there
    ➥ are 3 images
End Sub

Private Sub Form_Load()

Timer1.Enabled=True

Timer1.Interval=50

End Sub
```

Analysis

Before you can continue with this routine, you must first create three or more animation images. Save them in your application directory before you continue. In form1, you must create a control array. For this example create three arrays of images, `Image1(0)`, `Image1(1)`, `Image1(2)`. Load one icon image into each `Image1` control. After this, remember to change the `Visible` property to `False`. Similarly, you can use the ImageList control to load images into the control. Finally, add a timer control to Form1. Remember to add the code as shown to start the timer control.

Now you can type the preceding routine. Run the program, and you will see that the icon at the taskbar button starts to animate.

There are a few things to note before you start using this routine in your program. Do not use a very big icon because Windows will shrink the icon to fit in the taskbar button, making it look meaningless. 16×16 pixel icons should be enough. Next, try not to overdo the animation. Too much animation can be annoying to the user. Three to five animation images are good enough.

This routine can be useful when you need to convey important messages to the user. You can create an animated virus warning, a printing-in-progress animation, a warning before closing the application animation, or an alarm system animation. Here, creativity comes into play. Have fun!

3.10 EASTER EGGS

by Then Nam Kheong

Description

You might be familiar with Easter eggs. Basically, they are extra unnecessary routines added to an existing program for many reasons, such as the following:

- To show off a developer's programming skills
- To thank the team effort made
- To give a programmer his own credit because his company doesn't want to put his name in the program
- Just for fun

Truthfully, Easter eggs serve no purpose in programs other than for fun or to display a programmer's imagination. (Perhaps one day you will find this useful.) Easter eggs are triggered by a combination of keypresses or mouse clicks, or both. A more complex one would monitor the `KeyDown` events for several controls. What you see in Easter eggs is purely the author's creation. Windows 3.11 and Windows 95 have not-too-exciting Easter eggs, but the Easter egg in Excel 5 is actually a 3D game!

Syntax

None.

Code Listing

```
'**********************************************
'* Submitted by Then Nam Kheong
'**********************************************

Sub Form_KeyDown(KeyCode As Integer, Shift As Integer)

Dim ShiftDown As Boolean, CtrlDown As Boolean
 ShiftDown = (Shift And vbShiftMask) > 0
 CtrlDown = (Shift And vbCtrlMask) > 0
  If KeyCode = vbKeyT Then    'Here, user will need to press
 ➡Shift+Ctrl+T at the same time
     If ShiftDown And CtrlDown = True Then
         Picture1.Visible = True
         Timer1.Enabled = True
         Timer1.Interval = 1000
     End If
  End If
End Sub


Sub Timer1_Timer()
Static i As Integer
i = (i + 1) Mod 5    'Cycles thru 0 to 4
  If i = 0 Then
     Label1.Caption = "This is my Easter Egg!"
  ElseIf i = 1 Then
     Label1.Caption = "Nice, isn't it?"
  ElseIf i = 2 Then
     Label1.Caption = "You can make different " + Chr(10) +
     ➡"kinds of eggs."
  ElseIf i = 3 Then
     Label1.Caption = "And animations."
  Else
     Label1.Caption = "Good Bye."
  End If
End Sub
```

Analysis

To program an Easter egg you simply add code to KeyDown() events. Picture1 is set invisible while the Timer1 control is disabled. When the user presses the required keys (Shift+Ctrl+T) Picture1 is set to visible and enables the timer. Remember to set Form1's KeyPreview properties to True.

The third line tests for a condition by first comparing Shift or Ctrl to a bit mask by using the And operator. If the Shift key is pressed, the variable ShiftDown will be greater than 0:

```
ShiftDown = (Shift And vbShiftMask) > 0
```

The KeyDown event will test for pressed Shift, Ctrl, and Alt keypresses. Type the following code if you want to test for Ctrl and Alt keys:

```
CtrlDown = (Shift And vbCtrlMask) > 0
AltDown = (Shift And vbAltMask) > 0
```

Your Easter egg will start in the `Timer1` control. What you code under the `Timer1_Timer()` is entirely up to your imagination. Here, my Easter egg displays a bitmap and text. You also can use VB animation to display your Easter egg.

3.11   DELAYING A VISUAL BASIC PROGRAM

by James Limm

Description

This code suspends the execution of a Visual Basic program for a defined number of milliseconds. The delay it produces is not dependent on clock speed, so it is much more accurate than any delays that are based on loops. However, due to the multitasking environment, delays using `Sleep` cannot be guaranteed to be accurate.

Syntax

```
Call Sleep(time)
```

Part	Description
time	Required. The number of milliseconds that the function should delay.

Code Listing

```
'Copy this code into the declarations section of the project.
Private Declare Sub Sleep Lib "kernel32" (ByVal dwMilliseconds As Long)
```

Analysis

This code sample is based on the API call `Sleep`. The `Sleep` function accepts a time in milliseconds and halts execution of all code for the time defined in its parameters. There are 1000 milliseconds in a second, so the function is capable of producing quite accurate delays. When the delay is complete, Windows resumes running the code from the line after the `Sleep` command is called. This is very useful if you are waiting for an external process to complete. It could also be used inside loops to slow them down if you want to create a stopwatch or timer.

Because the `Sleep` function is part of the Windows API, the delays it produces are not dependent on the processor speed. However, the delay can vary because Windows is a multitasking operating system. If Windows has allocated processing time away from the thread that the Visual Basic program uses, the `Sleep` function might not be very accurate.

It is important to realize that the `Sleep` function really does send the program to sleep. It receives no processing time and will not process any events, including `Paint`, until the `Sleep` function returns control to the program. With this in mind, it is important to use `Sleep` for very short delays only, in conjunction with the `DoEvents` method, which allows the program to process any pending events.

In most cases, the timer control is better for delays because it does not tie up the program as much as the `Sleep` function.

3.12 GET USER REGISTRATION INFORMATION

by Mike Shaffer

Description

The `GetRegistration` routine obtains the username and company name entered when Windows was installed on the machine.

Note that this routine uses the `GetRegEntry` routine, also included with this book.

Syntax

```
GetRegistration strUser$, strCompany$
```

Part	*Description*
strUser$	Required. A string that will receive the registered username.
strCompany$	Required. A string that will receive the registered company name.

Code Listing

```
'**********************************************
'* Submitted by Mike Shaffer
'**********************************************
Sub GetRegistration(RegUser As String, RegCompany As String)
    '
    Dim USER As String, org As String
    Dim lngType As Long
    Dim strTemp As String
    Dim varRetString As Variant
    '
    '
    ' First we get the country/language specifics
    '
    If GetOSVersion = 2 then
        VarRatString = GetRegEntry("HKEY_LOCAL_MACHINE", _
```

```
      "SOFTWARE\Microsoft\Windows NT\CurrentVersion", "RegisteredOrganization",
   ➡ lngType)
         RegCompany = varRetString
         '
         VarRetString = GetRegEntry("HKEY_LOCAL_MACHINE", _
   "SOFTWARE\Microsoft\Windows NT\CurrentVersion", "RegisteredOwner", lngType)
         RegUser = varRetString
      Else
         varRetString = GetRegEntry("HKEY_LOCAL_MACHINE", _
   "SOFTWARE\Microsoft\Windows\CurrentVersion", "RegisteredOrganization", lngType)
         RegCompany = varRetString
         '
         varRetString = GetRegEntry("HKEY_LOCAL_MACHINE", _
   "SOFTWARE\Microsoft\Windows\CurrentVersion", "RegisteredOwner", lngType)
         RegUser = varRetString
      End if
      '
   End Sub
```

Analysis

This routine is useful in obtaining default username and company name information. This information might be useful in your own software's licensing, warranty, and setup routines (to automatically provide default username and company name). See also the `GetRegEntry` routine.

3.13 GET THE OS VERSION

by Mike Shaffer

Description

The `GetOSVersion` function returns the Windows platform currently running. The value returned by this function will correspond to the following:

0	Pre-Windows 95 (such as Windows 3.1 or WFW)
1	Windows 95
2	Windows NT 4.0
3	Windows 98
4	Windows NT 3.51

Syntax

```
If GetOSVersion = 0 then MsgBox "Can't run on pre-Windows 95 systems!"
```

Part	Description
GetOSVersion	The integer function

Code Listing

```
'************************************************
'* Submitted by Mike Shaffer
'************************************************
Declare Function GetVersionEx Lib "kernel32" Alias "GetVersionExA" _
(lpVersionInformation As OSVERSIONINFO) As LongPrivate Type OSVERSIONINFO
    dwOSVersionInfoSize As Long
    dwMajorVersion As Long
    dwMinorVersion As Long
    dwBuildNumber As Long
    dwPlatformId As Long
    szCSDVersion As String * 128
End Type
Dim OSV As OSVERSIONINFO              ' allocate struct

Public Function GetOSVersion() As Integer
    '
    Dim result As Long
    '
    OSV.dwOSVersionInfoSize = Len(OSV)
    '
    result = GetVersionEx(OSV)
    '
    GetOSVersion = OSV.dwPlatformId
    Select case GetOSVersion
        Case 1
            If OSV.dwMinorVersion = 10 then GetOSVersion = 3
        Case 2
            If OSV.dwMinorVersion = 51 then GetOSVersion = 4
    End Select
    '
End Function
```

Analysis

This code returns the high-level Windows platform information. The Windows API call `GetVersionEX` provides this information in the following format:

	Win95	*Win98*	*Win NT 3.51*	*Win NT 4.0*
dwPlatformID	1	1	2	2
dwMajorVersion	4	4	3	4
dwMinorVersion	0	10	51	0

3.14   GET LOCALE INFORMATION

by Mike Shaffer

Description

The GetLocale function obtains the default language and currency symbol in use with the current Windows configuration. Note that this function uses the GetRegEntry routine, also included with this book.

Syntax

RC = GetLocale(Lang$, CurrSym$)

Part	Description
RC	Required. Long result code, 0 if failure, otherwise it is the Windows language code.
Lang$	Required. A string that will receive the human-readable description (name) of the language in use.
CurrSym$	Required. A string that will receive the currency symbol in use.

Code Listing

```
'***********************************************
'* Submitted by Mike Shaffer
'***********************************************
Declare Function GetLocaleInfo Lib "kernel32" Alias "GetLocaleInfoA"
➥ (ByVal Locale As Long, _
ByVal LCType As Long, ByVal lpLCData As String, ByVal cchData As Long)
➥As Long

 Function GetLocale(CtryLang As String, CurrSym As String) As Long
    '
    Dim lngType As Long
    Dim varRetString As Variant
    Dim strTemp As String
    Dim Buffer As String * 100
    Dim dl as long
    '
    ' First we get the country/language specifics
    '
    varRetString = GetRegEntry("HKEY_LOCAL_MACHINE", _
      "System\CurrentControlSet\Control\Nls\Locale", "", lngType)
    If IsNumeric(varRetString) Then
       GetLocale = CLng(varRetString)
    Else
```

```
        GetLocale = 0
    End If
    '
    strTemp = varRetString
    varRetString = GetRegEntry("HKEY_LOCAL_MACHINE", _
  "System\CurrentControlSet\Control\Nls\Locale", strTemp, lngType)
    CtryLang = varRetString
    '
    dl = GetLocaleInfo(LOCALE_USER_DEFAULT, LOCALE_SCURRENCY, Buffer, 100)
    CurrSym = Left$(Buffer, dl-1)
    '
End Function
```

Analysis

See also the GetRegEntry routine in section 3.12, "Get User Registration Information."

3.15   GET AN APPLICATION'S PATH

by Mike Shaffer

Description

The GetAppPath function is an improvement on VB's App.Path. It fixes an inconsistency with trailing backslashes. For example, an application located in the root subdirectory of drive C: would return an App.Path of C:\ (note the trailing backslash), whereas an application located in the Windows directory might return an App.Path of C:\WINDOWS (note the lack of a trailing backslash). This routine simply ensures a consistent response to finding your application's path.

Syntax

GetAppPath

Code Listing

```
'***********************************************
'* Submitted by Mike Shaffer
'***********************************************
Function GetAppPath() As String
    '
    Dim tmp As String
    '
    tmp = App.Path
    If Right$(tmp, 1) = "\" Then tmp = Left$(tmp, Len(tmp) - 1)
    '
```

```
    GetAppPath = tmp
    '
End Function
```

Analysis

This routine makes retrieving the application path more consistent. The function simply retrieves the application's path using the VB function App.Path, and then strips a trailing backslash if it exists.

3.16   ACTIVATE PARTIAL

by Mike Shaffer

Description

The AppActivatePartial routine is a vast improvement on the Visual Basic AppActivate function. One of the problems with AppActivate is that it will not restore the program it is activating if that program is in a minimized state. There are various methods to try and force AppActivate to work (most involve using SendKeys), but they cannot be guaranteed to function under all conditions and Windows platforms. This set of routines will work correctly under Windows 95, Windows 98, and Windows NT.

AppActivatePartial actually consists of two separate routines. They could be consolidated into one routine, but you might find the individual functions useful on their own.

To use the AppActivatePartial function in your application, you might use code similar to this in your MAIN routine or your FORM_LOAD event (note the reference to UnloadAllForms, which is also included in this book):

```
If App.PrevInstance Then
    ' Save the app's title to restore other instance
    SaveTitle$ = App.Title
    ' Set title to something else momentarily
    App.Title = "... duplicate instance."
    ' Activate it
    RC = AppActivatePartial(Trim$(SaveTitle$), 0&, False)
    UnloadAllForms ""
    End
End If
```

Syntax

```
RC= AppActivatePartial(AppTitle$, FindType&, CaseSensitive)
```

Part	Description
RC	Required. The resulting code of the function (0 if failed, handle if successful).
AppTitle$	Required. A string expression that specifies the title of the application you want to activate. This may be a partial name.
FindType&	Optional. This may be any of the following:
	0 Title starts with string AppTitle$
	1 Title contains string AppTitle$
	2 Title matches AppTitle$ exactly
CaseSensitive	Optional. A Boolean value that makes the application title comparison case-sensitive (TRUE) or case-insensitive (FALSE).

Code Listing

```
Private stchWnd As Long
Private stcMethod As FindWindowPartialTypes
Private stcCase As Boolean
Private m_Visible As Boolean
Private stcApplicationTitle As String
'
' Constants used by FindWindowPartial
'
Public Enum FindWindowPartialTypes
    FwpStartsWith = 0
    FwpContains = 1
    FwpMatches = 2
End Enum
Declare Function IsIconic Lib "USER32" (ByVal hWnd As Long) As Long
Declare Function ShowWindow Lib "USER32" (ByVal hWnd As Long, _
        ByVal nCmdShow As Long) As Long
Declare Function SetForegroundWindow Lib "USER32" (ByVal hWnd As Long)
➡As Long
Declare Function EnumWindows Lib "USER32" (ByVal lpEnumFunc As Long, _
        ByVal lParam As Long) As Long
Declare Function IsWindowVisible Lib "USER32" (ByVal hWnd As Long)
➡As Long
Private Declare Function GetStrCaption Lib "USER32" Alias
➡"GetWindowTextA" (ByVal hWnd As Long, _
ByVal lpString As String, ByVal cch As Long) As Long

Public Function AppActivatePartial(AppTitle As String, _
        Optional Method As FindWindowPartialTypes = FwpStartsWith, _
        Optional CaseSensitive As Boolean = False) As Long
    ':::::::::::::::::::::::::::::::::::::::::::::::::::::::::::::::::::'
    ':::                                                          :::'
    ':::    Retrieve window handle for first top-level window      :::'
    ':::    that starts with or contains the passed string.        :::'
    ':::                                                          :::'
    ':::::::::::::::::::::::::::::::::::::::::::::::::::::::::::::::::::'
```

```
    '
    Dim hWndApp As Long
    '
    AppActivatePartial = 0
    '
    hWndApp = FindWindowPartial(AppTitle, Method, CaseSensitive, True)
    If hWndApp Then
        '
        ' Switch to it, restoring if necessary (minimized)
        '
        If IsIconic(hWndApp) Then Call ShowWindow(hWndApp, SW_RESTORE)
        '
        Call SetForegroundWindow(hWndApp)
        AppActivatePartial = hWndApp
        '
    End If
    '
End Function

Public Function FindWindowPartial(AppTitle As String, _
    Optional Method As FindWindowPartialTypes = FwpStartsWith, _
    Optional CaseSensitive As Boolean = False, _
    Optional MustBeVisible As Boolean = False) As Long
    '
    ':::::::::::::::::::::::::::::::::::::::::::::::::::::::::::::::::::::::'
    ':::                                                             :::'
    ':::    Retrieve window handle for first top-level window         :::'
    ':::    that starts with or contains the passed string.          :::'
    ':::                                                             :::'
    ':::::::::::::::::::::::::::::::::::::::::::::::::::::::::::::::::::::::'
    '
    ' Reset all search parameters.
    '
    stchWnd = 0
    stcMethod = Method
    stcCase = CaseSensitive
    stcApplicationTitle = AppTitle
    '
    ' Upper-case search string if case-insensitive.
    '
    If stcCase = False Then stcApplicationTitle =
    ➥UCase$(stcApplicationTitle)
    '
    ' Fire off enumeration, and return stchWnd when done.
    '
    Call EnumWindows(AddressOf EnumWindowsProc, MustBeVisible)
    FindWindowPartial = stchWnd
End Function

Private Function EnumWindowsProc(ByVal hWnd As Long, ByVal lParam As Long)
➥ As Long
    '
```

```
':::::::::::::::::::::::::::::::::::::::::::::::::::::::::::::::::::::::::'
':::                                                                ::::'
':::    Function to enumerate all windows procs                     ::::'
':::                                                                ::::'
':::::::::::::::::::::::::::::::::::::::::::::::::::::::::::::::::::::::::'
'
'
Static StrCaption As String
Static lngRC As Long
'
' Make sure we meet visibility requirements.
'
If lParam Then EnumWindowsProc = (IsWindowVisible(hWnd) = False)
'
' Retrieve the caption
'
StrCaption = Space$(256)
lngRC = GetStrCaption(hWnd, StrCaption, Len(StrCaption))
'
If lngRC Then
    '
    ' Clean up window text and prepare for comparison.
    '
    StrCaption = Left$(StrCaption, lngRC)
    If stcCase = False Then
        StrCaption = UCase$(StrCaption)
    End If
    '
    ' See if caption matches in desired way
    '
    Select Case stcMethod
       Case FwpMatches
          If StrCaption = stcApplicationTitle Then stchWnd = hWnd
       Case FwpStartsWith
          If InStr(StrCaption, stcApplicationTitle) = 1 Then
          ➥stchWnd = hWnd
       Case FwpContains
          If InStr(StrCaption, stcApplicationTitle) <> 0 Then
          ➥stchWnd = hWnd
    End Select
    '
End If
'
' Continue enumeration if necessary
'
EnumWindowsProc = (stchWnd = 0)
'
End Function
```

Analysis

This routine is a bit involved, but its interface is fortunately very simple. It is useful as a direct, enhanced replacement for the VB AppActivate function.

3.17   PARSE COMMAND PARAMETERS

by Tom Honaker

Description

The CommandLineParamParser is a command-line argument handler consisting of a sub and two functions (with no requirement for API calls). It permits easy handling of command-line switches, and command-line parameter passing to applications.

Windows and Windows NT users might not be aware that command-line parameters can be passed to graphical applications as well as to their text-based cousins. Of course, DOS users are intimately familiar with command-line parameter passing because a large number of DOS programs can accept at least one switch. (For example, try typing command.com /? at a DOS prompt. /? is the command-line switch to invoke the built-in help text.)

Exploiting this behavior can lead to interesting, useful additions that could enhance an application. It can, for example, be exploited to grant the capability to turn little-used or infrequently needed features on or off via shortcuts.

The three routines combine to grant flexible, powerful, expandable code for handling most types of command-line arguments. With creative use of this code, it is possible to add almost any switch to a program and invoke its corresponding code by adding the appropriate switch's text to a shortcut pointing to the compiled executable. The code can also accept data passed with a switch (for example, /score:500, /sys-dir:c:\windows\system or /password:letmein) and parse it, returning the data in either string or numeric form (or both) that can be copied into program variables for easy use by code elsewhere in the program.

After it is added to a project by way of a module, the core routine (ParseCLSwitches) is called from the beginning of program code (in Sub_Main or in the Form_Load event of the first form that loads). That way, anything passed to the program via the command line can be interpreted and dealt with before other code in the program that can interfere with the same functions is run.

The code is remarkably well behaved, ignoring anything not starting with a specific character or group of characters. Most DOS command-line switches started with either a hyphen (-) or a forward slash (/).

Because Windows 95 and NT can accept filenames that contain hyphens but do not permit a forward slash in a filename, this is the default choice. This can, of course, be changed. Command-line parameters that start with the correct character but have not had detect code sections installed are copied into a variable to be dealt with as the programmer sees fit. Switches that are not intended to be used with parameters (such as the /debug example earlier) but have them tacked on anyway are dealt with as normal, and the parameters added to that switch are ignored.

Any number of command-line switches can be detected by adding a small section of code (8–10 lines usually) for each switch to look for. The order in which the switches appear on the command line is not important; all switches that have matches in code will be detected in the order in which they appear on the command line. The operating system imposes a length limit on a command line of 256 characters, so plan accordingly.

Because this code is very flexible and expandable, and can be readily adapted to practically any command-line data passing that should be needed, the code is fairly complex. As a result, it has been heavily commented. Reading the comments and stepping through execution is recommended.

Syntax

Call the sub ParseCLSwitches without any arguments as soon in the execution of the program as possible.

Code Listing

```
' Paste this into a module and call it from the first
' executing sub.

Public ReturnedString$
Public ParameterText$
Public ParameterValue

Sub ParseCLSwitches()

    Dim unksw$, comm$, nop%, checkchar, functreturn

    ' Check to see if any command-line data was passed to
    ' the program. After all, if nothing was passed there's
    ' not much point in running this sub.
    '
    If Command = "" Then Exit Sub

    ' Get the command line arguments passed to the program...
    '
    comm$ = Command


    ' ***
    '
    ' Default on-off variable values for each item go first...
    ' Make sure to declare each in your project's global
```

```
' declarations if you want to use the variable(s)
' project-wide...
'
' Replace the examples with variables appropriate to your
' needs.
'
'


' Our rhetorical switch, Switch1. Its variable is 'Switch1%'
' and the switch we look for is '/switch1'
'
Switch1% = False

' Our rhetorical parameter passer, Switch2. This one can accept
' a value that trails the switch and a colon. What we look for
' in this case is '/switch2:<value>' where <value> can be any
' numeric integer value. (Use the appropriate data type for
' a storage variable for non-integer numbers.)
'
Switch2% = False
Switch2Value = 0

' Our demonstration switch, '/test', which triggers a MsgBox
' when the command-line switch is passed.

TestMode% = 0


'
'
' ***


' Time to start parsing the CL... This code assumes that the
' switch-identifying character is a forward-slash. You can
' substitute whatever character(s) you'd prefer. If it does
' not begin with this particular character(s) the parser
' will ignore it, which is useful for passing filenames
' to your program.
'
' IMPORTANT! Select characters for command-line switches
' that won't occur in filenames, etc. A forward slash is
' a good choice, as is a pipe (shift-backslash.)
'
Do Until InStr(1, comm$, "/", 1) = 0

    ' ***
    ' Sections to detect each CL switch go here...
    '



    ' ***
    ' This is a section for detecting one switch. Use one
```

```
' such section with the appropriate changes for each
' switch you'd like to trap and act upon. This particular
' section is intended to deal with switches that turn
' something on or off. For passing values, examine the
' next demonstration section.

If Switch1% <> True Then
' ...meaning that as long as the value hasn't
'     been set by another pass, check to see if
'     it's there. If it HAS been detected, don't
'     bother rechecking. This saves some processing
'     time in some situations.

     ' The text to check. In this case, we're
     ' looking for '/switch1' We'll pass this to
     ' the checking function to see if it finds
     ' the string.
     '
' Notice too that we include the switch character,
     ' in this case a forward slash, in this function call.
     '
     a$ = GetCLSwitch(comm$, "/switch1")

     If a$ <> "NotFound" Then

          ' Okay, that switch exists. Set the appropriate
          ' variable. (Feel free to add any extra code.)
          '
          Switch1% = True

          ' If there are parameters attached to this switch,
          ' we need to find and remove them so we do not have
          ' any source of confusion later for switches that
          ' actually do have parameters we need to be worried
          ' about.
          '
          ' We do this by calling the StripParams function
          ' and ignore its returned data.
          '
          functreturn = StripParams(a$)

          ' Use the returned string (which is the
          ' command-line arguments passed to the
          ' program, with the switch we're looking
          ' for replaced with spaces) for next time...
          '
          comm$ = ReturnedString$

     End If
End If
'
' End of this section. Repeat as desired for each switch.
```

```
' If you'd like to compress the source a bit, edit out the
' comments from all but one such section. Doing so will reduce
' a section to around a dozen lines of code.
' ***


' ***
' This section is slightly different from the first in
' that it will receive a numeric value. In this case we
' want to pass a value to the program through the command
' line. In this case, we can accept things like
' '/switch2:255' and so forth.
'
If Switch2% <> True Then

        ' Now to look for the switch. DO NOT include the colon
        ' that separates the switch from the value.
        '
        a$ = GetCLSwitch(comm$, "/switch2")
        If a$ <> "NotFound" Then

            ' Yes, the switch is present.
            '
            Switch2% = True

            ' Now that we've established that the switch
            ' exists, we call the StripParams function to
            ' find and process any parameters that were
            ' attached to the switch.
            '
            functreturn = StripParams(a$)

            ' Since we only care about the numeric value
            ' of this particular switch, we read the value
            ' returned in ParameterValue into our variable
            ' and ignore the ParameterChars$ data.
            '
            Switch2Value = ParameterValue

comm$ = ReturnedString$

        End If
    End If
    ' ***

    ' This is what these two example sections would look like
    ' without any comments:
    '
    ' If Switch1% <> True Then
    '     a$ = GetCLSwitch(comm$, "/switch1")
    '     If a$ <> "NotFound" Then
    '         Switch1% = True
```

```
'           functreturn = StripParams(a$)
'           comm$ = ReturnedString$
'      End If
' End If
'
' ...And for the switch that carried a value the
' section is only one line longer:
'
' If Switch2% <> True Then
'     a$ = GetCLSwitch(comm$, "/switch2")
'     If a$ <> "NotFound" Then
'         Switch2% = True
'         functreturn = StripParams(a$)
'         Switch2Value% = ParameterValue
'         comm$ = ReturnedString$
'     End If
' End If
'
'
' Not very big. As a result you can add switch
' handling for practically any number of switches.


' Now to test for our demonstration switch '/test'÷

If TestMode% <> True Then
    a$ = GetCLSwitch(comm$, "/test")
    If a$ <> "NotFound" Then
        MsgBox "Test Mode activated! (/test command-line _
        switch detected)" , vbInformation, "Command-line _
        switch detected"
        TestMode% = True
        functreturn = StripParams(a$)
        comm$ = ReturnedString$
    End If
End If



'
'
' ***
' End of switch detector sections.


' ***
' This section MUST follow AFTER all of the other
' CL switch detectors above.
'
If (a$ = comm$) And (comm$ <> "") And _
  (InStr(1, comm$, "/", 1) <> 0) Then
```

```
             ' Okay, we've stripped off everything that we
             ' recognize. Now we need to strip off any
             ' command-line arguments we DON'T recognize.
             '
             comm$ = Trim(comm$)
             checkchar = InStr(1, comm$, "/", 1)
             nop% = checkchar
             Do Until (Mid$(comm$, nop%, 1) = " ") _
               Or (nop% > Len(comm$))
                  nop% = nop% + 1
             Loop
             unksw$ = unksw$ + Mid$(comm$, checkchar, _
               nop% - checkchar) + " "
             Mid(comm$, checkchar, nop% - checkchar) = _
               Space(nop% - checkchar)
             comm$ = Trim(comm$)
        End If


        ' Repeat until we find no more command-line
        ' text that starts with our designated command
        ' character(s).
        '
    Loop



        ' At this point, we're left with these variables:
        '
        ' comm$,   which holds the remaining parameters. (You can parse
        '          this for filenames, etc. if your program accepts
        '          filenames and you'd like drag-and-drop activation,
        '          etc.)
        ' unksw$, which contains anything that started with our
        '          favorite command character(s) that is not found in
        '          the sections above. This traps out typo'ed switches,
        '          etc. You could alert the user to these errant
        '          switches if desired.
        '
        ' You can move the contents of these to globally declared
        ' variables if you'd like to pass them out of this sub for
        ' whatever reason.

End Sub

Function GetCLSwitch(commandlineargs As String, _
  commandtosearchfor As String) As String

        ' This function checks to see if a certain string exists within
        ' another string. If so, it replaces it with spaces so that the
        ' command-line checker routine doesn't loop infinitely.
```

```
' Pretty basic.

Dim whereargstarts, arglength

' Find the substring's (the command-line switch we want to
' check for) starting location...
'
whereargstarts = InStr(1, commandlineargs$, _
 commandtosearchfor$, 1)

' Is it in there?
'
If whereargstarts <> 0 Then

    ' Yes. Replace it with spaces...
    '
    arglength = Len(commandtosearchfor$)
    Mid(commandlineargs$, whereargstarts, arglength) _
      = Space(arglength)

    ' Pass the resulting string out of the function for
    ' the next pass.
    '
    GetCLSwitch = commandlineargs$

Else

    ' No. Pass 'NotFound' out of the function.
    '
    GetCLSwitch = "NotFound"

End If

End Function

Function StripParams(source As String)

    If InStr(1, source$, "  :", 1) = 0 Then
        ReturnedString$ = source$
        Exit Function
    End If

    checkchar = InStr(1, source$, "  :", 1) + 2

    nop% = 0
    Do Until (Mid(source$, checkchar + nop%, 1) = " ") _
      Or (checkchar + nop% > Len(source$))
        nop% = nop% + 1
    Loop

    ParameterChars$ = Mid$(source$, checkchar + 1, nop% - 1)
    ParameterValue = Val(Mid$(source$, checkchar + 1, nop%))
```

```
Mid(source$, checkchar, checkchar + nop%) = Space(nop%)
ReturnedString$ = source$

End Function
```

Analysis

Because the code is complex, it is more helpful to read through the comments and step through program execution with a few dummy (or real) command-line parameters being passed to the program from VB directly. (Open the project's Properties window from the Project menu, click the Make tab, and add items to the Command Line Arguments box to do this.)

Essentially, in the beginning of `ParseCLSwitches` the program will check for any command-line arguments and exit the sub if none are found. Then, a variable (`comm$`) is filled with the arguments in the form of one long string. Each switch has a small section of code that checks for that switch's text. If the switch text is found within `comm$`, appropriate code is executed, the `GetCLSwitches` function replaces it with spaces, and the `StripParams` function checks for and replaces any data attached to the switch. The process repeats until nothing is found that begins with the command-line switch character (a forward slash, although this can be changed). The remaining contents of `comm$` are then trimmed to remove leading and trailing spaces that were left from the replacement process.

At the end, the routine leaves two variables that might still be holding data. One is `comm$`, which by this point only holds any remaining data that doesn't look to the parser like a switch (for example, no words that begin with the command character, a forward slash). The other is `unksw$`, which holds any words that started with the forward slash but were not defined as switches to look for by code sections. Erroneous switches will be dumped into `unksw$`, making discovery of incorrectly spelled switches easy, especially of this variable's contents are presented to the user in a dialog box to let him know of the bad switches.

Adding a new switch is as simple as defining a variable to hold its state, adding a section of code to look for that switch's text, and coding whatever actions throughout the program to take if the switch is invoked. The only limits to switch count are the physical size of the program and the fact that command-line arguments cannot exceed 255 characters in length, including the path to the file in question.

There are two known limitations.

- Switches cannot contain substrings that match other complete switches. If this occurs, the first match of the two will be used regardless of whether this is intended. For example, assume that the code has been installed to look for both `/switch1` and `/switch11` and the `/switch1` code appears first. The user passes `/switch11` as the command-line parameter. The code looking for `/switch1` will activate and remove all the switches, while code for `/switch11` will see nothing. Using two complete switches that share substrings is accepted, such as `/switch1` and `/switch2`. To simplify, similarities like `/switch1` and `/switch11` are not advised, but similarities like `/switch1` and `/switch2` are acceptable.

- Switch data cannot contain spaces. For example, the switch `/file:c:\Program Files\myapp\blah.exe` would produce erroneous results because of the space between `Program` and `Files`. The reason for this is that spaces in the command line are used by the operating system as delimiters, separating each item. As a result, this code also looks for spaces as delimiters and assumes that a space marks the end of the entry. The workaround is simply to not use spaces within switch data. In the case of filenames, pass them in MS-DOS 8.3 format instead of as long filenames to eliminate this problem.

This code was intended for Visual Basic 5 but should work well with no to little modification in Visual Basic 4 because commands common to both versions have been employed.

3.18   RED, GREEN, AND BLUE

by Fredrik Bodin

Description

These three functions return the color components of a selected region of the screen. You can use them when you create a color dialog box. For example, if the user clicks on a brown box, three text boxes can indicate the levels of red, green, and blue that are used. The opposite of this function is the RGB function.

Syntax

```
colorRed = Red(Color)
colorGreen = Green(Color)
colorBlue = Blue(Color)
```

Part	Description
Color	Required. Specifies the color of, for example, a picture box. It can also describe the color of a point using the point command. The function returns a value within the range of 0 to 255.

Code Listing

```
Private Function Red(ByVal Color As Long) As Integer
        Red = Color Mod &H100
End Function

Private Function Green(ByVal Color As Long) As Integer
        Green = (Color \ &H100) Mod &H100
End Function

Private Function Blue(ByVal Color As Long) As Integer
            Blue = (Color \ &H10000) Mod &H100
End Function
```

Analysis

This routine calculates the color of a selected region on the screen. Each pixel on the screen is filled with a specific color, which is determined by the levels of red, green, and blue present. The three colors mix together to form a color.

As an example, the level of red is returned by dividing the color by 256 (hexadecimal 100), and the excess from 255 is the specific value. Green is the same thing, but then you divide the color value twice, and so on. This is how the RGB system is constructed in Windows.

3.19   BETTER SPACE FILL

by David Berube

Description

The SpaceEx function enables you to create a string full of spaces. The string can be as long as you want. Additionally, you can substitute another character for the space. Visual Basic provides a simple way to accomplish this through the Space function, but it does not easily allow characters other than the space to be used. The SpaceEx routine provided here performs such tasks with ease.

Using this function in your application is simple; just call SpaceEx with the number of characters to return and the character to repeat as arguments.

Syntax

```
ReturnString  = SpaceEx(Number, Character)
```

Part	Description
ReturnString	Required. A string returned containing characters.
Number	Required. A numerical expression that specifies the number of characters to return.
Character	Optional. A string expression that denotes the character to repeat.

Code Listing

```
Public Function SpaceEx(Number As Long, Optional Character As String)
➥As String

    'Declare our variables
    Dim I As Long
    Dim Temp As String
```

```
        if IsMissing(Character) then Character = " "
        'If we were not passed a character to use in place of a
        'space, then use a space.

        For I = 1 To Number
            Temp = Temp & Character
                'For every number between 1 and the Number of
                'characters to return, add one character to the
                'temporary  string.
        Next

        'Return our temporary string
        SpaceEx = Temp

End Function
```

Analysis

This routine is not complicated. It appends repeatedly to the `Temporary` string, and then returns the result. Using the `Character` parameter is optional; if no `Character` parameter is present, it assumes you want to use the space.

Notice the line

```
if IsMissing(Character) then Character = " "
```

The `IsMissing` function detects whether a certain optional parameter has been passed. It returns `TRUE` if the parameter has not been passed (for example, it is "missing"), and `FALSE` if it has. In VB5, you could simply say

```
Optional Character As String =" "
```

3.20 LAUNCHING A FILE WITH AN ASSOCIATED APPLICATION

by Kamal A. Mehdi

Description

The `LaunchFile` function will launch a file of any extension type with the Windows-registered associated application, opening the file in that application. There is no need to know the application with which the file type is associated. You also don't need to know the application name or the name and location of its executable file on disk.

When you call the `LaunchFile` function specifying, for example, the file c:\mydoc.doc for the function `FileName` argument, the function will open the specified file in Word. If you specify the file c:\mytext.txt, the function will open the file in Notepad. If the specified file is associated with an application other than the default application, it will be opened in the currently associated application. For example, if files with the .doc extension are associated with Wordpad, they will be opened in Wordpad rather than in Word.

Using the LaunchFile function, you can also specify which action to perform on the specified file. You can choose either to open the file in the associated application, or you can print the file through the associated application directly by calling the function.

If the function is called with a specified filename whose extension is not associated with an application, the function will return the error code 31, which informs the user that no application currently is associated with this file type.

The LaunchFile function also enables you to specify the window state of the application when the file is opened. The file can be opened inside the application in a normal window, in a minimized window, or in a maximized window.

The LaunchFile function can also be used to launch an application directly by specifying its executable filename. Calling the function with calc.exe specified for the filename will launch your Windows calculator. The LaunchFile function also supports long filenames on Windows 95/98 and Windows NT platforms.

The sample code listing demonstrates the functionality of the LaunchFile function. The code incorporates conditional compilation and API declarations for both 16-bit and 32-bit Windows platforms.

Syntax

```
RetVal = LaunchFile(FileName, Action, WindowState)
```

Part	Description
RetVal	Required. A numeric expression that receives the value returned by the function. The function return values are described below. The data type is Long.
FileName	Required. A string expression that specifies the full path and name of the file to launch with the associated application. The data type is String.
Action	Optional. A numeric expression that specifies the action to perform when the file is launched with the application. The Action settings are described below. The data type is Integer.
WindowState	Optional. A numeric expression that specifies the state of the window in which the file is opened. The WindowState settings are described below. The data type is Integer.

The LaunchFile function returns on success the window handle of the window in which the file has opened. Normally, this window is the launched application window. Other values returned by the function through the RetVal variable are the same error codes returned by the ShellExecute API function, as described here:

Value	Description
0	The system is out of memory. Also returned if the specified file is an executable file and could not be run (the file is corrupt).
2	The specified file was not found.
5	A sharing error or network protection error. Also returned if the function tried to link dynamically to a task.
6	The library required separate data segments for each task.
8	There was insufficient memory to launch the associated application.
10	An incorrect version of Windows.
11	An invalid or non-Windows executable file.
12	The application was designed for a different operating system.
13	The application was designed for MS-DOS version 4.0.
14	The type of the executable file is unknown.
15	An attempt was made to load a real-mode application that was developed for an earlier version of Windows.
16	An attempt was made to load a second instance of an executable file containing multiple data segments not marked read-only.
19	The EXE file is a compressed executable. The file must be decompressed before it can be loaded.
20	One of the dynamic-link libraries (DLLs) required to run this application was corrupt or the DLL file was invalid.
21	The EXE file requires Microsoft Windows 32-bit extensions to run.

The following are the settings for the `Action` argument:

Setting	Description
0	Opens the specified file in the associated application window (the default).
1	Prints the specified file using the associated application.

The following are the settings for the `WindowState` argument:

Setting	Description
1	The file is launched in the application window with normal window state (the default).
2	The file is launched in the application window minimized.
3	The file is launched in the application window maximized.

If the `WindowState` argument is not specified, the file is launched in a normal window (the default).

Modules and Controls Required

The following code demonstrates the use of the `LaunchFile` function. You will need the following modules and controls to build the sample project:

Module/Control	Description
Module1	A standard Visual Basic module (.BAS)
Form1	A standard non-MDI Visual Basic form (.FRM) with the `Caption` property set to Launching a File with the Associated Application
Frame1	A frame control with the `Caption` property set to Enter File Name
Frame2	A frame control with the `Caption` property set to Window State
Frame3	A frame control with the `Caption` property set to Action
Command1	A command button with the `Caption` property set to Launch File with Associated Application
Command2	A command button with the `Caption` property set to Browse...
Command3	A command button with the `Caption` property set to Exit
Text1	A text box control
CommonDialog1	A common dialog control
Option1	An option button with the `Caption` property set to Normal
Option2	An option button with the `Caption` property set to Minimized
Option3	An option button with the `Caption` property set to Maximized
Option4	An option button with the `Caption` property set to Open
Option5	An option button with the `Caption` property set to Print
Label1	A label control with the `Caption` property set to Function Return Value:
Label2	A label control

Follow these steps to draw controls:

1. Start a new standard EXE project. Form1 will be created by default. Set the form's `Height` and `Width` properties to approximately 4000 and 6000, respectively, and set its `Caption` property as shown earlier.
2. Draw `Frame1` at the top side of the form and set its width to approximately the width of the form. Set its height to almost one-third the form's height and set its `Caption` property as shown earlier.
3. Draw `Text1` and `Command2` inside `Frame1`. Set the `Command2` `Caption` property as shown earlier.
4. Draw `Frame2` under `Frame1` at the left side of the form and draw `Frame3` to the right of `Frame2`. Adjust the size of both frames so that they cover almost one-third of the form's height and approximately the entire form width.

5.   Draw Option1, Option2, and Option3 option buttons inside Frame1 and set their Caption property as shown earlier.

6.   Draw Option4 and Option5 inside Frame3 and set their Caption property as shown earlier.

7.   Draw Label1 and Label2 label controls under Frame2 with Label2 to the right of Label1. Set Label1's Caption property as shown earlier.

8.   Draw Command1 and Command2 at the bottom side of the form and set their Caption properties as shown earlier.

9.   Draw the CommonDialog1 common dialog control anywhere on the form.

Note

The common dialog control is not included on the toolbox by default. You can add it to the toolbox by selecting the Components submenu from the Project menu and adding the control.

Code Listing

```
'Code in Module1

'Conditional compilation for 16-bit and 32-bit platforms

#If Win32 Then
    '32-bit API declarations
    Declare Function ShellExecute Lib _
    "shell32.dll" Alias "ShellExecuteA" _
    (ByVal hwnd As Long, _
    ByVal lpOperation As String, _
    ByVal lpFile As String, _
    ByVal lpParameters As String, _
    ByVal lpDirectory As String, _
    ByVal nShowCmd As Long) As Long

#Else
    '16-bit API declarations
    Declare Function ShellExecute Lib _
    "shell.dll" _
    (ByVal hwnd As Integer, _
    ByVal lpOperation As String, _
    ByVal lpFile As String, _
    ByVal lpParameters As String, _
    ByVal lpDirectory As String, _
    ByVal nShowCmd As Integer) As Integer
#End If

    'Constant declarations
    Const SW_SHOWNORMAL = 1
    Const SW_SHOWMINIMIZED = 2
    Const SW_SHOWMAXIMIZED = 3
```

```
Function LaunchFile(FileName As String, Optional Action As Integer,
➥Optional WindowState As Integer) As Long

    Dim RetVal As Long
    Dim LAction As String

    'If window state is not specified, set to normal
    If WindowState = 0 Then WindowState = SW_SHOWNORMAL

    'Assign action
    If Action = 0 Then
        LAction = "Open"
    Else
        LAction = "Print"
    End If

    'Call the function
    RetVal = ShellExecute(0&, _
        LAction, _
        FileName, _
        vbNullString, _
        vbNullString, _
        WindowState)

        LaunchFile = RetVal

End Function
'Code in Form1

Private Sub Command1_Click()

    Dim RetVal As Long
    Dim WindowState As Integer
    Dim Action As Integer

    'Check the style of window state
    If Option1.Value = True Then
        WindowState = 1     'Normal window
    ElseIf Option2.Value = True Then
        WindowState = 2     'Minimized window
    ElseIf Option3.Value = True Then
        WindowState = 3     'Maximized window
    End If

    'Check which action is required
    If Option4.Value = True Then
        Action = 0     'Open file
    ElseIf Option5.Value = True Then
        Action = 1     'Print file
    End If

    'Call the function
```

```
        RetVal = LaunchFile(Text1, Action, WindowState)
        Label2 = RetVal

End Sub

Private Sub Command2_Click()

        'Show the common dialog
        CommonDialog1.FileName = ""
        CommonDialog1.ShowOpen
        Text1 = CommonDialog1.FileName

End Sub

Private Sub Command3_Click()

        Unload Me

End Sub

Private Sub Form_Load()

        'Initialize
        Text1 = ""
        Label2.Caption = ""
        Option1.Value = True      'WindowState=1
        Option4.Value = True      'Action=open

End Sub
```

Enter the code into the appropriate form, module, or control events as indicated and run the project. Enter the filename you want to launch with the associated application in the text box, or click the browse button to select the file from the Explorer-like file open dialog and click the Launch File with Associated Application button. If the file type is registered, it will be opened with the appropriate application. `Label2` will display the value returned from the function. If the operation was successful, the value will be the window handle of the launched application window. You can also select the window style and the action to perform from the appropriate option buttons before launching the file with the associated application.

Analysis

The `LaunchFile` function is notably useful in cases in which you want to open a file of a specific type without knowing the name of the associated application and where its executable is located on the user's machine. For example, when you distribute your application that might contain an HTML document file which will show the user some information about your application and enable him to go directly to your Web site, you do not need to figure out whether the user has the Internet Explorer browser, Netscape Navigator browser, or both installed on his machine and in which folder they are installed. The `LaunchFile` function will do the job for you by launching your HTML document file in the default Web browser registered on the user's machine.

The `LaunchFile` function not only enables you to launch the specified file and open it in the associated application, it also enables you to print the file using that application without the need to click the appropriate commands in the application to print the file. However, not all applications support the print action—but most of them do. For example, Word supports the print action sent by the `LaunchFile` function.

The `LaunchFile` function also enables you to determine whether there is an application installed on the user's machine that supports and is associated with the file type specified by the `FileName` argument. You just call the function and check the return code. If you receive the error code 13 from the function, you can conclude that the specified file type has no association.

The `LaunchFile` function is based on the `ShellExecute` API function but is easier to use in your applications than `ShellExecute`. You just specify the filename and call the function, and it will adjust the remaining parameters for you and launch the file in the associated application.

Note that in Windows 95/98 and Windows NT, when you run the sample project provided here and call the function without specifying a filename, an Explorer-style window will open and show you the contents of the current drive. If you specify only a drive name or a folder name in the FileName text box, the window will show you the contents of that drive or folder.

The sample project LNCHFILE.VBP on the CD-ROM that accompanies this book demonstrates the application of the `LaunchFile` function.

3.21 COMMUNICATING WITH THE PC SERIAL PORT

by Kamal A. Mehdi

Description

The computer serial ports, also known as COM ports, are one of the principal means of communicating with external devices such as modems or control devices from within applications. The sample code presented here enables you to communicate with and send or receive data to and from any device connected to the COM ports by using the MSComm communications control shipped with Visual Basic.

This sample code enables you to communicate with your modem by sending modem commands that you enter and receiving feedback data (an answer) from the modem using the computer's COM port. The project implements two methods for reading incoming data from the COM port: the MSComm event-driven method and the plain port-polling method. The event-driven method is a powerful method that uses the MSComm control `OnComm` event to handle data transmission and reception tasks to and from the COM port. In the event-driven method, an event is generated by the MSComm control whenever a certain number of characters arrives at the COM port, a certain number of characters is sent through the COM port, or when a certain COM event or COM error occurs. The COM events and errors generated by the MSComm control are described later in detail.

In the port-polling method, the COM port buffer is read in a continuous manner or at specific time intervals. Your application checks the COM port receive buffer through the use of the `InBufferCount` property of the MSComm control to determine whether characters have arrived at the buffer and the number of these characters. When characters are read using the `Input` property of the control, the receive buffer is flushed (emptied).

The MSComm control also enables implementation of various standard communication protocols such as the XON/XOFF handshaking, RTS/CTS (Request To Send/Clear To Send) handshaking, both, or none. It also supports different communication speeds (baud rates) and parity error detection.

COM Events and Errors

The following are the COM event and error codes generated by the MSComm control.

Events

Constant	Code	Description
comEvSend	1	The number of characters in the transmit buffer is less than the `SThreshold` value.
ComEvReceive	2	The `RThreshold` number of characters was received. This event is generated continuously until the `Input` property is used to get the data from the receive buffer.
ComEvCTS	3	The Clear To Send line state has changed.
comEvDSR	4	The Data Set Ready line state has changed. This event occurs only when the DSR line state changes from 1 to 0.
comEvCD	5	The Carrier Detect line state has changed.
comEvRing	6	A phone line ring signal is detected.
comEvEOF	7	End-Of-File (character 26) was received.

Errors

Constant	Code	Description
comEventBreak	1001	A break signal was received.
comEventCTSTO	1002	Clear To Send signal timeout. The Clear To Send line state was low for the specified time interval while trying to transmit a character.
comEventDSRTO	1003	Data Set Ready signal timeout. The Data Set Ready line state was low for the specified time interval while trying to transmit a character.
ComEventFrame	1004	Framing error. The hardware detected a framing error.
ComEventOverrun	1006	Port overrun. A character was not read from the hardware before the next character arrived and was lost.

Constant	Code	Description
ComEventCDTO	1007	Carrier Detect signal timeout. The Carrier Detect line state was low for the specified time interval while trying to transmit a character.
ComEventRxOver	1008	Receive-buffer overflow. There is no space in the receive buffer to receive more data.
ComEventRxParity	1009	Parity error. The hardware detected a parity error.
ComEventTxFull	1010	Transmit-buffer full. There was no space in the transmit buffer while trying to append a character.
ComEventDCB	1011	Unexpected error retrieving Device Control Block (DCB) for the port.

Modules and Controls Required

You will need the following modules and controls to build the sample project:

Module/Control	Description
Form1	Standard non-MDI Visual Basic form (.FRM) with the following property settings:
	Caption = Communicating with the PC COM ports
	BorderStyle = 3-Fixed Dialog
Frame1	Frame control with the Caption property set to COM Read Method
Frame2	Frame control with the Caption property set to COM Port
Frame3	Frame control with the Caption property set to Enter Command to Send to Modem
Frame4	Frame control with the Caption property set to Data Received from Modem
Command1	Command button with the Caption property set to Send Command
Command2	Command button with the Caption property set to Clear
Command3	Command button with the Caption property set to Exit
Command4	Command button with the Caption property set to Open Port
Command5	Command button with the Caption property set to Close Port
Text1	Text box control
Text2	Text box control with the MultiLine property set to True
Option1	Option button with the Caption property set to Event Driven
Option2	Option button with the Caption property set to Port Polling
Option3	Option button with the Caption property set to COM1
Option4	Option button with the Caption property set to COM2
MSComm1	MSComm communication control

Follow these steps to draw controls:

1. Start a new standard EXE project. Form1 will be created by default. Set the form's Height and Width properties to approximately 6000 and 5000, respectively, and set its Caption and BorderStyle properties as shown earlier.

2. Draw Frame1 and Frame2 at the top of the form with Frame1 to the left and Frame2 to the right. Set their Caption properties as shown earlier.

3. Draw Option1 and Option2 option buttons inside Frame1 and set their Caption properties as shown earlier.

4. Draw Option3 and Option4 option buttons and Command4 and Command5 command buttons inside Frame2. Set their Caption properties as shown earlier.

5. Draw Frame3 under Frame1 and Frame2 and set its width to approximately the width of the form. Set its height to accommodate a single-line text box. Set its Caption property as shown earlier.

6. Draw Text1 inside Frame3 and set its size to fill the entire frame area.

7. Draw Command1 under Frame3 and set its Caption property as shown earlier.

8. Draw Frame4 on the form and set its width to approximately the width of the form. Set its height to accommodate a multiple-line text box. Set its Caption property as shown earlier.

9. Draw Text2 inside Frame4 and adjust its size so that it fills almost two-thirds of the entire frame area. Set its MultiLine property as shown earlier. Draw Command2 inside the frame control and set its Caption property as shown earlier.

10. Draw Command3 under Frame4 and set its Caption property as shown earlier.

11. Draw the MSComm1 communications control anywhere on the form.

Note

The MSComm1 communications control is not included on the toolbox by default. You can add it to the toolbox by selecting Project, Components and adding the control. (The control name in the components list is shown as Microsoft Comm Control 5.0, where 5.0 is the version number. You might have another version on your system.)

Code Listing

```
'General form declarations
    Dim ComPort As Integer
    Dim PortIsOpen As Boolean

Private Sub Command2_Click()
    'Clear the text box
    Text2.Text = ""
End Sub

Private Sub Command3_Click()
    'End the program
    Unload Me
End Sub
```

```
Private Sub Command4_Click()
    'This is required to detect if another application uses the com port
    On Error GoTo ErrorHandler

    'Open the com port, enable and disable the appropriate controls
    MSComm1.CommPort = ComPort
    MSComm1.PortOpen = True
    Command4.Enabled = False
    Command5.Enabled = True
    Option3.Enabled = False
    Option4.Enabled = False
    Command1.Enabled = True
    PortIsOpen = True
    Exit Sub

ErrorHandler:
    MsgBox "COM" & ComPort & " is already used by another application." & _
    ➥ Chr(10) & "Could not open port.", vbInformation
    Exit Sub

End Sub

Private Sub Command5_Click()

    'Close the com port, enable and disable the appropriate controls
    MSComm1.PortOpen = False
    Command4.Enabled = True
    Command5.Enabled = False
    Option3.Enabled = True
    Option4.Enabled = True
    Command1.Enabled = False
    PortIsOpen = False

End Sub

Private Sub MSComm1_OnComm()

    'Use the comm event comEvReceive to read data whenever one
    'character is received from the com port
    If MSComm1.CommEvent = comEvReceive Then
        'Append the character to the modem data text box
        Text2.Text = Text2.Text + MSComm1.Input
    End If

End Sub

Private Sub Command1_Click()

    Dim ModemResponded As Boolean
    Dim ModemData As String

        'Flush the input and output buffers
```

```
            MSComm1.InBufferCount = 0
            MSComm1.OutBufferCount = 0

            'Send command to the modem
            MSComm1.Output = Text1.Text + Chr(13)

            'Check the com read method
            If Option1.Value = True Then
                'If the selected read method is event driven, then exit
                Exit Sub
            Else
                'If the read method is com polling, then write 'wait'
                'in the text box and continue
                Text2.Text = Text2.Text + "WAIT....." + Chr(13) + Chr(10)
            End If

            'Poll the com port for 3 seconds and read every character
            'coming back from the modem
            X = Timer
            Do
                'Yield to other processes
                dummy = DoEvents()

                'If there is data in the buffer, read it
                If MSComm1.InBufferCount Then
                    ModemResponded = True
                    ModemData = ModemData + MSComm1.Input
                End If
            Loop Until Timer >= X + 3

        'If modem did not respond, inform the user, otherwise show the data
        If ModemResponded Then
            Text2.Text = Text2.Text + ModemData
        Else
            Text2.Text = Text2.Text + "No responce received from modem!"
        End If

        'Note: the modem appends chr(10)+chr(13) to the end of its data string

End Sub

Private Sub Form_Load()

    'Initialize controls
    Text1.Text = ""
    Text2.Text = ""
    Command1.Enabled = False
    Command5.Enabled = False

    'Select 'event-driven' as the default method
    Option1.Value = True
```

```
    'Select COM2 as the default port
    Option4.Value = True
    ComPort = 2

    'Specify the com port settings
    'Baud rate=9600, no parity, 8 data bits, 1 stop bit
    MSComm1.Settings = "9600,n,8,1"

End Sub

Private Sub Form_Unload(Cancel As Integer)

    'Close the com port when form is unloaded
    If PortIsOpen Then MSComm1.PortOpen = False

End Sub

Private Sub Option1_Click()

    'Set the RThreshold and SThreshold to 1 in order to get
    'a read event whenever one character arrives at the com
    'port buffer
    MSComm1.RThreshold = 1
    MSComm1.SThreshold = 1

End Sub

Private Sub Option2_Click()

    'Set the RThreshold and SThreshold to 0 to disable the com events
    MSComm1.RThreshold = 0
    MSComm1.SThreshold = 0

End Sub

Private Sub Option3_Click()

    'Specify COM1 to be opened
    ComPort = 1

End Sub

Private Sub Option4_Click()

    'Specify COM2 to be opened
    ComPort = 2

End Sub
```

Enter the code into the appropriate form and control events as indicated and run the project. Select the COM port and the method for reading the COM port, and click the Open Port command button. If the

COM port is used by another application, you will be notified. In this case, select another port and click the Open Port button again. Enter the command to send to the modem. For example, enter ATZ to reset the modem, AT&F to restore the factory settings, or AT&V to view the stored modem profile. Click the Send Command button and notice the modem answer displayed in the Text2 text box.

Analysis

The code demonstrates how you can use the MSComm control that comes with Visual Basic to communicate with external devices through your computer COM ports.

The code actually specifies the COM port to work with, specifies the settings for the COM port, opens the COM port, and sends and receives characters to and from the port. The COM port is opened and closed by using the PortOpen property of the MSComm control and specifying either True to open the port or False to close the port. While the COM port is open, you can switch between the event-driven method and the port-polling method for reading incoming data. This is implemented in the code by changing the value of the RThreshold and SThreshold properties of the control. Setting either of these two properties to 0 disables the event-driven mode. In both methods, the Input property of the MSComm control is used to read incoming data while the Output property is used to send data to the port.

The COM port settings are actually represented by a string containing four different parts: the baud rate, the parity, the number of data bits, and the number of stop bits. The baud rate specifies the speed of data transmission and reception to and from the COM port measured in bits per second. The baud rate can be set between 110 and 256000 bps depending on the UART chip used in your system and the speed that can be handled by the modem or the external device.

The COM port driver also plays an important role when high speeds are used (a fast driver is required). The parity setting specifies whether error detection is implemented, and can be set to either even , odd (O), mark (M), space (S), or none (N), which is the default.

Data bits represents the number of bits contained in each sent/received byte and can be set between 4 and 8 (8 is the default value). The stop bits represents the number of bits that separates each data byte from the other and can be set to 1, 1.5, or 2 (1 is the default). These settings are specified using the Settings property of the MSComm control in the form BBBB,P,D,S where BBBB is the baud rate, P is the parity, D is the number of data bits, and S is the number of stop bits.

The code easily can be modified to communicate with any other external device connected to your system through the COM port. You just have to know what settings to use, the protocol to communicate, and what data to send to the device.

The sample project COMPORT.VBP on the CD-ROM that accompanies this book demonstrates the functionality of the presented code.

3.22   RETRIEVING THE SYSTEM'S INSTALLED FONTS

by Kamal A. Mehdi

Description

It is sometimes necessary to know whether a certain font or fonts are installed on the user's machine for the Visual Basic application to work correctly. You might also need to know this to install some fonts that do not exist on the user's machine and are required by the application.

This sample code retrieves the font names of all fonts installed on the system that are available for the current display device or active printer, and populates a list box with the font names. The code uses the `Screen` object's `FontCount` and `Fonts` properties to retrieve the number of installed fonts and their names.

Note that fonts that have the same name but different properties, such as Bold or Italic, will be retrieved as one font name and not as separate font names, as shown in the Windows Control Panel font viewer, where the different names are displayed.

Modules and Controls Required

You will need the following modules and controls to build the sample project:

Module/Control	Description
Form1	A standard non-MDI Visual Basic form (.FRM) with the following properties set:
	Caption = Retrieving the system installed fonts
	BorderStyle = 1-Fixed Single
Frame1	A frame control with the `Caption` property set to Fonts Installed
Frame2	A frame control with the `Caption` property set to Font Preview
List1	A list-box control with the `Sorted` property set to True
Command1	A command button with the `Caption` property set to Retrieve Installed Fonts
Command2	A command button with the `Caption` property set to Exit
Check1	A check-box control with the `Caption` property set to Bold
Check2	A check-box control with the `Caption` property set to Italic
Label1	A label control

Follow these steps to draw controls:

1. Start a new standard EXE project. `Form1` will be created by default. Set the form's `Height` and `Width` properties to approximately 4300 and 4000, respectively, and set its `Caption` and `BorderStyle` properties as shown earlier.
2. Draw `Frame1` on the top of the form and adjust its size to cover approximately one-half of the form area. Set its `Caption` property as shown earlier.
3. Draw the `List1` list box inside `Frame1` and adjust its size to fill the entire frame area. Set the `Sorted` property of the list box as shown earlier.
4. Draw `Frame2` under `Frame1` and adjust its width to approximately the width of the form. Set its `Caption` property as shown earlier.
5. Draw the `Check1` and `Check2` check boxes inside `Frame2` and set their `Caption` properties as shown earlier. Draw `Label1` on the remaining area of the frame.
6. Draw the `Command1` and `Command2` buttons under `Frame2` and set their `Caption` properties as shown earlier.

Code Listing

```
Private Sub Check1_Click()

    'Set the font bold property
    If Check1.Value = 0 Then
        Label1.Font.Bold = False
    Else
        Label1.Font.Bold = True
    End If

End Sub

Private Sub Check2_Click()

    'Set the font italic property
    If Check2.Value = 0 Then
        Label1.Font.Italic = False
    Else
        Label1.Font.Italic = True
    End If

End Sub

Private Sub Command1_Click()

    'Retrieve the installed font names and append them to the list box
    For I = 0 To Screen.FontCount - 1
        List1.AddItem Screen.Fonts(I)
    Next

    'select the first font in the list
    List1.ListIndex = 0
```

```
End Sub

Private Sub Command2_Click()

    'Exit
    Unload Me

End Sub

Private Sub Form_Load()

    'Initialize properties
    Label1.AutoSize = True
    Label1.Caption = "AaBbCc"

End Sub

Private Sub List1_Click()

    'Set the font name to the selected font in the list
    Label1.Font.Name = List1

    'Reset the font size (some fonts may change the font
    'size, so we must reset it)
    Label1.Font.Size = 14

End Sub
```

Enter the code in the appropriate form or control events as indicated. Run the project and click the Retrieve Installed Fonts button. The list box will be populated with the names of all available fonts installed on the system. Click one of the font names shown in the list to see the font preview displayed in the `Label1` caption. Click the Bold and Italic check boxes to see the font preview in bold and italic.

Analysis

The code demonstrates an easy method to retrieve the font names of all fonts installed on the user's system by using the Visual Basic `Screen` object. The number of fonts is retrieved by reading the `FontCount` property of the `Screen` object. The font names are retrieved from the `Fonts` property by enumerating all the values from 0 to `FontCount` - 1 for the index (`Screen.Fonts(Index)`). The font names retrieved by the `Screen` object represent all the fonts that are available for the current display device or active printer.

The sample code can be used as a simple, yet efficient, font viewer that will display the selected font in different typefaces as regular, bold, italic, and so on, as well as in any combination of these typefaces. You can modify it to view the entire character set of the selected font.

The sample project FONTS.VBP on the CD-ROM that accompanies this book demonstrates the functionality of the presented code.

3.23   ADDING AND REMOVING ITEMS IN THE CONTROL MENU

by Kamal A. Mehdi

Description

In the Windows environment, every window displayed on the screen has a standard default menu that can be pulled down by clicking the top-left corner of the window (the left edge of the title bar). This menu is known as the control menu or system menu and contains items that can be used to minimize, maximize, size, move, restore, and close the window.

You can add or remove items in the control menu of a Visual Basic form or any other application window using two API functions, RemoveMenu and AppendMenu. By knowing the handle of the window, you can add or remove any specific item from its control menu.

This code listing demonstrates how you can remove some items from the existing control menu of your Visual Basic form and then add some new items to it. Without any modifications, the code can be used to add new items or remove specific items from the control menu of any other application window just by specifying the handle of that window.

The *RemoveMenu* Function Syntax

```
RetVal = RemoveMenu (hMenu, nPosition, wFlags)
```

Part	Description
RetVal	Required. A numeric expression that receives the value returned from the function. Its data type is Long.
hMenu	Required. A numeric expression passed by value specifying the window handle where the menu exists. Its data type is Long.
nPosition	Required. A numeric expression passed by value specifying the ordinal position of the particular item to remove from the menu. Its data type is Long.
wFlags	Required. A numeric expression passed by value specifying the flags. The default value MF_BYPOSITION (or &H400) can be used to remove the required item. Its data type is Long.

The *AppendMenu* Function Syntax

```
RetVal = AppendMenu (hMenu, wFlags, wIDNewItem, lpNewItem)
```

Part	Description
RetVal	Required. A numeric expression that receives the value returned from the function. Its data type is `Long`.
hMenu	Required. A numeric expression passed by value specifying the window handle where the menu exists. Its data type is `Long`.
wFlags	Required. A numeric expression passed by value specifying the flags as described below. Its data type is `Long`.
wIDNewItem	Required. A numeric expression passed by value specifying the item ID of the new menu item. The item ID is passed in the `WM_COMMAND` message when the menu is clicked. Its data type is `Long`.
lpNewItem	Required. A string expression passed by value specifying the caption string of the new menu item. Its data type is `Long`.

The following are the settings for the `wFlags` argument in the `AppendMenu` function:

Setting	Description
MF_BITMAP	Uses a bitmap as the item. The `lpNewItem` parameter contains the handle to the bitmap.
MF_CHECKED	Places a check mark next to the item. If the application provides check mark bitmaps, this flag displays the check mark bitmap next to the menu item.
MF_DISABLED	Disables the menu item so that it cannot be selected but the flag does not gray it.
MF_ENABLED	Enables the menu item so that it can be selected and restores it from its grayed state.
MF_GRAYED	Disables the menu item and grays it so it cannot be selected.
MF_MENUBARBREAK	Functions the same as the `MF_MENUBREAK` flag except for pop-up menus, where the new column is separated from the old column by a vertical line.
MF_MENUBREAK	Places the item on a new line (for menu bars) or in a new column (for pop-up menus) without separating columns.
MF_OWNERDRAW	Specifies that the item is an owner-drawn item. Before the menu is displayed for the first time, the window that owns the menu receives a `WM_MEASUREITEM` message to retrieve the width and height of the menu item. The `WM_DRAWITEM` message is then sent to the window procedure of the owner window whenever the appearance of the menu item must be updated.
MF_POPUP	Specifies that the menu item is a pop-up item; that is, selecting it activates a pop-up menu. The `wIDNewItem` parameter specifies the handle to the pop-up menu. This flag is used to add a pop-up item to a menu bar or to a pop-up menu.
MF_SEPARATOR	Draws a horizontal dividing line. This flag is used only in a pop-up menu. The line cannot be grayed, disabled, or highlighted. The `lpNewItem` and `wIDNewItem` parameters are ignored.
MF_STRING	Specifies that the menu item is a text string; the `lpNewItem` parameter points to the string.
MF_UNCHECKED	Does not place a check mark next to the item (default). If the application supplies check mark bitmaps, this flag displays the unchecked bitmap next to the menu.

Modules and Controls Required

You will need the following modules and controls to build the sample project:

Module/Control	Description
Form1	A standard non-MDI Visual Basic form with controls as shown later in this section.
Command1()	A control array of three command buttons with the Caption property set as shown here:
	Index = 0, Caption = Remove items from the control menu
	Index =1, Caption = Add new items to the control menu
	Index = 2, Caption = Exit

To draw controls, start a new standard EXE project. Form1 will be created by default. Draw one command button anywhere on the form and create the control array from the button. Set the Caption property of the buttons as shown earlier in this section.

Note

You can create control arrays by inserting one control on the form and copying and pasting the control on the form using either the right mouse button or the Edit menu. When you paste the control on the form, Visual Basic will prompt you whether to create a control array; choose Yes.

Code Listing

```
'API declarations
    Private Declare Function RemoveMenu Lib "user32" (ByVal hMenu As Long,
    ➥ ByVal nPosition As Long, ByVal wFlags As Long) As Long
    Private Declare Function GetSystemMenu Lib "user32" (ByVal hWnd As Long,
    ➥ ByVal bRevert As Long) As Long
    Private Declare Function AppendMenu Lib "user32" Alias "AppendMenuA"
    ➥ (ByVal hMenu As Long, ByVal wFlags As Long, ByVal wIDNewItem
    ➥ As Long, ByVal lpNewItem As String) As Long

    'Constants
    Const MF_BYPOSITION = &H400
    Const MF_STRING = &H0&
    Const MF_BYCOMMAND = &H0&

Private Sub Command1_Click(Index As Integer)

    Dim hWnd As Long
    Dim J As Integer
    Dim RemoveMe As Long
    Dim AddIMe As Long
    Dim NewItem As String

    'Get the window handle of the form
```

```
        hWnd = GetSystemMenu(Form1.hWnd, 0)

    Select Case Index
        Case Is = 0      'Remove 4 items from the menu
            For J = 3 To 0 Step -1
                RemoveMe = RemoveMenu(hWnd, J, MF_BYPOSITION)
            Next J
            MsgBox "Four items removed from the Control menu", vbInformation

        Case Is = 1
            For J = 1 To 10     'Add 10 items to the menu
                NewItem = "&New Item" + Str(J)
                AddMe = AppendMenu(hWnd, MF_STRING, 0&, NewItem)
            Next
            MsgBox "Ten items added to the Control menu", vbInformation

        Case Is = 2
            'End
            Unload Me

    End Select

End Sub

Private Sub Form_Load()

    'Center form on the screen
    Me.Top = (Screen.Height - Me.Height) / 2
    Me.Left = (Screen.Width - Me.Width) / 2

End Sub
```

Enter the code in the appropriate form and control events as indicated. Run the project and click the control menu of the form. You will see the menu with the six normal items: Restore, Move, Size, Minimize, Maximize, and Close. Click the Remove Items From The Control Menu button and look again at the control menu. You will see the first four top items removed from the menu. Now click the Add New Items To The Control Menu button and recheck the control menu again. You will see that 10 new items have been added to the menu.

Analysis

Removing items from the control menu of a particular window is sometimes useful when you need to force the window not to be moved or resized by the user, for example. On the other hand, appending new items to the control menu of a Visual Basic form or another application window is useful when you must add some additional functionality to that window through its control menu. However, the newly added items can be accessed only by using subclassing.

The sample code demonstrates how easily you can add new items or remove existing items from the control menu of a specific window using two API functions, AppendMenu and RemoveMenu. To remove a specific item from the menu, just provide the handle of the window, the ordinal position of the item in the menu, and specify that the item is to be removed by position and call the RemoveMenu function. Note that although the control menu appears to have six items, it actually contains seven items. This is because the separating bar shown over the Close command is a normal menu item but is nonselectable.

You add a new item to the menu by calling the AppendMenu function while specifying the window handle of the particular window and the caption string of the new item. You specify that the new item is a text string using MF_STRING in the wFlags argument. You can also add an item as a bitmap or place a check mark next to the item by using the appropriate settings for the wFlags argument.

The sample project CTRLMENU.VBP on the CD-ROM that accompanies this book demonstrates the use of these two functions.

3.24 INSTALLING FONTS FROM VISUAL BASIC

by Kamal A. Mehdi

Description

This sample code installs a new TrueType font on the system and adds it to the list of available fonts to the Windows applications. The code installs the new font by calling the AddNewFont procedure while passing both the font name and the font filename to the appropriate arguments.

The AddNewFont procedure installs the new font by calling the AddFontResource API function to add the font to the list of font resources for the current Windows session. It then calls the RegSetValueEx API function to register the font key value in the Windows Registry to permanently add the font to the Windows font resources.

Note that you must first copy the font file to the \Fonts directory located under your Windows directory before calling the AddNewFont procedure.

Before installing the new font, you can determine whether the font already exists on the system by implementing the procedure described in section 3.22, "Retrieving the System's Installed Fonts."

Syntax

AddNewFont (FontName, FontFile)

Part	Description
FontName	Required. A string expression specifying the real name of the font to be added. The font will be registered in the Windows Registry using the specified name, and the font will appear in all Windows applications under this name.

Part	Description
FontFile	Required. A string expression that specifies the font filename. No path name is required. The font file must be located in the \Windows\Fonts directory (your Windows directory name might be different).

Code Listing

You will need one Visual Basic standard module (.BAS), one non-MDI form (.FRM), and one command button to be able to use the code.

```
'Code in module1

'Module-level API declarations
Declare Function FormatMessage Lib "kernel32" Alias "FormatMessageA" _
        (ByVal dwFlags As Long, lpSource As Any, _
        ByVal dwMessageId As Long, ByVal dwLanguageId As Long, _
        ByVal lpBuffer As String, ByVal nSize As Long, Arguments As Long)
        ➥ As Long

'Constants
Public Const FORMAT_MESSAGE_ALLOCATE_BUFFER = &H100
Public Const FORMAT_MESSAGE_IGNORE_INSERTS = &H200
Public Const FORMAT_MESSAGE_FROM_STRING = &H400
Public Const FORMAT_MESSAGE_FROM_HMODULE = &H800
Public Const FORMAT_MESSAGE_FROM_SYSTEM = &H1000
Public Const FORMAT_MESSAGE_ARGUMENT_ARRAY = &H2000
Public Const FORMAT_MESSAGE_MAX_WIDTH_MASK = &HFF
Public Const LANG_USER_DEFAULT = &H400&


Function GetLastErrorStr(dwErrCode As Long) As String

'This will return the system error string associated with the given
➥ error code.

'Let VB allocate the buffer. If FORMAT_MESSAGE_ALLOCATE_BUFFER
'was used, the lpBuffer param (sMsgBuf) would have to be a long pointer
'to the buffer & would then have to be freed when we're done.
'256 chars is the maximum length for a resource string (+ 1 for the
➥ null char)
Static sMsgBuf As String * 257, dwLen As Long

'Fill sMsgBuf with the system error string and return it's length.
'FORMAT_MESSAGE_IGNORE_INSERTS must be used as there are many system error
'strings that contain inserts (replaceable parameters).
'There are also a few random length multi-line error strings,
'FORMAT_MESSAGE_MAX_WIDTH_MASK returns them as one line
dwLen = FormatMessage(FORMAT_MESSAGE_FROM_SYSTEM _
                Or FORMAT_MESSAGE_IGNORE_INSERTS _
                Or FORMAT_MESSAGE_MAX_WIDTH_MASK, ByVal 0&, _
                dwErrCode, LANG_USER_DEFAULT, _
```

```
                    ByVal sMsgBuf, 256&, 0&)

   If dwLen Then
      GetLastErrorStr = Left$(sMsgBuf, dwLen)
   Else
      GetLastErrorStr = "Unknown error."
   End If

End Function

'Code in Form1

'API declarations
Private Declare Function GetLastError Lib "kernel32" () As Long

Private Declare Function PostMessage Lib "user32" _
        Alias "PostMessageA" (ByVal hWnd As Long, ByVal _
        wMsg As Long, ByVal wParam As Long, ByVal _
        lParam As Long) As Long

Private Declare Function AddFontResource Lib "gdi32" _
        Alias "AddFontResourceA" (ByVal lpFilename As _
        String) As Long

Private Declare Function GetWindowsDirectory Lib _
        "kernel32" Alias "GetWindowsDirectoryA" (ByVal _
        lpBuffer As String, ByVal nSize As Long) As Long

'API functions for writing to the windows registry
Private Declare Function RegSetValueEx Lib _
        "advapi32.dll" Alias "RegSetValueExA" (ByVal _
        hKey As Long, ByVal lpValueName As String, _
        ByVal Reserved As Long, ByVal dwType As Long, _
        lpData As Any, ByVal cbData As Long) As Long

Private Declare Function RegOpenKey Lib _
        "advapi32.dll" Alias "RegOpenKeyA" (ByVal hKey _
        As Long, ByVal lpSubKey As String, phkResult _
        As Long) As Long

Private Declare Function RegCloseKey Lib _
        "advapi32.dll" (ByVal hKey As Long) As Long


'Declare constants
Private Const HWND_BROADCAST = &HFFFF&
Private Const WM_FONTCHANGE = &H1D
Private Const MAX_PATH = 260
Private Const HKEY_LOCAL_MACHINE = &H80000002
Private Const REG_SZ = 1 ' Unicode null terminated string
```

```vb
Private Sub AddNewFont(FontName As String, FileName As String)

'Declare variables
    Dim lResult As Long
    Dim WinFontPath As String, FontFile As String
    Dim hKey As Long

    'Specify the font file name and path
    WinFontPath = Space$(MAX_PATH)
    FontFile = FileName

    'Call the GetWindowsDirectory API to get the Windows directory
    'and the fonts path '\windows\fonts'
    lResult = GetWindowsDirectory(WinFontPath, MAX_PATH)

    If lResult <> 0 Then
        Mid$(WinFontPath, lResult + 1) = "\fonts\"
            WinFontPath = RTrim$(WinFontPath)
    End If

    'This actually adds the font to the list of available
    'fonts for the current Windows session
    lResult = AddFontResource(WinFontPath + FontFile)

    'Check the returned value and show the error if any
    If lResult = 0 Then
        MsgBox "Error Occured When Calling AddFontResource" & Chr(10) & _
                GetLastErrorStr(GetLastError)
        Exit Sub
    End If

     'Write the font name and file name to the registry value
     'to permanently install the font

    '1. Open the registry key
    lResult = RegOpenKey(HKEY_LOCAL_MACHINE, _
    "software\microsoft\windows\currentversion\" & _
    "fonts", hKey)

    '2. Write the registry key value
    lResult = RegSetValueEx(hKey, FontName & " " & FontFile & _
    " (TrueType)", 0, REG_SZ, ByVal FontFile, _
    Len(FontFile))

    '3. Close the registry key
    lResult = RegCloseKey(hKey)

    'This will broadcast a message to let all top-level
    'windows know that a font change has occured so they
    'can reload their font list
    lResult = PostMessage(HWND_BROADCAST, WM_FONTCHANGE, _
    0, 0)
```

```
        'Inform user on success
        MsgBox "New font added successfully!"

End Sub


Private Sub Command1_Click()

'Call the procedure to install the new font
'Note: The font file must be copied to the '\windows\fonts'
'directory first.
'Change the arguments below to show the correct font name
'and file name of the font you are installing
Call AddNewFont("Algerian", "ALGER.TTF")

End Sub
```

Enter the code into the appropriate form, module, or control events as indicated, specify the font name and the font filename in the `Command1_Click` event, and run the project. Click the command button to install the new font.

Analysis

The `AddNewFont` procedure uses the `AddFontResource` API function to add the new font to the list of Windows font resources. It takes two arguments. One specifies the font name under which the TrueType font is to be registered in the Windows Registry and shown in all Windows applications. The second argument is the font filename that was previously copied to the \Fonts directory located under the Windows directory.

Making the new font permanently available to the Windows applications requires creation of a new key value for the new font in the Windows Registry under the `HKEY_LOCAL_MACHINE\Software\Microsoft\Windows\Currentversion\Fonts` section. This is accomplished by the `AddNewFont` procedure through the use of the three API functions: `RegOpenKey` to open the above Registry key, `RegSetValueEx` to create the new key value for the added font, and `RegCloseKey` to close the opened Registry key. After the Registry key is created for the new font, the font is permanently installed on the system.

`AddNewFont` also supports error handling. If any error occurs during the font installation process, the error description will be reported.

By default, Windows keeps all its fonts and installs the new fonts added to the system using the Control Panel, Fonts under the \Fonts folder (directory). So it is convenient that you copy your new font file to this folder before installing the font using the preceding code.

Note that the `AddNewFont` procedure described earlier is suitable for installing new fonts on systems running the Windows 95 operating system. In Windows 98, the new fonts will be automatically installed and registered by Windows when they are copied to the \Fonts folder located under the Windows directory.

The sample project ADDFONT.VBP on the CD-ROM that accompanies this book demonstrates the use of the described procedure.

3.25 HOW TO TURN ON OR OFF NUM LOCK, SCROLL LOCK, AND CAPS LOCK KEYS

by Kamal A. Mehdi

Description

The state of the special keyboard keys Num Lock, Caps Lock, and Scroll Lock can be retrieved and set from within your Visual Basic application with the help of the Windows API.

This code uses three Visual Basic functions to read the state of these special keys and three Visual Basic subroutines to set their state to either `True` (on) or `False` (off). The functions that retrieve the specific key state use the API function `GetKeyState`. The subroutines used to set the key states are based on the `GetKeyboardState` and `SetKeyboardState` API functions.

The 16-bit API declarations are also provided.

Functions Syntax

The following three functions are used to retrieve the current key state:

```
KeyState = GetNumLock()

KeyState = GetCapsLock()

KeyState = GetScrollLock()
```

Part	Description
KeyState	Required. A numeric expression that returns the state of the specified key. If the key is currently turned on, 1 is returned, otherwise 0 is returned. Data type: `Integer`.

Subroutines Syntax

The following three procedures are used to set the key state:

```
SetNumLock(KeyValue)

SetCapsLock(KeyValue)

SetScrollLock(KeyValue)
```

Part	Description
KeyValue	Required. A Boolean expression that sets the value (state) of the specified key. Specifying True sets the key state (turns the key on) while specifying False turns the key off. Data type: Boolean.

Modules and Controls Required

You will need the following modules and controls to build the sample project:

Module/Control	Description
Module1	A standard Visual Basic module (.BAS)
Form1	A standard non-MDI Visual Basic form (.FRM) with controls, as shown later in this section
Frame1	A frame control with the Caption property set to Get Key State
Frame2	A frame control with the Caption property set to Set Key State
Command1()	A control array of three command buttons with the properties set as the following:
	Index = 0, Caption = Num Lock
	Index = 1, Caption = Caps Lock
	Index = 2, Caption = Scroll Lock
Command2()	A control array of three command buttons with the properties set as shown for Command1()
Check1()	A control array of three check boxes
Check2()	A control array of three check boxes

Follow these steps to draw controls:

1. Start a new standard EXE project. Form1 will be created by default. Set the form's Height and Width properties to approximately 3000 and 5300, respectively, and set its Caption property as shown earlier in this section.
2. Draw Frame1 on the left half of the form and set its Caption property as shown earlier.
3. Draw Frame2 on the right half of the form and set its Caption property as shown earlier.
4. Draw the three Command1() buttons and the three Check1() check boxes inside Frame1 with each check box near the command button having the same index value, and set their Caption properties as shown earlier.
5. Repeat step 4 for Command2() and Check2() but inside Frame2.

Note

You can create control arrays by inserting one control on the form and copying and pasting the control on the form using either the right mouse button or the Edit menu. When you paste the control on the form, Visual Basic will prompt you whether to create a control array; choose Yes.

Code Listing

```
'32-bit API declarations (in module1)
Declare Function GetKeyboardState Lib "user32" (pbKeyState As Byte) As Long
Declare Function SetKeyboardState Lib "user32" (lppbKeyState As Byte)
➥ As Long
Declare Function GetKeyState Lib "user32" (ByVal nVirtKey As Long) As
➥ Integer

'16-bit API declarations (use only in VB 16-bit)
'Declare Sub GetKeyboardState Lib "User" (LpKeyState As Any)
'Declare Sub SetKeyboardState Lib "User" (lpKeyState As Any)
'Declare Function GetKeyState Lib "User" (ByVal nVirtKey As Integer) As
➥ Integer

'Form1 code
Private Sub Command1_Click(Index As Integer)

    Select Case Index

        Case Is = 0 'Get the Num Lock key state
            Check1(0).Value = GetNumLock()

        Case Is = 1 'Get the Caps Lock key state
            Check1(1).Value = GetCapsLock()

        Case Is = 2 'Get the Scroll Lock key state
            Check1(2).Value = GetScrollLock()

    End Select

End Sub

Private Sub Command2_Click(Index As Integer)

    Select Case Index

        Case Is = 0 'Set the Num Lock key state
            SetNumLock (CBool(Check2(0).Value))

        Case Is = 1 'Set the Caps Lock key state
            SetCapsLock (CBool(Check2(1).Value))

        Case Is = 2 'Set the Scroll Lock key state
            SetScrollLock (CBool(Check2(2).Value))

    End Select

End Sub

'Module1 code
Function GetCapsLock() As Integer
```

```
        'Returns the state of the CapsLock key
        GetCapsLock = GetKeyState(vbKeyCapital)

End Function

Function GetNumLock() As Integer

        'Returns the state of the NumLock key
        GetNumLock = GetKeyState(vbKeyNumlock)

End Function

Function GetScrollLock() As Integer

        'Returns the state of the ScrollLock key
        GetScrollLock = GetKeyState(vbKeyScrollLock)

End Function

Sub SetCapsLock(Value As Boolean)

        'Sets the state of the CapsLock key
        Call SetKeyState(vbKeyCapital, Value)

End Sub

Sub SetNumLock(Value As Boolean)

        'Sets the state of the NumLock key
        Call SetKeyState(vbKeyNumlock, Value)

End Sub

Sub SetScrollLock(Value As Boolean)

        'Sets the state of the ScrollLock key
        Call SetKeyState(vbKeyScrollLock, Value)

End Sub

Private Sub SetKeyState(KeyName As Integer, KeyValue As Boolean)

        'This code will retrieve the keyboard state, sets the particular
        'key state passed to the 'KeyName' argument with the value passed
        'to the 'KeyValue' argument, and then sets the entire keyboard
        'state back to the state it was before with the new value of the
        'key just changed
        Dim Buffer(0 To 255) As Byte
        GetKeyboardState Buffer(0)
        Buffer(KeyName) = CByte(Abs(KeyValue))
        SetKeyboardState Buffer(0)

End Sub
```

Enter the code in the appropriate form, module, and control events as indicated and run the project. Click any of the `Command1()` buttons to get the state of the specific key (it will be displayed in the adjacent `Check1()` box). To set the state of any of the keys, check or uncheck the appropriate `Check2()` check box and click the adjacent `Command2()` button.

Analysis

The standard computer keyboard keys Num Lock, Caps Lock, and Scroll Lock are special keys that can have two different states, `True` and `False`. The state of these keys can be read and set using API calls in Visual Basic.

Retrieving the key state is straightforward with the `GetKeyState` API function. Changing the key state requires you to retrieve the entire keyboard state using the `GetKeyboardState` API function, change the specific key value, and then set back the entire keyboard state with the only one key changed, using the `SetKeyboardState` API function.

This code demonstrates how this can be done using pure Visual Basic code without the need to use any custom controls like the MicroHelp Key State control shipped with Visual Basic, which performs this functionality. The code makes it easy for the VB programmer to implement the required functionality in his own projects by using any of the three custom procedures and the three custom functions provided without the need to get inside the API details.

The sample project KEYSTATE.VBP on the CD-ROM that accompanies this book demonstrates the use of the described functions and subroutines.

Chapter 4

DEBUGGING AND ERROR HANDLING, MEMORY FUNCTIONS, CONVERSION FUNCTIONS, AND DATA HANDLING

This chapter includes several functions designed to help with error handling, debugging, converting data, and memory management. If you are doing any API or advanced Visual Basic programming, this chapter should contain some very useful functions for you to use. Even though some of this code won't end up in the finished product, it certainly will speed up your development and debugging time.

4.1 CONTROL PRINT OUTPUT

by Mario Gentile

Description

The `PrintControl` routine enables you to microtune everything sent to the printer object. You will have control over the number of characters per line and the carriage return, and will be able to start a new page at any Y coordinate. All the printer object properties and methods apply. Although this code was written for Visual Basic 4 there are no known reasons why it should not work in later versions.

Place this code in a form's `General Declarations` area and add a command button and text box. Change the text box `MultiLine` property to `TRUE`.

Code Listing

```
'***********************************************
'Submitted by Mario Gentile
```

```
'***********************************************
Public Sub PrintControl()

Dim Scroll, Ready, MakeWord, Storage As String
Dim Start, Finish, LineEnd, PageEnd, TP As Integer

Scroll = Text1.Text
Start = 1
Finish = 1
Ready = ""
MakeWord = ""

'**********************************************************************
'Set the Tab position for the starting point of each new line.
TP = 5

'Set the length of the page by changing the TWIP count of the PageEnd
➥variable.
PageEnd = 14400

'Set the number of characters each line will hold by changing the LineEnd
➥ variable.
LineEnd = 74

'Please note that the settings I have given here will load text with
➥74 chr lines and a page length of
'14400 TWIPS which prints a 8 1/2" X 11" page, with a MS Sans Serif
➥size 8 font.
'**********************************************************************

Do Until Start > Len(Scroll)
    Storage = Mid(Scroll, Start, 1)
    If Storage <> vbCr Then
        MakeWord = MakeWord + Storage
        End If
    If Storage = vbCr Then
        If Ready = "" Then
            If Printer.CurrentY > PageEnd Then 'Set the CurrentY to any
            ➥length page.
                Printer.NewPage 'Start new page
                End If
            Printer.Print Tab(TP); MakeWord
            End If
        If Ready <> "" Then
            Ready = Ready + MakeWord
            If Printer.CurrentY > PageEnd Then 'Set the CurrentY to any
            ➥length page.
                Printer.NewPage 'Start new page
                End If
            Printer.Print Tab(TP); Ready
            End If
        Start = Start + 1
```

```
            Finish = 0
            MakeWord = ""
            Ready = ""
            End If
        If Finish = LineEnd Then 'Change the length of the printed line here.
            If Printer.CurrentY > PageEnd Then 'Set the CurrentY to any
            ➥length page.
                Printer.NewPage 'Start new page
                End If
            Printer.Print Tab(TP); Ready
            Finish = 0
            Ready = ""
            End If
        If Storage = Chr(32) Then
            Ready = Ready + MakeWord
            MakeWord = ""
            End If
        Start = Start + 1
        Finish = Finish + 1
        If Start > Len(Scroll) And (Ready <> "" Or MakeWord <> "") Then
            Ready = Ready + MakeWord
            If Printer.CurrentY > PageEnd Then 'Set the CurrentY to any
            ➥length page.
                Printer.NewPage 'Start new page
                End If
            Printer.Print Tab(TP); Ready
            End If
    Loop

Printer.EndDoc

End Sub

Public Sub Command1_Click ()
    PrintControl
End Sub
```

Analysis

I set the Tab position to 5 to add room on the left side for binder holes. You may tab to any position you want to start your sentence. If you want to change the tab position, simply give the TP variable the Tab value. Remember that tabular columns are fixed width and do not adjust for the variable-width fonts you might be using. Tab(0) is equal to the Y coordinate of zero; other than that the Tab(n) column will only be equal to the Tab(n) column.

You can change CurrentY to start a new page. Change the PageEnd variable to the twip setting at which you want the page to end. The default setting is 14,400 twips. This tells the printer object to invoke the NewPage method when the CurrentY value is greater than 14400. There are 1440 twips per logical inch, so this code will leave a 1 1/2-inch footer on an 11 1/2-inch printout. Multiply the length of the page you want printed by 1440 to get your desired page length. To print a document that is five inches top to bottom you would multiply 5×1440. Now set the `PageEnd` variable to 7200 and you're ready to print a five-inch page.

To set the line length, just change the value of the `LineEnd` variable. Because of variable-width fonts, determining how many characters to have per line is less scientific. You will need to adjust the line length by calculating your font size and paper width. Use my default settings as your comparison starting point, remembering that the settings I have given here will load text with 74 characters per line and a page length of 14,400 twips, which prints a 8 1/2×11-inch page, with a MS Sans Serif size 8 font.

The routine reads the text area one character at a time and stores it to the `Scroll` variable. Before printing a line it makes sure that the last word is complete. If not, that word is placed at the beginning of the next line. The code modifications are all located in the `PrintControl` subroutine, and they are defined within the asterisk lines. All you need to do is set the value of the `TP`, `PageEnd`, and `LineEnd` variables, or to print a standard letter keep the default settings. Click the command button and you will print a professional-looking document. The code is easy to understand, which makes it easy to troubleshoot.

4.2   RETRIEVE THE SYSTEM ERROR TITLE

by Brian Shea

Description

The `APIErrorDef` routine is mainly a collection of definitions for API error titles. It includes a function that accepts an error number and returns the appropriate title. This module was designed for use with the `APIErrorHandler` module.

The error definitions are from publicly available information provided by Microsoft. These definitions might change as new operating systems are released. New lists can be found in the Microsoft Knowledge Base and the Microsoft Developer's Network.

The `GetErrorTitle` function is the only function included in this module. It accepts an integer value error number and returns the title of this error.

Syntax

```
stTitleString = GetErrorTitle(inErrNum)
```

Part	Description
stTitleString	Required. The string that will contain the returned title.
inErrNum	Required. The integer value of the error code.

Code Listing

```
Option Explicit

'****************************************************************
'* APIErrorDef.bas
'* Created by Brian Shea
'* Defines Names to API Return Codes
'****************************************************************


'****************************************************************
'* The section below is a listing of API or system error titles
'* and numbers, commented with the text.
'****************************************************************
'* Clip the needed definitions out of this file and into your
'* project as needed to support the API calls that you are using
'* The PUBLIC declarations below should be placed into the
'* general declarations section of your code. If you place
'* them in a form, you will have to change them to PRIVATE
'****************************************************************


Public Const ERROR_SUCCESS = 0 'The operation completed successfully
Public Const ERROR_INVALID_FUNCTION = 1 'Incorrect function.
Public Const ERROR_FILE_NOT_FOUND = 2 'The system cannot find the file
➥ specified.
Public Const ERROR_PATH_NOT_FOUND = 3 'The system cannot find the path
➥ specified.
Public Const ERROR_TOO_MANY_OPEN_FILES = 4 'The system cannot open the file.
Public Const ERROR_ACCESS_DENIED = 5 'Access is denied.
Public Const ERROR_INVALID_HANDLE = 6 'The handle is invalid.
Public Const ERROR_ARENA_TRASHED = 7 'The storage control blocks were
➥ destroyed.
Public Const ERROR_NOT_ENOUGH_MEMORY = 8 'Not enough storage is available to
➥ process this_
      command.
Public Const ERROR_INVALID_BLOCK = 9 'The storage control block address is
➥ invalid.
Public Const ERROR_BAD_ENVIRONMENT = 10 'The environment is incorrect.
Public Const ERROR_BAD_FORMAT = 11 'An attempt was made to load a program with
➥ an _
      incorrect format.
Public Const ERROR_INVALID_ACCESS = 12 'The access code is invalid.
Public Const ERROR_INVALID_DATA = 13 'The data is invalid.
Public Const ERROR_OUTOFMEMORY = 14 'Not enough storage is available to
➥ complete this_
      operation.
Public Const ERROR_INVALID_DRIVE = 15 'The system cannot find the drive
➥ specified.
Public Const ERROR_CURRENT_DIRECTORY = 16 'The directory cannot be removed.
Public Const ERROR_NOT_SAME_DEVICE = 17 'The system cannot move the file to a
➥ different_
      disk drive.
Public Const ERROR_NO_MORE_FILES = 18 'There are no more files.
```

```
Public Const ERROR_WRITE_PROTECT = 19 'The media is write protected.
Public Const ERROR_BAD_UNIT = 20 'The system cannot find the device specified.
Public Const ERROR_NOT_READY = 21 'The device is not ready.
Public Const ERROR_BAD_COMMAND = 22 'The device does not recognize the command.
Public Const ERROR_CRC = 23 'Data error (cyclic redundancy check).
Public Const ERROR_BAD_LENGTH = 24 'The program issued a command but the
➥ command length_
    is incorrect.
Public Const ERROR_SEEK = 25 'The drive cannot locate a specific area or track
➥ on the_
    disk.
Public Const ERROR_NOT_DOS_DISK = 26 'The specified disk or diskette cannot be
➥ accessed.
Public Const ERROR_SECTOR_NOT_FOUND = 27 'The drive cannot find the sector
➥ requested.
Public Const ERROR_OUT_OF_PAPER = 28 'The printer is out of paper.
Public Const ERROR_WRITE_FAULT = 29 'The system cannot write to the specified
➥ device.
Public Const ERROR_READ_FAULT = 30 'The system cannot read from the specified
➥ device.
'**********************************************************************
'* It continues like this for a while
'* <CLIP>
'**********************************************************************

Public Function GetErrorTitle(inErrNum As Integer) As String
    '**********************************************************************
    '* This function receives the error number and returns the
    '* error title.
    '**********************************************************************
    Dim stTitle As String

    '**********************************************************************
    '* Compare the error number to ranges of integers to get to the
    '* correct range, then use Select Case to get the title
    '**********************************************************************
    '* Remember that Error Code 0 is success, you should handle this
    '* in your code or you may get error handling for successful calls
    '**********************************************************************
    If inErrNum = 0 Then
        '* Success
        stTitle = ERROR_SUCCESS
    ElseIf inErrNum < 0 Then
        stTitle = "Error Number Out Of Range (Less Than 0)"
    ElseIf inErrNum > 0 And inErrNum <= 200 Then
        '* Handle Range 1 - 200
        If inErrNum > 0 And inErrNum <= 100 Then
            '* Handle Range 1 to 100
            Select Case inErrNum
            Case 1
                stTitle = "ERROR_INVALID_FUNCTION"
            Case 2
```

```
                stTitle = "ERROR_FILE_NOT_FOUND"
            Case 3
                stTitle = "ERROR_PATH_NOT_FOUND"
            Case 4
                stTitle = "ERROR_TOO_MANY_OPEN_FILES"
            Case 5
                stTitle = "ERROR_ACCESS_DENIED"
            Case 6
                stTitle = "ERROR_INVALID_HANDLE"
            Case 7
                stTitle = "ERROR_ARENA_TRASHED"
            Case 8
                stTitle = "ERROR_NOT_ENOUGH_MEMORY"
            Case 9
                stTitle = "ERROR_INVALID_BLOCK"
            Case 10
                stTitle = "ERROR_BAD_ENVIRONMENT"
            Case 11
                stTitle = "ERROR_BAD_FORMAT"
            Case 12
                stTitle = "ERROR_INVALID_ACCESS"
            Case 13
                stTitle = "ERROR_INVALID_DATA"
            Case 14
                stTitle = "ERROR_OUTOFMEMORY"
            Case 15
                stTitle = "ERROR_INVALID_DRIVE"
            Case 16
                stTitle = "ERROR_CURRENT_DIRECTORY"
            Case 17
                stTitle = "ERROR_NOT_SAME_DEVICE"
            Case 18
                stTitle = "ERROR_NO_MORE_FILES"
            Case 19
                stTitle = "ERROR_WRITE_PROTECT"
            Case 20
                stTitle = "ERROR_BAD_UNIT"
            Case 21
                stTitle = "ERROR_NOT_READY"
            Case 22
                stTitle = "ERROR_BAD_COMMAND"
            Case 23
                stTitle = "ERROR_CRC"
            Case 24
                stTitle = "ERROR_BAD_LENGTH"
            Case 25
                stTitle = "ERROR_SEEK"
'*************************************************
'* Again, the code gets boring here
'* <CLIP>
'*************************************************
```

Analysis

This routine doesn't require much analysis; it simply defines the error codes and titles. The `GetErrorTitle` function checks the error number against a series of ranges of values, then runs it through a `Select Case` to determine the value of the `stTitle` variable. This variable is returned as the title. Several error codes are not defined or listed, and the title of these is Not Listed. Error values lower than 0 or greater than 6999 are listed as Out Of Range because Microsoft has not defined those error codes for system or API errors. Vendor- or application-specific errors might have error codes outside the range defined here.

4.3   RETRIEVE ERROR INFORMATION

by Brian Shea

Description

The `APIErrorHandler` routine is designed to give detailed error messages when using API and system calls in Windows. The bulk of this routine is definitions, and it is designed for use with the `APIErrorDef` file.

This routine defines and gathers all the information on an API error, including the title and text, and indicates when the error occurred. You can output this information to a `MsgBox`, `Debug.Print`, or `Log` file. You can use this information during the build and debug phases of development to ensure that you are handling all the API errors in your code.

`APIErrorHandler` includes two major parts, the `HandleAPIError` function and the `BuildErrorText` function. The `HandleAPIError` function is where you specify the error number to handle and the output mode that you want to use. It will then call the `BuildErrorText` function to get the text of the error.

This function is currently configured to use `APIErrorDef` as well, though this can be commented out if you don't want to use it.

Note

This routine will not prevent or trap API errors that lead to system crashes. Always save your work before testing API calls, and remember that errors that crash VB or the system will not be found in the log files generated by this routine.

Additionally, this routine traps the Error Code = 0 (Success). This is for feedback during debugging and can be removed or handled during your development separately.

Syntax

```
HandleAPIError inErrNum, stOutputMode
```

Part	Description
inErrNum	Required. This is the error number returned from the API call.
stOutputMode	Required. The string expression that specifies what the output should be directed to. Possible values are MBox, Debug, or Log.

stErrorText = BuildErrorText inErrNum

Part	Description
inErrNum	Required. The error number returned from the API call.
stErrorText	Required. The variable that will hold the returned text.

Code Listing

```
Option Explicit

'*****************************************************************
'* APIErrorHandler.bas
'* Created by Brian Shea
'* Based on information from Microsoft Developer's Network
'* Handles API Errors and send them to MsgBox, Debug, or Log File
'*****************************************************************

Public Sub HandleAPIError(inErrNum As Integer, stOutputMode As String)
    '* Handles the error to specified output mode
    Dim stText As String, stDateTime As String
    Dim stTitle As String, stMessage As String
    Dim stFilePath As String, inFileNum As Integer

    '* Set/Get Values for later use
    stDateTime = Now
    '* Comment out the following line if not using the APIErrorDef file
    stTitle = GetErrorTitle(inErrNum)

    stText = BuildErrorText(inErrNum)
    stMessage = ""

    '*********************************************************
    '* This is the output file for the Log selection
    '* Change this to the log file you wish to use
    '*********************************************************
    '* Use the full drive:\path\name.ext format in this name
    '*********************************************************
    stFilePath = "C:\temp\APIError.log"

    '*********************************************************
    '* The vbCRLF has been used to provide rudimentary formatting
    '* in the output.  You may modify to output to one line only
    '* By removing the vbCRLF.
    '*********************************************************
```

```vb
'* The # Character is also used for a marker on the Debug and
'* Log output modes.  You may change or remove this as desired
'***************************************************************
'* Remove references to stTitle if not using APIErrorDef
'***************************************************************
If stOutputMode = "MBox" Then
    '* Prepare output for MsgBox
    stMessage = "API Error #" & CStr(inErrNum) & " (" & stTitle & ")"
    stMessage = stMessage & vbCrLf & " occurred at " & stDateTime & "."
    stMessage = stMessage & vbCrLf & "The text of the error is:"
    stMessage = stMessage & vbCrLf & stText
    MsgBox stMessage, vbOKOnly + vbCritical, "API Error Occurred."
    Exit Sub
ElseIf stOutputMode = "Debug" Then
    '* Prepare Message for Debug.Print Output
    Debug.Print "####################"
    Debug.Print "API Error #" & CStr(inErrNum) & " (" & stTitle & ")"
    Debug.Print "at " & stDateTime & " with text:"
    Debug.Print stText
    Debug.Print "####################"
    Exit Sub
ElseIf stOutputMode = "Log" Then
    '* Send info to log file
    inFileNum = FreeFile
    Open stFilePath For Append As #inFileNum
    stMessage = stDateTime & ": API Error#" & CStr(inErrNum)
    stMessage = stMessage & " (" & stTitle & ")" & vbCrLf & " " & stText
    Print #inFileNum, "################"
    Print #inFileNum, stMessage
    Print #inFileNum, "################"
    Close #inFileNum
    Exit Sub
Else
    '* Message to user, output type not recognized
    stMessage = "The output type selected is not recognized."
    stMessage = stMessage & vbCrLf & "Please try again, or select another
    ➥ method."
    MsgBox stMessage, vbOKOnly + vbExclamation, "Unknown Output Type."
End If

End Sub


Function BuildErrorText(inErrNum As Integer) As String
    '* Builds the output text for the error handler
    Dim stErrText As String

    stErrText = ""

    If inErrNum = 0 Then
        '* Success
        stErrText = "The operation completed successfully."
    ElseIf inErrNum < 0 Then
        stErrText = "Error Number Out Of Range (Less Than 0)."
```

```
    ElseIf inErrNum > 0 And inErrNum <= 200 Then
        '* Handle Range 1 - 200
        If inErrNum > 0 And inErrNum <= 100 Then
            '* Handle Range 1 to 100
            Select Case inErrNum
            Case 1
                stErrText = "Incorrect function."
            Case 2
                stErrText = "The system cannot find the file specified."
            Case 3
                stErrText = "The system cannot find the path specified."
            Case 4
                stErrText = "The system cannot open the file."
            Case 5
                stErrText = "Access is denied."
            Case 6
                stErrText = "The handle is invalid."
            Case 7
                stErrText = "The storage control blocks were destroyed."
            Case 8
                stErrText = "Not enough storage is available to process"
                stErrText = stErrText & vbCrLf & "this command."
            Case 9
                stErrText = "The storage control block address is invalid."
            Case 10
                stErrText = "The environment is incorrect."
            Case 11
                stErrText = "An attempt was made to load a program with"
                stErrText = stErrText & vbCrLf & "an incorrect format."
            Case 12
                stErrText = "The access code is invalid."
            Case 13
                stErrText = "The data is invalid."
            Case 14
                stErrText = "Not enough storage is available to complete this"
                stErrText = stErrText & vbCrLf & "operation."
            Case 15
                stErrText = "The system cannot find the drive specified."
            Case 16
                stErrText = "The directory cannot be removed."
            Case 17
                stErrText = "The system cannot move the file to a different"
                stErrText = stErrText & vbCrLf & "disk drive."
            Case 18
                stErrText = "There are no more files."
            Case 19
                stErrText = "The media is write protected."
            Case 20
                stErrText = "The system cannot find the device specified."
'**********************************************************
'* The code continues like this for a while
'* <CLIP>
'**********************************************************
```

Analysis

This routine is very easy to use and the code is not very complex. The collection of the error code text is the bulk of the code file (there are about 5800 error codes currently defined by Microsoft). The HandleAPIError function simply gets the output mode and error number and then processes the information. The error code is returned from the API call (often in the form of a long integer). You might have to convert the return code to an integer using Cint() before passing it to HandleAPIError.

The function then fills the string values with the text and title (if using APIErrorDef) of the error, and gets the current date and time. The stFilePath variable holds the path to the log file, and is used only if Log is the selected output mode. You must include the drive:\path\file.ext style pathname in stFilePath for the routine to find the correct file. The file will be created if it doesn't exist, and will be appended to if it does exist. If you want to be safe, you can always create an empty file on the desired path to ensure that you don't get any errors when trying to resolve the path and filename for the log file. The path can also be verified or created using the "Create a Directory" function found in Section 7 of this book.

The Log and Debug.Print options have # characters used to provide visual separators for each entry. This is because both of those output methods simply append the new data to any existing data. I thought that this made the output more readable, but if you are not concerned with that, you may remove them from the code.

4.4   BUILD AN ERROR LOG FILE

by Martin Cordova

Description

This subroutine saves relevant error information to a log file residing in the application's directory. The information is appended to the log file, which is named error.log. This file is for information and support purposes mainly, but it could also be parsed (interpreted) by a utility program in order to collect all the log files and store them in a more structured way, maybe in a database file.

> **Note**
>
> This procedure requires the following procedures: SysGetComputerName, SysGetUserName, and SaveFile. These routines are needed to collect some important system information, such as the computer name and the current user (network logon). The procedure SaveFile is reused as a facility to save the log buffer in just one line of code.

Syntax

```
RegError Err.Number, "modDBUTILS.InsertRecord", Err.Description
```

The second parameter is the error source, but you can send any string you consider convenient, as in the preceding example.

Part	Description
Number	The error code (usually `Err.Number`)
Source	The code or module location of the error (usually `Err.Source`)
Description	The description of the error (usually `Err.Description`)

Code Listing

```
Public Sub RegError(ByVal Number, ByVal Source, ByVal Description)

    Dim Buffer As String
    Dim FName As String

    On Error Resume Next

    '---build error report
    Buffer = "date: " & Format$(Now, "dd/mm/yyyy hh:mm am/pm")
    Buffer = Buffer & "Number:" & CStr(Number)
    Buffer = Buffer & "Source:" & Source
    Buffer = Buffer & "Description:" & Description
    Buffer = Buffer & "UserID:" & SysGetUserName()
    Buffer = Buffer & "Computer:" & SysGetComputerName()
    Buffer = Buffer & "Application:" & App.Title
    Buffer = Buffer & "Version:" & App.Major & "." & App.Minor & "."
                    ➥ & App.Revision

    '---append report to log file in the App path
    FName = "error.log"

    SaveFile FName, Buffer, True

End Sub
```

Analysis

This procedure assembles a string buffer with the relevant information about the error and about the context of the application. `UserName` and `ComputerName` are two key pieces of information that can be useful when you try to investigate the source of the error. For example, does some kind of error always happen on the same computer? Maybe there is something wrong with the configuration. This file could be processed by a utility program, parsed (disassembled) and stored in a database file, and then it would be very easy to run some statistical queries against this valuable data. The log file is the first step in the organization of a support and defect control infrastructure.

For example, assuming that several log files from different computers have been imported into a database file, the following metrics can be produced:

- ■ Defects density by error source
- ■ Defects density by error code (which is also an error category)
- ■ Defects density by user and by PC
- ■ Defects grow rate by date

4.5   STACK ROUTINES

by Ian Ippolito

Description

A stack is a useful data structure when a program must store information in a last-in, first-out (LIFO) manner. A stack functions exactly like a stack of plates in a plate dispenser at a restaurant: The last plate put onto the stack by the bus boy is the first plate pulled off by the chef. Many mathematical applications must implement stacks to keep track of paired parentheses and the like, and VB itself uses a stack to keep track of which procedures and functions you have called.

The following stack routines, `Stack_Init`, `Stack_Push`, and `Stack_Pop`, allow for the easy creation and use of a stack.

To use these functions, first initialize the stack by calling `Stack_Init`. (It is absolutely essential that this step be completed first. Forgetting to do so can cause unpredictable behavior from the stack.) After this, the stack can be added to (pushed) and removed from (popped) the stack at any time by calling `Stack_Push` and `Stack_Pop`. The routine has built-in error handling to gracefully recover from a user attempting to pop the stack when it is empty.

Syntax

```
Stack_Init()
Result = Stack_Pop()
Stack_Push Value
```

Part	*Description*
`Value`	Required. A string value to push onto the stack.

Code Listing

```
Option Explicit
Dim mintTopOfStackIndex As Integer
```

```
Dim arrStack() As String

Public Sub Stack_Init()
    'note: must be called before pushing or popping
    'initialize stack index
    mintTopOfStackIndex = 0
End Sub

Public Function Stack_Pop() As String
    'check for no entries on stack
    If (mintTopOfStackIndex < 1) Then
        Stack_Pop = ""
        Exit Function
    End If
    'pop off of stack
    Stack_Pop = arrStack(mintTopOfStackIndex)

    'decrement counter by one
    mintTopOfStackIndex = mintTopOfStackIndex - 1
    ReDim Preserve arrStack(mintTopOfStackIndex)
End Function

Public Sub Stack_Push(ByVal strValue As String)
    'increment counter by one
    mintTopOfStackIndex = mintTopOfStackIndex + 1

    'push on stack
    ReDim Preserve arrStack(mintTopOfStackIndex)
    arrStack(mintTopOfStackIndex) = strValue
End Sub
```

Analysis

These routines utilize a dynamically allocated array of strings to implement the stack and an integer pointer to keep track of the topmost element. The pointer limits the stack to a size of 32,766. However, if an application requires a stack size larger than this, the routines can be upsized by changing the declaration of mintTopOfStackIndex from an integer to a long.

Stack_Init initializes the stack pointer to zero, which is the stack's starting point.

The Stack_Pop and Stack_Push routines accomplish their business by dynamically resizing the array with the Redim keyword. By additionally specifying the little-used Preserve keyword with this statement, these routines are capable of resizing the stack without destroying any data already existing on it.

This routine can be customized to accept other types of variables (such as integers, longs, or objects) by simply changing a few declarations. First, declare the variable arrStack to be of the new variable type. Then set the return values of the functions Stack_Pop() and Stack_Push() to match the new variable type as well.

For example, to customize the routine to accept longs, the following changes are all that would be required:

```
Dim arrStack() As long

Public Function Stack_Pop() As long

Public Sub Stack_Push(ByVal strValue As long)
```

4.6   CURRENCY TO STRING CONVERSION

by Larry Serflaten

Description

Use this function to convert currency values to words in a string. The resulting string is suitable for printing on checks or as text input to a speech synthesizing telephony application. A Boolean switch `CentsAsFraction` is provided to report the cents value as a fraction (1) for printing on a check, or as words (0) for a telephony application. `Unit` and `UnitFraction` constants are provided to allow easy localization of the monetary units for international use.

To see this function in action, place two text boxes and a command button on a new form. Enlarge `Text2` and set its `MultiLine` property to `True`. Then insert the following functions into the form's code section. In the `Click` event of the command button add `Text2 = CurrencyText(CCur(Text1))` and run the program. Enter currency values into `Text1` and press the command button to see the conversion to text. The valid range is from 0 to 922337203685477.58; anything else returns an empty string. In the example, the `CCur` function will fail if the value entered is not within the valid range.

This code is ready to drop in and use. It has been tested in VB 3 and VB 4/16 and should work in later versions.

Syntax

```
strAmount = CurrencyText(curAmount)
```

Part	Description
strAmount	The string variable to hold the returned text.
curAmount	Required. A Currency value intended to be represented in text.

Code Listing

```
Function CurrencyText (ByVal Amount As Currency) As String
    Dim Amt$, Tri$, Out$
    Dim Grp%, Dollars!, Cents%
    Const GroupNames = "TrillionBillion Million Thousand"
```

```
      Const Unit = "Dollar"
      Const UnitFraction = "Cent"
      'Switch
      Const CentsAsFraction = 0

          If Amount < 0# Then CurrencyText = "": Exit Function
          Amt = Format$(Amount, "000000000000000.00")
          Dollars = Fix(Val(Amt))
          For Grp = 0 To 4
              Tri = Left$(Amt, 3)
              Amt = Mid$(Amt, 4)
              If Val(Tri) Then
                  Out = Out & TriGroupText(Tri)
                  If Grp <4 Then Out = Out & Trim$(Mid$(GroupNames,
          ➥ Grp * 8 + 1, 8)) & " ">
              End If
          Next Grp
          If Dollars Then
              Out = Out & Unit
              If Dollars  1 Then Out = Out & "s"
          Else
              Out = Out & "Zero " & Unit & "s"
          End If
          Amt = "0" & Right$(Amt, 2)
          Cents = Val(Amt)
          If Cents Then
              Out = Out & " and "
              If CentsAsFraction then
                  Out = Out & Right$(Amt, 2) & "/100"
              Else
                  Out = Out & TriGroupText(Amt) & UnitFraction
                  If Cents  1 Then Out = Out & "s"
              End If
          Else
              If CentsAsFraction then
                  Out = Out & " and 00/100"
              Else
                  Out = Out & " even"
              End If
          End If
          Out = Trim$(Out)
          CurrencyText = UCase$(Left$(Out, 1)) & Mid$(Out, 2)
  End Function

  Function TriGroupText (Amt$) As String
      Dim Digit1%, Digit10%, Out$
      Const Ones = "one   two   threefour five six   seveneightnine "
      Const Tens = "ten     twenty thirty forty  fifty   sixty
  ➥seventyeighty ninety "
      Const Teens = "eleven   twelve    thirteen fourteen fifteen  sixteen
  ➥seventeeneighteen nineteen "
```

```
    If (Len(Amt) <> 3) Or (IsNumeric(Amt) = False)
    ➥ Then TriGroupText = "": Exit Function
    Digit1 = Val(Left$(Amt, 1))
    If Digit1 Then Out = Trim$(Mid$(Ones, Digit1 * 5 - 4, 5)) & " Hundred"
    Digit1 = Val(Right$(Amt, 2))
    Select Case Digit1
        Case 20 To 99, 10
            Digit10 = Digit1 \ 10
            Digit1 = Digit1 - (Digit10 * 10)
            If Digit10 Then Out = Out & " " & Trim$(Mid$(Tens,
            ➥ Digit10 * 7 - 6, 7))
            If Digit1 Then Out = Out & " " & Trim$(Mid$(Ones,
            ➥ Digit1 * 5 - 4, 5))
        Case 1 To 9
            Out = Out & " " & Trim$(Mid$(Ones, Digit1 * 5 - 4, 5))
        Case 11 To 19
            Out = Out & " " & Trim$(Mid$(Teens, (Digit1 - 11) * 9 + 1, 9))
    End Select
    TriGroupText = Trim$(Out) & " "
End Function
```

Analysis

This function works by dividing the currency value into groups of three digits. These groups are the Thousands, Millions, Billions, and Trillions groups. Each group is processed by the `TriGroupText` function, which converts a three-character string to words representing hundreds, tens, and ones.

Formatting the input amount to a fixed size that is large enough to handle all currency values, the output string can be built by stepping into the formatted input in groups of threes. If the numeric value of the three-character group is greater than zero, `TriGroupText` is called to convert the value into words, and that group's name is appended to the output string. It is interesting to note how the `GroupNames` constant was used to supply a virtual array of strings.

When processing gets down to the last three characters (the decimal point and pennies value), the monetary constant text (that is, `Dollar`) is added if there were dollars in the input. The phrase `Zero Dollars` is used if no dollars are in the input. If there is more than one, s is added to indicate the plural. Replacing the decimal point with a `0` yields the final three-character group, which can also be processed by the `TriGroupText` function. To avoid ambiguity of the last word in the text, the word `even` is added when there is no fractional value in the currency amount.

4.7   CONVERT A NUMBER FROM HEX TO DECIMAL

by Kamal A. Mehdi

Description

The HexToDec function converts a hexadecimal number represented by a string in the hexadecimal notation to its corresponding decimal value. The hexadecimal number passed to the function must be a positive number. Negative numbers can be passed without the sign, and the sign is added to the decimal value after the conversion.

The HexToDec function accepts very large values for the hexadecimal number, up to the maximum limit of the Long data type (2,147,483,647 or &H7FFFFFFF).

Syntax

```
DecNumber = HexToDec(HexNumber)
```

Part	Description
DecNumber	Required. A variant number that returns the decimal value of the hexadecimal number (string in hexadecimal notation).
HexNumber	Required. A string expression that represents the hexadecimal number to be converted to decimal. The hexadecimal number must be positive. Both &HXX... and XX... hexadecimal strings are recognized by the function (X=0 to 9 or A to F). The hexadecimal string is case insensitive.

Code Listing

```
Function HexToDec(HexNum As String)
    'HexNum is the hexadecimal string to be converted to decimal

    'Declare variables
    Dim TempValue As Integer
    Dim Digit As String
    Dim DecValue As Long

    'Trim the '&H' characters if exist
    If UCase(Left$(HexNum, 2)) = "&H" Then HexNum = Right$(HexNum,
    ➥ Len(HexNum) - 2)

    'Evaluate the decimal value from the Hex string by iterating through all
    'characters contained in the hexadecimal string and evaluating their value
    'depending on the character and its position in the string
    For x = Len(HexNum) To 1 Step -1
        Digit = Mid$(HexNum, x, 1)
```

```
            Select Case UCase(Digit)
                Case Is = "A"
                    TempValue = 10
                Case Is = "B"
                    TempValue = 11
                Case Is = "C"
                    TempValue = 12
                Case Is = "D"
                    TempValue = 13
                Case Is = "E"
                    TempValue = 14
                Case Is = "F"
                    TempValue = 15
                Case "0" To "9"
                    TempValue = Val(Digit)
                Case Else    'If the hex character is invalid, report it and exit
                    MsgBox "Error in Hex string! (" & HexNum & ")"
                    Exit Function
            End Select
            'Calculate the temporary decimal value by adding the current
            'hexadecimal character value multiplied by its weight
            DecValue = DecValue + TempValue * 16 ^ (Len(HexNum) - x)
        Next

        'Assign the value to the function and exit
        HexToDec = DecValue

End Function
```

Analysis

This simple function accepts one string argument as a hexadecimal number in the standard hexadecimal notation and evaluates its decimal value. The function analyzes the hexadecimal number by taking each character in the hexadecimal string separately and evaluates its significance depending on its value and its position within the string. Characters that are numbers (0 to 9) are calculated directly by multiplying their value by 16^X, where X represents the relative character position within the string, while those that are letters (A to F) are converted to numbers first (10 to 15, respectively) and are then evaluated. The following is the formal hexadecimal-to-decimal conversion formula:

$$D = (X_1 * (16 \wedge 0)) + (X_2 * (16 \wedge 1)) + \ldots + (X_n * (16 \wedge n\text{-}1))$$

where

- D is the decimal value of the hexadecimal number.
- X[1]...X[n] are the subsequent hexadecimal characters from right to left (least-significant bit to most-significant bit).
- n is the number of characters in the hexadecimal string.

The following example shows how you can call the HexToDec function from within your own code to convert the hexadecimal number &HF0CE to its corresponding decimal value 61,646.

```
'Actual code to call the HexToDec function
'Declare variables
Dim DecNumber As Variant
Dim HexNumber As String

'Specify the hexadecimal number (string)
HexNumber = "&HF0CE"

'Call the function
DecNumber = HexToDec(HexNumber)
'Now DecNumber has the value 61,646 (show it in a message box)
MsgBox DecNumber
```

The `HexToDec` function recognizes both the `&HFFFF` and `FFFF` hexadecimal strings (with or without the hexadecimal identification symbol) as the same. It also accepts both upper- and lowercase strings. In addition, it shows a message box reporting an error if any of the hexadecimal string characters are invalid.

The sample project HEX2DEC.VBP on the CD-ROM demonstrates the use of this function.

4.8   CONVERT A NUMBER FROM DECIMAL TO BINARY

by Kamal A. Mehdi

Description

The `DecToBin` function converts a decimal number to a string representing the binary value (comprising 0s and 1s) of the decimal number as well as to a Boolean array containing the actual bit values (`True`/`False`) of the binary number. The function automatically evaluates the smallest number of bits (digits) required to represent the binary value of the decimal number. However, the number of bits in the returned binary value can also be prespecified and passed as an argument to the function to return a fixed-length binary string and a fixed-size binary array when a certain fixed number of bits is required.

The binary data is returned by the function through a string and Boolean array variable passed to the appropriate function arguments, while the function itself returns the number of bits contained in the evaluated binary value.

The `DecToBin` function accepts very large values for the decimal number, up to the maximum limit of the Long data type (`2,147,483,647`).

Syntax

```
Bits = DecToBin(DecNumber, BinString, BinData(), NumOfBits)
```

Part	Description
Bits	Required. A variant (number) that returns the number of bits contained in the evaluated binary data.
DecNumber	Required. A numeric expression representing the decimal number to be converted to binary. The decimal number must be positive. The data type is Long.
BinString	Required. The variable name passed to the function. It will return the binary value of the decimal number in string format. The data type is String.
BinData()	Required. An array variable name passed to the function. It will return the binary data bit values of the decimal number. The data type is Boolean.
NumOfBits	Optional. A numeric expression that specifies the required number of bits contained in the returned binary string and the binary data array. The data type is Integer.

Code Listing

```
Function DecToBin(DecNum As Long, BinStr As String, BinData() As Boolean,
➥ Optional NumOfBits As Integer)

    'DecNum is the decimal number to be converted to binary
    'BinStr is the string variable that will hold the string-representation
    'of the binary value
    'BinData() is the Boolean array that will hold the real bit-values of the
    'binary number
    'NumOfBits is the required number of bits in the returned binary number
    '(not required in the conversion process but is required only if you want
    'to get a fixed bit-length binary numbers - example 8-bit numbers)

    Dim TempValue As Integer
    Dim BinValue As String
    Dim BinLength As Integer

    'If the received decimal number is less than 0, make it 0.
    If DecNum < 0 Then DecNum = 0

    'Generate the binary string by continuously dividing the decimal
    'number by 2 and evaluating the remainder which represents the
    'current binary-bit value
    Do
        TempValue = DecNum Mod 2
        BinValue = CStr(TempValue) + BinValue
        DecNum = DecNum \ 2
    Loop Until DecNum = 0

    'Append zeros to the left of the binary string if it is less than the
    'NumOfBits argument value
    'Note: If the binary string is already longer that 'NumOfBits',
    'the complete number will be returned
    Do While Len(BinValue) < NumOfBits
        BinValue = "0" + BinValue
```

```
Loop

'Write the binary string in the BinStr argument
BinStr = BinValue

BinLength = Len(BinValue)

'Fill the passed BinData() array with the binary bit values after
'redimentioning it to the size (number of bits) of the evaluated
'binary value
ReDim BinData(BinLength)

For x = 1 To BinLength
    BinData(x - 1) = CBool(Mid$(BinValue, BinLength - x + 1, 1))
Next

'Assign the evaluated number of bits of the binary value to the
'function return value
DecToBin = BinLength

End Function
```

Analysis

The `DecToBin` function performs a true binary conversion of decimal numbers. The binary value of the decimal number is returned in two formats: string and real bit-value array. The returned binary string and binary array will always contain the minimum number of bits (digits) required to appropriately represent the binary value. For example, converting the decimal number 15 without specifying the number of digits will return the 4-digit string 1111 and the 4-element bit array with all elements having the Boolean value True. However, converting the decimal number 16 will return the 5-digit binary number (string) **10000** and the 5-element bit array with the most significant bit (MSB) element value being True (1) and all the other elements being False (0) as shown in the following examples.

Example 1

Input values:

Decimal number to convert: 15

```
'Declare variables
Dim Bits As Variant
Dim DecNumber As Long
Dim BinString As String
Dim BinData() As Boolean

'Specify the decimal number to convert
DecNumber = 15

'Call the function
Bits = DecToBin(DecNumber, BinString, BinData())
```

```
'Print results in the debug window
Debug.Print "BinString="; BinString
Debug.Print "Bits="; Bits
Debug.Print "Binary array element values:"
For I%= 0 To Bits - 1
    Debug.Print "Element: "; I%; "  Value: "; BinData(I%)
Next
```

Results:

- Returned binary string (`BinString`): 1111
- Returned number of bits (`Bits`): 4
- Returned bit array (`BinData()`):

Element	Value (Boolean)
0 (LSB)	1 (True)
1	1 (True)
2	1 (True)
3 (MSB)	1 (True)

Example 2

Input values:

Decimal number to convert: 16

Use the same code above replacing the value 15 with 16 for the `DecNumber` variable

Results:

- Returned binary string (`BinString`): "10000"
- Returned number of bits (`Bits`): 5
- Returned bit array (`BinData()`):

Element	Value (Boolean)
0 (LSB)	0 (False)
1	0 (False)
2	0 (False)
3	0 (False)
4 (MSB)	1 (True)

The number of bits (contained in the binary number) returned by the function in the `Bits` variable is actually needed because the size of the binary data array `BinData()` can be determined only from the `Bits` variable value.

In many cases however, you might need to get a fixed bit-length representation of the binary data (4-bit, 8-bit, and so on). This can be achieved by specifying the required number of bits for the `NumOfBits` argument. For example, if the binary value is required to be represented by an 8-bit number, the value 8 is passed to the NumOfBits argument, returning 00001111 for the decimal number 15, while 00010000 is returned for the decimal number 16. The binary data array will contain eight elements with the actual bit values of the number as shown in the following example.

Example 3

Input values:

Decimal number to convert: 15

Number of bits required: 8

```
'Declare variables
    Dim Bits As Variant
    Dim DecNumber As Long
    Dim BinString As String
    Dim BinData() As Boolean
    Dim NumOfBits As Integer

    'Specify the decimal number to convert and the required number of bits
    DecNumber = 15
    NumOfBits = 8

    'Call the function
    Bits = DecToBin(DecNumber, BinString, BinData(), NumOfBits)

    'Print results in the debug window
    Debug.Print "BinString="; BinString
    Debug.Print "Bits="; Bits
    Debug.Print "Binary array element values:"
    For I%= 0 To Bits - 1
        Debug.Print "Element: "; I%; "  Value: "; BinData(I%)
    Next
```

Results:

- Returned binary string (BinString): "00001111"
- Returned number of bits (Bits): 8
- Returned bit array (BinData()):

Element	Value (Boolean)
0 (LSB)	1 (True)
1	1 (True)
2	1 (True)
3	1 (True)
4	0 (False)
5	0 (False)
6	0 (False)
7 (MSB)	0 (False)

Note that if the number assigned to the NumOfBits argument is smaller than the minimum number of bits required to appropriately represent the binary value, the function will automatically evaluate and return the correct number of bits.

The sample project DEC2BIN.VBP on the CD-ROM demonstrates the use of this function.

4.9   CONVERT A NUMBER FROM HEX TO BINARY

by Kamal A. Mehdi

Description

The HexToBin function converts a hexadecimal number (represented by a string in hexadecimal notation) to a string representing the binary value (comprising 0s and 1s) of the hexadecimal number as well as to a Boolean array containing the actual bit values (True/False) of the binary number. The function automatically evaluates the smallest number of bits required to represent the binary value of the hexadecimal number. However, the number of bits in the returned binary value can also be prespecified and passed as an argument to the function to return a fixed-length binary string and a fixed-size binary array when a certain fixed number of bits is required.

The binary data is returned by the function through a string and a Boolean array variable passed to the appropriate function arguments, while the function itself returns the number of bits contained in the evaluated binary value.

The HexToBin function accepts very large values for the hexadecimal number, up to the maximum limit of the Long data type (2,147,483,647 or &H7FFFFFFF).

Syntax

Bits = HexToBin(HexNumber, BinString, BinData(), NumOfBits)

Part	Description
Bits	Required. A variant (number) that returns the number of bits contained in the evaluated binary data.
HexNumber	Required. A string expression that represents the hexadecimal number to be converted to binary. The hexadecimal number must be positive. Both &HXX... and XX... hexadecimal strings are recognized by the function (X = 0 to 9 or A to F). The hexadecimal string is case insensitive.
BinString	Required. A variable name passed to the function. It will return the binary value of the hexadecimal number in string format. The data type is String.

Part	Description
BinData()	Required. An array variable name passed to the function. It will return the binary data bit values of the converted hexadecimal number. The data type is Boolean.
NumOfBits	Optional. A numeric expression that specifies the required number of bits contained in the returned binary string and the binary data array. The data type is Integer.

Code Listing

```
Function HexToBin(HexNum As String, BinStr As String, BinData() As Boolean,
➡ Optional NumOfBits As Integer)
    'HexNum is the hexadecimal string to be converted to binary
    'BinStr is the string variable that will hold the string-representation
    'of the binary value
    'BinData() is the Boolean array that will hold the real bit-values of the
    'binary number
    'NumOfBits is the required number of bits in the returned binary number
    '(not required in the conversion process but is required only if you want
    'to get a fixed bit-length binary numbers - example 8-bit numbers)

    Dim TempValue As Integer
    Dim BinValue As String
    Dim BinLength As Integer
    Dim Digit As String
    Dim DecValue As Long

    'Trim the '&H' characters if exist
    If UCase(Left$(HexNum, 2)) = "&H" Then HexNum = Right$(HexNum,
    ➡ Len(HexNum) - 2)

    'Evaluate the decimal value from the Hex string by iterating through all
    'characters contained in the hexadecimal string and evaluating their value
    'depending on the character and its position in the string
    For x = Len(HexNum) To 1 Step -1
        Digit = Mid$(HexNum, x, 1)
        Select Case UCase(Digit)
            Case Is = "A"
                TempValue = 10
            Case Is = "B"
                TempValue = 11
            Case Is = "C"
                TempValue = 12
            Case Is = "D"
                TempValue = 13
            Case Is = "E"
                TempValue = 14
            Case Is = "F"
                TempValue = 15
            Case "0" To "9"
                TempValue = Val(Digit)
```

```
            Case Else    'If the hex character is invalid, report it and exit
                MsgBox "Error in Hex string! (" & HexNum & ")"
                Exit Function
        End Select
        'Calculate the temporary decimal value by adding the current
        'hexadecimal character value multiplied by its weight
        DecValue = DecValue + TempValue * 16 ^ (Len(HexNum) - x)
    Next

    'Generate the binary string by continuously dividing the decimal
    'number by 2 and evaluating the remainder which represents the
    'current binary-bit value
    Do
        TempValue = DecValue Mod 2
        BinValue = CStr(TempValue) + BinValue
        DecValue = DecValue \ 2
    Loop Until DecValue = 0

    'Append zeros to the left of the binary string if it is less than
    'the NumOfBits argument value
    'Note: If the binary string is already longer that 'NumOfBits',
    'the complete number will be returned
    Do While Len(BinValue) < NumOfBits
        BinValue = "0" + BinValue
    Loop

    'Write the binary string in the BinStr argument
    BinStr = BinValue

    BinLength = Len(BinValue)

    'Fill the passed BinData() array with the binary bit values after
    'redimentioning it to the size (number of bits) of the evaluated
    'binary value
    ReDim BinData(BinLength)

    For x = 1 To BinLength
        BinData(x - 1) = CBool(Mid$(BinValue, BinLength - x + 1, 1))
    Next

    'Assign the evaluated number of bits of the binary value to the
    'function return value
    HexToBin = BinLength

End Function
```

Analysis

The HexToBin function performs a true binary conversion of hexadecimal numbers. The binary value of the hexadecimal number is returned in two formats: string and real bit-value array format. The function first evaluates the decimal value of the hexadecimal number by analyzing the hexadecimal string, taking each character in the string separately and evaluating its significance depending on its value and position within the string. Characters that are numbers (0 to 9) are calculated directly by multiplying their value by 16^X, where X represents the relative character position within the string, whereas those that are letters (A to F) are converted to numbers first (10 to 15 respectively) and are then evaluated. The binary value of the hexadecimal number is then evaluated by continuously dividing the decimal number by 2 and considering the remainder.

The evaluated binary string and binary data array will always contain the minimum number of bits required to appropriately represent the binary value. For example, converting the hexadecimal number 0F without specifying the number of bits (NumOfBits argument) will return the 4-digit string 1111 and the 4-element bit array with all elements having the value True. Converting the hexadecimal number 10 will return the 5-digit number 10000 and a 5-element bit array with the most significant bit (MSB) being True (1) and all the other elements being False (0) as shown in the following examples.

Example 1

Input values:

Hexadecimal number to convert: &H0F

```
'Declare variables
Dim Bits As Variant
Dim HexNumber As String
Dim BinString As String
Dim BinData() As Boolean

'Specify the hexadecimal number to convert
HexNumber = "&H0F"

'Call the function
Bits = HexToBin(HexNumber, BinString, BinData())

'Print results in the debug window
Debug.Print "BinString="; BinString
Debug.Print "Bits="; Bits
Debug.Print "Binary array element values:"
For I%= 0 To Bits - 1
    Debug.Print "Element: "; I%; "  Value: "; BinData(I%)
Next
```

Results:

- Returned binary string (BinString): 1111
- Returned number of bits (Bits): 4
- Returned bit array (BinData()):

Element	Value (Boolean)
0 (LSB)	1 (True)
1	1 (True)
2	1 (True)
3 (MSB)	1 (True)

Example 2

Input values:

Hexadecimal number to convert: &H10

Use the same code above replacing the value &H0F with &H10 for the HexNumber variable.

Results:

- ■ Returned binary string (BinString): 10000
- ■ Returned number of bits (Bits): 5
- ■ Returned bit array (BinData()):

Element	Value (Boolean)
0 (LSB)	0 (False)
1	0 (False)
2	0 (False)
3	0 (False)
4 (MSB)	1 (True)

The number of bits (contained in the binary number) returned by the function in the Bits variable is actually needed because the size of the binary data array BinData() can be determined only from the Bits variable value.

In cases in which a specific fixed number of bits is required in the binary data, it can be specified and passed to the NumOfBits argument when the function is called. For example, when converting the hexadecimal number F8 to a 12-bit binary number, the value 12 is passed to the NumOfBits argument, returning the 12-digit binary string 000011111000 and a 12-element binary array data as shown in the following example.

Example 3

Input values:

Hexadecimal number to convert: &HF8

Number of bits required: 12

```
'Declare variables
Dim Bits As Variant
Dim HexNumber As String
Dim BinString As String
```

```
Dim BinData() As Boolean
Dim NumOfBits As Integer

'Specify the hexdecimal number to convert and the required number of bits
HexNumber = "&HF8"
NumOfBits = 12

 'Call the function
Bits = HexToBin(HexNumber, BinString, BinData(), NumOfBits)

 'Print results in the debug window
Debug.Print "BinString="; BinString
Debug.Print "Bits="; Bits
Debug.Print "Binary array element values:"
For I%= 0 To Bits - 1
     Debug.Print "Element: "; I%; "  Value: "; BinData(I%)
Next
```

Results:

- Returned binary string (`BinString`): `000011111000`
- Returned number of bits (`Bits`): `12`
- Returned bit array (`BinData()`):

Element	*Value (Boolean)*
0 (LSB)	0 (False)
1	0 (False)
2	0 (False)
3	1 (True)
4	1 (True)
5	1 (True)
6	1 (True)
7	1 (True)
8	0 (False)
9	0 (False)
10	0 (False)
11 (MSB)	0 (False)

Note that if the value passed to the `NumOfBits` argument is smaller than the minimum number of bits required to appropriately represent the binary value, the function will automatically evaluate and return the correct number of bits.

The function recognizes both `&HFFFF` and `FFFF` hexadecimal strings (with or without the hexadecimal identification symbol) as the same. It also accepts both upper- and lowercase strings. In addition, it shows a message box reporting an error if any of the hexadecimal string characters are invalid.

The sample project HEX2BIN.VBP on the CD-ROM demonstrates the use of this function.

4.10 RETRIEVE THE RADIAN VALUE OF A NUMBER OF DEGREES

by Fredrik Bodin

Description

This is a function that returns the radian value of a number in degrees. The definition of 360 degrees in radians is 2pi. Therefore, Radians = Degrees * (2pi/360), or Radians = Degrees * (pi/180).

This function is useful when you are using cos, sin, and other trigonometry functions because they operate in radians.

Syntax

```
Radians = fnRad(valDegrees )
```

Part	Description
Radians	A double that returns the function's value in radians.
valDegrees	Required. A number representing degrees.

Code Listing

```
Function fnRad ( valDegrees as integer ) as currency
    Const pi = 3.1415
    FnRad = valDegrees * (pi / 180)
End function
```

Analysis

Radians is a unit used by COS, SIN, and TAN operations. This routine makes your code more "nice," as shown in the following example:

```
aX = COS(fnRad(Angle))
```

This is better than writing

```
aX = COS(Angle * (Pi / 180))
```

In radians, 2pi are 360 degrees.

4.11 RETRIEVE THE VALUE OF A RADIAN IN A NUMBER OF DEGREES

by Fredrik Bodin

Description

This routine calculates the degree value of a number that is in radians. The definition of 360 degrees in radians is 2pi. Therefore, Degrees = Radians * (360/2pi), or Degrees = Radians * (180/pi). This is useful when you are using cos, sin, and other trigonometry functions because they often operate in radians.

You might want to use a constant to do this, but that usually messes up the code and makes it harder to follow.

Syntax

```
Degrees = fnDeg(valRadians )
```

Part	Description
Degrees	An integer or double that returns the value of the procedure.
valRadians	Required. A number representing the radian value.

Code Listing

```
Function fnDeg ( valRadians as double ) as currency
    Const pi = 3.1415
    FnDeg = valRadians * (180 / pi)
End function
```

Analysis

Radians is a unit used by COS, SIN, and TAN operations. This routine makes your code more "nice," as shown in the following example:

```
aX = fnDeg(COS(Angle))
```

This is better than writing

```
aX = COS(Angle) * (180 / Pi)
```

In radians, 2pi is 360 degrees.

4.12   THE LOG MANAGER

by Larry Serflaten

Description

When you're in charge of creating and supporting applications for a large group of people, or any time you are separated from the people that use your program, you can't look over their shoulders when they have problems. In many cases, the user simply must be better educated in using the program, but in a few cases, she might actually find a bug. When that time comes, knowing what the program did in response to user input goes a long way in tracking down the problem.

One solution is to have the user describe what he or she did that caused the problem while you try to re-create the problem on your system, running the same program. Another solution, presented here, is to have the program log execution activity so that its steps can be traced right to the problem area. The log feature might be turned on by a menu option or a command-line switch. Once engaged, the user would then re-create the problem on his or her own system. After the problem appears, the user can stop momentarily and retain a copy of the log file to send to you. With the log file data in hand, your search for the offending code can be narrowed down to a few procedures.

The LogManager routine that follows is a subroutine that creates or amends a log file as needed. It keeps track of called procedures and optionally reports whether each procedure that calls it ends in the normal manner. This helps locate unforeseen errors that might invoke an error handler that wasn't intended to handle that type of unforeseen error.

The following is an example of the log generated when a program starts up in SubA, which calls SubB. Unfortunately, SubB caused an error for which no error handler was present.

```
[08/28/98 14:18:18] SAMPLE - VERSION: 1 0 0
[08/28/98 14:18:19]          START: SubA( 3.5 )
[08/28/98 14:18:20]               START: SubB( 55309, "Big Lake,
➥Minnesota" )
[08/28/98 14:18:20]               ERROR: 13, Type mismatch
[08/28/98 14:18:20]          LOGICAL ERROR: Handler/Exit calls missing
[08/28/98 14:18:21]          __END:SubA
```

The LogManager lists the application title and version number when the file is created, and optionally includes integer and string parameters passed to each routine. From this report you can verify the version number and see that SubA and SubB, with their parameters, were called just before the trouble started. The LOGICAL ERROR indicates that SubB did not end properly, so that would be the best place to start. Supplying the same parameters to SubB as listed in the log and stepping through the procedure might lead you right to the problem, with a minimum amount of time and resources.

All this help comes at a price; you must include a call to the `LogManager` at the beginning of your major procedures, in all your error handlers, and optionally at the end of these same procedures. During each call to the `LogManager` there is some disk activity, that is why it is recommended to be able to turn it off and on. The call to `LogManager` should be made conditionally on the state of a global flag. Set this flag any time you want to log the execution steps:

```
Private Sub MyRoutine(Param1, Param2)
Dim a%, b%

    If gLogEnabled Then LogManager logStart, "MyRoutine", Param1, Param2
    On Error Goto MyRoutineError
    '...
    'Your routine's code
    '...
    If gLogEnabled Then LogManager logEnd, "MyRoutine"
    Exit Sub
MyRoutineError:
    If gLogEnabled Then LogManager Err.Number, Err.Description
    '...
    'Your error routine code
    '...
    If gLogEnabled Then LogManager logMessage, "Error was
    ➥handled successfully"
    If gLogEnabled Then LogManager logEnd, "MyRoutine"
End Sub
```

As previously revealed, the Log Manager comes with a few options or features. After placing the routine in a module accessible to your project, you must decide whether you plan to use the optional procedure end calls. The optional procedure end calls are the ones you add at the end of your major procedures and error-handler code. You must use them in all or none of the procedures that use a start call to the Log Manager. If you otherwise use them only in some, `LOGICAL ERROR:` will appear after each routine that uses an ending call and has called a routine that does not. If you want the full benefit of having your errors logged, you should use ending calls for every procedure that uses a starting call. If you do not want to use ending calls, you need only set the `Indent_Spacing` constant to zero.

Calling the `LogManager` routine is simple. There are four types of calls you can make to it. Each are identified by an integer value: `-2` indicates a procedure ending call, `-1` indicates a procedure starting call, `0` indicates the message is to be logged, and all positive numbers indicate all positive error codes. You might make the first three (`-2`, `-1`, `0`) global constants—`logEnd`, `logStart`, `logMessage`, as used in the previous example.

The type of call is followed by the logged message and optional parameters. The message will be the name of the procedure for the start and end calls, the message to be logged for message calls, or the error description for error message calls. Be sure to use identical procedure names for both the start and end calls. The optional parameters can be anything, but only strings and numerical values are recognized. Any number of optional parameters can be used after the message parameter, each separated by a comma.

Two switches, provided as constants, enable you to control the log file's indent spacing and the routine's own memory use. As shown previously, procedure calls are nested by indents, making the beginning and ends more obvious. The amount of indent is governed by the INDENT_SPACING constant. Each start call stores the procedure name in a static string. Before the name is stored it is trimmed, or padded, to a specific length. This makes the relationship between the stored procedure name and the amount of indexing proportional.

The specific length the procedure names are trimmed or padded to is governed by the MESSAGE_SIZE constant. Set this constant small enough to hold several calls in available string memory and large enough to identify each procedure name. If you set this constant to the length of the largest procedure name in your application, you should get satisfactory results. The MESSAGE_SIZE constant also determines the length of string parameters logged to the file. Some string parameters can become quite long, so to avoid an oversized log entry, string parameters longer than MESSAGE_SIZE are trimmed.

Syntax

```
LogManager ErrorCode, Message [, Params]
```

Part	Description
ErrorCode	Required. Positive numbers that print the error code and message. When zero, only Message is printed. When it is -1 the beginning of the procedure is processed, and when it is -2 the procedure end is processed.
Message	Required. The error description or message.
Params	Optional. One or more procedure parameters to be included in the log.

Code Listing

```
Sub LogManager(ErrCode%, Msg$, ParamArray Prm())
Const INDENT_SPACING = 8
Const MESSAGE_SIZE = 25
Const TimeFormat = "mm/dd/yy hh:nn:ss"
Static Indents%, Calls$, LogStarted%
Dim FileChannel%, CallIndex%
Dim LogFile$, Info$, FixedCall As String * MESSAGE_SIZE

    FileChannel = FreeFile

    'Intialization code starts here
        'GetFilename
        LogFile = App.Path
        If Right$(LogFile, 1) <> "\" Then LogFile = LogFile & "\"
        LogFile = LogFile & App.EXEName & ".LOG"
        'Test for file
        If Len(Dir(LogFile)) = 0 Then
            Info = "[" & Format$(Now, TimeFormat) & "] " & App.Title &
            ➥ " - VERSION:"
```

```
        Info = Info & Str$(App.Major) & Str$(App.Minor) &
        ➡ Str$(App.Revision)
        Open LogFile For Output As FileChannel
        Print #FileChannel, Info
        Close FileChannel
        Info = ""
        LogStarted = True
    ElseIf LogStarted = False Then
        Info = vbCrLf & "[" & Format$(Now, TimeFormat) & "]
        ➡NEW SESSION" & vbCrLf
        LogStarted = True
    End If
'End initialization code

FixedCall = Msg
CallIndex = InStr(Calls, Msg)

'Build Output
Info = Info & "[" & Format$(Now, TimeFormat) & "] " &
➡ Space$(Indents * INDENT_SPACING)
If ErrCode   0 Then
    Info = Info & "ERROR: " & CStr(ErrCode) & ", " & Msg
ElseIf ErrCode = -1 Then
    Calls = Calls & FixedCall
    Indents = Indents + 1
    Info = Info & Space(INDENT_SPACING) & "START: " & Msg
    'For Param array
    If UBound(Prm)   -1 Then
        Info = Info & "("
        For CallIndex = 0 To UBound(Prm)
        If TypeName(Prm(CallIndex)) = "String" Then
            Info = Info & " """
            'Limiting string parameter size
            If Len(CStr(Prm(CallIndex)))   MESSAGE_SIZE Then
                Info = Info & Left(CStr(Prm(CallIndex)),
                ➡ MESSAGE_SIZE - 3) & "..."
            Else
                Info = Info & CStr(Prm(CallIndex))
            End If
            Info = Info & """"
        ElseIf IsNumeric(Prm(CallIndex)) Then
            Info = Info & Str(Prm(CallIndex))
        Else
            Info = Info & " [Type Unknown]"
        End If
        If CallIndex <> UBound(Prm) Then Info = Info & ","
        Next CallIndex
        Info = Info & " )"
    End If
    'End of Parameter array code
ElseIf ErrCode = -2 Then
    If (CallIndex \ MESSAGE_SIZE) = (Indents - 1) Then
```

```
                Info = Info & "__END: " & Msg
            If Indents Then
                Indents = Indents - 1
                Calls = Left$(Calls, Indents * MESSAGE_SIZE)
            End If
        Else
            If CallIndex Then
                Indents = (CallIndex \ MESSAGE_SIZE) + 1
                Info = Trim(Info) & " " & Space(Indents * INDENT_SPACING) &
            ➥ "LOGICAL ERROR: Handler/Exit calls missing" & vbCrLf
                Info = Info & "[" & Format$(Now, TimeFormat) & "] " &
            ➥ Space$(Indents * INDENT_SPACING)
                Info = Info & "__END: " & Msg
                Indents = Indents - 1
                Calls = Left(Calls, Indents * MESSAGE_SIZE)
            Else
                Info = Info & "LOGICAL ERROR: Unknown exit message"
            End If
        End If
    Else
        Info = Info & Msg
    End If
    'Limiting static string size when end calls are not used
    If (INDENT_SPACING = 0) And (Len(Calls)  16000) Then Calls = ""
    'Print
    Open LogFile For Append As FileChannel
    Print #FileChannel, Info
    Close FileChannel
End Sub
```

Analysis

At the beginning of this routine is a section of code that is needed but not necessarily required each time the Log Manager is invoked. Finding the filename and testing to see whether it must be created should be done in the initialization code with the filename stored in a variable for the Log Manager to use. It was included here to provide working code. To move the initialization code to your own initialization procedure, move the LogFile string variable to the module level, delete the indented initialization code in the LogManager procedure, and add this code to your initialization sequence:

```
Public Sub InitLogManager()
Const TimeFormat = "mm/dd/yy hh:nn:ss"
Dim Info$
Dim FileChannel%

    FileChannel = FreeFile
    'GetFilename
    LogFile = App.Path
    If Right$(LogFile, 1) <> "\" Then LogFile = LogFile & "\"
    LogFile = LogFile & App.EXEName & ".LOG"
    'Test for file
```

```
    If Len(Dir(LogFile)) = 0 Then
        Info = "[" & Format$(Now, TimeFormat) & "] " & App.Title & " -
        ➥VERSION:"
        Info = Info & Str$(App.Major) & Str$(App.Minor) &
        ➥Str$(App.Revision)
        Open LogFile For Output As FileChannel
    Else
        Info = vbCrLf & "[" & Format$(Now, TimeFormat) & "] NEW SESSION"
        Open LogFile For Append As FileChannel
    End If
    Print #FileChannel, Info
    Close FileChannel
End Sub
```

After the filename is created and its existence determined, the work of the `LogManager` begins by fixing the size of the message parameter and locating that text in the `Calls` string. The `Calls` string is a variable-length static string that holds the message part of all the start calls. By assigning the message to a fixed-length string before adding it to `Calls`, all the messages in `Calls` will be equally spaced from each other. The position of the message in `Calls` is used to determine how many indents there should be, which is compared to how many indents there are. In an end call, these should match or something is wrong. Memory used by `Calls` will grow quickly if the constant `MESSAGE_SIZE` is set too large. It should be set to the least amount of characters needed to uniquely identify each of your procedure names. `Calls` is limited to 16000 bytes to avoid Out of Memory problems when end calls are not used.

`Info` is used as the output string. In building this string, the first element added is the current date and time to verify when the error was logged. Also, in all cases the amount of spacing needed for indents is added before processing the `ErrCode` parameter. When processing start calls, the fixed-length message is saved in `Calls`, then additional indents and the word `START:` are added to `Info`. If the call has parameters they must also be added to the `Info` string.

The `ParamArray` elements are variants that can contain just about anything. For this reason the `LogManager` must determine the type of each element so that it can be properly included in the output string. Only strings and numerical parameters were provided for. If you must include other types you may use the `TypeName` function to help you determine what type of parameter was passed. Extra long strings are reduced to the `MESSAGE_SIZE` number of characters to maintain the log in an easy-to-read format. In this section, the `CallIndex` variable is reused in favor of dimensioning another variable. It normally holds the position in which the procedure name was found in the `Calls` string. In this parameter section it is used to hold the value of the loop in looping through the parameter array.

In the ending section, the position of the procedure name message and the number of calls processed should be proportional. When they are, the procedure ends properly and the most recent procedure name should be removed from `Calls`. When there is a mismatch, two things might have happened: the procedure name was not the last name stored in `Calls` or the procedure name was not found in `Calls`. Both of these conditions are handled and recorded in `Info` for later printing. After the output string is complete, it is printed to the log file.

VB3 users can modify this routine to run in VB3. VB3 does not have parameter arrays, so all the code associated with them should be removed. Remove the optional `ParamArray` parameter, as well as the section of code following the remark `For Param array`, down to and including the `End of parameter array code`. Also the intrinsic (later version) VB constant `vbCrLf` must be declared as a string variable made up of the characters `Chr(13) & Chr(10)`. Finally, the program file's last modified date can be substituted for version information, which is also not available in VB3. Use the `FileDateTime` function to get the file's creation or last modified date.

4.13 CHECKING INPUT

by Then Nam Kheong

Description

Developers spend a good amount of time checking a user's input. One type of checking is to see whether the user has typed the correct data type. For example, if the input requires the user to type numeric input but he types something else, this is not good, especially for database entry.

The routine checks whether the input is the needed data type, in this case numeric. The routine also adds the interaction between two input boxes. This will be useful when it comes to database data entry.

Syntax

None.

Code Listing

```
'*********************************************
'* Submitted by Then Nam Kheong
'*********************************************

(In declaration)
Public Sub FocusMe(ctlName As Control)
    With ctlName
        .SelStart = 0
        .SelLength = Len(ctlName)
    End With
End Sub

(In Form1)
Private Sub Command1_Click()
 End
End Sub
```

```
Private Sub Text1_GotFocus()
 FocusMe Text1
End Sub

Private Sub Text1_LostFocus()
   If Text1.Text <> "" Then
    If Not IsNumeric(Text1.Text) Then
     MsgBox "Not a numeric number!" + Chr(10) + "Remember, no alphabets!"
     Text1.SetFocus
    End If
   End If
End Sub

Private Sub Text2_GotFocus()
   FocusMe Text2
End Sub

Private Sub Text2_Lostfocus()
   If Text2.Text <> "" Then
    If Not IsNumeric(Text2.Text)Then
     MsgBox "Not a numeric number!" + Chr(10) + "Remember, no alphabets!"
     Text2.SetFocus
    End If
 End If
End Sub
```

Analysis

This routine uses `GotFocus` and `LostFocus` events. The `LostFocus` event of the `Text1` control checks for two occurrences:

■ Is the input text empty? If the input is empty, then none of the code will be executed. The text box control will lose the focus and the focus will move on to the next.

■ Is the input numeric? If the input is not empty, then it checks to see whether the input is in numeric format. If it is not in numeric format, it will display a message box and the program will refocus on the same text box by using the `SetFocus` method. When this text box gets the focus, the `GotFocus` event is triggered and highlights the last text input.

```
Private Sub Text1_LostFocus()
   If Text1.Text <> "" Then
    If Not IsNumeric(Text1.Text) Then
     MsgBox "Not a numeric number!" + Chr(10) + "Remember,
    ➡no alphabets!"
     Text1.SetFocus
    End If
   End If
End Sub

Private Sub Text1_GotFocus()
   FocusMe Text2
End Sub
```

4.14   DATE ENTRY

by Then Nam Kheong

Description

Many times you must create an input box for users to type a date. But you might design in a way that the user must type both the numeric figures and the forward slash (/), which indicates the day, month, and year divider. This is not a very good method of date input because the / key is quite a distance away from the numeric keys.

This routine eases that problem. The user will need to type only the day, month, and year without using the forward slash key. Basically, you will create three text box arrays and add some code to them. The user will see the cursor jumping from one box to another. This looks very professional and is great for data-entry purposes.

Syntax

None.

Code Listing

```
'*********************************************
'* Submitted by Then Nam Kheong
'*********************************************

In declaration form)
Public Sub FocusMe(ctlName As Control)
    With ctlName
        .SelStart = 0
        .SelLength = Len(ctlName)
    End With
End Sub

In Form1)
Private Sub txtDate_Change(Index As Integer)
Dim strDate As Date       'Defines a date variable

'Check if the input is numeric or alphabetic
   If Not IsNumeric(txtDate(Index).Text) And txtDate(Index).Text <>
   ➡"" Then
     MsgBox "Not a numeric input! Please try again."
     FocusMe txtDate(Index)
     Exit Sub
   End If
```

```
'Check if the length of txtDate is longer than the specified length
 If Len(txtDate(Index).Text) = txtDate(Index).MaxLength Then
    If Index + 1 <> 3 Then        'Check if Index is 3, if it is 3 then
    ➥it is not the year field
     txtDate(Index + 1).SetFocus    'Sets the next txtDate to be focused
    End If
 End If
'If Index is 2 and that this txtDate is been filled up, the
➥program will change
'the format to date format.
 If Index = 2 And Len(txtDate(Index).Text) =
 ➥txtDate(Index).MaxLength Then
  strDate = DateSerial(txtDate(2).Text, txtDate(1).Text, txtDate(0).Text)
  Label3.Caption = "The date entered is: " + Str(strDate)
 End If
End Sub


Private Sub txtDate_GotFocus(Index As Integer)
   FocusMe txtDate(Index)
End Sub
```

Analysis

Before you begin you must insert three text box arrays. To create them, first click the text box control and insert it into the form. Then copy this control and paste again. It will prompt if you want to create a control array. Click Yes and you will have another text box. (Note that the array starts from 0 and not from 1.) Align them, insert two labels, and change their caption to /. Add another label and change the caption to dd/mm/yyyy. This label prompts the user to enter the entry beginning with the day, followed by the month and year. Finally, set the MaxLength property for the day and month to 2 and set the year MaxLength property to 4.

A routine called FocusMe highlights any text in the text box.

```
Public Sub FocusMe(ctlName As Control)
    With ctlName
        .SelStart = 0
        .SelLength = Len(ctlName)
    End With
End Sub
```

Most of the work is in the txtDate_Change() event. If there are any changes in the text box, they will trigger this event. You will use this event to create your date entry.

The following line checks whether the text typed into the text box is equal to the maximum length allowed in this text box. If the allowed length of the box is reached, the cursor will jump to the next text box array by increasing the index number. Here use the SetFocus method to change the focus of the box:

```
If Len(txtDate(Index).Text) = txtDate(Index).MaxLength Then
 If Index + 1 <> 3 Then       'Check if Index is 3, if it is 3 then it is
 ➥ not the year field
```

```
    txtDate(Index + 1).SetFocus    'Sets the next txtDate to be focused
  End If
End If
```

The FocusMe routine comes into play when the user types the wrong day in the date but the cursor has jumped to the month text box. The user can use the mouse or Shift+Tab to move back to the last text box. When the user does that, this text box will receive the focus and the text will be automatically highlighted. This is where you use the GotFocus event. In this event, you add one line to highlight the entire selection of text. To see the difference, delete the following line:

```
Private Sub txtDate_GotFocus(Index As Integer)
FocusMe txtDate(Index)
End Sub
```

Finally, you must change the input to data that is useful to you. Use the DateSerial() function to return a date data type.

```
strDate = DateSerial(txtDate(2).Text, txtDate(1).Text, txtDate(0).Text)
```

This date entry routine is just one of the methods introduced to make it look professional. I personally used it for my own database programming and it looks really good.

Chapter 5

DATABASE FUNCTIONS

Visual Basic has had a long history of being a great way to access databases. This chapter shows you some more tricks to add to your database connectivity collection. Many different methods are shown here to give a broad feel for the options and methods that you can use to get at your data. This chapter includes an entire wrapper class for the ODBC API, examples of DAO, RDO, and ADO as well as several supporting functions to help you work with databases.

5.1   RDO APEX GRID

by Andy Carrasco

Description

The RDO Abstraction Class can be very useful to ease access to an ODBC data source, such as Microsoft SQL Server. Although Microsoft's Remote Data Objects are simple to use, it can be cumbersome for developers who have used the DAO/Jet database engines to familiarize themselves with the new standard. It might also take longer than expected to write code in an application to utilize the Remote Data Objects.

The RDO Abstraction Class attempts to ease these situations by providing a ready-to-use class that handles all the RDO objects internally. RDO, a multiple object architecture, requires you to create and destroy multiple objects representing anything from the actual database server to individual resultsets. The RDO Abstraction Class can be used as a single database object within your Visual Basic project because it creates and destroys all the required RDO objects internally. You must simply create a single RDO Abstraction Class object within your project, then using the simple methods and properties defined on it, you can quickly write an application that accesses an RDO/ODBC data source.

This class also contains some useful functions that would normally require you to write extra code in order to implement them in your own projects, but which were standard in the DAO/Jet database access packages.

The Find method enables you to search the resultset for a specific record matching the search criteria. In addition to providing the standard search capabilities on a key column, you can also specify multiple column searches, in which all specified columns must match the defined values.

The RDO Abstraction Class also contains properties that let you determine which columns in a resultset have been defined as unique indexes or primary keys. This is particularly useful when the RDO Abstraction Class is used in applications that import large amounts of data into the remote server, and manual data integrity checks must be performed.

This class also contains complete error handling for each method and provides a trappable error condition whenever an error occurs. The class retrieves a rather descriptive error string from the database server and provides the information via the Visual Basic Err object.

Any table or resultset generated with this class must be defined with at least one unique index to ensure that certain operations performed on the resultset, such as in the Find method, will be executed correctly. This should never be a problem because the rules of good database design dictate that all tables should have at least one unique index or primary key.

Syntax

```
Dim objDatabase As New RDODatabase
```

Part	Description
objDatabase	Required. The name of a variable that will contain the newly created instance of the RDO Abstraction Class.
RDODatabase	Required. The name of the RDO Abstraction Class after it has been placed in the project.

You can add this class to your project using the Project, Add Class Module menu item in VB5. Select the Existing tab in the resulting dialog, and browse for the file RDODatabase.cls on the included CD.

The following code examples use the RDODatabase class to connect to a remote database server, read from and write to a table on that server, then disconnect from the server:

```
Sub ReadFromAuthors()
'ReadFromAuthors will connect to a remote database server and
'send the results of a query to the Immediate window.

    'First, connect to the remote database server
    RDODatabase.Connect "ODBCDSN", "DatabaseName", "UserName", "Password"

    'Execute a simple select query
    RDODatabase.Execute "SELECT * FROM Authors"
```

```
    'Loop through each record returned until the end of
    'the recordset has been reached. Note: If you would
    'like to know how many records were returned, check the
    'RowCount property after an Execute statement.
    Do Until RDODatabase.EOF
        'Print the value in the column AuthorName for the
        'current record to the Immediate window.
        Debug.Print RDODatabase("AuthorName")
        'The MoveNext method must be used to retrieve a new
        'record. If you leave this out, this loop will become
        'infinite.
        RDODatabase.MoveNext
    Loop

    'Close the connection to the remote database server
    RDODatabase.Disconnect

    'Its a good idea to destroy your objects when you are
    'done with them.
    Set RDODatabase = Nothing

End Sub

Sub WriteToAuthors()
'WriteToAuthors will open a connection on the remote database server,
'then add a new Author to the Authors table.

    'Connect to the remote database server
    RDODatabase.Connect "ODBCDSN", "DatabaseName", "UserName", "Password"

    'Open the Authors table
    RDODatabase.OpenTable "Authors"

    'Add a new record
    RDODatabase.AddNew

    'Modify the new record
    RDODatabase("AuthorName") = "Guy, Mystery"
    RDODatabase("Address") = "1515 N. Sherlock Circle"

    'Save this record
    RDODatabase.Update

    'Close the connection
    RDODatabase.Disconnect

    'Again, we manually destroy the object
    Set RDODatabase = Nothing

End Sub
```

You can find the complete syntax and description for each of the class methods and properties in the "Analysis" section immediately following the code listing.

Code Listing

```
Option Explicit

DEFAULT_LOGINTIMEOUT

Sets the number of seconds to wait for the server to respond to a login
request before generating a timeout error.
Const DEFAULT_LOGINTIMEOUT = 30

DEFAULT_QUERYTIMEOUT

Sets the number of seconds to wait for the server to respond to a query
request before generating a timeout error.
Const DEFAULT_QUERYTIMEOUT = 60

QSQL

This object only generates a single query object per instance. RDO
supports multiple query objects indexed by name. This option merely
defines the name to use for our single query object. You should never
need to change it.
Const QSQL = "PREPAREDQUERY"

SQL_OPENTABLE

This is the query to use to open a table with the OpenTable method. You
should never need to change this, but if you do, remember that the
StrReplace identifyer (%1) will contain the name of the table to open.
Const SQL_OPENTABLE = "SELECT * FROM %1"

ERROR_SOURCE

On locally generated OLE errors, this option specifies the
string to use for the Err.Source property of the Err object.
Again, only change if you change the name of the library.
Const ERROR_SOURCE = "RDODatabase"

ERRMSG_NOPRIMARYKEY

The descriptive error message that is generated when the developer attempts
to use the OpenTable method on a table which has no unique index defined.
Const ERRMSG_NOPRIMARYKEY = "The table %1 has no primary key or unique index
➥ defined. Please define a primary key before using it with
➥ the OpenTable method."

- - - - - - - - - - - - - - - - - - - - - - - - - - - - - - - - - - - - - - - - -
YOU SHOULDN'T NEED TO CHANGE ANYTHING BELOW THIS LINE...
- - - - - - - - - - - - - - - - - - - - - - - - - - - - - - - - - - - - - - - - -
```

Values which represent the return code passed back from the Connect method.
This is a public enumeration and is contained in the type library.

```
Public Enum CONNECT_ERRORS
        Connection was established.
    CONNECT_SUCCESS
        Unable to establish connection
    CONNECT_FAIL
        User cancelled an ODBC dialog (obsolete)
    CONNECT_CANCEL
        An unknown error occured
    CONNECT_UNKNOWN
End Enum
```

Values which represent the type of dataset to open.
This is a public enumeration and is contained in the type library.

```
Public Enum DATASETTYPES
        For simple roll through algorithms, the Forward-Only
        dataset will only accept the MoveNext method for
        cursor movement. Forward-Only datasets are Read-Only.
FORWARD_ONLY
        The Dynamic dataset can accept all cursor processing
        methods such as MoveNext and MovePrevious. Dynamic
        datasets are Read/Write. Dynamic datasets can be
        slower than Forward-Only datasets.
    DYNAMIC
End Enum


Private lErrorNumber As Long
Private sErrorMessage As String
Private DataErr As rdoError

Private mvarUsername As String
Private mvarPassword As String
Private mvarServerName As String
Private mvarDatabaseName As String
Private mvarLoginTimeout As Integer
Private mvarQueryTimeout As Integer
Private mvarColumns As New Collection

Private ConLiveFlag As Boolean
Private boolResultsAvailable As Boolean
Private MyConnectionNumber As Long

Private mvarQueryObject As rdoQuery
Private mvarRDOResults As rdoResultset
Private mvarRDOConnection As New rdoConnection

Private DTCache As Long

Private QBuffer As Variant
Dim IndexFieldNames As New Collection
```

```
Public Property Let UserName(vData As String)
    mvarUsername = vData
End Property

Public Property Get UserName() As String
    UserName = mvarUsername
End Property

Public Property Let Password(vData As String)
    mvarPassword = vData
End Property

Public Property Get Password() As String
    Password = mvarPassword
End Property

Public Property Let DSN(vData As String)
    mvarServerName = vData
End Property

Public Property Get DSN() As String
    DSN = mvarServerName
End Property

Public Property Let Databasename(vData As String)
    mvarDatabaseName = vData
End Property

Public Property Get Databasename() As String
    Databasename = mvarDatabaseName
End Property

Public Property Let LoginTimeout(vData As Integer)
    mvarLoginTimeout = vData
End Property

Public Property Get LoginTimeout() As Integer
    LoginTimeout = mvarLoginTimeout
End Property

Public Property Let QueryTimeout(vData As Integer)
    mvarQueryTimeout = vData
End Property

Public Property Get QueryTimeout() As Integer
    QueryTimeout = mvarQueryTimeout
End Property

Public Function Connect(Optional strDSN As String, Optional strDatabaseName
➥ As String, Optional strUserName As String,
➥ Optional strPassword As Variant) As Long
Call connect to attach to an RDO/ODBC datasource and be happy.
```

```
    If ConLiveFlag Then Exit Function

    On Error GoTo Connect_Error

    If strDSN <> "" Then mvarServerName = strDSN
    If strDatabaseName <> "" Then mvarDatabaseName = strDatabaseName
    If strUserName <> "" Then mvarUsername = strUserName
    If Not IsMissing(strPassword) Then mvarPassword = strPassword
    If mvarQueryTimeout = 0 Then mvarQueryTimeout = DEFAULT_QUERYTIMEOUT
    If mvarLoginTimeout = 0 Then mvarLoginTimeout = DEFAULT_LOGINTIMEOUT

    If ConLiveFlag Then Call Disconnect

    With mvarRDOConnection
        .Connect = ODBCConnectionString
        .LoginTimeout = mvarLoginTimeout
        .CursorDriver = rdUseOdbc
        On Error Resume Next
        .QueryTimeout = mvarQueryTimeout
        On Error GoTo Connect_Error
        .EstablishConnection rdDriverNoPrompt
    End With

    DoEvents

    ConLiveFlag = True
    Connect = 0
Exit Function
Connect_Error:

    Call HandleError

End Function

Public Sub Disconnect()

On Error GoTo Disconnect_Error

    If ConLiveFlag Then
        Dim X As Integer
        Set mvarQueryObject = Nothing
        For X = 1 To mvarRDOConnection.rdoQueries.Count
            mvarRDOConnection.rdoQueries(X - 1).Close
        Next X
        mvarRDOConnection.Close

    End If

    ConLiveFlag = False
Exit Sub
Disconnect_Error:
```

```
        Call HandleError

End Sub

Private Function ODBCConnectionString() As String

ODBCConnectionString = "DSN=" + mvarServerName + "; UID=" + mvarUsername + ";
➡ PWD=" + mvarPassword + "; DATABASE=" + mvarDatabaseName + ";"

End Function

Private Sub Class_Terminate()
    On Error Resume Next
    If ConLiveFlag Then mvarRDOConnection.Close
    Set mvarQueryObject = Nothing
    Set mvarRDOResults = Nothing
    Set mvarRDOConnection = Nothing
End Sub

Public Sub Execute(sSQL As String, Optional DatasetType As Variant,
➡ Optional Mute As Boolean)
If the Mute param is True, then no dataset is returned from the server,
➡ as in an INSERT query or
DROP query.
On Error GoTo Execute_Error

    If mvarRDOConnection.rdoQueries.Count Then mvarQueryObject.Close
    Set mvarQueryObject = mvarRDOConnection.CreateQuery(QSQL, sSQL)
    If IsMissing(DatasetType) Then DatasetType = DATASETTYPES.DYNAMIC

    If we are mute, execute without results
    If Mute Then
        mvarQueryObject.Execute
    Else
        If DatasetType = DATASETTYPES.FORWARD_ONLY Then
            Set mvarRDOResults = mvarQueryObject.OpenResultset
                    ➡(rdOpenForwardOnly, rdConcurReadOnly)
        ElseIf DatasetType = DATASETTYPES.DYNAMIC Then
            Set mvarRDOResults = mvarQueryObject.OpenResultset
                    ➡(rdOpenKeyset, rdConcurRowVer)
        End If
        DoEvents
        boolResultsAvailable = True
    End If

Exit Sub

Execute_Error:

    Call HandleError

End Sub
```

```
Public Property Get Columns(sKey As String) As Variant
Returns the data from a column. sKey is the column name, or number.
Although a select case statement here is more eloquent, the current
ugly if-elseif constructs are much faster.

On Error GoTo Columns_Get_Error

    QBuffer = mvarRDOResults(sKey)
    DTCache = VarType(QBuffer)

    If DTCache = vbString Then
        Columns = CStr(QBuffer)
    ElseIf DTCache = vbInteger Then
        Columns = CInt(QBuffer)
    ElseIf DTCache = vbLong Then
        Columns = CLng(QBuffer)
    ElseIf DTCache = vbSingle Then
        Columns = CSng(QBuffer)
    ElseIf DTCache = vbDouble Then
        Columns = CDbl(QBuffer)
    ElseIf DTCache = vbDate Then
        Columns = CDate(QBuffer)
    ElseIf DTCache = vbBoolean Then
        Columns = CBool(QBuffer)
    ElseIf DTCache = vbByte Then
        Columns = CByte(QBuffer)
    ElseIf DTCache = vbNull Then
        Columns = ""
    Else
        We don't know what this is so we will just return a string instead!
        Columns = CStr(QBuffer)
    End If

Exit Property

Columns_Get_Error:

    Call HandleError

End Property

Public Property Let Columns(sKey As String, vData As Variant)
Sets the data in a column. vData is variant to promote the use of strict
datatypes when writing data to the database.
Although a select case statement here is more eloquent, the current
ugly if-elseif constructs are much faster.

On Error GoTo Columns_Let_Error

    DTCache = VarType(vData)

    If DTCache = vbString Then
        mvarRDOResults(sKey) = CStr(vData)
```

```
        ElseIf DTCache = vbInteger Then
            mvarRDOResults(sKey) = CInt(vData)
        ElseIf DTCache = vbLong Then
            mvarRDOResults(sKey) = CLng(vData)
        ElseIf DTCache = vbSingle Then
            mvarRDOResults(sKey) = CSng(vData)
        ElseIf DTCache = vbDouble Then
            mvarRDOResults(sKey) = CDbl(vData)
        ElseIf DTCache = vbDate Then
            mvarRDOResults(sKey) = CDate(vData)
        ElseIf DTCache = vbBoolean Then
            mvarRDOResults(sKey) = CBool(vData)
        ElseIf DTCache = vbByte Then
            mvarRDOResults(sKey) = CByte(vData)
        Else
            Err.Raise 13
        End If

Exit Property

Columns_Let_Error:

    Call HandleError

End Property

Public Sub MoveFirst()
On Error GoTo MoveFirst_Error
    mvarRDOResults.MoveFirst
Exit Sub
MoveFirst_Error:
    Call HandleError
End Sub

Public Sub MoveLast()
On Error GoTo MoveLast_Error
    mvarRDOResults.MoveLast
Exit Sub
MoveLast_Error:
    Call HandleError
End Sub

Public Sub MoveNext()
On Error GoTo MoveNext_Error
    mvarRDOResults.MoveNext
Exit Sub
MoveNext_Error:
    Call HandleError
End Sub

Public Sub MoveBack()
```

```
On Error GoTo MoveBack_Error
    mvarRDOResults.MovePrevious
Exit Sub
MoveBack_Error:
    Call HandleError
End Sub

Public Property Get EOF() As Boolean
Returns true is the row pointer is after the last row in the recordset.
    EOF = mvarRDOResults.EOF
End Property

Public Property Get BOF() As Boolean
Returns true if the row pointer is before the first row of the recordset.
    BOF = mvarRDOResults.BOF
End Property

Public Sub Edit()
On Error GoTo Edit_Error
    mvarRDOResults.Edit
Exit Sub
Edit_Error:
    Call HandleError
End Sub

Public Sub Update()
On Error GoTo Update_Error
    mvarRDOResults.Update
Exit Sub
Update_Error:
    Call HandleError
End Sub

Public Sub CancelUpdate()
On Error GoTo CancelUpdate_Error
    mvarRDOResults.CancelUpdate
Exit Sub
CancelUpdate_Error:
    Call HandleError
End Sub

Public Sub Delete()
On Error GoTo Delete_Error
    mvarRDOResults.Delete
Exit Sub
Delete_Error:
    Call HandleError
End Sub

Public Sub AddNew()
On Error GoTo AddNew_Error
    mvarRDOResults.AddNew
```

```
Exit Sub
AddNew_Error:
    Call HandleError
End Sub

Public Property Get RowCount()
    RowCount = mvarRDOResults.RowCount
End Property

Public Property Get RowsAffected() As Long
    RowsAffected = mvarRDOConnection.RowsAffected
End Property

Public Function Find(ParamArray sSearchString() As Variant) As Integer

On Error GoTo Find_Error

    If Not mvarRDOResults.Bookmarkable Then
        Find = 0
        Exit Function
    ElseIf (UBound(sSearchString) + 1) Mod 2 Then
        Err.Raise 64001, "DBDatabaseAbstractionLayer:Find",
                    ➡ "Incorrect number of arguments"
        Exit Function
    End If

    Dim CurRow As Variant
    Dim SeekRow As Variant
    Dim Conditions() As String
    Dim Found As Boolean

 Step 1: Parse out the field names and values from the paramarray

    Dim X As Integer
    Dim Y As Integer
    ReDim Conditions((UBound(sSearchString) - 1) / 2, 1)
    Do Until X > UBound(sSearchString)
        Conditions(Y, 0) = sSearchString(X)
        Conditions(Y, 1) = sSearchString(X + 1)
        X = X + 2
        Y = Y + 1
    Loop


    CurRow = mvarRDOResults.Bookmark

    mvarRDOResults.MoveFirst

    Do While Not mvarRDOResults.EOF

        For X = 0 To UBound(Conditions, 1)
            If mvarRDOResults(Conditions(X, 0)) = Conditions(X, 1) Then
```

```
                    Found = True
            Else
                    Found = False
                    Exit For
            End If
        Next X

        If Found Then
            SeekRow = mvarRDOResults.Bookmark
            Found = True
            Exit Do
        Else
            Found = False
        End If
        mvarRDOResults.MoveNext
    Loop

    If Found Then
        mvarRDOResults.Bookmark = SeekRow
        Find = True
    Else
        If mvarRDOResults.RowCount <> 0 Then mvarRDOResults.Bookmark = CurRow
        Find = False
    End If

Exit Function

Find_Error:

    If Err.Number = 40022 Then              Result set is empty
        Find = 0
    Else
        Call HandleError
    End If

End Function

Public Function OpenTable(sTablename As String) As Boolean
On Error GoTo OpenTable_Error

    Get the unique indexes, which will help to decide whether or not to Edit
    an existing record or add a new one.
    Dim Column As rdoColumn
    Dim IndexResults As rdoResultset
    If mvarRDOConnection.rdoQueries.Count Then mvarQueryObject.Close
    Set mvarQueryObject = mvarRDOConnection.CreateQuery(QSQL,
    ➥ "{call sp_helpindex(" + sTablename + ")}")
    mvarQueryObject.Prepared = False
    Set IndexResults = mvarQueryObject.OpenResultset()

    Dim TempFieldNames As Variant
    Dim X As Integer
```

```
    Set IndexFieldNames = Nothing

    On Error GoTo OpenTable_NoKey_Error
    Do Until IndexResults.EOF
        If InStr(IndexResults("index_description"), "unique") Then
            TempFieldNames = Tokenize(IndexResults("index_keys"), ",")
            For X = 0 To UBound(TempFieldNames)
                IndexFieldNames.Add TempFieldNames(X), TempFieldNames(X)
            Next X
        End If
    IndexResults.MoveNext
    Loop

    On Error GoTo OpenTable_Error

    IndexResults.Close
    Set IndexResults = Nothing


    Ok, now we must open the actual table
    Dim sSQL As String
    sSQL = StrReplace(SQL_OPENTABLE, sTablename)

    mvarQueryObject.Close
    Set mvarQueryObject = mvarRDOConnection.CreateQuery(QSQL, sSQL)
    mvarQueryObject.Execute
    Set mvarRDOResults = mvarQueryObject.OpenResultset(rdOpenKeyset,
                    ➥ rdConcurValues)

    On Error Resume Next
    If mvarRDOResults.RowCount = 0 Then mvarRDOResults.MoveLast


Exit Function
OpenTable_Error:

    Call HandleError

Exit Function
OpenTable_NoKey_Error:

    Err.Number = 40000
    Err.Description = StrReplace(ERRMSG_NOPRIMARYKEY, sTablename)
    Call HandleError

Exit Function
End Function

Public Property Get ErrorNumber() As Long
    ErrorNumber = lErrorNumber
End Property
```

```
Public Property Get ErrorMessage() As String
    ErrorMessage = sErrorMessage
End Property

Private Sub GenDatabaseError()


Dim MSG As String
MSG = Err.Description + "¦"

For Each DataErr In rdoErrors
    MSG = MSG + "[" & DataErr.Number & "]" & DataErr.Description
Next DataErr

lErrorNumber = Err.Number
sErrorMessage = MSG

Err.Raise lErrorNumber, ERROR_SOURCE, sErrorMessage

End Sub

Private Sub HandleError()

    Dim lErrNum As Long
    Dim sErrMsg As String

    lErrNum = Err.Number
    sErrMsg = Err.Description

    If lErrNum = 40002 Then
        Call GenDatabaseError
    Else
        Err.Raise lErrNum, ERROR_SOURCE, sErrMsg
    End If

End Sub

Public Sub BeginTrans()
On Error GoTo BeginTrans_Error
    mvarRDOConnection.BeginTrans
Exit Sub
BeginTrans_Error:
    Call HandleError
End Sub

Public Sub CommitTrans()
On Error GoTo CommitTrans_Error
    mvarRDOConnection.CommitTrans
Exit Sub
CommitTrans_Error:
    Call HandleError
End Sub
```

```
Public Sub RollbackTrans()
On Error GoTo RollbackTrans_Error
    mvarRDOConnection.RollbackTrans
Exit Sub
RollbackTrans_Error:
    Call HandleError
End Sub

Public Property Get Bookmark() As Variant
    Bookmark = mvarRDOResults.Bookmark
End Property

Public Property Let Bookmark(vData As Variant)
On Error GoTo Bookmark_Let_Error
    mvarRDOResults.Bookmark = vData
Exit Property
Bookmark_Let_Error:
    Call HandleError
End Property

Public Property Get Bookmarkable() As Boolean
    Bookmarkable = mvarRDOResults.Bookmarkable
End Property

Public Sub Requery()
On Error GoTo Requery_Error
    mvarRDOResults.Requery
Exit Sub
Requery_Error:
    Call HandleError
End Sub

Public Property Get UniqueColumns() As Collection
    Set UniqueColumns = IndexFieldNames
End Property

Public Function FindB(Parameters As Variant) As Boolean

On Error GoTo FindB_Error

    If Not mvarRDOResults.Bookmarkable Then
        FindB = 0
        Exit Function
    ElseIf (UBound(Parameters) + 1) Mod 2 Then
        Err.Raise 64001, "DBDatabaseAbstractionLayer:FindB",
                     ➥ "Incorrect number of arguments"
        Exit Function
    End If

    Dim CurRow As Variant
    Dim SeekRow As Variant
```

```
    Dim Conditions() As String
    Dim Found As Boolean

Step 1: Parse out the field names and values from the paramarray

    Dim X As Integer
    Dim Y As Integer
    ReDim Conditions((UBound(Parameters) - 1) / 2, 1)
    Do Until X > UBound(Parameters)
        Conditions(Y, 0) = Parameters(X)
        Conditions(Y, 1) = Parameters(X + 1)
        X = X + 2
        Y = Y + 1
    Loop

    CurRow = mvarRDOResults.Bookmark

    mvarRDOResults.MoveFirst

    Do While Not mvarRDOResults.EOF

        For X = 0 To UBound(Conditions, 1)
            If mvarRDOResults(Conditions(X, 0)) = Conditions(X, 1) Then
                Found = True
            Else
                Found = False
                Exit For
            End If
        Next X

        If Found Then
            SeekRow = mvarRDOResults.Bookmark
            Found = True
            Exit Do
        Else
            Found = False
        End If
        mvarRDOResults.MoveNext
    Loop

    If Found Then
        mvarRDOResults.Bookmark = SeekRow
        FindB = True
    Else
        If mvarRDOResults.RowCount <> 0 Then mvarRDOResults.Bookmark = CurRow
        FindB = False
    End If

Exit Function
FindB_Error:
```

```
    If Err.Number = 40022 Then          Result set is empty
        FindB = 0
    Else
        Call HandleError
    End If

End Function
```

Analysis

The following explains the properties and methods in the code.

Properties

UniqueColumns: A collection of strings that contain the name of each unique column in the current record-set. Use this property to determine which columns in the recordset have been defined as unique and are related to the primary key. It is populated only if the recordset has been opened with the `OpenTable` method because a recordset opened with a SQL statement using the `Execute` method could be related to multiple tables. This property can be iterated through with the `For..Each` syntax. It also contains all the default methods and properties of a standard Visual Basic collection. It is always read-only.

BOF: Returns `True` if the cursor has been moved to a position immediately before the first record in the resultset.

EOF: Returns `True` if the cursor has been moved to a position past the last record in the resultset.

Bookmarkable: Returns `True` if bookmarks can be used in the current resultset.

Bookmark: Returns or sets the bookmark of a specific column in the database. Useful when you would like to return to the record you were on before the `AddNew` method was called. Simply place the value of the `Bookmark` property into a temporary variable, execute the `AddNew` method, and then set the value of the `Bookmark` property to the value of the temporary variable. Not all resultsets support this property, and you should examine the value of the `Bookmarkable` property before you attempt to set the `Bookmark` value.

Columns: This property provides an easy way to set and retrieve the values of the columns in the current recordset. It is also the default property, which allows a simpler syntax to be used when referring to a specific column in the database. Usage:

```
RDODatanase(ColumnName) = Value
Value = RDODatabase(ColumnName)
```

DSN: Returns or sets the name of the ODBC DSN to use when connecting to the remote database server. You can either set this value in the property or pass it as a parameter to the `Connect` method.

DatabaseName: Returns or sets the name of the database to use on the remote database server. You may either set this value in the property or pass it as a parameter to the `Connect` method.

Password: Returns or sets the password to use when connecting to the remote database server. You may either set this value in the property or pass it as a parameter to the `Connect` method.

UserName: Returns or sets the user name to use when connecting to the remote database server. You may either set this value in the property or pass it as a parameter to the `Connect` method.

QueryTimeout: Returns or sets the length of time, in seconds, that a query will be allowed to run before an error is generated.

RowCount: Returns the number of rows in the current recordset.

RowsAffected: Returns the number of rows affected by an action query such as an `INSERT`, `UPDATE`, or `DELETE`.

ErrorNumber: Returns the error number of the last raised error.

ErrorMessage: Returns the error message of the last raised error.

Methods

Connect: Establishes a connection with the remote database server. `Connect` attempts to establish a connection with the remote database server. All parameters are optional, and if a parameter has been left out, the corresponding property will be used instead. See "Properties" for more information. The following are the parameters:

Part	Description
strDSN	Optional. A string specifying a DSN to use for this connection.
strDatabaseName	Optional. A string containing the name of the database to open on the remote server.
strUserName	Optional. A string containing the user name to use when connecting to the remote server.
strPassword	Optional. A string containing the password to use when connecting to the remote server.

It returns a value corresponding to the public enumeration `CONNECT_ERRORS`.

Disconnect: Disconnect from the remote database server. The `Disconnect` method disconnects from the remote database server only if the `RDODatabase` class is connected. It will also destroy any existing query objects you might have opened.

ODBCConnectionString: This function builds an ODBC connection string for use with RDO connection methods. It has been placed inside its own function to make changing it easier in the event Microsoft ever changes the convention. This function is private to the class, but might be useful in your own projects where you must generate a DSN connection string.

Execute: Execute a SQL statement on the remote database server. You must use the `Execute` method whenever you need a dataset to process. `Execute` also enables you to send muted (a statement that returns no dataset) SQL statements to the server such as an `INSERT` or `DROP` statement. `Execute` can open both dynamic and forward-only type datasets. The following are the parameters:

Part	*Description*
sSQL	Required. A string that contains a SQL statement to execute on the remote server. For action queries that do not return a resultset, see the Mute parameter.
DatasetType	Optional. An integer that specifies the desired type of resultset. These values are available in the public enumeration DATASETTYPES defined in the Declarations section of the class. If this parameter has been left out, the Execute method defaults to DATASETTYPES.DYNAMIC.
Mute	Optional. A Boolean value that specifies whether the query defined in the parameter sSQL will return a resultset. If this value is True, no resultset will be created (such as an INSERT query). If no value is specified, the function will assume the query will return a resultset.

MoveFirst: Moves the cursor to the first record in the resultset. If no resultset has been opened, or the resultset type is DATASETTYPES.FORWARD_ONLY, MoveFirst will raise an error.

MoveLast: Moves the cursor to the last record in the dataset. If no resultset has been opened, or if the resultset type is DATASETTYPES.FORWARD_ONLY, then MoveLast will raise an error.

MoveNext: Moves the cursor forward one record in the dataset. If no resultset has been opened, MoveNext will raise an error. This is the only cursor positioning method that will work with resultsets opened as DATASETTYPES.FORWARD_ONLY.

MoveBack: Moves the cursor back one record in the dataset. If no resultset has been opened, or if the resultset type is DATASETTYPES.FORWARD_ONLY, then MoveBack will raise an error.

Edit: Activates editing for the record currently selected by the cursor. Use Edit when you would like to change column values for the current record. Also see the related methods AddNew, Update, and Delete.

You must activate editing mode before you can write a value to the Columns property. When editing has been completed, you must call the Update method before moving the cursor, otherwise your edit will not be saved. You can use the CancelUpdate method to cancel the edit if necessary.

Update: Sends the updated version of the currently selected record to the database server. Also see the related methods Edit and Delete.

Use the Update method to save the currently selected record to the database. You must first activate editing mode by calling the Edit or the AddNew method before calling the Update method.

CancelUpdate: Cancels editing mode and discards changes to the currently selected record.

Delete: Deletes the entire record currently selected by the cursor. Also see the related methods Edit, AddNew, and Update.

AddNew: Creates a new blank record in the dataset and activates editing mode. AddNew moves the cursor to the newly created record. You must use the Bookmark property to return to the record you were on before you called the AddNew method. You must use the Update method to save your changes to the database. Use the CancelUpdate method to abort any changes you have made.

Find/FindB: Moves the cursor to the record in the dataset matching the specified criteria. Call this function to force the class to seek a specific record in the current recordset. If the record exists, the Find methods will place the cursor on it and return a value of `True`. You can check for multiple conditions using the following syntax:

`Find(Fieldname, Value, [Fieldname], [Value]...)`

The only difference between the two versions of the `Find` method, `Find` and `FindB`, is how you pass the search criteria to the method.

The following is the syntax for the `Find` method:

Part	Description
sSearchString	Required. A parameter array that contains the search criteria. Please keep in mind that this single argument is a Visual Basic parameter array. Although it appears as though you are passing multiple parameters to the function, the parameters you pass are actually converted into a variant array called `sSearchString`. This way, you can have a variable number of parameters in a function. Note that the parameter definition for this function declaration appears as `ParamArray sSearchString As String`. The function will read the parameters as `FieldName, Value, FieldName, Value, ...`

The syntax for the `FindB` method is almost the same, except that the `FieldName/Value` pairs are passed using a two-dimensional array of strings. This allows you to dynamically generate the search criteria in code.

Returns `True` if the record specified in the search criteria was found, otherwise, `Find` and `FindB` will return `False`.

OpenTable: Opens the specified table on the remote database. Opens the specified table as a `DATASET-TYPES.DYNAMIC` type dataset. The following is the parameter:

Part	Description
sTableName	Required. A string containing the name of the table, located on the remote database server, to open.

True if the table was successfully opened, otherwise, `OpenTable` will return `False`.

GenDatabaseError: Internally used to raise database-specific errors to the parent object. The `RDODatabase` class assumes that a 40002 (ODBC) error was raised. This method will generate a possibly huge string containing a series of error messages that might have occurred immediately before the fatal error. This method will try to filter out any noncritical error messages. The entire string will be prefixed by the actual ODBC VB error number and message, then separated from the rest of the error string by a pipe character (¦).

BeginTrans: Begins a transaction on the remote database server.

CommitTrans: Commits a transaction on the remote server. See `BeginTrans`.

Caveat: I haven't been able to figure out why, when using the RDO transaction methods with Microsoft SQL Server 6.5, calling the `CommitTrans` method will close the current resultset. The transaction appears to work fine. If this happens to you, you simply must call the `Requery` method immediately following the call to the `CommitTrans` method.

RollbackTrans: Aborts a transaction on the remote server.

Requery: Forces the object to re-execute the original query the current resultset is based on. You should execute the `Requery` method after deleting or adding large amounts of data to the recordset or if you have deleted all the records in the recordset and are about to execute the `Find` method. `Requery` will ensure that the resultset and the `RowCount` property are up to date.

5.2   STORE A SQL QUERY RESULT

by Lenard Dean with Brian Shea

Description

This function fills a combo or list box with the results of a SQL query. It's a handy routine to use for lookup tables. The function uses the Data Access Object model for database access. You must add one of the DAO libraries to your project to get this function to operate correctly.

Syntax

```
DAOFillComboList dbs As Database, ComboList As Control, strSQL As String
```

Part	Description
dbs	The database object.
ComboList	The ComboBox or ListBox control.
strSQL	The SQL statement with which to fill the control.

Code Listing

```
Public Sub DAOFillComboList(dbs As Database, ComboList As Control,
➥ strSQL As String)

  On Local Error Resume Next

  Dim Rst As Recordset
  Dim blnIDFound As Boolean

  blnIDFound = InStr(strSQL, ",") > 0


  Set Rst = dbs.OpenRecordset(strSQL, dbOpenForwardOnly)

  With ComboList
    .Clear
    If Not Rst Is Nothing Then
      If blnIDFound Then
        Do Until Rst.EOF
```

```
            .AddItem Rst(1)
            .ItemData(.NewIndex) = Rst(0)
            Rst.MoveNext
        Loop
    Else
        Do Until Rst.EOF
            .AddItem Rst(0)
            Rst.MoveNext
        Loop
    End If
  End If
End With


End Sub
```

Analysis

The routine shown here takes a SQL SELECT statement and collects the resulting recordset into a ComboBox or ListBox control. The function goes through the normal declarations and error handling, then checks the SQL statement for commas. bInIDFound holds the Boolean value for whether the SQL statement is looking for two values (True) or just one (False). The target control is cleared to prevent multiple uses conflicting with one another, and then the recordset is checked to ensure that the SQL query brought back some data. If it returned data, the function processes the results.

The first section handles the condition in which a two-value recordset is returned. The values are added one at a time to the combo or list box and the ItemData property is set to the first field of the recordset. The second section simply adds the item to the combo or list box one at a time.

To use, do as follows:

```
DAOFillComboList dbs, cboNames, "Select ID, Description From Customers"
```

This assumes that the first field contains the ID information and second the description (that is, text) information. When the item is selected from the combo box or list box, the ItemData property will contain the ID. If the ID is not specified, ItemData will not be set. For example:

```
DAOFillComboList dbs, cboNames, "Select Description From Customers"
```

5.3 LOOK UP A DAO DATABASE RECORD

by Lenard Dean with Brian Shea

Description

You can use this function to look up a specific record in a database table. It uses the DAO model for database access, so the project that uses this function must have one of the DAO libraries referenced for this function to work. You can do this by going to the Projects menu and selecting References, then adding a check next to one of the DAO libraries. Click OK, and you should be ready.

The following examples better describe what this function does. First, assume there is a database called Customers, with the fields ID, Name, Address, Phone, Description, and Comments. You could use DAOLookupID in the following ways:

```
vaRetVal = DAOLookupID(dbs, "Select ID From Customers
➥ Where Description='Ferrari'")

vaRetVal = DAOLookupID(dbs, "Select Description From Customers Where ID=5")
```

The first example retrieves the value from the ID field for the record that has a description of Ferrari. The second example gets the value of the description field for the record with an ID of 5. The return value ID is a variant, so you can get values from integer, date/time, or string (VarChar) fields. You might need to use the CInt, CDate, or CStr functions to ensure that you don't receive any Type Mismatch errors.

Syntax

```
vaReturnValue = DAOLookupID(dbs As Database, strSQL As String)
```

Part	Description
vaReturnValue	Required. This is the value that is returned from the function.
dbs	Required. The database object. In addition, you should already have opened the connection to the database object before using DAOLookupID.
strSQL	Required. The SQL statement to retrieve a record based on a specific field.

Code Listing

```
Public Function DAOLookupID(dbs As Database, strSQL As String) As Variant

  On Local Error Resume Next

  Dim Rst As Recordset
  Dim strField As String
  Dim intSPos As Integer
  Dim intEPos As Integer

  Set Rst = dbs.OpenRecordset(strSQL, dbOpenSnapshot)
  intSPos = InStr(strSQL, " ") + 1

  If InStr(strSQL, ",") Then
    intEPos = InStr(intSPos, strSQL, ",")
  Else
    intEPos = InStr(intSPos, strSQL, " ")
  End If
```

```
      strField = Mid(strSQL, intSPos, intEPos - intSPos)
      DAOLookupID = Rst(strField)

End Function
```

Analysis

The `DAOLookupID` function is used to get the value of a specified field from a database. This function uses the DAO model for its database access, so when you use this function in a project, you must go to Project, References and select a DAO library for the project to use.

The function itself is very simple. It opens a recordset object based on the results of the SQL query. It then gets the field name being asked for and sets the return value to the values of that field. The function will look up only the value of the first field in the SQL query, so it is best suited for use with a query that returns one record and looks for only one field.

5.4 DEALING WITH NULL STRINGS IN ACCESS DATABASE FIELDS

by James Limm

Description

Access database fields by default contain `NULL` values unless a value has been assigned to them, such as an open string. Unfortunately, reading in these `NULL` values from the database recordset into string variables usually causes a runtime error. There is a way around this problem. When you read in a value from the database, make sure you add an open string (`""`) value before assigning the data to a string variable. Note that the (`""`) value is different from the Visual Basic constant `vbNullString`. This constant means a string with the value of `0`, which is usually used to call external procedures.

Code Listing

Here is an example of how to read in a `NULL` database value without causing a runtime error:

```
Dim DB As Database
Dim RS As Recordset
Dim sYear As String
Set DB = OpenDatabase("Biblio.mdb")
Set RS = DB.OpenRecordset("Authors")
sYear = "" & RS![Year Born]
```

Analysis

This code prevents runtime errors by adding an open string to the field being read from the database and then assigning it to a string variable. Because string variables cannot normally handle `NULL` values, this prevents errors. NULL values are different from the open string value. NULL means "no data," whereas " " is data. It is important to realize that the problem of NULL values in database fields occurs only when reading in from the database. After some data has been assigned to the field, the field no longer will be NULL. Also, numerical database fields do not suffer from the NULL data problem, so you should not read in a number field with a " " value because a data type conversion error will occur.

5.5   CONVERT A STRING TO A SQL QUERY

by Mike Shaffer

Description

The StrToQuery function can help you construct valid SQL queries. In particular, this function will accept any string and change all single quote marks to two single quote marks.

As an example, assume that an application enables users to type the last name of a person in order to look him or her up within a database. Standard code to create the SQL statement and recordset might look something like this:

```
StrSQL = "SELECT * FROM Guests WHERE LastName = '" & trim$(Text1.Text) & "' "
Set rs1 = db1.OpenRecordset(strSQL, dbOpenDynaset)
```

The only problem with this code is that it would generate a SQL error if the user happened to enter the name O'Malley, because that name has an embedded single quote. To correct this problem, use the StrToQuery routine like this:

```
StrSQL = "SELECT * FROM Guests WHERE LastName = '" &
➥trim$(StrToQuery(Text1.Text)) & "' "
```

Note that this function also removes embedded nulls from the passed string.

Syntax

```
StrToQuery(strValue$)
```

Part	Description
StrValue$	Required. The string to be made "SQL-safe."

Code Listing

```
'*********************************************
'* Submitted by Mike Shaffer
'*********************************************
Function strToQuery(QryString As String) As String
```

```
    '
    ':::::::::::::::::::::::::::::::::::::::::::::::::::::::::::::::::::::'
    ':::                                                             :::'
    ':::    This function makes a string safe for SQL query (replaces all  :::'
    ':::    single quotes with two single quotes).                    :::'
    ':::                                                             :::'
    ':::::::::::::::::::::::::::::::::::::::::::::::::::::::::::::::::::::'
    '

    Dim st As Integer
    '
    If InStr(QryString, "'") <> 0 Then
        st% = 1
        While st% <= Len(QryString) And InStr(st%, QryString, "'") > 0
            st% = InStr(st%, QryString, "'")
            QryString = Left$(QryString, st%) & "'" & Mid$(QryString, st% + 1)
            st% = st% + 2
        Wend
    End If
    '
    While InStr(QryString, Chr$(0))
        st% = InStr(QryString, Chr$(0))
        QryString = Left$(QryString, st% - 1) & Mid$(QryString, st% + 1)
    Wend
    '
    strToQuery = QryString
    '
End Function
```

Analysis

This routine can also be used (with little modification) in your VBScript routines to help when using databases in Active Server Pages.

5.6 CLOSE ALL RECORDSETS AND DATABASES

by Mike Shaffer

Description

The DBCloseAll routine will close all open recordsets and databases within an application. This routine came about as a way to ensure that rogue recordsets and databases were not being left open when a form was being unloaded, which would cause memory resource leaks (as well as possibly undesirable side effects within your database). Although using it is not as good a practice as explicitly closing and setting to Nothing, this routine can help quickly cure problems in code you might have inherited.

Note

Because this routine simply executes the Close method on each recordset and database, all VB standard database rules regarding pending transactions, record locking, and so on, would apply.

In your main form's unload event, you could simply include the following line, and all your recordsets and databases would be closed and set to Nothing:

```
DBCloseAll
```

Syntax

```
DBCloseAll
```

Code Listing

```
'************************************************
'* Submitted by Mike Shaffer
'************************************************
Sub DBCloseAll()
    '
    Dim WSTemp as Workspace
    Dim DBTemp As Database
    Dim RSTemp As Recordset
    '
    On Error Resume Next
    For Each WSTemp in Workspaces
       For Each DBTemp In WSTemp.Databases
             For Each RSTemp In DBTemp.Recordsets
                RSTemp.Close
             Next
             DBTemp.Close
       Next
    Next
    '
End Sub
```

Analysis

This routine is useful when you prematurely end a program (due to a critical error condition, for example) and want to ensure that all open recordsets and databases are closed and deallocated.

5.7 IMPLEMENTING "BAG" MECHANICS

by Martin Cordova

Description

Distributed (multitier) applications are today's hot topic, and DCOM (distributed COM) is a vital Microsoft technology that enables the construction of powerful distributed applications using the foundations of ActiveX components. Visual Basic is a very powerful tool to build this kind of application, but some design issues specific to client/server projects must be considered when you create such systems. One of the most critical is network traffic, and the other is a good object-oriented design.

This class module is a reusable component that encapsulates the mechanics of a *bag*, a facility to store items of any native VB type for easy packaging and unpackaging. This is a vital technique in distributed applications that must save as much traffic as possible between clients and transaction servers. For example, you must avoid as many round trips as possible in a Microsoft transaction server (MTS) application, and because of this you will use stateless objects on the server side. But you don't have to resign to use high-level, well-structured classes to maintain your objects on the client side because you can easily package them using bags and then send them to the server in just one trip. This class module makes that packaging and unpackaging very easy.

In other words, you are going to use stateful objects on the client side to make programming easier and more object oriented. However, on the server side the aim is to save traffic (as much as possible), so stateless objects are the preferred way to go. The problem is how to pack stateful objects into variant arrays and send them in one shot to the server-side stateless objects, and how to make it easy for those server methods to unpack those properties stored in the variant arrays. This is the basic tradeoff of distributed applications written with Visual Basic and DCOM.

The following is an example on the client side:

```
Dim Bag As New clsBag

Bag.Add "CustomerID", oCust.ID
Bag.Add "LastName", oCust.LastName
Bag.Add "FirstName", oCust.FirstName
Bag.Add "Orders", oCust.ArrayOfOrderData

MyRemoteServer.Save Bag.Package
```

The following is an example on the server side:

```
Public Sub Save(v As Variant)

    Dim Bag As New clsBag

    Bag.Unpack v
    ...
    Rs.AddNew
    Rs!CustID = Bag("CustomerID")
    Rs!Lastname = Bag("Lastname")
    ...
    Rs.Update

End Sub
```

This component exposes three services:

```
Public Sub Add(ItemName As String, Value); add an item to the bag
Public Property Package; returns the bag as an array of variants ready
➡ for transmission via DCOM
Public Sub Unpack(Data As Variant); transform an array of variants into
➡a Bag (the opposite of Package)
Public Proeprty Get Item(ItemName As String) As Variant; return an item
➡value by its name (defaut property)
```

To reuse this code, create an empty class module called clsBag and paste the following code.

Code Listing

```
Option Explicit

'---error constants
Public Enum clsPropertyBagError
    pbBadFormat = vbObjectError + 1000
    pbNotFound = vbObjectError + 1001
    pbIsEmpty = vbObjectError + 1002
End Enum

'---items counter
Private m_ItemCount As Integer

'---field names array
Private m_Fields As Variant

'---field values array
Private m_Values As Variant

'---add an item to the bag
Public Sub Add(ByVal Field As String, ByVal Value As Variant)

    If m_ItemCount = 0 Then

        ReDim m_Fields(0)
```

```
            ReDim m_Values(0)

        Else

            ReDim Preserve m_Fields(0 To m_ItemCount)

            ReDim Preserve m_Values(0 To m_ItemCount)

        End If

        m_Fields(m_ItemCount) = LCase(Field)

        m_Values(m_ItemCount) = Value

        m_ItemCount = m_ItemCount + 1

End Sub

'---return an item value given its name
Public Property Get Item(ByVal Field As String) As Variant

        Dim i As Integer

        Field = LCase(Field)

        If IsArray(m_Fields) Then

            For i = 0 To m_ItemCount - 1
                If m_Fields(i) = Field Then
                    Item = m_Values(i)
                    Exit Property
                End If
            Next

            Err.Description = "Item '" & Field & "' not found in
            ➥Property Bag."
            Err.Raise pbNotFound

        Else

            Err.Description = "Property Bag is empty."
            Err.Raise pbIsEmpty

        End If

End Property

'---return bag's data as an array of variants
'---element(0) = field names
'---element(1) = field values
Public Property Get Package() As Variant
```

```
    Dim Bag(0 To 1) As Variant

    If IsArray(m_Fields) Then

        Bag(0) = m_Fields
        Bag(1) = m_Values

        Package = Bag

    Else

        Err.Description = "Property Bag is empty."
        Err.Raise pbIsEmpty

    End If

End Property

'---unpack a variant arrays and transform it into a bag
Public Sub Unpack(ByVal Package As Variant)

    If Not IsArray(Package) Then

        Err.Description = "Invalid package format."

        Err.Raise pbBadFormat

    Else

        If UBound(Package) <> 1 Then

            Err.Description = "Invalid package format."

            Err.Raise pbBadFormat

        End If

        m_Fields = Package(0)

        m_Values = Package(1)

        If UBound(m_Fields) <> UBound(m_Values) Then

            Err.Description = "Invalid package format."

            Err.Raise pbBadFormat

        End If
```

```
        m_ItemCount = UBound(m_Fields) + 1

    End If

End Sub
```

Analysis

Internally the class implements the bag as two variant arrays, one for the property names and the other for the values. Variant arrays are very appropriate for DCOM, not only because they are naturally marshaled by DCOM (transmitted over TCP/IP), but also because a variant can represent the exact semantics of VB data types. For example, a date stored in a variant will remain a date when it arrives at the server, no matter what the international configurations are in the client and server machines. So native data types and marshaling are two of the main benefits of using variants for DCOM intercommunications.

This class also provides a handy method for adding a new element to the bag. The bag gets resized automatically. When it's time for "transmission," the `Package` property returns the two variant arrays as just one variant variable (which is also an array), making all the data manipulation very simple for the programmer, on the client and the server side.

In order to "unpackage" a variant originally produced by a `Bag` object, this class provides the `Unpack` method, which will verify the format of the data passed in order to determine whether it's compatible with a `Bag` object. If the test is passed, the data in raw form will be converted to the very usable form of a bag.

This component is completely self-contained (no external dependencies) and exposes its own error codes.

GRAPHICS AND SCREEN SAVER FUNCTIONS

This chapter contains some fun routines for creating graphic effects and screen savers. These functions are valuable because these graphic effects can really add visual appeal to your program. The animation, graphic effects in forms, and general graphic file functions included here can help you add spice to your project quickly and easily.

6.1 PAINT A GRADIENT BACKGROUND ONTO A FORM

by Tom Honaker

Description

The `PaintForm` sub will paint any form's background with a gradient based on parameters supplied by the code that calls it. Gradient step rates for each primary color (red, green, blue) as well as how many steps to sweep across the form are also controllable. Orientation can be horizontal, vertical, or diagonal from the upper-left corner outward. With some careful selection of values, you can achieve interesting and eye-catching or subtle and hardly noticeable background gradients.

The code is reasonably fast on most Pentium-class systems, and will produce an acceptable appearance even on 256-color systems, although the higher the color depth setting the better.

This code should be called from within a form's `Form_Paint()` event so that the form's gradient background can be repainted when needed. Also, the form's `ClipControl` property should be set to `True` and its `AutoRedraw` property set to `False`.

Syntax

```
PaintForm(FormName, Orientation%, RStart%, GStart%, _
   BStart%, Rinc!, Ginc!, Binc!, [StepRate%])
```

Part	Description
FormName	Required. The name of the form (as defined in the form's Name property) to paint.
Orientation%	Required. A string expression that specifies the source file name. Can include directory or folder and drive.
RStart%, GStart%, BStart%	Required. Integer expressions that set red, green, and blue components of the starting color.
RInc!, BInc!, GInc!	Required. A single-precision expression that determines the change to apply to the red, green, and blue components of each step's color.
StepRate%	Optional. An integer that determines how many steps of gradient are to be applied to a form. Higher numbers will produce smoother results, but at the cost of slower repaint speed and much more sensitivity to changes in the RInc!, BInc!, and GInc! parameters. If not specified, StepRate% is automatically set to 32.

Code Listing

```
' Paste all of this into a module, preferably the one
' that holds your global variable/function/whatever declarations.

Global RS%, GS%, BS%, RI!, GI!, BI!, Direction%, Step%

Declare Function GetDeviceCaps Lib "gdi32" _
   (ByVal hDC As Long, ByVal nIndex As Long) As Long

Declare Function CreateSolidBrush Lib "gdi32" _
    (ByVal crColor As Long) As Long

Declare Function DeleteObject Lib "gdi32" _
   (ByVal hObject As Long) As Long

Declare Function FillRect Lib "user32" _
   (ByVal hDC As Long, lpRect As RECT, _
   ByVal Hbrush As Long) As Long

Type RECT
        Left As Long
        Top As Long
        Right As Long
        Bottom As Long
End Type
Global fillarea As RECT



Sub PaintForm(FormName As Form, Orientation%, RStart%, _
   GStart%, BStart%, Rinc!, Ginc!, Binc!, Optional StepRate%)
```

```
On Error Resume Next
Dim X As Integer, Y As Integer, Z As Integer, Cycles As Integer,
➥Cycles2 As Integer
Dim R!, G!, B!, RgnCnt, ColorBits, BitsPerPixel, _
  NbrPlanes, Hbrush, qwerty, prevScaleMode
R! = RStart%: G! = GStart%: B! = BStart%

prevScaleMode = FormName.ScaleMode 'save the current scalemode
FormName.ScaleMode = 3 'set to pixel

RgnCnt = StepRate%
If RgnCnt = 0 Then RgnCnt = 32

Select Case Orientation%
        Case 0
                Cycles = FormName.ScaleHeight \ RgnCnt
        Case 1
                Cycles = FormName.ScaleWidth \ RgnCnt
        Case 2
                Cycles = FormName.ScaleHeight \ RgnCnt
                Cycles2 = FormName.ScaleWidth \ RgnCnt
End Select

fillarea.Left = 0
fillarea.Top = 0
fillarea.Right = FormName.ScaleWidth
fillarea.Bottom = FormName.ScaleHeight

X = 0
Y = 0
For Z = 1 To RgnCnt ñ 1
        ' Time to create a brush to paint the form withÖ
        Hbrush = CreateSolidBrush(RGB(R!, G!, B!))

        Select Case Orientation
            Case 0: 'Top to Bottom
                If X > FormName.ScaleHeight Then Exit For
                fillarea.Top = X
            Case 1: 'Left to Right
                If X > FormName.ScaleWidth Then Exit For
                fillarea.Left = X
            Case 2: 'Diagonal
                If X > FormName.ScaleHeight Then Exit For
                If Y > FormName.ScaleWidth Then Exit For
                fillarea.Top = X
                fillarea.Left = Y
        End Select
        ' Now we paint a rectangle on the form with our
        ' brush...
        qwerty = FillRect(FormName.hDC, fillarea, Hbrush)

        ' Time to unload the brush. Brushes consume resources
```

continues

```
        ' that are needed elsewhere.
        qwerty = DeleteObject(Hbrush)

        X = X + Cycles + 1
        Y = Y + Cycles2 + 1
        R! = R! + Rinc!
        G! = G! + Ginc!
        B! = B! + Binc!

        If R! > 255 Then R! = 255
        If R! < 0 Then R! = 0

        If G! > 255 Then G! = 255
        If G! < 0 Then G! = 0

        If B! > 255 Then B! = 255
        If B! < 0 Then B! = 0
    Next Z

    FormName.ScaleMode = prevScaleMode

End Sub
```

Analysis

This routine can be called from anywhere in a project. The easiest mistake to make is not to specify the form's name in the call, especially when pasting the code to call this sub in other forms. If called from a form's `Form_Paint()` event, the gradient can be automatically redrawn whenever needed.

How it works is simple. When called, the starting values are used to draw a rectangle the same height and width as the target form via API calls. A `for...next` loop steps through the number of steps determined by the `StepRate%` parameter, reducing the rectangle's size proportionately. With each step the rectangle's color is altered slightly as well, and the end result is a smooth gradient effect that can be easily controlled at run-time.

Some minor limitations do exist. As is the case with all such form-level graphics routines, this routine has no effect on MDI parent forms' background areas. However, it can be put to good use in the child forms themselves. Also, increasing the `StepRate%` parameter too high might make for uncomfortably long repaint times for compiled executables, especially on slower systems or systems with less advanced video hardware. Finally, the refresh time is longer when the area to paint is larger; therefore, maximized forms at higher resolutions will increase the paint time enough to be noticeable. This code lends itself best to smaller windows, such as non-maximizable MDI child forms.

The routine is designed as listed for Visual Basic 5.0, but with proper changes to the API declarations it should also function properly in 4.0 (32- or 16-bit, again with proper declarations).

6.2   FILLING A FORM WITH A GRADIENT

by Kamal A. Mehdi

Description

The sample code in this section fills a form's background with a gradient color similar to that which appears on an application's setup screen. The code uses the Line method to draw multiple rectangle areas on the form and fill each rectangle with the appropriate color using the RGB function. The rectangle fill color values are adjusted according to the relative position of the particular rectangle on the form to produce the gradient appearance of the form's background.

The sample code enables you to select one of three default gradient color patterns to fill the form's background: Black-to-blue, black-to-green, and black-to-red gradient color patterns are implemented. However, you can specify a color offset for each of the red, green, and blue colors separately to implement any gradient fill pattern. Up to 16.7 million different color patterns are possible.

Modules and Controls Required

You will need the following modules and controls to build the sample project:

Module/Control	Description
Form1	A standard non-MDI Visual Basic form (.FRM) with the Caption property set to Fill Form With Gradient Color
Frame1	A frame control with the Caption property set to Color Pattern
Frame2	A frame control with the Caption property set to Offset
Option1	An option button with the Caption property set to Gradient Red
Option2	An option button with the Caption property set to Gradient Green
Option3	An option button with the Caption property set to Gradient Blue
Label1	A label control with the Caption property set to Red
Label2	A label control with the Caption property set to Green
Label3	A label control with the Caption property set to Blue
Text1	A text box control
Text2	A text box control
Text3	A text box control
Command1	A command button with the Caption property set to Redraw Form

To draw controls, follow these steps:

1. Start a new standard EXE project. `Form1` will be created by default. Set the form's `Height` and `Width` properties to `2600` and `4300`, respectively, and set its `Caption` property as shown above.
2. Draw `Frame1` on the left side of the form and set its `Caption` property as shown above. Draw the three option buttons inside the frame control with `Option1` on the top, `Option2` in the middle, and `Option3` on the bottom. Set their `Caption` properties as shown above.
3. Draw `Frame2` on the right side of the form and set its `Caption` property as shown above. Draw the three label controls inside the frame control with `Label1` on the top-left side of the frame, `Label2` in the middle-left side, and `Label3` in the bottom-left side. Set their `Caption` properties as shown above. Draw the three text boxes on the right side of the frame with `Text1` to the right of `Label1`, `Text2` to the right of `Label2`, and `Text3` to the right of `Label3`. Make the size of all text boxes big enough to enter three characters.
4. Draw `Command1` on the bottom of the form and set its `Caption` property as shown above.

Code Listing

```
'Form global variables
    Dim btnTop As Integer
    Dim btnLeft As Integer

Private Sub Form_Load()

    'Maximize form window
    Me.WindowState = 2

    'Set default color offsets to 0
    Text1.Text = 0
    Text2.Text = 0
    Text3.Text = 0

    'Select the black-to-blue pattern as default
    Option3.Value = True

    'Store the current position of Command1
    btnTop = Command1.Top
    btnLeft = Command1.Left

End Sub

Private Sub Command1_Click()

    Static NewFill As Boolean

    'Error handling is important here in case values may
    'exceed the allowable range
    On Error Resume Next
```

```
'The NewFill flag is used to know whether to hide controls
'and fill the form or to show the controls and try another fill
If NewFill Then      'Show the controls and exit
    NewFill = False
    Frame1.Visible = True
    Frame2.Visible = True
    Command1.Top = btnTop
    Command1.Left = btnLeft
    Command1.Caption = "Redraw Form"
    Exit Sub
Else      'Hide controls and fill the form
    Frame1.Visible = False
    Frame2.Visible = False
    Command1.Caption = "Try another fill pattern"
    Command1.Top = 0
    Command1.Left = 0
    DoEvents
End If

'Set the autoredraw property to true because otherwise
'the form will lose its fill if another window may get
'in front of it
Me.AutoRedraw = True

'Specify the desired R, G, B color offsets
'Restrict values to be between 0-255
Roffset = Abs(Val(Text1) Mod 256)
Goffset = Abs(Val(Text2) Mod 256)
Boffset = Abs(Val(Text3) Mod 256)

'Start the color filling loop
For I% = 0 To Me.Height / Screen.TwipsPerPixelY

    'Draw a rectangle and fill it with the calculated
    'RGB color depending on the selected option button
    'and the current vertical drawing position relative to
    'the form's top
    Line (0, Y%)-(Me.Width, Y% + 15), RGB( _
    Abs(CInt(Option1.Value)) * I% + Roffset, _
    Abs(CInt(Option2.Value)) * I% + Goffset, _
    Abs(CInt(Option3.Value)) * I% + Boffset), BF

    'Increment the current Y drawing position by 30
    Y% = Y% + 30

Next I%

'Set the NewFill flag to true
NewFill = True

End Sub
```

Enter this code in the appropriate events of the form module and the form's controls. Run the project, select one of the gradient color patterns by clicking the appropriate option button, and click the Redraw Form button to fill the form with the selected pattern. Click the command button again to show the controls and select another color pattern or enter different offsets for one or more of the three colors (RGB). Click the Redraw Form button again. Notice the new gradient color pattern based on the selected pattern or the new color offset values.

Analysis

The code is fairly simple. It uses the RGB function to fill rectangle areas drawn on the form with a gradually increasing value of the red, green, or blue color. The starting fill color value is always 0 (black) if no offset is specified for the particular color used in the corresponding gradient fill. If an offset is specified, it will be used as the starting fill color value. However, if an offset is specified for a color other than the one used for the selected gradient fill, the color offset value will be consistently used in the appropriate RGB function argument during the fill process.

The rectangle drawing method draws and fills a 15-twip high rectangle to ensure both speed in drawing as well as uniform color fill on the entire form.

Note that the form's AutoRedraw property must be set to True before filling the form; otherwise, the form will lose its filled appearance if another window covers the form's window after the drawing process. This is done at runtime by the code.

The sample code can be used without any modifications for gradient filling of a picture box by specifying the picture box as the object for the Line method. In addition, the color pattern and the offsets can be specified in the code to fill the form with the required gradient without using controls.

The sample project GRADCOLR.VBP on the CD-ROM that accompanies this book demonstrates the functionality of the presented code.

6.3   TILE THE BACKGROUND OF AN MDI PARENT FORM

by Tom Honaker

Description

Windows permits a potentially useful interface layout called multiple document interface (MDI). This child-windows-within-a-parent-window enables you to have several usage-specific windows in an application without cluttering the screen much. Also, this approach keeps all the application windows in one easy-to-manage package.

MDI parent forms are different from other form types in areas other than simply the support for child windows. Most notably, although it is easy to tile a background image on a non-MDI form or any MDI child form, tiling a background onto the (typically dark gray) child container area of an MDI parent form is tough.

This routine uses a separate form as a palette to create the background, and then the whole background is transferred at once to the MDI parent form. Therefore, using this code requires the following elements:

- The MDI parent form on which to place a background. Its name will be passed in the call to the routine that performs the background effect.
- A standard form. Its name can be anything you want because this will also be passed to the routine. No other controls should be placed on this form, and it should not be used for anything else because it will not be held resident in memory unless needed. Some parameters must be set as follows:

Property	Value
AutoRedraw	True
BorderStyle	0 - None
Caption	(No caption)
ClipControls	True
ControlBox	False
Visible	False

- A PictureBox control on the form. Some parameters must be set as follows:

Property	Value
Name	Picture1
AutoRedraw	True
AutoSize	True
BorderStyle	0 - None
ClipControls	True
Visible	False

- A background image that can be supported by a Visual Basic PictureBox control. The formats this control accepts are graphics interchange format (GIF), JPEG compressed (JPG), Windows bitmap (BMP), and Windows enhanced metafile (WMF). The image must be passed by way of its full path to the routine.

The code should be called from the MDI parent form's Form_Load() event.

Syntax

```
TileMDIBkgd(MDIForm, bkgdtiler, bkgdfile)
```

Part	Description
MDIForm	Required. A string expression holding the name given to the receive the tiled backMDI parent form that will ground.
bkgdtiler	Required. A string expression holding the name given to the form that will be used to generate the background before it is moved to the MDI form named in MDIForm.
bkgdfile	Required. A string expression holding the full path and filename pointing to an image file to tile. This image must be a BMP, non-interlaced GIF (interlaced GIFs will produce banding in some cases), JPG, or WMF only, and should be designed with tiling in mind.

Code Listing

```
Sub TileMDIBkgd(MDIForm As Form, bkgdtiler As Form, _
  bkgdfile As String)

    Dim ScWidth%, ScHeight%, countn%, counto%

    ' Get the actual screen resolution...
    ScWidth% = Screen.Width / Screen.TwipsPerPixelX
    ScHeight% = Screen.Height / Screen.TwipsPerPixelY
    ' ScWidth% and ScHeight% hold the screen resolution.

    ' Load the form we'll use as a container to build
    ' the background in...
    Load bkgdtiler
    bkgdtiler.Height = Screen.Height
    bkgdtiler.Width = Screen.Width
    bkgdtiler.ScaleMode = 3 ' Set ScaleMode to Pixels...

    ' Set up the Picture1 control created on that form...
    bkgdtiler!Picture1.Top = 0
    bkgdtiler!Picture1.Left = 0
    bkgdtiler!Picture1.Picture = LoadPicture(bkgdfile)
    bkgdtiler!Picture1.ScaleMode = 3 ' Pixels again...

    ' Tile the image into the PictureBox control Picture1...
    For countn% = 0 To ScHeight% Step _
      bkgdtiler!Picture1.ScaleHeight
        For counto% = 0 To ScWidth% Step _
          bkgdtiler!Picture1.ScaleWidth
            bkgdtiler.PaintPicture _
              bkgdtiler!Picture1.Picture, counto%, countn%
        Next counto%
    Next countn%
```

```
' Transfer the completed background to the MDI
' form and unload the temporary form...
MDIForm.Picture = bkgdtiler.Image
Unload bkgdtiler

End Sub
```

Analysis

This code is pretty straightforward. You create a form and create on it a PictureBox control. The form is used to create the whole tiled background, while the PictureBox is used to preload the image once and determine its size for the tiling loops. When the tile operation is complete, you set the MDI parent form's `Picture` property to the image of the form that you tiled and unload the form that you now no longer need.

This call must be made only once because Windows automatically refreshes the background along with the rest of the MDI parent form. (There is no `Paint` event for MDI forms as a result of Windows handling them the way it does.)

If you set up some means for a user to select a file to use as a background, you can implement this code to permit custom user-selected backgrounds for your MDI-based applications.

There are two primary limitations of this code: There is a momentary CPU and memory drain caused by having to load a form and tile it and then transfer that to the MDI parent form. Also, the background is tiled to approximately the same area as the screen's resolution even if the visible area that will be tiled is smaller. The first limitation shouldn't be too much of a concern as long as the user's resolution is not exceedingly high. The second will reveal itself only on systems whose video hardware supports a virtual desktop, and this will depend on how the drivers for the video card report the screen resolution to the system.

Also, it is suggested that images to tile should be no smaller than 75×75 pixels but no larger than 250×250 pixels. A smaller image takes longer to paint, and holding a copy of a larger one eats more memory.

To use a tiled-image background on a non-MDI parent form (such as an MDI child form for the application that uses this code), use the non-MDI parent version of this code.

This code can be used for all Visual Basic versions with little or no changes.

6.4 TILE AN IMAGE ONTO A FORM AS A BACKGROUND

by Tom Honaker

Description

This fairly simple routine will enable you to use a tiled image as the background of a form. With proper image selection, excellent effects can be introduced into forms, including the possibility of making a form that resembles a Web page.

The non-MDI parent (although MDI child forms are acceptable) is the form to paint the background tile on. Its name can be anything you want because this will also be passed to the routine.

The following are required elements for this code:

- A PictureBox control on the form. You can name it what you want because this too is passed in the routine call. No controls should be placed within this PictureBox, and it should not be used for anything else because it will be used when needed to repaint the form. Some parameters must be set as follows:

Property	Value
AutoRedraw	True
AutoSize	True
BorderStyle	0 - None
ClipControls	True
Visible	False

- A background image that can be supported by a Visual Basic PictureBox control. This control accepts the graphics interchange format (GIF), JPEG compressed (JPG), Windows bitmap (BMP), and Windows enhanced metafile (WMF) formats. The image must be passed by way of its full path to the routine.

The code should be called from the form's `Form_Paint()` event.

Syntax

`TileBkgd(frm, picholder, bkgdfile)`

Part	Description
frm	Required. A string expression holding the name given to the form that will receive the tiled background.
picholder	Required. A string expression holding the name given to the PictureBox that will serve as a temporary holder for the image to tile. This PictureBox will not be visible.
bkgdfile	Required. A string expression holding the full path and filename pointing to an image file to tile. This image must be a BMP, non-interlaced GIF (interlaced GIFs will produce banding in some cases), JPG, or WMF only, and should be designed with tiling in mind.

Code Listing

```
Sub TileBkgd(frm As Form, picholder As PictureBox, bkgdfile As String)
    ' Make sure to pass the Form's name (frm), Placeholder
    ' PictureBox name (picholder), and Image file with
    ' full path (bkgdfile) to the sub!

    If bkgdfile = "" Then Exit Sub
    Dim ScWidth%, ScHeight%, ScMode%, countn%, counto%

    ' Prepare the form by setting its ScaleMode to pixels...
    ScMode% = frm.ScaleMode
    picholder.ScaleMode = 3
    frm.ScaleMode = 3

    ' Prepare the PictureBox the same way...
    picholder.Picture = LoadPicture(bkgdfile)
    picholder.ScaleMode = 3

    ' Paint the form with the image...
    For countn% = 0 To frm.Height Step picholder.ScaleHeight
        For counto% = 0 To frm.Width Step picholder.ScaleWidth
            frm.PaintPicture picholder.Picture, counto%, countn%
        Next counto%
    Next countn%

    ' Set the ScaleMode back to what it was...
    frm.ScaleMode = ScMode%
End Sub
```

Analysis

This code is pretty straightforward. A PictureBox holds the image to tile, and the routine paints it onto the form, offsetting it according to its size as it goes. The result is the tiled background.

If you set up some means for a user to select a file to use as a background, you can implement this code to permit custom user-selected backgrounds for your applications.

There are two primary concerns of this code. There is a brief CPU resource drain caused by having to load a form and tile it, and the background is tiled to at least the same area as the form's size at each repaint of the form. These become a concern only on 486-class systems or applications that are trying to tile a very large form.

Also, it is suggested that images to tile be no smaller than 75×75 pixels but no larger than 250×250 pixels. A smaller image takes longer to paint, and holding a copy of a larger one eats more memory.

To tile-background an MDI parent form, use the MDI version of this code.

This code can be used for all VB versions with little or no changes.

6.5   ACTIVATE A SCREEN SAVER

by Ian Ippolito

Description

The Windows screen saver feature is useful for preventing an image from staying on the user's monitor too long, resulting in "burning in" a permanent shadow into the circuitry. If your Visual Basic application runs for a long time, you might want to force the Windows screen saver to turn on to avoid this problem. Your users certainly will thank you!

Note

The 16-bit version of this function will not work in Windows NT (if this is your case, use the 32-bit version instead).

Syntax

```
Activate_Screen_Saver()
```

Code Listing

```
Option Explicit
#If Win16 Then
    Declare Function SendMessage Lib "User" (ByVal hwnd As Integer, _
        ByVal wMsg As Integer, ByVal wParam As Integer, _
        lParam As Any) As Long
#Else
    Declare Function SendMessage Lib "user32" Alias "SendMessageA" _
        (ByVal hwnd As Long, ByVal wMsg As Long, _
        ByVal wParam As Long, lParam As Any) As Long
#End If

    Const WM_SYSCOMMAND = &H112
    Const SC_SCREENSAVE = &HF140

Sub Activate_Screen_Saver()
Dim lngReturn As Long

    'send message to top level windows
    lngReturn = SendMessage(-1, WM_SYSCOMMAND, SC_SCREENSAVE, 0&)

End Sub
```

Analysis

This routine uses the Windows API function `SendMessage` to send the `SC_SCREENSAVE` command to all the top-most windows active in the system. One of these windows in turn will activate the screen saver.

The routine also uses the `Alias` keyword to map the 32-bit `SendMessageA` API call to the same name as the 16-bit `SendMessage` API call, allowing a single line of code to call either function.

6.6 SET WINDOWS WALLPAPER

by Ian Ippolito

Description

One of the nicer features about Windows is its capability to customize its appearance to a user's personal preferences. The wallpaper feature of the Windows desktop enables a user to change the background of the desktop to appear as any custom .BMP wanted.

It would be very useful to be able to change this setting from inside a Visual Basic program, but there is no command in VB to do so. Fortunately, it can be done with a single function call using this routine that harnesses the power of the Windows API.

Syntax

`Set_Windows_Wallpaper BmpFile, Permanent`

Part	Description
BmpFile	Required. The bitmap file to use to wallpaper the desktop.
Permanent	Required. Set to TRUE to make the desktop wallpaper change take effect in subsequent Windows sessions. Set to FALSE to make only a temporary change.

Note

When used under Windows NT, only the TRUE setting functions properly. Attempting to set this parameter to FALSE will still have a permanent effect.

Code Listing

```
Option Explicit
#If Win16 Then
Const SPI_SETDESKWALLPAPER = 20
```

continues

```
Const SPIF_SENDWININICHANGE = &H2
Const SPIF_UPDATEINIFILE = &H1
Declare Function SystemParametersInfo Lib "User" (ByVal uAction _
    As Integer, ByVal uParam As Integer, lpvParam As Any, _
    ByVal fuWinIni As Integer) As Integer
#Else
Declare Function SystemParametersInfo Lib "user32" _
    Alias "SystemParametersInfoA" (ByVal uAction As Long, _
    ByVal uParam As Long, ByVal lpvParam As Any, _
    ByVal fuWinIni As Long) As Long
Public Const SPI_SETDESKWALLPAPER = 20
Public Const SPIF_SENDWININICHANGE = &H2
Public Const SPIF_UPDATEINIFILE = &H1

#End If

Sub Set_Windows_Wallpaper(ByVal strWallpaperBmpFile As String, _
    ByVal boolPermanent As Boolean)

#If Win16 Then
'16 bit
Dim intOptions As Integer
Dim intReturn As Integer

    If (boolPermanent = True) Then
        'permanenet
        intOptions = SPIF_UPDATEINIFILE Or SPIF_SENDWININICHANGE
    Else
        'this session only
        intOptions = 0
    End If

    intReturn = SystemParametersInfo(SPI_SETDESKWALLPAPER, _
        0, ByVal strWallpaperBmpFile, intOptions)
#Else
'32 bit
Dim lngOptions As Long
Dim lngReturn As Long

    If (boolPermanent = True) Then
        'permanenet
        _lngOptions = SPIF_UPDATEINIFILE Or SPIF_SENDWININICHANGE
    Else
        'this session only
        lngOptions = 0
    End If

    lngReturn = SystemParametersInfo(SPI_SETDESKWALLPAPER, _
        0, ByVal strWallpaperBmpFile, lngOptions)
#End If
End Sub
```

Analysis

This routine first determines whether the calling function wants to make the desktop wallpaper setting a permanent change. If the change is to be permanent, it sets the options variable equal to two Windows API constants: SPIF_UPDATEINIFILE or SPIF_SENDWININICHANGE. These constants will inform Windows to first update the settings and then to notify the system (as well as other applications) about the change. If the calling function wants only a temporary desktop change, this parameter is set to nothing (0).

After this determination is made, the SystemParametersInfo Windows API function is called, passing in the SPI_SETDESKWALLPAPER API constant to indicate that the system parameter to be changed is the desktop wallpaper.

Finally, the ByVal keyword being passed in as the last parameter to the API function might look out of place. It is actually required because the API parameter is declared as type Any rather than as a Visual Basic string.

6.7 OBTAINING BITMAP IMAGE INFORMATION

by Kamal A. Mehdi

Description

Bitmap image files can be displayed by applications or by your Visual Basic picture box or the image control after the bitmap information is read from the bitmap file headers. The bitmap file actually contains two headers, one identifying the bitmap file information and the other identifying the specific bitmap image information. The image is actually displayed by retrieving and processing the bitmap image information header.

The bitmap data contained in the information header includes the image header size, image width, image height, number of planes, color depth, compression method, image size, X and Y pixels per meter, colors used, and colors important for displaying the bitmap. The 40-byte bitmap information header consists of 11 binary data segments that hold the various bitmap attributes, which can be represented by the BITMAPINFOHEADER type variable as shown here:

Table 6.7.1

BITMAPINFOHEADER **type-defined variable structure**

Subtype	Bytes	Description
biSize	4	Image header size in bytes
biWidth	4	Image width in pixels
biHeight	4	Image height in pixels
biPlanes	2	Number of planes

continues

Table 6.7.1, continued

Subtype	Bytes	Description
biBitCount	2	Image color depth in bits
biCompression	4	Image compression method
biSizeImage	4	Image size in bytes
biXPelsPerMeter	4	Number of X pixels per meter
biYPelsPerMeter	4	Number of Y pixels per meter
biClrUsed	4	Number of colors used in the bitmap
biClrImportant	4	Number of colors important to display the bitmap

The code listing retrieves the bitmap information header of the selected bitmap file and displays the various bitmap data attributes as well as the bitmap image itself. The sample project can be used as a simple bitmap image browser but can be modified to display other image formats.

Modules and Controls Required

You will need the following modules and controls to build the sample project:

Module/Control	Description
Form1	A standard non-MDI Visual Basic form (.FRM) with the `Caption` property set to Bitmap Image Information
Frame1	A frame control with the `Caption` property set to Select Bitmap Image
Command1	A command button with the `Caption` property set to Exit
Image1	An image control
Drive1	A drive list box
Dir1	A directory list box
File1	A file list box
Label1()	A control array of nine label controls with the `Caption` property set to the following:

Index	Caption
0	Image information:
1	Width:
2	Height:
3	Image size:
4	Planes:
5	Bits per pixel:
6	Compression:
7	Colors used:
8	Colors important:
Label2()	A control array of eight label controls

To draw controls, follow these steps:

1. Start a new standard EXE project. `Form1` will be created by default. Set the form's `Height` and `Width` properties to `6000` and `7000`, respectively, and set its `Caption` property as shown above.

2. Draw `Frame1` on the form so that it covers almost the entire form, and set its `Caption` property as shown above.

3. Draw the `Drive`, `Dir`, and `File` list boxes inside the frame control in the top-left region with the `Drive` list box on the top, the `Dir` list box in the middle, and the `File` list box on the bottom. Adjust the width and height of the controls by dragging their resize handles with the mouse so that they cover almost half the width and half the height of the frame control (they will cover nearly one-fourth of the total frame area). Note that the `Drive` list box does not allow the adjustment of its height.

4. Draw `Image1` inside `Frame1` in the top-right region so that it covers nearly one-fourth of the frame area.

5. Draw `Command1` under the bottom-right corner of `Image1` and set its `Caption` property as shown above.

6. Draw `Label1` under the bottom-left corner of the `File` list box. Copy the `Label1` control and paste it eight times on the frame control to create a control array of a total of nine elements. Arrange the `Label1()` array elements one under the other with `Label1(0)` on the top and `Label1(8)` on the bottom. Set their `Caption` properties as shown above.

7. Draw `Label2` to the right of `Label1(1)` and create a control array of eight elements from `Label2` the same way you did with `Label1`. Arrange the `Label2()` array elements so that `Label2(0)` is located to the right of `Label1(1)`, `Label2(1)` is located to the right of `Label1(2)`, and so on. Adjust the width of all elements of `Label2()` to the maximum width possible. Adjust the height of `Label2(6)` and `Label2(7)` so that they can display two lines of text. The default captions of all `Label2()` array elements will be removed at runtime.

Code Listing

```
'Global declarations in the general-declarations section of Form1
'Declare constants
Private Const BI_RGB = 0&
Private Const BI_RLE8 = 1&
Private Const BI_RLE4 = 2&
Private Const BI_bitfields = 3&

'Declare type variables
Private Type BITMAPINFOHEADER    '40 bytes total
    biSize          As Long     '4 bytes
    biWidth         As Long     '4 bytes
    biHeight        As Long     '4 bytes
    biPlanes        As Integer    '2 bytes
    biBitCount      As Integer    '2 bytes
    biCompression   As Long     '4 bytes
    biSizeImage     As Long     '4 bytes
    biXPelsPerMeter As Long     '4 bytes
    biYPelsPerMeter As Long     '4 bytes
```

continues

```
    biClrUsed            As Long     '4 bytes
    biClrImportant       As Long     '4 bytes
End Type

Private Type BITMAPFILEHEADER     '14 bytes total
    bfType               As Integer   '2 bytes
    bfSize               As Long      '4 bytes
    bfReserved1          As Integer  '2 bytes
    bfReserved2          As Integer  '2 bytes
    bfOffBits            As Long      '4 bytes
End Type

Private Sub Command1_Click()

'Unload form and exit
Unload Me

End Sub

Private Sub Dir1_Change()

    'Change path of File1 and refresh it
    File1.Path = Dir1.Path
    File1.Refresh

End Sub

Private Sub Drive1_Change()

    'Change path of Dir1 and refresh it
    Dir1.Path = Drive1.Drive
    Dir1.Refresh

End Sub

Private Sub File1_Click()

    'Declare general variables
    Dim ffile As Integer
    Dim MyString As String

    'Declare type variables that will hold the bitmap info
    Dim FileHeader As BITMAPFILEHEADER
    Dim InfoHeader As BITMAPINFOHEADER

    'Handle errors that may occure during displaying the image or
    ➥reading the headers
    On Error GoTo ErrorHandler

    'Load the bitmap in the image control
    If Right$(Dir1.Path, 1) = "\" Then
        ImageFile = Dir1.Path & File1.filename
```

```
Else
    ImageFile = Dir1.Path & "\" & File1.filename
End If
Image1.Picture = LoadPicture(ImageFile)
DoEvents

'Get the first free file handle available
ffile = FreeFile

'Open the file and read the header info

Open ImageFile For Binary Access Read As #1
    Get #ffile, , FileHeader
    Get #ffile, , InfoHeader
Close #1

'Display the BMP file info
'Show the image width in pixels
Label2(0) = InfoHeader.biWidth & " pixels"

'Show the image height in pixels
Label2(1) = InfoHeader.biHeight & " pixels"

'Show the image size in bytes
Select Case InfoHeader.biSizeImage

    Case Is = 0
        MyString = "BI_RGB bitmap; size variable not specified."

    Case Else
        MyString = Format$(InfoHeader.biSizeImage, "#,###,###") &
        ➥" bytes"

End Select

Label2(2) = MyString

'Show number of planes
Label2(3) = InfoHeader.biPlanes

'Show number of colors
Label2(4) = InfoHeader.biBitCount & " (" & 2 ^ InfoHeader.biBitCount &
    ➥ " colors)"

'Show bitmap compression based on the value of biCompression
Select Case InfoHeader.biCompression

    Case BI_RGB
        MyString = "Uncompressed bitmap."

    Case BI_RLE8
        MyString = "Run-length encoded (RLE) format for bitmaps
        ➥ with 8 bits per pixel."
```

continues

```
    Case BI_RLE4
        MyString = "Run-length encoded (RLE) format for bitmaps
        ➥with 4 bits per pixel."

    Case BI_bitfields
        MyString = "Uncompressed 16- or 32-bit-per-pixel format."

End Select

Label2(5) = MyString


'Show the bitmap colors used based on the value of biClrUsed
Select Case InfoHeader.biClrUsed

    Case Is = 0

        MyString = "The bitmap image uses maximum number of colors
        ➥ corresponding to the"

        MyString = MyString & " bits-per-pixel for the specified
        ➥ compression mode."


    Case Is <> 0 And InfoHeader.biBitCount = 16

        MyString = "The size of the color table used to optimize
        ➥ performance "

        MyString = MyString & "of Windows color palettes is " &
        ➥ CStr(InfoHeader.biClrUsed) & "."

End Select

Label2(6) = MyString


'Show the colors important based on the value of biClrImportant

Select Case InfoHeader.biClrImportant

    Case Is = 0

        MyString = "All " & 2 ^ InfoHeader.biBitCount &
        ➥" color indices are"

        MyString = MyString & " considered important for displaying
        ➥ this bitmap."

    Case Is <> 0
```

```
                MyString = "The number of colors considered important for
                ➥ displaying"

                MyString = MyString & " this bitmap are " &
                ➥ CStr(InfoHeader.biClrImportant) & "."

        End Select

        Label2(7) = MyString

        Exit Sub


'Error handler
ErrorHandler:
    'Show error details for the corresponding error code
    MsgBox "Error! " & Chr(10) & Error$(Err), vbInformation

End Sub

Private Sub Form_Load()

    'Center form on screen
    Me.Move (Screen.Width - Me.Width) \ 2, (Screen.Height -
    ➥Me.Height) \ 2

    'Initialize the image control
    Image1.Stretch = True
    Image1.BorderStyle = 1

    'Delete the captions from all label2 control array elements
    For Each element In Label2
        element.Caption = ""
    Next

    'Set the File1 list box pattern property to show only bitmap files
    File1.Pattern = "*.bmp"

    Label1(0).Font.Underline = True

End Sub
```

Enter this code into the appropriate events of the form module and the form's controls and run the project. Select any bitmap image file from the file list box. The image will be displayed inside the image control and all the bitmap image information will be shown. Note that the file list box will show only files with the .BMP extension because its `Pattern` property is set to *.BMP in the code.

Analysis

By knowing the various attributes of the bitmap image, you can draw or process any bitmap image through your code without the need to use a picture box or image control. For example, you can draw the bitmap dithered or inverted or even with effects on your form or on a picture box by writing the appropriate code. You can also read the bitmap file, convert the bitmap as needed, and save it to the file or to a new file without using any image controls.

The code demonstrates how you can retrieve the information of a bitmap image from the image file headers through the use of BITMAPINFOHEADER and BITMAPFILEHEADER type-defined variables. Actually, only the BITMAPINFOHEADER variable is required and is used to retrieve the image information. You read the information from the bitmap file by opening the file in binary mode as you normally open any other file and reading the two file headers. There is no need to load the bitmap into a picture box to get its information.

The sample project BMPINFO.VBP on the CD-ROM that accompanies this book demonstrates the functionality of the presented code.

6.8   ICON ANIMATION

by Then Nam Kheong

Description

Icons are usually listless and boring, but you can make them come alive whenever the mouse pointer passes over them. This creates attention and can delight your users.

Syntax

None.

Code Listing

```
'**********************************************
'* Submitted by Then Nam Kheong
'**********************************************
Private Sub Image1_MouseMove(Button As Integer, Shift As Integer,
➥ X As Single, Y As Single)
 Image2.Left = Image2.Left ñ 100   ' A simple animation
 Delay 0.1
 Image2.Left = Image2.Left + 100   'A simple animation
End Sub

In the declaration section of Form1, add this subroutine:

Sub Delay(secs!)
```

```
    Dim start!

    ' Get the current seconds since midnight
    start! = Timer

    ' Wait for seconds to elapse
    While (Timer < (start! + secs!))
    Wend

End Sub
```

Analysis

Two images are created for this example: Image1 and Image2. `Image1_MouseMove()` is used for our purpose. Whenever the mouse pointer is over Image1 (that is, the icon), it will activate this routine. Load an image (usually an icon from the \icons directory) in both Image1 and Image2 before you continue.

This routine is fairly simple. The subroutine `Image1_MouseMove()` is activated whenever the mouse pointer is over the icons. I have added a simple animation to illustrate as you will see when it runs.

```
Image2.Left = Image2.Left ñ 100   ' A simple animation
Delay 0.1
Image2.Left = Image2.Left + 100   'A simple animation
```

The following routine is used to slow down the animation. Another function similar to this is the `Sleep()` function. See section 6.16, "Kaleidoscope," for the use of this function.

```
Delay 0.1
```

You can add more animation to this routine, but note that too much can cause some problems during run-time, so make your icon animation simple like I did. Of course, you can add some text in `tooltiptext` under "Properties" for elaborate explanations of your icons (for VB5 only).

6.9   STARFIELD SIMULATIONS

by Then Nam Kheong

Description

Visual Basic has the capability to create 3D images. One example of 3D is the starfield simulation, similar to the Windows 95 screen saver. It uses a 3D algorithm, explained later in this section.

Syntax

None.

Code Listing

```
'**********************************************
'* Submitted by Then Nam Kheong
'**********************************************
(Declarations)

Private Type stars          ' declare a user type stars
 x As Double
 y As Double
 z As Double
End Type


Const maxstar = 300     ' We will have 300 stars in the screen. Customizable
➡ to any amount of stars
Dim star(maxstar) As stars     ' Recording of the stars position, used in
➡ calculation of nstars() position
Dim ostar(maxstar) As stars     ' Recording of the stars drawn before, used
➡ in deleting "old" stars
Dim nstar(maxstar) As stars     ' Recording of the newly calculated stars,
➡ used in drawing the stars to screen
Dim Speed              ' Determines how fast the stars will travel

Private Sub Form_Load()
Randomize              ' Randomizing all numbers
ScaleMode = 3
BackColor = QBColor(0)     ' Make sure that the background is black in color,
➡ because the star is white in color
ScaleWidth = 320
ScaleHeight = 200
Speed = 4                      'Determines how fast the stars will travel

For i = 1 To maxstar      'Initalises the variables
    star(i).x = Rnd * ScaleWidth - 160
    star(i).y = Rnd * ScaleHeight - 100
    star(i).z = i
Next
Timer1.Interval = 10     'Sets the timer and thus starts the motion
End Sub


Private Sub Timer1_Timer()
colour = QBColor(15)     ' color of the stars are white

For f = 1 To maxstar      'Draws the stars
 PSet (ostar(f).x, ostar(f).y), 0
 PSet (nstar(f).x, nstar(f).y), colour
Next
```

```
For e = 1 To maxstar      'Calculates the next position of each star
    If star(e).z < 22 Then
      star(e).z = maxstar
    Else
      star(e).z = star(e).z - Speed
    End If
    div_x = (256 * star(e).x) / star(e).z
    div_y = (256 * star(e).y) / star(e).z
    ostar(e).x = nstar(e).x    ' The last position of each star is recorded
    ➥ in ostar() for deleting
    ostar(e).y = nstar(e).y
    nstar(e).x = div_x + 160     ' The newly calculated star position is
    ➥ recorded in nstar() for drawing
    nstar(e).y = div_y + 100
Next
End Sub
```

Analysis

How the starfield works is quite simple. To understand the 3D concept, note that the x and y values are the x and y axis you would see on a graph. The z coordinate is the third dimension, pointing toward or away from you. Now think of each star as having an x, y, and z coordinate. As the star moves toward you, the z value of the stars decreases. In easier terms, as the z value decreases the stars become closer to you. Thus, by following this algorithm you will have the effect of stars on the x and y scale passing by you in a 3D manner. Note that the middle of the screen has the coordinates of 0,0,0. Here, no stars are created.

To code this, the program starts creating a data type called Stars, with data members x, y, and z. The x value is randomly selected between –160 and 160, and the y value is selected between –100 and 100. Each z value is assigned to each star sequentially so that the stars look spread out on the screen.

It is my habit to create the screen 320×200 pixels in size because I am more comfortable with it. You can create a different screen size but note that as you create a different screen size, the x and y value are randomly selected by half the screen value (that is, in a 320 pixel screen size, the x value selection range is 320/2=160).

`Timer1_Timer()` is where all the action starts:

1. Create the 3D coordinates by converting them to 2D coordinates. This is done by dividing the x and y value by z.
2. Clear away the old stars using the last coordinates.
3. Draw the new star coordinates according to the calculated value in step 1.
4. If the star's z value has become negative, place it back at the beginning so that it will come out again.

That's it! Now that you know how to create a basic starfield, there are many things you can do with it. You can make the stars move away from you or move to the left or right. What can a starfield do for an application? How about creating a menu or dialog box with the starfield as a background? Many ideas can come out of this little effect—have fun with it.

6.10 CARTOON ANIMATIONS

by Then Nam Kheong

Description

If you think it is not possible to create cartoon-like animations in VB, the following example will prove you wrong. You will realize how easy it is to create a simple and yet sophisticated animation.

Syntax

None.

Code Listing

```
'***********************************************
'* Submitted by Then Nam Kheong
'***********************************************
Private Sub Timer1_Timer()
Static idx As Integer, Counter As Integer
idx = (idx + 1) Mod 6      '6 Frames to work with.
If idx = 0 Then idx = 1    'Imagelist doesn't give me Index 0, so I
➡ have to make idx=0 to idx=1
Picture1.Picture = ImageList1.ListImages(idx).Picture
Label1.Left = Label1.Left - 100
Counter = Counter + 1
If Counter >= 20 Then      'When timer event was called 20 times, Label2 is
➡ activated
 Label2.Visible = True
 Label2.Left = Label2.Left + 100
End If
If Label2.Left > Form1.Width Then Timer1.Enabled = False
End Sub
```

Analysis

To start this example, you will have to place a Timer control, Imagelist control, two Label controls, and a PictureBox control. Load the Imagelist control with the images and make the `Label2` visible property `False`. Type some text in both labels and finish with the code in the `Timer` event, and you can start.

The animation relies on the Timer control, where all the actions begin. You can think of each `Timer` event as a "move": What is the next number? Which picture is to be displayed? These questions can be answered every time the program calls for the `Timer` event.

What makes the animation? The secret lies in this algorithm:

```
idx = (idx + 1) Mod 6
```

Basically, this algorithm cycles through a range of numbers, in this case numbers 0 to 5. Based on the number, the program will load the appropriate image into the PictureBox control. Thus, the algorithm is actually looping through the images to create the visual effect that the animation is constantly moving. To see the numbers running in series, type `Debug.Print idx` to see the results of `idx`. Note that if you have six images to display you will `Mod 6`, if you have three images, you will `Mod 3`.

The first part of the animation begins with a tiger running with a text scrolling from right to left. At a certain point in the animation, the program will display Label2, scrolling from left to right. When Label2 has finished, the program will disable the timer.

6.11 MCI AND sndPlaySound LAYERING

by Then Nam Kheong

Description

The Windows environment can play many sound and music files, of which .WAV and .MID are two of the most common. Windows provides a way to play .WAV files by using the Windows API `sndPlaySound()` or MCI control.

However, if you want to layer sounds (that is, play two sounds simultaneously), you can't do so by using only `sndPlaySound` or the MCI control. You can't use the WaveMix library, supplied by Microsoft, because it is too code-intensive. So what can you do? Many programmers want to layer sound and music together, so I combined both the `sndPlaySound` function and the MCI control to create that idea. It is easier to code, as you will see later.

Definitely, there are limitations. You can layer a sound file only with a music file—you can't layer sound with sound or music with music.

Syntax

None.

Code Listing

```
'**********************************************
'* Submitted by Then Nam Kheong
'**********************************************
(In Module file)
Public Const SND_SYNC = &H0              ' Don't return to control until
➡ sound ends(This is the default)
Public Const SND_ASYNC = &H1        ' Return to control after sound starts
Public Const SND_NODEFAULT = &H2    ' If file not found, do not play default
➡ sound
```

continues

```
Public Const SND_MEMORY = &H4          ' Play sound loaded in memory
Public Const SND_LOOP = &H8              ' Loop sound
Public Const SND_NOSTOP = &H10         ' Don't stop this sound to play another

Public SoundString As String     'Global variable so that
➥all procedure can access
Public PlayLoop As Boolean

Declare Function sndPlaySound Lib "winmm.dll" Alias "sndPlaySoundA" (ByVal
➥ lpszSoundName As String, ByVal uFlags As Long) As Long

(In Form1)
Private Sub Command1_Click()
   RetVal = sndPlaySound(dogsound, SND_MEMORY Or SND_ASYNC)

End Sub

Private Sub Command2_Click()
   MMControl1.Command = "Play"
   PlayLoop = False
End Sub

Private Sub Command3_Click()
   MMControl1.Command = "Play"
   PlayLoop = True
End Sub

Private Sub Command4_Click()
   MMControl1.Command = "Stop"
   PlayLoop = False
   MMControl1.Command = "Seek" 'Goes back to the beginning
End Sub

Private Sub Form_Load()
   dogsound = StrConv(LoadResData(101, "SOUND"), vbUnicode)
   MMControl1.filename = App.Path + "\cat.mid"
   MMControl1.DeviceType = "Sequencer"
   MMControl1.Command = "Open"
End Sub

Private Sub MMControl1_StatusUpdate()
   If MMControl1.Mode = mciModeStop And PlayLoop Then

       MMControl1.Command = "Seek"
       MMControl1.Command = "Play"
   End If
End Sub
```

Analysis

To begin, you must place an MCI control in the form. If you can't find one, go to Project, Components and click Microsoft Multimedia Control 5.0.

Now look at the sndPlaySound function.

The sndPlaySound Function

The following constants are declared for the purpose of using sndPlaySound:

```
Public Const SND_SYNC = &H0                    ' Don't return to control until
➥ sound ends(This is the default)
Public Const SND_ASYNC = &H1              ' Return to control after sound starts
Public Const SND_NODEFAULT = &H2     ' If file not found, do not play default
➥ sound
Public Const SND_MEMORY = &H4            ' Play sound loaded in memory
Public Const SND_LOOP = &H8                  ' Loop sound
Public Const SND_NOSTOP = &H10           ' Don't stop this sound to play another
```

The usage of sndPlaySound is as follows:

```
Results=sndPlaySound("C:\WINDOWS\Media\The Microsoft Sound.wav",
➥ SND_ASYNC Or SND_NODEFAULT)
```

The first parameter is clear. The second parameter sets the flag. Using SND_ASYNC means that the function will play sound and then return the control to the program. If you use SND_LOOP, the function will loop the sound.

You might be tempted to combine both SND_LOOP and SND_ASYNC in order to create a continuous background sound effect, but this will create a situation in which the sound will loop forever! Thus, you will need another function called sndStopSound to stop the sound.

```
Declare Function sndStopSound Lib "winmm.dll" Alias "sndPlaySoundA"
➥ (ByVal ANull As Long, ByVal Flags As Integer) As Integer
```

To stop the sound, place a 0 value in both parameters:

```
results= sndStopSound(0,0)
```

Soon you might realize that playing wave files might be slow because you will need to load the files, which can take quite some time. Thus you might need to preload them into memory first. I would recommend that you load the .WAV files into the resource file and load the .WAV as a resource.

```
SoundString = StrConv(LoadResData(101, "SOUND"), vbUnicode)
```

The preceding LoadResData function will load the .WAV file into the SoundString variable. As such, the file is loaded into memory. Next, activate the sound by using the sndPlaySound function with the SND_MEMORY flag:

```
RetVal = sndPlaySound(SoundString, SND_MEMORY Or SND_ASYNC)
```

You will usually load the .WAV file into memory at the beginning of the program and activate the sound in the later part of the program. Note, however, that you cannot load more than 64KB of .WAV file into memory because the file has been loaded into a string variable. Thus, it is better to keep the wave file short. A wave file that produces sound for about one second is safe.

The MCI Control

To be able to use the MCI control, you must place the control into the form. Next, the following code is placed in Form1_Load():

```
MMControl1.filename = App.Path + "\cat.mid"
MMControl1.DeviceType = "Sequencer"
MMControl1.Command = "Open"
```

This code loads the file into the control, giving the control a sequencer type. It then opens the file, ready to play.

The second button will play the music by using the Play command:

```
MMControl1.Command = "Play"
```

The third button stops the playing. However, when you stop the music, the control pointer will point to the spot where you stop the music. If you play the music again, it will continue from where it stopped. Thus, to rewind it, use the Seek command:

```
MMControl1.Command = "Stop"
MMControl1.Command = "Seek"                'Goes back to the beginning
```

MMControl1_StatusUpdate is where it will check for any update. When the control plays, stops, seeks, opens, and so on, it will activate this routine. Here we will check whether the user has clicked looping music, which sets the variable PlayLoop to True. Here the program will check whether the music has stopped and is set to PlayLoop. If so, it will Seek to the beginning and play again:

```
Private Sub MMControl1_StatusUpdate()
  If MMControl1.Mode = mciModeStop And PlayLoop Then
    MMControl1.Command = "Seek"
    MMControl1.Command = "Play"
  End If
End Sub
```

Run the sample program and enjoy the sound and music.

6.12   LOADING RESOURCES FROM A .RES FILE

by Then Nam Kheong

Description

Sometimes when you distribute your application you will find some files, such as .WAV or .BMP, hanging in the directory. Definitely, you don't want the user to use your artwork. Thus, it is best to keep all the files in a resource file, which has a .RES extension. Programmers keep all these files in .RES for the following reasons:

- Users will not be able to use your files unless they have the utilities to extract the files.
- The files are compacted into a single file, saving space.
- The lesser files are listed in the directory, giving the user the impression that you know how to keep your stuff.

In this section you will use the Resource Editor, an add-in program provided by Microsoft. The old method of writing out .RC files and then compiling them might not work well in VB (I tried it; it gave me nightmares). Thus, I strongly recommend that you go to Microsoft's Owner's Area and get a copy of the program. This program is free for all registered users of VB5.

The Microsoft Owner's Area's address is `http://www.microsoft.com/vstudio/owner/default.asp`.

Syntax

`LoadResData(index, format)`

Loads the data of several possible types from a resource (.RES) file.

`LoadResPicture(index, format)`

Loads a bitmap, icon, or cursor from a resource (.RES) file.

`LoadResString(index)`

Loads a string from a resource (.RES) file.

Please see the Visual Basic 5.0 Help file for a detailed explanation of the syntax.

Code Listing

```
'**********************************************
'* Submitted by THEN NAM KHEONG
'**********************************************
(In Module file)

Public Const SND_MEMORY = &H4     ' To be used in sndPlaySound
Public Const SND_ASYNC = &H1

Public dogsound As String     'Global variable so that all procedure can access

Declare Function sndPlaySound Lib "winmm.dll" Alias "sndPlaySoundA" (ByVal
➥ lpszSoundName As String, ByVal uFlags As Long) As Long
(In Form1)
Private Sub Command1_Click()
    dogsound = StrConv(LoadResData(101, "SOUND"), vbUnicode)
```

continues

```
        retval = sndPlaySound(dogsound, SND_MEMORY Or SND_ASYNC)
End Sub


Private Sub Command2_Click()
    Form1.MouseIcon = LoadResPicture(101, vbResCursor)
    Form1.MousePointer = 99
End Sub

Private Sub Command3_Click()
    Form1.Icon = LoadResPicture(101, vbResIcon)
End Sub

Private Sub Command4_Click()
    Label1.Caption = LoadResString(101)
End Sub

Private Sub Command5_Click()
    Picture1.Picture = LoadResPicture(101, vbResBitmap)

End Sub
```

Analysis

In this example, you will learn how to load .WAV, .BMP, .ICO, and .CUR files, and strings from .RES files. Before you proceed to learn how to code it, let me turn your attention to using the Resource Editor.

The Resource Editor

The Resource Editor is available in the Owner's Area located on Microsoft's Web site. It exists as an .EXE setup program—just run the program and follow the installation instructions. After you have installed the program, run VB5 and you will find a small icon at the top-right corner of the programming environment.

The Resource Editor environment is presented with a fixed toolbar on top and a tree list view with Resource File as the head of the tree.

To load a resource (such as a bitmap or cursor), click the appropriate button on the toolbar. You are presented with a dialog box prompting you to click a file to load as a resource. Click the file you want and select Open. The tree list will extend out with the newly loaded icon.

Beside the icon is the number 101, which is the resource ID. An ID automatically will be assigned to a resource when a resource is loaded. This ID is important because the functions will need to know which ID to look for in order to load the resource. It is like looking up a person's social security code. To change the ID, double-click the ID number and you are presented with Edit Properties dialog box. Type your new ID and click OK to save it.

After you have finished loading all the resources you want, remember to click Save, otherwise the .RES will not be saved. In your Project Explorer, you will find an additional item called Related Document, which contains the .RES file. If the file is not there, right-click the Project Explorer and select Add, Resource File.

That is all for using the Resource Editor. Now move on to the code itself.

This program must have the following public data in the module file so that it can be accessed by the sndPlaySound function:

```
Public Const SND_MEMORY = &H4    ' To be used in sndPlaySound
Public Const SND_ASYNC = &H1
Public dogsound As String    'Global variable so that all procedure can access

Declare Function sndPlaySound Lib "winmm.dll" Alias "sndPlaySoundA"
➥ (ByVal lpszSoundName As String, ByVal uFlags As Long) As Long
```

The preceding constants and declared functions are used to demonstrate how to load a .WAV file. To study more on playing .WAV files, please refer to section 6.11, "MCI and sndPlaySound Layering."

On the form itself are five buttons to demonstrate loading cursors, icons, bitmap, sounds, and strings.

The first button demonstrates the loading of .WAV. The explanation of playing .WAV can be found in section 6.11.

```
Private Sub Command1_Click()
    dogsound = StrConv(LoadResData(101, "SOUND"), vbUnicode)
    retval = sndPlaySound(dogsound, SND_MEMORY Or SND_ASYNC)
End Sub
```

The next three buttons demonstrate how to load a mouse cursor, icon, and bitmap by using the LoadResPicture() function. When you load a mouse icon, be sure to set the mouse pointer of Form1 to 99, which means that a custom icon has been specified by the MouseIcon property.

```
Form1.MouseIcon = LoadResPicture(101, vbResCursor)
Form1.MousePointer = 99
Form1.Icon = LoadResPicture(101, vbResIcon)
Picture1.Picture = LoadResPicture(101, vbResBitmap)
```

The last button demonstrates the loading of a string, which is easily done by specifying the ID:

```
Label1.Caption = LoadResString(101)
```

6.13 WALLPAPER (LOGO) ON AN MDI FORM

by Jesper Madsen

Description

This code provides two different ways to put a picture (logo) as wallpaper on an MDI form. The first function stretches the picture to fit the MDI client area at all times, such as when it is resized. The second function centers your picture on the MDI client area at all times. For the latter it's possible to choose any color to be painted around your picture. For transparent effects you choose a color that is the same as the background on your picture, or make the background of your picture the same as the MDI client area. Normal color for the MDI client area is RGB(130,130,130). For the best result your picture should be the size you want when the MDI form is maximized.

Using one of the two functions in your own MDI application is simple. Just add two picture boxes to your MDI form. Draw them in the toolbar area so you won't have any trouble finding them. Then put your picture in picture1 and leave picture2 empty. Set the properties AutoRedraw = true and AutoSize = true for the two picture boxes. Finally, add the code to the MDI form.

Syntax

None.

Code Listing

```
'************************************************
'* Submitted by Jesper Madsen.
'************************************************

' ************** Put these declarations in a module **************
Public Declare Function StretchBlt Lib "gdi32" (ByVal hdc As Long,
➥ByVal x As Long, ByVal y As Long, ByVal nWidth As Long,
➥ByVal nHeight As Long, ByVal hSrcDC As Long, ByVal xSrc As Long,
➥ByVal ySrc As Long, ByVal nSrcWidth As Long, ByVal nSrcHeight As Long,
➥ByVal dwRop As Long) As Long
Public Declare Function GetWindowRect Lib "user32" (ByVal hwnd As Long,
➥ lpRect As RECT) As Long
Public Declare Function FindWindowEx Lib "user32" Alias "FindWindowExA"
➥ (ByVal hWnd1 As Long, ByVal hWnd2 As Long, ByVal lpsz1 As String,
➥ ByVal lpsz2 As String) As Long
Public Declare Function FillRect Lib "user32" (ByVal hdc As Long,
➥ lpRect As RECT, ByVal hBrush As Long) As Long
Public Declare Function SelectObject Lib "gdi32" (ByVal hdc As Long,
➥ ByVal hObject As Long) As Long
Public Declare Function GetObject Lib "gdi32" Alias "GetObjectA"
➥ (ByVal hObject As Long, ByVal nCount As Long, lpObject As Any) As Long
Public Declare Function CreateSolidBrush Lib "gdi32" (ByVal crColor As Long)
➥ As Long
Public Declare Function DeleteObject Lib "gdi32" (ByVal hObject As Long)
➥ As Long
Public Declare Function SetStretchBltMode Lib "gdi32" (ByVal hdc As Long,
➥ ByVal nStretchMode As Long) As Long


Type BITMAP
        bmType As Long
        bmWidth As Long
        bmHeight As Long
        bmWidthBytes As Long
        bmPlanes As Integer
        bmBitsPixel As Integer
        bmBits As Long
```

```
End Type

Type RECT
        Left As Long
        Top As Long
        Right As Long
        Bottom As Long
End Type

Public Const STRETCH_ANDSCANS = 1     ' BlackOnWhite
Public Const STRETCH_ORSCANS = 2      ' WhiteOnBlack
Public Const STRETCH_DELETESCANS = 3 ' ColorOnColor
' **************************************************

' ************ Put this in your MDI form code **************

Private Sub MDIForm_Load()
' Other initialization

  Picture2.Left = 0
  Picture2.Top = 0
  Picture1.Left = 0
  Picture1.Top = 0
  Picture1.ScaleMode = vbPixels
End Sub


Private Sub MDIForm_Resize()
'   ResizeFitWallpaper
'     OR
  ResizeCenterWallpaper
End Sub


Public Sub ResizeFitWallpaper()
  Dim Rc As RECT

' Find and get the size of the client area
  hMDIClientwnd& = FindWindowEx(Me.hwnd, 0, "MDIClient", vbNullString)
  GetWindowRect hMDIClientwnd&, Rc

  iWidth% = Rc.Right - Rc.Left  ' = rc.Width
  iHeight% = Rc.Bottom - Rc.Top ' = rc.Height

  Picture2.Width = iWidth% * Screen.TwipsPerPixelX
  Picture2.Height = iHeight% * Screen.TwipsPerPixelY
' Set the Stretch mode that gives the best results for your picture
  SetStretchBltMode Picture2.hdc, STRETCH_DELETESCANS
' Stretch Picture to fit size of the MDI Client area
  StretchBlt Picture2.hdc, 0, 0, iWidth%, iHeight%, Picture1.hdc, 0, 0, _
                      Picture1.ScaleWidth, Picture1.ScaleHeight, vbSrcCopy
```

continues

```
    Me.Picture = Picture2.Image ' Set the new Picture
End Sub


Public Sub ResizeCenterWallpaper()
    Dim Rc As RECT
    Dim bmWallpaper As BITMAP
    Dim iSX As Integer, iSY As Integer, iX As Integer
    Dim iY As Integer, iWidth As Integer, iHeight As Integer
    Dim dAspect As Double

' Find and get the size of the client area
    hMDIClientwnd& = FindWindowEx(Me.hwnd, 0, "MDIClient", vbNullString)
    GetWindowRect hMDIClientwnd&, Rc
    hdc& = Picture2.hdc

    iWidth = (Rc.Right - Rc.Left) ' = rc.Width
    iHeight = (Rc.Bottom - Rc.Top) ' = rc.Height

    Picture2.Width = iWidth * Screen.TwipsPerPixelX
    Picture2.Height = iHeight * Screen.TwipsPerPixelY
' Get the size of the currently displayed picture
    GetObject Picture1.Image, 24, bmWallpaper

    iSX = bmWallpaper.bmWidth ' The current width of the picture
    iSY = bmWallpaper.bmHeight ' The current height of the picture
' dAspect will make the picture shrink faster when it's to big to fit the
➡ client area.
    dAspect = iSX / iSY

    If (iSX > iWidth) Then
      iSX = iWidth
      iSY = iWidth / dAspect ' Start squeezing the height
    End If

    If (iSY > iHeight) Then
      iSX = iHeight * dAspect ' Start squeezing the width
      iSY = iHeight
    End If

    iX = ((iWidth - iSX) / 2)  ' Left of wallpaper picture
    iY = ((iHeight - iSY) / 2) ' Top of wallpaper picture

    hBrush& = CreateSolidBrush(RGB(130, 130, 130)) ' Select a background color
    hOldBrush& = SelectObject(hdc&, hBrush&) ' Replace the old brush with the
➡ new one

' When running from VB, there can be some side effects where slower machines
➡ may not be able to
' paint fast enough. The effect should disappear running  your app. outside VB.

' Fill Top of wallpaper
```

```
        Rc.Left = 0
        Rc.Top = 0
        Rc.Right = iWidth
        Rc.Bottom = iY
        FillRect hdc&, Rc, hBrush&

    ' Fill Bottom of wallpaper
        Rc.Left = 0
        Rc.Top = iY + iSY
        Rc.Right = iWidth
        Rc.Bottom = iHeight
        FillRect hdc&, Rc, hBrush&

    ' Fill Left of wallpaper
        Rc.Left = 0
        Rc.Top = iY
        Rc.Right = iX
        Rc.Bottom = iY + iSY
        FillRect hdc&, Rc, hBrush&

    ' Fill Right of wallpaper
        Rc.Left = iX + iSX
        Rc.Top = iY
        Rc.Right = iWidth
        Rc.Bottom = iY + iSY
        FillRect hdc&, Rc, hBrush&

        SelectObject hdc&, hOldBrush& ' Reset Brush
        DeleteObject hBrush& ' Delete the created brush

    ' Set the Stretch mode that gives the best results for your picture
        SetStretchBltMode Picture2.hdc, STRETCH_DELETESCANS
    ' Position and/or stretch the picture to the new coordinates.
        StretchBlt hdc&, iX, iY, iSX, iSY, Picture1.hdc, 0, 0, _
                            bmWallpaper.bmWidth, bmWallpaper.bmHeight, vbSrcCopy

        Me.Picture = Picture2.Image ' Set the new Picture
    End Sub
```

Analysis

The first function (`ResizeFitWallpaper`) starts by finding and getting the size of the MDI client area. You can use the API call `GetClientRect` instead, but remember to subtract the toolbar height from the MDI client area. The client area is then assigned to the destination picture box, before the stretch is performed. The stretch mode that is set before the actual stretch depends on your picture color schemes. The following are the modes:

■ STRETCH_ANDSCANS, also called `BlackOnWhite`—Performs a Boolean AND operation using the color values for the eliminated and existing pixels. If the bitmap is a monochrome bitmap, this mode preserves black pixels at the expense of white pixels.

■ STRETCH_ORSCANS, also called WhiteOnBlack—Performs a Boolean OR operation using the color values for the eliminated and existing pixels. If the bitmap is a monochrome bitmap, this mode preserves white pixels at the expense of black pixels.

■ STRETCH_DELETESCANS, also called ColorOnColor—Deletes the pixels. This mode deletes all eliminated lines of pixels without trying to preserve their information.

Set the stretch mode that gives the best results for your picture. After the stretch, the newly stretched picture is then assigned to the MDI form's picture property.

The second function (ResizeCenterWallpaper) differs from the first in two ways. First, it centers the picture in the MDI client area in its original size. Second, it doesn't start the stretch before the picture is bigger than the MDI client area. The API call FillRect is used to fill the area around your picture, with a color of your choice. Another difference is that when the MDI form is resized from one side, the picture is automatically sized from the other side as well. This makes the picture look "good" at all times.

6.14   PRINTING 3D TEXT

by Then Nam Kheong

Description

The PrintText function prints 3D text on the screen in a specified location. It looks nice on the screen when you are working with graphics or games programming. VB provides only the basic printing of text on the form. You can, however, use this shortfall to print 3D text just by using font size, font color, and text location.

Syntax

PrintText Form,Text,X,Y

Part	Description
Form	Required. Specifies the form on which the text will be displayed.
Text	Required. A string expression that specifies the text to be displayed.
X	Required. An integer that specifies the x coordinate of the text.
Y	Required. An integer that specifies the y coordinate of the text.

Code Listing

```
'**********************************************
'* Submitted by THEN NAM KHEONG
'**********************************************
```

```
Public Sub PrintText(frm As Form, Text As String, X As Integer, Y As Integer)
    frm.ForeColor = RGB(32, 32, 32) 'Color for the shadow
    frm.Font.Name = "Arial"
    frm.Font.Size = 48
    frm.CurrentX = X                     ' Positioning of the text, add numbers here
    frm.CurrentY = Y                     ' to make shadows
    frm.Print Text
    frm.ForeColor = vbYellow             'forecolor changed to yellow
    frm.CurrentX = X - 20
    frm.CurrentY = Y - 30
    frm.Print Text
    End Sub

Private Sub Form_Load()
 Form1.Show
 PrintText Me, "Hello!", 150, 150
End Sub
```

Analysis

The routine simply uses Visual Basic's `Print` method and starts shifting the printing position. First, you must define the background color, font, size, and position. Then you must print the text using the `Print` method:

```
frm.ForeColor = RGB(32, 32, 32) 'Color for the shadow
frm.Font.Name = "Arial"
frm.Font.Size = 48
frm.CurrentX = X                     ' Positioning of the text, add numbers here
frm.CurrentY = Y                     ' to make shadows
frm.Print Text
```

Next change the color to yellow, shifting the position to the upper-left portion of the form:

```
frm.ForeColor = vbYellow  'forecolor changed to yellow, or any color you wish
frm.CurrentX = X - 20
frm.CurrentY = Y - 30
frm.Print Text
```

Next you must activate it by using the syntax mentioned earlier. For this example, show the form and print Hello! in the defined x and y position:

```
Form1.Show
PrintText Me, "Hello!", 150, 150
```

Remember, this routine simply makes repeated calls to the `Print` method with the text's position moved slightly. This is the part where your creativity works. You can modify this function to make text with shadows by printing black text, and then printing the same text again in another color in the upper-left position.

6.15   FLASHING WINDOWS

by Then Nam Kheong

Description

The FlashWindows routine will make the title bar of a window flash, which is a good attention grabber. It is an API routine that is very useful for programs that must grab a user's attention, such as an anti-virus program or error trapping.

Syntax

```
RetVal=FlashWindow hWnd,bInvert
```

Part	Description
hWnd	Required. The name of the window handle.
bInvert	Required. This is to be set True.

Code Listing

```
'**********************************************
'* Submitted by NAME HERE
'**********************************************
(In Module file)
Declare Function FlashWindow Lib "user32" (ByVal hwnd As Long,
➥ ByVal bInvert As Long) As Long

(In Form1)
Private Sub Timer1_Timer()
 RetVal = FlashWindow(Me.hwnd, True)
End Sub
```

Analysis

This routine uses the Timer control. The FlashWindow function will flash only once, so to keep it going you must call this API in a Timer event. The speed of the flash depends on the Timer's interval. Setting the Interval property from 10–50 creates a faster flashing rate, whereas an interval of 200–300 makes a slow flashing rate.

Set the first parameter to the form you want to flash and set the second parameter to True.

```
RetVal = FlashWindow(Me.hwnd, True)
```

Note that you can flash only windows of a form, not a control. As far as I know, this API can be used only in forms.

What can you do with this routine? Remember the animated taskbar icon? You can combine both routines to form a super attention grabber.

6.16 KALEIDOSCOPE

by Then Nam Kheong

Description

A kaleidoscope can be a great screen saver idea, or it can provide a way to relieve stress from work by watching the lines fill up the entire screen.

Syntax

```
Sleep Milliseconds
```

Part	Description
Milliseconds	Required. Will pause the program by a number of milliseconds.

Code Listing

```
'********************************************
'* Submitted by THEN NAM KHEONG
'********************************************
(In Declaration Section)
Private Declare Sub Sleep Lib "kernel32" (ByVal dwMilliseconds As Long)

(In Form1)
Sub Timer1_Timer()
Dim X1 As Integer, X2 As Integer, X3 As Integer, X4 As Integer
Dim Y1 As Integer, Y2 As Integer, Y3 As Integer, Y4 As Integer
Dim StepX1 As Integer, StepX2 As Integer
Dim StepY1 As Integer, StepY2 As Integer
Dim MaxRandomX As Integer, MaxRandomY As Integer, times As Integer
Static LineCol As Long, TimesCol As Integer

Randomize                              'seed random number generator
MaxRandomX = ScaleWidth / 2                    'half width (starts at 0)
MaxRandomY = ScaleHeight / 2                    'half height (starts at 0)

TimesCol = TimesCol + 1
LineCol = RGB(Rnd * 255, Rnd * 255, Rnd * 255)   'Randomly sets the color
X1 = Rnd * MaxRandomX             'set X1 to a random (0 to max)
Y1 = Rnd * MaxRandomY             'ditto for Y1
```

continues

```
X2 = Rnd * MaxRandomX              'ditto for X2
Y2 = Rnd * MaxRandomY              'ditto for Y2

StepX1 = Rnd * 4 - 3              'set StepX1 to random (-2 to 2)
StepY1 = Rnd * 4 - 3              'ditto for StepY1
StepX2 = Rnd * 4 - 3              'ditto for StepX2
StepY2 = Rnd * 4 - 3              'ditto for StepY2

       For times = 1 To 80               'do 80 sets of lines

            X3 = ScaleWidth - X1              'calculate points for
            X4 = ScaleWidth - X2              '4 lines
            Y3 = ScaleHeight - Y1             '4 X values
            Y4 = ScaleHeight - Y2             '4 Y values

            Line (X1, Y1)-(X2, Y2), LineCol     'draw the lines
            Line (X3, Y1)-(X4, Y2), LineCol
            Line (X1, Y3)-(X2, Y4), LineCol
            Line (X3, Y3)-(X4, Y4), LineCol
            Sleep 0.8

            X1 = X1 + StepX1              'adjust with step value
            Y1 = Y1 + StepY1             'ditto
            X2 = X2 + StepX2             'ditto
            Y2 = Y2 + StepY2            'ditto
       Next
   End Sub
```

Analysis

The kaleidoscope is easy to create. First, you must load a `Sleep()` subroutine from Kernel32.dll. Next, create a `Timer` control in Form1. Set the following properties:

- `BackColor`—Any black color
- `Caption`—An empty string
- `ClipControls`—False
- `ControlBox`—False

Note that you must not set the `AutoRedraw` property to `True` or the effect of fanning out the lines will not be seen. You are now ready for the code. Look at the `Sleep` API routine.

```
Private Declare Sub Sleep Lib "kernel32" (ByVal dwMilliseconds As Long)
```

The `Sleep` routine is used in this way:

```
Sleep 0.8
```

This routine creates a slow, smooth fanning-out motion of lines being drawn with an interval of 0.8 milliseconds. As the number gets closer to zero, the lines are drawn faster. As the number gets closer to 1 or more, the lines are drawn slower. As a guideline, 1000 milliseconds is equal to one second.

Next, the entire preceding code is coded in `Timer1_Timer()`. The algorithm should be easily understood. However, note the following lines of code, which can be customized to enhance the display:

```
StepX1 = Rnd * 4 +1              'set StepX1 to random (-2 to 2)
StepY1 = Rnd * 4 +1              'ditto for StepY1
StepX2 = Rnd * 4 +1              'ditto for StepX2
StepY2 = Rnd * 4 +1              'ditto for StepY2
```

This code sees how far apart the lines are between each other. This code has them at +1. The larger the number, the further apart the lines are. If you use -1 or smaller, the lines are very packed together.

```
For times = 1 To 80             'do 80 sets of lines
        .
        .
        .
        .
        Next
```

The preceding code draws the number of lines, in this case 80. You can customize it to the number of lines to be drawn.

```
LineCol = RGB(Rnd * 255, Rnd * 255, Rnd * 255)   'Randomly sets the color
        .
        .
        .

Line (X1, Y1)-(X2, Y2), LineCol     'draw the lines
        .
        .
        .
```

The preceding code determines what color is to be displayed when the lines are being drawn. You can set different colors here. Also, you can set a gradient of color in the `Line` method by modifying the `LineCol` variable.

$$Chapter\ 7$$

FILE MANIPULATION

This chapter focuses on a very important part of Visual Basic programming, file access and manipulation. It includes functions for finding files, reading and saving files, zipping and unzipping files, and even how to split and reassemble them. This should give any programmer the tools required to build file access and manipulation into their applications quickly and easily.

7.1 READING AND WRITING INI FILES

by Kamal A. Mehdi

Description

It is often necessary to store some important information about your application on the user's system so that you can reconfigure your application each time it is started by retrieving these settings. For example, you might have some check boxes in your application that represent various options the user can change, and you want to save and then restore these option settings as last modified by the user the next time your application is launched. You can do this by creating an initialization (.INI) file in which you store the profiles and retrieve them when needed. You can also retrieve and modify some Windows settings by manipulating the different profiles stored in the WIN.INI and SYSTEM.INI files located under the Windows directory.

Profiles written to an INI file consist of three parts: the section name (or application name), the key name, and the key value. The format of the profile and organization of the different profiles within the initialization file is as follows:

```
[Section1 Name]
Key1 name= Key1 value
Key2 name= Key2 value
...
```

```
[Section2 Name]
Key1 name= Key1 value
Key2 name= Key2 value
...
```

The following example better clarifies the topic:

```
[Desktop]
Wallpaper=C:\WIN95\PLUS!.BMP
TileWallpaper=0
WallpaperStyle=0
Pattern=(None)
```

The section name in the example refers to the Windows desktop settings section. Each key refers to a particular setting for the desktop and stores its current value.

The following code listing demonstrates how to store and retrieve profiles to and from INI files in Visual Basic. It uses the `WritePrivateProfileString` API function to create a new profile or write to an existing profile. The `GetPrivateProfileString` API is used to retrieve the specific key value in a particular profile. Both 16-bit and 32-bit API functions are provided. Conditional compilation is also implemented so that the code can be run on both platforms without any modifications.

Syntax

```
RetVal= WritePrivateProfileString (lpApplicationName, lpKeyName, lpString,
➥ lpFileName)
```

```
RetVal= GetPrivateProfileString (lpApplicationName, lpKeyName, lpDefault,
➥ lpReturnedString, nSize, lpFileName)
```

Part	Description
RetVal	Required. A numeric expression that receives the value returned by the function. 1 is returned on success, 0 is returned on failure. Data type: Long.
lpApplicationName	Required. A string expression that specifies the section name under which the key name and value is to be written to or read from.
lpKeyName	Required. A string expression that specifies the key name from which the value is to be read from or written into. Data type: Variant.
lpString	Required. A string expression that specifies the value to be written to the specified key. Data type: Variant.
lpFileName	Required. A string expression that specifies the full path and name of the INI file.
lpDefault	Required. A string expression that specifies the default value for the specified key if the key cannot be found in the INI file.
lpReturnedString	Required. A string expression specifying the buffer that will receive the value read from the key. The buffer size must be 128 characters.
nSize	Required. A numeric expression that specifies the maximum number of characters (including the last null character) to be copied to the buffer. Data type: Long.

Modules and Controls Required

You will need the following modules and controls to build the sample project:

Module/Control	Description
Form1	A standard non-MDI Visual Basic form (.FRM) with the following properties set:
	`Caption = Read/Write INI Files`
	`BorderStyle = 1-Fixed Single`
	`MinButton = True`
Frame1	A frame control with the `Caption` property set to Read/Write Sample Profile Strings
Frame2	A frame control with the `Caption` property set to Read/Write Custom Profile Strings
Command1	A command button with the `Caption` property set to Write Profile Strings
Command2	A command button with the `Caption` property set to Read Profile Strings
Command3	A command button with the `Caption` property set to Write Profile Strings
Command4	A command button with the `Caption` property set to Read Profile Strings
Command5	A command button with the `Caption` property set to Browse
Command6	A command button with the `Caption` property set to Exit
List1	A list box control
Text1	A text box control
Text2	A text box control
Text3	A text box control
Text4	A text box control
Label1	A label control with the `Caption` property set to File Name:
Label2	A label control with the `Caption` property set to Section Name:
Label3	A label control with the `Caption` property set to Key Name:
Label4	A label control with the `Caption` property set to Key Value:
CommonDialog1	A common dialog control

Follow these steps to draw controls:

1. Start a new standard EXE project. `Form1` will be created by default. Set the form's `Height` and `Width` properties to approximatcly `3000` and `7700`, respectively, and set its `Caption`, `BorderStyle`, and `MinButton` properties as shown earlier in this section.

2. Draw `Frame1` at the left side of the form and adjust its size so that it covers almost half the form area. Set its `Caption` property as shown earlier.
3 . Draw `Command1` and `Command2` buttons inside `Frame1` at the bottom side of the frame and set their `Caption` properties as shown earlier.
4. Draw `List1` inside `Frame1` and adjust its size so that it fills the remaining area of the frame control.
5. Draw `Frame2` at the right side of the form and adjust its size so that it covers almost the other half of the form area. Set its `Caption` property as shown earlier.
6. Draw `Command3` and `Command4` buttons inside `Frame2` at the bottom of the frame. Set their `Caption` properties as shown earlier.
7. Draw the four label controls inside `Frame2` at the left side of the frame with `Label1` at the top, `Label2` and `Label3` in the middle, and `Label4` at the bottom. Set their `Caption` properties as shown earlier.
8. Draw the four text boxes inside `Frame2` at the middle, with `Text1` to the right of `Label1`, `Text2` to the right of `Label2`, `Text3` to the right of `Label3`, and `Text4` to the right of `Label4`. Adjust the width of all text boxes to about 1700.
9. Draw `Command5` inside `Frame2` to the left of `Text1` and set its `Caption` property as shown earlier.
10. Draw `Command6` under the bottom-right edge of `Frame2` and set its `Caption` property as shown earlier.
11. Draw the `CommonDialog1` common dialog control anywhere on the form.

Note

The common dialog control is not shown on the toolbox by default. You can add it to the toolbox by selecting the Components submenu from the Project menu and adding the control.

Code Listing

```
'API declarations in the general-declarations section of the form
'Platform-dependent conditional compilation
#If Win32 Then
    '32-bit API declarations for read/write INI file profiles
    Private Declare Function GetPrivateProfileString Lib "kernel32" Alias _
            "GetPrivateProfileStringA" (ByVal lpApplicationName As String, _
            ByVal lpKeyName As Any, ByVal lpDefault As String, _
            ByVal lpReturnedString As String, ByVal nSize As Long, _
            ByVal lpFileName As String) As Long

    Private Declare Function WritePrivateProfileString Lib "kernel32" Alias _
            "WritePrivateProfileStringA" (ByVal lpApplicationName As String, _
            ByVal lpKeyName As Any, ByVal lpString As Any, _
            ByVal lpFileName As String) As Long

#Else
    '16-bit API declarations
    Private Declare Function GetPrivateProfileString Lib "Kernel" _
            (ByVal lpApplicationName As String, lpKeyName As Any, _
            ByVal lpDefault As String, ByVal lpReturnedString As String, _
            ByVal nSize As Integer, ByVal lpFileName As String) As Integer
```

```
        Private Declare Function WritePrivateProfileString Lib "Kernel" _
                (ByVal lpApplicationName As String, lpKeyName As Any, _
                 lpString As Any, ByVal lplFileName As String) As Integer
#End If

Private Sub Command1_Click()

        'Declare variables
        Dim RetVal As Long
        Dim X As Integer, Y As Integer

        'Specify the file name (sample file)
        lpFileName$ = App.Path & "\Myfile.ini"

        'Specify the default key value if not specified
        lpDefault$ = ""

        'Enter a loop to write multiple sections and keys
        For X = 1 To 2

            'Specify the section name to write
            lpAppName$ = "MySection" & CStr(X)

            For Y = 1 To 3

                'Specify the key name to write
                lpKeyName$ = "MyKey" & CStr(X) & "-" & CStr(Y)

                'Specify the new value to write to the key
                WriteValue$ = "Hello " & CStr(X) & "-" & CStr(Y)

                RetVal = WritePrivateProfileString(lpAppName$, lpKeyName$,
                ➥ WriteValue$, lpFileName$)

                'On success, 1 must be returned. If not, display a message
                If RetVal < 1 Then MsgBox "An error occured while writing
                ➥ profile!", vbInformation

            Next Y

        Next X

End Sub

Private Sub Command2_Click()

        'Declare variables
        Dim RetVal As Long
        Dim X As Integer, Y As Integer

        'Clear the list box
```

continues

```
    List1.Clear

    lpDefault$ = ""

    'Specify the string variable that will receive the key value
    'We must also specify its size
    ReturnValue$ = Space$(128)
    Size& = Len(ReturnValue$)      'Must be short integer in 16-bit platforms

    'Specify the file name (the sample file)
    lpFileName$ = App.Path & "\Myfile.ini"

    'Enter a loop to read all the sections and keys previously written
    For X = 1 To 2

        'Specify the section name
        lpAppName$ = "MySection" & CStr(X)

        'Add it to the list
        List1.AddItem lpAppName$

        For Y = 1 To 3

            'Specify the key name
            lpKeyName$ = "MyKey" & CStr(X) & "-" & CStr(Y)

            'Call the function to read the key value
            RetVal = GetPrivateProfileString(lpAppName$, lpKeyName$,
            ➥ lpDefault$, ReturnValue$, Size&, lpFileName$)

            'On success, 1 must be returned. If not, display a message
            If RetVal < 1 Then MsgBox "An error occured while reading
            ➥profile!", vbInformation

            'Add the key name and value to the list
            List1.AddItem "       " & lpKeyName$ & "= " & ReturnValue$

        Next Y

    Next X

End Sub

Private Sub Command3_Click()

    'Declare variables
    Dim RetVal As Long
    Dim Answer As String

    'Specify the INI file name
    lpFileName$ = Text1.Text
```

```
    'Specify the default value to write if non is specified
    lpDefault$ = ""

    'Specify the section name
    lpAppName$ = Text2.Text

    'Specify the key name
    lpKeyName$ = Text3.Text

    'Specify the value to write to the key
    WriteValue$ = Text4.Text

    'Warn the user if the INI file is not the sample file
    If lpFileName$ <> App.Path & "\Myfile.ini" Then
        Answer = MsgBox("Are you sure you want to write to the file " &
        ➥ lpFileName$, vbYesNo)
        If Answer = 7 Then Exit Sub
    End If

    'Call the function to write the key value
    RetVal = WritePrivateProfileString(lpAppName$, lpKeyName$, WriteValue$,
    ➥ lpFileName$)

    'On success, 1 must be returned. If not, display a message
    If RetVal < 1 Then MsgBox "An error occurred while writing profile!",
    ➥ vbInformation

End Sub

Private Sub Command4_Click()

    'Declare variables
    Dim RetVal As Long

    'Specify the INI file name
    lpFileName$ = Text1.Text

    'Specify the default key value if not specified
    lpDefault$ = ""

    'Specify the name and size of the variable to receive the
    ➥returned key value
    ReturnValue$ = Space$(128)
    Size& = Len(ReturnValue$)        'Must be short integer in 16-bit platforms

    'Specify the section name
    lpAppName$ = Text2.Text

    'Specify the key name
    lpKeyName$ = Text3.Text

    'Call the function to read the key
```

continues

```
    RetVal = GetPrivateProfileString(lpAppName$, lpKeyName$, lpDefault$,
    ➥ ReturnValue$, Size&, lpFileName$)

    'On success, 1 must be returned. If not, display a message
    If RetVal < 1 Then MsgBox "An error occured while reading profile!",
    ➥ vbInformation

    'Show the retrieved key value
    Text4.Text = ReturnValue$

End Sub

Private Sub Command5_Click()

    'Initialize the common dialog properties and specify INI files
    'for the filter (will show only INI files)
    CommonDialog1.filename = ""
    CommonDialog1.Filter = "INI Files (*.INI)¦ *.ini"

    'Show the open dialog
    CommonDialog1.ShowOpen

    'Get the file name
    If CommonDialog1.filename <> "" Then Text1.Text = CommonDialog1.filename

End Sub

Private Sub Command6_Click()
    'Exit
    Unload Me
End Sub

Private Sub Form_Load()

    'Initialize
    Text2.Text = ""
    Text3.Text = ""
    Text4.Text = ""

    'Center form on the screen
    Me.Top = (Screen.Height - Me.Height) / 2
    Me.Left = (Screen.Width - Me.Width) / 2

    'Specify the default sample file name located in the project directory
    Text1.Text = App.Path & "\Myfile.ini"

End Sub
```

Enter the code into the appropriate events of the form module and the form's controls and run the project. Click the Write Profile Strings button located on the left side of the form (inside Frame1) to write sample profiles of two sections, each with three keys, to the file Myfile.ini located under the project directory. If the file does not exist, it will be created. Now click the adjacent Read Profile Strings button to read the profiles just created from the file. The list box will be populated with the section names and all the key names and values that were just written to the file.

Click the Browse button to show the Windows File Open dialog box, and select the file Win.ini located under the Windows directory. Specify Desktop for the section name and Wallpaper for the key name in the appropriate text boxes. Click the Read Profile Strings button located under the text boxes (inside `Frame2`). The Key Value text box displays the value (current setting) of the Windows wallpaper key. If no value is returned in the text box, the key value is not specified in the Win.ini file. You can also try retrieving profile settings from other INI files that exist on your system.

Analysis

The sample code listing demonstrates how you can create new profiles or modify existing ones in your INI files as well as how to retrieve these profiles.

To write a profile, specify the name of the INI file, the section name, the key name, and the key value and call the `WritePrivateProfileString` API function with these values as arguments. The function will first search the INI file for the specified section name and key name. If the section name is not found, it will be created and the key name is added as an entry under the created section and assigned the value specified. However, if both the section and the key names are found, the current key value will be modified using the new value specified. If the specified key name does not exist in the section, it will be added as a new entry with the specified value. In addition, if the specified file does not exist, it will also be created.

Reading an existing profile from the INI file is just as simple as writing a profile. You must specify the filename, the section and key names, and assign a buffer to receive the retrieved key value and call the `WritePrivateProfileString` API function to get the key setting.

Both `WritePrivateProfileString` and `GetPrivateProfileString` functions return the value 1 on success, otherwise 0 is returned. The code listing incorporates error-handling code and will display a message box if an error occurs during the profile read or write process.

The sample project INIFILES.VBP on the CD-ROM that accompanies this book demonstrates the functionality of the presented code.

7.2   SPLITTING A FILE

by Kamal A. Mehdi

Description

The `SplitFile` function splits a file into multiple segments (files) with a specified segment size while providing means to update a percent progress bar. The `SplitFile` function uses a fast "decremental chunk-size read/write" method to read bytes from the source file and write them to the destination segment file. The function automatically calculates the required number of file segments to be generated based on the specified segment size passed to the appropriate function argument. It will update an optional argument with the resulting number of segments to inform the user. The last generated segment might not necessarily contain the number of bytes specified by the segment size argument but will depend on the remaining bytes to read from the source file.

File segments generated by the `SplitFile` function will have the incremental numbering format .001, .002, and so on, for the file extension and will reside in the same directory in which the source file exists. The file segments can be merged back to re-create the original file using the complementary `MergeFiles` function presented elsewhere in this chapter.

The `SplitFile` function automatically updates a standard Visual Basic progress bar control or any other control that has a `Value` property to inform the user of the process's progress. The control is simply passed to the appropriate function argument as a `Control` object, and the function will automatically populate the progress bar without the need to write additional code.

The `SplitFile` function also involves several error-handling routines and error notification. The actual return value from the function will contain one of the error codes described later in this section on failure, and `0` is returned on success.

Using the `SplitFile` function in your own applications is simple. Call the function and provide the necessary arguments, including the full path or name of the file to split, the segment size in bytes, and the control name of the progress bar to update on your form. Also, you can optionally specify a variable and pass it to the `NumOfSegments` argument to be informed of the number of resulting segment files.

The code listing demonstrates the application of the `SplitFile` function.

Syntax

```
RetVal = SplitFile(FileName, SegmentSize, PercentShow, NumOfSegments)
```

Part	Description
RetVal	Required. A numeric expression that receives the value returned by the function as described later. Data type: `Integer`.
FileName	Required. A string expression that specifies the full path/name of the file to split. It must include the drive and directory names. Data type: `String`.
SegmentSize	Required. A numeric expression that specifies the required size of the resulting segment file in bytes. Data type: `Long`.
PercentShow	Required. An object expression that specifies the name of the control to be updated with the percent progress value. The control must have a `Value` property. Data type: `Object`.
NumOfSegments	Optional. A numeric expression that returns the number of the resulting file segments to which the source file was split. Data type: `Integer`.

The following are the `SplitFile` function return values:

Value	Description
0	No error. The operation was successfully completed.
1	The file path/name specified by the `FileName` argument was not found. Also returned if the `FileName` argument is empty (no filename is specified).
2	Invalid number specified for the `SegmentSize` argument (number <= 0).
3	The ratio of file size in bytes of the source file to the specified `SegmentSize` argument value resulted in 1000 or more segment files (will cause incorrect file extensions, especially on 16-bit platforms).
4	Unknown error. Might be caused by a Disk Full situation, Unable to Create File situation, or Write Protect error.

Modules and Controls Required

The following code demonstrates the use of the `SplitFile` function. You will need the following modules and controls to build the project:

Module/Control	Description
`Module1`	A standard Visual Basic module (.BAS)
`Form1`	A standard non-MDI Visual Basic form (.FRM) with the `Caption` property set to Split a File
`Frame1`	A frame control with the `Caption` property set to File to Split
`Frame2`	A frame control with the `Caption` property set to Status
`Command1`	A command button with the `Caption` property set to Split File
`Command2`	A command button with the `Caption` property set to Browse
`Command3`	A command button with the `Caption` property set to Exit
`Text1`	A text box control
`Text2`	A text box control
`CommonDialog1`	A common dialog control
`ProgressBar1`	A progress bar control
`Label1`	A label control with the `Caption` property set to File Name:
`Label2`	A label control with the `Caption` property set to Segment Size:
`Label3`	A label control with the `Caption` property set to Error Code:
`Label4`	A label control

Follow these steps to draw controls:

1. Start a new standard EXE project. `Form1` will be created by default. Set the form's `Height` and `Width` properties to approximately `3600` and `5500`, respectively, and set its `Caption` property as shown earlier in this section.

2. Draw `Frame1` at the top of the form and adjust its size so that it covers almost two-thirds of the form area. Set its `Caption` property as shown earlier.

3. Draw `Label1` and `Label2` label controls inside `Frame1` at the left side of the frame, with `Label2` under `Label1`. Set their `Caption` properties as shown earlier.

4. Draw `Text1` and `Text2` text boxes inside `Frame1` to the right of `Label1` and `Label2`, respectively, and set their width to approximately `2600`.

5. Draw `Command1` inside `Frame1` under `Text2`, and set its `Caption` property as shown earlier.

6. Draw `Command2` inside `Frame1` to the right of `Text1`. Set its `Caption` property as shown earlier.

7. Draw `Label3` under the bottom-left edge of `Frame1` and set its `Caption` property as shown earlier. Draw `Label4` to the right of `Label3`.

8. Draw `Command3` under the bottom-right edge of `Frame1` and set its `Caption` property as shown earlier.

9. Draw `Frame2` at the bottom side of the form and adjust its size so that it covers almost one-fourth of the form area. Set its `Caption` property as shown earlier.

10. Draw the `ProgressBar1` progress bar control inside `Frame2` and adjust its size to fill the entire frame area.

11. Draw the `CommonDialog1` common dialog control anywhere on the form.

Note

The common dialog control is not shown on the toolbox by default. You can add it to the toolbox by selecting the Components submenu from the Project menu and adding the control.

Code Listing

```
'Code in Module1

    'Type declaration for ChunkSize variable
    Type ChunkSize
        S12000 As String * 12000
        S6000 As String * 6000
        S3000 As String * 3000
        S1500 As String * 1500
        S500 As String * 500
        S100 As String * 100
        S25 As String * 25
        S5 As String * 5
        S1 As String * 1
    End Type
```

```
    'Declare the variable Bytes as of ChunkSize type
    Dim Bytes As ChunkSize

Function SplitFile(FileName As String, SegmentSize As Long,
➡ PercentShow As Control, Optional NumOfSegments As Integer) As Integer

    Dim SourceBytes As Long
    Dim SourceFile As String
    Dim DestinationFile As String
    Dim SegmentNumber As Integer
    Dim BytesDone As Long
    Dim FPath As String
    Dim FName As String
    Dim FNameNoExt As String
    Dim ErrorCode As Integer

    On Error GoTo ErrorHandler

    'Make sure the file exists
    If FileName = "" Or Dir(FileName) = "" Then
        ErrorCode = 1
        GoTo ErrorHandler
    End If

    'Ensure that the segment size is valid
    If SegmentSize = 0 Then
        ErrorCode = 2
        GoTo ErrorHandler
    End If

    'Retrieve the path name where file exists
    Do
        I = I + 1
        'Find the first occurance of the "\" in the FileName string
        'from the right side
        J = InStr(Len(FileName) - I, FileName, "\", vbTextCompare)
    Loop Until J > 0

    'Extract the file name
    FName = Right$(FileName, Len(FileName) - J)

    'Extract the path name
    FPath = Left$(FileName, J)

    'Find the file name without extension
    'Find the first occurance of the '.' in the FileName string
    J = InStr(1, FName, ".", vbTextCompare)
    If J = 0 Then    'File name does not contain a '.' character
        FNameNoExt = FName
    Else     'File name does contain the '.' character
        FNameNoExt = Left$(FName, J - 1)
    End If
```

continues

```
'Get total number or bytes in the source file
SourceBytes = FileLen(FileName)

'Ensure that the resultant segments will not exceed 999 segments
'because otherwise we will have incorrect file extensions
If SourceBytes / SegmentSize >= 1000 Then
    ErrorCode = 3
    GoTo ErrorHandler
End If

'Open the source file for binary read
Open FileName For Binary Access Read As #1 Len = 1

Do
    'Increase the number of segments counter by 1
    SegmentNumber = SegmentNumber + 1

    'Compose the file name of the new file to be created (file segment)
    Select Case SegmentNumber
        Case Is < 10
            DestinationFile = FPath & FNameNoExt & ".00"
                            ➥ & CStr(SegmentNumber)
        Case 10 To 99
            DestinationFile = FPath & FNameNoExt & ".0" &
                            ➥ CStr(SegmentNumber)
        Case 100 To 999
            DestinationFile = FPath & FNameNoExt & "." &
        ➥ CStr(SegmentNumber)
    End Select

    'Create the new file segment and open it for binary write
    Open DestinationFile For Binary Access Write As #2 Len = 1

    'Check whether the remaining bytes to process in the source file are
    'less than Segment bytes
    If SourceBytes - BytesDone < SegmentSize Then
        RemainingBytes = SourceBytes - BytesDone
    Else
        RemainingBytes = SegmentSize
    End If

'Read bytes from the source file and write them to the destination
'file (the current segment file)
'Depending on the remaining bytes to read and write, the routine
'below will read the largest possible chunk of data
Do

        Select Case RemainingBytes
            Case Is >= 12000
                'Read 12000 bytes of data from the source file
                Get #1, , Bytes.S12000
```

```
        'Write the bytes to the destination file
        Put #2, , Bytes.S12000
        'Decrease the number of remaining bytes by 12000
        RemainingBytes = RemainingBytes - 12000
        'Update the bytes done counter
        BytesDone = BytesDone + 12000
        'Yield to windows and other processes to do their jobs
        'Also, this helps fulshing the disk buffers to the file
        DoEvents
Case 6000 To 11999
        Get #1, , Bytes.S6000
        Put #2, , Bytes.S6000
        RemainingBytes = RemainingBytes - 6000
        BytesDone = BytesDone + 6000
        DoEvents
Case 3000 To 5999
        Get #1, , Bytes.S3000
        Put #2, , Bytes.S3000
        RemainingBytes = RemainingBytes - 3000
        BytesDone = BytesDone + 3000
        DoEvents
Case 1500 To 2999
        Get #1, , Bytes.S1500
        Put #2, , Bytes.S1500
        RemainingBytes = RemainingBytes - 1500
        BytesDone = BytesDone + 1500
        DoEvents
Case 500 To 1499
        Get #1, , Bytes.S500
        Put #2, , Bytes.S500
        RemainingBytes = RemainingBytes - 500
        BytesDone = BytesDone + 500
        DoEvents
Case 100 To 499
        Get #1, , Bytes.S100
        Put #2, , Bytes.S100
        RemainingBytes = RemainingBytes - 100
        BytesDone = BytesDone + 100
        DoEvents
Case 25 To 99
        Get #1, , Bytes.S25
        Put #2, , Bytes.S25
        RemainingBytes = RemainingBytes - 25
        BytesDone = BytesDone + 25
        DoEvents
Case 5 To 24
        Get #1, , Bytes.S5
        Put #2, , Bytes.S5
        RemainingBytes = RemainingBytes - 5
        BytesDone = BytesDone + 5
        DoEvents
Case 1 To 4
```

continues

```
                        Get #1, , Bytes.S1
                        Put #2, , Bytes.S1
                        RemainingBytes = RemainingBytes - 1
                        BytesDone = BytesDone + 1
                        DoEvents
                    Case Is = 0
                        'When the loop enters here, the segment bytes are completed.
                        'Close the segment file and exit the loop
                        Close 2
                        DoEvents
                        Exit Do
                End Select

                'Update the percent control on the form
                PercentShow = Int((BytesDone / SourceBytes) * 100)
                'Refresh the form and yield to windows
                DoEvents
            Loop

    Loop Until BytesDone = SourceBytes
    'Close the source file
    Close 1

    'When the code reaches this point, everything went OK.
    'Acknowledge the number of segments, assign the value '0' to
    'the function and exit
    NumOfSegments = SegmentNumber
    SplitFile = 0
    Exit Function

ErrorHandler:

'This is entered only when an error occurs

    Select Case ErrorCode
        Case Is = 0     'Unknown error
            Reset     'Close any open files
            SplitFile = 4     'Assign error code 4 to the function
        Case Else    'Assign error code value to the function (1 to 3)
            SplitFile = ErrorCode
    End Select

    Exit Function

End Function

'Code in Form1

Private Sub Command1_Click()

    Dim X As Integer
    Dim Segments As Integer
```

```
    'Call the function
    X = SplitFile(Text1, Val(Text2), ProgressBar1, Segments)

    'Inform the user about the call success or failure
    Label4 = X
    If X = 0 Then
        MsgBox "The process completed successfully." & Chr(10) &
        ➥ "The file was split to " & Segments & " segments.
        ➥", vbInformation
    Else
        MsgBox "An error occured!", vbInformation
    End If

End Sub

Private Sub Command2_Click()

    'Initialize the common dialog control and show it
    CommonDialog1.DialogTitle = "Select file to split"
    CommonDialog1.FileName = ""
    CommonDialog1.ShowOpen
    Text1 = CommonDialog1.FileName

End Sub

Private Sub Command3_Click()
    Unload Me
End Sub

Private Sub Form_Load()
    'Initialize
    Label4.Caption = ""
    Text1 = ""
    Text2 = ""
End Sub
```

Enter the code into the appropriate form, module, or control events as indicated and run the project. Enter the filename to split, or click the Browse button to select the file from the Explorer-like file open dialog box. Enter the size of the segment you want in the Text2 text box and click the Split File button. The file will be split to the appropriate number of segments, and a message box will appear to inform you of the process's success and the number of resulting segments. Label4 will display the error code returned from the function (0 will be displayed on success). Also notice how the progress bar is continuously updated throughout the process to display the percent completed (the ratio of the number of bytes processed to the total number of bytes in the source file).

Analysis

The SplitFile function is useful when you want to split a large file into smaller segments. These segments can be transferred to a removable media, such as floppy or zip disks, or transferred to another person through the Internet where there might be some limitation for the maximum file size to be transferred.

The function can be incorporated into your own applications and can be used very simply. Just call the function after specifying the filename to split, the segment file size, and the percent control to update. The file will be split into multiple segments, each with the size specified by the `SegmentSize` argument.

When called, the `SplitFile` function will verify that both the specified filename and the segment size given are valid. It then extracts the pathname, the filename, and the file extension and verifies that the specified segment size will not generate more than 999 files. Anything higher might cause problems with the file extensions on 16-bit platforms where no more than three characters are allowed for the file extension. The function will then open the source file for binary read, compose the new filename of the current segment file, open the segment file for binary write, and start transferring variable-size chunks of data from the source file to the destination file.

The data transfer is significantly accelerated by using a "decremental chunk-size read/write" transfer method where the size of the current chunk to read from the source file depends on the number of remaining bytes required to write to the destination file (current segment file). For example, if the remaining bytes to write to the destination file are more than 12000 bytes, the chunk size is adjusted to 12000 bytes. However, when the number of remaining bytes to write goes just below 12000 bytes, the chunk size is adjusted to 6000 bytes. Similarly, the chunk size is decreased gradually to 3000, 1500, 500, 100, 25, 5, and 1 bytes dynamically throughout the process. This ensures fast data transfer that does not depend on the source file size or the segment file size but only depends on the remaining bytes to write to the destination file. However, when the specified segment file size is less than X bytes (X=12000 for example), the read/write process starts with the next largest possible chunk size, which in this case is 6000.

The `SplitFile` function also supports progress notification of the process by updating the `Value` property of a progress bar or any other control passed to the function without the need to write additional code. Error handling is also supported in the function.

The sample project SPLTFILE.VBP on the CD-ROM that accompanies this book demonstrates the use of the `SplitFile` function.

7.3   MERGING A SPLIT FILE

by Kamal A. Mehdi

Description

The `MergeFiles` function joins the group of file segments of a split file to reconstruct the original source file. The `MergeFiles` function is complementary to the `SplitFile` function presented earlier in this chapter.

The `MergeFiles` function uses a fast decremental chunk-size read/write method to read bytes from the segmented files and writes them to the destination file (original file). The function automatically detects and processes the segmented files required to reconstruct the original file, provided that all files exist in the same directory and have the file extension format .001, .002, and so on, as generated by the complementary `SplitFile` function. However, the function can be easily modified to join any number of files with different extensions.

The `MergeFiles` function automatically updates a standard Visual Basic progress bar control, or any other control that has a `Value` property, to inform the user of the process's progress. The control is simply passed to the appropriate function argument as a `Control` object, and the function automatically populates the progress bar without the need to write additional code.

Using the `MergeFiles` function in your own applications is simple. Call the function and provide the necessary arguments, including the full path or name of any member of the file segment group, and the control name of the progress bar to update on your form. You also can specify a variable and pass it to the `NumOfSegments` argument to be informed of the number of segment files that were detected and joined.

The `MergeFiles` function also implements various error-handling routines and error notification. The actual return value from the function will contain one of the error codes described later in this section on failure, and `0` is returned on success.

The code listing demonstrates the application of the `MergeFiles` function.

Syntax

```
RetVal = MergeFiles(SourceFile, PercentShow, NumOfSegments)
```

Part	Description
RetVal	Required. A numeric expression that receives the value returned by the function, as described later in this section. Data type: `Integer`.
SourceFile	Required. A string expression that specifies the full path or name of any member of the file segment group to join. Must include the drive and directory names. Data type: `String`.
PercentShow	Required. An object expression that specifies the name of the control to be updated with the percent progress value. The control must have a `Value` property. Data type: `Object`.
NumOfSegments	Optional. A numeric expression that returns the number of file segments that were joined to reconstruct the source file. Data type: `Integer`.

The following are the `MergeFiles` function's return values:

Value	Description
0	No error. The operation was successfully completed.
1	The file path or name specified by the `SourceFile` argument was not found. Also returned if the `SourceFile` argument is empty (no filename is specified).

continues

Value	*Description*
2	The filename specified by the `SourceFile` argument is not a valid segment file.
3	The destination file already exists in the same directory in which the group of segments are located.
4	Unknown error. Might be caused by a Disk Full situation, Unable to Create File situation, or Write Protect error.

Modules and Controls Required

The following code demonstrates the use of the `MergeFiles` function. You will need the following modules and controls to build the project:

Module/Control	*Description*
`Module1`	A standard Visual Basic module (.BAS)
`Form1`	A standard non-MDI Visual Basic form (.FRM) with the `Caption` property set to Merge a Split File
`Frame1`	A frame control with the `Caption` property set to File to Merge
`Frame2`	A frame control with the `Caption` property set to Status
`Command1`	A command button with the `Caption` property set to Merge Files
`Command2`	A command button with the `Caption` property set to Browse...
`Command3`	A command button with the `Caption` property set to Exit
`Text1`	A text box control
`CommonDialog1`	A common dialog control
`ProgressBar1`	A progress bar control
`Label1`	A label control with the `Caption` property set to Segment File Name:
`Label2`	A label control with the `Caption` property set to Error Code:
`Label3`	A label control

Follow these steps to draw controls:

1. Start a new standard EXE project. `Form1` is created by default. Set the form's `Height` and `Width` properties to approximately `3600` and `5500`, respectively, and set its `Caption` property as shown earlier in this section.
2. Draw `Frame1` at the top of the form and adjust its size so that it covers almost half the form area. Set its `Caption` property as shown earlier.
3. Draw `Label1` inside `Frame1` at the left side of the frame, and set its `Caption` property as shown earlier.
4. Draw `Text1` inside `Frame1` to the right of `Label1`, and set its width to approximately `2100`.

5. Draw `Command1` inside `Frame1` under `Text1`, and set its `Caption` property as shown earlier.
6. Draw `Command2` inside `Frame1` to the right of `Text1`. Set its `Caption` property as shown earlier.
7. Draw `Label2` under the bottom-left edge of `Frame1`, and set its `Caption` property as shown earlier. Draw `Label3` to the right of `Label2`.
8. Draw `Command3` under the bottom-right edge of `Frame1` and set its `Caption` property as shown earlier.
9. Draw `Frame2` at the bottom side of the form and adjust its size so that it covers almost one-fourth of the form area. Set its `Caption` property as shown earlier.
10. Draw the `ProgressBar1` progress bar control inside `Frame2` and adjust its size to fill the entire frame area.
11. Draw the `CommonDialog1` common dialog control anywhere on the form.

Note

The common dialog control is not shown on the toolbox by default. You can add it to the toolbox by selecting the Components submenu from the Project menu and adding the control.

Code Listing

```
'Code in Module1

'Type declaration for ChunkSize variable
    Type ChunkSize
        S12000 As String * 12000
        S6000 As String * 6000
        S3000 As String * 3000
        S1500 As String * 1500
        S500 As String * 500
        S100 As String * 100
        S25 As String * 25
        S5 As String * 5
        S1 As String * 1
    End Type

    'Declare the variable Bytes as of ChunkSize type
    Dim Bytes As ChunkSize

Function MergeFiles(SourceFile As String, PercentShow As Control,
➥ Optional NumOfSegments As Integer) As Integer

    Dim TotalBytes As Long
    Dim DestinationFile As String
    Dim SegmentFile As String
    Dim SegmentNumber As Integer
    Dim Segments As Integer
    Dim BytesDone As Long
    Dim FPath As String
    Dim FName As String
    Dim FNameNoExt As String
```

continues

```
Dim ErrorCode As Integer

On Error GoTo ErrorHandler

'Make sure the source file name is given and is valid (exists)
If SourceFile = "" Or Dir(SourceFile) = "" Then
    ErrorCode = 1
    GoTo ErrorHandler
End If

'Find the number of segments of the split file
'Retrieve the path name where files exist
Do
    I = I + 1
    'Find the first occurance of the "\" in the SourceFile string
    'from the right side
    J = InStr(Len(SourceFile) - I, SourceFile, "\", vbTextCompare)
Loop Until J > 0

'Extract the file name
FName = Right$(SourceFile, Len(SourceFile) - J)

'Extract the path name
FPath = Left$(SourceFile, J)

'Find the file name without extension
'Find the first occurance of the '.' in the SourceFile string
J = InStr(1, FName, ".", vbTextCompare)
If J = 0 Then      'File name does not contain a '.' character
    FNameNoExt = FName
Else      'File name does contain the '.' character
    FNameNoExt = Left$(FName, J - 1)
End If

'Now find the number of segments of the split file that reside in
'the same directory where the source file is
'Also count the total number of bytes in the segments (this will be
'used for the calculation of the percent done value
Do
    'Increase the number of segments counter by 1
    Segments = Segments + 1

    'Compose the segment file name and check
    Select Case SegmentNumber
        Case Is < 10
            SegmentFile = FPath & FNameNoExt & ".00" & CStr(Segments)
        Case 10 To 99
            SegmentFile = FPath & FNameNoExt & ".0" & CStr(Segments)
        Case 100 To 999
            SegmentFile = FPath & FNameNoExt & "." & CStr(Segments)
    End Select
    If Dir(SegmentFile) = "" Then Exit Do
```

```
        TotalBytes = TotalBytes + FileLen(SegmentFile)
Loop

Segments = Segments - 1 'This is the number of segments found

'Check the detected number of segments. If is =0, then the given
'file name is not a segment file
If Segments = 0 Then
    ErrorCode = 2
    GoTo ErrorHandler
End If

'Check if the destination file to be created does exist in the same dir
'If yes, return error in the function return value
DestinationFile = FPath & FNameNoExt & ".src"
If Dir(DestinationFile) <> "" Then
    ErrorCode = 3
    GoTo ErrorHandler
End If

'Open the destination file for binary write
Open DestinationFile For Binary Access Write As #1 Len = 1

Do
    'Increase the number of segments counter by 1
    SegmentNumber = SegmentNumber + 1

    'Compose the file name of the new segment file to be opened and read
    Select Case SegmentNumber
        Case Is < 10
            SourceFile = FPath & FNameNoExt & ".00" & CStr(SegmentNumber)
        Case 10 To 99
            SourceFile = FPath & FNameNoExt & ".0" & CStr(SegmentNumber)
        Case 100 To 999
            SourceFile = FPath & FNameNoExt & "." & CStr(SegmentNumber)
    End Select

    'Open the source file segment for binary read
    Open SourceFile For Binary Access Read As #2 Len = 1

    'Get the total number of bytes in the current segment file
    RemainingBytes = FileLen(SourceFile)

    'Read bytes from the source file (the current segment file) and
    'write them to the destination file
    'Depending on the remaining bytes to read and write, the routine
    'below will read the largest possible
    'chunk of data
    Do

        Select Case RemainingBytes
            Case Is >= 12000
```

continues

```
                    'Read 12000 bytes of data from the source file
                    Get #2, , Bytes.S12000
                    'Write the bytes to the destination file
                    Put #1, , Bytes.S12000
                    'Decrease the number of remaining bytes by 12000
                    RemainingBytes = RemainingBytes - 12000
                    'Update the bytes done counter
                    BytesDone = BytesDone + 12000
                    'Yield to windows and other processes to do their jobs
                    'Also, this helps fulshing the disk buffers to the file
                    DoEvents
                Case 6000 To 11999
                    Get #2, , Bytes.S6000
                    Put #1, , Bytes.S6000
                    RemainingBytes = RemainingBytes - 6000
                    BytesDone = BytesDone + 6000
                    DoEvents
                Case 3000 To 5999
                    Get #2, , Bytes.S3000
                    Put #1, , Bytes.S3000
                    RemainingBytes = RemainingBytes - 3000
                    BytesDone = BytesDone + 3000
                    DoEvents
                Case 1500 To 2999
                    Get #2, , Bytes.S1500
                    Put #1, , Bytes.S1500
                    RemainingBytes = RemainingBytes - 1500
                    BytesDone = BytesDone + 1500
                    DoEvents
                Case 500 To 1499
                    Get #2, , Bytes.S500
                    Put #1, , Bytes.S500
                    RemainingBytes = RemainingBytes - 500
                    BytesDone = BytesDone + 500
                    DoEvents
                Case 100 To 499
                    Get #2, , Bytes.S100
                    Put #1, , Bytes.S100
                    RemainingBytes = RemainingBytes - 100
                    BytesDone = BytesDone + 100
                    DoEvents
                Case 25 To 99
                    Get #2, , Bytes.S25
                    Put #1, , Bytes.S25
                    RemainingBytes = RemainingBytes - 25
                    BytesDone = BytesDone + 25
                    DoEvents
                Case 5 To 24
                    Get #2, , Bytes.S5
                    Put #1, , Bytes.S5
                    RemainingBytes = RemainingBytes - 5
                    BytesDone = BytesDone + 5
```

```
                        DoEvents
                    Case 1 To 4
                        Get #2, , Bytes.S1
                        Put #1, , Bytes.S1
                        RemainingBytes = RemainingBytes - 1
                        BytesDone = BytesDone + 1
                        DoEvents
                    Case Is = 0
                      'When the loop enters here, the segment bytes are completed.
                      'Close the segment file and exit the loop
                      Close 2
                      DoEvents
                      Exit Do
                End Select

                'Update the percent control on the form
                PercentShow = Int((BytesDone / TotalBytes) * 100)
                'Refresh the form and yield to windows
                DoEvents
            Loop

    Loop Until SegmentNumber = Segments
    'Close the destination file
    Close 1

    'When the code reaches this point, everything went OK.
    'Acknowledge the number of segments, assign the value '0' to
    'the function and exit
    NumOfSegments = Segments
    MergeFiles = 0
    Exit Function

ErrorHandler:

    'This is entered only when an error occures
    Select Case ErrorCode
        Case Is = 0      'Unknown error
            Reset      'Close any open files
            MergeFiles = 4     'Assign error code 4 to the function
        Case Else     'Assign error code value to the function
            MergeFiles = ErrorCode
    End Select

    Exit Function

End Function

'Code in Form1

Private Sub Command1_Click()

    Dim X As Integer
```

continues

```
    Dim Segments As Integer

    'Call the function
    X = MergeFiles(Text1, ProgressBar1, Segments)

    'Inform the user about the call success or failure
    Label3 = X
    If X = 0 Then
        MsgBox "The process completed successfully." & Chr(10) & Segments &
        ➡" file segments were merged.", vbInformation
    Else
        MsgBox "An error occured!", vbInformation
    End If

End Sub

Private Sub Command2_Click()

    'Initialize the common dialog control and show it
    CommonDialog1.DialogTitle = "Select file segment to merge"
    CommonDialog1.filename = ""
    CommonDialog1.ShowOpen
    Text1 = CommonDialog1.filename

End Sub

Private Sub Command3_Click()
    Unload Me
End Sub

Private Sub Form_Load()
    'Initialize
    Label3.Caption = ""
    Text1 = ""
End Sub
```

Enter the code into the appropriate form, module, or control events as indicated and run the project. Enter the filename of one of the members of a split file group or click the Browse button to select the file from the Explorer-like file open dialog box. Click the Merge Files button. The file segments are merged to reconstruct the original file, and a message box appears to inform you of the process's success and the number of segments detected and processed. Label3 displays the error code returned from the function (0 is displayed on success). Also notice how the progress bar is continuously updated throughout the process to display the percent completed (the ratio of the number of bytes processed to the total number of bytes to process).

Analysis

Files split using the SplitFile function and transferred to removable media or through the Internet can be merged back to re-create the original file using the complementary MergeFiles function.

The function can be incorporated into your own applications and used very simply. Just call the function after specifying the filename of any segment of the split group of files and the percent control to update, and the file segments will be merged back to reconstruct the original file. The resulting original file will always have the default extension .SRC (source), but any other file extension can be specified by modifying the function code.

When the `MergeFiles` function is called, it will verify that the specified filename is valid and the file actually exists and is a segment file. The function then tries to detect and determine the actual number of segments to be merged by searching the directory in which the specified segmented file is located. The function determines the number of segments by looking for all files with the extension format .001, .002, and so on. The function then opens the source file (first segment file) for binary read, creates and opens the destination file (original file) for binary write, and starts transferring variable-size chunks of data from the source file to the destination file. After the entire data is read and transferred from the first segment file, the file is closed and the second segment is opened and data is read and transferred. The operation continues until the last file segment data is transferred to the destination file.

The data transfer is significantly accelerated by using a decremental chunk-size read/write transfer method where the size of the current chunk to read from the source file depends on the number of remaining bytes to read from that file (the current segment file). For example, if the remaining bytes to read are more than 12000 bytes, the chunk size is adjusted to 12000 bytes. However, when the number of remaining bytes to read goes below 12000 bytes, the chunk size is adjusted to 6000 bytes. Similarly, the chunk size is decreased gradually to 3000, 1500, 500, 100, 25, 5, and 1 bytes dynamically throughout the process. This ensures fast data transfer that does not depend on the source file size or the destination file size. It depends only on the remaining bytes to read from the source file. However, if the segment file size is less than X bytes (X=12000, for example), the read/write process starts with the next largest possible chunk size, which in this case is 6000.

The `MergeFiles` function also supports progress notification of the process by updating the `Value` property of a progress bar or any other similar control passed to the function without the need to write additional code. Error handling is also supported in the function.

The sample project MERGFILE.VBP on the CD-ROM that accompanies this book demonstrates the use of the `MergeFiles` function.

7.4 FINDING A FILE ON DISK

by Kamal A. Mehdi

Description

This sample code demonstrates a simple, yet powerful, file search utility based on the developed `FindFile` function. It searches the disk or the specified directory or folder for a given filename and returns the number of files found. It also returns the full pathnames of the files that match the search criteria.

The `FindFile` function populates a string array and optionally a list box control passed as arguments to the function with the path and name of the files. It also updates a label control passed as an argument with the number of files found. Both the list box and the label control are updated continuously while the search process is progressing.

The `FindFile` function also supports directory recursion and will search the entire directory tree for the specified search criteria if the appropriate argument is specified. It also supports wildcards such as `*.*`, `*.XXX`, `XXX*`, and `XXX??.*`. Long folder and filenames are also supported.

Process interruption is supported in the `FindFile` function by using a special global module variable assigned for this task. This is particularly useful when a large disk with thousands of files is to be searched, because the user might need to terminate the search process at any time.

The function implements fast search and recurse methods using the Visual Basic collection object without the need for any API calls. Error handling is also implemented in the function.

Syntax

```
RetVal = FindFile(sPath, sFileName, fArray(), RecurseDirs, nfLabel, fList)
```

Part	Description
RetVal	Required. A numeric expression that receives the value returned by the function. Data type: Long.
sPath	Required. A string expression that specifies the parent path in which to search. Both the drive name and folder name must be specified. If the folder is the root directory, only the drive name is specified.
sFileName	Required. A string expression that specifies the filename or criteria to search for. Standard wildcard formats (`*.*`, `*.XXX`, `XXX*`, and `XXX??.*`) can also be specified.
fArray()	Required. An array expression that specifies the name of the array to populate with the search results (filenames) of the files found that match the specified search criteria. Data type: String.
RecurseDirs	Optional. A Boolean expression that specifies whether all subdirectories under the specified folder name are to be recursed into. If not specified, no recursion will be performed.
nfLabel	Optional. An object expression that evaluates to a reference of a label control that will be continuously updated with the number of files currently found during the search process.
fList	Optional. An object expression that evaluates to a reference of a list-box control that will be continuously updated with the filenames of the files currently found that match the search criteria during the search process.

Modules and Controls Required

You will need the following modules and controls to build the sample project:

Module/Control	*Description*
Module1	A standard Visual Basic module (.BAS)
Form1	A standard non-MDI Visual Basic form (.FRM) with the following properties set: Caption = Find files on disk BorderStyle = 1-Fixed Single MinButton = True
Drive1	A drive list box
Dir1	A Dir list box
List1	A list box
Command1	A command button with the Caption property set to Search
Command2	A command button with the Caption property set to Terminate Search
Command3	A command button with the Caption property set to Exit
Label1	A label control with the Caption property set to Files Found:
Label2	A label control
Label3	A label control with the Caption property set to Status:
Label4	A label control
Frame1	A frame control with the Caption property set to Select Search Path
Frame2	A frame control with the Caption property set to Search Criteria
Frame3	A frame control with the Caption property set to Search Results
Text1	A text box control
Check1	A check box control with the Caption property set to Recurse Subdirectories

Follow these steps to draw controls:

1. Start a new standard EXE project. Form1 is created by default. Set the form's Height and Width properties to approximately 4400 and 7600, respectively, and set its Caption, BorderStyle, and MinButton properties as shown earlier in this section.
2. Draw Frame1 at the top-left side of the form and adjust its size so that it covers almost half the form width and two-thirds of the form height. Set its Caption property as shown earlier.
3. Draw the Drive1 drive list box inside Frame1 at the top of the frame and adjust its width to approximately the width of the frame.

4. Draw the `Dir1` Dir list box under the `Drive1` list box and adjust its width to approximately the | width of the frame and its height to approximately two-thirds of the frame height.

5. Draw the `Check1` check box inside `Frame1` under the `Dir1` list box, and set its `Caption` property as shown earlier.

6. Draw `Frame2` under `Frame1` and set its width as of `Frame1` and its height enough to accommodate a single-line text box. Set its `Caption` property as shown earlier.

7. Draw `Text1` inside `Frame2` and set its size to cover the entire frame area.

8. Draw `Frame3` at the right side of the form and adjust its size so that it covers almost the second half of the form area. Set its `Caption` property as shown earlier.

9. Draw `Label1` inside `Frame3` at the top-left side of the frame and set its `Caption` property as shown earlier. Draw `Label2` to the right of `Label1`.

10. Draw `Label3` inside `Frame3` at the bottom-left side of the frame and set its `Caption` property as shown earlier. Draw `Label4` to the right of `Label3`.

11. Draw the `List1` list box inside `Frame3` and adjust its size to fill the remaining area of the frame control.

12. Draw the `Command1` and `Command2` buttons under `Frame2` and set their `Caption` properties as shown earlier.

13. Draw `Command3` under `Frame3` and set its `Caption` property as shown earlier.

Code Listing

```
'Code in module1

'Declare global and private variables
Public Terminate As Boolean      'Flag used to terminate the search

Private numfFound As Long     'Total number of files found
'matching the search criteria

Private Loops As Long     'Flag used in conjunction with the
''FirstInstance' local procedure-variable to distinguish the
'first instance of function call

Function FindFile(ByVal sPath As String, ByVal sFileName As String,
➥ fArray() As String, Optional RecurseDirs As Boolean,
➥ Optional nfLabel As Label, Optional fList As ListBox) As Long

'Declare local variables
Dim sFile As String
Dim colItem As Variant
Dim colDir As New Collection
Dim FirstInstance As Boolean

'Set the FirstInstance flag to true if the function has just
'entered for the first time (because the function will be
'called recursively)
If Loops > 0 Then
```

```
        FirstInstance = False
Else
        FirstInstance = True
End If

'Set error handling. This is very important if any of the
'optional arguments are not specified or are of incorrect type
On Error Resume Next

DoEvents        'Important here to enable search interruption

'If the user terminates the process, erase the colDir collection
'and exit the function. The function will return the number of
'files found from its first call instance
If Terminate Then
        Set colDir = Nothing
        Exit Function
End If

'Find all files matching the search criteria in the current
'specified (or passed) directory and add them to the fArray()
'The size of the array will increased as needed
'Also increment the number of files found counter and update
'the label and list controls passed to the procedure
sFile = Dir$(sPath & sFileName)
While sFile <> ""
        If Left$(sFile, 1) <> "." Then
            'Increment counter by 1
            numfFound = numfFound + 1

            If numfFound = 1 Then
                'Dimension the array for the first time
                ReDim fArray(numfFound - 1)
            Else
                'Increase the array size and preserve its contents
                ReDim Preserve fArray(numfFound - 1)
            End If

            'Add the file path/name to the array
            fArray(numfFound - 1) = sPath & sFile

            'Update the list and the label controls
            fList.AddItem sPath & sFile
            nfLabel.Caption = numfFound
            DoEvents
        End If
        sFile = Dir$
Wend

'At this point, all the files that match the search criteria
'has been found. If the RecurseDirs argument is not specified,
'then update the function return value and exit
```

continues

```
If Not RecurseDirs Then GoTo ExitFunction

'If the sFile variable is a directory, add it to the colDir collection
sFile = Dir$(sPath, vbDirectory)
While sFile <> ""
    If Left$(sFile, 1) <> "." Then
        If GetAttr(sPath & sFile) And vbDirectory Then
            colDir.Add sPath & sFile & "\"
        End If
    End If
    sFile = Dir$
Wend


'Now call the function recursively for each member of the collection
'If the member directory include sub-directories, the function will
'recursively be called until all the sub-directory tree is checked
For Each colItem In colDir
    Loops = Loops + 1
    FindFile colItem, sFileName, fArray(), RecurseDirs, nfLabel, fList
Next colItem

ExitFunction:

'Erase the colDir collection
Set colDir = Nothing

'If this is the first instance of the function call, assign the function
'return value, reset variables and exit
If FirstInstance Then
    FindFile = numfFound
    numfFound = 0
    Loops = 0
    FirstInstance = False
End If

End Function

'Code in Form1

Option Explicit

Private Sub Command1_Click()

'Declare local variables
Dim colItem As Variant
Dim MyPath As String
Dim FileCriteria As String
Dim FilesFound() As String
Dim Recurse As Boolean
Dim RetVal As Long
```

```
'Set the 'Terminate' public variable to false
Terminate = False

'Initialize controls
List1.Clear
Label2.Caption = "0"
Label4.Caption = "Searching..."


'Trim the '\' character from the path name if it is
'the root directory
If Right$(Dir1.Path, 1) = "\" Then
    MyPath = Dir1.Path
Else
    MyPath = Dir1.Path & "\"
End If

'Specify the search criteria
FileCriteria = Text1.Text

'Specify whether to recurse subdirectories
Recurse = CBool(Check1.Value)

'Call the function and pass the appropriate arguments
'Both Label2 and List1 are passed as controls to be
'updated with the search results by the function while
'the search is progressing
RetVal = FindFile(MyPath, Text1.Text, FilesFound(), Recurse, Label2, List1)

'Enable the following lines to see the number of files found
'and their names stored in the FilesFound() array
'MsgBox RetVal
'For Each colItem In FilesFound
'    MsgBox colItem
'Next colItem

'Update status label and make a beep sound
Label4.Caption = "Done"
Beep

End Sub

Private Sub Command2_Click()

    'Terminate the search. The variable 'Terminate' is public
    'and will be checked continuously by the search function
    'if the search is in progress
    Terminate = True

End Sub

Private Sub Command3_Click()
```

continues

```
        'EXit
        Unload Me

End Sub

Private Sub Drive1_Change()

        'Error handling is required in case a floppy drive
        'or CD-ROM drive with no media is accessed
        On Error Resume Next

        'Synchronize the path of the Dir1 list box with the
        'drive name of Drive1 list box and refresh it
        Dir1.Path = Drive1.Drive
        Dir1.Refresh

End Sub

Private Sub Form_Load()

        'Initialize controls
        Label2.Caption = ""
        Label4.Caption = ""
        Text1.Text = ""

End Sub
```

Enter the code in the appropriate form, module, or control events as indicated and run the project. Select the drive and folder to search into, enter the filename or the search criteria in the `Text1` text box, check or uncheck the Recurse Subdirectories check box, and click the Search button. The list box is populated with the filenames that match the search criteria while the search process is progressing. `Label2` also displays the total number of files currently found in the specified folder and subfolders.

Analysis

The `FindFile` function takes the path name and filename or the search criteria passed as arguments and searches the specified path for the existence of the filename given. A string array passed as a third argument is populated with the path/names of all files found that match the search criteria. If the optional argument `RecurseDirs` is specified, the entire subdirectory tree located under the specified path will be searched.

The logic of the `FindFile` function is fairly simple. It first checks all the entries under the specified path and distinguishes between file entries and directory entries. It then checks whether any file entries match the specified criteria. If there is a match, the entry is appended to the passed array. Entries that evaluate to folders or directories are appended to a new collection so that they will be searched later if the recurse directories option was specified. The function then calls itself recursively for each directory entry and repeats exactly the same process until no more files are found under the last directory level in each directory entry.

During the search process, the list-box control optionally passed to the function is populated and continuously updated by the function with the full path and names of the files found that match the search criteria. The number of files currently found is displayed in the label control passed to the appropriate argument.

When all recursive function calls are completed, the function assigns the number of files found to its return value, resets the module variables, and terminates.

Although the search method implemented is fast, the time required to search an entire disk of several gigabytes in size might be lengthy. Therefore, the `FindFile` function can be terminated at any time by incorporating the module-level `Terminate` variable. This variable can be set at any time by your calling application during the search process.

The sample project FINDFILE.VBP on the CD-ROM demonstrates the application of the described function through a sample file-search utility.

7.5 SAVE A VALUE INTO AN .INI KEY

by Martin Cordova

Description

This function saves the value of a key into an .INI file. The value must be formatted as a string. .INI files are text files with some internal structure, and have been used for years by Windows applications to store configuration information. Windows itself uses two very important .INI files, Win.INI and System.INI.

You can also use .INI files—the Windows API provides some functions to save numeric and string values into these files. This function encapsulates one of those API functions in one easy-to-use function that provides a unique and uniform way to store numbers and text, but always using strings, so you don't have to deal with one function for strings and another for saving numeric values. .INI files still represent a very practical alternative to the more sophisticated (and complicated) Windows Registry file.

An .INI file looks like this:

```
[MyServer]
Database=pubs
userid=sa
password=
```

The text between brackets (`[MyServer]`) represents a section. The text to the left of the equal sign (=) represents a key. The text to the right of the equal sign represents the key value.

Syntax

```
Dim File As String
Dim Section As String
```

```
Dim Key As String
Dim MyValue As String

File = "myfile.ini"
Section = "startup"
Key = "lastuser"
MyValue = "john_doe"

SaveIniKey File, Section, Key, MyValue
```

Part	Description
File	The full name of the file. If the path is not included the Windows directory is assumed.
Section	The section inside the .INI file (don't include the brackets [ ]).
Key	The name of the key in the given section.
Value	The value to be saved unser that key. Must be formated as a string.

Code Listing

```
'---paste this code in the declarations section of a module or class
Private Declare Function WritePrivateProfileString Lib "kernel32"
➥ Alias "WritePrivateProfileStringA" (ByVal lpApplicationName As String,
➥ ByVal lpKeyName As Any, ByVal lpString As Any, ByVal lpFileName
➥ As String) As Long

Public Sub SaveIniKey(ByVal File As String, ByVal Section As String, ByVal Key
➥ As String, ByVal Value As String)

    Dim fRet As Long

    fRet = WritePrivateProfileString(Section, Key, Value, File)

End Sub
```

Analysis

This function encapsulates the API call to use private profiles and simplifies the calling interface, presenting the subroutine as a natural extension to VB. As you can see, there is little work to do because the API call receives the same number of parameters, but you must call it as a function because it returns a value. The VB wrapper avoids the function call syntax and presents a simpler interface.

7.6   RETRIEVE A VALUE FROM AN .INI KEY

by Martin Cordova

Description

This function returns the value of a key from an .INI file. The value returns as a string. .INI files are text files with some internal structure, and have been used for years by Windows applications to store configuration information. Windows itself uses two very important .INI files, Win.INI and System.INI. You can also use .INI files—the Windows API provides some functions to retrieve numeric and string values from these files. This functions encapsulates one of those API functions in one easy-to-use function that always returns a string, even if the value is numeric, providing a uniform and unique mechanism to read from .INI files.

An .INI file looks like this:

```
[MyServer]
Database=pubs
userid=sa
password=
```

The text between brackets ([MyServer]) represents a section. The text to the left of the equal sign (=) represents a key. The text to the right of the equal sign represents the key value.

Syntax

```
Dim MyKeyValue As String
Dim szFile As String
Dim szSection As String
Dim szKey As String

szFile = "windows.ini"
szSection = "windows"
szKey = "device"

'---read Windows 95 default printer name, port and driver...
MyKeyValue = GetIniKey(szFile, szSection, szKey)
```

Part	Description
szFile	The full name of the file. If the path is not included, the Windows directory is assumed.
szSection	The section inside the .INI file (don't include the brackets [ ]).
szKey	The name of the key in the given section.

Code Listing

```
'---paste this code in the declarations section of a module or class
Private Declare Function GetPrivateProfileString Lib "kernel32" Alias
➡ "GetPrivateProfileStringA" (ByVal lpApplicationName As String,
➡ ByVal lpKeyName As Any, ByVal lpDefault As String,
➡ ByVal lpReturnedString As String, ByVal nSize As Long,
➡ ByVal lpFileName As String) As Long
```

continues

```
Function GetIniKey(ByVal szFile As String, ByVal szSection As String,
➥ ByVal szKey As String) As String

    Dim szValue As String
    Dim szDefault As String
    Dim nLen As Integer

    '---prepare string buffers
    szValue = Space$(250)
'---default return value will be always "" ñempty string-
    szDefault = ""

    '---call WINAPI
    nLen = GetPrivateProfileString(szSection, ByVal szKey, szDefault, szValue,
    ➥ Len(szValue), szFile)

    '---trim null char
'---this function returns the real lengh of the Key value,
➥without the null char
    If nLen = 0 Then
        GetIniKey = ""
    Else
        GetIniKey = Trim$(Left$(szValue, nLen))
    End If

End Function
```

Analysis

This function encapsulates the API call to use private profiles and simplifies the calling interface because you pass fewer parameters to this function. If a value is not found, an empty string is returned.

It also provides access to the Windows standard profiles (Win.INI and System.INI) as well as to any .INI file. Please note that the default value parameter is assumed as an empty string in order to minimize the number of parameters in the function call.

The `GetPrivateProfileString` function returns the key value in the `szValue` parameter, but it comes packed as a C string—not a VB string—which always includes a NULL character at the end. Fortunately, the function returns the length of the string without the NULL char, so trimming this NULL char from the key value is easy.

7.7 CHECK FOR FILE EXISTENCE

by Martin Cordova

Description

This function detects the existence of a file, given a full filename (drive, path, and filename with extension). It also accepts UNCs (network share names, such as \\server\data\biblio.mdb). If the file is found, it returns TRUE, otherwise it returns FALSE.

Syntax

```
Dim Found As Boolean
Dim szFileName As String

szFileName = "c:\config.sys"

Found = FileExist(szFileName)
```

Part	Description
szFileName	The full name of the file, including the path.
Returns	TRUE if the file exists, FALSE if it does not.

Code Listing

```
Function FileExist(ByVal szFileName As String) As Boolean

    Dim nFileNumber As Integer

    On Error Resume Next

    nFileNumber = FreeFile

    '---try to open file
    Open szFileName For Input As nFileNumber

    '---if fails the file does not exist
    If Err.Number <> 0 Then
        FileExist = False
    Else
        FileExist = True
    End If

    Close nFileNumber

End Function
```

Analysis

This function encapsulates the native VB file management functions to provide an easy-to-use function that can test in one call the existence of a file. It uses the popular technique of trying to open the file and test for an error. If there is no error then the file was found and the function returns TRUE.

If the `szFileName` parameter does not contain the full path name, the current directory is assumed. If the filename is not a valid Windows filename, the function returns `FALSE`. This function does not perform any syntax validation on filenames.

7.8   READ A FILE INTO A BUFFER

by Martin Cordova

Description

This function returns a whole text file in just one call. It is very fast. It relies on the native VB file I/O commands, and encapsulates them in this function, including error handling.

Syntax

```
Dim Buffer As String
Dim MyFile as String

MyFile = InputBox("Enter File Name (including full path)")

Buffer = GetFile(MyFile)
```

Part	*Description*
File	The full name of the file. If a path is not included, the variable `App.Path` is used.
Returns	A string representing the contents of the text file specified in the File parameter.

Code Listing

```
Public Function GetFile(ByVal File As String) As String

    Dim Path As String
    Dim Fnum As Integer

    On Error GoTo ErrorHandler

    '---filename includes path?
    If InStr(File, "\") = 0 Then
        '---otherwise use App.Path
        Path = App.Path
        If Right(Path, 1) <> "\" Then
            File = Path & "\" & File
        Else
```

```
            File = Path & File
        End If
    End If

    '---read file in one pass!
    Fnum = FreeFile
    Open File For Input As #Fnum
        GetFile = Input(LOF(Fnum), Fnum)
    Close Fnum

    Exit Function

ErrorHandler:
    Err.Description = "GetFile: " & Err.Description & " -> " & File
    Err.Raise Err.Number

End Function
```

Analysis

This function encapsulates the native VB file management functions to read in just one pass the whole file into a string buffer. Note the use of the native VB `Input()` function. Please note the use of the VB command `Input(LOF(Fnum), Fnum)`, where the size of the file is the first parameter and the file handle is the second. The function's internal code is very easy to follow, but not very reusable if you must type it every time you want to read a file.

This function is very useful because it encapsulates all those tedious file I/O commands in just one call. You don't even have to worry about opening or closing the file, you just need to provide a valid filename. In case of error, a full error description, including the filename used, is raised to the caller, which is useful for debugging purposes.

7.9 SAVE A BUFFER TO A FILE

by Martin Cordova

Description

This subroutine saves a string buffer in just one call. It is very fast. Optionally, you can append the buffer to an existing file. If the file does not exist, it will be created; otherwise it will be overwritten if you don't use the append mode.

If the path is not included in the specified filename, the procedure will assume the `App.Path` property. This procedure won't test the syntax of the filename, so if a bad filename is passed the procedure will fail and raise an error using standard VB error-handling techniques.

This procedure is very useful to mantain log files, and there is no practical limit to the size of the file (other than the inherent operating system limitations). This procedure can make your code faster and easier to read.

Syntax

```
Dim Buffer As String

Buffer = "Hello world ñ do not append"
SaveFile "my log file.log", Buffer

Buffer = "Hello world #2 ñappend"
SaveFile "my log file.log", Buffer, True
```

Parameter	Description
File	The full name of the file. If the path is not included, the variable App.Path is used.
Buffer	The string buffer to be saved.
UseAppend	Optional. If TRUE, then Buffer will be appended to the file.

Code Listing

```
Public Sub SaveFile(ByVal File$, ByVal Buffer$,
➥ Optional ByVal UseAppend = False)

    Dim Path As String
    Dim Fnum As Integer

    On Error GoTo ErrorHandler

    '---file includes path?
    If InStr(File$, "\") = 0 Then
        '---otherwise use App.Path
        Path = App.Path
        If Right(Path, 1) <> "\" Then
            File$ = Path & "\" & File$
        Else
            File$ = Path & File$
        End If
    End If

    Fnum = FreeFile

    If Not UseAppend Then
        Open File$ For Output As #Fnum
    Else
        Open File$ For Append As #Fnum
    End If
```

```
        Print #Fnum, Buffer$
    Close Fnum

    Exit Sub

ErrorHandler:
    Err.Description = "SaveFile: " & Err.Description & " -> " & File$
    Err.Raise Err.Number

End Sub
```

Analysis

This function encapsulates the native VB file management functions to save in just one pass a string buffer. An optional variable is used to make it more flexible and allow the same interface to be used for appends, which is useful for creating log files.

The procedure examines the filename in order to determine whether it includes the path. If it does not, then App.Path is assumed. Standard error-handling techniques have been implemented into this procedure to make it more robust, despite the fact that it does not include any filename syntax validation.

7.10 COMPRESS FILES USING ZIP32

by Raymond King

Description

The VBZip32 routine will zip up files. It includes built-in error handling. Before calling the Zip32 function you must set all the parameters, which are included in the module source code along with an explanation of what each one does. The module now supports a zip file password.

I would like to thank the Info-Zip group for letting me use their public domain Zip32 and Unzip32 DLLs. Also, a very special thanks to Mr. Mike White, Mr. Mike Le Voi, and Deepu Chandy Thomas, author of *Easy Zip 98*, for their hard work and time to get this working for me in Visual Basic 5.0.

The source code to the DLLs and Visual Basic 5.0 are free from the Info-Zip Group at ftp://ftp.cdrom.com/pub/infozip/infozip.html. These are the latest DLLS, but you should check their Web site for updates. Please note that zip32.dll must be in your Windows/System directory.

Syntax

VBZip32

Code Listing

```
Option Explicit



Option Explicit

'----------------------------------------------------------------
'-- Please Do Not Remove These Comments!!!
'----------------------------------------------------------------
'-- Sample VB 5 code to drive zip32.dll
'-- Contributed to the Info-Zip project by Mike Le Voi
'--
'-- Contact me at: mlevoi@modemss.brisnet.org.au
'--
'-- Visit my home page at: http://modemss.brisnet.org.au/~mlevoi
'--
'-- Use this code at your own risk. Nothing implied or warranted
'-- to work on your machine :-)
'----------------------------------------------------------------
'--
'-- The Source Code Is Freely Avaiable From Info-Zip At:
'-- http://www.cdrom.com/pub/infozip/infozip.html
'--
'-- A Very Special Thanks To Mr. Mike Le Voi
'-- And Mr. Mike White Of The Info-Zip
'-- For Letting Me Use And Modify His Orginal
'-- Visual Basic 5.0 Code! Thank You Mike Le Voi.
'----------------------------------------------------------------
'--
'-- Contributed To The Info-Zip Project By Raymond L. King
'-- Modified June 21, 1998
'-- By Raymond L. King
'-- Custom Software Designers
'--
'-- Contact Me At: king@ntplx.net
'-- ICQ 434355
'-- Or Visit Our Home Page At: http://www.ntplx.net/~king
'--
'----------------------------------------------------------------

'-- C Style argv
'-- Holds The Zip Archive Filenames
Public Type ZIPnames
    zFiles(0 To 99) As String
End Type

'-- Call Back "String"
Public Type ZipCBChar
    ch(4096) As Byte
End Type

'-- ZPOPT Is Used To Set The Options In The ZIP32.DLL
```

```
Public Type ZPOPT
    fSuffix          As Long    ' Include Suffixes (Not Yet Implemented!)
    fEncrypt         As Long    ' 1 If Encryption Wanted, Else 0
    fSystem          As Long    ' 1 To Include System/Hidden Files, Else 0
    fVolume          As Long    ' 1 If Storing Volume Label, Else 0
    fExtra           As Long    ' 1 If Including Extra Attributes, Else 0
    fNoDirEntries    As Long    ' 1 If Ingoring Directory Entries, Else 0
    fExcludeDate     As Long    ' 1 If Excluding Files Earlier Than Specified
    ➥ Date, Else 0
    fIncludeDate     As Long    ' 1 If Including Files Earlier Than Specified
    ➥ Date, Else 0
    fVerbose         As Long    ' 1 If Full Messages Wanted, Else 0
    fQuiet           As Long    ' 1 If Minimum Messages Wanted, Else 0
    fCRLF_LF         As Long    ' 1 If Translate CR/LF To LF, Else 0
    fLF_CRLF         As Long    ' 1 If Translate LF To CR/LF, Else 0
    fJunkDir         As Long    ' 1 If Junking Directory Names, Else 0
    fRecurse         As Long    ' 1 If Recursing Into Sub-Directories, Else 0
    fGrow            As Long    ' 1 If Allow Appending To Zip File, Else 0
    fForce           As Long    ' 1 If Making Entries Using DOS File Names, Else 0
    fMove            As Long    ' 1 If Deleting Files Added Or Updated, Else 0
    fDeleteEntries   As Long    ' 1 If Files Passed Have To Be Deleted, Else 0
    fUpdate          As Long    ' 1 If Updating Zip File-Overwrite Only If Newer,
    ➥ Else 0
    fFreshen         As Long    ' 1 If Freshing Zip File-Overwrite Only, Else 0
    fJunkSFX         As Long    ' 1 If Junking SFX Prefix, Else 0
    fLatestTime      As Long    ' 1 If Setting Zip File Time To Time Of Latest
    ➥ File In Archive, Else 0
    fComment         As Long    ' 1 If Putting Comment In Zip File, Else 0
    fOffsets         As Long    ' 1 If Updating Archive Offsets For SFX Files,
    ➥ Else 0
    fPrivilege       As Long    ' 1 If Not Saving Privileges, Else 0
    fEncryption      As Long    ' Read Only Property!!!
    fRepair          As Long    ' 1 = Fix Archive, 2 = Try Harder To Fix, Else 0
    flevel           As Byte    ' Compression Level - 0 = Stored 6 = Default
    ➥ 9 = Max
    Date             As String  ' US Date (8 Bytes Long) "12/31/98"?
    szRootDir        As String  ' Root Directory Pathname (Up To 256 Bytes Long)
End Type

'-- This Structure Is Used For The ZIP32.DLL Function Callbacks
Public Type ZIPUSERFUNCTIONS
    ZDLLPrnt      As Long       ' Callback ZIP32.DLL Print Function
    ZDLLCOMMENT   As Long       ' Callback ZIP32.DLL Comment Function
    ZDLLPASSWORD  As Long       ' Callback ZIP32.DLL Password Function
    ZDLLSERVICE   As Long       ' Callback ZIP32.DLL (Currently Not Used!!!)
End Type

'-- Local Declarations
Public ZOPT  As ZPOPT
Public ZUSER As ZIPUSERFUNCTIONS

'-- This Assumes ZIP32.DLL Is In Your \Windows\System Directory!
```

continues

```
Private Declare Function ZpInit Lib "zip32.dll" _
    (ByRef Zipfun As ZIPUSERFUNCTIONS) As Long '-- Set Zip Callbacks

Private Declare Function ZpSetOptions Lib "zip32.dll" _
    (ByRef Opts As ZPOPT) As Long '-- Set Zip Options

Private Declare Function ZpGetOptions Lib "zip32.dll" _
    () As ZPOPT '-- Used To Check Encryption Flag Only

Private Declare Function ZpArchive Lib "zip32.dll" _
    (ByVal argc As Long, ByVal funame As String, _
     ByRef argv As ZIPnames) As Long '-- Real Zipping Action


'---------------------------------------------------------
'-- Public Variables For Setting The ZPOPT Structure...
'-- (WARNING!!!) You Must Set The Options That You
'-- Want The ZIP32.DLL To Do!
'-- Before Calling VBZip32!
'--
'-- NOTE: See The Above ZPOPT Structure Or The VBZip32
'--       Function, For The Meaning Of These Variables
'--       And How To Use And Set Them!!!
'-- These Parameters Must Be Set Before The Actual Call
'-- To The VBZip32 Function!
'---------------------------------------------------------
Public zSuffix       As Integer
Public zEncrypt      As Integer
Public zSystem       As Integer
Public zVolume       As Integer
Public zExtra        As Integer
Public zNoDirEntries As Integer
Public zExcludeDate  As Integer
Public zIncludeDate  As Integer
Public zVerbose      As Integer
Public zQuiet        As Integer
Public zCRLF_LF      As Integer
Public zLF_CRLF      As Integer
Public zJunkDir      As Integer
Public zRecurse      As Integer
Public zGrow         As Integer
Public zForce        As Integer
Public zMove         As Integer
Public zDelEntries   As Integer
Public zUpdate       As Integer
Public zFreshen      As Integer
Public zJunkSFX      As Integer
Public zLatestTime   As Integer
Public zComment      As Integer
Public zOffsets      As Integer
Public zPrivilege    As Integer
Public zEncryption   As Integer
Public zRepair       As Integer
```

```
Public zLevel        As Integer
Public zDate         As String
Public zRootDir      As String

'-- Public Program Variables
Public zArgc         As Integer      ' Number Of Files To Zip Up
Public zZipFileName  As String       ' The Zip File Name ie: Myzip.zip
Public zZipFileNames As ZIPnames     ' File Names To Zip Up
Public zZipInfo      As String       ' Holds The Zip File Information

'-- Public Constants
'-- For Zip & UnZip Error Codes!
Public Const ZE_OK = 0               ' Success (No Error)
Public Const ZE_EOF = 2              ' Unexpected End Of Zip File Error
Public Const ZE_FORM = 3             ' Zip File Structure Error
Public Const ZE_MEM = 4              ' Out Of Memory Error
Public Const ZE_LOGIC = 5            ' Internal Logic Error
Public Const ZE_BIG = 6              ' Entry Too Large To Split Error
Public Const ZE_NOTE = 7             ' Invalid Comment Format Error
Public Const ZE_TEST = 8             ' Zip Test (-T) Failed Or Out Of Memory
➥ Error
Public Const ZE_ABORT = 9            ' User Interrupted Or Termination Error
Public Const ZE_TEMP = 10            ' Error Using A Temp File
Public Const ZE_READ = 11            ' Read Or Seek Error
Public Const ZE_NONE = 12            ' Nothing To Do Error
Public Const ZE_NAME = 13            ' Missing Or Empty Zip File Error
Public Const ZE_WRITE = 14           ' Error Writing To A File
Public Const ZE_CREAT = 15           ' Could't Open To Write Error
Public Const ZE_PARMS = 16           ' Bad Command Line Argument Error
Public Const ZE_OPEN = 18            ' Could Not Open A Specified File To Read
➥ Error

'-- These Functions Are For The ZIP32.DLL
'--
'-- Puts A Function Pointer In A Structure
'-- For Use With Callbacks...
Public Function FnPtr(ByVal lp As Long) As Long

    FnPtr = lp

End Function

'-- Callback For ZIP32.DLL - DLL Print Function
Public Function ZDLLPrnt(ByRef fname As ZipCBChar, ByVal x As Long) As Long

    Dim s0 As String
    Dim xx As Long

    '-- Always Put This In Callback Routines!
    On Error Resume Next

    s0 = ""
```

continues

```
    '-- Get Zip32.DLL Message For Displaying
    For xx = 0 To x
        If fname.ch(xx) = 0 Then
            xx = 99999
        Else
            s0 = s0 + Chr(fname.ch(xx))
        End If
    Next

    '--------------------------------------------------
    '-- This Is Where The DLL Passes Back Messages
    '-- To You! You Can Change The Message Printing
    '-- Below Here!
    '--------------------------------------------------

    '-- Dispaly Zip File Information
    '-- zZipInfo = zZipInfo & s0
    Form1.Print s0;

    DoEvents

    ZDLLPrnt = 0

End Function

'-- Callback For ZIP32.DLL - DLL Password Function
Public Function ZDLLPass(ByRef p As ZipCBChar, _
    ByVal n As Long, ByRef m As ZipCBChar, _
    ByRef Name As ZipCBChar) As Integer

    Dim prompt      As String
    Dim xx          As Integer
    Dim szpassword As String

    '-- Always Put This In Callback Routines!
    On Error Resume Next

    ZDLLPass = 1

    '-- If There Is A Password Have The User Enter It!
    '-- This Can Be Changed
    szpassword = InputBox("Please Enter The Password!")

    '-- The User Did Not Enter A Password So Exit The Function
    If szpassword = "" Then Exit Function

    '-- User Entered A Password So Proccess It
    For xx = 0 To 255
        If m.ch(xx) = 0 Then
            Exit For
        Else
```

```
                prompt = prompt & Chr(m.ch(xx))
        End If
    Next

    For xx = 0 To n - 1
        p.ch(xx) = 0
    Next

    For xx = 0 To Len(szpassword) - 1
        p.ch(xx) = Asc(Mid(szpassword, xx + 1, 1))
    Next

    p.ch(xx) = Chr(0) ' Put Null Terminator For C

    ZDLLPass = 0

End Function

'-- Callback For ZIP32.DLL - DLL Comment Function
Public Function ZDLLComm(ByRef s1 As ZipCBChar) As ZipCBChar

    '-- Always Put This In Callback Routines!
    On Error Resume Next

    '-- Not Supported Always Return \0
    s1.ch(0) = vbNullString

    ZDLLComm = s1

End Function

'-- Main ZIP32.DLL Subroutine.
'-- This Is Where It All Happens!!!
'--
'-- (WARNING!) Do Not Change This Function!!!
'--
Public Function VBZip32() As Long

    Dim retcode As Long

    On Error Resume Next '-- Nothing Will Go Wrong :-)

    retcode = 0

    '-- Set Address Of ZIP32.DLL Callback Functions
    '-- (WARNING!) Do Not Change!!!
    ZUSER.ZDLLPrnt = FnPtr(AddressOf ZDLLPrnt)
    ZUSER.ZDLLPASSWORD = FnPtr(AddressOf ZDLLPass)
    ZUSER.ZDLLCOMMENT = FnPtr(AddressOf ZDLLComm)
    ZUSER.ZDLLSERVICE = 0& '-- Not Coded Yet :-) FnPtr(AddressOf DLLServ)

    '-- Set ZIP32.DLL Callbacks
```

continues

```
    retcode = ZpInit(ZUSER)

    '-- Setup ZIP32 Options
    '-- (WARNING!) Do Not Change!
    ZOPT.fSuffix = zSuffix             ' Include Suffixes (Not Yet Implemented)
    ZOPT.fEncrypt = zEncrypt           ' 1 If Encryption Wanted
    ZOPT.fSystem = zSystem             ' 1 To Include System/Hidden Files
    ZOPT.fVolume = zVolume             ' 1 If Storing Volume Label
    ZOPT.fExtra = zExtra               ' 1 If Including Extra Attributes
    ZOPT.fNoDirEntries = zNoDirEntries ' 1 If Ignoring Directory Entries
    ZOPT.fExcludeDate = zExcludeDate   ' 1 If Excluding Files Earlier Than A
    ➥ Specified Date
    ZOPT.fIncludeDate = zIncludeDate   ' 1 If Including Files Earlier Than A
    ➥ Specified Date
    ZOPT.fVerbose = zVerbose           ' 1 If Full Messages Wanted
    ZOPT.fQuiet = zQuiet               ' 1 If Minimum Messages Wanted
    ZOPT.fCRLF_LF = zCRLF_LF           ' 1 If Translate CR/LF To LF
    ZOPT.fLF_CRLF = zLF_CRLF           ' 1 If Translate LF To CR/LF
    ZOPT.fJunkDir = zJunkDir           ' 1 If Junking Directory Names
    ZOPT.fRecurse = zRecurse           ' 1 If Recursing Into Subdirectories
    ZOPT.fGrow = zGrow                 ' 1 If Allow Appending To Zip File
    ZOPT.fForce = zForce               ' 1 If Making Entries Using DOS Names
    ZOPT.fMove = zMove                 ' 1 If Deleting Files Added Or Updated
    ZOPT.fDeleteEntries = zDelEntries  ' 1 If Files Passed Have To Be Deleted
    ZOPT.fUpdate = zUpdate             ' 1 If Updating Zip File-Overwrite Only
    ➥ If Newer
    ZOPT.fFreshen = zFreshen           ' 1 If Freshening Zip File-Overwrite
    ➥ Only
    ZOPT.fJunkSFX = zJunkSFX           ' 1 If Junking SFX Prefix
    ZOPT.fLatestTime = zLatestTime     ' 1 If Setting Zip File Time To Time Of
    ➥ Latest File In Archive
    ZOPT.fComment = zComment           ' 1 If Putting Comment In Zip File
    ZOPT.fOffsets = zOffsets           ' 1 If Updating Archive Offsets For SFX
    ➥ Files
    ZOPT.fPrivilege = zPrivilege       ' 1 If Not Saving Privelages
    ZOPT.fEncryption = zEncryption     ' Read Only Property!
    ZOPT.fRepair = zRepair             ' 1 = Fix Archive, 2 = Try Harder To Fix
    ZOPT.flevel = zLevel               ' Compression Level - (0 To 9) Should Be
    ➥ 0!!!
    ZOPT.Date = zDate                  ' "12/31/79"? US Date?
    ZOPT.szRootDir = zRootDir          ' Root Directory Pathname

    '-- Set ZIP32.DLL Options
    retcode = ZpSetOptions(ZOPT)

    '-- Go Zip It Them Up!
    retcode = ZpArchive(zArgc, zZipFileName, zZipFileNames)

    '-- Return The Function Code
    VBZip32 = retcode

End Function
```

Program Example:

Option Explicit

```
'-----------------------------------------------------------------
'-- Please Do Not Remove These Comments!!!
'-----------------------------------------------------------------
'-- Sample VB 5 code to drive zip32.dll
'-- Contributed to the Info-Zip project by Mike Le Voi
'--
'-- Contact me at: mlevoi@modemss.brisnet.org.au
'--
'-- Visit my home page at: http://modemss.brisnet.org.au/~mlevoi
'--
'-- Use this code at your own risk. Nothing implied or warranted
'-- to work on your machine :-)
'-----------------------------------------------------------------
'--
'-- The Source Code Is Freely Avaiable From Info-Zip At:
'-- http://www.cdrom.com/pub/infozip/infozip.html
'--
'-- A Very Special Thanks To Mr. Mike Le Voi
'-- And Mr. Mike White Of The Info-Zip
'-- For Letting Me Use And Modify His Orginal
'-- Visual Basic 5.0 Code! Thank You Mike Le Voi.
'-----------------------------------------------------------------
'--
'-- Contributed To The Info-Zip Project By Raymond L. King
'-- Modified June 21, 1998
'-- By Raymond L. King
'-- Custom Software Designers
'--
'-- Contact Me At: king@ntplx.net
'-- ICQ 434355
'-- Or Visit Our Home Page At: http://www.ntplx.net/~king
'--
'-----------------------------------------------------------------

Private Sub Form_Click()

    Dim retcode As Integer   ' For Return Code From ZIP32.DLL

    Cls

    '-- Set Options - Only The Common Ones Are Shown Here
    '-- These Must Be Set Before Calling The VBZip32 Function
    zDate = vbNullString
    zJunkDir = 0         ' 1 = Throw Away Path Names
    zRecurse = 0         ' 1 = Recurse -R 2 = Recurse -r 2 = Most Useful :)
```

continues

```
    zUpdate = 0        ' 1 = Update Only If Newer
    zFreshen = 0       ' 1 = Freshen - Overwrite Only
    zLevel = Asc(9)    ' Compression Level (0 - 9)
    zEncrypt = 1       ' Encryption = 1 For Password Else 0

    '-- Select Some Files - Wildcards Are Supported
    '-- Change The Paths Here To Your Directory
    '-- And Files!!!
    zArgc = 2              ' Number Of Elements Of mynames Array
    zZipFileName = "c:\copy\testzip.zip"
    zZipFileNames.zFiles(0) = "c:\copy\zip32\vbzipbas.bas"
    zZipFileNames.zFiles(1) = "c:\copy\zip32\zip32.dll"
    zRootDir = "c:\"      ' This Affects The Stored Path Name

    '-- Go Zip Them Up!
    retcode = VBZip32

    '-- Display The Retuned Code Or Error!
    Print "Return code:" & Str(retcode)

End Sub

Private Sub Form_Load()

    Me.Show

    Print "Click me!"

End Sub
```

Analysis

This module is fairly simple. It will make a zip file given the source files and destination zip file name. The structure parameters must be set before calling the Zip32 function. The module has some nice functions that demonstrate the use of byte arrays and how to use callbacks using the AddressOf operator. The source code to zip32.dll and unzip32.dll is free from the Info-Zip Group (see the URL in the code comments). You should check their Web site for updates to the DLLs. The original Visual Basic 5.0 source code was written by Mike Le Voi and modified by me to make it easy to use. I would like to thank him and Mike White of the Info-Zip also Deepu Chandy Thomas for allowing me to use this code for this book.

The difference between zip32 and unzip32 is that Zip32 will zip files and unzip32 will unzip files.

7.11 UNCOMPRESS FILES USING UNZIP32

by Raymond King

Description

The VBUnZip32 routine will unzip a zip file. The VBUnZip32 routine is in the vbunzip.bas module along with supporting routines and functions.

Visual Basic provides no simple way to unzip files. But thanks to the fine people at Info-Zip for a public domain DLL (and to Mr. Mike Le Voi and Deepu Chandy Thomas, who worked very hard to make this possible and gave me permission to modify the original Visual Basic 5.0 code), Visual Basic 5.0 users can now include Unzip in their applications. The orginal source code is avaiable from Info-Zip at `ftp://ftp.cdrom.com/pub/infozip/infozip.html`. Please check there for updated DLLs and Visual Basic source code. This module now supports a zip file password. Please note that the unzip32.dll must be in your Windows/System directory.

Syntax

```
Call VBUnZip32
```

Code Listing

```
Option Explicit

'-- Please Do Not Remove These Comment Lines!
'----------------------------------------------------------------
'-- Sample VB 5 code to drive unzip32.dll
'-- Contributed to the Info-Zip project by Mike Le Voi
'--
'-- Contact me at: mlevoi@modemss.brisnet.org.au
'--
'-- Visit my home page at: http://modemss.brisnet.org.au/~mlevoi
'--
'-- Use this code at your own risk. Nothing implied or warranted
'-- to work on your machine :-)
'----------------------------------------------------------------
'--
'-- This Source Code Is Freely Avaiable From The Info-Zip At:
'-- http://www.cdrom.com/pub/infozip/infozip.html
'--
'-- A Very Special Thanks To Mr. Mike Le Voi
'-- And Mr. Mike White
'-- And The Fine People At The Info-Zip
'-- For Letting Me Use And Modify Their Orginal
'-- Visual Basic 5.0 Code! Thank You Mike Le Voi.
'-- For Your Hard Work In Helping Me Get This To Work!!!
'----------------------------------------------------------------
'--
'-- Contributed To The Info-Zip Project By Raymond L. King.
'-- Modified June 21, 1998
'-- By Raymond L. King
'-- Custom Software Designers
'--
```

continues

```vbnet
'-- Contact Me At: king@ntplx.net
'-- ICQ 434355
'-- Or Visit Our Home Page At: http://www.ntplx.net/~king
'--
'----------------------------------------------------------------

'-- C Style argv
Private Type UNZIPnames
    uzFiles(0 To 99) As String
End Type

'-- Callback Large "String"
Private Type UNZIPCBChar
    ch(32800) As Byte
End Type

'-- Callback Small "String"
Private Type UNZIPCBCh
    ch(256) As Byte
End Type

'-- UNZIP32.DLL DCL Structure
Private Type DCLIST
    ExtractOnlyNewer   As Long      ' 1 = Extract Only Newer, Else 0
    SpaceToUnderscore  As Long      ' 1 = Convert Space To Underscore, Else 0
    PromptToOverwrite  As Long      ' 1 = Prompt To Overwrite Required, Else 0
    fQuiet             As Long      ' 2 = No Messages, 1 = Less, 0 = All
    ncflag             As Long      ' 1 = Write To Stdout, Else 0
    ntflag             As Long      ' 1 = Test Zip File, Else 0
    nvflag             As Long      ' 0 = Extract, 1 = List Zip Contents
    nUflag             As Long      ' 1 = Extract Only Newer, Else 0
    nzflag             As Long      ' 1 = Display Zip File Comment, Else 0
    ndflag             As Long      ' 1 = Honor Directories, Else 0
    noflag             As Long      ' 1 = Overwrite Files, Else 0
    naflag             As Long      ' 1 = Convert CR To CRLF, Else 0
    nZIflag            As Long      ' 1 = Zip Info Verbose, Else 0
    C_flag             As Long      ' 1 = Case Insensitivity, 0 = Case Sensitivity
    fPrivilege         As Long      ' 1 = ACL, 2 = Privileges
    Zip                As String    ' The Zip Filename To Extract Files
    ExtractDir         As String    ' The Extraction Directory,
    ➥ NULL If Extracting To Current Dir
End Type

'-- UNZIP32.DLL Userfunctions Structure
Private Type USERFUNCTION
    UZDLLPrnt      As Long      ' Pointer To Apps Print Function
    UZDLLSND       As Long      ' Pointer To Apps Sound Function
    UZDLLREPLACE   As Long      ' Pointer To Apps Replace Function
    UZDLLPASSWORD  As Long      ' Pointer To Apps Password Function
    UZDLLMESSAGE   As Long      ' Pointer To Apps Message Function
    UZDLLSERVICE   As Long      ' Pointer To Apps Service Function (Not Coded!)
    TotalSizeComp  As Long      ' Total Size Of Zip Archive
```

```
    TotalSize        As Long      ' Total Size Of All Files In Archive
    CompFactor       As Long      ' Compression Factor
    NumMembers       As Long      ' Total Number Of All Files In The Archive
    cchComment       As Integer   ' Flag If Archive Has A Comment!
End Type

'-- UNZIP32.DLL Version Structure
Private Type UZPVER
    structlen        As Long           ' Length Of The Structure Being Passed
    flag             As Long           ' Bit 0: is_beta  bit 1: uses_zlib
    beta             As String * 10    ' e.g., "g BETA" or ""
    date             As String * 20    ' e.g., "4 Sep 95" (beta) or
    ➡ "4 September 1995"
    zlib             As String * 10    ' e.g., "1.0.5" or NULL
    unzip(1 To 4)    As Byte           ' Version Type Unzip
    zipinfo(1 To 4)  As Byte           ' Version Type Zip Info
    os2dll           As Long           ' Version Type OS2 DLL
    windll(1 To 4)   As Byte           ' Version Type Windows DLL
End Type

'-- This Assumes UNZIP32.DLL Is In Your \Windows\System Directory!
Private Declare Function windll_unzip Lib "unzip32.dll" _
    (ByVal ifnc As Long, ByRef ifnv As UNZIPnames, _
     ByVal xfnc As Long, ByRef xfnv As UNZIPnames, _
     dcll As DCLIST, Userf As USERFUNCTION) As Long

Private Declare Sub UzpVersion2 Lib "unzip32.dll" (uzpv As UZPVER)

'-- Private Variables For Structure Access
Private UZDCL   As DCLIST
Private UZUSER  As USERFUNCTION
Private UZVER   As UZPVER

'-- Public Variables For Setting The
'-- UNZIP32.DLL DCLIST Structure
'-- These Must Be Set Before The Actual Call To VBUnZip32
Public uExtractNewer     As Integer   ' 1 = Extract Only Newer, Else 0
Public uSpaceUnderScore  As Integer   ' 1 = Convert Space To Underscore, Else 0
Public uPromptOverWrite  As Integer   ' 1 = Prompt To Overwrite Required, Else 0
Public uQuiet            As Integer   ' 2 = No Messages, 1 = Less, 0 = All
Public uWriteStdOut      As Integer   ' 1 = Write To Stdout, Else 0
Public uTestZip          As Integer   ' 1 = Test Zip File, Else 0
Public uExtractList      As Integer   ' 0 = Extract, 1 = List Contents
Public uExtractOnlyNewer As Integer   ' 1 = Extract Only Newer, Else 0
Public uDisplayComment   As Integer   ' 1 = Display Zip File Comment, Else 0
Public uHonorDirectories As Integer   ' 1 = Honor Directories, Else 0
Public uOverWriteFiles   As Integer   ' 1 = Overwrite Files, Else 0
Public uConvertCR_CRLF   As Integer   ' 1 = Convert CR To CRLF, Else 0
Public uVerbose          As Integer   ' 1 = Zip Info Verbose
Public uCaseSensitivity  As Integer   ' 1 = Case Insensitivity,
➡ 0 = Case Sensitivity
Public uPrivilege        As Integer   ' 1 = ACL, 2 = Privileges, Else 0
```

continues

```vb
Public uZipFileName       As String    ' The Zip File Name
Public uExtractDir        As String    ' Extraction Directory,
➥ Null If Current Directory

'-- Public Program Variables
Public uZipNumber     As Long          ' Zip File Number
Public uNumberFiles   As Long          ' Number Of Files
Public uNumberXFiles  As Long          ' Number Of Extracted Files
Public uZipMessage    As String        ' For Zip Message
Public uZipInfo       As String        ' For Zip Information
Public uZipNames      As UNZIPnames    ' Names Of Files To Unzip
Public uExcludeNames  As UNZIPnames    ' Names Of Zip Files To Exclude
Public uVbSkip        As Integer       ' For DLL Password Function

'-- Puts A Function Pointer In A Structure
'-- For Callbacks.
Public Function FnPtr(ByVal lp As Long) As Long

    FnPtr = lp

End Function

'-- Callback For UNZIP32.DLL - Receive Message Function
Public Sub UZReceiveDLLMessage(ByVal ucsize As Long, _
    ByVal csiz As Long, _
    ByVal cfactor As Integer, _
    ByVal mo As Integer, _
    ByVal dy As Integer, _
    ByVal yr As Integer, _
    ByVal hh As Integer, _
    ByVal mm As Integer, _
    ByVal c As Byte, ByRef fname As UNZIPCBCh, _
    ByRef meth As UNZIPCBCh, ByVal crc As Long, _
    ByVal fCrypt As Byte)

    Dim s0     As String
    Dim xx     As Long
    Dim strout As String * 80

    '-- Always Put This In Callback Routines!
    On Error Resume Next

    '------------------------------------------------
    '-- This Is Where The Received Messages Are
    '-- Printed Out And Displayed.
    '-- You Can Modify Below!
    '------------------------------------------------

    strout = Space(80)

    '-- For Zip Message Printing
    If uZipNumber = 0 Then
```

```
        Mid(strout, 1, 50) = "Filename:"
        Mid(strout, 53, 4) = "Size"
        Mid(strout, 62, 4) = "Date"
        Mid(strout, 71, 4) = "Time"
        uZipMessage = strout & vbCrLf
        strout = Space(80)
    End If

    s0 = ""

    '-- Do Not Change This For Next!!!
    For xx = 0 To 255
        If fname.ch(xx) = 0 Then xx = 99999 Else s0 = s0 & Chr(fname.ch(xx))
    Next

    '-- Assign Zip Information For Printing
    Mid(strout, 1, 50) = Mid(s0, 1, 50)
    Mid(strout, 51, 7) = Right("       " & Str(ucsize), 7)
    Mid(strout, 60, 3) = Right("0" & Trim(Str(mo)), 2) & "/"
    Mid(strout, 63, 3) = Right("0" & Trim(Str(dy)), 2) & "/"
    Mid(strout, 66, 2) = Right("0" & Trim(Str(yr)), 2)
    Mid(strout, 70, 3) = Right(Str(hh), 2) & ":"
    Mid(strout, 73, 2) = Right("0" & Trim(Str(mm)), 2)

    ' Mid(strout, 75, 2) = Right(" " & Str(cfactor), 2)
    ' Mid(strout, 78, 8) = Right("        " & Str(csiz), 8)
    ' s0 = ""
    ' For xx = 0 To 255
    '     If meth.ch(xx) = 0 Then xx = 99999 Else s0 = s0 & Chr(meth.ch(xx))
    ' Next xx

    '-- Do Not Modify Below!!!
    uZipMessage = uZipMessage & strout & vbCrLf
    uZipNumber = uZipNumber + 1

End Sub

'-- Callback For UNZIP32.DLL - Print Message Function
Public Function UZDLLPrnt(ByRef fname As UNZIPCBChar, ByVal x As Long) As Long

    Dim s0 As String
    Dim xx As Long

    '-- Always Put This In Callback Routines!
    On Error Resume Next

    s0 = ""

    '-- Gets The UNZIP32.DLL Message For Displaying.
    For xx = 0 To x
        If fname.ch(xx) = 0 Then xx = 99999 Else s0 = s0 & Chr(fname.ch(xx))
    Next
```

continues

```
        '-- Assign Zip Information
        uZipInfo = uZipInfo & s0

        UZDLLPrnt = 0

End Function

'-- Callback For UNZIP32.DLL - Password Function
Public Function UZDLLPass(ByRef p As UNZIPCBCh, _
    ByVal n As Long, ByRef m As UNZIPCBCh, _
    ByRef Name As UNZIPCBCh) As Integer

    Dim prompt      As String
    Dim xx          As Integer
    Dim szpassword As String

    '-- Always Put This In Callback Routines!
    On Error Resume Next

    UZDLLPass = 1

    If uVbSkip = 1 Then Exit Function

    '-- Get The Zip File Password
    szpassword = InputBox("Please Enter The Password!")

    '-- No Password So Exit The Function
    If szpassword = "" Then
        uVbSkip = 1
        Exit Function
    End If

    '-- Zip File Password So Proccess It
    For xx = 0 To 255
        If m.ch(xx) = 0 Then
            Exit For
        Else
            prompt = prompt & Chr(m.ch(xx))
        End If
    Next

    For xx = 0 To n - 1
        p.ch(xx) = 0
    Next

    For xx = 0 To Len(szpassword) - 1
        p.ch(xx) = Asc(Mid(szpassword, xx + 1, 1))
    Next

    p.ch(xx) = Chr(0)  ' Put Null Terminator For C
```

```
        UZDLLPass = 0

End Function

'-- Callback For UNZIP32.DLL - Report Function To Overwrite Files.
'-- This Function Will Display A MsgBox Asking The User
'-- If They Would Like To Overwrite The Files.
Public Function UZDLLRep(ByRef fname As UNZIPCBChar) As Long

    Dim s0 As String
    Dim xx As Long

    '-- Always Put This In Callback Routines!
    On Error Resume Next

    UZDLLRep = 100 ' 100 = Do Not Overwrite - Keep Asking User
    s0 = ""

    For xx = 0 To 255
        If fname.ch(xx) = 0 Then xx = 99999 Else s0 = s0 & Chr(fname.ch(xx))
    Next

    '-- This Is The MsgBox Code
    xx = MsgBox("Overwrite " & s0 & "?", vbExclamation & vbYesNoCancel, _
                "VBUnZip32 - File Already Exists!")

    If xx = vbNo Then Exit Function

    If xx = vbCancel Then
        UZDLLRep = 104         ' 104 = Overwrite None
        Exit Function
    End If

    UZDLLRep = 102             ' 102 = Overwrite 103 = Overwrite All

End Function

'-- ASCIIZ To String Function
Public Function szTrim(szString As String) As String

    Dim pos As Integer
    Dim ln  As Integer

    pos = InStr(szString, Chr(0))
    ln = Len(szString)

    Select Case pos
        Case Is > 1
            szTrim = Trim(Left(szString, pos - 1))
        Case 1
            szTrim = ""
        Case Else
```

continues

```
                szTrim = Trim(szString)
        End Select

End Function

'-- Main UNZIP32.DLL UnZip32 Subroutine
'-- (WARNING!) Do Not Change!
Public Sub VBUnZip32()

    Dim retcode As Long

    '-- Set The UNZIP32.DLL Options
    '-- (WARNING!) Do Not Change
    UZDCL.ExtractOnlyNewer = uExtractNewer        ' 1 = Extract Only Newer
    UZDCL.SpaceToUnderscore = uSpaceUnderScore    ' 1 = Convert Space To
    ➥ Underscore
    UZDCL.PromptToOverwrite = uPromptOverWrite    ' 1 = Prompt To Overwrite
    ➥ Required
    UZDCL.fQuiet = uQuiet                         ' 2 = No Messages 1 = Less
    ➥ 0 = All
    UZDCL.ncflag = uWriteStdOut                   ' 1 = Write To Stdout
    UZDCL.ntflag = uTestZip                       ' 1 = Test Zip File
    UZDCL.nvflag = uExtractList                   ' 0 = Extract 1 = List Contents
    UZDCL.nUflag = uExtractOnlyNewer              ' 1 = Extract Only Newer
    UZDCL.nzflag = uDisplayComment                ' 1 = Display Zip File Comment
    UZDCL.ndflag = uHonorDirectories              ' 1 = Honour Directories
    UZDCL.noflag = uOverWriteFiles                ' 1 = Overwrite Files
    UZDCL.naflag = uConvertCR_CRLF                ' 1 = Convert CR To CRLF
    UZDCL.nZIflag = uVerbose                      ' 1 = Zip Info Verbose
    UZDCL.C_flag = uCaseSensitivity               ' 1 = Case insensitivity,
    ➥ 0 = Case Sensitivity
    UZDCL.fPrivilege = uPrivilege                 ' 1 = ACL 2 = Priv
    UZDCL.Zip = uZipFileName                      ' ZIP Filename
    UZDCL.ExtractDir = uExtractDir                ' Extraction Directory,
    ➥ NULL If Extracting

                                                  ' To Current Directory

    '-- Set Callback Addresses
    '-- (WARNING!!!) Do Not Change
    UZUSER.UZDLLPrnt = FnPtr(AddressOf UZDLLPrnt)
    UZUSER.UZDLLSND = 0&     '-- Not Supported
    UZUSER.UZDLLREPLACE = FnPtr(AddressOf UZDLLRep)
    UZUSER.UZDLLPASSWORD = FnPtr(AddressOf UZDLLPass)
    UZUSER.UZDLLMESSAGE = FnPtr(AddressOf UZReceiveDLLMessage)
    UZUSER.UZDLLSERVICE = 0& '-- Not Coded Yet :)

    '-- Set UNZIP32.DLL Version Space
    '-- (WARNING!!!) Do Not Change
    With UZVER
        .structlen = Len(UZVER)
        .beta = Space(9) & vbNullChar
        .date = Space(19) & vbNullChar
```

```
        .zlib = Space(9) & vbNullChar
    End With

    '-- Get Version
    Call UzpVersion2(UZVER)

    '------------------------------------
    '-- You Can Change This For Displaying
    '-- The Version Information!
    '------------------------------------
    VBUnzFrm.Print "DLL Date: " & szTrim(UZVER.date)
    VBUnzFrm.Print "Zip Info: " & Hex(UZVER.zipinfo(1)) & "." &
    ➡ Hex(UZVER.zipinfo(2)) &     Hex(UZVER.zipinfo(3))
    VBUnzFrm.Print "DLL Version: " & Hex(UZVER.windll(1)) & "." &
    ➡ Hex(UZVER.windll(2)) & Hex(UZVER.windll(3))
    VBUnzFrm.Print "-------------"
    '-- End Of Version Information.

    '-- Go UnZip The The Files! (Do Not Change Below!!!)
    '-- This Is The Actual UnZip Routine
    retcode = windll_unzip(uNumberFiles, uZipNames, uNumberXFiles, _
                               uExcludeNames, UZDCL, UZUSER)
    '------------------------------------------------------------

    '-- If Theres An Error Display A MsgBox!
    If retcode <> 0 Then MsgBox retcode

    '-- You Can Change This As Needed!
    '-- For Compression Information
    VBUnzFrm.Print "Only Shows If uExtractList = 1 List Contents"
    VBUnzFrm.Print "-------------"
    VBUnzFrm.Print "Comment          : " & UZUSER.cchComment
    VBUnzFrm.Print "Total Size Comp : " & UZUSER.TotalSizeComp
    VBUnzFrm.Print "Total Size        : " & UZUSER.TotalSize
    VBUnzFrm.Print "Compress Factor : %" & UZUSER.CompFactor
    VBUnzFrm.Print "Num Of Members   : " & UZUSER.NumMembers
    VBUnzFrm.Print "-------------"

End Sub


Program Example:


Option Explicit

'-------------------------------------------------
'-- Please Do Not Remove These Comment Lines!
'-----------------------------------------------------------
'-- Sample VB 5 code to drive unzip32.dll
'-- Contributed to the Info-Zip project by Mike Le Voi
'--
```

continues

```vb
'-- Contact me at: mlevoi@modemss.brisnet.org.au
'--
'-- Visit my home page at: http://modemss.brisnet.org.au/~mlevoi
'--
'-- Use this code at your own risk. Nothing implied or warranted
'-- to work on your machine :-)
'-----------------------------------------------------------------
'--
'-- This Source Code Is Freely Avaiable From The Info-Zip At:
'-- http://www.cdrom.com/pub/infozip/infozip.html
'--
'-- A Very Special Thanks To Mr. Mike Le Voi
'-- And Mr. Mike White
'-- And The Fine People At The Info-Zip
'-- For Letting Me Use And Modify Their Orginal
'-- Visual Basic 5.0 Code! Thank You Mike Le Voi.
'-- For Your Hard Work In Helping Me Get This To Work!!!
'-----------------------------------------------------------------
'--
'-- Contributed To The Info-Zip Project By Raymond L. King.
'-- Modified June 21, 1998
'-- By Raymond L. King
'-- Custom Software Designers
'--
'-- Contact Me At: king@ntplx.net
'-- ICQ 434355
'-- Or Visit Our Home Page At: http://www.ntplx.net/~king
'--
'-----------------------------------------------------------------

Private Sub Form_Click()

    Cls

    '-- Init Global Message Variables
    uZipInfo = ""
    uZipNumber = 0      ' Holds The Number Of Zip Files

    '-- Select UNZIP32.DLL Options - Change As Required!
    uPromptOverWrite = 1  ' 1 = Prompt To Overwrite
    uOverWriteFiles = 0   ' 1 = Always Overwrite Files

    '-- Change The Next Line To Do The Actual Unzip!
    uExtractList = 1         ' 1 = List Contents Of Zip 0 = Extract
    uHonorDirectories = 1  ' 1 = Honour Zip Directories

    '-- Select Filenames If Required
    '-- Or Just Select All Files
    uZipNames.uzFiles(0) = vbNullString
    uNumberFiles = 0

    '-- Select Filenames To Exclude From Processing
```

```
    ' Note UNIX convention!
    '    vbxnames.s(0) = "VBSYX/VBSYX.MID"
    '    vbxnames.s(1) = "VBSYX/VBSYX.SYX"
    '    numx = 2

    '-- Or Just Select All Files
    uExcludeNames.uzFiles(0) = vbNullString
    uNumberXFiles = 0

    '-- Change The Next 2 Lines As Required!
    '-- These Should Point To Your Directory
    uZipFileName = "c:\copy\testzip.zip"
    uExtractDir = "c:\copy"

    '-- Let's Go And Unzip Them!
    Call VBUnZip32

    '-- Tell The User What Happened
    If Len(uZipMessage) > 0 Then Print uZipMessage

    '-- Display Zip File Information.
    If Len(uZipInfo) > 0 Then
        Print "uZipInfo is:"
        Print uZipInfo
    End If

    '-- Display The Number Of Extracted Files!
    If uZipNumber > 0 Then Print "Number Of Files: " & Str(uZipNumber)

End Sub

Private Sub Form_Load()

    Me.Show

    Print "Click me!"

End Sub
```

Analysis

This routine is fairly simple. You set the `Public` variables in the `DCLIST` user-defined type using the `Public` variable `UZDCL.variable`. The `DCLIST` user-defined type are flags for the unzip options. They are commented in the `DCLIST` user-defined type. This module also shows how to work with byte arrays and the `AddressOf` function for pointers to callbacks. You should not modify any of the callback functions except where noted. Error handling is built into the functions. Also included is a sample program to show you how to use the routine. The module now supports a password for Zip files.

7.12   CREATE A DIRECTORY

by Lenard Dean with Brian Shea

Description

The `CreateDir` function creates a directory or directory structure using the
`MakeSureDirectoryPathExists` function from the imagehlp.dll file. The purpose of this function is to
ensure that a particular directory path exists for later use in the program. If the directory or directory path
does not exist, the function will create it. The directory path passed to this function should end with a trailing \ character. You can use the `NormalizePath` function found in Chapter 8 to accomplish this.

This function can be useful for confirming the existence or creation of temp directories for use by the application later. There are, of course, many other uses for this function. You could find or create a
\Windows\apps\logs\ directory tree to store application error logs. Later, other applications could store their
logs in that same directory, and if the user hasn't installed the first application, no worries—this function
would automatically create it and move on without any error.

Syntax

`boGoodCreate = CreateDir(ByVal strPath As String) As Boolean`

Part	Description
boGoodCreate	Optional. This is the return value for the function. `True` indicates the direc-tory exists or was created. `False` indicates that an error occurred.
strPath	Required. The directory structure to create.

Code Listing

```
Private Declare Function MakeSureDirectoryPathExists Lib "imagehlp.dll"
➡ (ByVal DirPath As String) As Long

Public Function CreateDir(ByVal strPath As String) As Boolean

    On Local Error Resume Next

    CreateDir = MakeSureDirectoryPathExists(strPath)

End Function
```

Analysis

The `CreateDir` function is a wrapper for the imagehlp.dll function `MakeSureDirectoryPathExists`. This
function will confirm or create the directory path that is passed to it. Unlike `MKDIR`, `CreateDir` can also
create a directory structure like c:\temp\download\programs\.

7.13   PARSE A DIRECTORY PATH

[VB 5]

by Lenard Dean with Brian Shea

Description

This function extracts the specified portion of a pathname from the string that is passed to the function. You should use fully qualified paths when passing a string to this function. That means that if the path is to a directory, you should make sure the path ends with a trailing \. If you do not do this, the function will interpret the last directory name as a filename with no extension.

This function does not attempt to determine whether the parsed path elements are valid or not; it simply parses the elements out of the string it is given. It is up to other functions to do the data validation of the path, either before or after it is passed to this function.

Syntax

```
stReturnStr =  ParsePath(ByVal strPath As String, intPart As ParseParts)
  ➥ As String
```

Part	Description
strReturnStr	Required. This is the returned string value for the path part that is parsed out of the full path.
strPath	Required. The pathname to parse.
intPart	Required:
	DrvOnly: Drive only (with colon).
	DirOnly: Directory only.
	DirOnlyNoSlash: Same as above but not terminated with backslash.
	DrvDir: Drive and directory.
	DrvDirNoSlash: Same as above but not terminated with backslash.
	FileNameBase: Filename base.
	FileNameExt: Filename extension.
	FileNameBaseExt: Filename base and extension.
	FileNameExtNoDot: Same as above but without the dot.
	DrvDirFileNameBase: Drive, directory, and filename base.

Code Listing

```
Public Enum ParseParts
   DrvOnly = 1
   DirOnly = 2
   DirOnlyNoSlash = -2
   DrvDir = 3
   DrvDirNoSlash = -3
   FileNameBase = 4
   FileNameExt = 5
   FileNameExtNoDot = -5
   FileNameBaseExt = 6
   DrvDirFileNameBase = 7
End Enum

Public Function ParsePath(ByVal strPath As String, intPart As ParseParts)
 ➥ As String

On Local Error Resume Next

Dim intCPos As Integer
Dim intLPos As Integer
Dim intTemp As Integer
Dim intPathStart As Integer
Dim intPathLen As Integer
Dim strPart1 As String
Dim strPart2 As String
Dim strPart4 As String
Dim strPart5 As String

intPathLen = Len(strPath)

'-----------------
' Get drive portion.
'-----------------
intCPos = InStr(strPath, ":")

If intCPos Then
    strPart1 = Left(strPath, intCPos)
End If

'-----------------
' Get path portion.
'-----------------
intLPos = InStr(1, strPath, "\")
If Right(strPath, 1) = "\" Then

   '---------------------------
   ' strPath contains no filename.
   '---------------------------
   If intPathLen > intLPos Then
     If intPart < 0 Then
       strPart2 = Mid(strPath, intLPos, intPathLen - intLPos)
```

```
      Else
        strPart2 = Mid(strPath, intLPos)
      End If
    Else
      strPart2 = "\"
    End If

  Else

    If intLPos Then

      '----------------------------
      'strPath must contain a filename.
      '----------------------------
      intPathStart = intLPos
      intLPos = intLPos + 1

      Do
        intCPos = InStr(intLPos, strPath, "\")
        If intCPos Then
          intLPos = intCPos + 1
        End If
      Loop While intCPos

        If intPart < 0 Then
          strPart2 = Mid(strPath, intPathStart, intLPos - intPathStart - 1)
        Else
          strPart2 = Mid(strPath, intPathStart, intLPos - intPathStart)
        End If

    Else
        '------------------
        ' No path was found.
        '------------------

      If Len(strPart1) Then

        '-----------------------------------------------------------------
        ' If drive spec, start at position 3 when getting filename portion.
        '-----------------------------------------------------------------
        intLPos = 3

      Else
        intLPos = 1

      End If

    End If

    strPart4 = Mid(strPath, intLPos)

    '-------------------------------------
```

continues

```
' Check if filename base has extension.
'----------------------------------------
intCPos = 1
Do
   intTemp = InStr(intCPos + 1, strPart4, ".")
   If intTemp Then intCPos = intTemp
Loop While intTemp

If intCPos > 1 Then

    '----------------------------------
    ' Get filename extension portion.
    '----------------------------------
    If InStr(CStr(intPart), "-") Then ' Check if it's "negative".
      strPart5 = Mid(strPart4, intCPos + 1)
    Else
      strPart5 = Mid(strPart4, intCPos)
    End If

    '----------------------------
    ' Get filename base portion.
    '----------------------------
    strPart4 = Left(strPart4, intCPos - 1)

End If

End If

Select Case intPart

'----------------------
' Return drive portion.
'----------------------
Case DrvOnly
  ParsePath = strPart1

'---------------------
' Return path portion.
'---------------------
Case DirOnly, DirOnlyNoSlash
  ParsePath = strPart2

'------------------------------
' Return drive and path portion.
'------------------------------
Case DrvDir, DrvDirNoSlash
  ParsePath = strPart1 & strPart2

'------------------------------
' Return filename base portion.
'------------------------------
Case FileNameBase
```

```
    ParsePath = strPart4

  '..................................
  ' Return filename extension portion.
  '..................................
  Case FileNameExt, FileNameExtNoDot
    ParsePath = strPart5

  '............................................
  ' Return filename base and extension portion.
  '............................................
  Case FileNameBaseExt
    ParsePath = strPart4 & strPart5

  '............................................
  ' Return filename base and extension portion.
  '............................................
  Case DrvDirFileNameBase
    ParsePath = strPart1 & strPart2 & strPart4

End Select

End Function
```

Analysis

This function is very useful for processing file and directory operations within your application. It can be used to get the directory, filename, extension, drive, or combinations of those pieces and return the desired portion. Make sure when passing directories to terminate it with the \ character. The function uses this trailing \ to determine whether the last parameter in the string is a filename or a directory name, and errors in parsing the path can occur if the trailing \ is not present.

First, you declare the Enum that enables you to accept the intPart parameter as a named value instead of a number. This helps make the code more readable and more intuitive. The possible values for the intPart parameter are listed above, and each type specifies what data the function will return.

The bulk of the function then moves through the string and gathers the parts into the strPartsX variables. Most of this is done by using the InStr and Right, Left, and Mid Visual Basic functions. InStr is used to find the token character, usually a \ or a :, then the other functions gather the string value for the strPartX variable.

The last section of this function simply builds the return values from the gathered pieces, based on the intPart parameter that was passed into the function. The built value is then passed out of the function to the strReturnStr.

7.14   VALIDATE DRIVE, VALIDATE DIRECTORY, VALIDATE FILE

by Ian Ippolito

Description

The Visual Basic file controls are fantastic for allowing a user to quickly and easily specify a drive, file, and directory. However, they also make it easier than ever for a user to crash your program by specifying invalid information.

You can use the following routines to validate all the file information specified by the user and avoid nasty program crashes before they happen.

Syntax

```
Exists = Validate_Drive(Drive)
Exists = Validate_Directory(Path, Create)
Exists = Validate_File(FileName) As Integer
```

Part	*Description*
Drive	The drive to validate (example: c:/).
Path	The path to validate (example: c:/helpmake).
Create	TRUE to create a directory if it doesn't exist, otherwise FALSE to do nothing. Note that unlike the DOS mkdir command, this routine can create nested directories that have more than one subdirectory which doesn't yet exist.
FileName	The file to validate (example: c:/helpmake/helpmake.exe).
Exists	TRUE if exists, else FALSE.

Code Listing

```
Option Explicit
'return codes
    Global Const NO_DRIVE = "NO DRIVE"    'no drive found in Get_Drive_Name
    Global Const NO_PATH = "NO PATH"      'no path found in Get_Strict_Path_Name
    Global Const NO_FILE = "NO FILE"      'no file found in Get_File_Name

Function Validate_Drive(ByVal strDrive As String)
On Error GoTo BAD2
    Dim strOldDrive As String
    strOldDrive = Get_Drive_Name(CurDir$)
    ChDrive (strDrive)
    ChDrive (strOldDrive)
```

```
    On Error GoTo 0
    Validate_Drive = True
Exit Function

BAD2:
    Validate_Drive = False
    Resume Exit2

Exit2:
    Exit Function
End Function

Function Validate_Directory(ByVal strPath As String, _
    ByVal boolCreate)
Dim strDrive As String
Dim strDirectory As String
Dim strBuildDirectory As String

    'attempt to find directory
    On Error GoTo erhBAD_DIRECTORY
    If (Dir(strPath, 16) = "") Then
        GoTo erhBAD_DIRECTORY
    End If
    On Error GoTo 0

    'directory found
    Validate_Directory = True

Exit Function
erhBAD_DIRECTORY:

    'directory not found
    Validate_Directory = False

    'check if directory should be created
    If (boolCreate = True) Then

        'directory should be created

        'get drive/directory
        strDrive = Get_Drive_Name(strPath)

        'make sure directory name has \ at end
        If (Right$(strPath, 1) <> "\") Then
            strDirectory = strPath & "\"
        End If
        strDirectory = Get_Strict_Path_Name(strDirectory) & "\"


        'build directory recursively
        strBuildDirectory = ""
        'get next \ (if any)
```

continues

```
            While (InStr(2, strDirectory, "\") > 1)
                '\ found

                strBuildDirectory = strBuildDirectory & _
                    Left$(strDirectory, InStr(2, strDirectory, "\") - 1)
                strDirectory = Mid$(strDirectory, _
                    InStr(2, strDirectory, "\"))

                'determine if directory node exists
                If Dir(strDrive & strBuildDirectory, 16) = "" Then
                    'doesn't--create it
                    MkDir strDrive & strBuildDirectory
                End If
            Wend
        End If

End Function
Function Validate_File(ByVal FileName As String) As Integer
Dim fileFile As Integer
    '       'attempt to open file
    fileFile = FreeFile
    On Error Resume Next
    Open FileName For Input As fileFile

    '       'check for error
    If Err Then
        Validate_File = False
    Else
        '           'file exists
        '           'close file
        Close fileFile
        Validate_File = True
    End If
End Function
Function Get_Drive_Name(ByVal strString As String) As String
    'purpose:gets a drive name from a file
    'inputs:strString--drive name to extract
    'returns:see purpose
    'ex. c:\vb\programs\fred.exe returns c:\
    '        if no drive name is specified, returns NO_DRIVE


    If (InStr(strString, ":") > 0) Then
        Get_Drive_Name = Left$(strString, InStr(strString, ":"))
    Else
        Get_Drive_Name = NO_DRIVE
    End If

End Function

Function Get_File_Name(ByVal strString As String) As String
    'purpose:Searches from right to left in strString and returns string
```

```
'to the right of "\"
'if no file name was found--returns NO_FILE
'ex. c:\vb\programs\it.exe returns it.exe
'      it.exe                   returns it.exe
'      c:\                      returns NO_FILE
'      c:                       returns NO_FILE
'inputs:strString--file path and name
'returns:see purpose
Dim intIndex As Integer
For intIndex = Len(strString) To 1 Step -1
    If ((Mid$(strString, intIndex, 1) = "\") Or (Mid$(strString,
  ➥ intIndex, 1) = ":")) Then
        Get_File_Name = Mid$(strString, intIndex + 1)
        If (Len(Mid$(strString, intIndex + 1)) = 0) Then
            Get_File_Name = NO_FILE
        End If
        Exit Function
    End If
Next intIndex


'no ":" or "\" found so return entire string
Get_File_Name = strString

End Function

Function Get_Path_Name(ByVal strString As String) As String
    'purpose:gets a file path from a complete string   (drive is included)
    'i.e. c:\vb\icons\accessories\office01.ico
    'returns c:\vb\icons\accessories
    'inputs:strString--path and name of file
    'returns:see purpose
    Dim intIndex As Integer
    For intIndex = Len(strString) To 1 Step -1
        If (Mid$(strString, intIndex, 1) = "\") Then
            Get_Path_Name = Left(strString, intIndex - 1)

            'if c:--change to c:\
            If (Len(Left(strString, intIndex - 1)) = 2) Then
                Get_Path_Name = Left(strString, intIndex - 1) & "\"
            End If
            Exit Function
        End If
    Next intIndex
    'no path--default to root
    Get_Path_Name = "\"

End Function
Function Create_File_Name(ByVal strPath As String, ByVal strFile As String)
  ➥ As String
    'purpose:concatenates a file path and name properly together
    'ex c:\vb\windows and progman.exe
```

continues

```
'   returns c:\vb\windows\progman.exe
'inputs:strPath--path of file
'        strFile--file name
'returns:see purpose

If (Right$(strPath, 2) = ":\") Then
    Create_File_Name = strPath & strFile
Else
    Create_File_Name = strPath & "\" & strFile
End If
End Function
Function Get_Strict_Path_Name(ByVal strString As String) As String
    'gets a strict file path from a complete string (i.e. no drive)
    'i.e. 1)c:\vb\icons\accessories\office01.ico returns \vb\icons\accessories
    '     2)c:\vb\exe\ returns \vb\exe
    '     3)c:icons.exe returns NO_PATH
    '     4)icons.exe returns NO_PATH
    '     5)c:\ returns \
    '     6)c:\*.* return \

    'check for case 5
    If ((Len(strString) = 3) And (Mid$(strString, 3, 1) = "\")) Then
        Get_Strict_Path_Name = "\"
        Exit Function
    End If

    'check for case 6
    If (Mid$(strString, 4, 1) = "*") Then
        Get_Strict_Path_Name = "\"
        Exit Function
    End If

    Dim intIndex As Integer
    For intIndex = Len(strString) To 1 Step -1

        'look for first \
        If (Mid$(strString, intIndex, 1) = "\") Then
            'found first \

            'check for c:\
            'If (intIndex = Len(strString)) Then
                'Get_Strict_Path_Name = "\"
            'Else
                Get_Strict_Path_Name = Mid$(strString, InStr(strString, ":")
                ➥ + 1, intIndex - InStr(strString, ":") - 1)
            'End If
            Exit Function
        End If
    Next intIndex

    'no path--default to root
    Get_Strict_Path_Name = NO_PATH

End Function
```

Analysis

`Validate_Drive` determines whether a drive exists by actually attempting to change to that drive with the Visual Basic `ChDrive` command. If this attempt is successful, it knows that the drive exists. Otherwise, the routine invisibly traps the error using the `ON ERROR GOTO` command, so as not to alert the user, and then changes the drive back to the current drive before returning `FALSE`.

`Validate_Directory` performs in a similiar fashion to `Validate_Drive` by using the Visual Basic `Dir` command. If the directory passed in is found not to exist and the user has denoted that it should be created, this routine does so. Rather than using the familiar VB `Mkdir` command, which is unable to create directories that have more than one node that doesn't exist, this routine manually parses the directory string node by node, creating each node individually and bypassing this problem.

`Validate_File` determines whether a file exists by opening it. This approach is efficient and works well for most applications. However, if a program must check a network file, this routine will erroneously indicate that the file doesn't exist if another user happens to have the file opened exclusively. If your application must handle this scenario, the routine can be modifed to use the visual Basic `Dir` command instead.

7.15 GET SPACE AVAILABLE ON DISK

by Mike Shaffer

Description

The `GetDiskSpace` function returns the amount of free space on any drive. If the function is passed an invalid drive specification, the return value will be –1.

Syntax

```
if GetDiskSpace(strDrive) < 100000 then end
```

Part	Description
`strDrive`	Required. The drive name (in the form X:\) for which to report the available free space.
`Returns`	The disk space value (in bytes) as a currency data type (used to hold a larger number).

Code Listing

```
'*********************************************
'* Submitted by Mike Shaffer
'*********************************************
```

continues

```
Declare Function GetDiskFreeSpace Lib "kernel32" Alias "GetDiskFreeSpaceA" _
  (ByVal lpRootPathName As String, lpSectorsPerCluster As Long, _
  lpBytesPerSector As Long, lpNumberOfFreeClusters As Long, _
  lpTotalNumberOfClusters As Long) As Long


Public Function GetDiskSpace(Drive As String) As Currency
    '
    ':::::::::::::::::::::::::::::::::::::::::::::::::::::::::::::::::::::::::'
    ':::                                                               :::'
    ':::     Function to return disk free space. Pass disk name (e.g. C:\) :::'
    ':::     Works regardless of file system (e.g. FAT16 or FAT32)       :::'
    ':::     If an invalid drive designation is passed, the value '-1' will :::'
    ':::     will be returned.                                           :::'
    ':::                                                               :::'
    ':::::::::::::::::::::::::::::::::::::::::::::::::::::::::::::::::::::::::'
      '
      Dim nSectorsPerCluster As Long
    Dim nBytesPerSector As Long
    Dim nNumberOfFreeClusters As Long
    Dim nTotalNumberOfClusters As Long
      '
    If Len(Drive) < 3 Then Drive = Drive & "\"
    If GetDiskFreeSpace(UCase$(Drive), nSectorsPerCluster, nBytesPerSector, _
nNumberOfFreeClusters, nTotalNumberOfClusters) Then
        DiskFree = nNumberOfFreeClusters * nSectorsPerCluster
        DiskFree = DiskFree * nBytesPerSector
    Else
        DiskFree = -1
    End If
End Function
```

Analysis

A single Windows API call (GetDiskFreeSpace) does most of the work here. This routine simply multiplies the values returned to come up with a value that normal users can understand (that is, bytes free). The drive value passed should be in the form C:\ (use the colon and the initial backslash because that is what the Windows API expects).

7.16   MOVE A FILE BETWEEN DIRECTORIES

by Fredrik Bodin

Description

This is a subroutine that moves a selected file from one directory to another. The routine does not look to see whether the destination directory exists or if the filename is correct.

Syntax

```
Movefile(StartName, EndName)
```

Part	Description
StartName	Required. Specifies the file you want to move. For example, the string could be "C:\WINDOWS\TEST.TXT".
EndName	Required. Specifies the destination for the file. For example, "A:\TEST.TXT".

Code Listing

```
Private Sub MoveFile(StartName, EndName As String)
    FileCopy StartName, EndName
    Kill StartName
End Sub
```

Analysis

This routine works by first copying the original file to the destination and then deleting the file at the previous location. This moves the file from one position to another. If the destination isn't valid, the program breaks at the FileCopy line.

Chapter 8

STRING MANIPULATION

Even though Visual Basic is pretty good at handling strings, there are still several areas that could use some improvement. We have collected some of those improvements and some additional functions that you can add to your string toolbox in this chapter. Functions for searching backward through a string, setting the proper case on string data, and search and replace all can be found here.

8.1 BREAKING A STRING INTO INDIVIDUAL ELEMENTS

by Andy Carrasco

Description

`Tokenize` breaks up a delimited string into elements of an array. It is particularly useful when reading comma-delimited text files, in which each unique value is separated by a comma, or for specifying a list constant within your code.

Syntax

```
Array = Tokenize(sList, sDelimiter)
```

Part	Description
Array	Required. A variant variable that will hold the array generated from the value of sList.
sList	Required. A string containing a list of values, delimited by a character (usually a comma). It doesn't matter whether this value contains a trailing delimiter or not.
sDelimiter	Required. A single character string that contains the delimiter character used.

Code Listing

```
Public Function Tokenize(sList As String, sDelimiter As String) As Variant
'Tokenize a comma delimited string, store as string array, and return it
Dim LocalArray() As String
Dim iLoc As Integer
Dim Bound As Integer

sList = Trim$(sList)

If Right$(sList, 1) <> sDelimiter Then sList = sList + sDelimiter

iLoc = InStr(sList, sDelimiter)

Do Until iLoc = 0
    Bound = Bound + 1
    ReDim Preserve LocalArray(Bound)
    LocalArray(Bound - 1) = Trim$(Left$(sList, iLoc - 1))
    sList = Right$(sList, Len(sList) - iLoc)
    iLoc = InStr(sList, sDelimiter)
Loop

ReDim Preserve LocalArray(Bound - 1)

Tokenize = LocalArray
End Function
```

Analysis

This function loops through the string sList looking for the character specified in the variable sDelimiter. When found, the element is extracted from the string and placed into the variable LocalArray. LocalArray is dynamically resized as necessary to accommodate each element found in the variable sList. When all elements have been extracted, the function will return the array contained in the variable LocalArray.

8.2 FIXED FONT WORD WRAP

by Andy Carrasco

Description

LineWrap inserts a carriage return and line feed at specified intervals within a string. This is useful for displaying neatly formatted text based on column position. LineWrap receives as its arguments the string to process and the desired column at which to begin wrapping. It returns the processed string.

Syntax

```
NewString = LineWrap( sString, Interval )
```

Part	Description
NewString	Required. A variable to hold the processed string.
sString	Required. The string to format for word wrapping.
iInterval	Required. An integer specifying the general column to begin wrapping at. Usually 80.

Code Listing

```
Public Function LineWrap(sString As String, iInterval As Integer) As String

Dim lPos As Long
Dim iPosCounter As Long
Dim lFinalLen As Long
Dim lBeginPos As Long
Dim lEndPos As Long
Dim iWordLen As Long
Dim iWordPos As Long
Dim dWrapThresh As Integer

lFinalLen = Len(sString)

Const WRAP_CHAR = vbCrLf

Do Until lPos >= lFinalLen
    'ok, we hit the wrap point
    If iPosCounter = iInterval Then
        'Reset the interval counter
        iPosCounter = 0

        'Get the beginning position of the current word
        For lBeginPos = lPos To 0 Step -1
            If Mid$(sString, lBeginPos, 1) = " " Then Exit For
        Next lBeginPos

        'Get the ending position of the current word
        For lEndPos = lPos To lFinalLen
            If Mid$(sString, lEndPos, 1) = " " Then Exit For
        Next lEndPos

        'Get the length of the current word
        iWordLen = (lEndPos - 1) - (lBeginPos + 1)

        'Find out at which character we are located in the word
        iWordPos = lPos - (lBeginPos + 1)
```

continues

```
        'If we are over half way, then we move forward,
        'otherwise we move back
        dWrapThresh = iWordLen / 2

        If lEndPos > Len(sString) Then Exit Do

        If iWordPos >= dWrapThresh Then 'Wrap at end of word
            sString = Left$(sString, lEndPos) + WRAP_CHAR +  _
        Right$(sString, lFinalLen - lEndPos)
        Else                            'Wrap at beginning of word
            sString = Left$(sString, lBeginPos) + WRAP_CHAR + _
        Right$(sString, lFinalLen - lBeginPos)
        End If

        lFinalLen = Len(sString)

    End If
iPosCounter = iPosCounter + 1

'Reset if new line already
If lPos > 0 Then If Mid$(sString, lPos, 2) = vbCrLf Then iPosCounter = 0

lPos = lPos + 1
Loop

LineWrap = sString

End Function
```

Analysis

This function generates a nicely formatted string. Although most simple line wrapping algorithms insert a line feed based solely on the column, this algorithm never breaks a word in the middle. Instead, it uses a more intelligent technique.

The function loops through the string, incrementing `iPosCounter` for each character encountered. When `iPosCounter` is equal to `iInterval`, you know that the line feed must be placed around where you are in the string. First check to see whether you are currently somewhere in the middle of a word; if not, your job is easy. Simply insert the line feed at the current position. If you are in the middle of a word, things become slightly more complicated.

The first task is to determine the position of the word's first and last characters within the string. This is accomplished with two small loops that search for a space character before and after the current position in the string. After you have the start and end positions of the word, you can determine the length of the word and your current position within the word. The line feed must be placed either before or after the current word. To determine this, simply check to see whether your current position in the word is before or after the middle. If your current position is before the middle character of the word, insert the line feed before the current word; otherwise, it is placed after it.

8.3   INSERT WORD WRAP

VB
5

by Lenard Dean with Brian Shea

Description

The insert word wrap function simply adds a word wrap on a text string to a specified width. You can pass the function a string value and an integer representing the length of the desired line (in characters) and the function will insert carriage return/line feed characters to wrap the text to that length.

If the wrap length is shorter than any word in the string, the function prompts the user with that information and asks whether the function should continue. If the user responds Yes, the function adds a hyphen to the end of the current line and continues at the next letter of the word. If the user responds No the function quits at the current execution point and the WordWrap function returns a NULL string.

Syntax

```
strReturnStr = WordWrap(ByVal strText As String, ByVal intWidth As Integer)
➥ As String
```

Part	Description
strReturnStr	Required. This is the variable that will hold the returned string with the wrap characters in it.
strText	Required. The text to word wrap.
intWidth	Required. The text length per line.

Code Listing

```
Public Function WordWrap(ByVal strText As String, ByVal intWidth As Integer)
➥ As String

   Dim intTextLen As Integer
   Dim intPointer As Integer, inResponse As Integer
   Dim intN As Integer, I As Integer
   Dim strTemp As String, stNote As String

   On Local Error Resume Next

   intPointer = 1
   intTextLen = Len(strText)
   I = 0

   Do
     For intN = intPointer + intWidth To intPointer Step -1
```

continues

```
        If I = intWidth Then
            '* Remove the following lines for no user prompt on Wrap error
            stNote = "The String Contains A Word Longer Than The Wrapped Length"
            stNote = stNote & Chr$(13) & "Do you want to continue?"
            inResponse = MsgBox(stNote, vbYesNo, "Continue Wrapping Text?")
            If inResponse = vbNo Then
                WordWrap = ""
                Exit Function
            End If
            '* The lines below are needed to add the hyphen and continue the
            ➥ function
            strTemp = strTemp & Mid(strText, intPointer, intWidth) & "-" & vbCrLf
            intPointer = intPointer + intWidth
            I = 0
            Exit For
        End If
        If Mid(strText, intN, 1) = " " Or intN = intTextLen + 1 Then
            strTemp = strTemp & Mid(strText, intPointer, intN - intPointer) &
            ➥ vbCrLf
            intPointer = intN + 1
            Do While Mid(strText, intPointer, 1) = " "
              intPointer = intPointer + 1
            Loop
            I = 0
            Exit For
        Else
            I = I + 1
        End If
    Next
  Loop While intPointer < intTextLen

  WordWrap = strTemp

End Function
```

Analysis

This function is pretty easy to follow. It parses through the string and inserts vbCRLF characters at the desired wrap length or at the end of the word just before the wrap length. This function can be very useful for formatting text that will be printed or displayed for reports or in a known fixed format.

Here's what is happening in this function. It takes the first intWidth + 1 characters and looks to see whether the last character is a space. If it is, the function breaks here; if it isn't, the function walks backward through the first section until it finds a space and inserts the break at that point. A pointer to the break position is then updated from 1 to the end of the last string + 1 and the function does the process again. It continues until it has reached the length of the string.

This function also prompts the user if a word is longer than the wrap length. The user may choose to continue or not. If the user does not continue, WordWrap returns a NULL string, and if he or she does continue, the word is hyphenated and the function continues. You might need to change this behavior for automated routines that shouldn't have user interaction on the word wrap function; the code is commented to show which lines should be removed.

Note

The function as it is currently written doesn't check to see whether the text string was previously wrapped. This can cause problems if you plan to use the function to let users wrap text to custom sizes, because they might wrap the text more than once and get strange results. You could extend this code to check for and strip out all vbCRLF or Chr$(13) characters before doing the wrapping function, and that should correct for that condition.

8.4   SEARCH AND REPLACE

by Andy Carrasco

Description

StrInStr replaces all occurrences of a string within a string, similar to the search and replace feature of popular word processors. This function is especially useful for filtering unwanted characters from within strings and replacing bad tags within an HTML document.

If you are using Visual Basic 6, it now contains an intrinsic function (**Replace**) that performs the same operation.

To use, pass the function the original string, the value you are searching for, and the value you want to replace it with.

Syntax

NewString = StrInStr(sOriginalString, sSearchValue, sReplaceValue)

Part	Description
sOriginalString	Required. The string in which the find and replace will be performed.
sSearchValue	Required. A string containing the value to be replaced.
sReplaceValue	Required. A string containing the value that will replace sSearchValue within the string.

Code Listing

```
Public Function StrInStr(sOriginalString As String, sSearchValue As String,
➡ sReplaceValue As String) As String

Dim iLoc As Long
Dim LastLoc As Long
Dim iSearchLen As Integer

iLoc = InStr(1, sOriginalString, sSearchValue, vbBinaryCompare)
iSearchLen = Len(sSearchValue)
LastLoc = iLoc

Do Until iLoc = 0
    sOriginalString = Left$(sOriginalString, iLoc - 1) + sReplaceValue +
    ➡ Right$(sOriginalString, Len(sOriginalString) -
    ➡ (iLoc - 1 + iSearchLen))
    iLoc = InStr(LastLoc + Len(sReplaceValue), sOriginalString, sSearchValue,
    ➡ vbBinaryCompare)
    LastLoc = iLoc
Loop

StrInStr = sOriginalString

End Function
```

Analysis

This function loops through sOriginalString looking for occurrences of sSearchString. When one is found, the old value is replaced by sReplaceValue. When all replacements have been made, the new processed string is returned.

8.5   REPLACE A STRING TOKEN

by Lenard Dean with Brian Shea

Description

You use this function to replace a string or specific characters within a string. This routine can also be used to strip characters out of a string. The function returns the new string whether the original was modified or not. The blnUpdated variable is updated to True if the string is updated by this function.

Syntax

```
strReturnStr = ReplaceCS(ByVal strWork As String, ByVal strOld As String,
➡ ByVal strNew As String, Optional ByVal intOPMode As OpMode,
➡ Optional blnUpdated As Boolean)
```

Part	Description
strReturnStr	Required. The returned string value for the function.
strWork	Required. The string to work on.
strOld	Required. If intOPMode is negative, defines the characters to replace. If intOPMode is positive, defines the string to replace. Otherwise this should be the character to replace.
strNew	Required. The new character (or string) to substitute. To strip a string or characters, set vbNullString or "".
intOPMode	Optional. Sets the operation mode by defining the replace mode (string or character) and compare mode (binary, text, or database). Valid parameters are
	StringBinaryCompare (the default if not specified)
	StringTextCompare
	StringDataBaseCompare
	CharacterBinaryCompare
	CharacterTextCompare
	CharacterDataBaseCompare
blnUpdated	Optional. Returns True if the string was modified.

Note

A note about OPModes. The OPMode for this function defines both the replace mode and the compare mode. The replace mode can be a character or string. Although a string can be only one character, it can sometimes increase a code's readability and clarity if you ensure you use the character mode when working with character data. The compare mode of binary is a case-sensitive compare. Text mode is not case-sensitive. Database mode is used when operating on data from Access databases.

Code Listing

```
Public Enum OpMode
    StringBinaryCompare = vbBinaryCompare + 1
    StringTextCompare = vbTextCompare + 1
    StringDataBaseCompare = vbDatabaseCompare + 1
    CharacterBinaryCompare = -(vbBinaryCompare + 1)
    CharacterTextCompare = -(vbTextCompare + 1)
    CharacterDataBaseCompare = -(vbDatabaseCompare + 1)
End Enum
```

continues

```
Public Function ReplaceCS(ByVal strWork As String, ByVal strOld As String,
  ➥ ByVal strNew As String, Optional ByVal intOPMode As OpMode,
  ➥ Optional blnUpdated As Boolean) As String

On Error Resume Next

Dim intOldLen As Integer
Dim intNewLen As Integer
Dim intSPos As Long
Dim intN As Integer

If intOPMode = 0 Then
  intOPMode = StringBinaryCompare
End if

intNewLen = Len(strNew)
intOldLen = Len(strOld)

intSPos = 1
blnUpdated = False

If intOPMode < 0 Then
  intOPMode = Abs(intOPMode) - 1
  For intN = 1 To intOldLen
    intSPos = 1
    Do
      intSPos = InStr(intSPos, strWork, Mid(strOld, intN, 1), intOPMode)
      If intSPos Then
        strWork = Left(strWork, intSPos - 1) & strNew & Mid(strWork,
          ➥ intSPos + 1)
        intSPos = intSPos + intNewLen
        blnUpdated = True
      End If
    Loop While intSPos
  Next
Else
  intOPMode = intOPMode - 1
  Do
    intSPos = InStr(intSPos, strWork, strOld, intOPMode)
    If intSPos Then
      strWork = Left(strWork, intSPos - 1) & strNew & Mid(strWork, intSPos +
          ➥ intOldLen)
      intSPos = intSPos + intNewLen
      blnUpdated = True
    End If
  Loop While intSPos
End If

ReplaceCS = strWork

End Function
```

Analysis

The replace string token function is pretty easy to analyze. It simply replaces the specified string or character with the new string or character. The function also lets you specify the mode of operation and compare mode by setting the OpMode parameter. This value defaults to string mode and text compare if not specified.

First, the function defines the OpModes used, and this section of code should be placed in the global declaration section of your project. This will allow you to use the OpModes referred to throughout this listing.

The function then reads the OpMode and determines whether the mode is string or character replacement. It will then read through the string and find the target string. The function then replaces the target with the new string specified, and in the string replace or character replace mode. The blnUpdated variable is updated if the string is modified, and the resulting string is returned.

Note

Be careful to specify the correct mode when you replace strings. If you specify character mode and tell it to use a string as the new value, the string will be inserted in place of every character of the target string.

8.6 PARSE STRING TOKENS

by Lenard Dean with Brian Shea

Description

This function enables you to retrieve a specified token of a string. (A *string token* is a string or segment of a string that you want to treat as a single unit.) This function can be used to easily get values out of delimited text or get specific words out of strings. The function returns the string token, and if the token is not found it will return an empty string (""). This routine requires ReplaceCS to work when using encapsulation characters, but you will need to include it or comment out the ReplaceCS line for the function to operate.

The function will return the token number that you specify in the intTokenNum parameter, or it will return all the tokens in the string when run in automode. You set the function to automode by setting intTokenNum to 0. If you are processing more than one string in automode, be sure to reset the function between uses by using ParseStr ("", 0, "").

For example, assume you are parsing the third token in strWork:

```
John Doe, 1998/03/01, Calgary, Canada
```

If you set up the function as ParseStr(strWork, 3, ","), it returns Calgary.

When defining a `strWork` string that might contain characters in the token which also define the delimiter for that string, it is important to set the `strEncapChar` or the wrong token will be returned. For example:

`"Doe, John", 1998/03/01, Calgary, Canada`

If you set the function as `ParseStr(strWork, 1, ",", Chr(34))`, it will return `John Doe`.

If you want to retrieve all the tokens in the string shown above, you can do it a couple of ways.

Method 1:

```
For intN = 1 to 4
    strToken(intN) = ParseStr(strWork, intN, ",", Chr(34))
Next
```

Method 2: (Faster)

```
Call ParseStr("", 0, "")    ' Reset auto-mode counter.

For intN = 1 to 4
    strToken(intN) = ParseStr(strWork, 0, ",", Chr(34))
Next
```

Syntax

```
strRetVal = ParseStr(ByVal strWork As String, intTokenNum As Integer,
➥ strDelimitChr As String, Optional ByVal strEncapChr As String)
```

Part	*Description*
strRetVal	Required. This is the returned value for the function.
strWork	Required. The string to work on.
intTokenNum	Required. If greater than zero, returns the specified token in the string. If zero, returns the next token in the string each time the function is called. (If no more tokens are found, the function will return zero.)
strDelimitChr	Required. The token delimiter.
strEncapChr	Optional. Allows tokens to return strings encapsulated with `strDelimitChr` characters.

Code Listing

```
Public Function ParseStr(ByVal strWork As String, intTokenNum As Integer,
➥ strDelimitChr As String, Optional ByVal strEncapChr As String)
➥ As String

On Local Error Resume Next

Dim blnExitDo As Boolean
Dim intDPos As Integer
```

```
Dim intSPtr As Integer
Dim intEPtr As Integer
Dim intCurrentTokenNum As Integer
Dim intWorkStrLen As Integer
Dim intEncapStatus As Integer
Static intSPos As Integer
Dim strTemp As String
Static intDelimitLen As Integer

intWorkStrLen = Len(strWork)

If Len(strEncapChr) Then
  intEncapStatus = Len(strEncapChr)
End If

If intWorkStrLen = 0 Or (intSPos > intWorkStrLen And intTokenNum = 0) Then
  intSPos = 0
  Exit Function
ElseIf intTokenNum > 0 Or intSPos = 0 Then
  intSPos = 1
  intDelimitLen = Len(strDelimitChr)
End If

Do

  intDPos = InStr(intSPos, strWork, strDelimitChr)

  If intEncapStatus Then
    intSPtr = InStr(intSPos, strWork, strEncapChr)
    intEPtr = InStr(intSPtr + 1, strWork, strEncapChr)
    If intDPos > intSPtr And intDPos < intEPtr Then
      intDPos = InStr(intEPtr, strWork, strDelimitChr)
    End If
  End If

  If intDPos < intSPos Then
    intDPos = intWorkStrLen + intDelimitLen
  End If

  If intDPos Then
    If intTokenNum Then
      intCurrentTokenNum = intCurrentTokenNum + 1
      If intCurrentTokenNum = intTokenNum Then
        strTemp = Mid(strWork, intSPos, intDPos - intSPos)
        blnExitDo = True
      Else
        blnExitDo = False
      End If
    Else
      strTemp = Mid(strWork, intSPos, intDPos - intSPos)
```

continues

```
        blnExitDo = True
    End If
    intSPos = intDPos + intDelimitLen
  Else
    intSPos = 0
    blnExitDo = True
  End If
Loop Until blnExitDo

If intEncapStatus Then
  ParseStr = ReplaceCS(strTemp, strEncapChr, "", StringBinaryCompare)
Else
  ParseStr = strTemp
End If
End Function
```

Analysis

First, you declare the variables and determine whether an encapsulation character is being used. Next, the function determines whether the string being tokenized is empty, sets the length of the delimiter, and sets the start position.

The function then finds the first delimiter string and checks for the encapsulation character. It then loops through the string, finding the token values between the delimiter or encapsulation characters. The VB Mid and InStr functions are heavily used to accomplish this task.

The last thing the function does is to remove the encapsulation characters from the returned string if they are present. This is the part of the function that really requires the ReplaceCS function. If you don't think you'll ever have to use the encapsulation characters, you can leave out the ReplaceCS function and comment out the IF, ELSE, END IF, and ReplaceCS lines.

8.7   TOKEN COUNT

by Lenard Dean with Brian Shea

Description

This function counts the number of tokens in a string based on the delimiter that you specify. It can also be used to determine the number of delimiter characters found in the string by subtracting 1 from the returned value.

This function currently is coded to count null or blank tokens along with tokens that have values. Additionally, you should be careful not to use a delimiter that might appear in the actual string data. The function will not be able to discern that character from an actual delimiter, and the count will come back as inaccurate.

This function can be used to check comma-delimited files for the correct number of fields before importing the data into a database or Excel file, or counting the number of words in a string or text file. It can also be used to determine how many directories are in a path statement.

Syntax

```
lgRetVal =  TokenCount(strWork As String, strDelimiter As String)
```

Part	Description
lgRetVal	Required. The returned value for the number of tokens (including blank or null ones) in the string.
strWork	Required. The string to work on.
strDelimiter	Required. The string delimiter. This character should not appear anywhere in the string data except as a delimiter.

Code Listing

```
Public Function TokenCount(strWork As String, strDelimiter As String) As Long

  On Local Error Resume Next

  Dim lngN As Long
  Dim lngCPos As Long
  Dim lngSPos As Long
  Dim lngCharLen As Long

  If Len(strWork) = 0 Then Exit Function

  lngCharLen = Len(strDelimiter)
  lngSPos = 1

  Do
    lngCPos = InStr(lngSPos, strWork, strDelimiter)
    If lngCPos Then
      lngN = lngN + 1
      lngSPos = lngCharLen + lngCPos
    End If
  Loop While lngCPos

  If Right(strWork, lngCharLen) <> strDelimiter Then
    TokenCount = lngN + 1
  Else
    TokenCount = lngN
  End If

End Function
```

Analysis

This function is fairly simple. It checks the string to see whether it's empty, and exits the function if it is. If it's not empty, the function proceeds to check the string for delimiter characters and then increments a count by one. The last step checks to see whether the last character is a delimiter, and adds one to the token count if not, or simply returns the token count if it is.

That's all there is to it, but despite its simplicity this is a very useful function.

8.8 CALCULATE SIGNIFICANT DIGITS

by Lenard Dean with Brian Shea

Description

This function calculates the significant digits of a string value. The string value should represent a decimal, single, or double value, which can be converted to a string by using CStr(NUMERIC VALUE). Converting the value to a string enables you to do the functions on the properties of the number instead of operating on the number itself. Typically, these decimal, single, or double values will be trimmed to their significant digits by Visual Basic before they are converted to a string.

Syntax

```
intRetVal = GetSigDigits(ByVal strValue As String) As Integer
```

Part	Description
intRetVal	Required. The returned value for the significant digits.
strValue	This is the value to check (passed as a string).

Code Listing

```
Private Function GetSigDigits(ByVal strValue As String) As Integer

    Dim intCPos As Integer
    Dim strLeftSide As String
    Dim strRightSide As String
    Dim intSPos As Integer
    Dim intEPos As Integer
    Dim intN As Integer
    Dim strChar As String

    On Error Resume Next
```

```
    strValue = Trim(strValue)
    intCPos = InStr(strValue, ".")

    If intCPos Then
      strLeftSide = CStr(Fix(strValue))
      If strLeftSide = "0" Then strLeftSide = ""
      If Len(strLeftSide) Then
        strRightSide = CStr(Mid(strValue, intCPos + 1))
      Else
        strRightSide = CStr(Fix(Mid(strValue, intCPos + 1)))
      End If
      intEPos = InStr(1, strRightSide, "0")
      strRightSide = Left(strRightSide, intEPos - 1)
      GetSigDigits = Len(strLeftSide) + Len(strRightSide)
    Else
      For intN = 1 To Len(strValue)
        strChar = Mid(strValue, intN, 1)
        If strChar <> "0" And intSPos = 0 Then
          intSPos = intN
        End If
        If strChar <> "0" Then
          intEPos = intN
        End If
      Next
      GetSigDigits = intEPos - intSPos + 1
    End If

End Function
```

Analysis

This function determines the number of significant digits in a numeric value. To accomplish this, though, the numeric value is converted to a string before using the function. You can use `CStr` to accomplish the conversion.

The first thing the function does is to determine the presence of a decimal point. If a decimal point is present, the function checks the left and right sides of the decimal point for significant digits, and then adds those numbers together to get the actual value.

If no decimal is present, the function simply walks through each character and determines whether it is a number or a 0. It counts the number of nonzero values and returns that as the significant digits.

8.9 FORMAT A NUMBER WITH SIGNIFICANT DIGITS

5

by Lenard Dean with Brian Shea

Description

This function can be used to format a value to the specified number of significant digits. As with the "Calculate Significant Digits" section, the value you use to set the significant digits should be converted to a string value when passed into this function. Doing this enables you to do more manipulations on the format of the data than you can when the number is in its native (decimal, single, or double) format.

Syntax

```
strRetVal = SetSigDigits(ByVal strValue As String, ByVal intSigDigits As
➥ Integer)
```

Part	Description
strRetVal	Required. This is the returned string value, which represents the numeric data set to the correct significant digits.
strValue	Required. The string that represents the numeric value to format.
intSigDigits	Required. The number of significant digits to use for the returned string.

Code Listing

```
Public Function SetSigDigits(ByVal strValue As String, ByVal intSigDigits
➥ As Integer) _
    As String

  Dim intTemp As Integer
  Dim strTemp As String
  Dim intDigits As Integer
  Dim intCPos As Integer
  Dim strValueLen As Integer

  On Local Error Resume Next

  strTemp = String(intSigDigits, "0")
  strValue = CDbl(Format(CDbl(strValue), strTemp & "e-" & strTemp))
  strValueLen = Len(strValue)

  intTemp = InStr(strValue, ".")

  If intTemp Then
    If Fix(strValue) Then
      strValue = strValue & String(intSigDigits - strValueLen + 1, "0")
    Else
      strValue = strValue & String(intSigDigits - Len(Fix(Mid(strValue,
      ➥ intTemp + 1))), _
          "0")
    End If
  Else
```

```
      If intSigDigits <> strValueLen Then
        strValue = strValue & "." & String(intSigDigits - strValueLen, "0")
      End If
   End If

   SetSigDigits = strValue

End Function
```

Analysis

You can use this function to set the number of significant digits in a number. Because string data is easier to format, though, you must first convert the numeric data (decimal, single, or double) to a string. You can then call the `SetSigDigits` function.

The function then sets a temp string to contain the correct number of significant digits and fills it with zeros. The format function is then used to format the string to the correct significant digits. The value of `intTemp` is then set to the position of the decimal.

Sounds like you're finished, right? Well, normally this would be all, but you haven't checked to ensure that the correct number of significant digits is displayed. If the number of significant digits is more than the number of nonzero digits in the string, the value can be truncated. The next section corrects for this by padding the value with trailing zeros and sets a decimal place as needed. This ensures that the correct value is returned whether or not the original value had enough.

8.10 LOAD A TEXT FILE INTO A STRING ARRAY

VB 5

by Lenard Dean with Brian Shea

Description

The load text file into string array function does exactly that: it loads the contents of a text file into a string array. Each line of the text file is loaded into one item of the array. This function uses the get file EOL indicator function, which can also be found in this section. This function also provides a progress indicator that updates as the function progresses. You may choose to not use this part of the function if you don't need this functionality.

Note

The function places the data in a local string array as written. If you want to make the data available to other functions, you can make the string array a public array or you must handle the data from within the function. You can also modify the function slightly to add the data to a control such as a list or text box if you want.

Syntax

```
lgRetVal = GetFileStrArray(strFileName As String, strFileArray() As String,
➥ ctlProgress As Control)
```

Part	Description
lgRetVal	Required. The returned value for the number of lines processed into the array.
strFileName	Required. The full path of the file to load.
strFileArray	Required. The array into which to load the file.
ctlProgress	Required. The desired progress object, such as a label or text control. Pass NOTHING if not needed.

Code Listing

```
Public Function GetFileStrArray(strFileName As String, strFileArray()
➥ As String, _
    ctlProgress As Control) As Long

  On Error Resume Next

  Dim lngN As Long
  Dim lngMaxDim As Long
  Dim fh As Integer
  ReDim strFileArray(1 To 1) ' Just incase it is not defined
  Dim lngFileSize As Long

  Dim strBuffer As String
  Dim lngLastBlockSize As Long
  Dim intBlocks As Integer
  Dim intBlock As Integer
  Dim intSPos As Integer
  Dim intBuffPtr As Integer
  Dim strEOLChar As String
  Dim intEOLCharLen As Integer
  Dim lngFilePtr As Long
  Dim intMinDim As Integer

  Const kintArraySize As Integer = 31744
  Const kintBlockSize As Integer = 31744

  strEOLChar = FileEOLChars(strFileName)
  intEOLCharLen = Len(strEOLChar)
  strBuffer = Space(kintBlockSize)
  intMinDim = LBound(strFileArray)

  fh = FreeFile
  Open strFileName For Input As #fh
```

```
If Err = 0 Then
  lngFileSize = LOF(fh)
  lngFilePtr = 1
  ' Determine number of blocks
  intBlocks = (lngFileSize \ kintBlockSize) + 1
  'Read each block
  For intBlock = 1 To intBlocks
    ctlProgress = Format(lngFilePtr / lngFileSize * 100, " 0.0") & "%"
    DoEvents
    If intBlock = intBlocks Then
     lngLastBlockSize = lngFileSize - Seek(fh) + 1
     strBuffer = Input(lngLastBlockSize, fh)
   Else
      strBuffer = Input(kintBlockSize, fh)
    End If
    intSPos = 1
    Do
      intBuffPtr = InStr(intSPos, strBuffer, strEOLChar)
      If intBuffPtr Then
        If lngN = lngMaxDim Then
          lngMaxDim = lngMaxDim + kintArraySize
          ReDim Preserve strFileArray(intMinDim To lngMaxDim)
        End If
        lngN = lngN + 1
        strFileArray(lngN) = Mid(strBuffer, intSPos, intBuffPtr - intSPos)
        intSPos = intBuffPtr + intEOLCharLen
      ElseIf intBlock = intBlocks Then ' Check if this is the Last block
     ➥ and if so, _
          make note of it.
        If intBuffPtr = 0 Then
          lngN = lngN + 1
          strFileArray(lngN) = Right(strBuffer, lngLastBlockSize -
       ➥ intSPos + 1)
          If Len(strFileArray(lngN)) = 0 Then lngN = lngN - 1 ' Don't include
       ➥ blank _
              line if file ends with CRLF.
        End If
      Else
        lngFilePtr = lngFilePtr + intSPos - 1
        Seek #fh, lngFilePtr
      End If
    Loop While intBuffPtr
  Next

  Close #fh

  If lngN Then
    ReDim Preserve strFileArray(intMinDim To lngN)
    GetFileStrArray = lngN
  End If
```

continues

```
    ctlProgress = " 100%"
    DoEvents
  Else
    Debug.Print Err.Description
  End If

End Function
```

Analysis

This function takes the contents of a text file and enters it into a string array. This functionality can be very useful, so look at what happens in the course of the function. The first thing you see, as usual, is the declarations of the variables. The string array is set to one item for now, and the array item size and text buffer size are set to 31744.

Next, the end of line (EOL) character is found, the buffer is set, and the minimum array boundary is set. Then the function opens the text file and proceeds if there is no error. The `Debug.Print` line near the end of the function should catch any errors that occur. You can change this to a `MsgBox` or whatever method you prefer for catching errors.

You now see the block size is determined and the function loops through all the blocks, adding each to a line in the array. You can see that the function uses `InStr` and `Mid` functions to accomplish much of the string manipulation work. Additionally, this function won't include the last blank line if the text file ends with a carriage return/line feed character.

The function ends by returning the number of lines read out of the file into the array. The progress control is also set to 100% at the end of this function if the progress control is being used.

8.11 ENCAPSULATE A STRING IN QUOTES

by Lenard Dean with Brian Shea

Description

This function encapsulates a string with the specified character by adding that character to the beginning and ending of the string. The default character is double quotes, but you can change that to single quotes or any character you choose. It's a handy routine if you work with SQL statements.

With a little modification, this function could be used to add HTML tags to text from a text box or RichText control.

Syntax

```
strRetStr = QQ(ByVal strWork As String, Optional varQuoteChr As Variant)
```

Part	Description
strRetStr	Required. The returned string contained in the encapsulating characters.
strWork	Required. The string to encapsulate.
varQuoteChr	Optional. The encapsulation character. 1 = singe quote, 2 = double quote (the default). You also can define a specific character. When not specified, the default is 2.

Code Listing

```
Public Function QQ(ByVal strWork As String, Optional varQuoteChr As Variant)
➡ As String

 On Error Resume Next

  If IsMissing(varQuoteChr) Then ' Set default
    QQ = Chr(34) & strWork & Chr(34)
  ElseIf IsNumeric(varQuoteChr) Then
    If varQuoteChr = 1 Then
      QQ = "'" & strWork & "'"
    Else
      QQ = Chr(34) & strWork & Chr(34)
    End If
  Else
    QQ = varQuoteChr & strWork & varQuoteChr
  End If

End Function
```

Analysis

This routine puts a string between two characters that you specify. These characters can be any that you choose, but one common use is single or double quotes.

The function simply checks the value of varQuoteChr to find out the value of the encapsulating character. If it is not passed to the function, double quotes are used. It also handles the values of 1 for single quotes and 2 for double quotes. You could add any string values to this list that you need.

If you needed to, you could also add a varQuoteChr1 and varQuoteChr2 (replacing the varQuoteChr parameter) and have a different starting character and ending character wrapped around the string. Using this type of technique, you could add HTML tags to text easily.

8.12 GET A FILE EOL INDICATOR

by Lenard Dean with Brian Shea

Description

This function checks what the end of line (EOL) character is in a file (for example, `vbCrLf`, `vbCr`, or `vbLf`). The function will go out, open a file, and try to determine the EOL character. It is capable of detecting only `vbCrLf` (carriage return/line feed), `vbCr` (carriage return), or `vbLf` (line feed). The return value is an empty string if the character is not recognized.

You can extend the capability of this function by adding values to the list for which it checks. This way, if you have a special file format that you want to use, the function can be altered to recognize it.

Syntax

```
strRetVal = FileEOLChars(strFile As String)
```

Part	Description
strRetVal	Required. The returned string value for the end of line character. This will be an empty string if the character is not recognized.
strFile	Required. The path and filename of the file to check.

Code Listing

```
Public Function FileEOLChars(strFile As String) As String

  On local Error Resume Next

  Dim fh As Integer
  Dim lngBufSize As Long
  Dim strLineBuf As String

  fh = FreeFile
  Open strFile For Input As #fh

  lngBufSize = LOF(fh)

  If lngBufSize > 1024 Then
    strLineBuf = Input(1024, #fh)
  Else
    strLineBuf = Input(lngBufSize, #fh)
  End If
```

```
    If InStr(strLineBuf, vbCrLf) Then
        FileEOLChars = vbCrLf
    ElseIf InStr(strLineBuf, vbCr) Then
        FileEOLChars = vbCr
    ElseIf InStr(strLineBuf, vbLf) Then
        FileEOLChars = vbLf
    Else
        FileEOLChars = vbNullString
    End If

    Close #fh

End Function
```

Analysis

This function is easy to understand. It gets a file number for the file you are about to open, and then opens that file. The length of the file is checked, and if it exceeds 1024 bytes, the function buffers the first 1024 bytes for use. There should be no need to check the entire file. Next, the InStr function is used to determine whether the known culprit is the EOL character. If not, an empty string is returned. The returned string values you get back can then be used while parsing the string, or (with the Len() or LenB() functions) used to increment position pointers when moving through the string.

If you want to check for additional characters, you can add them to the If statement located before the Close statement.

This function might not operate on a file that is already opened.

8.13   GET A FILE LINE COUNT

by Lenard Dean with Brian Shea

Description

This function can be used to get the total number of lines in a text file. This entry uses the FileEOLChars that is described elsewhere in this section to get the end of line (EOL) character and then determines how many lines the text file has in it based on that count. If the file ends in a blank line containing only an EOL character, the function doesn't count that line.

Syntax

```
lgRetVal = FileLineCount(strFileName As String)
```

Part	Description
lgRetVal	Required. The returned line count.
strFileName	Required. The file to check.

Code Listing

```
'* by Lenard Dean

Public Function FileLineCount(strFileName As String) As Long

  On Local Error Resume Next

  Dim intN As Long
  Dim intSPos As Integer
  Dim intCPos As Integer
  Dim fh As Integer
  Dim strBuffer As String
  Dim lngBlocks As Long
  Dim lngBlock As Long
  Dim lngLastBlockSize  As Long
  Dim strEOLChars As String
  Dim intEOLCharsLen As Integer
  Dim lngFilePtr As Long
  Dim lngFileSize As Long

  Const kintBlockSize As Integer = 31477

  strEOLChars = FileEOLChars(strFileName)
  intEOLCharsLen = Len(strEOLChars)
  strBuffer = Space(kintBlockSize)

  fh = FreeFile
  Open strFileName For Input As #fh

  lngFileSize = LOF(fh)
  lngFilePtr = 1

  ' Determine number of blocks and size of last (short) block
  lngBlocks = (lngFileSize \ kintBlockSize) + 1

  'Read each block
  For lngBlock = 1 To lngBlocks
    If lngBlock = lngBlocks Then
      lngLastBlockSize = lngFileSize - Seek(fh) + 1
      strBuffer = Input(lngLastBlockSize, fh)
    Else
      strBuffer = Input(kintBlockSize, fh)
    End If
    DoEvents
```

```
      intSPos = 1
      Do
        intCPos = InStr(intSPos, strBuffer, strEOLChars)
        If intCPos Then
          intN = intN + 1
          intSPos = intCPos + intEOLCharsLen
        Else
          lngFilePtr = lngFilePtr + intSPos - 1
          Seek #fh, lngFilePtr
        End If
      Loop While intCPos
    Next

    Close #fh

    'Add one to count if last line does not end with a CrLf.
    If Right(strBuffer, intEOLCharsLen) <> strEOLChars Then intN = intN + 1

    FileLineCount = intN

End Function
```

Analysis

This function is pretty straightforward. It simply gets the number of lines in a text file by counting the number of EOL characters in the file. This function will not count a line if the text file wraps but there is no EOL character. It also will not count an empty last line if the file contains one.

8.14 GET FILES OR DIRECTORIES

VB5

by Lenard Dean with Brian Shea

Description

You can use this function to retrieve all files or directories from a specified path. This function also requires the NormalizePath routine, which can be found in this section. In addition to returning the total number of files or directories, the function also stores all the file or directory names in a string array for later use if needed.

Syntax

```
intRetVal = GetDirFiles(strPath As String, strArray() As String,
➥intMode As Integer)
```

Part	Description
`intRetVal`	Required. The returned number of target files or directories.
`strPath`	Required. The path to check to get files or directories.
`strArray`	Required. The array containing the files or directories.
`intMode`	Required. The retrieve mode:
	`vbNormal`: Get files. Can include wildcards such as * and ?.
	`vbDirectory`: Get directories.

Code Listing

```
'* by Lenard Dean

Public Function GetDirFiles(strPath As String, strArray() As String,
➥ intMode As Integer) As Integer

On Local Error Resume Next

  Dim strFDName As String
  Dim intN As Integer

' Don't normalize if we are passing wildcards or filename.
  If InStr(strPath, "*") = 0 And InStr(strPath, "?") = 0 And intMode =
➥ vbDirectory Then
    '* Otherwise normalize the path to ensure consistent handling
    strPath = NormalizePath(strPath)
  End If

'* Check the mode and handle the vbDirectory condition to get directories
  If intMode = vbDirectory Then
    strFDName = Dir(strPath, intMode)
    '* Get each Directory and repeat until you have them all
    Do While strFDName <> ""
      '* Don't get the Current Dir and Parent Dir
      If strFDName <> "." And strFDName <> ".." Then
        '* If this is a Directory, add it to the count and list
        If GetAttr(strPath & strFDName) And intMode Then
          intN = intN + 1
          ReDim Preserve strArray(1 To intN)
          strArray(intN) = strFDName
        End If
      End If
      strFDName = Dir
    Loop
  Else
```

```
      '* We have files to deal with, get the items with the archive bit set
      strFDName = Dir(strPath, intMode + vbArchive)
      '* While we have files in the list, increment the count and list by 1
      Do While strFDName <> ""
        intN = intN + 1
        ReDim Preserve strArray(1 To intN)
        strArray(intN) = strFDName
        strFDName = Dir
      Loop
   End If

'* Return either 0 (and blank the array) or the number of requested items
 If intN = 0 Then
   ReDim strArray(0)
 Else
   GetDirFiles = intN
 End If

End Function
```

Analysis

As you can see, this function relies on the DIR Visual Basic function to get the directory of filenames from the path specified. This function also gets all the files or directories and stores their names in an array for later use. The array used in the function shown is a local scope array, and will not carry the contents outside the function. If you need access to this data from other functions you could declare the array using a Public scope or store the array contents in a control.

8.15 LOCATE A SUBSTRING BACKWARD

by Lenard Dean with Brian Shea

Description

This function operates the same as InStr, but can also start the search from the other end of the string. This function returns the position of the first occurrence of one string within another, or enables you to specify the occurrence number of the string being searched for.

For example, you could search for the second occurrence of the word "be" in Hamlet's soliloquy "To be, or not to be" or the fifth occurrence from the end of "Sam I Am" in *Green Eggs and Ham*. (Assuming, of course, you have a string containing "Hamlet" or "Green Eggs and Ham" <G>.)

Syntax

```
lgRetVal = InstrBak(lngStartPos As Long, strSource As String,
➥ strSearch As String, Optional ByVal lngSearchCount As Long)
```

Part	Description
lgRetVal	Required. The returned position of the search string.
lngStartPos	Required. The position from which to start the search (–1 starts from the end).
strSource	Required. The source string.
strSearch	Required. The search string.
lngSearchCount	Optional. Enables you to define which strSearch to return. For example, if you are reverse searching the \ character but want the position of the second one found, you would set this value to 2. If not specified, the position of the first occurrence is returned.

Code Listing

```
'* by Lenard Dean

Public Function InstrBak(lngStartPos As Long, strSource As String,
➥ strSearch As String, _
    Optional ByVal lngSearchCount As Long) As Long

   On Local Error Resume Next

   Dim lngI As Long
   Dim lngCurPos As Long
   Dim lngSourceLen As Long
   Dim lngN As Long
   Dim intCounter As Integer
   Dim lngPrevI As Long

'* Get the source string length
   lngSourceLen = Len(strSource)

'* Set the starting position of the search
   If lngStartPos = -1 Then
     lngCurPos = lngSourceLen
   Else
     lngCurPos = lngStartPos
   End If

'* Step backwards through the string, starting at the start position
   For lngN = lngCurPos To 1 Step -1
     '* Find the first occurance of the search string
```

```
      lngI = InStr(lngN, strSource, strSearch, vbTextCompare)
      If lngI Then
        '* If no Search Count specified, return this value
        If lngSearchCount = 0 Then
          Exit For
        '* Otherwise, keep going until the item found is the
          ➥correct one specified
        ElseIf lngI <> lngPrevI Then
          intCounter = intCounter + 1
          If lngSearchCount = intCounter Then
            Exit For
          Else
            lngPrevI = lngI
          End If
        End If
      End If
    Next

  '* Return the position of the specified item
    InstrBak = lngI

End Function
```

Analysis

This function should be pretty easy to figure out as you go through it. First you determine the direction in which you're going to move through the string, and set the start position accordingly. If the start position is a positive number, the function behaves exactly like InStr. However, if the start position is listed as -1, the function moves backward through the string and finds the search string in the reverse order. The function returns the integer value of the position of the desired occurrence.

8.16 NORMALIZE A PATH

by Lenard Dean with Brian Shea

Description

This routine adds a backslash to the end of a path if one is not already present. It comes in handy when you don't know whether a path ends with a backslash. Using this function always makes sure the path does end in a backslash. The function will not add a second backslash if one is already present.

This can be very useful when you are parsing directory paths or Registry keys and must ensure that the path ends in a backslash before appending the filename or key name.

Syntax

```
strRetVal = NormalizePath(ByVal strPath As String)
```

Part	Description
strRetVal	Required. The returned string value for the normalized path.
strPath	Required. The path on which to work.

Code Listing

```
'* by Lenard Dean

Public Function NormalizePath(ByVal strPath As String) As String

  On Local Error Resume Next

'* Remove the leading or trailing spaces
  strPath = Trim(strPath)

  If Len(strPath) Then
    If Right(strPath, 1) <> "\" Then
      NormalizePath = strPath + "\"
    Else
      NormalizePath = strPath
    End If
  End If

End Function
```

Analysis

This routine is very simple. It starts by trimming off any spaces that might be present. Then it checks to see whether a trailing \ is already present and adds one if it is not. The value returned is the normalized string with a trailing \ character.

8.17 PAD A STRING

by Lenard Dean with Brian Shea

Description

This function can be used to pad a string with a specified character to the specified width. You can also specify the alignment of the string within the new, padded string, but the default is left alignment if not specified. You can specify the character that you want to use for a padding character, which can be very useful. The padding character used, if not specified, is the space character.

If you must undo the padding that you add using this function, you will have to use Left, Right, or Trim functions. If you specify spaces, Trim is a good choice to remove the extra space characters when you want to.

Syntax

```
strRetVal = PadString(ByVal strWorkStr As String, ByVal intWidth As _
Integer, Optional ByVal strAlign As String, Optional ByVal varCharCode
➥ As Variant)
```

Part	Description
strRetVal	Required. The returned string with padding and justification.
strWorkStr	Required. The string to pad.
intWidth	Required. The length to which to pad the string.
strAlign	Optional. Specifies the alignment of the original string within the new string. L = left (default), R = right, C = center.
varCharCode	Optional. Character code like * or 42 to pad the string with. If not specified, padding will occur with the space character.

Code Listing

```
'* by Lenard Dean

Public Function PadString(ByVal strWorkStr As String,
➥ByVal intWidth As Integer,
➥ Optional ByVal strAlign As String,
➥Optional ByVal varCharCode As Variant) As String

  On Local Error Resume Next

  Dim strTemp As String
  Dim intWorkStr As Integer
  Dim intN As Integer

'* Set the temp string length, and woking string length
  strTemp = Space(intWidth)
  intWorkStr = Len(strWorkStr)
'* Set the character to use and alignment, if not specified
  If IsMissing(varCharCode) Then varCharCode = 32
  If strAlign = "" Then strAlign = "L"

  If strAlign = "L" Then
    '* If the string is shorter than the length, pad the string
```

continues

```
      If intWidth > intWorkStr Then
        strTemp = strWorkStr & String(intWidth - intWorkStr, varCharCode)
      '* Otherwise, trim the string to the length specified
      Else
        strTemp = Left(strWorkStr, intWidth)
      End If
  '* Repeat the same steps, but pad to the left side for Right Alignment
  ElseIf strAlign = "R" Then
    If intWidth > intWorkStr Then
      strTemp = String(intWidth - intWorkStr, varCharCode) & strWorkStr
    Else
      '* Always keep the leftmost characters, even on a right alignment
      strTemp = Left(strWorkStr, intWidth)
    End If
  Else
      '* On Center align, determine if we need to pad or trim
    If intWorkStr < intWidth Then
      '* Determine the number of characters to pad on either side
      intN = Fix((intWidth - intWorkStr) / 2)
      '* Add the same amount to either side
      If (intWidth - intWorkStr) Mod 2 = 0 Then
        strTemp = String(intN, varCharCode) & strWorkStr & String(intN,
        ➥ varCharCode)
      '* Otherwise, add the extra character to the left side
      Else
        strTemp = String(intN + 1, varCharCode) & strWorkStr & String(intN,
        ➥ varCharCode)
      End If
    Else
      '* We still get the leftmost characters when trimming
      strTemp = Left(strWorkStr, intWidth)
    End If
  End If

'* Return the altered string
  PadString = strTemp

End Function
```

Analysis

This function pads a string value with the specified character and aligns the string in the new string to left, right, or center. Working through the code is fairly easy; it primarily uses the & operator to accomplish its functionality.

First the function sets a temporary string and determines the length of the working string. It also sets the values of the optional variables here if they haven't already been set.

Next, the function handles the left- and right-aligned string by using the & operator and "adding" the string values together in the correct order to get a new string aligned in the desired way. If the starting string is longer than the desired width, the string is trimmed to include the most characters it can from the original string. No padding characters are added at all in this case.

The Center alignment condition is handled last; it simply splits the padding between the left and right sides of the string and uses the & operator to "add" the strings together. If the original string is longer than the target string, the original is cut off to the desired length.

8.18 REGULAR EXPRESSIONS

by Paolo Bonzini

Description

This class module implements regular expression matching. A regular expression is similar to the right-hand operand of the Like operator.

I'll refer to the components of a regular expression as *atoms* and *modifiers*. An atom can be a dot (which matches all characters), a character (which matches only that character) optionally preceded by the backslash escape character (which allows you to match dots, brackets, and other special characters), or ranges (which are enclosed in brackets and work the same way as in the Like operator). A modifier is placed after an atom and can be a +, *, or ? character. A modifier is optional: A plus matches one or more occurrences of the atom it follows, a star matches zero or more occurrences, and a question mark matches zero or one occurrences.

Sample regular expressions are [!A-Za-z]+ (which matches nonalphabetic sequences) or [A-Za-z0-9][A-Za-z0-9_]* (which matches Visual Basic identifiers); the classic "match all files" *.* becomes ".*\..*". As you can see, regular expressions are easier to use than to describe, and they are very powerful, too.

A regular expression also might begin with a caret, indicating that a match is not valid unless it begins in the first character of a string, or it might end with a dollar, indicating that a valid match must end in the last character of string. For example, 0abcdef$123 matches [a-f]+, but it does not match ^[a-f]+, ^[a-f]$, or [a-f]+$. It matches [a-f]+\$, however, because the dollar is preceded by an escape character.

Here is a quick reference on regular expressions:

Pattern	Notation
^	Matches the beginning of a line.
$	Matches the end of a line.
.	Matches any single character.
[\]char	Matches the specified character. The slash is mandatory if char is a special character: *, +, ?, ., ^, $, \, or [.
[*string*]	Matches any single character in *string*.
pattern*	Matches a sequence of zero or more matches of the pattern.
pattern+	Matches a sequence of one or more matches of the pattern.
pattern?	Matches a sequence of zero or one matches of the pattern.

To use this class, put this code in a new class module. Then use the `Init` method to precompile a regular expression (parsing it and dividing it into atoms). Use the `Match` method to match a string to a regular expression.

Syntax

```
regexpobj.Init RegExp
result = regexpobj.Match(FromX, ToX, Text)
```

Part	Description
regexpobj	Required. An object expression evaluating to an instance of `RegularExpression`.
RegExp	Required. A string expression evaluating to a valid regular expression.
result	Required. A returned value indicating whether a match was found.
FromX	Required. An integer expression evaluating to the first character position to search. On return, if result is true, it indicates the position of the first character in the match. You will want to pass to `Match` a `Long` variable, usually setting it to 1 before the call.
ToX	Required. On return, if result is true, it indicates the position of the last character in the match. You will usually want to pass to `Match` a `Long` variable.

Code Listing

```
Option Explicit

'? = edOptional; + = edMulti; * = edOptional or edMulti
Private Enum RegExpAtomTypes
    edOptional = 65536
    edMulti = 131072
    edModifierMask = edOptional Or edMulti
```

```
      edCharacter = 0
      edBracketed = 262144        'for example, [a-z]
      edAny = 524288
End Enum

Private Type StateStack
    Atom As Long
    Posi As Long
    MinPosi As Long
End Type

Private mStack() As StateStack
Private mCompiled() As Long
Private mNAtoms As Long
Private mPattern As String
Private mAnchorBeginning As Boolean
Private mAnchorEnd As Boolean
Private mMinLength As Long


Private Sub AddAtom(ByVal Flags As Long, _
    ByVal CharOrPosi As Long)

If mNAtoms = UBound(mCompiled) Then
    ReDim Preserve mCompiled(1 To mNAtoms + 10) As Long
End If
mNAtoms = mNAtoms + 1
mCompiled(mNAtoms) = CharOrPosi Or Flags

End Sub

Public Sub Init(RegExp As String)

Dim StackSize As Long, Posi As Long, EndPosi As Long

'Initialize member variables
mPattern = RegExp
mNAtoms = 0
mMinLength = 0
ReDim mCompiled(1 To 10) As Long

Posi = 1
EndPosi = Len(RegExp)

If Left(mPattern, 1) = "^" Then
    Posi = Posi + 1
    mAnchorBeginning = True
End If
If Right(mPattern, 1) = "$" Then
    If Right(mPattern, 2) <> "\$" Then
        EndPosi = EndPosi - 1
```

continues

```
                mAnchorEnd = True
        End If
End If

Do Until Posi > EndPosi
    Select Case Mid$(mPattern, Posi, 1)
        Case "."
            AddAtom edAny, 0
            Posi = Posi + 1
        Case "\"
            Posi = Posi + 1
            AddAtom edCharacter, Asc(Mid$(mPattern, Posi, 1))
            Posi = Posi + 1
        Case "["
            AddAtom edBracketed, Posi
            Posi = RangeParse(Posi)
            If Posi = -1 Then Err.Raise 5
        Case Else
            AddAtom edCharacter, Asc(Mid$(mPattern, Posi, 1))
            Posi = Posi + 1
    End Select

    'check for modifiers (?, +, *)
    Select Case Mid$(mPattern, Posi, 1)
        Case "?"
            mCompiled(mNAtoms) = mCompiled(mNAtoms) _
                Or edOptional
            StackSize = StackSize + 1
            Posi = Posi + 1
        Case "+"
            mCompiled(mNAtoms) = mCompiled(mNAtoms) _
                Or edMulti
            StackSize = StackSize + 1
            Posi = Posi + 1
            mMinLength = mMinLength + 1
        Case "*"
            mCompiled(mNAtoms) = mCompiled(mNAtoms) _
                Or edMulti Or edOptional
            StackSize = StackSize + 1
            Posi = Posi + 1
        Case Else
            mMinLength = mMinLength + 1
    End Select
Loop

'Minimize wasted memory by dimensioning exact arrays
ReDim Preserve mCompiled(1 To mNAtoms) As Long
If StackSize = 0 Then StackSize = 1
ReDim mStack(1 To StackSize) As StateStack

End Sub
```

```
Public Function Match(ByRef FromX As Long, ByRef ToX As Long, _
    Text As String) As Boolean

Dim Matched As Boolean
Dim CurAtom As Long
Dim Atom As Long
Dim SP As Long
Dim LenText As Long
Dim LastFromX As Long


LenText = Len(Text)
LastFromX = IIf(mAnchorBeginning, 1, LenText - mMinLength + 1)
For FromX = FromX To LastFromX
    ToX = FromX
    Atom = 1
    SP = 0
    Do
        If Atom <= mNAtoms Then
            GoSub MatchAtom
        ElseIf (Not mAnchorEnd) Or (ToX > LenText) Then
            'ToX is pointing the first character
            'PAST the matched string
            ToX = ToX - 1
            Match = True
            Exit For
        Else
            'Set CurAtom to 0, to make all the IFs fail
            'and force backtracking
            CurAtom = 0
            Matched = False
        End If
        If Matched Then
            If CurAtom And edModifierMask Then
                'create a new item in the backtrack stack
                SP = SP + 1
                If CurAtom And edOptional Then
                    mStack(SP).MinPosi = ToX
                Else
                    mStack(SP).MinPosi = ToX + 1
                End If
                If CurAtom And edMulti Then
                    '+ or *, try to get as far as possible
                    If CurAtom And edAny Then
                        'When matching .* and .+, the longest
                        'sequence reaches the end of the string
                        ToX = LenText + 1
                    Else
                        Do
                            ToX = ToX + 1
                            GoSub MatchAtom
                        Loop Until Not Matched
                    End If
```

continues

```
                Else
                    '?, look just one character ahead
                    ToX = ToX + 1
                End If
                Atom = Atom + 1
                mStack(SP).Posi = ToX
                mStack(SP).Atom = Atom
            Else
                'no +, *, nor ?, advance to the next atom
                ToX = ToX + 1
                Atom = Atom + 1
            End If
        ElseIf CurAtom And edOptional Then
            'not matched, but it was optional... no problem
            Atom = Atom + 1
        Else
            'backtrack: find the next usable item in the stack
            For SP = SP To 1 Step -1
                If mStack(SP).Posi > mStack(SP).MinPosi Then
                    Exit For
                End If
            Next SP
            If SP = 0 Then Exit Do
            mStack(SP).Posi = mStack(SP).Posi - 1
            ToX = mStack(SP).Posi
            Atom = mStack(SP).Atom
        End If
    Loop
Next FromX
Exit Function

MatchAtom:
    CurAtom = mCompiled(Atom)
    If ToX > LenText Then
        Matched = False
    ElseIf CurAtom And edAny Then
        Matched = True
    ElseIf CurAtom And edBracketed Then
        Matched = _
            RangeMatch(CurAtom And 65535, Mid$(Text, ToX, 1))
    Else
        Matched = _
            (CurAtom And 65535) = Asc(Mid$(Text, ToX, 1))
    End If
    Return

End Function

Private Function RangeMatch(Posi As Long, ch As String) _
    As Boolean
```

```
RangeMatch = ch Like _
    Mid$(mPattern, Posi, InStr(Posi, mPattern, "]") - Posi + 1)

End Function


'Return the end of the range (e.g. [a-z]) starting at position Posi.
'Return -1 if the regular expression is not well formed.
Private Function RangeParse(Posi As Long) As Long

Dim EndPosi As Long

EndPosi = InStr(Posi, mPattern, "]")

'Try using operator Like and check if an error occurs
On Error Resume Next
If "a" Like Mid(mPattern, Posi, EndPosi - Posi + 1) Then:
If Err Then
    RangeParse = -1
    Err.Clear
Else
    RangeParse = EndPosi + 1
End If

End Function
```

Analysis

Let's start with `Init`, which is the simplest function. It scans the string for atoms and stores information about them in the `mCompiled` member variable. Items of `mCompiled` are Longs in which bits 0–15 are used for various data (for characters, the ASCII value; for ranges, the position of the open bracket in the regular expression). Bits 16–17 contain information about modifiers, and bits 18–19 contain the type of atom (dot, character, or range).

When a range is found, the matching closed bracket is found with `InStr`, the range is extracted, and then `RangeParse` checks for errors in its syntax. To do so, simply pass the range to operator `Like` and check whether VB itself raises an error. If so, `RangeParse` answers `-1` and `Init` raises an Illegal Function Call error.

`Init` also assigns values to other variables: `mPattern` contains the whole regular expression (which must be saved in order to parse ranges), `mNAtoms` keeps a count of the atoms, `mAnchorBeginning` and `mAnchorEnd` save whether there are carets or dollars in the regular expression, `mMinLength` contains the minimum length of a match and is used to limit the amount of job done in `Match`. `mMinLength` is incremented whenever an atom is found that is not followed by a star or question mark.

In addition, `Init` dimensions a `Stack` variable, of type `StateStack`, which leads to the hairy topic of backtracking. Every regular expression-parsing algorithm uses it because matching regular expressions must be done by trial and error: Whenever you find a modifier after an atom, push your state on the stack and try to match that atom with the longest possible sequence. If you find yourself locked, you must try with a slightly shorter sequence. When you cannot have a shorter sequence, pop a state from stack and try shortening another sequence. If no sequences are on the stack, the matching has failed.

Here's an example: Suppose you're matching the regular expression [a-z]+d4 to abcd4efgh. First [a-z]+ is matched with abcd; however, as soon as you try to match the second atom (d) you find a 4. So [a-z]+ is matched with abc, which allows the matching to be completed. Note that efgh can be discarded because there was no dollar at the end of the regular expression.

Another example: The regular expression is .+-[a-e]+d-e, the string is abcd-abcd-e. First .+ is matched to the whole string, but this does not allow - to match. So .+ is matched to abcd-abcd—this allows - to match, and [a-e]+ matches to the last e. However, d cannot match anything. Because the sequence that matches [a-e]+ cannot be shortened, try shortening the sequence that matched .+. After a few iterations, .+ will be correctly matched to abcd, [a-e]+ will be matched to abcd, and the matching will succeed.

As you can see, backtracking is a complex but mechanical process—perfect for a computer. If you understood it, you will easily grasp the algorithm used by Match.

The outer loop is a For loop that tries every possible value of FromX. Inside it is a Do loop that ends when the backtracking stack is empty and you must try another value of FromX. When the last state is matched successfully and the matching satisfies the anchoring rules given by dollars, use Exit For to jump out of both loops.

At the beginning of the Do loop is a GoSub to MatchAtom. This is used to match a single character to an atom; in case of ranges, use Like to match the character (function RangeMatch). MatchAtom sets the Matched variable to true or false, depending on whether the match was successful.

Now, there are five possibilities:

- The atom was matched and it had no modifier. Update ToX and proceed with the next atom.
- The atom was matched and it had a ? modifier. Update ToX and push an item on the state stack, with its MinPosi (the beginning of the shortest possible sequence) equal to the old value of ToX. Then proceed with the next atom.
- The atom was matched and it had a * or + modifier. First push an item on the state stack; the MinPosi is ToX for a star, ToX + 1 for a plus. Then repeatedly update ToX and call MatchAtom to get the longest possible sequence. When MatchAtom fails, proceed with the next atom. The code has a small optimization for the .* and .+ cases. There is no need to call MatchAtom because you already know that the longest possible sequence is the whole remaining part of the string.
- The atom could not be matched but it was optional (modified by * or ?). Just skip it and proceed with the next.
- The atom could not be matched and it was mandatory. You find an item of the state stack for which Posi—that is, the position where to restart—is greater than MinPosi. If none can be found (that is, if SP is 0 at the end of the For SP = SP To 1 Step -1 loop), exit and try with another value of FromX.

Actually there is another way to implement regular expression matching: by using recursion. Recursion hides the details of backtracking but does not eliminate it. Instead, the state stack is replaced by the CPU stack, where Visual Basic saves the local variables so that they can assume different values for different instances of the recursive subroutine. Recursion, however, can be slower and requires CPU stack space.

All other variations on regular expression matching are refinements of this basic algorithm. For example, they might extend the concept of *atom* so that a regular expression like [0-9]*VisualBasic is made of two atoms ([0-9]* and VisualBasic) instead of 12 ([0-9]*, plus one atom per character). *Dr. Dobb's Journal*, Nov. 1997, has an interesting article about advanced regular expression algorithms.

As an exercise, you might want to extend the algorithm by making it smarter (as hinted earlier) or more powerful. For example, (abc)* could match abcabcabc, and {abcd¦ef+gh} could match abcd, efgh, and effffgh.

8.19 COUNT STRING OCCURRENCES

by David Berube

Description

The CountStr routine counts the number of occurrences one string has within another. It receives a source string and a search string. If the search string is found 80 times in the source string, then 80 is returned. If an error occurs, 0 is returned. This capability is not intrinsic to Visual Basic.

Using this routine in your application is simple. Just call the sCount routine with your string as the first parameter and the string to search for as the second.

Syntax

val = Count Source, Countee

Part	Description
Source	Required. A string expression that specifies the string within which occurrences are counted.
Countee	Required. A string expression that specifies the string to count within the Source string.
Val	Required. A numerical expression denoting the number of occurrences found.

Code Listing

```
Public Function Count(Source As String, Countee As String) As Long

    'Declare our variables

    Dim I As Long, iCount As Integer

    'Initialize our variables
    iCount = 0
    I = 1

    Do
            'If we've gone past the end of the string, exit

            If (I > Len(Source)) Then Exit Do

            'Look for the next occurrence, and store it in I.

              I = InStr(I, Source, Countee, vbTextCompare)

            'If we've found another occurrence, add one to iCount and two to
            ' our current position(I)
              If I Then
                'Increment our "found" count
                        iCount = iCount + 1
                'Increment our position
                        I = I + 1
                'This code is in here so that we don't eat up all available
                ' CPU time
                        DoEvents
              End If

    Loop While I

        sCount = iCount
    Exit Function


CountError:

        sCount = 0
        Exit Function

End Function
```

Analysis

This routine simply loops through the code, incrementing the i counter as it goes. When i is equal to zero (that is, no more strings are found), then the loop exits, returning iCount, and leaves. If an error occurs, it jumps to CountError, returns zero, and leaves.

The `vbTextCompare` constant is one of the two available searching modes. In text compare mode, VB does not discriminate between upper- and lowercase letters. The strings `AA` and `aa` are identical as far as `InStr` is concerned. In `vbBinaryCompare` mode, or binary mode, aa, AA, Aa, and aA are all different.

8.20 CONCATENATE STRINGS

by Martin Cordova

Description

This class module is a reusable component that encapsulates an optimized technique to concatenate strings. It's a very useful add-on for Web programming, log file management, report writers, and so on. Often, VB programmers use the popular string concatenation operator (&) to accomplish all sort of tasks, such as building dynamic Web pages. However, this technique (illustrated next) is very inefficient:

```
For I = 1 to 100
    B$ = Space(1000)
A$ = A$ & B$
Next I
```

VB will consume a lot of time when it must allocate string space (A$ = A$ & B$)

The class `clsString` allows for much faster string concatenation through an easy-to-use interface:

```
Dim Buf As New clsString

For I = 1 to 100
    Buf.Add Space(1000)
Next i
SaveFile "Test.txt", Buf.Data
```

This component exposes three services, two methods, and one property (read only):

```
Public Sub Add(Buffer As String);
```

adds a string to the buffer.

```
Public Sub Clear;
```

clears the internal buffer.

```
Public Property Get Data() As String;
```

returns the resulting string buffer.

This component relies on the technique of preallocating big buffers in order to avoid wasting time each time a string is appended to a buffer. Internally, the buffer's empty space is filled with each concatenation until the buffer size must be readjusted. The component uses a default buffer size of 10000 characters.

To reuse this code, create an empty class module called clsString and paste the following code.

Code Listing

```
Option Explicit

'---position inside buffer to append string data
Private m_Pos As Long

'---internal buffer
Private m_Data As String

'---append string data
Public Sub Add(s As String)

    Dim sLen As Long

    sLen = Len(s)

    If (m_Pos + sLen) > Len(m_Data) Then
        m_Data = m_Data & Space(10000)
    End If

    Mid(m_Data, m_Pos, sLen) = s
    m_Pos = m_Pos + sLen

End Sub

'---return whole data
Public Function Data() As String

    Data = Left(m_Data, m_Pos - 1)

End Function

'---initialize internal variables
Private Sub Class_Initialize()

    Clear

End Sub

Public Sub Clear()

    m_Pos = 1
    m_Data = Space(10000) 'allocate buffer for speed

End Sub
```

Analysis

The class uses two private modular variables to store the concatenated buffer and track the position of the last valid character. When an object of this class is created, the `Class_Initialize` subroutine is called (by VB's runtime) and the initial string space is preallocated (using the default of 10000 characters—about 10KB).

When the `Add` method is called, the passed string is "inserted" into the preallocated buffer, and here relies on the "speed trick" because there is no need to waste time allocating string space each time the `Add` method is invoked. This method is intelligent enough that if the preallocated buffer gets exhausted, then additional space will be allocated at once (another 10KB).

When you want to retrieve your concatenated data, just call the `Data` property. It returns just the actual data, without the filler spaces present on the right side of the buffer.

This technique can be much faster than traditional BASIC concatenation, and is specially well suited for tasks such as building Web pages or generating tabular reports (as those required by the popular VideoSoft's control `VSView`).

8.21 SOUNDEX FUZZY LOGIC TEXT MATCHING

by Andy Carrasco

Description

The `SoundEx` function generates code based on the sound of a word. This soundex code will match the soundex codes of words that sound similar when pronounced. It is especially useful when searching through a large list of words, such as subjects, book titles, and names, when the user might not know the exact spelling of the word.

Original Word	Soundex Code
Eric	E6200
Erik	E6200
Erack	E6200
Ehrhick	E6200

In this example, each spelling of the word Eric produces the same soundex code because when all the spellings are pronounced they sound similar.

To use, simply call the `SoundEx` function, passing it the string you would like to be converted into a soundex code, and compare the returned value with the soundex code of another word.

Syntax

```
CodeString = SoundEx( Word )
```

Part	Description
CodeString	Required. A string variable that will hold the generated SoundEx code.
Word	Required. A string that contains the word used to generate the SoundEx code.

Code Listing

```
Public Function SoundEx(sString As String) As String

Dim x As Long
Dim CharCode As String * 1
Dim Code As String

Const SOUNDEX_ALPHABET = "01230120022455012623010202"
sString = UCase(sString)

Code = Left$(sString, 1)
sString = Right$(sString, Len(sString) - 1)

'Generate the basic soundex code
For x = 1 To Len(sString)
    CharCode = Mid$(SOUNDEX_ALPHABET, Asc(Mid$(sString, x)) - 64)
    If (Val(CharCode) And CharCode <> Mid$(Code, Len(Code))) Then _
    Code = Code + CharCode
Next x

'Truncate and pad out the code if nessesary
If Len(Code) >= 5 Then
    Code = Left$(Code, 5)
Else
    For x = Len(Code) To 4
        Code = Code + "0"
    Next x
End If

SoundEx = Code

End Function
```

Analysis

The SoundEx algorithm is surprisingly simple. To generate a soundex code for any word you simply must follow a series of arbitrary rules. You must convert all letters within the string to numbers based on the following table:

0	A, E, I, O, U, H, Y
1	B, F, P, V
2	C, G, J, K, Q, S, X, Z
3	D, T
4	L
5	M, N
6	R

Note that the constant SOUNDEX_ALPHABET, defined at the top of the function, contains the entire English alphabet converted to numerical values based on this table. Convert all the characters in the original string to uppercase before you begin generating the soundex code. The ASCII values for all the uppercase letters in the English alphabet fall between 65 and 90. For each character in the original string, you must find the ASCII value, then subtract 64. The resulting number is the index to use in conjunction with the Mid$ function to find the correct soundex code in the string constant SOUNDEX_ALPHABET. This number is then concatenated with the string variable Code, which will eventually contain the completely generated soundex code.

All vowels, and the letters H and Y, are given a value of zero, which eliminates them from the resulting soundex code. You never want to repeat the same number twice in a row. Therefore, if the soundex number for the next nonzero character in the original string is the same as the soundex number for the nonzero character that preceded it, the soundex number for that character will not be added to the variable Code.

A proper soundex code is exactly five characters in length. The first character in the soundex code is always the same as the first character in the original string, even if that character is a vowel or the letters H and Y. Then the soundex code contains a maximum of four generated numbers from the original string. If the resulting code is less than five characters in length, pad it out with zeros.

It is truly uncanny how well this simple algorithm can generate the exact same codes for words that sound familiar. The only caveat involved is that, when generating a soundex code for a word that is spelled phonetically, the first character of the phonetically spelled word must be the same as the first letter of the correctly spelled word; otherwise, the soundex codes will not match.

One possible way to solve this problem is to modify the soundex algorithm to use a number as the first character in the soundex code, instead of the actual character. Then, you could write the matching algorithm to consider the first character in the soundex code, and to allow matches for numbers that fall within a specified range from each other.

Chapter 9

INTERNET AND HTML FUNCTIONS

The Internet is quickly becoming the medium of choice for most communication, and as programmers it would be nice to able to make our programs take advantage of that fact. With the functions shown here you can do just that. You can check to see whether the user is already connected to the Internet, connect and use the IRC, send mail, and even build HTML documents from delimited text files.

9.1 CONNECTED TO NET

by Xtreme Software

Description

The `Connected_To_Net` function returns `True` or `False` depending on whether a remote access (RAS) connection is open. In many cases this will indicate whether you are connected to the Internet. If you use a proxy server or firewall-based network connection this function would suggest you're not connected. If you use a dial-up RAS connection you'll receive a misleading result because you might not have a live Internet connection.

Windows stores Internet connection information in the `System\CurrentControlSet\Services\RemoteAccess` area of the Registry. Visual Basic doesn't provide a way to access all Registry keys; therefore, `Connected_To_Net` must call on the API to open the needed key and return its value to your application.

Using the `Connected_To_Net` function in your own applications is simple:

```
If Connected_To_Net Then
     msgbox "You're Online!"
Else
     msgbox "Sorry, No Connection!"
End If
```

Syntax

```
Connected = Connected_To_Net
if Connected_To_Net then …
```

Part	*Description*
Connected	Required. Stores the current connection status.

Code Listing

```
'Registry Access Declarations
Private Declare Function RegOpenKey Lib "advapi32.dll" Alias "RegOpenKeyA"
➡ (ByVal hKey As Long, ByVal lpSubKey As String,
➡phkResult As Long) As Long

Private Declare Function RegCloseKey Lib "advapi32.dll" (ByVal hKey
➡ As Long) As Long

Private Declare Function RegQueryValueEx Lib "advapi32.dll" Alias
➡ "RegQueryValueExA" (ByVal hKey As Long, ByVal lpValueName As String,
➡ ByVal lpReserved As Long, lpType As Long, lpData As Any, lpcbData
➡ As Long) As Long


Public Function Connected_To_Net() As Boolean
        Dim phkResult As Long, lpData As Long, lpcbData As Long
     Dim ReturnCode As Long
        Connected_To_Net = False
    ReturnCode = RegOpenKey(&H80000002, _
    "System\CurrentControlSet\Services\RemoteAccess", phkResult)

    If ReturnCode = 0& Then
            lpData = 0&
            lpcbData = 0&
            ReturnCode = RegQueryValueEx(phkResult, _
        "Remote Connection", 0&, 0&, ByVal lpData, lpcbData)
            lpcbData = Len(lpData)
            ReturnCode = RegQueryValueEx(phkResult, _
        "Remote Connection", 0&, 0&, lpData, lpcbData)
            If ReturnCode = 0& And lpData <> 0 _
        Then Connected_To_Net = True
            RegCloseKey (phkResult)
        End If
End Function
```

Analysis

This routine is fairly simple. It first checks the Registry key System\CurrentControlSet\Services\ RemoteAccess. If RemoteAccess is a viable key and no errors occur, the RemoteAccess subkey is probed for its value. This value is then passed to your application as the value of the `Connected_To_Net` function. The Registry has many areas like this that change continuously with current information.

9.2 GET RGB COLOR VALUES

by Gary A. Wiley

Description

The `Get_RGB` function converts decimal and hexadecimal numbers to RGB colors such as those used in HTML for the body, font, and table tags. You can use the `ShowColor` method of the CommonDialog control to obtain a color. For example:

```
CommonDialog.ShowColor
sRGB = Get_RGB(CommonDialog.Color, True)
```

Or

```
sRGB = Get_RGB(Hex(CommonDialog.Color), False)
```

Syntax

```
sRGB = Get_RGB (RGBNOT, NumType)
```

Part	Description
sRGB	Required. A string expression returned with the RGB number.
RGBNOT	Required. A decimal or hexadecimal number to be converted.
NumType	Required. The type of number passed to the function.

The following are the ranges for `RGBNOT`:

Number type	Range
Hexadecimal	0 to FFFFFF
Decimal	0 to 16,777,215

The following are the settings for `NumType`:

Value	Type
False	Hexadecimal number
True	Decimal number

Code Listing

```
Function Get_RGB (RGBNOT As Variant, NumType As Boolean) As String
    Dim Zeros As String
    On Error Resume Next
    'Out of range or invalid characters error
    If RGBNOT > 16777215 Or RGBNOT < 0 Then
        Dim ans As Long, msg As String
        msg = "Number out of range or invalid characters." & vbCrLf
        msg = msg & "Range for decimal numbers: 0 to 16,777,215" & vbCrLf
        msg = msg & "Range for hexadecimal numbers: 0 to FFFFFF" & vbCrLf
        msg = msg & "Valid characters are: 0 to 9 and A to F."
ans = MsgBox (msg, vbOKOnly + vbInformation, "Get_RGB")
        Exit Function
    End If
    Zeros = "00000"
TryAgain:
    'Check for decimal number and convert to hex
    If NumType  Then RGBNOT = Hex(RGBNOT)
    If Err Then Err.Clear
    'Pad hex number with 0's if length is not 6
    RGBNOT = Mid$(Zeros, 1, 6 - Len(RGBNOT)) + RGBNOT
    If Err Then NumType = True: Err.Clear: GoTo TryAgain
    'Convert hex to rgb by swapping 2 leftmost char with 2 rightmost
    Get_RGB = Right$(RGBNOT, 2) + Mid$(RGBNOT, 3, 2) + Left$(RGBNOT, 2)
End Function
```

Analysis

This routine is fairly simple. It receives a decimal or hexadecimal number and returns a string with the RGB color used in HTML documents. Decimal numbers are first converted to hexadecimal. Hexadecimal numbers are converted to RGB format by swapping the first two characters with the last two. Passing decimal numbers to the function with NumType set to False hexadecimal will be converted correctly. However, passing a hexadecimal number with NumType set to True decimal will be converted correctly only if the hexadecimal number contains a letter in the range A to F. A message box is displayed if RGBNOT is out of range or contains invalid characters.

9.3   DISCONNECTING FROM THE INTERNET

by James Limm

Description

This code disconnects all dial-up networking connections that are running on the system. Most Internet connections are initiated with the Windows dial-up networking functions, so disconnecting all these connections usually disconnects the computer from the Internet.

Syntax

```
Call Hangup
```

Code Listing

```
'Declare the following in the declarations section of your code
Public Const RAS_MAXENTRYNAME As Integer = 256
Public Const RAS_MAXDEVICETYPE As Integer = 16
Public Const RAS_MAXDEVICENAME As Integer = 128
Public Const RAS_RASCONNSIZE As Integer = 412

Public Type RasEntryName
    dwSize As Long
    szEntryName(RAS_MAXENTRYNAME) As Byte
End Type

Public Type RasConn
    dwSize As Long
    hRasConn As Long
    szEntryName(RAS_MAXENTRYNAME) As Byte
    szDeviceType(RAS_MAXDEVICETYPE) As Byte
    szDeviceName(RAS_MAXDEVICENAME) As Byte
End Type

Public Declare Function RasEnumConnections Lib "rasapi32.dll"
➥ Alias "RasEnumConnectionsA" (lpRasConn As Any, lpcb As Long,
➥ lngConnections As Long) As Long

Public Declare Function RasHangUp Lib "rasapi32.dll" Alias "RasHangUpA"
➥ (ByVal hRasConn As Long) As Long
Public lngResult As Long

'Hangup Procedure
Public Sub HangUp()
Dim lngCurCon As Long
Dim lpRasConn(255) As RasConn
Dim lpcb As Long
Dim lngConnections As Long
Dim hRasConn As Long
lpRasConn(0).dwSize = RAS_RASCONNSIZE
lpcb = RAS_MAXENTRYNAME * lpRasConn(0).dwSize
lngConnections = 0
lngResult = RasEnumConnections(lpRasConn(0), lpcb, _
lngConnections)

If lngResult = ERROR_SUCCESS Then
    'enumerate through all active connections
    For lngCurCon = 0 To lngConnections - 1
        hRasConn = lpRasConn(lngCurCon).hRasConn
        'hang up the connection
```

continues

```
            lngResult = RasHangUp(ByVal hRasConn)
        Next
    End If

    End Sub
```

Analysis

This code example takes advantage of the set of remote access services API functions that Windows uses to perform dial-up networking requests. The `HangUp` procedure enumerates through all the active connections and sends a message instructing Windows to disconnect them one at a time. You could use this code in a program that regulates the amount of time the computer is online, or even as part of an Internet "nanny" system that disconnects the system if the browser accesses a site that contains unsuitable content.

9.4   LOAD THE BROWSER AND DO A URL JUMP

by Mike Shaffer

Description

`BrowserJump` loads the user's standard Internet browser when passed a URL. This is done by launching whatever application Windows has associated with the .HTM or .HTML file extension (for example, if a user's system is set up to launch WordPad instead, that is actually what will happen). If no association exists, this routine does nothing.

Syntax

`BrowserJump URL`

Part	Description
URL	Required. The URL to load after the browser is launched. If you are attempting to load a Web page, be sure to include the full URL with protocol specifier (for example, `http://www.microsoft.com`).

Code Listing

```
'**********************************************
'* Submitted by Mike Shaffer
'**********************************************
Declare Function ShellExecute Lib "shell32.dll" Alias "ShellExecuteA" _
(ByVal hWnd As Long, ByVal lpOperation As String, ByVal lpFile As String, _
```

```
ByVal lpParameters As String, ByVal lpDirectory As String,
➥ ByVal nShowCmd As Long) As Long

Public Sub BrowserJump(ByVal URL As String)
  '
  '::::::::::::::::::::::::::::::::::::::::::::::::::::::::::::::::::::::::'
  ':::                                                             :::'
  ':::    Launches the user's 'default' web browser and loads the    :::'
  ':::    specified URL                                             :::'
  ':::                                                             :::'
  '::::::::::::::::::::::::::::::::::::::::::::::::::::::::::::::::::::::::'
    '
    '
  Call ShellExecute(0&, vbNullString, URL, vbNullString, _
                      vbNullString, vbNormalFocus)
                                        ' Perform via association
    '
End Sub
```

Analysis

This routine performs its magic by calling the Windows API function `ShellExecute`. The URL is passed as the second parameter of the `ShellExecute` call, and Windows simply launches the associated application, passing the URL as a target for that application. Note that this technique might be adapted for other purposes. For example, pass it a URL of `C:\TEST.DOC`, and you might end up launching a word processor.

9.5 USING WEB PAGES FOR DOCUMENTATION

by Tom Honaker

Description

Windows includes a help system that provides useful features such as annotation, fast searching, and so on. It's also annoying, slow, memory-intensive, and requires a recompile of the help files with every edit. So why not use Web pages (HTML files) for help instead?

Although this method results in a help system that can't be searched for keywords without using an ActiveX control, Java applet, and so on, building a help system out of Web pages is much easier than compiling a WinHelp-compatible help file. Making changes is much easier as well because HTML files can, in a pinch, be created or edited in a simple text editor.

The following code invokes help by means of the `ShellExecute` API call. The API call is made with reference to the HTML file itself, not to any program to display it. As a result of an association between HTML files and a Web browser, the Web browser program is invoked and the Web page is displayed. This takes advantage of the fact that Windows includes a browser (Internet Explorer), and the overwhelming majority of systems running Windows 95, 98, and NT will have a Web browser installed, even if it is not in use.

With modifications, this code can be used to invoke any program, or any file that is associated with a program. Therefore, its uses extend far beyond the use outlined here, although this use would be of the most immediate interest.

As a fringe benefit, this code can invoke a browser to look at Web pages that are posted on the Internet, as long as the filename passed is a full URL pointing to a Web page. This should be used only if the user is connected, however, or the browser will return an error when it tries to connect to the server holding the page in question.

This code can be called from any control in a project. If successful, the function returns the handle (hWnd) of the newly launched file or associated viewer program. (It returns zero if the function fails.) The handle returned can be used elsewhere for functions such as SetWindowPos.

Syntax

```
Temp& = StartDoc(Filename)
```

Part	Description
Filename	Required. A string expression holding the name of the file to open. If the file is not in a directory listed in the PATH environment variable or in the same directory as the program that invokes this call, the full path must be included.

Code Listing

```
' Paste this section into a module...

Declare Function ShellExecute Lib "shell32.dll" _
  Alias "ShellExecuteA" (ByVal hwnd As Long, _
  ByVal lpOperation As String, ByVal lpFile As String, _
  ByVal lpParameters As String, ByVal lpDirectory As String, _
  ByVal nShowCmd As Long) As Long

Declare Function GetDesktopWindow Lib "user32" () As Long

Global Const SW_SHOWNORMAL = 1


Function StartDoc(DocName As String) As Long
        Dim Scr_hDC As Long
        Scr_hDC = GetDesktopWindow()
        StartDoc = ShellExecute(Scr_hDC, "Open", DocName, _
```

```
            "", "C:\", SW_SHOWNORMAL)
End Function



' Paste this section into the control (menu, button, etc.)
' that will invoke the help...

dim tempvar&, filetoopen$
' Use the filename that you need for the context in question.
' Note that this reference includes App.Path, which is the
' path to the application.
filetoopen$ = App.Path +"\index.html"
tempvar& = StartDoc(filetoopen$)
```

Analysis

The code is straightforward. A call to the `StartDoc` function will trigger two API calls. The first, `GetDesktopWindow`, gets the handle to the Desktop window of the system. The second invokes the help file (in this application, a Web page) and with it the associated viewer (a Web browser).

Placing the control code into a Help menu entry and setting its keyboard shortcut to F1 will enable users to invoke help from the Windows "universal" help keyboard shortcut.

There are many potential uses for this code, such as displaying any file on command. Experiment and see what you can come up with.

9.6   SENDING EMAIL USING WINSOCK

by Kamal A. Mehdi

Description

This sample code demonstrates how to use the Winsock control shipped with Visual Basic to send an email message through an SMTP (Simple Mail Transport Protocol) server. The sample code makes a connection with the SMTP remote host via TCP on port 25 and sends the email message data containing the sender name, sender email address, recipient name, recipient email address, message subject, and the message body text. It checks for the appropriate response code to be sent by the SMTP server in each data-segment transmission to verify that data is correctly received by the server.

The core of the code is represented by the `SendEmail` procedure, which is explained later in detail. The sample code will only send simple text email messages to SMTP mail servers; no attachments are possible.

Syntax

```
SendEmail(MailServerName, SenderName, SenderEmail, RecipientName,
➥RecipientEmail, EmailSubject, EmailBody)
```

Part	Description
MailServerName	Required. A string expression specifying the name of the SMTP server.
SenderName	Required. A string expression specifying the name of the email sender.
SenderEmail	Required. A string expression specifying the email address of the sender.
RecipientName	Required. A string expression specifying the name of the email recipient.
RecipientEmail	Required. A string expression specifying the email address of the recipient.
EmailSubject	Required. A string expression specifying the email message subject.
EmailBody	Required. A string expression specifying the body of the message text.

Modules and Controls Required

Module/Control	Description
Form1	A standard non-MDI Visual Basic form (.FRM) with the Caption property set to Send E-Mail Using the Winsock Control
Winsock1	A Winsock control
Command1	A command button with the Caption property set to &Send E-Mail
Command2	A command button with the Caption property set to &Exit
StatusLabel	A label control with the Caption property set to ""
Frame1	A frame control with the Caption property set to Status:
Text1()	A control array of seven text boxes with the Text1(6) MultiLine property set to True
Label1()	A control array of seven label controls with the Caption property set as shown:
	Index = Caption
	0 = Your Name
	1 = From (Your e-mail address)
	2 = Recipient's Name
	3 = To (Recipient's e-mail address)
	4 = E-Mail (SMTP) server Name
	5 = Subject
	6 = Message Body

·Follow these steps to draw controls:

1. Start a new standard EXE project. Form1 is created by default. Set the form's Height and Width properties to approximately 6100 and 7200, respectively, and set its Caption property as shown earlier in this section.

2. Draw Label1 on the top-left side of the form. Create the other six label control array elements from the label control and position them under Label1(0) so that they are arranged according to their Index property value (0, 1,..., 6 from top to bottom). Set the Caption property of each of the label control array elements as shown earlier.

3. Draw Text1 to the right of Label1(0). Create the other six text box control array elements from the text box and position them to the right of each label control created in step 2, with each text box to the right of the label control that has the same Index property value. Adjust the width of all text boxes so that they extend up to the right edge of the form. Adjust the height of the last text box (Text1(6)) so that it can accommodate multiple lines, and set its MultiLine property to True.

4. Draw Command1 and Command2 command buttons under Text1(6) and set their Caption properties as shown earlier.

5. Draw Frame1 below the command buttons and set its Caption property as shown earlier.

6. Draw the StatusLabel label control inside Frame1, and adjust its size so that it fills the entire frame area.

7. Draw the Winsock1 Winsock control anywhere on the form.

Note

The Winsock control is not included on the toolbox by default. You can add it to the toolbox by selecting the Components submenu from the Project menu and adding the control.

You can create control arrays by inserting one control on the form and copying and pasting the control on the form using either the right mouse button or the Edit menu. When you paste the control on the form, Visual Basic will prompt you whether to create a control array; choose Yes.

Code Listing

```
'General form declarations
    Dim Response As String

Sub SendEmail(MailServerName As String, SenderName As String,
➥ SenderEmailAddress As String, RecipientName As String,
➥ RecipientEmailAddress As String, EmailSubject As String,
➥ EmailBodyOfMessage As String)

    'Declare variables
    Dim Data1 As String, Data2 As String
    Dim Data3 As String, Data4 As String
```

continues

```
Dim Data5 As String, Data6 As String
Dim Data7 As String, Data8 As String
Dim CurrentDate As String
Dim TimeDifference As String

'Set the Winsock control's local port to 0, because otherwise
'you may not be able to send more than one e-mail message
'every time the program runs
Winsock1.LocalPort = 0

'Start composing the required data strings, but first check
'if the Winsock socket is closed
If Winsock1.State = sckClosed Then

    'Compose the current date and time string
    TimeDifference = " -200"      'Your zone time-difference

    CurrentDate = Format(Date, "Ddd") & ", " & Format(Date, "dd Mmm YYYY")
    ➡& " " & Format(Time, "hh:mm:ss") & TimeDifference

    'Set the program name used to send this e-mail message (you can
    'put your program name here)
    AppName = "X-Mailer: " + "My Mail Program V1.0" + Chr(13) + Chr(10)

    'Set the e-mail address of the sender
    Data1 = "mail from:" + Chr(32) + SenderEmailAddress + Chr(13) +
    ➡Chr(10)

    'Set the e-mail address of the recipient
    Data2 = "rcpt to:" + Chr(32) + RecipientEmailAddress + Chr(13) +
    ➡Chr(10)

    'Set the date string
    Data3 = "Date:" + Chr(32) + CurrentDate + Chr(13) + Chr(10)

    'Set the name of the sender
    Data4 = "From:" + Chr(32) + SenderName + Chr(13) + Chr(10)

    'Set the name of the recipient
    Data5 = "To:" + Chr(32) + Text1(2) + Chr(13) + Chr(10)

    'Set the subject of the E-Mail message
    Data6 = "Subject:" + Chr(32) + EmailSubject + Chr(13) + Chr(10)

    'Set the E-mail message body string
    Data7 = EmailBodyOfMessage + Chr(13) + Chr(10)

    'Combine the whole string for proper SMTP syntax
    Data8 = Data4 + Data3 + AppName + Data5 + Data6
```

```
'Set the Winsock protocol
Winsock1.Protocol = sckTCPProtocol

'Set the remote host name (of SMTP server)
Winsock1.RemoteHost = MailServerName

'Set the SMTP Port to the default port 25
Winsock1.RemotePort = 25

'Start the connection
Winsock1.Connect

'Wait for response from the remote host
WaitForResponse ("220")

'Report status
StatusLabel.Caption = "Connecting...."
StatusLabel.Refresh

'Send your computer name or company name
Winsock1.SendData ("HELO mycomputername" + Chr(13) + Chr(10))

'Wait for response from the remote host
WaitForResponse ("250")

'Update status
StatusLabel.Caption = "Connected"
StatusLabel.Refresh

'Send the first string
Winsock1.SendData (Data1)

'Update status
StatusLabel.Caption = "Sending Message"
StatusLabel.Refresh

'Wait for response from the remote host
WaitForResponse ("250")

'Send the second string
Winsock1.SendData (Data2)

'Wait for response from the remote host
WaitForResponse ("250")

'Tell the SMTP server that you want to send data now
Winsock1.SendData ("data" + Chr(13) + Chr(10))

'Wait for response from the remote host
WaitForResponse ("354")
```

continues

```
            'Send the data
            Winsock1.SendData (Data8 + Chr(13) + Chr(10))
            Winsock1.SendData (Data7 + Chr(13) + Chr(10))
            Winsock1.SendData ("." + Chr(13) + Chr(10))

            'Wait for response from the remote host
            WaitForResponse ("250")

            'Send quitting acknowledgment
            Winsock1.SendData ("quit" + Chr(13) + Chr(10))

            'Update status
            StatusLabel.Caption = "Disconnecting"
            StatusLabel.Refresh

            'Wait for response from the remote host
            WaitForResponse ("221")

            'Close the connection
            Winsock1.Close

    Else

            'Report error
            MsgBox (Str(Winsock1.State))

    End If

End Sub

Sub WaitForResponse(ResponseCode As String)

    Dim Start As Single
    Dim TimeToWait As Single

    Start = Timer

    'Start a loop checking for response from SMTP host
    While Len(Response) = 0

        TimeToWait = Start - Timer
        DoEvents
        'If TimeToWait expires, report timeout error

        If TimeToWait > 50 Then
            MsgBox "SMTP timeout error, no response received", 64, App.Title
            Exit Sub
        End If

    Wend
```

```
        While Left(Response, 3) <> ResponseCode
            DoEvents

            If TimeToWait > 50 Then
                'Report error if incorrect code is received
                MsgBox "SMTP error, improper response code received!" + Chr(10) +
                ➥"Correct code is: " + ResponseCode + ", Code received: " +
                ➥Response, 64, App.Title
                Exit Sub

            End If

        Wend

        'Set response to nothing
        Response = ""

End Sub

Private Sub Command1_Click()

    'Call the SendEmail procedure and pass the arguments: MailServerName,
    ' SenderName, SenderEmailAddress, RecipientName, RecipientEmailAddress,
    ' EmailSubject, EmailBodyOfMessage)
    SendEmail Text1(4), Text1(0), Text1(1), Text1(2), Text1(3), Text1(5),
    ➥Text1(6)

    'Update status
    StatusLabel.Caption = "Mail Sent"
    StatusLabel.Refresh

End Sub

Private Sub Command2_Click()

    Unload Me

End Sub

Private Sub Form_Unload(Cancel As Integer)

    Set Form1 = Nothing

    End

End Sub

Private Sub Winsock1_DataArrival(ByVal bytesTotal As Long)

    'Check for response from the remote host
    Winsock1.GetData Response

End Sub
```

Enter the code into the appropriate form or control events as indicated, and run the project. Fill the text boxes with the appropriate data and click the Send E-Mail button. Watch the status label for the email session progress.

Analysis

The SendEmail procedure uses the Winsock control to send a simple plain text email message to an SMTP mail server. The use of the procedure is simple: you just need to send the necessary email message data as arguments, including the sender name, sender email address, recipient's name and email address, and the email message subject and body text.

The SendEmail procedure starts the email session by composing the necessary email message data segments, initializing the Winsock control, connecting to the SMTP remote server, sending the sender's and recipient's email addresses, transferring the message data, and disconnecting from the remote server and closing the session. In each step of the email session, the SendEmail procedure calls another procedure, WaitForResponse, which checks the response code received from the remote server to verify whether the response is correct.

While the SendEmail procedure sends the email message, it updates a status label with the progress of the entire process. It reports the status when it first starts to connect to the remote host, when it gets connected, when the message is successfully sent, and when it disconnects. It also displays a message box when an error occurs during the email transfer process, such as a server reply time out, incorrect response code received from the SMTP server, and so on. It also displays a message box if the user tries to send an email while the Winsock socket is still open from a previous email session.

The sample project SMTPMAIL.VBP on the CD-ROM that accompanies this book demonstrates how to send an email message using this code.

Chapter 10

MISCELLANEOUS FUNCTIONS

This chapter contains the grab bag of functions that didn't easily fit into other categories. But don't let that make you think they are just the leftovers. Here are functions for data encryption, accessing the Registry, sorting functions, and math functions. So be sure to take a look through these functions because you're likely to find some very useful routines here.

10.1 DYNAMIC FACTORIALS

by Larry Serflaten

Description

This function returns the factorial of the supplied root. The factorial of 4 is 4 * 3 * 2 * 1, or 24. Factorials are commonly used in calculations involving probability. Factorials can be calculated using a simple recursive routine:

```
Function Fac (Value%)
    If (Value And &H7FFE) = 0 Then Fac = Value Else Fac = Fac(Abs(Value) - 1)
    ➥ * Abs(Value)
End Function
```

However, when using large factorials, calculating a factorial each time it is needed becomes a time-consuming task. This is especially true when you use them inside loops where these same calculations must be performed over and over, hundreds or thousands of times. The method introduced here can be used in place of this and other lengthy calculations. As shown in the example, using an array to hold previously calculated values can increase execution speed considerably.

The first two elements, `Fac(0)` and `Fac(1)`, are assigned when the function is first called. There is some contention over what the factorial of 0 should be—this example uses 0 as the factorial of 0. Except for the first two array elements, the factorials are calculated when the next larger factorial is requested. For requests of a factorial that has already been calculated, it is located in the array and returned, bypassing the need for recalculation.

The input parameter to this function is validated to be in the range of 0–170. The array space is dynamically allocated and used only if needed. The return value is a double precision type. The following factorial code was tested in VB3 and VB4/16. It will also work in other versions of VB but was not tested.

Because the array is dynamic, the `Factorial` array must be declared at the module level. The first line in the code listing must be placed in the `General Declarations` section of the code module in which this function will reside.

Syntax

```
dblFactorial = Fac(intNumber)
```

Part	Description
dblFactorial	A double precision variable to hold the returned result.
intNumber	Required. The integer to find the factorial of. The range as supplied is 0 to 170.

Code Listing

```
Dim Factorial() As Double

Function Fac (ByVal Value%) As Double
Dim UB As Integer
Const MyMax = 170

    'Test for valid data
    If Value  MyMax Then Error 6

    On Error Resume Next
    UB = UBound(Factorial)

    'The first time called UB will be 0.
    If UB          ReDim Factorial(0 To 1) As Double
        Factorial(0) = 0
        Factorial(1) = 1
        UB = 1
    End If

    'Test for array size increase
    If Value  UB Then
        ReDim Preserve Factorial(Value) As Double
        Dim i As Integer
```

```
        'Calculate factorials for the new elements
            For i = UB + 1 To Value
                Factorial(i) = Factorial(i - 1) * i
            Next i
    End If

    'Look up factorial
    Fac = Factorial(Value)
End Function
```

Analysis

After input validation, the last element allocated is determined using the `UBound` function. When first called, the array has no size and the `UBound` function will error. This condition causes the function to initialize the array for indexes 0 and 1. You can avoid using the error condition by placing `Dim Factorial(0)` as `Double` in the load or initialize event of the local module, then removing the `On Error` statement.

If the input value is larger than the index of the last element, this function will increase the size of the dynamic array up to the input value and calculate the factorials for the new elements created. If the input value is equal to or less than the index of the last element, this function must only look up the factorial in the array.

Visual Basic limits the range of the returned value. The largest factorial that VB can represent using a `Double Precision` type is 7.25741561530799E+306, which is the factorial of 170. An input value less than 0 or larger than 170 will cause a trappable Overflow error. Until a higher precision data type is made available, calculations needing larger factorials might be able to employ the `Log` and `Exp` functions to reduce the large numbers to a more workable range. If a higher precision data type is made available, this function can easily be rewritten to include the more precise type; change the declarations from `Double` to the new data type, and increase `MyMax` to the highest factorial root allowed.

Parts of this algorithm can also be modified for use in other array-based occasions where either dynamically allocated arrays or index validation is wanted. If the need arises, this function could also release the memory used by the dynamic array. Before input validation, a test for a special value, (perhaps `Fac(-1)`) could indicate that the array should be erased.

10.2 ROUND UP TO A SELECTED RANGE

by Mike Shaffer

Description

The `RoundMe` function is useful for rounding to the nearest *X* multiple. For example, when dealing with money, suppose you wanted to round to the nearest quarter or the nearest half dollar. This routine makes that type of rounding quite straightforward. Other examples might be sales of lumber, where cuts must be rounded up to the nearest foot, or calculations for weight requirements that must be rounded to the nearest 1,000 pounds.

Syntax

```
RoundMe(Amount, RoundTo)
```

Part	Description
Amount	Required. The amount to round.
RoundTo	Required. The multiple to round to (for example, 5 would be 5 cents, 100 would be 1 dollar).
	The returned value is a double (although you can modify this to meet your needs) that consists of the original value rounded to the multiple you specified in RoundTo.

Code Listing

```
'*********************************************
'* Submitted by Mike Shaffer
'*********************************************
Public Function RoundMe(amount, RoundTo) As Double
  '
  ':::::::::::::::::::::::::::::::::::::::::::::::::::::::::::::::::::::::::::::::'
  ':::                                                                      :::'
  ':::     Rounds any amount (AMOUNT) to any rounding value (RoundTo)       :::'
  ':::                                                                      :::'
  ':::::::::::::::::::::::::::::::::::::::::::::::::::::::::::::::::::::::::::::::'
  ':::                                                                      :::'
  ':::   Passed:                                                            :::'
  ':::                                                                      :::'
  ':::      amount     :=     The amount                                    :::'
  ':::      RoundTo    :=     Value to round to (e.g. 5 would be 5 cents):::'
  ':::                                                                      :::'
  ':::::::::::::::::::::::::::::::::::::::::::::::::::::::::::::::::::::::::::::::'
   '
   Dim tempAmt As Double
   If RoundTo = 0 then
      RoundMe = Amount
      Exit Function
   End if
   tempAmt = amount
   tempAmt = tempAmt * 100#
     ' for IRS/ISO/Banker's rules rounding, use   tempAmt = RoundTo *
     ➡((tempAmt + (RoundTo / 2#)) \ RoundTo)
   tempAmt = RoundTo * Int(((tempAmt + (RoundTo / 2#)) / RoundTo))
   tempAmt = tempAmt / 100#
   RoundMe = tempAmt
End Function
```

Analysis

The `RoundTo` function can be especially useful in financial calculations. Pay particular attention to the commented line within the routine. If you want ISO standard rounding (which is typically what banks and the IRS use), uncomment that line and delete or comment the line below it. This function can help to standardize results and alleviate much of the confusion surrounding the (seemingly inconsistent) ways in which VB itself sometimes rounds results (for example, `INT`, `VAL`, `CINT/CLNG`, `FIX`, and so on).

10.3 RETURN A PERCENTAGE

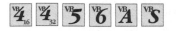

by David Berube

Description

The `Percent` routine will return a percentage of a number. To use it in VB, just call with the number and percentage in the first and second arguments, respectively.

Syntax

```
Result  = Percent(Number, Percentage)
```

Part	Description
Result	Required. The result of the calculation.
Number	Required. The number on which to perform the calculation.
Percentage	Required. The percentage of the first number to return.

Code Listing

```
Public Function Percent(Number As Double, Percentage As Double) As Double
        dim i as double
    I = (Number / 100) * Percent
    Percent = I
End Function
```

Analysis

This routine receives two values, the number and the percentage, and returns the percentage of the number.

10.4 ACCESSING THE WINDOWS REGISTRY

by Raymond King

Description

The `VbRegMod` module is made up of five routines for accessing the Windows Registry. Visual Basic provides a simple way to save parameters to the Registry using the `SaveSettings` and `GetSettings` functions, but it limits you to saving to the VBA section of the Registry. `VbRegMod` enables you to save and retrieve Registry entries from anywhere in the Registry.

Syntax

```
VbRegDeleteKey(RootKey, KeyName, SubKey)
VbRegCreateKey(RootKey, KeyName)
lRtn = VbRegQueryValue(RootKey, KeyName, ValueName)
VbRegSetValue(RootKey, KeyName, ValueName, KeyType, KeyValue)
VbRegDeleteValue(RootKey, KeyName, ValueName)
```

Part	Description
RootKey	Required. A Long value specifying the Registry root key `HKEY_LOCAL_MACHINE`.
KeyName	Required. A string expression that specifies the new key name `MySoftware`.
SubKey	Required. A string expression that specifies the new subkey `Top`.
ValueName	Required. A string expression that specifies the new value name.
KeyValue	Required. A `Variant` value that specifies the value to be set under the value name.
KeyType	Required. A Long value that specifies the key type `REG_SZ` and so on.

Code Listing

```
Option Explicit

'--------------------------------------------------
'-- VbRegMod.Bas
'-- A Visual Basic 32-Bit Module For Accessing
'-- The Windows Registry.
'--
'-- Date: Sunday, May 17, 1998
'-- By Custom Software Designers.
'-- Programmer Raymond L. King
'--------------------------------------------------
```

```
'-- Windows Registry Root Key Constants.
Public Const HKEY_CLASSES_ROOT = &H80000000
Public Const HKEY_CURRENT_CONFIG = &H80000005
Public Const HKEY_CURRENT_USER = &H80000001
Public Const HKEY_DYN_DATA = &H80000006
Public Const HKEY_LOCAL_MACHINE = &H80000002
Public Const HKEY_USERS = &H80000003

'-- Windows Registry Key Type Constants.
Public Const REG_OPTION_NON_VOLATILE = 0        ' Key is preserved when system
➥ is rebooted
Public Const REG_EXPAND_SZ = 2                  ' Unicode nul terminated string
Public Const REG_DWORD = 4                      ' 32-bit number
Public Const REG_SZ = 1                         ' Unicode nul terminated string
Public Const REG_BINARY = 3                     ' Free form binary
Public Const REG_DWORD_BIG_ENDIAN = 5           ' 32-bit number
Public Const REG_DWORD_LITTLE_ENDIAN = 4        ' 32-bit number (same as
➥ REG_DWORD)

'-- Function Error Constants.
Public Const ERROR_SUCCESS = 0
Public Const ERROR_REG = 1

'-- Registry Access Rights.
Public Const SYNCHRONIZE = &H100000
Public Const READ_CONTROL = &H20000
Public Const STANDARD_RIGHTS_ALL = &H1F0000
Public Const STANDARD_RIGHTS_READ = (READ_CONTROL)
Public Const STANDARD_RIGHTS_WRITE = (READ_CONTROL)
Public Const KEY_QUERY_VALUE = &H1
Public Const KEY_SET_VALUE = &H2
Public Const KEY_CREATE_LINK = &H20
Public Const KEY_CREATE_SUB_KEY = &H4
Public Const KEY_ENUMERATE_SUB_KEYS = &H8
Public Const KEY_NOTIFY = &H10
Public Const KEY_READ = ((STANDARD_RIGHTS_READ Or KEY_QUERY_VALUE
➥ Or KEY_ENUMERATE_SUB_KEYS Or KEY_NOTIFY) And (Not SYNCHRONIZE))
Public Const KEY_ALL_ACCESS = ((STANDARD_RIGHTS_ALL Or KEY_QUERY_VALUE
➥ Or KEY_SET_VALUE Or  KEY_CREATE_SUB_KEY Or KEY_ENUMERATE_SUB_KEYS
➥ Or KEY_NOTIFY Or KEY_CREATE_LINK) And (Not SYNCHRONIZE))
Public Const KEY_EXECUTE = ((KEY_READ) And (Not SYNCHRONIZE))
Public Const KEY_WRITE = ((STANDARD_RIGHTS_WRITE Or KEY_SET_VALUE
➥ Or KEY_CREATE_SUB_KEY) And (Not SYNCHRONIZE))

'-- Windows Registry API Declarations.
'-- Registry API To Open A Key.
Private Declare Function RegOpenKeyEx Lib "advapi32.dll"
➥ Alias "RegOpenKeyExA" _
    (ByVal hKey As Long, ByVal lpSubKey As String, ByVal ulOptions As Long, _
    ByVal samDesired As Long, phkResult As Long) As Long
```

continues

```
'-- Registry API To Create A New Key.
Private Declare Function RegCreateKeyEx Lib "advapi32.dll"
➡ Alias "RegCreateKeyExA" _
    (ByVal hKey As Long, ByVal lpSubKey As String, ByVal Reserved As Long, _
    ByVal lpClass As String, ByVal dwOptions As Long,
    ➡ ByVal samDesired As Long, _
    ByVal lpSecurityAttributes As Long, phkResult As Long,
    ➡ lpdwDisposition As Long) As Long

'-- Registry API To Query A String Value.
Private Declare Function RegQueryValueExString Lib "advapi32.dll"
➡ Alias "RegQueryValueExA" _
    (ByVal hKey As Long, ByVal lpValueName As String, ByVal lpReserved
    ➡ As Long, _
    lpType As Long, ByVal lpData As String, lpcbData As Long) As Long
    ' Note that if you declare the lpData parameter as String, you must
    ➡ pass it By Value.

'-- Registry API To Query A Long (DWORD) Value.
Private Declare Function RegQueryValueExLong Lib "advapi32.dll"
➡ Alias "RegQueryValueExA" _
    (ByVal hKey As Long, ByVal lpValueName As String, ByVal lpReserved
    ➡ As Long, _
    lpType As Long, lpData As Long, lpcbData As Long) As Long

'-- Registry API To Query A NULL Value.
Private Declare Function RegQueryValueExNULL Lib "advapi32.dll"
➡ Alias "RegQueryValueExA" _
    (ByVal hKey As Long, ByVal lpValueName As String,
    ➡ ByVal lpReserved As Long, _
    lpType As Long, ByVal lpData As Long, lpcbData As Long) As Long

'-- Registry API To Set A String Value.
Private Declare Function RegSetValueExString Lib "advapi32.dll"
➡ Alias "RegSetValueExA" _
    (ByVal hKey As Long, ByVal lpValueName As String, ByVal Reserved As Long, _
    ByVal dwType As Long, ByVal lpValue As String, ByVal cbData As Long)
    ➡ As Long
    ' Note that if you declare the lpData parameter as String, you must pass
    ➡ it By Value.

'-- Registry API To Set A Long (DWORD) Value.
Private Declare Function RegSetValueExLong Lib "advapi32.dll"
➡ Alias "RegSetValueExA" _
    (ByVal hKey As Long, ByVal lpValueName As String, ByVal Reserved As Long, _
    ByVal dwType As Long, lpValue As Long, ByVal cbData As Long) As Long

'-- Registry API To Delete A Key.
Private Declare Function RegDeleteKey Lib "advapi32.dll"
➡ Alias "RegDeleteKeyA" _
    (ByVal hKey As Long, ByVal lpSubKey As String) As Long
```

```
'-- Registry API To Delete A Key Value.
Private Declare Function RegDeleteValue Lib "advapi32.dll"
➡ Alias "RegDeleteValueA" _
    (ByVal hKey As Long, ByVal lpValueName As String) As Long

'-- Registry API To Close A Key.
Private Declare Function RegCloseKey Lib "advapi32.dll" (ByVal hKey As Long)
➡ As Long

'-- Constants For Error Messages.
Public Const OpenErr = "Error: Opening Registry Key!"
Public Const DeleteErr = "Error: Deleteing Key!"
Public Const CreateErr = "Error: Creating Key!"
Public Const QueryErr = "Error: Querying Value!"

'-------------------------------------------------------------
'-- Procedure    : Public Method VbRegDeleteKey
'-- Programmer   : Raymond L. King
'-- Created On   : Sunday, May 17, 1998 11:03:04 AM
'-- Module       : VbRegMod
'-- Module File  : VbRegMod.bas
'-- Project      : Project1
'-- Project File : Project1.vbp
'-- Parameters   :
'-- RootKey      : The Root Key To Open, EG: HKEY_CURRENT_USER
'-- KeyName      : The Key Name To Open
'--              : Example: MySettings\Settings
'-- SubKey       : The Sub Key Under KeyName To Delete
'-------------------------------------------------------------
'
Public Sub VbRegDeleteKey _
        (RootKey As Long, KeyName As String, SubKey As String)

    Dim lRtn    As Long        '-- API Return Value
    Dim hKey    As Long        '-- Handle Of Key

    '-- Open The Specified Registry Key.
    lRtn = RegOpenKeyEx(RootKey, KeyName, 0&, KEY_ALL_ACCESS, hKey)

    '-- Check For An Error.
    If lRtn <> ERROR_SUCCESS Then
        MsgBox OpenErr
        RegCloseKey (hKey)
        Exit Sub
    End If

    '-- Delete The Registry SubKey.
    lRtn = RegDeleteKey(hKey, SubKey)

    '-- Check For An Error.
    If lRtn <> ERROR_SUCCESS Then
```

continues

```
            MsgBox DeleteErr
        End If

        '-- Close The Registry Key.
        RegCloseKey (hKey)

End Sub

'-------------------------------------------------------------
'-- Procedure   : Public Method VbRegCreateKey
'-- Programmer  : Raymond L. King
'-- Created On  : Sunday, May 17, 1998 11:03:18 AM
'-- Module      : VbRegMod
'-- Module File : VbRegMod.bas
'-- Project     : Project1
'-- Project File: Project1.vbp
'-- Parameters  :
'-- RootKey     : The Root Key To Open, EG: HKEY_CURRENT_USER
'-- KeyName     : The New Key Name To Create
'--             : Example: MySettings\Settings
'-------------------------------------------------------------
'
Public Sub VbRegCreateKey(RootKey As Long, KeyName As String)

    Dim lRtn    As Long       '-- Registry API Return Value
    Dim hKey    As Long       '-- Handle Of Open Key

    '-- Create The New Registry Key.
    lRtn = RegCreateKeyEx(RootKey, KeyName, 0&, vbNullString, _
    ➡ REG_OPTION_NON_VOLATILE, _
                          KEY_ALL_ACCESS, 0&, hKey, lRtn)

    '-- Check For An Error.
    If lRtn <> ERROR_SUCCESS Then
        MsgBox CreateErr
    End If

    '-- Close The Registry Key.
    RegCloseKey (hKey)

End Sub

'-------------------------------------------------------------
'-- Procedure   : Public Method VbRegQueryValue
'-- Programmer  : Raymond L. King
'-- Created On  : Sunday, May 17, 1998 11:03:29 AM
'-- Module      : VbRegMod
'-- Module File : VbRegMod.bas
'-- Project     : Project1
'-- Project File: Project1.vbp
'-- Parameters  :
```

```
'-- RootKey      : The Root Key To Open, EG: HKEY_CURRENT_USER
'-- KeyName      : The Key Name To Open
'--              : Example: MySettings\Settings
'-- ValueName    : The Value Name To Query
'------------------------------------------------------------
'
Public Function VbRegQueryValue _
        (RootKey As Long, KeyName As String, ValueName As String) As Variant

    Dim lRtn     As Long     '-- API Return Code
    Dim hKey     As Long     '-- Handle Of Open Key
    Dim lCdata   As Long     '-- The Data
    Dim lValue   As Long     '-- Long (DWORD) Value
    Dim sValue   As String   '-- String Value
    Dim lRtype   As Long     '-- Type Returned String Or DWORD

    '-- Open The Registry Key.
    lRtn = RegOpenKeyEx(RootKey, KeyName, 0&, KEY_ALL_ACCESS, hKey)

    '-- Check For An Error.
    If lRtn <> ERROR_SUCCESS Then
        MsgBox OpenErr
        RegCloseKey (hKey)
        Exit Function
    End If

    '-- Query Registry Key For Value Type.
    lRtn = RegQueryValueExNULL(hKey, ValueName, 0&, lRtype, 0&, lCdata)

    '-- Check For An Error.
    If lRtn <> ERROR_SUCCESS Then
        MsgBox QueryErr
        RegCloseKey (hKey)
        Exit Function
    End If

    '-- Get The Key Value By Type.
    Select Case lRtype
        Case 1      '-- REG_SZ (String)
            sValue = String(lCdata, 0)
            '-- Get Registry String Value.
            lRtn = RegQueryValueExString(hKey, ValueName, 0&, lRtype,
            ➥ sValue, lCdata)
            '-- Check For Error.
            If lRtn = ERROR_SUCCESS Then
                VbRegQueryValue = sValue
            Else
                VbRegQueryValue = Empty
            End If
        Case 4      '-- REG_DWORD
            '-- Get Registry Long (DWORD) Value.
```

continues

```
            lRtn = RegQueryValueExLong(hKey, ValueName, 0&, lRtype, _
          ➥ lValue, lCdata)
            '-- Check For Error.
            If lRtn = ERROR_SUCCESS Then
                VbRegQueryValue = lValue
            Else
                VbRegQueryValue = Empty
            End If
    End Select

    '-- Close The Registry Key.
    RegCloseKey (hKey)

End Function

'----------------------------------------------------------------
'-- Procedure    : Public Method VbRegSetValue
'-- Programmer   : Raymond L. King
'-- Created On    : Sunday, May 17, 1998 11:03:42 AM
'-- Module       : VbRegMod
'-- Module File  : VbRegMod.bas
'-- Project      : Project1
'-- Project File : Project1.vbp
'-- Parameters   :
'-- RootKey      : The Root Key To Open, EG: HKEY_CURRENT_USER
'-- KeyName      : The Key Name To Open
'--              : Example: MySettings\Settings
'-- ValueName    : The Value Name To Open
'-- KeyType      : The Key Type, EG: REG_SZ Or REG_DWORD
'-- KeyValue     : The Value To Set Under ValueName
'----------------------------------------------------------------
'
Public Sub VbRegSetValue _
        (RootKey As Long, KeyName As String, _
         ValueName As String, KeyType As Integer, _
         KeyValue As Variant)

    Dim lRtn    As Long      '-- Returned Value From API Registry Call
    Dim hKey    As Long      '-- Handle Of The Opened Key
    Dim lValue  As Long      '-- Setting A Long Data Value
    Dim sValue  As String    '-- Setting A String Data Value
    Dim lSize   As Long      '-- Size Of String Data To Set

    '-- Open The Registry Key.
    lRtn = RegOpenKeyEx(RootKey, KeyName, 0, KEY_ALL_ACCESS, hKey)

    '-- Check For An Error.
    If lRtn <> ERROR_SUCCESS Then
        MsgBox OpenErr
        RegCloseKey (hKey)
        Exit Sub
    End If
```

```
    '-- Select The Key Type.
    Select Case KeyType
        Case 1      '-- REG_SZ (String)
            sValue = KeyValue           '-- Assign Key Value
            lSize = Len(sValue)         '-- Get Size Of String
            '-- Set String Value.
            lRtn = RegSetValueExString(hKey, ValueName, 0&, REG_SZ, _
            ➥ sValue, lSize)
            '-- Check For An Error.
            If lRtn <> ERROR_SUCCESS Then
                MsgBox "Error Setting String Value!"
                RegCloseKey (hKey)
                Exit Sub
        End If
        Case 4      '-- REG_DWORD
            lValue = KeyValue       '-- Assign The Long Value.
            '-- Set The Long Value (DWORD).
            lRtn = RegSetValueExLong(hKey, ValueName, 0&, REG_DWORD, lValue, 4)
            '-- Check For An Error.
            If lRtn <> ERROR_SUCCESS Then
                MsgBox "Error Setting Long (DWORD) Value!"
            End If
    End Select

    '-- Close The Registry Key.
    RegCloseKey (hKey)

End Sub

'-------------------------------------------------------------
'-- Procedure    : Public Method VbRegDeleteValue
'-- Programmer   : Raymond L. King
'-- Created On   : Sunday, May 17, 1998 11:03:49 AM
'-- Module       : VbRegMod
'-- Module File  : VbRegMod.bas
'-- Project      : Project1
'-- Project File : Project1.vbp
'-- Parameters   :
'-- RootKey      : The Root Key To Open, EG: HKEY_CURRENT_USER
'-- KeyName      : The Key Name To Open
'--              : Example: MySettings\Settings
'-- ValueName    : The Value Name To Delete
'-------------------------------------------------------------
'
Public Sub VbRegDeleteValue _
        (RootKey As Long, KeyName As String, ValueName As String)

    Dim lRtn    As Long         '-- API Call Returned Value
    Dim hKey    As Long         '-- Handle Of Opened Key

    '-- Open Registry Key...
    lRtn = RegOpenKeyEx(RootKey, KeyName, 0&, KEY_ALL_ACCESS, hKey)
```

continues

```
'-- Check For An Error.
If lRtn <> ERROR_SUCCESS Then
    MsgBox OpenErr
    RegCloseKey (hKey)
    Exit Sub
End If

'-- Delete Opened Key Value Name...
lRtn = RegDeleteValue(hKey, ValueName)
'-- Check For An Error.
If lRtn <> ERROR_SUCCESS Then
    MsgBox DeleteErr
End If

'-- Close The Registry Key.
RegCloseKey (hKey)

End Sub


Example Program:


Option Explicit

Private Sub Form_Load()

    Dim NewKey As String
    Dim NewValue As Variant
    NewKey = "Custom Software Designers\MySettings"

    '-- Create A New Key
    VbRegCreateKey HKEY_LOCAL_MACHINE, NewKey

    '-- Create A Key Under MySettings
    NewKey = NewKey & "\Settings"
    VbRegCreateKey HKEY_LOCAL_MACHINE, NewKey

    '-- Create A Key Value Name String
    VbRegSetValue HKEY_LOCAL_MACHINE, NewKey, "REG_SZ", REG_SZ, "String"

    '-- Create A Key Value Name DWORD
    VbRegSetValue HKEY_LOCAL_MACHINE, NewKey, "REG_DWORD", REG_DWORD, 123456

    '-- Delete A Value
    'VbRegDeleteValue HKEY_LOCAL_MACHINE, NewKey, "REG_SZ"
```

```
'-- Delete A Key
'VbRegDeleteKey HKEY_LOCAL_MACHINE, "Custom Software Designers\MySettings",
➥ "Settings"

    Text1 = VbRegQueryValue(HKEY_LOCAL_MACHINE, NewKey, "REG_DWORD")

End Sub
```

Analysis

This module is fairly simple. You use the routines in this module to access the Windows Registry. A sample program shows how to use the routines.

You must first create a new key using **VbRegCreateKey**. Then you use **VbRegCreateKey** to create a subkey under your main key above. You would then use **VbRegSetValue** to assign a value to the subkey. To delete a key value use **VbRegDeleteValue**; to delete a key use **VbRegDeleteKey**.

To query a key value use the **VbRegQueryValue** function, which will return the key value to your program.

10.5 GET A REGISTRY ENTRY

by Mike Shaffer

Description

The **GetRegEntry** function will query the System Registry for any value using human-readable values for parameters (this aids program readability and documentation). For example, calling the API directly to get a value contained within the **HKEY_CURRENT_CONFIG** section of the Registry would require that you remember the numeric key (which happens to be **&H80000005**). Clearly, it is more advantageous (both for you and for the person who will be reading your code three years from now) to be able to use human-readable Registry parameters. For example, this line returns the Windows-registered owner name (see the **GetRegistration** function for more information on this particular Registry entry):

```
varRetString = GetRegEntry("HKEY_LOCAL_MACHINE", _
"SOFTWARE\Microsoft\Windows\CurrentVersion", _
"RegisteredOwner", lngType)
```

Syntax

```
GetRegEntry(strKey$, strSubkey$, strValuename$, lngType),
```

Part	Description
StrKey$	Required. The Windows Registry key.
StrSubKey$	Required. The Windows Registry subkey.
StrValueName$	Required. The Windows Registry value name.
LngType	Required. A Long value indicating the data type within the Registry. (Returns −1 if an error occurred).
	The return value is a string corresponding to the data contained within the requested Registry key.

Code Listing

```
'**********************************************
'* Submitted by Mike Shaffer
'**********************************************
Declare Function RegOpenKeyEx Lib "advapi32.dll" Alias "RegOpenKeyExA"
➨(ByVal hKey As Long, _
ByVal lpSubKey As String, ByVal ulOptions As Long, ByVal samDesired As Long, _
phkResult As Long) As Long
Declare Function RegQueryValueEx Lib "advapi32.dll" Alias "RegQueryValueExA" _
(ByVal hKey As Long, ByVal lpValueName As String, ByVal lpReserved As Long, _
lpType As Long, lpData As Any, lpcbData As Long) As Long
Declare Function RegCloseKey Lib "advapi32.dll" (ByVal hKey As Long) As Long
Public Const REG_BINARY = 3              ' Binary data
Public Const REG_DWORD = 4              ' 32-Bit long
Public Const REG_DWORD_BIG_ENDIAN = 5        ' 32-bit long (big endian)
Public Const REG_DWORD_LITTLE_ENDIAN = 4     ' 32-bit long (little endian)
Public Const REG_EXPAND_SZ = 2          ' Unexpanded environment string
Public Const REG_LINK = 6              ' Symbolic link
Public Const REG_MULTI_SZ = 7            ' list of strings
Public Const REG_NONE = 0              ' Undefined
Public Const REG_RESOURCE_LIST = 8         ' Resource list (for device drivers)
Public Const REG_SZ = 1               ' String with null terminator

Function GetRegEntry(strKey As String, strSubKeys As String,
➨strValName As String, _
lngType As Long) As String
    '
    On Error GoTo GetRegEntry_Err
    '
    Dim lngResult As Long, lngKey As Long
    Dim lngHandle As Long, lngcbData As Long
    Dim strRet As String
    '
    ' Take the human-readable key class and convert it to a WIN95 reserved
    ' numeric constant
    Select Case strKey
      Case "HKEY_CLASSES_ROOT"
        lngKey = &H80000000
```

```
        Case "HKEY_CURRENT_CONFIG"
            lngKey = &H80000005
        Case "HKEY_CURRENT_USER"
            lngKey = &H80000001
        Case "HKEY_DYN_DATA"
            lngKey = &H80000006
        Case "HKEY_LOCAL_MACHINE"
            lngKey = &H80000002
        Case "HKEY_PERFORMANCE_DATA"
            lngKey = &H80000004
        Case "HKEY_USERS"
            lngKey = &H80000003
        Case Else
            Exit Function
    End Select
        '
    If Not ERROR_SUCCESS = RegOpenKeyEx(lngKey, strSubKeys, 0&, KEY_READ,
    ➥lngHandle) Then
        Exit Function
                End If
        '
    lngResult = RegQueryValueEx(lngHandle, strValName, 0&, lngType,
    ➥ByVal strRet, lngcbData)
    strRet = Space$(lngcbData)
    lngResult = RegQueryValueEx(lngHandle, strValName, 0&, lngType,
    ➥ByVal strRet, lngcbData)
        '
    If Not ERROR_SUCCESS = RegCloseKey(lngHandle) Then lngType = -1&
        '
    GetRegEntry = strRet
        '
GetRegEntry_Exit:
    On Error GoTo 0
    Exit Function
        '
GetRegEntry_Err:
    lngType = -1&
    MsgBox Err & "> " & Error$, 16, "Common/GetRegEntry"
    Resume GetRegEntry_Exit
        '
End Function
```

Analysis

This function makes retrieving any Windows Registry value fairly simple. You might want to comment out the MsgBox within the GetRegEntry_Err section of code and handle notifying the user outside this function. Notice that the main function of this routine is to provide an intermediary between your human-readable keys and the Windows API key numbers. The API call RegQueryValueEx actually does all the work within the Registry in this routine.

10.6 STRING ARRAY SORT

by Andy Carrasco

Description

The `InsertSort` function sorts a single-dimensional array in ascending or descending order. This function works with both numerical arrays and string arrays. You must pass a variant containing a single-dimensional array of strings or numbers, and the function will return a variant containing the sorted array.

Syntax

```
NewArray = InsertSort( ValueList, [SortDescending] )
```

Part	Description
`NewArray`	Required. A variant variable that will hold the sorted array.
`ValueList`	Required. The unsorted array variable.
`SortDescending`	Optional. By default, `InsertSort` will sort the array specified in `ValueList` in ascending order. If you want the array to be sorted in descending order, set the value of the `SortDescending` parameter to `True`.

Code Listing

```
Public Function InsertSort(ValueList As Variant, Optional SortDescending
➥ As Boolean) As Variant

Dim RipVal As Variant
Dim RipOrdinal As Long
Dim RipDescent As Long
Dim PrivateBuffer As Variant
Dim Placed As Boolean
Dim x As Long
Dim y As Long

PrivateBuffer = ValueList

'Ok, we start at the second position in the array and go
'from there

RipOrdinal = 1
RipDescent = 1
```

```
    For y = 1 To UBound(PrivateBuffer)
        RipVal = PrivateBuffer(y)
        If y <> 1 Then RipDescent = y
        Do Until Placed
            If IIf(SortDescending, (PrivateBuffer(RipDescent - 1) <= RipVal), _
        (PrivateBuffer(RipDescent - 1) >= RipVal)) Then

                RipDescent = RipDescent - 1
                If RipDescent = 0 Then
                    For x = y To RipDescent Step -1
                        If x = 0 Then Exit For
                        PrivateBuffer(x) = PrivateBuffer(x - 1)
                    Next x
                PrivateBuffer(RipDescent) = RipVal
                Placed = True
                End If
            Else
                'shift the array to the right
                For x = y To RipDescent Step -1
                    If x = 0 Then Exit For
                    PrivateBuffer(x) = PrivateBuffer(x - 1)
                Next x
                'insert the ripped value
                PrivateBuffer(RipDescent) = RipVal
                Placed = True
            End If
        Loop
        Placed = False
    Next y

'return the sorted array
InsertSort = PrivateBuffer

End Function
```

Analysis

This function uses a simple algorithm to sort arrays and is fairly quick when working with arrays that contain a few thousand elements or less. The structure of the function consists of one main loop and a smaller internal loop. The main loop begins at the second element of the array and performs the smaller loop for each element of the original array.

The actual work of the sort is performed by the smaller loop. As each new element of the array is encountered, the smaller loop works backward through the array looking for a value which, depending on the selected sort order, is greater than or less than the current element. When that condition is true, it will insert the current element into the array at that position, and then shift the remaining elements in the array to the right.

Suppose you have a numerical array that contains four values:

`{20,5,15,10}`

You want to sort the array in ascending order. To accomplish this, the function begins the main loop at the second element of the array, which in this case is 5.

The smaller loop will begin to work backward, examining each element encountered to determine whether that element is larger than the element you are trying to place. In this array, the first element is 20, which is larger than the value you are trying to place (5), so the function will insert the value you want to place into the first element of the array and shift the remaining values to the right.

`{5,20,15,10}`

This process continues for the third element in the array, 15. The second element in the array, 20, is larger than 15, so the function will insert the 15 into the second element, and then shift the remaining element to the right again.

`{5,15,20,10}`

This process continues once again until the function achieves the sorted array.

`{5,10,15,20}`

Note

This code is designed to operate on Option Base 0. If it's run under Option Base 1 you will receive a subscript error message.

10.7 QUICK SORT STRING ARRAY

by Lenard Dean with Brian Shea

Description

This function can be used to quick sort a string array or sections of a string array. You can specify the element within the array to use as a starting point and the one to use for an ending point, which enables you to sort sections without sorting the entire array. This can be used to provide speed or granularity in your sorting.

This function can also sort by only sections of the array elements rather than just sorting on the entire string stored in each element. This enables you to optimize the sorts for speed and enables you to sort on the second word or other criteria that you might want to use.

If you are going to sort the entire array or start at a specific point and continue to the end of the array, you might want to use the Shell Sort String Array function, also found in this section. It is a slightly faster function for the sorting, but it doesn't stop until the end of the array is reached.

Syntax

```
SortStrArrayQuick strArray() As String, ByVal lngFirst As Long,
➥ ByVal lngLast As Long, Optional ByVal varStrPosOffset As Variant,
➥ Optional ByVal varStrOffsetLen As Variant
```

Part	Description
strArray	Required. The array to sort.
lngFirst	Required. The start element to sort.
lngLast	Required. The end element to sort.
varStrPosOffset	Optional. The start position of the element to sort.
varStrOffsetLen	Optional. The length of string to sort.

Code Listing

```
'* by Lenard Dean

Public Sub SortStrArrayQuick(strArray() As String, ByVal lngFirst As Long,
➥ ByVal lngLast As Long, Optional ByVal varStrPosOffset As Variant,
➥ Optional ByVal varStrOffsetLen As Variant)

  On Local Error Resume Next

  Dim lngI As Long
  Dim lngJ As Long
  Dim strSplit As String
  Dim strTemp As String
  Dim blnCompareOffset As Boolean
  Dim intStrPosOffset As Integer
  Dim intStrOffsetLen As Integer

  If IsMissing(varStrPosOffset) Then
    blnCompareOffset = False ' This is done for speed
  Else
    intStrPosOffset = varStrPosOffset ' This is done for speed
    If varStrPosOffset < 2 Then
      blnCompareOffset = False
    Else
      blnCompareOffset = True
      If IsMissing(varStrOffsetLen) Then
        intStrOffsetLen = Len(strArray(1)) - intStrPosOffset + 1
      Else
```

continues

```
            intStrOffsetLen = varStrOffsetLen
        End If
      End If
    End If

    lngI = lngFirst
    lngJ = lngLast
    strSplit = strArray((lngFirst + lngLast) \ 2)

    Do While lngI <= lngJ

      If blnCompareOffset Then
        Do While (StrComp(Mid(strArray(lngI), intStrPosOffset, intStrOffsetLen),
➥ Mid(strSplit, intStrPosOffset, intStrOffsetLen), 1) < 0 And
➥lngI < lngLast)
          lngI = lngI + 1
        Loop

        Do While (StrComp(Mid(strArray(lngJ), intStrPosOffset, intStrOffsetLen),
➥ Mid(strSplit, intStrPosOffset, intStrOffsetLen), 1) > 0 And
➥lngJ > lngFirst)
          lngJ = lngJ - 1
        Loop
      Else
        Do While (StrComp(strArray(lngI), strSplit, 1) < 0 And lngI < lngLast)
          lngI = lngI + 1
        Loop

        Do While (StrComp(strArray(lngJ), strSplit, 1) > 0 And lngJ > lngFirst)
          lngJ = lngJ - 1
        Loop
      End If

      If lngI <= lngJ Then
        strTemp = strArray(lngI)
        strArray(lngI) = strArray(lngJ)
        strArray(lngJ) = strTemp
        lngI = lngI + 1
        lngJ = lngJ - 1
      End If

    Loop

    DoEvents

    If lngFirst < lngJ Then SortStrArrayQuick strArray(), lngFirst, lngJ,
➥ varStrPosOffset, varStrOffsetLen
    If lngI < lngLast Then SortStrArrayQuick strArray(), lngI, lngLast,
➥ varStrPosOffset, varStrOffsetLen

End Sub
```

Analysis

The first section of code determines whether the function will be comparing by offsets or not. If you are comparing by offsets, the array element length should all be the same. You can use the `Pad String` function from the string manipulation section to set the length of each element to the length of the longest one.

Next, the function walks through the array and uses `StrComp` to compare and move elements of the string up or down within the specified range of elements. The function continues to the end, then calls itself if the sort is not completed. This enables the function to operate until it is finished.

Note

Because the function calls itself, it might in rare cases cause resource allocation problems. This would occur only on extremely large arrays, so be careful. I have never observed this condition, but it is (in theory) possible.

10.8 SHELL SORT STRING ARRAY

by Lenard Dean with Brian Shea

Description

This function enables you to sort the contents of an array to either ascending or descending order. You can also specify the position of the strings (within each element) on which to sort and the length of the sort string within the array. If you choose to sort on any part of an element rather than the whole element, the array elements must all be the same size. You can use Pad String, found in Chapter 8, "String Manipulation," to accomplish this task.

If you do not need to sort all the elements of the array, you might want to use the quick sort string array function, also found in this chapter. It will enable you to specify regions within the array to sort.

Syntax

```
SortStrArrayShell strArray() As String, ByVal intOrder As Integer,
➥Optional ByVal varStrPosOffset As Variant,
➥Optional ByVal varStrOffsetLen As Variant
```

Part	Description
strArray()	Required. The array to sort.
intOrder	Required. Use 0 for ascending and -1 for descending order.
varStrPosOffset	Optional. The position within the string elements from which to start the sort.
varStrOffsetLen	Optional. The string position from which to start the compare. The string array must be fixed in length.

Code Listing

```
'* by Lenard Dean

Public Sub SortStrArrayShell(strArray() As String, ByVal intOrder As Integer,
➥Optional ByVal varStrPosOffset As Variant, Optional ByVal varStrOffsetLen
➥As Variant)

  On Local Error Resume Next

  Dim lngDistance As Long
  Dim strTemp As String
  Dim lngNextElement As Long
  Dim lngSize As Long
  Dim lngIndex As Long
  Dim lngN As Long
  Dim lngArrayStart As Long
  Dim lngArrayEnd As Long
  Dim blnCompareOffset As Boolean
  Dim intStrPosOffset As Integer
  Dim intStrLenOffset As Integer

  If IsMissing(varStrPosOffset) Then
    blnCompareOffset = False
  Else
    intStrPosOffset = varStrPosOffset
    If varStrPosOffset < 2 Then
      blnCompareOffset = False
    Else
      blnCompareOffset = True
      If IsMissing(varStrOffsetLen) Then
        intStrLenOffset = Len(strArray(1)) - intStrPosOffset + 1
      Else
        intStrLenOffset = varStrOffsetLen
      End If
    End If
  End If

  lngArrayStart = LBound(strArray)
  lngArrayEnd = UBound(strArray)
```

```
lngSize = lngArrayEnd - lngArrayStart + 1
lngDistance = 1

Do While lngDistance <= lngSize
  lngDistance = lngDistance * 2
Loop

lngDistance = (lngDistance \ 2) - 1

Do While lngDistance > 0
  lngNextElement = lngArrayStart + lngDistance
  Do While lngNextElement <= lngArrayEnd
    lngIndex = lngNextElement
    Do
      If lngIndex >= lngArrayStart + lngDistance Then
        If intOrder = -1 Then ' Descending
          lngN = lngIndex - lngDistance
          If blnCompareOffset Then
            If StrComp(Mid(strArray(lngN), intStrPosOffset, intStrLenOffset),
            ➥ Mid(strArray(lngIndex), intStrPosOffset,
            ➥intStrLenOffset), 1) = -1 Then
              strTemp = strArray(lngIndex)
              strArray(lngIndex) = strArray(lngN)
              strArray(lngN) = strTemp
              lngIndex = lngN
            Else
              Exit Do
            End If
          Else
            If StrComp(strArray(lngN), strArray(lngIndex), 1) = -1 Then
              strTemp = strArray(lngIndex)
              strArray(lngIndex) = strArray(lngN)
              strArray(lngN) = strTemp
              lngIndex = lngN
            Else
              Exit Do
            End If
          End If
        Else   ' Ascending
          lngN = lngIndex - lngDistance
          If blnCompareOffset Then
            If StrComp(Mid(strArray(lngN), intStrPosOffset, intStrLenOffset),
            ➥ Mid(strArray(lngIndex), intStrPosOffset,
            ➥intStrLenOffset), 1) >= 0 Then
              strTemp = strArray(lngIndex)
              strArray(lngIndex) = strArray(lngN)
              strArray(lngN) = strTemp
              lngIndex = lngN
            Else
              Exit Do
            End If
          Else
```

continues

```
                If StrComp(strArray(lngN), strArray(lngIndex), 1) >= 0 Then
                  strTemp = strArray(lngIndex)
                  strArray(lngIndex) = strArray(lngN)
                  strArray(lngN) = strTemp
                  lngIndex = lngN
                Else
                  Exit Do
                End If
              End If
            End If
          Else
            Exit Do
          End If
        Loop
        lngNextElement = lngNextElement + 1
      Loop
      lngDistance = (lngDistance - 1) / 2
    Loop

End Sub
```

Analysis

This function is very simple. It uses the `StrComp` function to sort array elements either up or down in comparison to their neighboring elements. The function loops through half the unsorted array elements, loops back and gets the other half, and so on until it gets down to the last element.

10.9 QUICK SORT

by Mike Shaffer

Description

The `QSort` routine uses a Quicksort algorithm to arrange all elements of a string array into proper (sorted) order. This is a much faster, general-purpose sort than the `SelSort` routine (see the next section). Quicksort generally performs better than a Selection sort unless your list of values to be sorted includes many duplicates. The Quicksort algorithm uses a recursive "divide-and-conquer" technique. It operates by dividing your list of data into smaller and smaller subgroups, which it recursively sorts.

Syntax

```
Qsort List(), Lower, Upper
```

Part	Description
List()	Required. A string array containing the data to be sorted.
Lower	Required. The beginning element for the sort.
Upper	Required. The ending element for the sort.

Code Listing

```
'***********************************************
'* Submitted by Mike Shaffer
'***********************************************
Public Sub QSort(strList() As String, lLbound As Long, lUbound As Long)
':::::::::::::::::::::::::::::::::::::::::::::::::::::::::::::::::::::::::'
':::                                                               :::'
':::    Routine:    QSort                                          :::'
':::    Author:     Mike Shaffer (after Rod Stephens, et al.)      :::'
':::    Date:       21-May-98                                      :::'
':::    Purpose:    Very fast sort of a string array              :::'
':::    Passed:     strList    String array                       :::'
':::                lLbound    Lower bound to sort (usually 1)     :::'
':::                lUbound    Upper bound to sort (usually ubound())):::'
':::    Returns:    strList    (in sorted order)                  :::'
':::    Revisions:  22-May-98 Added and then dropped revision      :::'
':::                using CopyMemory rather than the simple swap    :::'
':::                when it was found to not provide much benefit.  :::'
':::                                                               :::'
':::::::::::::::::::::::::::::::::::::::::::::::::::::::::::::::::::::::::'

    Dim strTemp As String
    Dim strBuffer As String
    Dim lngCurLow As Long
    Dim lngCurHigh As Long
    Dim lngCurMidpoint As Long

    ' Start current low and high at actual low/high
    lngCurLow = lLbound
    lngCurHigh = lUbound

    ' Error!
    If lUbound <= lLbound Then Exit Sub:

    ' Find the approx midpoint of the array
    lngCurMidpoint = (lLbound + lUbound) \ 2

    ' Pick as a starting point (we are making
    ' an assumption that the data *might* be
```

continues

```
' in semi-sorted order already!
strTemp = strList(lngCurMidpoint)

Do While (lngCurLow <= lngCurHigh)

    Do While strList(lngCurLow) < strTemp
        lngCurLow = lngCurLow + 1
        If lngCurLow = lUbound Then Exit Do
    Loop

    Do While strTemp < strList(lngCurHigh)
        lngCurHigh = lngCurHigh - 1
        If lngCurHigh = lLbound Then Exit Do
    Loop

    ' if low is <= high then swap
    If (lngCurLow <= lngCurHigh) Then
        strBuffer = strList(lngCurLow)
        strList(lngCurLow) = strList(lngCurHigh)
        strList(lngCurHigh) = strBuffer
        '
        lngCurLow = lngCurLow + 1
        lngCurHigh = lngCurHigh - 1
    End If

Loop

' Recurse if necessary
If lLbound < lngCurHigh Then
    QSort strList(), lLbound, lngCurHigh
End If

' Recurse if necessary
If lngCurLow < lUbound Then
    QSort strList(), lngCurLow, lUbound
End If

End Sub
```

Analysis

This function is useful for sorting string arrays of any size. It is quite fast, and capable of sorting more than 10,000 10-byte strings in less than 1/5th of a second (on a Pentium 200 running Windows 95). With very few exceptions (see above), Quicksort will serve as the most important sorting routine in your programming arsenal.

10.10 SELECTION SORT

by Mike Shaffer

Description

The SelSort routine uses a selection sort to arrange all elements of a string array into proper (sorted) order. Selection sorts work by searching the entire list for the smallest value within the list. After it is found, that item is swapped with the first item in the list. Then, the next smallest item is searched for (starting at the second item in the list, because it already knows that the first one is the smallest), and the process continues until the entire list is sorted. This sort works best for items that are in relatively random or somewhat ordered arrays. For arrays that are already sorted in relatively reverse order, this sort is not as efficient. The primary benefits of the selection sort are that it is fast and fairly easy to understand.

Syntax

```
SelSortString List()
```

Part	Description
List()	Required. A string array containing the data to be sorted.

Code Listing

```
'***********************************************
'* Submitted by Mike Shaffer
'***********************************************
Sub SelSortString(list() As String)
    '
    '::::::::::::::::::::::::::::::::::::::::::::::::::::::::::::::::::::::::'
    ':::
    ':::    This routine performs a selection sort on an array of
    ':::    strings (list()).
    ':::
    '::::::::::::::::::::::::::::::::::::::::::::::::::::::::::::::::::::::::'
    '
    Dim j As Long, i As Long
    Dim best_value As String, best_j As Long
    '
    Min = LBound(list)
    max = UBound(list)
    '
    ' Create an array reference and dimension it to proper size
    Dim index() As Long
```

continues

```
ReDim index(Min To max)
'
' Fill it with array ponters
For x& = Min To max
    index(x&) = x&
Next
'
' Do the sort!
For i = Min To max - 1
    best_value = list(index(i))
    best_j = i
    For j = i + 1 To max
        If list(j) < best_value Then
            best_value = list(index(j))
            best_j = j
        End If
    Next j
    list(best_j) = list(i)
    list(i) = best_value
Next
'

End Sub
```

Analysis

This function is useful for sorting small arrays of strings. For a more robust (and faster) sorting routine, see the "Quick Sort" section, earlier in this chapter.

10.11 THAYER ENCRYPTION

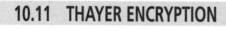

by Asgeir Bjarni Ingvarsson

Description

The Crypt routine uses an algorithm created by Rodney Thayer. This algorithm can use keys of various sizes. With a 40-bit key (5 characters) it can be freely exported from the U.S. The cipher is considered robust with 128 bits of key material but can use up to 2048 bits. This algorithm is compatible with RSA's RC4.

For more information on RSA's algorithms and an F.A.Q on cryptography you can go to http://www.rsa.com.

Syntax

```
ReturnValue = Crypt(Inp , Key)
```

Part	Description
Inp	Required. The input field. It must contain data to be either encrypted or decrypted. The data can be text from text files or data from picture files, .EXE files, and so on.
Key	Required. The key field. It must contain the same data for encryption and decryption. For better security, the data contained here should be random.

Code Listing

```
Public Function Crypt(inp As String, Key As String) As String
Dim Sbox(0 To 255) As Byte
Dim Sbox2(0 To 255) As Byte
Dim j As Long, i As Long, t As Double
Dim K As Long, temp As Long, Outp As String

        For i = 0 To 255 'Create SBox #1
                Sbox(i) = i  'and fill with
        Next i              'successive values

        j = 1
        For i = 0 To 255                        'Create SBox #2
                If j > Len(Key) Then j = 1      'And fill with key
                Sbox2(i) = Asc(Mid(Key, j, 1)) 'data, repeatedly
                j = j + 1                       'until the SBox is
        Next i                                  'full

        j = 0 'Initialize j
        For i = 0 To 255                            'Scramble SBox #1
                j = (j + Sbox(i) + Sbox2(i)) Mod 256 'with data from
                temp = Sbox(i)                       'SBox #2
                Sbox(i) = Sbox(j)
                Sbox(j) = temp
        Next i

        i = 0 'Initialize i
        j = 0 'Initialize j
        For x = 1 To Len(inp) 'Process the data passed on to us
                i = (i + 1) Mod 256 'Increment i
                j = (j + Sbox(i)) Mod 256 'Increment j
                temp = Sbox(i)      'Scramble SBox #1
                Sbox(i) = Sbox(j) 'further so that the encryptor
                Sbox(j) = temp    'will only repeat itself with a great
                ➥ interval. aprox. interval (distance between
                ➥ repetions) of 2 to the 1700th power
                t = (Sbox(i) + Sbox(j)) Mod 256 'Get ready to create pseudo
```

continues

```
    ➥ random   byte
    K = Sbox(t) 'Get   pseudo random byte

    Outp = Outp + Chr(Asc(Mid(inp, x, 1)) Xor K) 'Xor the data
    ➥with the pseudo random   byte
Next x
Crypt = Outp 'Return the Output Data
End Function
```

Analysis

This routine is fairly simple. It receives data to work on and a key to scramble or unscramble the data. It can be operated with 40 bits (5 characters) of key material, but this is not recommended. For very good security I recommend using 128 bits (16 characters) of key material. If you want optimal security you could use 2048 bits (256 characters) of key material (but this is usually considered an overkill).

This routine is constructed from a draft taken from Internet Engineering Task Force (IETF) at `http://www.ietf.cnri.reston.va.us/home.html`.

To check whether the implementation is right you can use these test vectors:

- Plain Text: &H00, &H00, &H00, &H00, &H00, &H00, &H00, &H00
- Key: &H01, &H23, &H45, &H67, &H89, &HAB, &HCD, &HEF
- Text: &H74, &H94, &HC2, &HE7, &H10, &H4B, &H08, &H79

If the test vectors come out incorrect, the implementation is incorrect. If they come out OK, you're set.

Note

The vectors are given on a byte-by-byte basis in hexadecimal values. For correct application they should first be translated into strings. This routine is extremely fast and is 100% error free if it is implemented correctly.

10.12 THE *BUMPDATE* FUNCTION

by Mike Shaffer

Description

The `BumpDate` function analyzes any date to determine whether it falls on a weekend. If it does, it will return the following Monday date. If it does not, it returns the original date passed.

Syntax

```
BumpDate(dtDate1)
```

Part	Description
dtDate1	Required. The date to test.

Code Listing

```
'***********************************************
'* Submitted by Mike Shaffer
'***********************************************
Public Function BumpDate(dtBump As Date) As Date
   '
  '::::::::::::::::::::::::::::::::::::::::::::::::::::::::::::::::::::::::::::'
  ':::                                                                  :::'
  ':::    Given a date, will ensure that it does not fall on a weekend  :::'
  ':::    by bumping it forward as needed.                              :::'
  ':::                                                                  :::'
  '::::::::::::::::::::::::::::::::::::::::::::::::::::::::::::::::::::::::::::'
    '
  BumpDate = dtBump
  While (WeekDay(BumpDate) Mod 6) = 1
     BumpDate = DateAdd("d", "1", BumpDate)
  Wend
    '
End Function
```

Analysis

This function is useful for determining whether calculated dates fall on business days (for example, payment term dates, insurance policy expiration dates, or library book due dates). For example, a video club that is closed on weekends would not want to calculate a return date that falls on a weekend, so it could use this routine to be sure the return date gets pushed to the following Monday. Or an appointment scheduler might be made more useful if it could automatically warn the end user that an auto-scheduled appointment was going to fall on a weekend.

10.13 BETTER *ATN*

by Paolo Bonzini

Description

This function calculates the arctangent of a passed value of a single parameter, just like the original function. If you pass two arguments, however (such as Atn(y,x)), this version calculates the arctangent of y/x, handling the case when x = 0. Because it is common to compute the arctangent of a ratio, and in such a computation the denominator will possibly be 0, error handling is necessary.

Syntax

```
Result = Atn(Y[, X])
```

Part	Description
Result	Required. The computed arctangent.
Y	Required. The numerator of the ratio whose arctangent is to be computed.
X	Optional, defaults to 1. The denominator of the ratio whose arctangent is to be computed.

Code Listing

```
'*********************************************
'* Submitted by Paolo Bonzini
'*********************************************
Function Atn(ByVal Y As Double, Optional ByVal X As Double = 1) As Double

    On Error Resume Next
    Atn = VBA.Atn(Y / X)
    If Err Then
        If X <> 0 Then
            Atn = Sgn(Y) * Sgn(X) * 1.570796326795
        Else
            Atn = Sgn(Y) * 1.570796326795
        End If
        Err.Clear
    End If
End Function
```

Analysis

The code is very simple. An arctangent is calculated using the version of Atn in the VBA library. If the computation raises an error, the error is cleared and the correct value is computed. The absolute value of the result is PI/2. The sign can be positive or negative: if x is zero, it is the same sign as y; otherwise, the sign of y/x is computed using Sgn(Y) * Sgn(X).

11

GAME PROGRAMMING AND MULTIMEDIA

How could we have a complete code library without game and multimedia functions? Here we have collected some functions that will help you build sound, video, and joystick support into your applications. You can use these functions to create games, or just enhance the appeal of your application.

11.1 JOYSTICK FUNCTIONS

by Raymond King

Description

The `JoyMod` module gives a Visual Basic program access to the joystick. Error handling is built into the joystick functions. Visual Basic provides no simple way to access the joystick, outside of using API calls.

Using the `JoyMod` module in your own applications is simple: simply add the `JoyMod` module to your application program. There are two functions in this module, `JoyStick_Init` and `JoyStick_GetPos`. These `JoyStick` routines use all Windows API calls to access the `JoyStick` functions.

Syntax

```
Call JoyStick_Init(JoyStickID)
Call JoyStick_GetPos(JoyStickID)
```

Part	Description
JoyStickID	Required. The joystick ID specifying the joystick you want to use. These are constants defined in the JoyMod module.

Code Listing

```
Option Explicit

'----------------------------------------------------------
'-- JoyMod.bas
'-- Programmer: Raymond L. King
'-- Custom Software Designers
'--
'-- Functions For Accessing The JoyStick
'--
'----------------------------------------------------------

'-- General Constants.
Public Const MAXPNAMELEN = 32   ' Max Product Name Length (Including NULL)
Public Const MAXOEMVXD = 160

'-- JoyStick ID Constants.
Public Const JOYSTICKID1 = 0
Public Const JOYSTICKID2 = 1

'-- JoyStick Flag Constants.
Public Const JOY_CAL_READ3 = &H40000
Public Const JOY_CAL_READ4 = &H80000
Public Const JOY_CAL_READ5 = &H400000
Public Const JOY_CAL_READ6 = &H800000
Public Const JOY_CAL_READALWAYS = &H10000
Public Const JOY_CAL_READRONLY = &H2000000
Public Const JOY_CAL_READUONLY = &H4000000
Public Const JOY_CAL_READVONLY = &H8000000
Public Const JOY_CAL_READXONLY = &H100000
Public Const JOY_CAL_READXYONLY = &H20000
Public Const JOY_CAL_READYONLY = &H200000
Public Const JOY_CAL_READZONLY = &H1000000
Public Const JOY_POVBACKWARD = 18000
Public Const JOY_POVCENTERED = -1
Public Const JOY_POVFORWARD = 0
Public Const JOY_POVLEFT = 27000
Public Const JOY_POVRIGHT = 9000
Public Const JOY_RETURNBUTTONS = &H80&
Public Const JOY_RETURNCENTERED = &H400&
Public Const JOY_RETURNPOV = &H40&
Public Const JOY_RETURNPOVCTS = &H200&
Public Const JOY_RETURNR = &H8&
Public Const JOY_RETURNRAWDATA = &H100&
Public Const JOY_RETURNU = &H10          ' Axis 5
Public Const JOY_RETURNV = &H20          ' Axis 6
Public Const JOY_RETURNX = &H1&
Public Const JOY_RETURNY = &H2&
Public Const JOY_RETURNZ = &H4&
Public Const JOY_USEDEADZONE = &H800&
Public Const JOY_RETURNALL = (JOY_RETURNX Or JOY_RETURNY Or JOY_RETURNZ _
```

```
                        Or JOY_RETURNR Or JOY_RETURNU Or JOY_RETURNV _
                        Or JOY_RETURNPOV Or JOY_RETURNBUTTONS)

'-- JoyStick Error Constants.
Public Const JOYERR_BASE = 160                        ' Error Base
Public Const JOYERR_NOCANDO = (JOYERR_BASE + 6)    ' Request Not Completed
Public Const JOYERR_NOERROR = (0)                  ' No Error
Public Const JOYERR_PARMS = (JOYERR_BASE + 5)      ' Bad Parameters
Public Const JOYERR_UNPLUGGED = (JOYERR_BASE + 7) ' JoyStick Is Unplugged


'-- JOYCAPS User Defined Type.
Public Type JOYCAPS
    wMid            As Integer  ' Manufacturer Identifier.
    wPid            As Integer  ' Product Identifier.
    szPname         As String * MAXPNAMELEN ' Null Terminated String -
    ➥ JoyStick Product Name.
    wXmin           As Long     ' Minimum X-coordinate.
    wXmax           As Long     ' Maximum X-coordinate.
    wYmin           As Long     ' Minimum Y-coordinate.
    wYmax           As Long     ' Maximum Y-coordinate.
    wZmin           As Long     ' Minimum Z-coordinate.
    wZmax           As Long     ' Maximum Z-coordinate.
    wNumButtons     As Long     ' Number Of JoyStick Buttons.
    wPeriodMin      As Long     ' Smallest Polling Frequency Supported By
    ➥ JoySetCapture.
    wPeriodMax      As Long     ' Largest Polling Frequency Supported By
    ➥ JoySetCapture.
    wRmin           As Long     ' Minimum Rudder Value. The Rudder Is A Fourth
    ➥ Axis Movement.
    wRmax           As Long     ' Maximum Rudder Value. The Rudder Is A Fourth
    ➥ Axis Movement.
    wUmin           As Long     ' Minimum U-coordinate (Fifth Axis) Values.
    wUmax           As Long     ' Maximum U-coordinate (Fifth Axis) Values.
    wVmin           As Long     ' Minimum V-coordinate (Sixth Axis) Values.
    wVmax           As Long     ' Maximum V-coordinate (Sixth Axis) Values.
    wCaps           As Long     ' JoyStick Capabilities.  Note: See JoyCaps
    ➥ Flags Below...
    wMaxAxes        As Long     ' Maximum Number Of Axes Supported By JoyStick.
    wNumAxes        As Long     ' Number Of Axes Currently In Use By JoyStick.
    wMaxButtons     As Long     ' Maximum Number Of Buttons Supported By The
    ➥ JoyStick.
    szRegKey        As String * MAXPNAMELEN ' Null-Terminated String Containing
    ➥ The Registry Key.
    szOEMVxD        As String * MAXOEMVXD ' Null-Terminated String Identifying
    ➥ The JoyStick Driver OEM.
End Type


'-- JOYINFOEX User Defined Type.
Public Type JOYINFOEX
    dwSize          As Long     ' Size, In Bytes, Of This User Defined Type.
    dwFlags         As Long     ' Flags See Below: JOYINFOEX Flags.
    dwXpos          As Long     ' Current X-coordinate.
```

continues

```
        dwYpos          As Long      ' Current Y-coordinate.
        dwZpos          As Long      ' Current Z-coordinate.
        dwRpos          As Long      ' Current Position Of The Rudder Or Fourth
        ➥ JoyStick Axis.
        dwUpos          As Long      ' Current Fifth Axis Position.
        dwVpos          As Long      ' Current Sixth Axis Position.
        dwButtons       As Long      ' Current State Of The 32 JoyStick Buttons.
        dwButtonNumber  As Long      ' Current Button Number That Is Pressed.
        dwPOV           As Long      ' Current Position Of The Point-Of-View
        ➥ Control.
        dwReserved1     As Long      ' Reserved; Do Not Use.
        dwReserved2     As Long      ' Reserved; Do Not Use.
End Type

'-- For Accessing The JoyStick User Defined Types.
Public JsCaps As JOYCAPS
Public JsInfo As JOYINFOEX

'-- JoyStick API Declarations.
Private Declare Function joyGetDevCaps Lib "winmm.dll" Alias "joyGetDevCapsA" _
    (ByVal id As Long, lpCaps As JOYCAPS, ByVal uSize As Long) As Long

Private Declare Function joyGetNumDevs Lib "winmm.dll" () As Long

Private Declare Function joyGetPosEx Lib "winmm.dll" _
    (ByVal uJoyID As Long, pji As JOYINFOEX) As Long

Private Declare Function joyGetThreshold Lib "winmm.dll" _
    (ByVal id As Long, lpuThreshold As Long) As Long

Private Declare Function joyReleaseCapture Lib "winmm.dll" (ByVal id As Long)
➥ As Long

Private Declare Function joySetCapture Lib "winmm.dll" _
    (ByVal Hwnd As Long, ByVal uID As Long, ByVal uPeriod As Long,
    ➥ByVal bChanged As Long) _
    As Long

Private Declare Function joySetThreshold Lib "winmm.dll" _
    (ByVal id As Long, ByVal uThreshold As Long) As Long

'-- Initialize The JoyStick Structures
Public Sub JoyStick_Init(JoyStick As Integer)

    Dim lRtn   As Long
    Dim luSize As Long

    '-- Size Of User Defined Type
    luSize = Len(JsCaps)
```

```
    '-- Get The JoyStick Capabilities...
    lRtn = joyGetDevCaps(JoyStick, JsCaps, luSize)

    '-- Check For Error...
    If lRtn <> JOYERR_NOERROR Then
        MsgBox "JoyStick Initialization Error! " & Str(lRtn)
    End If

End Sub

'-- Get JoyStick Position
Public Sub JoyStick_GetPos(JoyStick As Integer)

    Dim lRtn  As Long
    Dim lSize As Long

    '-- Size Of User Defined Type
    lSize = Len(JsInfo)

    JsInfo.dwSize = lSize

    '-- Set Flag To Return All
    JsInfo.dwFlags = JOY_RETURNALL

    '-- Get JotStick Position
    lRtn = joyGetPosEx(JoyStick, JsInfo)

    '-- Check For An Error
    If lRtn <> JOYERR_NOERROR Then
        MsgBox "A JoyStick Error Has Occurred! " & Str(lRtn)
    End If

End Sub


Example Program:

Option Explicit

Private Sub Form_Load()

    '-- Disable The Timer
    Timer1.Enabled = False

    '-- Initialize The JoyStick
    Call JoyStick_Init(JOYSTICKID1)
```

continues

```
        '-- Enable The Timer
        Timer1.Enabled = True

End Sub

Private Sub Timer1_Timer()

        '-- The Timer Interval Is Set To 100

        '-- Get JoyStick Positioning
        Call JoyStick_GetPos(JOYSTICKID1)

        Text1.Text = JsInfo.dwXpos    ' Assign X-Pos
        Text2.Text = JsInfo.dwYpos    ' Assign Y-Pos

End Sub
```

Analysis

This module is fairly simple. Giving the `JoyStickID` and calling the `JoyStick_Init` routine will initialize the joystick. The `JoyStick_GetPos` routine will fill the `JsInfo` user-defined type structure with all the joystick parameters. `JoyStick_GetPos` should be called only from a `Timer` event (see the example in the code). If there is an error a `MsgBox` is displayed that returns the joystick error number.

You can then access the variables in the `JsInfo` user-defined type structure for the joystick information, `JsInfo.variable`.

11.2   PLAY A .WAV FILE WITHOUT API CALLS

by Ian Ippolito

Description

In today's multimedia-enabled environment, an application that doesn't have sound simply can't compete favorably against a similar application that does.

However, Visual Basic's sound support—the `Beep` statement—is hardly state of the art. This statement merely provides the capability to beep the computer's speaker in a single tone and pitch. In order to produce quality sounds, a program normally must include yet another memory-hogging custom control (.OCX), which must be distributed to all users.

However, there is an alternative. This routine allows a program to play .WAV files as well as the standard sounds stored in the System Registry without the use of an .OCX.

Syntax

```
Success =  Play_Sound(SoundName,Paramaters)
```

Part	Description
SoundName	The name of the sound to play. This should be either the path and filename of an existing .WAV file or a Registry sound (specified by one of the el_ constants specified later).
Paramaters	Tells how the sound should be played.
	Pass in SND_FILENAME& if the sound is a .WAV file. Otherwise, pass in SND_ALIAS&. Additionally, any of the following SND_ paramaters can also be specified by using the + sign. (For example, SND_FILENAME& + SND_NOSTOP.)
	Note that the default values are SND_ASYNC + SND_NODEFAULT and cannot be changed.
Success	Returns TRUE if sound playing was succesful, otherwise returns FALSE.

Code Listing

```
Option Explicit
Private Declare Function PlaySound& Lib "winmm.dll" Alias _
        "PlaySoundA" (ByVal lpszName As String, ByVal hModule As Long, _
      ByVal dwFlags As Long)
    Global Const SND_SYNC = &H0 'play sound synchronously (return control
    ➥ after sound finishes)
    Public Const SND_ASYNC = &H1 'play sound asynchronously  (return control
    ➥ after sound begins)
    Global Const SND_NODEFAULT = &H2 'if sound/device unavailable--fail attempt
    Global Const SND_LOOP = &H8 'repeat the sound until the function is called
    ➥ again
    Global Const SND_NOSTOP = &H10 'if currently a sound is played the
    Global Const SND_NOWAIT& = &H2000 ' Do not use with SND_ALIAS or
    ➥ SND_FILENAME
    Global Const SND_RESOURCE& = &H40004
    Global Const SND_ALIAS& = &H10000
    Global Const SND_FILENAME& = &H20000

    ' registry sounds
    Public Const elDefault = ".Default"
    Public Const elGPF = "AppGPFault"
    Public Const elClose = "Close"
    Public Const elEmptyRecycleBin = "EmptyRecycleBin"
    Public Const elMailBeep = "MailBeep"
    Public Const elMaximize = "Maximize"
    Public Const elMenuCommand = "MenuCommand"
    Public Const elMenuPopUp = "MenuPopup"
    Public Const elMinimize = "Minimize"
```

continues

```
    Public Const elOpen = "Open"
    Public Const elRestoreDown = "RestoreDown"
    Public Const elRestoreUp = "RestoreUp"
    Public Const elSystemAsterisk = "SystemAsterisk"
    Public Const elSystemExclaimation = "SystemExclaimation"
    Public Const elSystemExit = "SystemExit"
    Public Const elSystemHand = "SystemHand"
    Public Const elSystemQuestion = "SystemQuestion"
    Public Const temStart = "SystemStart"


Public Function Play_Sound(strSoundName As String, _
    intParamaters As Long) As Boolean


    If (PlaySound(strSoundName, 0&, intParamaters + SND_ASYNC _
        + SND_NODEFAULT)) Then
        Play_Sound = True
    Else
        Play_Sound = False
    End If

End Function
```

Analysis

This routine uses the Windows API function PlaySound to perform sound generation. Applications that require synchronous sound or a default sound might want to change or remove the SND_ASYNC paramater or the SND_NODEFAULT paramater.

Use of this function requires either of the following:

■ A sound card, driver, and speakers
■ Use of the standard PC speaker via an installed speaker driver

11.3   DETECTING A SOUND CARD

by James Limm

Description

This code detects whether the system is capable of playing sounds or music though a sound card. The DetectSoundCard function returns TRUE if a sound card is present on the system, or FALSE if a card is not present.

Syntax

```
GotASoundCard = DetectSoundCard
```

Part	Description
GotASoundCard	If a sound card is present in the system, this parameter is set to TRUE. If a sound card is not present, this parameter is set to FALSE.

Code Listing

```
'Add the following code to the declarations section of the project.
Declare Function waveOutGetNumDevs Lib "winmm.dll"
➥ Alias "waveOutGetNumDevs" () As Long

'Detect Sound Card Function
Function DetectSoundCard() As Boolean
Dim i As Integer
i = waveOutGetNumDevs()
If i > 0 Then
    'the system has a sound card
    DetectSoundCard=True
Else
    'the system does not have a sound card
    DetectSoundCard=False
End If
End Function
```

Analysis

The DetectSoundCard function calls an API function that is built into the Windows multimedia DLL file, winmm.dll. If a sound card exists in the system, the DetectSoundCard function returns a Boolean TRUE value. If a sound card does not exist in the system, the DetectSoundCard function returns a Boolean FALSE value. This code could be used as part of a game setup program to warn the user if his system does not have the capability to play sounds.

11.4 PLAYING AVI FILES IN A SEPARATE WINDOW

by Kamal A. Mehdi

Description

This code demonstrates how you can play a video clip (AVI) file from your disk in your Visual Basic application but in a separate window. The code uses the Visual Basic MCI (Media Control Interface) multimedia control to play the video clip. The clip opens and plays in a separate window, and the window size automatically adjusts to the size of the video clip. The window is a normal window that can be minimized, maximized, and sized during the play session regardless of the original Visual Basic application window. The playing AVI clip can also be stopped, paused, rewound, fast forwarded, and stepped through frame by frame from the appropriate MCI control buttons. If the video clip contains a sound track, the sound will be heard through the sound card speakers.

When the form containing the MCI control loads, it initializes the necessary properties of the MCI control, assigns the appropriate device type to the control, and opens the MCI device. You then can play the video clip by pressing the Play button on the MCI control. The window in which the AVI clip will play is not shown until the MCI Play button is clicked.

The open MCI device must be closed when your application terminates so that Windows properly manages multimedia resources. This is done in the `Form_Unload()` event where the MCI device is closed using the MCI `Close` command.

Syntax

You can control the Visual Basic MCI multimedia control by sending various MCI command strings to the control from within your code at runtime. The following is the syntax for sending commands to the multimedia MCI control at runtime:

```
MMControl.Command = "MCIcommand"
```

Part	Description
MCIcommand	A string expression specifying the MCI command to execute. The MCI commands are described next. Data type: String.

MCI Commands

The following are the important MCI commands:

Command	Description
Open	Opens the MCI device specified in the DeviceType property of the MCI control.
Play	Plays the MCI device (the AVI file, for example).
Stop	Stops the playing of the MCI device.
Close	Closes the MCI device.
Pause	Pauses the playing MCI device.
Prev	Goes to the beginning of the current track or file.
Next	Goes to the beginning of the next track or the end of file.
Eject	Ejects the media from the device, such as the CD-ROM from the CD drive.

Note

More details on these MCI commands, as well as on other available commands, can be found in the MCI control help.

Modules and Controls Required

You will need the following modules and controls to build the sample project for playing AVI files in a separate window:

Module/Control	Description
Form1	A standard non-MDI Visual Basic form (.FRM) with controls as shown later in this section.
MMControl1	A multimedia (MCI) control.

To draw controls, place the MCI multimedia control anywhere on the form. The appropriate MCI control properties will be set at runtime. You must also provide an existing AVI filename (by default, the code will open and play the sample AVI file located under the project directory on the CD-ROM).

Note

The MCI multimedia control is not included on the toolbox by default. You can add it to the toolbox by selecting Project, Components, and adding the control. The control appears in the components list as Microsoft Multimedia Control 5.0, where 5.0 is the control version (you might have a different version on your system).

Code Listing

```
Private Sub Form_Load()

    'Set the Wait and Notify properties of the MCI control
    MMControl1.Wait = True
    MMControl1.Notify = False

    'Specify the Device type for the MCI control (AVI)
    MMControl1.DeviceType = "AVIVideo"

    'Specify the AVI file name
    MMControl1.filename = App.Path & "\fallfwd.avi"

    'Open the MCI device
    MMControl1.Command = "open"

    'Now the MCI control buttons are enabled, click the 'Play button
    'to play the video clip.
```

continues

```
        'You can click the 'Prev', 'Back', 'Stop', 'Pause', etc. to move
        'forward and backward or to pause or stop the play.

End Sub

Private Sub Form_Unload(Cancel As Integer)

        'You must close the MCI device before closing your application
        'to properly manage multimedia resources
        MMControl1.Command = "close"

End Sub
```

Analysis

The sample code demonstrates how you can play an AVI file from within your Visual Basic application using the multimedia MCI control. When you run the code, the form will load and initialize the appropriate MCI control properties for playing the AVI file. The AVI file will be played in a separate window with the window title set to the actual name of the AVI file.

You can customize the MCI control buttons at design time or at runtime to enable showing or hiding of the different buttons. You can also enable the Record button on the MCI control to be able to record and save portions or the entire playing video clip to a new file (this requires some additional code). In addition, you can set the MCI control's `Visible` property to `False` to hide the control on your form while still being able to manipulate the entire control functionality by sending the appropriate MCI commands to the control from within your code at runtime.

Remember that it is important to always close the MCI device using the MCI `Close` command whenever you quit your application to properly manage multimedia resources. This can be done in the `Form_Unload()` event of your form, as implemented in the preceding code.

The sample project PLAYAVI.VBP on the CD-ROM that accompanies this book demonstrates the use of the MCI control to play an AVI file. The project plays the sample AVI file located under the project directory. You can specify any other AVI file to play just by modifying the filename in the code.

11.5   PLAYING AVI FILES INSIDE VB FORMS

by Kamal A. Mehdi

Description

This code shows how you can play a video clip (AVI) file from your disk inside your Visual Basic form.

The code uses the Visual Basic MCI (Media Control Interface) multimedia control to play the video clip.

The clip opens and plays inside the Visual Basic form by using a picture box control. You can do this by setting the MCI control's `hWndDisplay` property to point to the window handle of the picture control (`Picture1.hWnd`).

The playing AVI clip can be stopped, paused, rewound, fast forwarded, and stepped through frame by frame from the appropriate MCI control buttons at any time. If the video clip contains a sound track, the sound will be heard through the sound card speakers.

When the form containing the MCI control loads, it initializes the necessary properties of the MCI control, assigns the appropriate device type to the control (`AVIVideo` for AVI files), and opens the MCI device. You then can play the video clip by clicking the Play button on the MCI control. The AVI clip will not show in the picture box until the MCI Play button is pressed.

The open MCI device must be closed when your application terminates in order to properly manage the multimedia resources. This is done in the `Form_Unload()` event where the MCI device is closed using the MCI `Close` command.

Syntax

You can control the Visual Basic MCI multimedia control by sending various MCI command strings to the control from within your code at runtime. The following is the syntax for sending commands to the multimedia MCI control at runtime:

```
MMControl.Command = "MCIcommand"
```

Part	*Description*
`MCIcommand`	A string expression specifying the MCI command to execute. The MCI commands are described later in this section. Data type: `String`.

MCI Commands

The following are the important MCI commands:

Command	*Description*
`Open`	Opens the MCI device specified in the `DeviceType` property of the MCI control.
`Play`	Plays the MCI device (the AVI file, for example).
`Stop`	Stops the playing of the MCI device.
`Close`	Closes the MCI device.
`Pause`	Pauses the playing MCI device.
`Prev`	Goes to the beginning of the current track or file.
`Next`	Goes to the beginning of the next track or end of file.
`Eject`	Ejects the media from the device, such as the CD-ROM from the CD drive.

Note

More details on these MCI commands, as well as on other available commands, can be found in the MCI control help.

Modules and Controls Required

You will need the following modules and controls to build the sample project for playing AVI files inside your VB form:

Module/Control	Description
Form1	A standard non-MDI Visual Basic form (.FRM) with controls as shown later
MMControl1	A multimedia (MCI) control
Picture1	A picture box control

To draw controls, place the MCI multimedia control and the picture box control anywhere on the form. Adjust the size of the picture box to accommodate the size (dimensions) of the AVI clip. The appropriate MCI control properties will be set at runtime. You must also provide an existing AVI filename (by default, the code will open and play the sample AVI file provided with the code on the CD-ROM).

Note

The MCI multimedia control is not included on the toolbox by default. You can add it to the toolbox by selecting Project, Components, and adding the control. The control appears in the components list as Microsoft Multimedia Control 5.0, where 5.0 is the control version (you might have a different version on your system).

Code Listing

```
Private Sub Form_Load()

    'Set the Wait and Notify properties of the MCI control
    MMControl1.Wait = True
    MMControl1.Notify = False

    'Specify the Device type for the MCI control (AVI)
    MMControl1.DeviceType = "AVIVideo"

    'Set the MCI hWndDisplay to be the Picture1.hWnd
    'This will play the AVI file inside the Picture1 control
    MMControl1.hWndDisplay = Picture1.hWnd
```

```
    'Specify the AVI file name
    MMControl1.filename = App.Path & "\fallfwd.avi"

    'Open the MCI device
    MMControl1.Command = "open"

    'Now the MCI control buttons are enabled, click the 'Play button
    'to play the video clip.
    'You can click the 'Prev', 'Back', 'Stop', 'Pause', etc. to move
    'forward and backward or to pause or stop the play.

End Sub

Private Sub Form_Unload(Cancel As Integer)

    'You must close the MCI device before closing your application
    'to properly manage multimedia resources
    MMControl1.Command = "close"

End Sub
```

Analysis

This code demonstrates how you can play an AVI file inside your Visual Basic form using the multimedia MCI control and a picture box control.

When you run the code, the form will load and initialize the appropriate MCI control properties for playing the AVI file inside the picture box by using the picture box window handle for the MCI window display. Note that the picture box will not be resized to the dimensions of the AVI file, nor can the video clip be stretched to the size of the picture box. Therefore, you must either adjust the size of the picture box to the size of the AVI clip if the dimensions of the clip are known, or you must retrieve the dimensions of the clip from the AVI file at runtime and adjust the picture box size accordingly before playing the clip.

You can customize the MCI control buttons at design time or at runtime to enable showing or hiding of the different buttons. You can also enable the Record button on the MCI control to be able to record and save portions or the entire playing video clip to a new file (this requires some additional code). In addition, you can set the MCI control's Visible property to False to hide the control on your form while still being able to manipulate the entire control functionality by sending the appropriate MCI commands to the control from within your code at runtime.

Remember that it is important to always close the MCI device using the MCI Close command whenever you quit your application to properly manage multimedia resources. This can be done in the Form_Unload() event of your form, as implemented in the code.

The sample project PLAYAVI1.VBP on the CD-ROM that accompanies this book demonstrates the use of the MCI control to play an AVI file inside the VB form. The project will play the sample AVI file located under the project directory. You can specify any other AVI file to play by modifying the filename in the code.

11.6 PLAYING AVI FILES IN FULL SCREEN

by Kamal A. Mehdi

Description

This code demonstrates how you can play a video clip (AVI) file from your disk in full-screen mode using the PlayAVIFullScreen function.

The PlayAVIFullScreen function is based on the mciSendString API function to play the video clip in full screen. The clip opens and plays in full-screen mode regardless of the actual dimensions of the AVI clip. Because the AVI clip is played in full screen, no other Windows applications are visible or accessible.

When you play an AVI file in full-screen mode, the color palette focus is set to the playing AVI file only. No dithering of colors will occur because there are no other windows in the background to capture the color palette.

Because the video clip is resized to the dimensions of the screen, the quality of the picture might be degraded depending on the actual size (dimensions) of the AVI clip. A significantly better picture quality can be obtained with AVI clips with larger dimensions.

You can terminate the playing AVI clip at any time by pressing the Esc key or the Space key. Pausing, fast-forwarding, rewinding, and stepping through the video clip are not possible in comparison with the corresponding functions available when using the MCI multimedia control to play AVI files. If the video clip contains a sound track, the sound will be heard through the sound card speakers.

When using the PlayAVIFullScreen function, there is no need to close any control to properly manage the multimedia resources as with the MCI multimedia control. All multimedia resources used will be recovered by Windows.

Syntax

RetVal = PlayAVIFullScreen (AVIFileName)

Part	Description
RetVal	Required. A numeric variable that receives the error value returned from the function, as described later in this section. Data type: Long.
AVIFileName	Required. A string expression specifying the full path/name of the AVI file to play. In Windows 95/98, the AVIFileName must have the short file path/name syntax. Data type: String.

The following are the function return values through `RetVal`:

Value	Description
0	The command completed successfully (the AVI file played and completed).
275	The AVI file specified by the `AVIFileName` was not found.

The return values are the same values returned by the `mciSendString` API function.

Code Listing

```
'Code in Module

'Win32 specific API declarations
    #If Win32 Then
        Private Declare Function mciSendString Lib "winmm.dll" Alias _
            "mciSendStringA" (ByVal lpstrCommand As String, ByVal _
            lpstrReturnString As Any, ByVal uReturnLength As Long, ByVal _
            hwndCallback As Long) As Long

    'Win16 specific API declarations
    #ElseIf Win16 Then
        Private Declare Function mciSendString Lib "mmsystem" (ByVal _
            lpstrCommand As String, ByVal lpstrReturnStr As Any, ByVal _
            wReturnLen As Integer, ByVal hCallBack As Integer) As Long
    #End If

Function PlayAVIFullScreen(FileName As String) As Long

    Dim CmdString As String

    'Compose the command string
    CmdString = "play " & FileName & " fullscreen"

    'Call the API function mciSendString passing the command string as argument
    PlayAVIFullScreen = mciSendString(CmdString, 0&, 0, 0&)

End Function

'Code to insert in your Form
Private Sub Command1_Click()

    Dim AVIFileName As String

    'Specify the AVI file name
    AVIFileName = "c:\fallfwd.avi"

    'Play the AVI file in full screen
    'the function will returen '0' on success and '275' if file is not found
    x = PlayAVIFullScreen(AVIFileName)

End Sub
```

Analysis

The sample code demonstrates how you can play an AVI file in full-screen mode using the `PlayAVIFullScreen` function. The function is based on the `mciSendString` API function, which communicates with the appropriate multimedia drivers installed on your system and sends the proper command strings to play the specified AVI file in full screen.

When you run the code and call the function while passing the AVI filename as argument, all open windows—including the desktop window—will hide, and the AVI file will open and play in full-screen mode with no dithering of colors. When the AVI file ends, all windows will show again, and the focus returns to the Visual Basic application.

This code incorporates platform-dependent declarations and compilation segments and will function in both 16-bit and 32-bit versions of Visual Basic. However, long filenames are not allowed in the 32-bit platforms (you must provide the MS-DOS short name format).

The sample project AVIFULSC.VBP on the CD-ROM that accompanies this book demonstrates the use of the function to play an AVI file in full screen. You can find a sample AVI file under the project directory on the CD-ROM.

11.7   SHOWING TEXT ON A PLAYING AVI CLIP

by Kamal A. Mehdi

Description

This code demonstrates how you can show text on a video clip (AVI) playing inside your Visual Basic form.

The code uses the Visual Basic MCI (Media Control Interface) multimedia control to play the video clip. The clip opens and plays inside the Visual Basic form in a picture box control. This can be accomplished by setting the MCI control's `hWndDisplay` property to point to the window handle of the picture control (`Picture1.hWnd`). Using the `TextOut` API function, a text string can be displayed inside the picture box and is refreshed using a continuous loop. The refresh rate of the text printed on the picture box is much higher than the rate at which the MCI control refreshes the picture box to view the consequent frames of the playing clip, resulting a flicker-free display of the text.

When the form containing the multimedia MCI control loads, it initializes the necessary properties of the MCI control, assigns the appropriate device type to the control (`AVIVideo`), and opens the MCI device. You then can play the video clip by clicking the Play button on the MCI control. The AVI clip will actually be invisible until the MCI Play button is clicked. The text in the picture box is continuously refreshed when the form becomes visible (performed in the `Form_Activate()` event). To stop the refreshing process of the text displayed inside the picture box and exit the loop, just click on the form. The refresh loop also terminates when you close the form.

The open MCI device must be closed when your application terminates in order to properly manage the multimedia resources. This is done in the `Form_Unload()` event where the MCI device is closed using the MCI `Close` command.

Syntax

```
RetVal = TextOut (hdc, X, Y, lpString, nCount)
```

Part	Description
RetVal	Required. A numeric variable that receives the value returned from the function. Data type: `Long`.
hdc	Required. A numeric expression specifying the device-context handle of the control where the text is to be displayed. Data type: `Long`.
X	Required. A numeric expression specifying the X coordinate where the text is to be displayed inside the control. Data type: `Long`.
Y	Required. A numeric expression specifying the Y coordinate where the text is to be displayed inside the control. Data type: `Long`.
lpString	Required. A string expression specifying the text string to be displayed inside the control. Data type: `String`.
nCount	Required. A numeric expression specifying the length of the text string. Data type: `Long`.

Modules and Controls Required

You will need the following modules and controls to build the sample project:

Module/Control	Description
Form1	A standard non-MDI Visual Basic form (.FRM) with controls as shown later in this section
MMControl1	A multimedia (MCI) control
Picture1	A picture box control

To draw controls, place the multimedia control and the picture box control anywhere on the form. Adjust the size of the picture box to accommodate the size (dimensions) of the AVI clip. The appropriate MCI control properties will be set at runtime. You must also provide an existing AVI filename (by default, the code will play the sample AVI file located under the project directory on the CD-ROM).

Note

The MCI multimedia control is not included on the toolbox by default. You can add it to the toolbox by selecting Project, Components, and adding the control. The control appears in the components list as Microsoft Multimedia Control 5.0, where 5.0 is the control version (you might have a different version on your system).

Code Listing

```
'Global form declarations
'API declarations
    Private Declare Function TextOut Lib "gdi32" Alias "TextOutA"
    ➥(ByVal hdc As Long, ByVal X As Long, ByVal Y As Long,
    ➥ByVal lpString As String, ByVal nCount As Long) As Long

    Dim EndRefresh As Integer

Private Sub Form_Activate()

    DoEvents
    Dim RetVal As Integer
    Dim X As Long, Y As Long
    Dim MyText As String, Characters As Long

    'Enter a loop and do not exit until the form is clicked or unloaded
    Do While EndRefresh = 0

        'Define the text to print on the picture box
        MyText = "Hello World"

        'Define the length of the text string
        Characters = Len(MyText)

        'Specify the X and Y coordinates from picture1 origin where to
        ' show the text
        X = 100
        Y = 100

        'Display the text (and refresh)
        RetVal = TextOut(Picture1.hdc, X, Y, MyText, Characters)
        DoEvents

    Loop

End Sub
```

```
Private Sub Form_Click()
    EndRefresh = 1
    End Sub

Private Sub Form_Load()

    'Set the Wait and Notify properties of the MCI control
    MMControl1.Wait = True
    MMControl1.Notify = False

    'Specify the Device type for the MCI control (AVI)
    MMControl1.DeviceType = "AVIVideo"

    'Set the MCI hWndDisplay to be the Picture1.hWnd
    'This will play the AVI file inside the Picture1 control
    MMControl1.hWndDisplay = Picture1.hWnd

    'Specify the AVI file name
    MMControl1.filename = App.Path & "\fallfwd.avi"

    'Open the MCI device
    MMControl1.Command = "open"

    'Now the MCI control buttons are enabled, click the 'Play button
    'to play the video clip.
    'You can click the 'Prev', 'Back', 'Stop', 'Pause', etc. to move
    'forward and backward or to pause or stop the play.

    'Set the text color for picture1 to white
    Picture1.ForeColor = &HFFFFFF

End Sub

Private Sub Form_Unload(Cancel As Integer)

    'You must close the MCI device before closing your application
    'to properely manage multimedia resources
    MMControl1.Command = "close"

    'Stop refreshing the text on the picture box
    EndRefresh = 1

End Sub
```

Analysis

The sample code demonstrates how you can display text on a playing AVI clip inside your Visual Basic form using the multimedia MCI control and a picture box control, and implementing the TextOut API function.

When you run the code, the form loads and initializes the appropriate MCI control properties for playing the AVI file inside the picture box and starts displaying the text on the picture box.

When the MCI control plays the AVI clip, it continuously repaints the picture box to display the consequent video frames, resulting in erasure of any text that exists on the picture box. By calling the `TextOut()` API function recursively, the text printed on the picture box is repainted at a higher refresh rate, resulting in steady display of the text. This is implemented through a loop in the `Form_Activate()` event, but can be inserted anywhere in your code and activated or deactivated when necessary.

The `TextOut()` API function prints the text on the picture box by using the `hdc` (device-context handle) of the picture box. Both the text string and its length in characters must be specified. The printing position is controlled by the `X` and `Y` argument values. Note that all function arguments are passed by value (using `ByVal`).

You can easily modify the code to show a different text string on the video clip from time to time, something like the film language translation you see on television. You can also control the color of the displayed text by changing the `ForeColor` property of the picture box at runtime.

Remember that it is important to always close the MCI device using the MCI `Close` command whenever you quit your application. This can be done in the `Form_Unload()` event, as implemented in the preceding code.

The sample project AVITEXT.VBP on the CD-ROM that accompanies this book demonstrates the code functionality. The project plays the sample AVI file located in the project directory. You can specify any other AVI file to play by modifying the filename in the code.

11.8   PLAYING MPEG VIDEO CLIPS

by Kamal A. Mehdi

Description

The new MPEG multimedia technology enables you to play MPEG-layer video clips on your system in true color mode with high frame rates. You can even play them in full screen, something that was almost impossible using the older multimedia techniques. This code shows how you can play an MPEG video clip file from your disk in a separate window using Visual Basic.

The code uses the Visual Basic MCI (Media Control Interface) multimedia control to play the MPEG video clip. The video clip opens and plays in a separate window, and the window size automatically is adjusted to the size of the video clip. The window is a normal window that can be minimized, maximized, resized, and so on during the play session regardless of the original Visual Basic application window (form). The playing MPEG video clip can be stopped, paused, rewound, fast forwarded, and stepped through frame by frame from the appropriate MCI control buttons. If the video clip contains a sound track, the sound will be heard through the sound card speakers.

When the form containing the MCI control loads, it initializes the necessary properties of the MCI control, assigns the appropriate device type to the control (MPEGVideo), and opens the MCI device. You then can play the video clip by clicking the Play button on the MCI control. The window in which the MPEG video clip will play is not shown until the MCI Play button is clicked.

The MPEG clip window can be maximized to show the video in full screen with the maximum number of colors supported by the system video adapter, without degrading the speed of the playing clip.

The open MCI control should be closed when your application terminates so that Windows properly manages multimedia resources. This is done in the Form_Unload() event where the MCI device is closed using the MCI Close command.

Syntax

You can control the Visual Basic MCI multimedia control by sending various MCI command strings to the control from within your code at runtime. The syntax for sending commands to the multimedia MCI control at runtime is

```
MMControl.Command = "MCIcommand"
```

Part	Description
MCIcommand	A string expression specifying the MCI command to execute. The MCI commands are described next. Data type: String.

MCI Commands

The following are the important MCI commands:

Command	Description
Open	Opens the MCI device specified in the DeviceType property of the MCI control.
Play	Plays the MCI device (the MPEG file, for example).
Stop	Stops the playing of the MCI device.
Close	Closes the MCI device.
Pause	Pauses the playing MCI device.
Prev	Goes to the beginning of the current track or file.
Next	Goes to the beginning of the next track or the end of file.
Eject	Ejects the media from the device, such as the CD-ROM from the CD drive.

More details on these MCI commands, as well as on other available commands, can be found in the MCI control help.

Modules and Controls Required

You will need the following modules and controls to build the sample project:

Module/Control	Description
Form1	A standard non-MDI Visual Basic form (.FRM) with controls, as shown next
MMControl1	A multimedia (MCI) control

To draw controls, place the MCI multimedia control anywhere on the form. The appropriate MCI control properties are set at runtime. You must also provide an existing MPEG filename *.MPG (by default, the code will open and play the sample MPEG file located under the project directory on the CD-ROM).

Note

The MCI multimedia control is not included on the toolbox by default. You can add it to the toolbox by selecting Project, Components, and adding the control. The control appears in the components list as Microsoft Multimedia Control 5.0, where 5.0 is the control version (you might have a different version on your system).

Code Listing

```
Private Sub Form_Load()

    'Set the Wait and Notify properties of the MCI control
    MMControl1.Wait = True
    MMControl1.Notify = False

    'Specify the Device type for the MCI control (MPEG video)
    MMControl1.DeviceType = "MPEGVideo"

    'Specify the MPEG clip file name
    MMControl1.filename = App.Path & "\sample.mpg"

    'Open the MCI device
    MMControl1.Command = "open"

    'Now the MCI control buttons are enabled, click the 'Play button
    'to play the video clip.
```

```
    'You can click the 'Prev', 'Back', 'Stop', 'Pause', etc. to move
    'forward and backward or to pause or stop the play.

End Sub

Private Sub Form_Unload(Cancel As Integer)

    'You must close the MCI device before closing your application
    'to properly manage multimedia resources
    MMControl1.Command = "close"

End Sub
```

Analysis

The sample code demonstrates how you can play an MPEG video file using the Visual Basic multimedia MCI control.

When you run the code, the form loads and initializes the MCI control properties for playing the MPEG file. The MPEG video clip is displayed in a separate window, with the window title set to the actual name of the MPEG file. You can maximize the window and watch the video clip in full screen with the normal frame rate of the clip. However, the quality of the picture will be slightly degraded because each pixel in the original video frames will be remapped to one or more pixels depending on the size (dimensions) in which the video clip was produced. The picture quality degradation decreases with the increased frame size of the video clip. If you watch the playing video from a distance, however, you will not see this degradation in the quality, and the picture will almost look as you see it on the television set.

You can customize the MCI control buttons at design time or at runtime to enable showing or hiding of the different buttons. You can also enable the Record button on the MCI control to be able to record and save portions or the entire playing video clip to a new file (this requires some additional code). In addition, you can set the MCI control's `Visible` property to `False` to hide the control on your form while still being able to manipulate the entire control functionality by sending the appropriate MCI commands to the control from within your code at runtime.

Remember that it is important to always close the MCI device using the MCI `Close` command whenever you quit your application to properly manage multimedia resources. This can be done in the `Form_Unload()` event of your form, as implemented in the code.

The sample project PLAYMPEG.VBP on the CD-ROM that accompanies this book demonstrates the use of the MCI control to play an MPEG file. The project plays the sample MPEG file located under the project directory. You can specify any other MPEG file to play by modifying the filename in the code.

Note

In order to be able to play the sample MPEG file or any similar *.MPG file, you must have the Microsoft ActiveMovie or an MPEG decompression codec installed on your system.

11.9 PLAYING MPEG LAYER-3 SOUND FILES

by Kamal A. Mehdi

Description

The new MPEG Layer-3 technique for audio encoding has made revolutionary changes in the field of digital audio processing. Using the MPEG Layer-3 compression technique, the total size of a 44100Hz, 16-bit stereo sound file can be brought down to as low as 1/10 without any noticeable loss in sound quality. The same file can even be compressed more with a lower sound quality, resulting in a file as small as 1/90 of the original sound file size.

Sound files compressed using the MPEG Layer-3 codec and saved with the .WAV extension (retaining the WAV file header) can be played in Visual Basic using the MCI (Media Control Interface) multimedia control. This code shows how you can play these files.

The code uses the MCI multimedia WaveAudio device on your system to play the MP3-format WAV file. The sound file plays in the normal quality in which it was produced. The playing sound file can be stopped, paused, rewound, and fast forwarded from the appropriate MCI control buttons.

When the form containing the MCI control loads, it initializes the necessary properties of the MCI control, assigns the appropriate device type to the control (WaveAudio), and opens the MCI device. You then can play the sound file by clicking the Play button on the MCI control.

The open MCI device must be closed when your application terminates so that Windows properly manages multimedia resources. This is done in the `Form_Unload()` event where the MCI device is closed using the MCI `Close` command.

Syntax

You can control the Visual Basic MCI multimedia control by sending various MCI command strings to the control from within your code at runtime. The syntax for sending commands to the multimedia MCI control at runtime is

```
MMControl.Command = "MCIcommand"
```

Part	Description
`MCIcommand`	A string expression specifying the MCI command to execute. The MCI commands are described next. Data type: `String`.

MCI Commands

The following are the important MCI commands:

Command	Description
Open	Opens the MCI device specified in the DeviceType property of the MCI control.
Play	Plays the MCI device (the sound file, for example).
Stop	Stops the playing of the MCI device.
Close	Closes the MCI device.
Pause	Pauses the playing MCI device.
Prev	Goes to the beginning of the current track or file.
Next	Goes to the beginning of the next track or the end of file.
Eject	Ejects the media from the device, such as an audio CD from the CD-ROM drive.

Note

More details on these MCI commands, as well as on other available commands, can be found in the MCI control help.

Modules and Controls Required

You will need the following modules and controls to be able to build the sample project for playing MPEG Layer-3 sound files:

Module/Control	Description
Form1	A standard non-MDI Visual Basic form (.FRM) with controls, as shown later in this section
MMControl1	A multimedia (MCI) control

To draw controls, place the MCI multimedia control anywhere on the form. The appropriate MCI control properties are set at runtime. You must also provide an existing AVI filename (by default, the code opens and plays the sample AVI file located under the project directory on the CD-ROM).

Note

The MCI multimedia control is not included on the toolbox by default. You can add it to the toolbox by selecting Project, Components, and adding the control. The control appears in the components list as Microsoft Multimedia Control 5.0, where 5.0 is the control version (you might have a different version on your system).

Code Listing

```
Private Sub Form_Load()

    'Set the Wait and Notify properties of the MCI control
    MMControl1.Wait = True
    MMControl1.Notify = False

    'Specify the Device type for the MCI control (WaveAudio)
    MMControl1.DeviceType = "WaveAudio"

    'Specify the MP3 audio file name (with the .WAV extension)
    MMControl1.filename = App.Path & "\mp3samp.wav"

    'Open the MCI device
    MMControl1.Command = "open"

    'Now the MCI control buttons are enabled, click the 'Play button
    'to play the sound file.
    'You can click the 'Prev', 'Back', 'Stop', 'Pause', etc. to move
    'forward and backward or to pause or stop the play.

End Sub

Private Sub Form_Unload(Cancel As Integer)

    'You must close the MCI device before closing your application
    'to properly manage multimedia resources
    MMControl1.Command = "close"

End Sub
```

Analysis

The sample code demonstrates how you can play an MPEG Layer-3 sound file saved with the .WAV extension (and header) using the Visual Basic multimedia MCI control. You can also play MPEG Layer-1 and Layer-2 sound files using the same code.

When you run the code, the form loads and initializes the appropriate MCI control properties for playing the sound file. Click the Play button on the MCI control to start playing the sound file. The sample code plays the MP3SAMP.WAV file located in the project directory. This file is a three-minute music sound sampled with the MP3 codec at 22KHz, 8-bit, mono, resulting in only about 700KB file size.

You can customize the MCI control buttons at design time or at runtime to enable showing or hiding the different buttons. You can also enable the Record button on the MCI control to be able to record and save portions or the entire playing sound file to a new file (you will need to write some additional code). In addition, you can set the MCI control's Visible property to False to hide the control on your form while still being able to manipulate the entire control functionality by sending the appropriate MCI commands to the control from within your code at runtime.

Remember that it is important to always close the MCI device using the MCI `Close` command whenever you quit your application to restore the multimedia resources. This is done in the `Form_Unload()` event of the form, as implemented in the preceding code.

The sample project MP3PLAY.VBP on the CD-ROM that accompanies this book demonstrates the use of the MCI control to play an MP3 sound file using the WaveAudio MCI device. You can compress your normal WAV files to the MP3 format while keeping the WAV file header, and use this code to play them. Many shareware and freeware utilities for MP3 sound compression are available from different Web sites.

Note

In order to be able to play the provided sample .WAV file compressed with the MP3 codec or any similar *.WAV file, you must have the Microsoft ActiveMovie or an MP3 decompression codec installed on your system.

11.10　PLAYING AUDIO CDS

by Kamal A. Mehdi

Description

You can play audio CD sound tracks in Visual Basic by using the MCI (Media Control Interface) multimedia control. This code listing demonstrates how you can play audio CD tracks on your system in Visual Basic.

The code uses the MCI CD-Audio device installed on your system to play the audio CD tracks. The sound tracks play in their normal CD sound quality (44100Hz, 16-bit, stereo). The playing sound track can be stopped, paused, rewound, and fast forwarded from the appropriate MCI control buttons. The audio CD media can also be ejected from the CD-ROM drive through the MCI control's Eject button.

When the form containing the MCI control loads, it initializes the necessary properties of the MCI control, assigns the appropriate MCI device type to the control (`CDAudio`), and opens the MCI device. You then can play the first sound track on the CD by clicking the Play button on the MCI control.

The code is a simple, yet efficient CD-player program. You can simply modify the form's appearance to make a professional-looking CD player. When the code runs, it displays the total number of sound tracks on the audio CD, the current sound track number, and the current MCI mode. An audio CD must be inserted in your CD-ROM drive in order for the MCI device to open when the form loads.

The open MCI device must be closed when your application terminates so that Windows properly manages multimedia resources. This is done in the `Form_Unload()` event where the MCI device is closed using the MCI `Close` command.

Syntax

You can control the Visual Basic MCI multimedia control by sending various MCI command strings to the control from within your code at runtime. The syntax for sending commands to the multimedia MCI control at runtime is

```
MMControl.Command = "MCIcommand"
```

Part	Description
MCIcommand	A string expression specifying the MCI command to execute. The MCI commands are described next. Data type: String.

MCI Commands

The following are the important MCI commands:

Command	Description
Open	Opens the MCI device specified in the DeviceType property of the MCI control.
Play	Plays the MCI device (the audio CD track, for example).
Stop	Stops the playing of the MCI device.
Close	Closes the MCI device.
Pause	Pauses the playing MCI device.
Prev	Goes to the beginning of the current track or file.
Next	Goes to the beginning of the next track or the end of file.
Eject	Ejects the media from the device, such as the audio CD from the CD drive.

Note

More details on these MCI commands, as well as on other available commands, can be found in the MCI control help.

Modules and Controls Required

The code listing demonstrates how to play an audio CD. You will need the following modules and controls to build the sample project for playing audio CDs:

Module/Control	*Description*
`Form1`	A standard non-MDI Visual Basic form (.FRM) with controls as shown next
`MMControl1`	A multimedia (MCI) control
`Command1`	A command button with the `Caption` property set to `Exit`
`Label1()`	A control array of three label controls with the `Caption` property as shown:
	`Index = 0`, `Caption` = Number of Tracks:
	`Index = 1`, `Caption` = Current Track:
	`Index = 2`, `Caption` = Status:
`Label2()`	A control array of three label controls

Follow these steps to draw controls:

1. Start a new standard EXE project. `Form1` is created by default. Set the form's `Height` and `Width` properties to approximately `2600` and `5400`, respectively, and set its `Caption` property as shown earlier in this section.

2. Draw `Label1` at the top-left side of the form and create the other two elements of the control array from it. Arrange the three label controls so that `Label1(0)` is at the top, `Label1(2)` is at the bottom, and `Label1(1)` is in between. Set the `Caption` property of the three labels as shown earlier.

3. Draw `Label2` to the right of `Label1(0)` and create the other two elements of the control array from it. Rearrange the `Label2()` array elements so that each element is located to the right of the corresponding `Label1()` control with the same index value.

4. Draw `Command1` anywhere on the form, and set its `Caption` property as shown earlier.

5. Draw the MCI multimedia control `MMControl1` at the bottom of the form.

All the necessary properties of the controls are set at runtime.

Note

You can create control arrays by inserting one control on the form and copying and pasting the control on the form using either the right mouse button or the Edit menu. When you paste the control on the form, Visual Basic will prompt you whether to create a control array; choose Yes.

The MCI multimedia control is not included on the toolbox by default. You can add it to the toolbox by selecting Project, Components, and adding the control. The control appears in the components list as Microsoft Multimedia Control 5.0, where 5.0 is the control version (you might have a different version on your system).

Code Listing

```
Function GetModeString(CurrentMode As Long) As String

    'Convert the Mode code to actual mode meaning
    Select Case CurrentMode

    Case mciModeNotOpen     'Device is not open
        GetModeString = "Not Open"

    Case mciModePlay     'Device is playing
        GetModeString = "Playing"

    Case mciModeStop     'Device is stopped
        GetModeString = "Stopped"

    Case mciModeSeek     'Device is seeking
        GetModeString = "Seeking"

    Case mciModeRecord     'Device is recording
        GetModeString = "Recording"

    Case mciModePause     'Device is paused
        GetModeString = "Paused"

    Case mciModeReady     'Device is ready
        GetModeString = "Ready"

    End Select

End Function

Private Sub Command1_Click()

    Unload Me

End Sub

Private Sub Form_Load()

    'Initialize the MCI control properties
    MMControl1.Notify = False
    MMControl1.Wait = True
    MMControl1.Shareable = False

    'Specify the device type (CDAudio)
    MMControl1.DeviceType = "CDAudio"

    'Specify the time format
    MMControl1.TimeFormat = MCI_FORMAT_TMSF
```

```
    'Open the MCI device
    MMControl1.Command = "Open"

End Sub

Private Sub Form_Unload(Cancel As Integer)

    'Close the MCI device to restore multimedia resources
    MMControl1.Command = "Close"

End Sub

Private Sub MMControl1_NextCompleted(Errorcode As Long)

    'Show the current track number
    Label2(1).Caption = Str$(MMControl1.Track)

End Sub

Private Sub MMControl1_StatusUpdate()

    Dim CurrentMode As Long

    'Display the number of tracks on the audio CD
    Label2(0).Caption = MMControl1.Tracks

    'Update the current track label
    Label2(1).Caption = Str$(MMControl1.Track)

    'Update the current Mode
    CurrentMode = MMControl1.Mode
    Label2(2).Caption = GetModeString(CurrentMode)

End Sub
```

MCI Mode Codes

The code incorporates a function that is used to retrieve the current mode of the MCI device. The GetModeString function converts the current mode code returned by the MCI control to a meaningful string that can be understood. The mode codes returned by the MCI control and their function conversion strings are as follows:

MCI Device Mode	Return Code	Function Return String
mciModeNotOpen	524	Not Open
mciModeStop	525	Stopped
mciModePlay	526	Playing
mciModeRecord	527	Recording
mciModeSeek	528	Seeking
mciModePause	529	Paused
mciModeReady	530	Ready

The `GetModeString` function is a generic function. It can be used in any application employing the multimedia MCI control to retrieve its current mode.

Analysis

The sample CD-Player code demonstrates how you can play a specific sound track from an audio CD using the `CDAudio` device of the Visual Basic multimedia MCI control.

When you run the code, the form loads and initializes the MCI control properties for playing the audio CD. The total number of tracks on the audio CD is displayed in `Label2(0)`, the current track (which is the first track on the CD) is displayed in `Label2(1)`, and the current CD-audio device status (Stopped) is displayed in `Label2(2)`.

Click the Play button on the MCI control to start playing the first audio track on the CD. You can click the Next or Prev buttons on the MCI control at any time to move to the next or previous track or to any other specific track.

You can customize the MCI control buttons at design time or at runtime to enable showing or hiding of the different buttons. You can also enable the Record button on the MCI control to be able to record and save portions or the entire playing sound track to a new file (you will need to write some additional code). In addition, you can set the MCI control's `Visible` property to `False` to hide the control on your form while still being able to manipulate the entire control functionality by sending the appropriate MCI commands to the control from within your code at runtime.

Remember that it is important to always close the MCI device using the MCI `Close` command whenever you quit your application. This can be done in the `Form_Unload()` event of the form, as shown in the code.

The sample project CDPLAYER.VBP on the CD-ROM that accompanies this book demonstrates the use of the MCI control to play an audio CD. To use the project, insert an audio CD in your CD-ROM drive, run the project, and click the Play button on the MCI control.

11.11 PLAYING A VIDEO CD

by Kamal A. Mehdi

Description

The new advances in multimedia technology enable you to play digital video tracks from a compact disc digital video (video CD) on personal computers in true-color mode with high frame rates and even in full screen, something that was impossible in the past with the older multimedia techniques. A video CD is actually a normal CD media (not a DVD disk) but differs from the CD-ROM in that video and sound tracks are written in a special format that is readable by video CD players. The standard MPEG compression codecs are used to compress video and audio streams written to a video CD.

This code shows how you can play a video CD track on your system using Visual Basic. The code uses the Visual Basic MCI (Media Control Interface) multimedia control to play the video CD tracks. The video track opens and plays in a separate window, and the window size is adjusted to the frame size of the video track. The window is a normal window that can be minimized, maximized, resized, and so on, during the play session regardless of the original Visual Basic application window (form). The playing video CD can be stopped, paused, rewound, fast forwarded, and stepped through frame by frame from the appropriate MCI control buttons. The video CD media can also be ejected from the CD-ROM drive through the MCI control's Eject button. If the video CD video track contains a sound track, the sound will be heard through the sound card speakers.

When the form containing the multimedia MCI control loads, it initializes the necessary properties of the MCI control, assigns the appropriate device type to the control (`VideoCD`), and opens the MCI device. You then can play the video CD track by clicking the Play button on the MCI control. The window in which the video track will be displayed is not shown until the MCI Play button is clicked.

The video display window can be maximized to show the video in full screen with the maximum number of colors supported by the system video adapter, without degrading the speed (frame rate) of the playing video track.

The open MCI control must be closed when your application terminates so that Windows properly manages multimedia resources. This can be done in the `Form_Unload()` event where the MCI device is closed using the MCI `Close` command.

Syntax

You can control the Visual Basic MCI multimedia control by sending various MCI command strings to the control from within your code at runtime. The syntax for sending commands to the multimedia MCI control at runtime is

```
MMControl.Command = "MCIcommand"
```

Part	Description
MCIcommand	A string expression specifying the MCI command to execute. The MCI commands are described next. Data type: String.

MCI Commands

The following are the important MCI commands:

Command	Description
Open	Opens the MCI device specified in the DeviceType property of the MCI control.
Play	Plays the MCI device (the video CD track, for example).
Stop	Stops the playing of the MCI device.
Close	Closes the MCI device.
Pause	Pauses the playing MCI device.
Prev	Goes to the beginning of the current track or file.
Next	Goes to the beginning of the next track or the end of file.
Eject	Ejects the media from the device, such as the video CD from the CD-ROM drive.

Note

More details on these MCI commands, as well as on other available commands, can be found in the MCI control help.

Modules and Controls Required

You will need the following modules and controls to build the sample project for playing video CDs:

Module/Control	Description
Form1	A standard non-MDI Visual Basic form (.FRM) with controls as shown later in this section
MMControl1	A multimedia (MCI) control

To draw controls, place the MCI multimedia control anywhere on the form. The appropriate MCI control properties will be set at runtime. You must also insert a video CD into your CD-ROM drive.

Note

The MCI multimedia control is not included on the toolbox by default. You can add it to the toolbox by selecting Project, Components, and adding the control. The control appears in the components list as Microsoft Multimedia Control 5.0, where 5.0 is the control version (you might have a different version on your system).

Code Listing

```
Private Sub Form_Load()

    'Set the Wait and Notify properties of the MCI control
    MMControl1.Wait = True
    MMControl1.Notify = False

    'Specify the Device type for the MCI control (VideoCD)
    MMControl1.DeviceType = "VideoCD"

    'Open the MCI device
    MMControl1.Command = "open"

    'Now the MCI control buttons are enabled, click the 'Play button
    'to play the video track.
    'You can click the 'Prev', 'Back', 'Stop', 'Pause', etc. to move
    'forward and backward or to pause or stop the play. You can also
    'click the 'Eject' button to eject the CD from the drive

End Sub

Private Sub Form_Unload(Cancel As Integer)

    'You must close the MCI device before closing your application
    'to properly manage multimedia resources
    MMControl1.Command = "close"

End Sub
```

Analysis

The sample code demonstrates how you can play a video CD track using the Visual Basic multimedia MCI control.

When you run the code, the form loads and initializes the MCI control properties for playing the video CD. The video track is displayed in a separate window, with the window title set to the actual name of the video track. You can maximize the window and watch the video clip in full screen with the normal track frame rate. However, you will notice a slight degradation in the picture quality because each pixel in the original video frames will be remapped to several pixels. If you watch the playing video from a distance, however, you will not see this degradation in quality, and the picture will almost look as you see it on the television set.

You can customize the MCI control buttons at design time or at runtime to enable showing or hiding of the different buttons. You can also enable the Record button on the MCI control to be able to record and save portions or the entire playing video clip to a disk file (you will need to write some additional code). In addition, you can set the MCI control's `Visible` property to `False` to hide the control on your form while still being able to manipulate the entire control functionality by sending the appropriate MCI commands to the control from within your code at runtime.

Remember that it is important to always close the MCI device using the MCI `Close` command whenever you quit your application. This can be done in the `Form_Unload()` event of the form as implemented in the code.

The sample project VIDEOCD.VBP on the CD-ROM that accompanies this book demonstrates the use of the MCI control to play a video CD. To use the project, insert a video CD in your CD-ROM drive, run the project, and click the Play button on the MCI control.

Note

In order to be able to play a video CD, you must have the Microsoft ActiveMovie or an MPEG decompression codec installed on your system. The Microsoft ActiveMovie can be downloaded from the Microsoft Web site.

11.12   PLAYING MIDI FILES

by Kamal A. Mehdi

Description

MIDI instrumental sound files are very popular because they are very small and light when they play, in terms of general system/CPU loading and disk activity. They also provide very good sound quality.

Sound contained in a MIDI file is actually represented by several codes that evaluate to sound tones of specific frequencies. The MIDI sequencer device installed on your system will process these codes and send the appropriate corresponding codes to the sound card to produce the tone for that code.

MIDI files (*.MID) can easily be played in Visual Basic using the MCI (Media Control Interface) multimedia control with the `Sequencer` device type. This code shows how you can play these files.

The code uses the MCI multimedia MIDI sequencer device installed on your system to play the MIDI file. The playing MIDI file can be stopped, paused, rewound, and fast forwarded from the appropriate MCI control buttons.

When the form containing the MCI control loads, it initializes the necessary properties of the MCI control, assigns the appropriate device type to the control (`Sequencer`), and opens the MCI device. You then can play the MIDI file by clicking the Play button on the MCI control.

The open MCI control must be closed when your application terminates so that Windows properly manages multimedia resources. This is done in the `Form_Unload()` event where the MCI device is closed using the MCI `Close` command.

Syntax

You can control the Visual Basic MCI multimedia control by sending various MCI command strings to the control from within your code at runtime. The syntax for sending commands to the multimedia MCI control at runtime is

```
MMControl.Command = "MCIcommand"
```

Part	Description
MCIcommand	A string expression specifying the MCI command to execute. The MCI commands are described next. Data type: `String`.

MCI Commands

The following are the important MCI commands:

Command	Description
Open	Opens the MCI device specified in the `DeviceType` property of the MCI control.
Play	Plays the MCI device (the sound file, for example).
Stop	Stops the playing of the MCI device.
Close	Closes the MCI device.
Pause	Pauses the playing MCI device.
Prev	Goes to the beginning of the current track or file.
Next	Goes to the beginning of the next track or end of file.
Eject	Ejects the media from the device, such as an audio CD from the CD-ROM drive.

Note

More details on these MCI commands, as well as on other available commands, can be found in the MCI control help.

Modules and Controls Required

You will need the following modules and controls to build the sample project for playing MIDI files:

Module/Control	Description
Form1	A standard non-MDI Visual Basic form (.FRM) with controls as shown later in this section
MMControl1	A multimedia (MCI) control

To draw controls, place the MCI multimedia control anywhere on the form. The appropriate MCI control properties are set at runtime. You must also provide an existing MIDI filename (by default, the code will open and play the sample MIDI file located under the project directory on the CD-ROM).

Note

The MCI multimedia control is not included on the toolbox by default. You can add it to the toolbox by selecting Project, Components, and adding the control. The control appears in the components list as Microsoft Multimedia Control 5.0, where 5.0 is the control version (you might have a different version on your system).

Code Listing

```
Private Sub Form_Load()

    'Set the Wait and Notify properties of the MCI control
    MMControl1.Wait = True
    MMControl1.Notify = False

    'Specify the Device type for the MCI control (Sequencer)
    MMControl1.DeviceType = "Sequencer"

    'Specify the MIDI file name (sample.mid exists in the project directory)
    MMControl1.filename = App.Path & "\sample.mid"

    'Open the MCI device
    MMControl1.Command = "open"

    'Now the MCI control buttons are enabled, click the 'Play button
    'to play the sound file.
    'You can click the 'Prev', 'Back', 'Stop', 'Pause', etc. to move
    'forward and backward or to pause or stop the play.

End Sub

Private Sub Form_Unload(Cancel As Integer)

    'You must close the MCI device before closing your application
    'to properly manage multimedia resources
    MMControl1.Command = "close"

End Sub
```

Analysis

The sample code demonstrates how you can play a MIDI sound file using the Visual Basic multimedia MCI control. When you run the code, the form loads and initializes the necessary MCI control properties for playing the MIDI file. Click the Play button on the MCI control to start playing the MIDI file. The sample code will play the SAMPLE.MID MIDI file located under the project directory on the CD-ROM. This file is a 90-second instrumental music sound that requires only 6KB of file size.

You can customize the MCI control buttons at design time or at runtime to enable showing or hiding of the different buttons. You can also enable the Record button on the MCI control to be able to record and save portions or the entire playing MIDI file to a new file (you will need to write some additional code). In addition, you can set the MCI control's `Visible` property to `False` to hide the control on your form, while still being able to manipulate the entire control functionality by sending the appropriate MCI commands to the control from within your code at runtime.

Remember that it is important to always close the MCI device using the MCI `Close` command whenever you quit your application to restore the multimedia resources. This can be done in the `Form_Unload()` event of the form, as shown in the code.

The sample project MIDIPLAY.VBP on the CD-ROM demonstrates the use of the MCI control to play a MIDI sound file using the `Sequencer` MCI device.

11.13 PLAYING SOUND FILES USING API CALLS

by Kamal A. Mehdi

Description

The `PlaySound` function plays sound files of wave type (*.WAV) using API calls without the need to have the MCI multimedia control in your Visual Basic project.

Using the `PlaySound` function is simple; you just specify the WAV filename and, optionally, the mode of play, and call the `PlaySound` function. You can choose to play the sound file and leave it to continue in the background while your code does other things, specify that the code stops executing until the sound play is completed, or even specify that the sound will play in a loop while your code does other things. This is accomplished by specifying the required mode of play for the function's `Mode` argument.

When the function is called, it first verifies that the sound file specified by the `FileName` argument actually exists. If the file does not exist, it shows a message box to report the error.

Syntax

```
RetVal = PlaySound (FileName, Mode)
```

Part	Description
RetVal	Required. A numeric variable that receives the value returned from the function. On success, RetVal returns True (-1), otherwise it returns False (0). Data type: Integer.
FileName	Required. A string expression that specifies the full path/name of the sound file to play. Data type: String.
Mode	Optional. A numeric expression that specifies the mode of play. The mode settings are described next. Data type: Integer.

The optional Mode argument takes the following settings:

Setting	Description
0	Plays the sound file in asynchronous mode. The function returns immediately after the sound starts playing (default).
1	Plays the sound file in synchronous mode. The function does not return until the sound stops playing.
2	Plays the sound file continuously in a loop until the function is called again. The function returns immediately after starting the sound.
3	If the sound is currently playing, the function does not play the specified file and returns False (0) immediately.

Code Listing

```
'API Declarations in your Module
Declare Function sndPlaySound Lib "winmm.dll" Alias "sndPlaySoundA"
➥ (ByVal lpszSoundName As String, ByVal uFlags As Long) As Long

'API Declaration for VB 16-bit only
'Declare Function sndPlaySound Lib "MMSYSTEM.DLL" (ByVal lpszSoundName As Any,
➥ ByVal wFlags%) As Integer

'Constants
    'Play sound synchronously (default)
    Const SND_SYNC = &H0

    'Play sound asynchronously
    Const SND_ASYNC = &H1

    'Loop the sound until the function sndPlaySound is called again
    Const SND_LOOP = &H8
```

```
        'If sound is playing, dont play it and return false
        Const SND_NOSTOP = &H10

'The PlaySound function
Function PlaySound(FileName As String, Optional Mode As Integer) As Integer

        Dim SoundMode As Integer

        'Check if the file does exist
        If Dir(FileName) = "" Then
            MsgBox "File not found", vbInformation
            Exit Function
        End If

        Select Case Mode

            Case Is = 0
                SoundMode = SND_ASYNC

            Case Is = 1
                SoundMode = SND_SYNC

            Case Is = 2
                SoundMode = SND_LOOP Or SND_ASYNC

            Case Is = 3
                SoundMode = SND_NOSTOP Or SND_ASYNC

            Case Else
                MsgBox "Invalid Mode received", vbInformation
                Exit Function

        End Select

        'Call the sndPlaySound API function
        PlaySound = sndPlaySound(ByVal FileName, SoundMode)

End Function
```

Analysis

The sample code demonstrates how you can play a WAV sound file using the `PlaySound` function. You just call the function from anywhere within your project, specifying the filename and optionally the mode of play, and the sound will play.

When you call the function, it checks to verify whether the specified file actually exists, and then plays the sound. If you do not specify the `Mode` argument, the function returns immediately after starting the sound play. Your code will continue to execute, performing other tasks while the sound is playing. You can also use the sound loop mode (Mode=2) when you want your application to have the sound playing in the background as long as your application is running, without calling the function each time to play the sound again.

The PlaySound function is based on the sndPlaySound API function but is easier to use within your Visual Basic applications. The 16-bit API declaration for the sndPlaySound is also provided in the code for compatibility.

The sample project PLAYSND.VBP on the CD-ROM that accompanies this book demonstrates the use of the PlaySound function.

11.14 DETERMINING WHETHER A SOUND CARD IS INSTALLED

by Kamal A. Mehdi

Description

Sometimes you must figure out whether the user has a sound card installed on his or her machine. For example, when you develop a multimedia application that involves speech or other sound data vital to the application, the user must have a sound card installed on his machine. Otherwise, your application might inform the user that it will not run properly due to the lack of a sound card.

The IsSoundCardInstalled function detects whether the user has a sound card installed on his machine. The function returns True to your application if it detects a sound card; otherwise it returns False.

The IsSoundCardInstalled function uses the waveOutGetNumDevs API function to determine whether a device capable of playing wave data is installed on the system. If the waveOutGetNumDevs function returns at least one device, the system should have a sound card installed.

Using the IsSoundCardInstalled function is very simple. Just call the function from your application without passing any parameters, and it will return either True or False. The IsSoundCardInstalled function will work on both 16-bit and 32-bit platforms because it contains conditional compilation and the appropriate API declarations for both platforms.

Syntax

RetVal = IsSoundCardInstalled()

Part	Description
RetVal	Required. A numeric variable that receives the value returned from the function, as described next. Data type: Boolean.

The following values are returned by the IsSoundCardInstalled function:

Value	Description
True	A sound card currently is installed on the system.
False	No sound card is installed.

Code Listing

```
'Code in Module

'Conditional compilation

#If Win16 Then
    '16-bit API declarations
    Declare Function waveOutGetNumDevs Lib "mmsystem.dll" () As Integer

#ElseIf Win32 Then
    '32-bit API declarations
    Declare Function waveOutGetNumDevs Lib "winmm.dll" () As Long

#End If

Function IsSoundCardInstalled() As Boolean

    'Call the waveOutGetNumDevs function and check if it returns
    'at-least one device capable of playing wave data
    If waveOutGetNumDevs() > 0 Then
        IsSoundCardInstalled = True
    Else
        IsSoundCardInstalled = False
    End If

End Function
```

Analysis

The IsSoundCardInstalled function demonstrates how you can determine whether the user has a sound card installed on his or her system. Just call the function from within your own application, and it will return either True or False, depending on whether a sound card was detected.

The IsSoundCardInstalled function uses the waveOutGetNumDevs API function to determine whether at least one device capable of playing wave data is installed on the user's machine.

The sample project SNDCARD.VBP on the CD-ROM that accompanies this book demonstrates the utility of the presented function.

11.15   SET THE AUDIO CD VOLUME

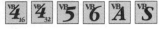

by Kamal A. Mehdi

Description

This code enables you to retrieve the current volume settings for the system's audio CD drive and set its volume. The sample code enables you to retrieve and set the volume of the left and right channels separately. It also detects whether the channels are synchronized (balanced) by retrieving and comparing their current volume settings.

When the form loads, the code searches for the existence of an audio CD device and informs you whether the device is not found. It also enumerates the sound card-available devices to retrieve the CD-audio device ID for subsequent use for volume retrieval and setting.

The sample code enables you to play an audio CD directly from your Visual Basic application by using the MCI (Media Control Interface) multimedia control. You will be able to play any sound track from the CD, jump to any specific track, and pause and stop the CD play. You can also open and close the door (tray) of the CD-ROM drive by using the MCI control's Eject button.

This code incorporates conditional compilation and API declarations for both 16-bit and 32-bit Windows platforms, and thus will function on both platforms without the necessity to make any modifications to the code.

Modules and Controls Required

You will need the following modules and controls to build a sample project:

Module/Control	Description
Module1	A standard Visual Basic module (.BAS)
Form1	A standard non-MDI Visual Basic form (.FRM) with the following property settings:
	Caption = Get/Set CD-ROM Drive Volume
	BorderStyle = 3-Fixed Dialog
Frame1	A frame control with the Caption property set to Set Volume
Command1	A command button with the Caption property set to Exit
MMControl1	An MCI multimedia control

Module/Control	Description
VScroll1	A vertical scrollbar with the following property settings:
	Min = 100
	Max = 0
Vscroll2	A vertical scrollbar with the following property settings:
	Min = 100
	Max = 0
Label1	A label control with the Caption property set to Left
Label2	A label control with the Caption property set to Right
Label3	A label control with the Caption property set to 0%
Label4	A label control with the Caption property set to 0%
Check1	A check box control with the Caption property set to Lock Channels

Follow these steps to draw controls:

1. Start a new standard EXE project. Form1 is created by default. Set the form's Height and Width properties to approximately 4800 and 4200, respectively, and set its Caption and BorderStyle properties as shown earlier in this section.
2. Draw Frame1 on the left side of the form and adjust its size so that it covers almost half the total form area. Set the frame's Caption property as shown earlier.
3. Draw the two vertical scrollbars VScroll1 and VScroll2 inside the frame control, with VScroll1 to the left and VScroll2 to the right. Leave some space above and below the scrollbars. Set their Min and Max properties as shown earlier.
4. Draw Label1 and Label2 inside the frame control under VScroll1 and VScroll2, respectively. Set the Caption property of the labels as shown earlier.
5. Draw Label3 and Label4 inside the frame control above VScroll1 and VScroll2, respectively. Set the Caption property of the labels as shown earlier.
6. Draw the Check1 check box inside the frame control at the bottom side and set its Caption property as shown earlier.
7. Draw the multimedia MCI control (MMControl1) at the bottom of the form.
8. Draw the Command1 button anywhere on the form, and set its Caption property as shown earlier.

Note

The MCI multimedia control is not included on the toolbox by default. You can add it to the toolbox by selecting Project, Components, and adding the control. The control appears in the components list as Microsoft Multimedia Control 5.0, where 5.0 is the control version (you might have a different version on your system).

Code Listing

```
'Code in Module1

Option Explicit

#If Win32 Then

    '32-bit API declarations
    Declare Function auxGetNumDevs Lib "winmm.dll" () As Long

    Declare Function auxGetDevCaps Lib "winmm.dll" Alias "auxGetDevCapsA"
    ➥ (ByVal uDeviceID As Long, lpCaps As AUXCAPS,
    ➥ByVal uSize As Long) As Long

    Declare Function auxGetVolume Lib "winmm.dll" (ByVal uDeviceID As Long,
    ➥ lpdwVolume As Long) As Long

    Declare Function auxSetVolume Lib "winmm.dll" (ByVal uDeviceID As Long,
    ➥ ByVal dwVolume As Long) As Long

#ElseIf Win16 Then

    '16-bit API declarations
    Declare Function auxGetDevCaps Lib "mmsystem.DLL" (ByVal wDeviceID As
    ➥ Integer, lpCaps As AUXCAPS, ByVal wSize As Integer) As Integer

    Declare Function auxGetVolume Lib "mmsystem.DLL" (ByVal wDeviceID As
    ➥ Integer, lpdwVolume As Long) As Integer

    Declare Function auxSetVolume Lib "mmsystem.DLL" (ByVal wDeviceID As
    ➥ Integer, ByVal dwVolume As Long) As Integer

    Declare Function auxGetNumDevs Lib "mmsystem.DLL" () As Integer
#End If

    'Flags for the wTechnology field in the AUXCAPS Structure
    Global Const AUXCAPS_CDAUDIO = 1     'Audio output from an
                                         ' internal CD-ROM drive
    Global Const AUXCAPS_AUXIN = 2       'Audio output from auxiliary
                                         ' input jacks

    'Flags for the dwSupport Field in the AUXCAPS Structure
    Global Const AUXCAPS_VOLUME = &H1     'Supports volume control
    Global Const AUXCAPS_LRVOLUME = &H2   'Supports separate left and
                                          ' right volume control

    Global Const MMSYSERR_BASE = 0
    Global Const MMSYSERR_BADDEVICEID = (MMSYSERR_BASE + 2)
                                         'Specified device ID is out of range
```

```
        Global Const MMSYSERR_NODRIVER = (MMSYSERR_BASE + 6)
                                    'The driver failed to install

    Type AUXCAPS
        wMid As Integer              'Manufacturer ID
        wPid As Integer              'Product ID
        vDriverVersion As Integer     'Version of the driver
        szPname As String * 80       'Product Name (NULL-Terminated String)
        wTechnology As Integer       'Type of device
        dwSupport As Long            'Functionality Supported by driver
    End Type

    Type CnvrtIVolumesType
        LeftVolume As Integer
        RightVolume As Integer
    End Type

    Type CnvrtLVolumeType
        Volume As Long
    End Type


'Code in Form1

'Form declarations
    Option Explicit
    Dim Loading As Boolean
    Dim DevID As Integer
    Dim LVol As Long
    Dim RVol As Long
    Dim VScroll1PrevVal As Integer
    Dim VScroll2PrevVal As Integer

Private Sub Command1_Click()

    Unload Me

End Sub

Private Function ConvertValue(LeftVol As Long, RightVol As Long) As Long

    Dim IVolumes As CnvrtIVolumesType
    Dim LVolume As CnvrtLVolumeType

    'Assign current volume settings to IVolumes
    IVolumes.LeftVolume = CInt("&H" & Hex$(LeftVol))
    IVolumes.RightVolume = CInt("&H" & Hex$(RightVol))
```

continues

```
    'Copy IVolume values to LVolume
    LSet LVolume = IVolumes
    ConvertValue = LVolume.Volume

End Function

Private Sub ReportError(ErrNum As Integer)

    Select Case ErrNum

        Case MMSYSERR_BADDEVICEID
            MsgBox "Bad device ID."

        Case MMSYSERR_NODRIVER
            MsgBox "Driver not installed."

    End Select

    End

End Sub

Private Sub Form_Load()

    'Declare variables
    Dim InitialVolume As Long
    Dim RetVal As Integer

    'Center form on screen
    Me.Left = (Screen.Width - Me.Width) / 2
    Me.Top = (Screen.Height - Me.Height) / 2

    'Form is loading (read volume values only)
    Loading = True

    'Get the CdAudio device ID
    DevID = GetCDAudioDevID()

    'Assign CDAudio to the DeviceType property of the MCI control
    MMControl1.DeviceType = "CDAudio"

    'Open the device
    MMControl1.Command = "Open"

    'Retrieve the current volume settings
    RetVal = auxGetVolume(DevID, InitialVolume)

    'If a value other than 0 is returned, report error and exit
    If RetVal <> 0 Then Call ReportError(RetVal)
```

```
    'Get left and right volume settings
    LVol = InitialVolume And &HFFFF&
    RVol = (InitialVolume And &HFFFF0000) / &H10000

    If RVol < 0 Then RVol = 2 ^ 16 + (InitialVolume And &HFFFF0000) / &H10000

    'Assign values to the scroll bars
    VScroll1.Value = Abs(CInt((LVol * 100&) / &HFFFF&))
    VScroll1PrevVal = VScroll1.Value

    VScroll2.Value = Abs(CInt((RVol * 100&) / &HFFFF&))
    VScroll2PrevVal = VScroll2.Value

    Loading = False

    'Check if both volumes are equal, then lock both scroll bars (synchronize)
    If LVol = RVol Then Check1.Value = 1

End Sub

Private Sub Form_Unload(Cancel As Integer)

    'Close the MCI device
    MMControl1.Command = "Close"

End Sub

Private Function GetCDAudioDevID()

    Dim NumAuxDevs As Integer
    Dim DevNum As Integer
    Dim DevCaps As AUXCAPS
    Dim RetVal As Integer, Pos As Integer

    'Retrieve the number of devices
    NumAuxDevs = auxGetNumDevs()
    GetCDAudioDevID = 0

    'Loop through all devices and find the device with string 'CD'
    For DevNum = 0 To (NumAuxDevs - 1)

        RetVal = auxGetDevCaps(DevNum, DevCaps, 92)
        If RetVal <> 0 Then Call ReportError(RetVal)
        Pos = InStr(DevCaps.szPname, "CD")

        If Pos <> 0 Then
```

continues

```
                'Get the device ID
                GetCDAudioDevID = DevNum
                Exit Function

        End If

    Next DevNum

End Function

Private Sub VScroll1_Change()

    Dim LeftScrollChange As Integer
    Dim VolumeChange As Long
    Dim RetVal As Integer

    'Synchronize the scroll bars
    If Check1.Value = 1 Then
        VScroll2.Value = VScroll1.Value
    End If

    'Show current left volume percent
    Label3.Caption = VScroll1.Value & "%"

    If Not Loading Then

        'Get the difference between current scroll bar value and previous value
        LeftScrollChange = VScroll1.Value - VScroll1PrevVal

        'Remember current value
        VScroll1PrevVal = VScroll1.Value
        VolumeChange = ((&HFFFF& * CLng(Abs(LeftScrollChange))) / 100&)

        If LeftScrollChange < 0 Then
            LVol = LVol - VolumeChange
            If LVol < &H0& Then LVol = &H0&

        Else

            LVol = LVol + VolumeChange
            If LVol > &HFFFF& Then LVol = &HFFFF&

        End If

        'Set the volume
        RetVal = auxSetVolume(DevID, ConvertValue(LVol, RVol))
```

```vb
                        'If a value other than 0 is returned, report error
                        If RetVal <> 0 Then Call ReportError(RetVal)

            End If

End Sub

Private Sub VScroll2_Change()

        Dim RightScrollChange As Integer
        Dim VolumeChange As Long
        Dim RetVal As Integer

        'Synchronize the scroll bars
        If Check1.Value = 1 Then
            VScroll1.Value = VScroll2.Value
        End If

        'Show current right volume percent
        Label4.Caption = VScroll2.Value & "%"

        If Not Loading Then

            'Get the difference between current scroll bar value and previous value
            RightScrollChange = VScroll2.Value - VScroll2PrevVal

            'Remember current value
            VScroll2PrevVal = VScroll2.Value
            VolumeChange = ((&HFFFF& * CLng(Abs(RightScrollChange))) / 100&)

            If RightScrollChange < 0 Then

                    RVol = RVol - VolumeChange
                    If RVol < &H0& Then RVol = &H0&

                    Else

                    RVol = RVol + VolumeChange
                    If RVol > &HFFFF& Then RVol = &HFFFF&

            End If

            'Set the volume
            RetVal = auxSetVolume(DevID, ConvertValue(LVol, RVol))

            'If a value other than 0 is returned, report error
            If RetVal <> 0 Then Call ReportError(RetVal)

        End If

End Sub
```

Enter the code into the appropriate form, module, or control events as indicated. Insert an audio CD in the CD-ROM drive and run the project. Notice that each scrollbar displays the particular channel volume setting for the CD-audio device (Label3 and Label4 will display the percent channel-volume setting). Click the speaker icon in the system tray (the area with icons located on the right side of the Windows task bar) and look at the volume settings of the CD-audio device in the sound card control panel. The settings should match the scrollbar values shown on your form. If both channel volume settings are equal, you will see the Check1 check box checked, which means that channels are locked (synchronized).

Now click the Play button on the MCI control to play the audio CD and try to change the volume settings using the scrollbars on your form. Notice the immediate change in the CD-Audio device volume, and you will see the corresponding change in the CD-Audio scrollbar position on your system's volume control panel of the sound card. You can change the left and right channel volume separately by unchecking the Lock Channels check box on your form, or you can change them simultaneously by checking the check box.

Analysis

The code demonstrates how you can retrieve and set the volume of your system's CD-Audio device independently of the master sound volume. The code first tries to detect whether your system has a CD-Audio device installed by enumerating all the devices exposed by the sound card using two API functions, auxGetNumDevs and auxGetDevCaps. It then retrieves the device ID for the CD-Audio device in order to be able to use it to retrieve and set the device volume.

You use the auxGetDeviceCaps API function when the device characteristics and capabilities for each auxiliary device installed on the system are to be retrieved. The function argument lpCaps is of AUXCAPS API-type variable, which provides the information in Table 11.1 for the specific device whose device ID is passed to the function's uDeviceID argument.

Table 11.15.1
AUXCAPS-Type Variable

Subtype	*Description*
wMid	Provides the manufacturer ID
wPid	Provides the product ID
vDriverVersion	Provides the version of the driver
szPname	Provides the product name
wTechnology	Provides the type of device
dwSupport	Provides the functionality supported by the driver

Retrieving the current volume setting for the CD-Audio device is actually done by calling the API function auxGetVolume. The volume is set by calling the auxSetVolume API function. The dwVolume argument in both functions represents a double-word data from which the left and right channel volume settings can be retrieved or set by separating and reading or writing the low-order and high-order words.

By specifying the device ID for the appropriate function argument, you can retrieve and set the volume of any sound device in your system using the `auxGetVolume` and `auxSetVolume` API functions.

The sample project CDVOL.VBP on the CD-ROM demonstrates the functionality of the presented code.

11.16   SET A SOUND CARD VOLUME

by Kamal A. Mehdi

Description

This code enables you to retrieve the current master volume setting of your system's sound card and adjust the master volume level. The sample code enables you to retrieve and set the volume of the left and right channels separately. It also detects whether the channels are synchronized (balanced) by retrieving and comparing their current volume settings.

When the form loads, the code enumerates the sound card–available devices to retrieve the master volume device ID for use in subsequent volume retrieval and setting. It also reads the current master volume setting to adjust the initial value of the scrollbars used to set the volume.

The code plays a sample MIDI sound file by using the MCI (Media Control Interface) multimedia control to enable you to hear the sound and monitor the volume level changes. The code incorporates conditional compilation and API function declarations for both 16-bit and 32-bit Windows platforms to enable functionality on both platforms without the necessity to make any modifications to the code.

Modules and Controls Required

You will need the following modules and controls to build the sample project:

Module/Control	Description
Module1	A standard Visual Basic module (.BAS)
Form1	A standard non-MDI Visual Basic form (.FRM) with the following property settings:
	`Caption` = Get/Set Sound Card Volume
	`BorderStyle` = 3-Fixed Dialog
Frame1	A frame control with the `Caption` property set to Set Volume
Command1	A command button with the `Caption` property set to Exit

continues

Module/Control	Description
MMControl1	An MCI multimedia control with the following properties set:
	BackVisible = False
	EjectVisible = False
	PauseVisible = False
	RecordVisible = False
	StepVisible = False
VScroll1	A vertical scrollbar with the following property settings:
	Min = 100
	Max = 0
Vscroll2	A vertical scrollbar with the following property settings:
	Min = 100
	Max = 0
Label1	A label control with the Caption property set to Left
Label2	A label control with the Caption property set to Right
Label3	A label control with the Caption property set to 0%
Label4	A label control with the Caption property set to 0%
Label5	A label control with the Caption property set to Play MIDI Sound
Check1	A check box control with the Caption property set to Lock Channels

Follow these steps to draw controls:

1. Start a new standard EXE project. Form1 is created by default. Set the form's Height and Width properties to approximately 5000 and 2300, respectively, and set its Caption and BorderStyle properties as shown earlier in this section.
2. Draw Frame1 on the top of the form and adjust its size so that it covers almost the upper two-thirds of the form area. Set the frame's Caption property as shown earlier.
3. Draw the two vertical scrollbars VScroll1 and VScroll2 inside the frame control, with VScroll1 to the left and VScroll2 to the right. Leave some space above and below the scrollbars. Set their Min and Max properties as shown earlier.
4. Draw Label1 and Label2 inside the frame control under VScroll1 and VScroll2, respectively. Set the Caption property of the labels as shown earlier.
5. Draw Label3 and Label4 inside the frame control above VScroll1 and VScroll2, respectively. Set the Caption property of the labels as shown earlier.
6. Draw the Check1 check box inside the frame control at the bottom side and set its Caption property as shown earlier.

7. Draw `Lable5` under the frame control and set its `Caption` property as shown earlier.
8. Draw the multimedia MCI control (`MMControl1`) below `Label5` and set its properties as shown earlier.
9. Draw the `Command1` command button under the MCI control and set its `Caption` property as shown earlier.

Note

The MCI multimedia control is not included on the toolbox by default. You can add it to the toolbox by selecting Project, Components, and adding the control. The control appears in the components list as Microsoft Multimedia Control 5.0, where 5.0 is the control version (you might have a different version on your system).

Code Listing

```
'Code in Module1

Option Explicit

#If Win32 Then

    '32-bit API declarations
    Declare Function auxGetNumDevs Lib "winmm.dll" () As Long

    Declare Function auxGetDevCaps Lib "winmm.dll" Alias "auxGetDevCapsA"
    ➡ (ByVal uDeviceID As Long, lpCaps As AUXCAPS,
    [ic:ccc[ByVal uSize As Long) As Long

    Declare Function auxGetVolume Lib "winmm.dll" (ByVal uDeviceID As Long,
    ➡lpdwVolume As Long) As Long

    Declare Function auxSetVolume Lib "winmm.dll" (ByVal uDeviceID As Long,
    ➡ByVal dwVolume As Long) As Long

#ElseIf Win16 Then

    '16-bit API declarations
    Declare Function auxGetDevCaps Lib "mmsystem.DLL" (ByVal wDeviceID As
    ➡Integer, lpCaps As AUXCAPS, ByVal wSize As Integer) As Integer

    Declare Function auxGetVolume Lib "mmsystem.DLL" (ByVal wDeviceID As
    ➡Integer, lpdwVolume As Long) As Integer

    Declare Function auxSetVolume Lib "mmsystem.DLL" (ByVal wDeviceID As
    ➡Integer, ByVal dwVolume As Long) As Integer

    Declare Function auxGetNumDevs Lib "mmsystem.DLL" () As Integer

#End If
```

continues

```
'Flags for the wTechnology field in the AUXCAPS Structure
Global Const AUXCAPS_CDAUDIO = 1      'Audio output from an internal
➥ CD-ROM drive
Global Const AUXCAPS_AUXIN = 2        'Audio output from auxiliary
➥ input jacks

'Flags for the dwSupport Field in the AUXCAPS Structure
Global Const AUXCAPS_VOLUME = &H1     'Supports volume control
Global Const AUXCAPS_LRVOLUME = &H2    'Supports separate left and
➥ right volume control

Global Const MMSYSERR_BASE = 0
Global Const MMSYSERR_BADDEVICEID = (MMSYSERR_BASE + 2)
➥ 'Specified device ID is out of range
Global Const MMSYSERR_NODRIVER = (MMSYSERR_BASE + 6)
➥ 'The driver failed to install

Type AUXCAPS
    wMid As Integer              'Manufacturer ID
    wPid As Integer              'Product ID
    vDriverVersion As Integer     'Version of the driver
    szPname As String * 80       'Product Name (NULL-Terminated String)
    wTechnology As Integer       'Type of device
    dwSupport As Long            'Functionality Supported by driver
End Type

Type CnvrtIVolumesType
    LeftVolume As Integer
    RightVolume As Integer
End Type

Type CnvrtLVolumeType
    Volume As Long
End Type

'Code in Form1

    'Form general declarations
    Option Explicit
    Dim Loading As Boolean
    Dim DevID As Integer
    Dim LVol As Long
    Dim RVol As Long
    Dim VScroll1PrevVal As Integer
    Dim VScroll2PrevVal As Integer

Private Sub Command1_Click()
```

```
    'Exit
    Unload Me

End Sub

Private Function ConvertValue(LeftVol As Long, RightVol As Long) As Long

    'Declare type-defined variables
    Dim IVolumes As CnvrtIVolumesType
    Dim LVolume As CnvrtLVolumeType

    'Assign current volume settings to IVolumes
    IVolumes.LeftVolume = CInt("&H" & Hex$(LeftVol))
    IVolumes.RightVolume = CInt("&H" & Hex$(RightVol))

    'Copy IVolume values to LVolume
    LSet LVolume = IVolumes
    ConvertValue = LVolume.Volume

End Function

Private Sub ReportError(ErrNum As Integer)

    'Show the error type
    Select Case ErrNum

        Case MMSYSERR_BADDEVICEID
            MsgBox "Bad device ID."

        Case MMSYSERR_NODRIVER
            MsgBox "Driver not installed."

    End Select

    End

End Sub

Private Sub Form_Load()

    'Declare variables
    Dim InitialVolume As Long
    Dim RetVal As Integer

    'Center form on screen
    Me.Left = (Screen.Width - Me.Width) / 2
    Me.Top = (Screen.Height - Me.Height) / 2

    'Form is loading (read volume values only)
    Loading = True
```

continues

```
    'Get the sound card master volume device ID
    DevID = GetMasterVolumeDevID()

    'Specify MIDI sequencer to the DeviceType property
    'of the MCI control
    MMControl1.DeviceType = "Sequencer"

    'Specify the file name (sample.mid in the project directory)
    MMControl1.filename = App.Path & "\sample.mid"

    'Open the MCI device
    MMControl1.Command = "Open"

    'Retrieve the current volume settings
    RetVal = auxGetVolume(DevID, InitialVolume)

    'If a value other than 0 is returned, report error and exit
    If RetVal <> 0 Then Call ReportError(RetVal)

    'Get left and right volume settings
    LVol = InitialVolume And &HFFFF&
    RVol = (InitialVolume And &HFFFF0000) / &H10000

    If RVol < 0 Then RVol = 2 ^ 16 + (InitialVolume And &HFFFF0000) / &H10000

    'Assign values to the scroll bars
    VScroll1.Value = Abs(CInt((LVol * 100&) / &HFFFF&))
    VScroll1PrevVal = VScroll1.Value

    VScroll2.Value = Abs(CInt((RVol * 100&) / &HFFFF&))
    VScroll2PrevVal = VScroll2.Value

    Loading = False

    'Check if both volumes are equal, then lock
    'both scroll bars (synchronize)
    If LVol = RVol Then Check1.Value = 1


End Sub

Private Sub Form_Unload(Cancel As Integer)

    'Close the MCI device so that windows can properely
    'manage multimedia resources
    MMControl1.Command = "Close"

End Sub

Private Function GetMasterVolumeDevID()

    'Declare variables
    Dim NumAuxDevs As Integer
```

```
        Dim DevNum As Integer
        Dim DevCaps As AUXCAPS
        Dim RetVal As Integer, Pos As Integer

        'Retrieve the number of devices
        NumAuxDevs = auxGetNumDevs()
        GetMasterVolumeDevID = 0

        'Loop through all sound devices and find the device
        'containing the 'Master' string (master volume)
        For DevNum = 0 To (NumAuxDevs - 1)

            RetVal = auxGetDevCaps(DevNum, DevCaps, 92)
            If RetVal <> 0 Then Call ReportError(RetVal)

            Pos = InStr(DevCaps.szPname, "Master")

            If Pos <> 0 Then

                'Get the device ID
                GetMasterVolumeDevID = DevNum
                Exit Function

            End If

        Next DevNum

End Function

Private Sub VScroll1_Change()

        'Declare variables
        Dim LeftScrollChange As Integer
        Dim VolumeChange As Long
        Dim RetVal As Integer

        'Synchronize the scroll bars
        If Check1.Value = 1 Then
            VScroll2.Value = VScroll1.Value
        End If

        'Show current left volume percent
        Label3.Caption = VScroll1.Value & "%"

        If Not Loading Then      'If form is not loading now

            'Get the difference between the current scroll bar value
            'and the previous value (left channel volume)
            LeftScrollChange = VScroll1.Value - VScroll1PrevVal

            'Remember current value
            VScroll1PrevVal = VScroll1.Value
```

continues

```
            'Calculate the left channel volume change
            VolumeChange = ((&HFFFF& * CLng(Abs(LeftScrollChange))) / 100&)

            If LeftScrollChange < 0 Then

                LVol = LVol - VolumeChange
                If LVol < &H0& Then LVol = &H0&

                Else

                LVol = LVol + VolumeChange
                If LVol > &HFFFF& Then LVol = &HFFFF&

            End If

            'Call the auxSetVolume API to set the volume to the new value
            RetVal = auxSetVolume(DevID, ConvertValue(LVol, RVol))

            'If a value other than 0 is returned, report error
            If RetVal <> 0 Then Call ReportError(RetVal)

        End If

End Sub

Private Sub VScroll2_Change()

    'Declare variables
    Dim RightScrollChange As Integer
    Dim VolumeChange As Long
    Dim RetVal As Integer

    'Synchronize the scroll bars
    If Check1.Value = 1 Then
        VScroll1.Value = VScroll2.Value
    End If

    'Show current right volume percent
    Label4.Caption = VScroll2.Value & "%"

    If Not Loading Then     'If form is not loading now

        'Get the difference between the current scroll bar value
        'and the previous value (right channel volume)
        RightScrollChange = VScroll2.Value - VScroll2PrevVal

        'Remember current value
        VScroll2PrevVal = VScroll2.Value
```

```
        'Calculate the right channel volume change
        VolumeChange = ((&HFFFF& * CLng(Abs(RightScrollChange))) / 100&)

        If RightScrollChange < 0 Then

            RVol = RVol - VolumeChange
            If RVol < &H0& Then RVol = &H0&

        Else

            RVol = RVol + VolumeChange
            If RVol > &HFFFF& Then RVol = &HFFFF&

        End If

        'Call the auxSetVolume API to set the volume to the new value
        RetVal = auxSetVolume(DevID, ConvertValue(LVol, RVol))

        'If a value other than 0 is returned, report error
        If RetVal <> 0 Then Call ReportError(RetVal)

    End If

End Sub
```

Enter the code into the appropriate form, module, or control events as indicated and run the project. Notice that each scrollbar displays the particular channel current volume setting for the master volume device (`Label3` and `Label4` will display the percent channel-volume setting). Click the speaker icon in the system tray (the area with icons located on the right side of the Windows task bar) and look at the master volume settings in the sound card control panel. The settings should match the scrollbar values shown on your form. If both channel volume settings are equal, you will see the Lock Channels check box checked, which means that channels are synchronized (left and right volume setting are balanced).

Now click the Play button on the MCI control to play the MIDI sound file (the sample.mid file located under the project directory on the CD-ROM plays). Try to change the volume settings using the scrollbars on your form. Notice the immediate change in the volume level and the corresponding change in the master volume scrollbar position on your system's volume control panel of the sound card. You can change the left and right channel volume separately by unchecking the Lock Channels check box on your form, or you can change them simultaneously by checking the check box.

Analysis

The code demonstrates how you can retrieve and set the level of your system's sound card master volume device. The code first tries to determine the device ID of the master volume device by enumerating all the devices exposed by the sound card using two API functions `auxGetNumDevs` and `auxGetDevCaps`, in order to be able to use it to retrieve and set the device volume. It then retrieves the initial (current) volume settings for both left and right channels of the master volume.

The `auxGetDeviceCaps` API function is used when the device characteristics and capabilities for each auxiliary device installed on the system are to be retrieved. The function argument `lpCaps` is of `AUXCAPS` API-type, which provides the information in Table 11.2 for the specific device whose device ID is passed to the function's `uDeviceID` argument.

Table 11.16.1
AUXCAPS-Type Variable

Subtype	Description
wMid	Provides the manufacturer ID
wPid	Provides the product ID
vDriverVersion	Provides the version of the driver
szPname	Provides the product name
wTechnology	Provides the type of device
dwSupport	Provides the functionality supported by the driver

Retrieving the current volume setting for the master volume device is actually done by calling the API function `auxGetVolume`. The volume level is set by calling the `auxSetVolume` API function. The `dwVolume` argument in both functions represents a double-word data from which the left and right channel volume settings can be retrieved or set by separating and reading or writing the low-order and high-order words.

By specifying the device ID for the appropriate function argument, you can retrieve and set the volume of any sound device in your system using the `auxGetVolume` and `auxSetVolume` API functions.

The sample project SOUNDVOL.VBP on the CD-ROM that accompanies this book demonstrates the functionality of the presented code.

Chapter 12

ADVANCED WINDOWS PROGRAMMING

This chapter contains functions that use the Windows API to accomplish their functionality. This enables you to get a bit deeper into the operating system and do things like add icons to the taskbar, get the user or computer name, and even shut down and restart Windows itself. These functions are a sampling of the power of the Windows API, and will give you a good start in building your API library.

12.1 SHUT DOWN AND REBOOT WINDOWS

by Ian Ippolito

Description

When you install a program you usually must copy many files to the user's PC. Often one or more of these files will be in use by Windows and cannot be updated. To get around this problem, professional installation programs shut down Windows to free up the files and then reinstall them when Windows starts up again.

You can duplicate this professional feature with the following routine. This code can also be used to reboot the entire system and log the current user off the PC (in 32-bit systems).

Note

Note that this function will not actually shut down Windows in a 16-bit program until the program is compiled into an executable.

Syntax

```
ShutdownWindows Parameters
```

Part	*Description*
Parameters	Required. Specify the action to perform when rebooting the system. The following are the 16-bit choices:
	EW_REBOOTSYSTEM: Reboot the system
	EW_RESTARTWINDOWS: Restart Windows
	EW_EXITWINDOWS: Exit Windows
	The following are the 32-bit choices:
	EWX_LOGOFF: Log off the current user
	EWX_SHUTDOWN: Shut down Windows
	EWX_REBOOT: Reboot Windows
	EWX_FORCE: Force reboot

Code Listing

```
Option Explicit
#If Win16 Then
    Declare Function ExitWindows Lib "User" (ByVal dwReturnCode _
        As Long, ByVal uReserved As Integer) As Integer

        Global Const EW_REBOOTSYSTEM = &H43
        Global Const EW_RESTARTWINDOWS = &H42
        Global Const EW_EXITWINDOWS = 0
#Else
    Declare Function ExitWindowsEx Lib "user32" (ByVal uFlags As Long, _
        ByVal dwReserved As Long) As Boolean

        Public Const EWX_LOGOFF = 0
        Public Const EWX_SHUTDOWN = 1
        Public Const EWX_REBOOT = 2
        Public Const EWX_FORCE = 4

#End If


Sub ShutdownWindows(ByVal intParamater As Integer)

#If Win16 Then
```

```
    '16 bit
    Dim intRetVal As Integer
    intRetVal = ExitWindows(intParamater, 0)

#Else

    '32 bit
    Dim blnReturn As Boolean
    blnReturn = ExitWindowsEx(intParamater, 0)

#End If
End Sub
```

Analysis

Depending on whether the program is being run in a 16- or 32-bit environment, this routine calls the appropriate Windows API subroutine, passing in the parameters specified by the subroutine's user.

Due to a quirk in the 16-bit API, the 16-bit version of this routine cannot shut down Windows while in the Visual Basic design-time environment. Instead, the program will display the dialog box saying Can't Shut Down at This Time. This problem can be circumnavigated by creating the program as an executable (.EXE) and running it.

12.2 GET WINDOWS DIRECTORIES

by Ian Ippolito

Description

The Windows directory and the Windows system directory are two of the most important directories on a Windows PC. Most application help files, .DLLs, .OCXs, .VBXs, and .INI files are placed in one of these locations.

However, getting to these directories from your Visual Basic program is not easy. Although Windows defaults the names of these directories to c:\windows and c:\windows\system, respectively, users are free to change these directories to any location that suits their fancy. Others are forced to change the default locations because they are either running multiple operating systems on a single PC or are using a networked version of Windows.

To reliably access these directories without crashing, you could use the Windows API. However, Windows API development is fraught with complexity and danger—even experienced programmers can crash their entire system while developing new code. A quicker and more reliable way is to use a Visual Basic function wrapper that works reliably and hides all the complexity of the API call "behind the scenes." The following wrapper functions will save you hours of headaches and aggravation.

Syntax

```
Directory = Get_Windows_Directory()
Directory = Get_Windows_System_Directory()
```

Part	Description
Directory	Returns the name of the directory requested.

Code Listing

```
Option Explicit
#If Win16 Then
Declare Function GetSystemDirectory Lib "Kernel" (ByVal lpBuffer As String, _
    ByVal nSize As Integer) As Integer
Declare Function GetWindowsDirectory Lib "Kernel" (ByVal lpBuffer As String, _
    ByVal nSize As Integer) As Integer
#Else
Declare Function GetWindowsDirectory32 Lib "Kernel32" Alias _
    "GetWindowsDirectoryA" (ByVal lpBuffer As String, ByVal nSize As Long) _
    As Long
Declare Function GetSystemDirectory32 Lib "Kernel32" Alias _
    "GetSystemDirectoryA" (ByVal lpBuffer As String, ByVal nSize As Long) _
    As Long
#End If

Function Get_Windows_Directory() As String
    Dim strBuffer As String * 256
#If Win16 Then
    '16 bit code
    Dim intReturn As Integer
    intReturn = GetWindowsDirectory(strBuffer, Len(strBuffer))
    ' Trim Buffer and return string
    Get_Windows_Directory = Left$(strBuffer, intReturn)

    #Else

    '32 bit code
    Dim lngReturn As Integer
    lngReturn = GetWindowsDirectory32(strBuffer, Len(strBuffer))
    ' Trim Buffer and return string
    Get_Windows_Directory = Left$(strBuffer, lngReturn)
    #End If

End Function
```

```
Function Get_Windows_System_Directory() As String
    Dim strBuffer As String * 256

    #If Win16 Then
    '16 bit code
    Dim intReturn As Integer
    intReturn = GetSystemDirectory(strBuffer, Len(strBuffer))
    'trim C style String
    Get_Windows_System_Directory = Left$(strBuffer, intReturn)

    #Else

    '32 bit code
    Dim lngReturn As Long
    lngReturn = GetSystemDirectory32(strBuffer, Len(strBuffer))
    'trim C style String
    Get_Windows_System_Directory = Left$(strBuffer, lngReturn)

    #End If

End Function
```

Analysis

These routines use the Windows API function `GetWindowsDirectory` (16-bit), `GetWindowsDirectoryA` (32-bit), `GetSystemDirectory` (16-bit), and `GetSystemDirectoryA` (32-bit) to obtain the names of the appropriate directory. All four API functions are unusual in that they require a fixed-length string to operate. To provide this, the functions first create one using the `As String * 256` syntax, and then pass it into the API routines as the first parameter.

When the directory name information is actually returned by these API routines, it is formatted as a C language string rather than as a Visual Basic string. If viewed at this point in the debugger, the string appears to contain garbage characters to the right of it. To fix this problem, the routines then truncate those garbage characters from the string and return the result.

When placing any API declaration in a Visual Basic project, it is important to insert it into the general declarations section of a code module. Attempting to place one in a class module or a form will cause Visual Basic to generate a compilation error.

12.3 MAKING YOUR APPLICATION WINDOW TOP-MOST

by Ian Ippolito

Description

Have you ever noticed how the Visual Basic toolbar floats above all the other windows in the VB environment? Did you ever wonder how Microsoft does it and if you could duplicate the same effect in your own programs? Well now you can! Just use the following function and you can instantly float a window over every other window on the PC desktop.

> **Note**
>
> Note that if you use this function in either Windows 95 or Windows NT in a 16-bit version of Visual Basic, the window will be made top-most only over other 16-bit program windows, not over 32-bit programs.

Syntax

```
Make_Window_TopMost Form, On
```

Part	Description
Form	Required. The form to change.
On	Set to TRUE to make the form top-most in the system. Set to FALSE to turn a top-most form back into a normal form.

Code Listing

```
Option Explicit
#If Win16 Then
    Declare Sub SetWindowPos Lib "User" (ByVal hWnd As Integer, _
        ByVal hWndInsertAfter As Integer, ByVal X As Integer, _
        ByVal Y As Integer, ByVal cx As Integer, ByVal cy As Integer, _
        ByVal wFlags As Integer)

#Else
    Declare Function SetWindowPos Lib "user32" (ByVal _
        hWnd As Long, ByVal hWndInsertAfter As Long, ByVal X _
        As Long, ByVal Y As Long, ByVal cx As Long, ByVal cy _
        As Long, ByVal wFlags As Long) As Long

#End If

Global Const SWP_NOMOVE = 2
Global Const SWP_NOSIZE = 1
Global Const FLAGS = SWP_NOMOVE Or SWP_NOSIZE
Global Const HWND_TOPMOST = -1
Global Const HWND_NOTOPMOST = -2
```

```
Sub Make_Window_TopMost(ByRef rfrmForm As Form, _
    ByVal vboolOn As Boolean)


#If Win32 Then
Dim lngReturn As Long
#End If

If (vboolOn = True) Then
    'make window topmost
    #If Win16 Then

        '16 bit
        SetWindowPos rfrmForm.hWnd, HWND_TOPMOST, _
            0, 0, 0, 0, FLAGS
    #Else

        '32 bit
        lngReturn = SetWindowPos(rfrmForm.hWnd, HWND_TOPMOST, _
            0, 0, 0, 0, FLAGS)
    #End If

Else
    'turn off topmost effect
    #If Win16 Then

        '16 bit
        SetWindowPos rfrmForm.hWnd, HWND_NOTOPMOST, _
        0, 0, 0, 0, FLAGS
    #Else

        '32 bit
        lngReturn = SetWindowPos(rfrmForm.hWnd, HWND_NOTOPMOST, _
            0, 0, 0, 0, FLAGS)
    #End If
End If

End Sub
```

Analysis

This routine utilizes the Windows API `SetWindowPos` to either make the form top-most in the system or to reset it back to normal status.

The problem mentioned earlier that occurs when executing this routine on a form in a 16-bit version of Visual Basic while running in either Windows 95, 98, and Windows NT systems is caused by the split nature of these operating systems. Both operating systems have separate 16- and 32-bit subsystems that don't communicate directly with each other. As a result, making a 16-bit application's window top-most in such a system affects only other 16-bit applications.

12.4   GET A USER NAME

by Martin Cordova

Description

This function returns a string containing the NetLogon user ID of the current user in the PC. If the user ID is not defined (you are not logged on to the network), the function returns an empty string (" ").

Syntax

```
Dim UserName As String
UserName = SYSGetUserName()
```

Code Listing

```
'---insert this code in the declarations section of a module or class
Private Declare Function GetUserName Lib "advapi32.dll" Alias "GetUserNameA"
➥ (ByVal lpBuffer As String, nSize As Long) As Long

Public Function SysGetUserName() As String

    Dim UserName As String
    Dim BufSize As Long
    Dim RetCode As Long
    Dim NullCharPos As Long

    UserName = Space(80)
    BufSize = Len(UserName)

    '---call WINAPI
    RetCode = GetUserName(UserName, BufSize)

    '---search for the end of the string
    NullCharPos = InStr(UserName, Chr(0))
    If NullCharPos > 0 Then
        UserName = Left(UserName, NullCharPos - 1)
    Else
        UserName = ""
    End If

    SysGetUserName = UserName

End Function
```

Analysis

This function encapsulates the call to the WINAPI function `GetUserName` in order to simplify the use of this service and present it in a more natural way to the VB programmer, just as an internal VB function. As you can see, in order to call `GetUserName` you must add some string parsing code. This function does that work for you, converting this service into a normal VB function call.

12.5 GET A COMPUTER NAME

by Martin Cordova

Description

This function returns a string containing the name of the computer in the network. If the computer name is not defined, the function returns an empty string (`""`). This can happen if the computer is not configured to be part of a network.

Syntax

```
Dim ComputerName As String
ComputerName = SYSGetComputerName()
```

Code Listing

```
'---insert this code in the declarations section of a module or class
Private Declare Function GetComputerName Lib "kernel32" Alias
➥"GetComputerNameA" (ByVal lpBuffer As String, nSize As Long) As Long

Public Function SysGetComputerName() As String

    Dim Computer As String
    Dim BufSize As Long
    Dim RetCode As Long
    Dim NullCharPos As Long

    Computer = Space(80)
    BufSize = Len(Computer)

    '---call WINAPI
    RetCode = GetComputerName(Computer, BufSize)

    '---search for the end of the string
    NullCharPos = InStr(Computer, Chr(0))
    If NullCharPos > 0 Then
```

continues

```
        Computer = Left(Computer, NullCharPos - 1)
    Else
        Computer = ""
    End If

    SysGetComputerName = Computer

End Function
```

Analysis

This function encapsulates the call to the WINAPI function `GetComputerName` in order to simplify the use of this service and present it in a more natural way to the VB programmer, just as an internal VB function. As you can see, some null checking must be made before retrieving the string with the computer name. However, through this function the programmer is relieved from this tedious string management task and can execute the function with a one-line call.

12.6   RETRIEVING A DISK'S SERIAL NUMBER

by James Limm

Description

When a disk is formatted, the operating system saves a random 32-bit number onto the disk. It is very unlikely that two disks would have the same number, so the serial number can be used to stop software piracy. You can retrieve this number in Visual Basic by using this code example.

Syntax

```
SerialNumber = GetSerialNumber(drive)
```

Part	Description
drive	Required. The disk drive from which to retrieve the serial number in *x*:\ format.

Code Listing

```
'Declare the following in the declarations section of your code
Private Declare Function GetVolumeInformation Lib "kernel32.dll"
➥ Alias "GetVolumeInformationA" (ByVal lpRootPathName As String,
➥ ByVal lpVolumeNameBuffer As String, ByVal nVolumeNameSize As Integer,
➥ lpVolumeSerialNumber As Long, lpMaximumComponentLength As Long,
➥ lpFileSystemFlags As Long, ByVal lpFileSystemNameBuffer As String,
➥ ByVal nFileSystemNameSize As Long) As Long
```

```
'GetSerialNumber Procedure ñ Put this in the module or form where it is called.
Function GetSerialNumber(strDrive As String) As Long
    Dim SerialNum As Long
    Dim Res As Long
    Dim Temp1 As String
    Dim Temp2 As String
    'initialise the strings
    Temp1 = String$(255, Chr$(0))
    Temp2 = String$(255, Chr$(0))
    'call the API function
    Res = GetVolumeInformation(strDrive, Temp1, Len(Temp1), SerialNum, 0, 0,
    ➥ Temp2, Len(Temp2))
    GetSerialNumber = SerialNum
End Function
```

Analysis

This code example retrieves the serial number of the disk specified in the parameters section of the function. It retrieves the serial number by calling the API function `GetVolumeInformation`, which retrieves information about the specified drive. The serial number it returns is a 32-bit Long that can be easily incorporated into the program.

This code example could be incorporated into the registration system so that the same enabling code cannot be used in more than one computer. It could also form part of a security system that prevents a program from being moved from computer to computer by checking the serial number on which it is installed.

12.7 OPENING AND CLOSING THE CD-ROM

by James Limm

Description

This example demonstrates how to open and close the CD-ROM drawer from Visual Basic.

Syntax

```
Call CDControl(action)
```

Part	Description
action	Required. Either TRUE to open the CD-ROM or FALSE to close it.

Code Listing

```
'Declare the following in the declarations section of your code
Declare Function mciSendString Lib "winmm.dll" Alias "mciSendStringA"
➥ (ByVal lpstrCommand As String, ByVal lpstrReturnString As String,
➥ ByVal uReturnLength As Long, ByVal hwndCallback As Long) As Long

'CDControl Procedure ñ Place this code into the form of module where it is
➥ called.
Sub CDControl(action as Boolean)
If action Then
    'open the CDROM
    retvalue = mciSendString("set CDAudio door open", returnstring, 127, 0)
Else
    'close the CDROM
    retvalue = mciSendString("set CDAudio door closed", returnstring, 127, 0)
End If
End Sub
```

Analysis

This procedure receives either a TRUE or a FALSE value depending on whether the code is going to open or close the CD-ROM. If you wanted to open the CD-ROM, you would use the following code:

```
Call CDControl(True)
```

If you wanted to close the CD-ROM, you would use this code:

```
Call CDControl(False)
```

This code example is basically a wrapper for the mciSendString API function that forms a part of the Windows multimedia control DLL, winmm.dll. This API function accepts a string as a command. The command can be anything to do with the multimedia system, such as playing a sound file or, in this case, opening the CD-ROM.

This code example can be used in a CD Player program or even in an installation program to complement a Please Insert CD message box.

12.8 SWAP MOUSE BUTTONS

by James Limm

Description

This code example demonstrates how to swap the operation of the mouse buttons from Visual Basic. This function could be used by a left-handed computer user who wants to temporarily swap the mouse buttons.

The SwapMouseButton function is used in this code example and affects the mouse buttons on a global scale, not just on the program that called the function.

Syntax

```
Call SwapMouseButton(swap)
```

Part	Description
swap	Required. Either TRUE to reverse the operation of the mouse buttons or FALSE to restore them to normal.

Code Listing

```
'Declare the following in the declarations section of a module.
Declare Function SwapMouseButton Lib "user32" (ByVal bSwap As Long) As Long
```

Analysis

This function is very simple; it is a direct call into the Windows API. It accepts one parameter that instructs it to either reverse the operation of the mouse buttons or restore them, depending on whether the parameter is TRUE or FALSE.

The SwapMouseButton function is just one of several API functions that influence the mouse. Others include SetDoubleClickTime, which alters the time between clicks that causes Windows to see the action as a double-click. You can retrieve the double-click time by using the GetDoubleClickTime function. Also, you can use the GetSystemMetrics function to find the number of buttons the mouse has. Finally, you can make the mouse cursor invisible by using the ShowCursor function.

12.9   GET THE NUMBER OF MOUSE BUTTONS

by James Limm

Description

This code example demonstrates how to retrieve the number of buttons on the mouse. It can also be used to detect whether a mouse is installed on the system. This code example uses the GetSystemMetrics function, which retrieves information about the system depending on which constant is specified in the API call. A wide range of information can be retrieved using this function, including whether a mouse is present, whether the mouse buttons have been swapped, and even whether the computer is too slow to run Windows 95. For a list of the most useful constants, see the following table:

Constant	Value	GetSystemMetrics *Results*
SM_MOUSEPRESENT	19	TRUE if a mouse is present
SM_SLOWMACHINE	73	TRUE if the computer is too slow to run Windows properly
SM_SWAPBUTTON	23	TRUE if the mouse buttons have been swapped
SM_CLEANBOOT	67	The mode in which Windows is running: 0 = normal, 1 = safe, 2 = safe with network installed

In order to use these constants properly, they must be declared in the program in the form

```
Public Const SM_CLEANBOOT = 67
```

You can then use the constant SM_CLEANBOOT in the GetSystemMetrics function. GetSystemMetrics can be used to retrieve information. SetSystemMetrics can be used to set the information.

Syntax

```
mousebuttons = GetSystemMetrics(SM_CMOUSEBUTTONS)
```

Part	Description
SM_CMOUSEBUTTONS	This is a constant that instructs the GetSystemMetrics function to retrieve the number of mouse buttons.
mousebuttons	When the function is called, the number of mouse buttons present is loaded into this variable.

Code Listing

```
'Declare the following in the declarations section of a module
Declare Function GetSystemMetrics Lib "user32" Alias "GetSystemMetrics"
➥(ByVal nIndex As Long) As Long
Public Const SM_CMOUSEBUTTONS = 43
```

Analysis

This function is very simple; it is a direct call into the Windows API. The function used is GetSystemMetrics, which can be used to retrieve information about many aspects of the system. In this case, we are passing the constant SM_CMOUSEBUTTONS, which instructs the function to return the number of buttons on the mouse. If there is no mouse installed, it returns 0 for no mouse buttons. This code could be used in a game to automatically check to see whether a mouse is installed—simply call this function and check to see whether the result is 0.

12.10   HIDE AND SHOW THE WINDOWS 95 TASKBAR

by James Limm

Description

This code demonstrates how to hide and show the Windows 95 taskbar. The taskbar is used to navigate between running programs and also acts as a home for the Start button and system tray. The taskbar is also used to quickly navigate between running programs. Running programs have a button on the taskbar that you can click to bring the program to the front of all other windows.

This code could be used as part of a security system that enables the supervisor of a computer to hide the taskbar to prevent users from altering the system clock.

Syntax

```
Call ShowTaskbar(bShow)
```

Part	Description
bShow	Required. Either True to show the taskbar or False to hide it.

Code Listing

```
'Declare the following in the declarations section of a module
Declare Function SetWindowPos Lib "user32" (ByVal hwnd _
As Long, ByVal hWndInsertAfter As Long, ByVal x As Long, _
ByVal y As Long, ByVal cx As Long, ByVal cy As Long, ByVal _
wFlags As Long) As Long

Declare Function FindWindow Lib "user32" Alias _
"FindWindowA" (ByVal lpClassName As String, ByVal _
lpWindowName As String) As Long

Const SWP_HIDEWINDOW = &H80
Const SWP_SHOWWINDOW = &H40
'ShowTaskbar procedure
'Add the following code to a module
Public Sub ShowTaskbar(bShow As Boolean)
Dim Thwnd As Long
Thwnd = FindWindow("Shell_traywnd", "")
If bShow Then
    'show taskbar
    Call SetWindowPos(Thwnd, 0, 0, 0, 0, 0, SWP_SHOWWINDOW)
Else
```

continues

```
    'hide taskbar
    Call SetWindowPos(Thwnd, 0, 0, 0, 0, 0, SWP_HIDEWINDOW)
End If
End Sub
```

Analysis

The ShowTaskbar procedure utilizes two API functions. First, the FindWindow function is called with the class name of the taskbar, Shell_traywnd. The function returns a long number called the handle, which is used in the other API function to send commands directly to the taskbar. The function that actually shows and hides the taskbar is SetWindowPos. The ShowTaskbar procedure passes the taskbar handle and a constant specifying whether to hide or show the taskbar to the ShowWindowPos function. The constant is either SWP_HIDEWINDOW or SWP_SHOWWINDOW.

Note

Hiding the taskbar does not disable the Start menu. If Ctrl+Escape is pressed, the Start menu will still appear, albeit with a gap where the taskbar usually is. In order to prevent the Start menu from appearing you must disable Ctrl+Escape.

12.11   DISABLING CTRL+ALT+DELETE

by James Limm

Description

This code disables the system key sequences of Ctrl+Alt+Delete and Ctrl+Escape. Ctrl+Alt+Delete is used to bring up the close program dialog box, from which all programs can be closed. The Ctrl+Escape key sequence causes a dialog box to appear that enables the user to navigate between running applications.

In all good security systems, the user has the option to disable these key sequences. The system does this by convincing Windows that a screen saver is running. This code example demonstrates how this can be done.

Syntax

```
Call DisableCtrlAltDelete(bDisabled)
```

Part	Description
bDisabled	Required. This Boolean property instructs the function to either disable Ctrl+Alt+Delete if it is TRUE or enable if it is FALSE.

Code Listing

```
'Copy this code into the declarations section of a module.
Private Declare Function SystemParametersInfo Lib _
"user32" Alias "SystemParametersInfoA" (ByVal uAction _
As Long, ByVal uParam As Long, ByVal lpvParam As Any, _
ByVal fuWinIni As Long) As Long

'DisableCtrlAltDelete procedure
Sub DisableCtrlAltDelete(bDisabled As Boolean)
    Dim X As Long
    X = SystemParametersInfo(97, bDisabled, CStr(1), 0)
End Sub
```

Analysis

This procedure calls the API function `SystemParametersInfo` and tells Windows that a screen saver is running. In response, Windows disables the system keys of Ctrl+Alt+Delete and Ctrl+Escape.

This code could be used in a security system that enables the user to enter Windows only if a correct password is entered. Disabling the system keys here would prevent the user from simply shutting the security program down.

12.12 FIND OUT HOW LONG WINDOWS HAS BEEN RUNNING

by James Limm

Description

This code returns the number of milliseconds that Windows has been running since it was started. Windows contains an internal timer that precisely tracks the amount of time it has been running. The `GetTickCount` function gives the Visual Basic program an interface to this internal timer.

The internal timer is much more precise than the Visual Basic timer, so programs that rely on precise measurements should use the `GetTickCount` function.

This program could be used as a security program that allows a user to log in only for a certain amount of time.

Syntax

```
TimeRunning = GetTickCount
```

Part	Description
TimeRunning	The `GetTickCount` function returns the number of milliseconds that Windows has been running and loads this value into the `TimeRunning` variable.

Code Listing

```
'Copy this code into the declarations section of the project.
Declare Function GetTickCount& Lib "kernel32" ()
```

Analysis

After calling the GetTickCount function, the length of time that Windows has been running, in milliseconds, is loaded into the TimeRunning variable as a long number. This number can then be used to calculate the total time that Windows has been running in seconds, minutes, and hours. There are 1000 milliseconds in each second.

12.13   ADDING SHORTCUTS TO THE START MENU

by James Limm

Description

This code example demonstrates how to add shortcuts to the Windows Start menu. Shortcuts are small (under 400 bytes) files that are used to redirect the computer to another file. They are effectively pointers, and offer a convenient way to link to a program or file. Shortcuts are usually found on the Start menu and desktop, although they can be placed anywhere on the system. This code example demonstrates how you can add a shortcut to the Start menu by using a function stored in the Visual Basic setup kit DLL, included in the setup disks that are generated by the VB Application Setup Wizard.

Syntax

```
Call fCreateShellLink(strTarget, strCaption, strPath, strAruments)
```

Part	Description
strTarget	Where to put the shortcut in relation to the Start menu Programs folder. To place the shortcut in the folder Accessories -> Game, the target would be Accessories\Games. To put the shortcut on the desktop, the target would be ..\..\Desktop.
StrCaption	The text to use for the shortcut when listed in the Start menu.
StrPath	The full path to the program to which the shortcut will point.
StrArguments	The arguments for the programs.

Code Listing

```
'Declare the following in the declarations section of a module
Declare Function fCreateShellLink Lib "STKIT432.DLL" _
(ByVal lpstrFolderName as String, ByVal lpstrLinkName _
as String, ByVal lpstrLinkPath as String, ByVal _
lpstrLinkArgs as String) As Long
```

Analysis

It is good practice in any installation program to add shortcuts to the Start menu so that the user will be able to use the application without having to search the disk to find the EXE file. The `fCreateShellLink` function makes it easy to do this, as long as the DLL file that contains the function is present.

The DLL used is included in the Visual Basic Setup Kit, which is used by the Application Setup Wizard to generate installation programs for VB programs. Therefore, if you have generated a setup routine by using the Setup Wizard, the required DLL will be installed on the end user's computer.

12.14 DISABLE THE TASKBAR

by Kamal A. Mehdi

Description

Sometimes you might need to disable the Windows 95/98 or Windows NT taskbar to restrict others from accessing the system when your Visual Basic application is running; for example, when the system is used for demonstrations or is operating in a public information terminal (InfoKiosk). Assume that the system does not have a keyboard so that the user cannot access the Windows task manager to terminate the application or switch between tasks. Note that your application must be running maximized when the system includes a mouse so that the desktop cannot be accessed using the mouse.

The `DisableTaskBar` function presented here enables you to disable the Windows taskbar by making a call to the function and specifying `True` for the function argument. You can call the function again, specifying `False` for the argument, and the taskbar is reenabled. You can easily incorporate the `DisableTaskBar` function in your own applications by entering the code in this section, along with the API declarations, and inserting them into your application module (.BAS) so that the function can be accessed from any of your application forms.

Syntax

```
RetVal = DisableTaskBar (ActionVal)
```

Part	Description
RetVal	Required. A numeric variable that receives the value returned by the function. The function return values are described next. Data type: Integer.
ActionVal	Required. A Boolean expression that specifies the action to perform on the taskbar. The ActionVal settings are described next. Data type: Boolean.

The following values are returned by the DisableTaskBar function through the RetVal variable:

Value	Description
0	Returned if the taskbar was enabled and is set disabled. Also returned if the taskbar was already enabled and an attempt to enable it was made.
8	Returned if the taskbar was disabled and is set enabled. Also returned if an attempt to disable it was made while it is already disabled.

The following are the settings for the ActionVal function argument:

Setting	Description
True	The taskbar is set disabled.
False	The taskbar is set enabled.

Modules and Controls Required

This code demonstrates the use of the DisableTaskBar function. You will need the following modules and controls to build the sample project:

Module/Control	Description
Module1	A standard Visual Basic module (.BAS)
Form1	A standard non-MDI Visual Basic form (.FRM) with the Caption property set to Disable/Enable the Windows Task Bar
Command1	A command button with the Caption property set to Disable Task Bar
Command2	A command button with the Caption property set to Enable Task Bar

Follow these steps to draw controls:

1. Start a new standard EXE project. Form1 is created by default. Set the form's Caption property as shown earlier.
2. Draw Command1 and Command2 buttons anywhere on the form and set their Caption properties as shown earlier.

Code Listing

```
'Code in Module1

'API declarations
    Declare Function EnableWindow Lib "user32" (ByVal hwnd As Long,
    ➥ ByVal fEnable As Long) As Long

    Declare Function FindWindow Lib "user32" Alias "FindWindowA" (ByVal
    ➥ lpClassName As String, ByVal lpWindowName As String) As Long


Function DisableTaskBar(Disable As Boolean) As Long

    'Declare variables
    Dim RetVal As Long
    Dim hwnd As Long
    Dim ClassName As String

    'Specify the class name of the task bar window
    ClassName = "Shell_TrayWnd"

    'Get the handle of the task bar window
    hwnd = FindWindow("Shell_TrayWnd", "")

    Select Case Disable

        Case Is = True
        'Disable the task bar:
        RetVal = EnableWindow(hwnd, False)

        Case Is = False
        'Enable the task bar:
        RetVal = EnableWindow(hwnd, True)

    End Select

    DisableTaskBar = RetVal

End Function


'Code in Form1

Private Sub Command1_Click()

    Dim RetVal As Long

    'Disable the task bar
    '0 is returned if task bar was enabled and is disabled
```

continues

```
    '8 is returned if the task bar is already disabled
    RetVal = DisableTaskBar(True)


End Sub

Private Sub Command2_Click()

    Dim RetVal As Long

    'Enable the task bar
    '8 is returned if task bar was disabled and is disabled
    '0 is returned if the task bar is already enabled
    RetVal = DisableTaskBar(False)

End Sub
```

Enter the code into the appropriate form, module, or control events as indicated and run the project. Click the Disable Task Bar button to disable the taskbar. Now try to click the Start button or any of the minimized applications (if any) on the taskbar. You will see that the Start button and all applications that might exist on the taskbar will not respond. In addition, clicking the taskbar with the right mouse button has no effect. Now click the Enable Task Bar button on your form to reenable the taskbar.

Analysis

The `DisableTaskBar` function uses two Windows API functions to disable and enable the Windows taskbar. It first calls the `FindWindow` function specifying the `Shell_TrayWnd` as the class name for the taskbar window to get its window handle (`hWnd`). It then calls the `EnableWindow` function, specifying the taskbar window handle retrieved by the `FindWindow` function, and sets the enabled or disabled state of the taskbar according to the value passed by the `ActionVal` argument. If `ActionVal` is `True`, the taskbar is set disabled. If `ActionVal` is `False`, the taskbar is set enabled.

Note that when the taskbar is set disabled, it will still be visible but will not respond to the mouse clicks, mouse movement, or the keyboard. If the taskbar has its auto-hide property set and is currently hidden (beyond the screen edge), it will not appear if it is set disabled until it is enabled again.

You can easily modify the function code to enable or disable any other application window by passing the value of its window handle to the `EnableWindow` API function argument.

The sample project TASKBAR.VBP on the CD-ROM that accompanies this book demonstrates the utility of the `DisableTaskBar` function.

12.15   FIND CHILD FUNCTIONS

by Langdon Oliver

Description

The find child functions easily enable you to access the handles of child windows for Microsoft Windows. Three routines are included: `FindChildByTitle`, `FindChildByClass`, and `FindChildByClassN`. The routines are fairly simple but require minimal knowledge of how the Windows API works.

`FindChildByTitle` enables you to find controls, such as command buttons, check boxes, and MDI child windows, using the text displayed on them.

`FindChildByClass` enables you to find any control by obtaining the control's class name.

`FindChildByClassN` works pretty much the same as `FindChildByClass`, but includes a feature to find the second or third index. For example, if you have five buttons on one window and would like to find the fourth, the call would be something like

`FindChildByClassN(hWnd&, "ThunderCommand", 4).`

Syntax

```
HWnd_Long = FindChildByTitle(Parent&, Caption$)

HWnd_Long = FindChildByClass(Parent&, ClassName$)

HWnd_Long = FindChildByClassN(Parent&, ClassName$, Index%)
```

Part	*Description*
Parent	Required. The handle of the parent window under which you want to search.
Caption	Required. The caption of the control you want to find under `Parent&`.
ClassName	Required. The class name of the control you want to find under `Parent&`. You can obtain class names by using tools such as IvySpy or SpyWin, or by using the function `GetClassName()`.
Index	Required for `FindChildByClassN`. Specifies the index of the control, or how many controls you want to skip.

Code listing

```
Option Explicit

'needed for finding parent windows...
Declare Function FindWindow Lib "user32" Alias "FindWindowA"
➡(ByVal lpClassName As String, ByVal lpWindowName As String) As Long

'needed for find child by class...
Declare Function GetWindow Lib "user32" (ByVal hwnd As Long,
➡ByVal wCmd As Long) As Long
Declare Function GetClassName Lib "user32" Alias "GetClassNameA"
➡(ByVal hwnd As Long, ByVal lpClassName As String,
➡ByVal nMaxCount As Long) As Long
```

continues

```
Declare Function GetNextWindow Lib "user32" Alias "GetWindow"
➥(ByVal hwnd As Long, ByVal wFlag As Long) As Long

'needed for find child by title...
Declare Function GetWindowText Lib "user32" Alias "GetWindowTextA"
➥(ByVal hwnd As Long, ByVal lpString As String, ByVal cch As Long)
➥ As Long


Function FindChildByClass&(parent&, ByVal class$)
Dim temp$, class_$, child&, child_&temp$ = String(255, 0)
➥'null string used for class name sring
child& = GetWindow(parent&, 5) 'obtain first child window of parent
 Do 'begin loop
  class_$ = Left$(temp$, GetClassName(child&, temp$, 255)) 'get class name of
  ➥ current window(child&)
   If LCase(class$) = LCase(class_$) Then FindChildByClass& = child&:
   ➥ Exit Function 'quit if window class matches recently found window
    If GetWindow(child&, 5) <> 0 Then 'checks for children under children
      child_& = FindChildByClass(child&, class$) 'gets sub-child
       If child_& <> 0 Then FindChildByClass& = child_&: Exit Function
       ➥ 'invoke recursion
    End If
 child& = GetNextWindow(child&, 2) 'obtain the next handle
 Loop Until child& = 0 'continue looping
FindChildByClass& = 0 'if no children found match the class name, return 0
End Function


Function FindChildByTitle&(ByVal parent&, ByVal title$)
Dim temp$, title_$, child&, child_&
temp$ = String(255, 0) 'null string used for title or caption
child& = GetWindow(parent&, 5) 'obtain first child window of parent
 Do 'begin loop
  title_$ = Left$(temp$, GetWindowText(child&, temp$, 255)) 'get caption of
  ➥ current window(child&)
   If title_$ <> "" And LCase(title$ & "*") Like LCase(title_$ & "*")
   ➥ Then FindChildByTitle& = child&: Exit Function
   ➥ 'quit if window title matches recently found title
    If GetWindow(child&, 5) <> 0 Then 'checks for children under children
      child_& = FindChildByTitle(child&, title$) 'gets sub-child
       If child_& <> 0 Then FindChildByTitle = child_&: Exit Function
       ➥ 'invoke recursion
    End If
 child& = GetNextWindow(child&, 2) 'obtain the next handle
 Loop Until child& = 0 'continue looping
FindChildByTitle& = 0 'if no children found match the title, return 0
End Function

Function FindChildByClassN&(parent&, handle$, num%)
Dim num_%, child&, temp$, handle_$
num_% = 1 'set index to 1
```

```
temp$ = String$(255, 0)
child& = FindChildByClass(parent&, handle$) 'obtain first handle
Do
 child& = GetNextWindow(child&, 2) 'obtain handle for 2nd window
  handle_$ = Left$(temp, GetClassName(child&, temp$, 255)) 'grab the handle of
 ➥ the window found
  If LCase(handle$) = LCase(handle_$) Then num_% = num_% + 1 'if the indicated
 ➥ handle matches the recently found handle, then add 1 to the count
Loop Until num% = num_% Or child& = 0 'stop then the index counter is equal to
➥ the indicated number
FindChildByClassN& = child& 'return the handle
End Function
```

Analysis

The functions are incredibly easy to use and are pretty much self-explanatory, although you should have some knowledge of how Windows API works. These functions are essential if you plan to create an add-on for any particular program. Something to keep in mind when using these functions is the speed of Visual Basic. Although the code itself is probably optimized for speed under Visual Basic, the VB compiler still is not very fast.

12.16 GET A DRIVE DESCRIPTION

by Mike Shaffer

Description

The GetDriveDesc function returns a type of disk drive when passed the letter of that drive.

Syntax

GetDriveDesc(strDrive)

Part	Description
strDrive	Required. A string containing the drive letter to examine (use the form C:\).

Code Listing

```
'************************************************
'* Submitted by Mike Shaffer
'************************************************
Private Declare Function GetDriveType Lib "kernel32" Alias "GetDriveTypeA" _
(ByVal sDrive As String) As Long
```

```
'- Drive Type Constants...
Const DRIVE_CDROM = 5
Const DRIVE_FIXED = 3
Const DRIVE_RAMDISK = 6
Const DRIVE_REMOTE = 4
Const DRIVE_REMOVABLE = 2

Public Function GetDriveDesc(strDrive as string) As String

  Dim RC as long

  rc = GetDriveType(strDrive)                              ' Get Drive Type

  Select Case RC
    Case DRIVE_CDROM
        GetDriveDesc = "[CD Rom Drive]"
    Case DRIVE_FIXED
        GetDriveDesc = "[Fixed Drive]"
    Case DRIVE_REMOTE
        GetDriveDesc = "[Network Drive]"
    Case DRIVE_RAMDISK
        GetDriveDesc = "[Ram Disk Drive]"
    Case DRIVE_REMOVABLE
        GetDriveDesc = "[Removable Disk Drive]"
    Case Else
        GetDriveDesc = "[Unknown drive type or error]"
    End Select

End Function
```

Analysis

This function is useful for determining whether a drive is fixed or removable. It can also be used as a rudimentary security function if, for example, you want to be sure that the user is running from a CD or from a non-network drive. To perform this test, your program could simply pass the drive portion of the App.Path property to this routine, giving an error message if the drive is REMOTE or CDROM.

12.17   GET A PROCESSOR TYPE

by Mike Shaffer

Description

The `GetProcessorType` subroutine returns the CPU type and speed. Generally, the speed is not attainable through any API call, but Windows 98 and Windows NT both create a Registry entry under

`\HKEY_LOCAL_MACHINE\HARDWARE\DESCRIPTION\System\CentralProcessor\0\~MHz`

which should contain the speed in MHz of CPU 0.

Syntax

`GetProcessorType ProcType$, Speed&`

Part	Description
ProcType$	A string that will contain the CPU description
Speed&	A long value containing the approximate CPU speed in Mhz (if present in the Registry)

Code Listing

```
'**********************************************
'* Submitted by Mike Shaffer
'**********************************************
Private Declare Sub GetSystemInfo Lib "kernel32" (lpSystemInfo As SYSTEM_INFO)

'- System Information Structure
Private Type SYSTEM_INFO
    dwOemID As Long
    dwPageSize As Long
    lpMinimumApplicationAddress As Long
    lpMaximumApplicationAddress As Long
    dwActiveProcessorMask As Long
    dwNumberOfProcessors As Long
    dwProcessorType As Long
    dwAllocationGranularity As Long
    dwReserved As Long
End Type

'-------------------------------------------------------------
' Processor Type Constants...
'-------------------------------------------------------------
Const PROCESSOR_INTEL_386 = 386
Const PROCESSOR_INTEL_486 = 486
Const PROCESSOR_INTEL_PENTIUM = 586
Const PROCESSOR_INTEL_860 = 860
Const PROCESSOR_MIPS_R2000 = 2000
Const PROCESSOR_MIPS_R3000 = 3000
Const PROCESSOR_MIPS_R4000 = 4000
```

continues

```
Const PROCESSOR_ALPHA_21064 = 210462
Const processor_ppc_601 = 601
Const processor_ppc_602 = 602
Const processor_ppc_603 = 603
Const processor_ppc_604 = 604

Private Sub GetProcessorType(ProcessorType as String, Speed as Long)
    Dim SysInfo As SYSTEM_INFO
    Dim strTemp as String
    Call GetSystemInfo(SysInfo)                ' Get System Information


    Select Case SysInfo.dwProcessorType
        Case PROCESSOR_INTEL_386
            ProcessorType = "80386"
        Case PROCESSOR_INTEL_486 = 486
            ProcessorType = "80486"
        Case PROCESSOR_INTEL_PENTIUM
            ProcessorType = "Pentium"
        Case PROCESSOR_INTEL_860
            ProcessorType = "860"
        Case PROCESSOR_MIPS_R2000
            ProcessorType = "MIPS R2000"
        Case PROCESSOR_MIPS_R3000
            ProcessorType = "MIPS R3000"
        Case PROCESSOR_MIPS_R4000
            ProcessorType = "MIPS R4000"
        Case PROCESSOR_ALPHA_21064
            ProcessorType = "ALPHA 21064"
        Case processor_ppc_601
            ProcessorType = "PPC 601"
        Case processor_ppc_602
            ProcessorType = "PPC 602"
        Case processor_ppc_603
            ProcessorType = "PPC 603"
        Case processor_ppc_604
            ProcessorType = "PPC 604"
        Case Else
            ProcessorType = "Unknown Processor Type"
    End Select
    '
    strTemp = GetRegEntry("HKEY_LOCAL_MACHINE",
    ➥"HARDWARE\DESCRIPTION\System\CentralProcessor\0", "~MHz", lngType)
    If Len(strTemp) > 0 then
        For x% = 1 To 4
            Speed = Speed + (Asc(Mid$(strTemp, x%, 1)) * (256^(x%-1)))
        Next
    Else
        Speed = 0
    End If
    '
End Sub
```

Analysis

This function is useful for determining the type of CPU installed. It can be used to see whether the user has enough horsepower to run your application. Naturally, other factors determine the power of any machine. You might also want to check available RAM, as well as disk swap area. Notice that if the Registry entry for ~MHz does not exist (it might not on some machines because there does not seem to be any guarantee) the speed reported by this function will be 0.

Note that this routine references the GetRegEntry function, which is also included in this book.

12.18   USING THE WIZARD CONTROL

by Trent Clarke

Description

This section focuses on the development of a form and two modules that can be reutilized in existing or new projects in the form of a wizard control. A wizard control is used by many software products to allow novice or moderate computer users to navigate through an ordered sequence of steps. An advantage of the wizard control is in explaining features and options as they are presented. Instead of visiting an online help file or printed resource, the necessary information is immediately on hand.

Wizard controls can be negative in the sense that users familiar with the flow of a program can be slowed down by the requirement to skip through all intermediary steps before reaching the final action step. Try to offer the user an alternative path as well as a wizard option. By building applications with both wizard controls and fast-path solutions, your applications will subscribe to all levels of computer and application expertise.

The following are examples of where using a wizard-type control would be beneficial:

- Contact management software—The wizard control could be used to guide the user through the process of entering a contact name into a contact management database.
- Print options in a decision support system—Rather than using one busy form to let the user select the output options from a decision support tool, a wizard control can guide a user through the option selection process while identifying what the options mean.

Three primary steps can describe the following wizard control:

- Introduction—Informs the user about what they are expected to accomplish by responding to the upcoming steps.

■ Information entry—Enables programmers to present a series of informational queries to the user. This step can contain as little as one question to the user, or it can contain an unlimited number of questions.

■ Finish—This final step enables the user to accept the entries he has made and complete the wizard process or cancel and abort any action.

Syntax

When executed, the wizard control calls the `modStart.Main()` subroutine. This subroutine populates the wizard variables with all the information the wizard control requires for execution.

The following code is extracted from the `modWizard` module. It demonstrates several important uses of naming conventions, constants, and user-definable data types using the `Type` statement.

```
Public Const WIZMAXSTEPS = 10
Public Const WIZMAXINPUTS = 10

Type Wizard
  intSteps As Integer 'Total number of steps in the wizard
  strTitle As String
End Type

Type WizardEntry
  strCaption As String   'Caption string
  strDefaultText As String  'Default value
  strUserText As String 'What the user entered
End Type

Type WizardStep
  strTitle As String
  strSubTitle As String
  strMemo As String 'Body of text
  intEntries As Integer 'Calculated by the wizard
  Entry(WIZMAXINPUTS) As WizardEntry   'What to enter
End Type

Public wizWizard As Wizard
Public wizSteps(WIZMAXSTEPS) As WizardStep
```

Tip

Note that the `WizardStep` user-defined variable must be defined after the `WizardEntry` user-defined variable because it contains a reference to the `WizardEntry` type.

Upon completion of execution (the user terminates or finishes the wizard control), the `modWizard.wizFinish` subroutine is called.

Creating Your Own Wizards

Copy the modStart.wizSample procedure and paste it into a new subroutine. Name the procedure wizAddContact in the example of a contact management system. Now modify the values in the subroutine to match your application's data requirements.

Code Listing

```
Public Sub wizSample()
   'Sample procedure

   'Cut and paste this subroutine into a new subroutine to create
   'alternate wizards.

   Dim LF As String

   LF = vbLf   'Linefeed

   'Number of wizard steps in total (include Introduction and Finish)
   wizWizard.intSteps = 5
   'Title to appear on wizard form
   wizWizard.strTitle = "Sample Wizard"

   '*** 1 - Introduction
   'Subtitle on first wizard step
   wizSteps(1).strTitle = "Introduction"
   wizSteps(1).strSubTitle = "Overview of the wizard."
   'Instructions to user for first step
   wizSteps(1).strMemo = "This wizard will guide you through the ...."
➥ & LF & LF & "Click on the 'Next' button to continue."
   '*** 2 - Information Entry
   wizSteps(2).strTitle = "Wizard Sample"
   wizSteps(2).strSubTitle = "Selection of the title of the project
➥ (or whatever)...."
   wizSteps(2).strMemo = "Enter the name of the whatever you wish to
➥ create." & LF & LF & "This name will show up as the ...."
   'Prompt the user with a single text box with caption Name:
   wizSteps(2).Entry(0).strCaption = "Name:"
   wizSteps(2).Entry(0).strDefaultText = "Sample"
   wizSteps(3).strTitle = "Sample"
   wizSteps(3).strSubTitle = "Sample value or whatever."
   wizSteps(3).strMemo = "This is the memo field for this entry point."
   wizSteps(3).Entry(0).strCaption = "Total # of values:"
   wizSteps(3).Entry(0).strDefaultText = "0"
   wizSteps(4).strTitle = "Sample"
   wizSteps(4).strSubTitle = "Sample subtitle."
   wizSteps(4).strMemo = "Type in the names of the sample values to be
➥ included in this ..." & LF & LF & "Just leave the section
➥ names blank when you are done."
   'In this step, we will have 4 text box entries
```

continues

```
wizSteps(4).Entry(0).strCaption = "Title Section 1:"
wizSteps(4).Entry(0).strDefaultText = ""
wizSteps(4).Entry(1).strCaption = "Title Section 2:"
wizSteps(4).Entry(1).strDefaultText = ""
wizSteps(4).Entry(2).strCaption = "Title Section 3:"
wizSteps(4).Entry(2).strDefaultText = ""
wizSteps(4).Entry(3).strCaption = "Title Section 4:"
wizSteps(4).Entry(3).strDefaultText = ""
wizSteps(4).Entry(4).strCaption = "Title Section 5:"
wizSteps(4).Entry(4).strDefaultText = ""
'*** 3 - Finish
wizSteps(5).strTitle = "Finished"
wizSteps(5).strSubTitle = "The wizard is now complete."
wizSteps(5).strMemo = "The wizard is now complete.  You may press the
➡ previous button to change any values you have entered.  To
➡ cancel, click on the windows 'x' on the title bar."
➡ & LF & LF & "Note: You may proceed to the...."
End Sub
```

The next step is to modify the `modWizard.wizFinish` subroutine. Add your wizard title to the `Select Case` clause within the subroutine.

```
Public Sub wizFinish()
  'The user clicked on the Wizard Finish command button
  Select Case wizWizard.strTitle
    Case "Sample Wizard"
        'Name
        MsgBox "Name= " & wizSteps(2).Entry(0).strUserText
        'Number of entries
        MsgBox "Number of Entries = " & wizSteps(3).Entry(0).strUserText
    Case "" '<- Insert the title of your wizard here
        'Insert your action code here
    Case Else
        MsgBox "Unknown wizard control - " & wizWizard.strTitle
  End Select
End Sub
```

If you want to insert information into a database, you could write an `Insert` query based on the user input into your wizard control.

Analysis

Obviously, this is a simple example of how a wizard control can be implemented. The following are some additional features you might want to add:

- Add a routine to obtain the wizard variable values from a SQL database.
- Allow for more than just text box entry with the introduction of radio buttons and check boxes by adding a `strControl` to the `WizardStep` variable type definition.
- Add data validation capabilities by adding `intLength`, `strDataType` to the `WizardStep` variable type definition and coding the required validation routines.

Tip

Converting VB5/VB6 forms to VB4 does not always have to be a complete rebuild. By modifying the .FRM file with an ASCII text editor, edit the first line VERSION 5.00 or VERSION 6.00 by changing it to VERSION 4.00. Also, you will have to remove any OCX/ActiveX declarations in the first few lines of code.

12.19 THE PRINT PREVIEW CONTROL

by Paolo Bonzini

Description

This user control implements the detail of printing and print previewing. It is similar to a standard picture box. It has no Paint event and no AutoSize, AutoRedraw, and Picture properties; in addition, it has the methods and events in the Syntax part.

The print-previewing technique is based on an old KnowledgeBase article that used version 2 of Visual Basic. I managed to turn that code into a Visual Basic 5 user control, and implemented some details in a much better way than the original article did.

The user control has no PSet, Scale, Print, or Circle methods. They are replaced by SetPixel, SetScale, PrintText, and DrawCircle because PSet, Scale, Print, and Circle are reserved words. (Curiously, Line is not a reserved word and you can use it as a method name. Instead, the ActiveX control wizard signals Line as a reserved keyword.) The only important lack of functionality is for PrintText, which does not enable you to use commas and semicolons, like the standard Print method, to format text. DrawCircle and SetPixel do not let you use the Step keyword. Also, you must remember not to use parentheses. For example, you must use DrawCircle 20, 30, 50 instead of Circle (20, 30), 50.

Syntax

Methods

- DrawCircle—Same parameters as Circle, but without the parentheses around the coordinates.
- SetScale—Same parameters as Scale, but without the parentheses around the coordinates.
- SetPixel—Same parameters as PSet, but without the parentheses around the coordinates.
- Line and PaintPicture—Same parameters as in a PictureBox.
- TextWidth and TextHeight—Same parameters as in a PictureBox.

```
PrintText stringexpression
PrintDoc([FirstPage[, [LastPage] [, [Copies] [, [Collate] ] ] ])
```

Events

```
DrawPage(Page As Integer, Printing As Boolean)
EndPrinting(Canceled As Boolean)
StatusUpdate(CurrentPage As Integer, TotalPages As Integer,
➥TotalCurrentPage As Long, Cancel As Boolean)
```

Part	Description
stringexpression	Required. A string expression indicating the text to be printed.
FirstPage	Optional, defaults to 1. The first page to be printed.
LastPage	Optional, defaults to the value of the **Pages** property. The last page to be printed.
Copies	Optional, defaults to 1. The number of copies to be printed.
Collate	Optional, defaults to **True**. If **True**, collate copies (page 1, page 2, page 3; page 1, page 2, page 3); else print, for example, two copies of page 1, two copies of page 2, and two copies of page 3.
Page	The parameter of the **DrawPage** event specifying which page must be displayed.
Printing	The parameter of the **DrawPage** event specifying whether the things drawn in the event are directed to the screen or to the printer. Note that the methods you use are exactly the same, but you might want (for example) to draw lines to simulate ruled paper when **Printing** is **False**.
Canceled	The parameter of the **DrawPage** event specifying whether the document printing was terminated.
CurrentPage	The parameter of the **StatusUpdate** event specifying the ordinal number of the last page printed.
TotalPages	The parameter of the **StatusUpdate** event specifying the total number of pages that will be printed.
TotalCurrentPage	The parameter of the **StatusUpdate** event specifying the total number of pages that have already been sent to the print spooler.
Cancel	The parameter of the **StatusUpdate** event specifying whether the printing process must be killed immediately.

Properties

In addition to these three properties, this control has all the properties that you find in a standard Visual Basic picture box.

Property	Description
Page	An integer. The page being shown on the screen.
Pages	An integer. The number of pages in the document
Ratio	A single. The ratio of the paper width to the control's width.

Code Listing

```
VERSION 5.00
Begin VB.UserControl PrintPreview
   ClientHeight    =    3600
   ClientLeft      =    0
   ClientTop       =    0
   ClientWidth     =    4800
   ScaleHeight     =    3600
   ScaleWidth      =    4800
   Begin VB.PictureBox picDraw
      Appearance    =    0   'Flat
      BackColor     =    &H80000005&
      BorderStyle   =    0   'None
      ForeColor     =    &H80000008&
      Height        =    1812
      Left          =    600
      ScaleHeight   =    1815
      ScaleWidth    =    2055
      TabIndex      =    0
      Top           =    600
      Width         =    2052
   End
End
Attribute VB_Name = "PrintPreview"
Attribute VB_GlobalNameSpace = False
Attribute VB_Creatable = True
Attribute VB_PredeclaredId = False
Attribute VB_Exposed = True
Option Explicit

'-------------------------
'Submitted by Paolo Bonzini
'-------------------------

'Default Property Values:
Const m_def_Pages = 1
Const m_def_Page = 1

'Property Variables:
Dim m_ScaleMode As ScaleModeConstants
Dim m_Page As Integer
Dim m_Pages As Integer
Dim m_Ratio As Single

'Other Variables:
Dim m_Initialized As Boolean
Dim m_Target As Object
Dim m_PageWidth As Single
Dim m_PageHeight As Single

'User events:
Event Click()
```

continues

```
Event DblClick()
Event MouseDown(Button As Integer, Shift As Integer, _
    x As Single, Y As Single)
Event MouseMove(Button As Integer, Shift As Integer, _
    x As Single, Y As Single)
Event MouseUp(Button As Integer, Shift As Integer, _
    x As Single, Y As Single)
Event Resize()

'Printing events:
Event DrawPage(Page As Integer, Printing As Boolean)
Event EndPrinting(Canceled As Boolean)
Event StatusUpdate(CurrentPage As Integer, TotalPages As _
    Integer, TotalCurrentPage As Long, Cancel As Boolean)

Private Declare Function GetTextExtentPoint Lib "gdi32" _
    Alias "GetTextExtentPointA" (ByVal hdc As Long, _
    ByVal lpszString As String, ByVal cbString As Long, _
    lpSize As size) As Long
Private Declare Function SetTextJustification Lib "gdi32" _
    (ByVal hdc As Long, ByVal nBreakExtra As Long, _
    ByVal nBreakCount As Long) As Long

Private Type size
    x As Long
    Y As Long
End Type


Public Sub DrawCircle(x As Single, Y As Single, _
    Radius As Single, Optional Color As Long = -1, _
    Optional StartPos, Optional EndPos, _
    Optional Aspect As Single = 1)

    'Fail if they did not set the size of the page
    If Not m_Initialized Then Err.Raise 5

    'Set the color to a default value if it was not provided
    If Color = -1 Then Color = m_Target.ForeColor

    If IsMissing(StartPos) Then
        'raise argument not optional errors if endpos found
        'else draw a full circle
        If Not IsMissing(EndPos) Then Err.Raise 449
        m_Target.Circle (x, Y), Radius, Color, , , Aspect
    Else
        'raise argument not optional errors if endpos missing
        'else draw an arc or a pie.
        If IsMissing(EndPos) Then Err.Raise 449
        m_Target.Circle (x, Y), Radius, Color, _
            StartPos, EndPos, Aspect
```

```
        End If
End Sub

Public Sub Line(Flags As Integer, X1 As Single, Y1 As Single, _
    X2 As Single, Y2 As Single, Color As Long)

    'Fail if they did not set the size of the page
    If Not m_Initialized Then Err.Raise 5

    'Note that, for some strange reason, Visual Basic rejects
    ' m_Target.[Line] Flags, X1, Y1, X2, Y2, Color

    If m_Target Is picDraw Then
        picDraw.[Line] Flags, X1, Y1, X2, Y2, Color
    Else
        Printer.[Line] Flags, X1, Y1, X2, Y2, Color
    End If
End Sub

Public Sub PaintPicture(Picture As IPictureDisp, _
    X1 As Single, Y1 As Single, Optional Width1 As Variant, _
    Optional Height1 As Variant, Optional X2 As Variant, _
    Optional Y2 As Variant, Optional Width2 As Variant, _
    Optional Height2 As Variant, Optional Opcode As Variant)

    'Fail if they did not set the size of the page
    If Not m_Initialized Then Err.Raise 5

    picDraw.PaintPicture Picture, X1, Y1, Width1, Height1, _
        X2, Y2, Width2, Height2, Opcode
End Sub

Public Function Point(x As Single, Y As Single) As Long
    'Fail if they did not set the size of the page. Warning:
    'using this method is dangerous. Pairs of coordinates that
    'on screen refer to the same pixel might not do the same
    'on printer, and vice versa.
    If Not m_Initialized Then Err.Raise 5
    Point = picDraw.Point(x, Y)
End Function

Public Sub PrintDoc(Optional ByVal FirstPage As Integer = 1, _
    Optional ByVal LastPage As Integer, _
    Optional ByVal Copies As Integer = 1, _
    Optional ByVal Collate As Boolean = True)

Dim i As Integer, j As Long, Kill As Boolean

'Fail if they did not set the size of the page
If Not m_Initialized Then Err.Raise 5
With Printer
```

continues

```
'get the hdc for the printer. This is necessary for the
'values that we give to the properties to be retained.
'If we would not use this dummy Print statement, Visual
'Basic would discard any assignment to the Printer
'object's graphic properties.
Printer.Width = m_PageWidth
Printer.Height = m_PageHeight
Printer.Print ""
Kill = False

If LastPage = 0 Then LastPage = Pages

'The properties are transferred so that the DrawPage event
'can assume know that properties that are never changed by
'the program retain the same value that they had in design
'mode. The user must not make any assumption on the value
'of any other property, though
Printer.ScaleLeft = picDraw.ScaleLeft
Printer.ScaleTop = picDraw.ScaleTop
Printer.ScaleWidth = picDraw.ScaleWidth
Printer.ScaleHeight = picDraw.ScaleHeight
Printer.ScaleMode = m_ScaleMode
Printer.DrawMode = picDraw.DrawMode
Printer.DrawWidth = picDraw.DrawWidth
Printer.DrawStyle = picDraw.DrawStyle
Printer.FillColor = picDraw.FillColor
Printer.FillStyle = picDraw.FillStyle
Printer.ForeColor = picDraw.ForeColor
Printer.FontTransparent = picDraw.FontTransparent
Set m_Target = Printer

i = FirstPage
For j = 1 To (LastPage - FirstPage + 1) * Copies
    RaiseEvent StatusUpdate(i - FirstPage + 1, _
        LastPage - FirstPage + 1, (j), Kill)
    If Kill Then Exit For

    If j <> 1 Then .NewPage
    If Collate Then
        'We are collating copies. This means that we output
        'an entire copy of the document at a time. Notice
        'the parentheses around i, needed to pass the
        'parameter by value.
        RaiseEvent DrawPage((i), True)
        If i = LastPage Then i = FirstPage Else i = i + 1
    Else
        'We are not collating copies. This means that we output
        'many copies of the same page before switching to
        'the next. Again, notice the parentheses.
        RaiseEvent DrawPage((i), True)
        If (j Mod Copies) = 0 Then i = i + 1
    End If
```

```
        Next j
        RaiseEvent EndPrinting((Kill))

        Set m_Target = picDraw

        If Kill Then .KillDoc Else .EndDoc
    End With

End Sub

Public Sub PrintText(Text As String)
    'Fail if they did not set the size of the page
    If Not m_Initialized Then Err.Raise 5

    If m_Target Is Printer Then
        m_Target.Print Text
        Exit Sub
    End If

    With picDraw
        Dim OldSize As Single
        Dim szBig As size, szSmall As size
        Dim Posi As Long, nBreak As Long

        'The text width in pixel must be exactly
        'm_Ratio * szBig, where szBig is the space used
        'by the text when using the same font that will
        'be used when printing.
        'We use SetTextJustification to add the
        'correct number of extra pixels
        GetTextExtentPoint hdc, Text, Len(Text), szBig
        OldSize = .Font.size
        .Font.size = .Font.size * m_Ratio
        GetTextExtentPoint .hdc, Text, Len(Text), szSmall

        Posi = InStr(Text, " ")
        Do Until Posi = 0
            nBreak = nBreak + 1
            Posi = InStr(Posi + 1, Text, " ")
        Loop
        SetTextJustification .hdc, szBig.x * m_Ratio - szSmall.x, nBreak
        m_Target.Print Text;
        SetTextJustification .hdc, 0, 0
        .Font.size = OldSize
    End With

End Sub


Public Sub Refresh()
    picDraw.Refresh
End Sub
```

continues

```
Public Property Get ScaleMode() As ScaleModeConstants
    ScaleMode = m_ScaleMode
End Property

Public Property Let ScaleMode(ByVal _
    New_ScaleMode As ScaleModeConstants)

    m_ScaleMode = New_ScaleMode
    If Ambient.UserMode = False Or Not m_Initialized Then
        'Either we are in design mode, or they did not tell
        'us anything about the size of the page, so we are
        'not print previewing anything.
        m_Target.ScaleMode() = New_ScaleMode
    ElseIf m_Target Is Printer Then
        'We are speaking to the printer, and the printer is
        'already using the correct page size, so we just set
        'the Printer object's ScaleMode to the one they asked
        'for.
        m_Target.ScaleMode() = New_ScaleMode
    ElseIf New_ScaleMode = vbUser Then
        'In User mode, we just use the ScaleWidth/ScaleHeight
        'supplied by the control container.
        m_Target.ScaleMode() = New_ScaleMode
    Else
        picDraw.ScaleMode = New_ScaleMode
        picDraw.Scale (0, 0)-( _
            picDraw.ScaleX(m_PageWidth, vbTwips), _
            picDraw.ScaleY(m_PageHeight, vbTwips))
    End If

    PropertyChanged "ScaleMode"
    PropertyChanged "ScaleHeight"
    PropertyChanged "ScaleWidth"
    PropertyChanged "ScaleLeft"
    PropertyChanged "ScaleTop"
End Property

Public Sub SetPaperSize(PaperWidth As Single, _
    PaperHeight As Single, _
    Optional PaperScale As ScaleModeConstants = vbInches)

    ' Set the physical page size:
    m_PageWidth = UserControl.ScaleX(PaperWidth, PaperScale)
    m_PageHeight = UserControl.ScaleY(PaperHeight, PaperScale)

    m_Initialized = True
    ScaleMode = ScaleMode
    UserControl_Resize
End Sub
```

```
Public Sub SetPixel(x As Single, Y As Single, Optional Color As Long = -1)
    'Fail if they did not set the size of the page
    If Not m_Initialized Then Err.Raise 5

    If Color = -1 Then Color = picDraw.ForeColor
    picDraw.PSet (x, Y), Color
End Sub

Public Sub SetScale(Optional X1 As Variant, _
    Optional Y1 As Variant, Optional X2 As Variant, _
    Optional Y2 As Variant)

    If IsMissing(X1) Then
        If Not IsMissing(X2) Then Err.Raise 449
        If Not IsMissing(Y1) Then Err.Raise 449
        If Not IsMissing(Y2) Then Err.Raise 449
        ScaleMode = vbTwips
    Else
        If IsMissing(X2) Then Err.Raise 449
        If IsMissing(Y1) Then Err.Raise 449
        If IsMissing(Y2) Then Err.Raise 449
        m_Target.Scale (X1, Y1)-(X2, Y2)
        m_ScaleMode = vbUser
    End If
End Sub

Public Function TextHeight(str As String) As Single

If Not m_Initialized Then Err.Raise 5

Dim sz As size
GetTextExtentPoint hdc, str, Len(str), sz
TextHeight = ScaleY((sz.Y), vbPixels)
If m_Target Is picDraw Then TextHeight = TextHeight * m_Ratio

End Function

Public Function TextWidth(str As String) As Single

If Not m_Initialized Then Err.Raise 5

Dim sz As size
GetTextExtentPoint hdc, str, Len(str), sz
TextWidth = ScaleX((sz.x), vbPixels)
If m_Target Is picDraw Then TextWidth = TextWidth * m_Ratio

End Function

Private Sub picDraw_Paint()
    Dim OldTarget As Object
```

continues

```
        If Ambient.UserMode And m_Initialized Then
            Set OldTarget = m_Target
            Set m_Target = picDraw
            RaiseEvent DrawPage((m_Page), False)
            Set m_Target = OldTarget
        End If
End Sub

Private Sub UserControl_Resize()
    If m_Initialized Then
        m_Ratio = UserControl.ScaleHeight / m_PageHeight

        'Don't set width unless it is absolutely necessary
        If Abs((m_PageWidth * m_Ratio) - Width) > _
            Screen.TwipsPerPixelX Then

            Width = m_PageWidth * m_Ratio
        End If
    End If
    picDraw.Move UserControl.ScaleLeft, UserControl.ScaleTop, _
        UserControl.ScaleWidth, UserControl.ScaleHeight
    ScaleMode = ScaleMode
    picDraw.Refresh
    RaiseEvent Resize
End Sub

'Start of wizard-generated code

Public Property Get ForeColor() As OLE_COLOR
Attribute ForeColor.VB_ProcData.VB_Invoke_Property = ";Misc"
    ForeColor = m_Target.ForeColor
End Property

Public Property Let ForeColor(ByVal NewForeColor As OLE_COLOR)
    m_Target.ForeColor() = NewForeColor
    PropertyChanged "ForeColor"
End Property

Public Property Get Enabled() As Boolean
    Enabled = UserControl.Enabled
End Property

Public Property Let Enabled(ByVal New_Enabled As Boolean)
    UserControl.Enabled() = New_Enabled
    PropertyChanged "Enabled"
End Property

Public Property Get Font() As IFontDisp
Attribute Font.VB_ProcData.VB_Invoke_Property = ";Font"
Attribute Font.VB_UserMemId = -512
```

```
        Set Font = m_Target.Font
End Property

Public Property Set Font(ByVal New_Font As IFontDisp)
        Set m_Target.Font = New_Font
        PropertyChanged "Font"
End Property

Public Property Get CurrentY() As Single
Attribute CurrentY.VB_MemberFlags = "400"
        CurrentY = m_Target.CurrentY
End Property

Public Property Let CurrentY(ByVal New_CurrentY As Single)
        m_Target.CurrentY() = New_CurrentY
        PropertyChanged "CurrentY"
End Property

Public Property Get CurrentX() As Single
Attribute CurrentX.VB_MemberFlags = "400"
        CurrentX = m_Target.CurrentX
End Property

Public Property Let CurrentX(ByVal New_CurrentX As Single)
        m_Target.CurrentX() = New_CurrentX
        PropertyChanged "CurrentX"
End Property

Public Property Get FontUnderline() As Boolean
Attribute FontUnderline.VB_MemberFlags = "400"
        FontUnderline = m_Target.FontUnderline
End Property

Public Property Let FontUnderline( _
        ByVal New_FontUnderline As Boolean)
        m_Target.FontUnderline() = New_FontUnderline
        PropertyChanged "FontUnderline"
End Property

Public Property Get FontTransparent() As Boolean
        FontTransparent = m_Target.FontTransparent
End Property

Public Property Let FontTransparent( _
        ByVal New_FontTransparent As Boolean)
        m_Target.FontTransparent() = New_FontTransparent
        PropertyChanged "FontTransparent"
End Property

Public Property Get FontStrikethru() As Boolean
Attribute FontStrikethru.VB_MemberFlags = "400"
```

continues

```
        FontStrikethru = m_Target.FontStrikethru
End Property

Public Property Let FontStrikethru(ByVal New_FontStrikethru As Boolean)
        m_Target.FontStrikethru() = New_FontStrikethru
        PropertyChanged "FontStrikethru"
End Property

Public Property Get FontSize() As Single
Attribute FontSize.VB_MemberFlags = "400"
        FontSize = m_Target.FontSize
End Property

Public Property Let FontSize(ByVal New_FontSize As Single)
        m_Target.FontSize() = New_FontSize
        PropertyChanged "FontSize"
End Property

Public Property Get FontName() As String
Attribute FontName.VB_MemberFlags = "400"
        FontName = m_Target.FontName
End Property

Public Property Let FontName(ByVal New_FontName As String)
        m_Target.FontName() = New_FontName
        PropertyChanged "FontName"
End Property


Public Property Get FontItalic() As Boolean
Attribute FontItalic.VB_MemberFlags = "400"
        FontItalic = m_Target.FontItalic
End Property

Public Property Let FontItalic(ByVal New_FontItalic As Boolean)
        m_Target.FontItalic() = New_FontItalic
        PropertyChanged "FontItalic"
End Property


Public Property Get FontBold() As Boolean
Attribute FontBold.VB_MemberFlags = "400"
        FontBold = m_Target.FontBold
End Property

Public Property Let FontBold(ByVal New_FontBold As Boolean)
        m_Target.FontBold() = New_FontBold
        PropertyChanged "FontBold"
End Property


Public Property Get FillStyle() As FillStyleConstants
Attribute FillStyle.VB_ProcData.VB_Invoke_Property = ";Misc"
```

```
        FillStyle = m_Target.FillStyle
End Property

Public Property Let FillStyle(ByVal New_FillStyle As FillStyleConstants)
        m_Target.FillStyle() = New_FillStyle
        PropertyChanged "FillStyle"
End Property


Public Property Get FillColor() As OLE_COLOR
Attribute FillColor.VB_ProcData.VB_Invoke_Property = ";Misc"
        FillColor = m_Target.FillColor
End Property

Public Property Let FillColor(ByVal NewFillColor As OLE_COLOR)
        m_Target.FillColor() = NewFillColor
        PropertyChanged "FillColor"
End Property


Public Property Get DrawWidth() As Integer
Attribute DrawWidth.VB_ProcData.VB_Invoke_Property = ";Misc"
        DrawWidth = m_Target.DrawWidth
End Property

Public Property Let DrawWidth(ByVal New_DrawWidth As Integer)
        m_Target.DrawWidth() = New_DrawWidth
        PropertyChanged "DrawWidth"
End Property

Public Property Get DrawStyle() As DrawStyleConstants
Attribute DrawStyle.VB_ProcData.VB_Invoke_Property = ";Misc"
        DrawStyle = m_Target.DrawStyle
End Property

Public Property Let DrawStyle(ByVal New_DrawStyle As DrawStyleConstants)
        m_Target.DrawStyle() = New_DrawStyle
        PropertyChanged "DrawStyle"
End Property

Public Property Get DrawMode() As DrawModeConstants
Attribute DrawMode.VB_ProcData.VB_Invoke_Property = ";Misc"
        DrawMode = m_Target.DrawMode
End Property

Public Property Let DrawMode(ByVal New_DrawMode As DrawModeConstants)
        m_Target.DrawMode() = New_DrawMode
        PropertyChanged "DrawMode"
End Property

Public Property Get hdc() As Long
Attribute hdc.VB_MemberFlags = "400"
```

continues

```
        hdc = m_Target.hdc
End Property

Public Property Get hwnd() As Long
Attribute hwnd.VB_MemberFlags = "400"
    hwnd = UserControl.hwnd()
End Property


Public Property Get MouseIcon() As Picture
    Set MouseIcon = UserControl.MouseIcon
End Property

Public Property Set MouseIcon(ByVal New_MouseIcon As Picture)
    Set UserControl.MouseIcon = New_MouseIcon
    PropertyChanged "MouseIcon"
End Property

Public Property Get MousePointer() As MousePointerConstants
    MousePointer = UserControl.MousePointer
End Property

Public Property Let MousePointer( _
    ByVal New_MousePointer As MousePointerConstants)
    UserControl.MousePointer() = New_MousePointer
    PropertyChanged "MousePointer"
End Property

Public Function ScaleY(Height As Single, _
    Optional FromScale As Variant, _
    Optional ToScale As Variant) As Single
    If Not m_Initialized Then Err.Raise 5
    If IsMissing(FromScale) Then FromScale = m_Target.ScaleMode
    If IsMissing(ToScale) Then ToScale = m_Target.ScaleMode
    ScaleY = m_Target.ScaleY(Height, FromScale, ToScale)
End Function


Public Function ScaleX(Width As Single, _
    Optional FromScale As Variant, _
    Optional ToScale As Variant) As Single
    If Not m_Initialized Then Err.Raise 5
    If IsMissing(FromScale) Then FromScale = m_Target.ScaleMode
    If IsMissing(ToScale) Then ToScale = m_Target.ScaleMode
    ScaleX = m_Target.ScaleX(Width, FromScale, ToScale)
End Function


Public Property Get ScaleWidth() As Single
Attribute ScaleWidth.VB_ProcData.VB_Invoke_Property = ";Scale"
```

```
        ScaleWidth = m_Target.ScaleWidth
End Property

Public Property Let ScaleWidth(ByVal New_ScaleWidth As Single)
        m_Target.ScaleWidth() = New_ScaleWidth
        m_ScaleMode = vbUser
        PropertyChanged "ScaleWidth"
        PropertyChanged "ScaleMode"
End Property


Public Property Get ScaleTop() As Single
Attribute ScaleTop.VB_ProcData.VB_Invoke_Property = ";Scale"
        ScaleTop = m_Target.ScaleTop
End Property

Public Property Let ScaleTop(ByVal New_ScaleTop As Single)
        m_Target.ScaleTop() = New_ScaleTop
        m_ScaleMode = vbUser
        PropertyChanged "ScaleTop"
        PropertyChanged "ScaleMode"
End Property

Public Property Get ScaleLeft() As Single
Attribute ScaleLeft.VB_ProcData.VB_Invoke_Property = ";Scale"
        ScaleLeft = m_Target.ScaleLeft
End Property

Public Property Let ScaleLeft(ByVal New_ScaleLeft As Single)
        m_Target.ScaleLeft() = New_ScaleLeft
        m_ScaleMode = vbUser
        PropertyChanged "ScaleLeft"
        PropertyChanged "ScaleMode"
End Property


Public Property Get ScaleHeight() As Single
Attribute ScaleHeight.VB_ProcData.VB_Invoke_Property = ";Scale"
        ScaleHeight = m_Target.ScaleHeight
End Property

Public Property Let ScaleHeight(ByVal New_ScaleHeight As Single)
        m_Target.ScaleHeight() = New_ScaleHeight
        m_ScaleMode = vbUser
        PropertyChanged "ScaleHeight"
        PropertyChanged "ScaleMode"
End Property

Public Property Get Page() As Integer
Attribute Page.VB_MemberFlags = "400"
```

continues

```
        Page = m_Page
End Property

Public Property Let Page(ByVal New_Page As Integer)
        m_Page = New_Page
        PropertyChanged "Page"
        If Ambient.UserMode Then Refresh
End Property

Public Property Get Pages() As Integer
Attribute Pages.VB_MemberFlags = "400"
        Pages = m_Pages
End Property

Public Property Let Pages(ByVal New_Pages As Integer)
        m_Pages = New_Pages
        PropertyChanged "Pages"
End Property

Public Property Get Ratio() As Single
Attribute Ratio.VB_MemberFlags = "400"
        If Not m_Initialized Then Err.Raise 5
        Ratio = m_Ratio
End Property

Private Sub picDraw_Click()
        RaiseEvent Click
End Sub

Private Sub picDraw_DblClick()
        RaiseEvent DblClick
End Sub

Private Sub picDraw_MouseDown(Button As Integer, _
        Shift As Integer, x As Single, Y As Single)
        RaiseEvent MouseDown(Button, Shift, x, Y)
End Sub

Private Sub picDraw_MouseMove(Button As Integer, _
        Shift As Integer, x As Single, Y As Single)
        RaiseEvent MouseMove(Button, Shift, x, Y)
End Sub

Private Sub picDraw_MouseUp(Button As Integer, _
        Shift As Integer, x As Single, Y As Single)
        RaiseEvent MouseUp(Button, Shift, x, Y)
End Sub

Private Sub UserControl_Initialize()
        Set m_Target = picDraw
```

```
    m_Page = m_def_Page
End Sub

'Initialize Properties for User Control
Private Sub UserControl_InitProperties()
    Set Font = Ambient.Font
    Pages = m_def_Pages
End Sub

'Load property values from storage
Private Sub UserControl_ReadProperties(PropBag As PropertyBag)
    On Error Resume Next

With PropBag
    MousePointer =.ReadProperty("MousePointer", 0)
    Set MouseIcon =.ReadProperty("MouseIcon", Nothing)
    ForeColor = .ReadProperty("ForeColor", &H80000012)
    Enabled = .ReadProperty("Enabled", True)
    Font = .ReadProperty("Font", Ambient.Font)
    FillStyle = .ReadProperty("FillStyle", 1)
    FillColor = .ReadProperty("FillColor", &H0&)
    DrawWidth = .ReadProperty("DrawWidth", 1)
    DrawStyle = .ReadProperty("DrawStyle", 0)
    DrawMode = .ReadProperty("DrawMode", 13)
    Pages = .ReadProperty("Pages", m_def_Pages)
    ScaleWidth = .ReadProperty("ScaleWidth", 4800)
    ScaleTop = .ReadProperty("ScaleTop", 0)
    ScaleLeft = .ReadProperty("ScaleLeft", 0)
    ScaleHeight = .ReadProperty("ScaleHeight", 3600)
    ScaleMode = .ReadProperty("ScaleMode", 1)
End With

End Sub

'Write property values to storage
Private Sub UserControl_WriteProperties(PropBag As PropertyBag)

With PropBag
    .WriteProperty "ForeColor", ForeColor, &H80000012
    .WriteProperty "Enabled", Enabled, True
    .WriteProperty "Font", Font, Ambient.Font
    .WriteProperty "FillStyle", FillStyle, 1
    .WriteProperty "FillColor", FillColor, &H0&
    .WriteProperty "Pages", Pages, m_def_Pages
    .WriteProperty "DrawWidth", DrawWidth, 1
    .WriteProperty "DrawStyle", DrawStyle, 0
    .WriteProperty "DrawMode", DrawMode, 13
    .WriteProperty "ScaleWidth", ScaleWidth, Null
    .WriteProperty "ScaleTop", ScaleTop, 0
    .WriteProperty "ScaleLeft", ScaleLeft, 0
```

continues

```
      .WriteProperty "ScaleHeight", ScaleHeight, Null
      .WriteProperty "ScaleMode", ScaleMode, 1
      .WriteProperty "MousePointer", MousePointer, 0
      .WriteProperty "MouseIcon", MouseIcon, Nothing
End With
```

Analysis

As you can see, most of the code for this control is boring wizard-generated code. This code is necessary to make the control's properties persistent (so that they don't lose their values when the form is closed and that, at runtime, they retain the values you set at design time) and to add to the control the properties and events that are simply delegated to one of the control's components.

For properties that are not simply delegated (for example, this control's `ScaleMode` property), you can use the wizard to write the persistency code and to write stubs that map the property to a private variable in the user control. All the other code, however, must be written manually.

One important thing about the wizard is that you must use it after you lay down in the designer window the components that make up your control (in this case, the `picDraw` picture box) and before you start writing your code. If you have already written some code for the properties or for the methods, the wizard will comment it and replace it with the stubs that it generates.

In conclusion, the wizard is indeed a useful tool when you use it to generate boring code, and using it for this is really easy. But don't expect it to do much more.

The rest of this analysis concentrates on the properties and methods that were not wizard-generated. These include the following:

- `DrawCircle`
- `TextHeight, TextWidth, PrintText`
- `ScaleMode, ScaleLeft, ScaleTop, ScaleWidth, ScaleHeight`
- `PrintDoc, picDraw_Paint`
- `UserControl_Resize, SetPaperSize`

What's important to note about `DrawCircle`'s implementation is that `Circle` does not support optional parameters. Not only can't you pass a `Missing` variant to accept the default aspect ratio of 1, you cannot even pass two `Missing` variants if you want to draw a circle (instead of an arc or wedge). So you must split the different cases for the `StartAngle` and `EndAngle` parameters. Passing just one parameter yields an error, while the cases for no parameters and both parameters use two different `Circle` statements. Note that `Scale` supports optional parameters, but the way `ScaleMode` is used here (see later in this analysis) forced me to split the code for `SetScale` in two different cases too.

The `TextHeight`, `TextWidth`, and `PrintText` functions are different than the original KnowledgeBase code, and they are the only functions that employ different algorithms when printing and when previewing. The original code only set a reduced font size (multiplying the normal font size by `Ratio`) before printing on the screen. This leads to approximation errors because it is generally not true that a font size that is x

times smaller than another will produce characters that are *x* times narrower. This problem is easy to solve for `TextHeight` and `TextWidth` because you simply multiply by `Ratio` the text height or width of the full-size text. Printing the text in the correct size (as required in `PrintText`), however, is a bit harder.

The algorithm employed here relies on the `SetTextJustification` API function. This function is intended to be used to produce justified text because it expands blank characters in the next call to a text printing function (including the `Print` method). Instead, it is used here to ensure that the printed text is exactly as wide as wanted; that is, that its width is really equal to the width of the text as printed on the printer, multiplied by `Ratio`.

First, call `GetTextExtentPoint` for the big font and save its result in `szBig`. Then multiply the font size by `Ratio` to set it to the size that will be used when drawing the text, and save in `szSmall` the new text width. The number of pixels to add, then, is given by (`szBig.x * Ratio – szSmall.x`). After tallying the blanks in the string, as needed by `SetTextJustification`, you can call `SetTextJustification`, print the text, and restore the old font size.

Tip

You might obtain a visually better result by using `SetTextCharacterExtra` together with `SetTextJustification`. When printing the text, Windows would add a few pixels between every character of the string, but still add more space between words to obtain text of exact size.

There are two important points about the `ScaleXXX` properties. One applies to every control exposing these properties; that is, the fact that you must call `PropertyChanged` for all the other scaling properties. The other is exclusive to the print-preview control because this property constitutes, so to speak, the heart of the print-previewing control.

No matter what `ScaleMode` you use, the picture box on which the user control draws its output is always in User mode. This is necessary because the `ScaleWidth` and `ScaleHeight` of the picture box are not equivalent to the control's width, but rather to the paper width. For example, if you set `ScaleMode` to `vbInches` for US letter paper size, `ScaleWidth` will be 8.5 and `ScaleHeight` will be 11, no matter the actual screen size of the picture box.

Because the `ScaleMode` of the picture box is always `vbUser`, it should be apparent that you must store the value of the `ScaleMode` property in a variable. This variable must be updated (setting it to `vbUser`) whenever the `ScaleLeft`, `ScaleTop`, `ScaleWidth`, and `ScaleHeight` properties are changed—or whenever `SetScale` is called—to reflect the behavior of a standard picture box.

`SetPaperSize` is used to set the paper size—which influences how the scaling mode for the picture box is set—and the ratio of the `UserControl`'s width to the `UserControl`'s height. This is because the only size property that you can change in a `PrintPreview` control is `Height`; setting the `Width` has no effect. Visual Basic enables you to do so, but the `UserControl_Resize` procedure will subvert your intention because it changes the `Width` property again to keep the width/height ratio constant. This behavior might cause a lot of flicker; to avoid it, hide the control before moving and sizing it, and show it again only after you changed the position of the control.

Note the `ScaleMode = ScaleMode` statements in `UserControl_Resize`. They are needed because when you change the size of a picture box its scale properties change, even if the `ScaleMode` is set to `vbUser`. If you double the size of a picture box, `ScaleWidth` and `ScaleHeight` will double and `ScaleTop` and `ScaleLeft` will remain the same. This funny behavior has a reason: You can ask the program to redraw only the newly visible part of a `PictureBox` without making the previous output refer to another coordinate system.

However, because you want the `ScaleWidth` and `ScaleHeight` properties to remain constant (Visual Basic, instead, will try to keep the size of a unit constant) you must do it manually, with that strange statement `ScaleMode = ScaleMode`. Note that you must refresh the whole control because your actions change the coordinate system.

The `Resize` event procedure fires a `Resize` event too. This event is intended, for example, to keep the control centered horizontally in a window.

Now look at `picDraw_Paint` and `PrintDoc`, where the real printing and previewing happens. Both of them raise the `DrawPage` event, so they effectively use the same code to draw the pages; that is, the code supplied for the event procedure). This is what makes this approach to preview so convenient. When printing, `StatusUpdate` events are raised too. This can be used to show a progress window that might also allow the user to cancel the print job before it is completely spooled.

Note the long sequence of property assignments in `PrintDoc`: it is needed to allow the program to use the defaults set in design mode when printing too. For example, you might want to always use a solid `FillStyle` while the default is transparent. For a `PictureBox`, you set `FillStyle` to solid in design mode. To achieve the same result when printing, you must somewhere set the `Printer` object's `FillStyle` to solid because this property's default value is, again, transparent. The best place to do so is before starting to print.

To add to this approach the zooming capabilities of standard Windows print preview, there is no need to change the (already complex) code for the control. Instead, you should place the zooming code in the form, using the control together with two scrollbars that implement a scrollable viewport (search the KnowledgeBase or MSDN for more information on scrollable viewports).

Chapter 13

NET API FUNCTIONS

This chapter on API functions concentrates on Windows NT functionality. These functions are designed to enable you to accomplish some of the Windows NT administration tasks through VB code. Presented here are several functions that enable you to do user and group management, and to discover information about users, groups, and the general environment.

Note ───

These functions are built to operate in a Windows NT networked environment. You must have access to a Windows NT primary domain controller, at a minimum, to be able to use these functions. Each function contains information about the level of access required to operate the function.

13.1 SUPPORTING FUNCTIONS

by Brian Shea

Description

The supporting functions section was written to provide more explanation about the functions, data types, and header information used by the NetAPI functions during their execution. These areas are necessary for the correct operation of the NetAPI, and serve to give insight into the overall operation of the API in the Windows NT environment.

Although I have tried to include all the areas that are relevant to the NetAPI functions presented in this book, several areas are not covered. You can find more information about these functions, data types, or variables in Microsoft Developer's Network, TechNet, and the Win32 SDK.

The header information listed is mainly variable definitions for the values referred to by the data types and functions. This data is listed as hexadecimal values, but they represent bit masks that can be set on the user account to alter a given property. The exception to this is the `Other Constant Declarations` and `ParmError Number Definitions`, which are covered in a moment.

An example of this is the `Server Type Definitions` used by `EnumerateServers` to determine which servers to retrieve. Each value can be combined with the other values to form custom bit masks, and these masks will determine the results of that function run. If I wanted to get a list of all domain controllers, I would select the values `SV_TYPE_DOMAIN_BAKCTRL` (for backup domain controllers) and add it to the `SV_TYPE_DOMAIN_CTRL` (domain controllers) value. This gives the hex value of &H18, which is 11000 in binary. This is how the function knows to return the information asked for, and each value or combination of values can still be unique. Many values must be `OR`ed with the other values, and others cannot be combined. The specific function will have the information on the exact methods that you should use for each one.

The `Other Constant Declarations` section is used to present the variables that didn't fit anywhere else easily. Most of these values are not bit mask values.

The `ParmError Number Definitions` section shows the number assigned to each parameter that can be passed to the NetAPI functions. This is used in conjunction with the functions that use the `lgParmError` parameter, and can be used to determine the first parameter that caused an error in the function call that didn't succeed.

Next let's look at the supporting functions themselves. The discussion of the functions and data types can be found in the "Analysis" section.

NetAPIBufferAllocate Syntax

```
lgResult = NetAPIBufferAllocate(lgByteCount, lgPointer)
```

Part	Description
lgResult	Required. The return value for this function.
lgByteCount	Required. The long integer value for the number of bytes of memory to allocate.
lgPointer	Required. The pointer to the location in memory in which the pointer to the allocated buffer is stored.

NetAPIBufferFree Syntax

```
lgResult = NetAPIBufferFree(lgPointer)
```

Part	Description
lgResult	Required. The return value for this function.
lgPointer	Required. The pointer to the buffer to be freed.

PtrToStr Syntax

```
lgResult = PtrToStr(btByteArray, lgPointer)
```

Part	Description
lgResult	Required. The return value for this function.
btByteArray	Required. The byte array that receives the string data. The byte array should be referenced at the first (0) element.
lgPointer	Required. The pointer to the location in memory where the string is stored.

Ptr2Str Syntax

```
stStringVal = Ptr2Str(lgPtrVal)
```

Part	Description
stStringVal	Required. The returned string value.
lgPtrVal	Required. The pointer to the string that you want to get.

StrToPtr Syntax

```
lgResult = StrToPtr(lgPointer, btByteArray)
```

Part	Description
lgResult	Required. The return value for this function.
lgPointer	Required. The long integer value for newly created pointer.
btByteArray	Required. The byte array that supplies the string data. The byte array should be referenced at the first (0) element.

Str2Ptr Syntax

```
lgPtrVal = Str2Ptr(stStringVal)
```

Part	Description
lgPtrVal	Required. The returned pointer to the string value.
stStringVal	Required. The string you need to get a pointer to.

PtrToInt Syntax

```
lgResult = PtrToInt(inInteger, lgPointer, lgCharCount)
```

Part	Description
lgResult	Required. The return value for this function.
inInteger	Required. The integer value that will receive the pointer's data.
lgPointer	Required. The pointer to the buffer that you want to dereference.
lgCharCount	Required. The maximum number of characters to return, including the terminating NULL.

StrLen Syntax

```
lgResult = StrLen(lgPointer)
```

Part	Description
lgResult	Required. The return value for this function, which contains the number of characters in the string.
lgPointer	Required. The pointer to the string data that you want to get the length of.

CopyMemory Syntax

```
CopyMemory(anDestination, lgSource, lgSize)
```

Part	Description
anDestination	Required. The Visual Basic type Any, and is the pointer to the destination of the returned data.
lgSource	Required. The pointer to the source data.
lgSize	Required. The long integer value for the length of the data to be copied.

Code Listing

```
'*******************************************************************************
'* Type Declarations for the NetAPI
'*******************************************************************************
Type TUser0                      '* Level 0 User Structure
    lgUsri0_name As Long
End Type

Type TUser1                      '* Level 1 User Structure
    lgUsri1_name As Long
    lgUsri1_password As Long
    lgUsri1_password_age As Long
```

```
    lgUsri1_priv As Long
    lgUsri1_home_dir As Long
    lgUsri1_comment As Long
    lgUsri1_flags As Long
    lgUsri1_script_path As Long
End Type

Type TUser2                      '* Level 2 User Structure
    lgUsri2_name As Long
    lgUsri2_password As Long
    lgUsri2_password_age As Long
    lgUsri2_priv As Long
    lgUsri2_home_dir As Long
    lgUsri2_comment As Long
    lgUsri2_flags As Long
    lgUsri2_script_path As Long
    lgUsri2_auth_flags As Long
    lgUsri2_full_name As Long
    lgUsri2_usr_comment As Long
    lgUsri2_parms As Long
    lgUsri2_workstations As Long
    lgUsri2_last_logon As Long
    lgUsri2_last_logoff As Long
    lgUsri2_acct_expires As Long
    lgUsri2_max_storage As Long
    lgUsri2_units_per_week As Long
    lgUsri2_logon_hours As Long
    lgUsri2_bad_pw_count As Long
    lgUsri2_num_logons As Long
    lgUsri2_logon_server As Long
    lgUsri2_country_code As Long
    lgUsri2_code_page As Long
End Type

Type TUser3                      '* Level 3 User Structure
    lgUsri3_name As Long
    lgUsri3_password As Long
    lgUsri3_password_age As Long
    lgUsri3_priv As Long
    lgUsri3_home_dir As Long
    lgUsri3_comment As Long
    lgUsri3_flags As Long
    lgUsri3_script_path As Long
    lgUsri3_auth_flags As Long
    lgUsri3_full_name As Long
    lgUsri3_usr_comment As Long
    lgUsri3_parms As Long
    lgUsri3_workstations As Long
    lgUsri3_last_logon As Long
    lgUsri3_last_logoff As Long
    lgUsri3_acct_expires As Long
    lgUsri3_max_storage As Long
```

continues

```
        lgUsri3_units_per_week As Long
        lgUsri3_logon_hours As Long
        lgUsri3_bad_pw_count As Long
        lgUsri3_num_logons As Long
        lgUsri3_logon_server As Long
        lgUsri3_country_code As Long
        lgUsri3_code_page As Long
        lgUsri3_user_id As Long
        lgUsri3_primary_group_id As Long
        lgUsri3_profile As Long
        lgUsri3_home_dir_drive As Long
        lgUsri3_password_expired As Long
End Type

Type TUser10
        lgUsri10_name As Long
        lgUsri10_comment As Long
        lgUsri10_usr_comment As Long
        lgUsri10_full_name As Long
End Type

Type TUser11
        lgUsri11_name As Long
        lgUsri11_comment As Long
        lgUsri11_usr_comment As Long
        lgUsri11_full_name As Long
        lgUsri11_priv As Long
        lgUsri11_auth_flags As Long
        lgUsri11_password_age As Long
        lgUsri11_home_dir As Long
        lgUsri11_parms As Long
        lgUsri11_last_logon As Long
        lgUsri11_last_logoff As Long
        lgUsri11_bad_pw_count As Long
        lgUsri11_num_logons As Long
        lgUsri11_logon_server As Long
        lgUsri11_country_code As Long
        lgUsri11_workstations As Long
        lgUsri11_max_storage As Long
        lgUsri11_units_per_week As Long
        lgUsri11_logon_hours As Long
        lgUsri11_code_page As Long
End Type

Type TUser20
        lgUsri20_name As Long
        lgUsri20_full_name As Long
        lgUsri20_comment As Long
        lgUsri20_flags As Long
        lgUsri20_user_id As Long
End Type
```

```
Type TUser1003
    lgUsri1003_password As Long
End Type

Type TUser1006
    lgUsri1006_home_dir As Long
End Type

Type TUser1007
    lgUsri1007_comment As Long
End Type

Type TUser1008
    lgUsri1008_flags As Long
End Type

Type TUser1009
    lgUsri1009_script_path As Long
End Type

Type TUser1011
    lgUsri1011_full_name As Long
End Type

Type TUser1014
    lgUsri1014_workstations As Long
End Type

Type TUser1020
    lgUsri1020_units_per_week As Long
    lgUsri1020_logon_hours As Long
End Type

Type TUser1052
    lgUsri1052_profile As Long
End Type

Type TGroup0
    lgGrpi0_name As Long
End Type

Type TGroup1
    lgGrpi1_name As Long
    lgGrpi1_comment As Long
End Type

Type TGroup2
    lgGrpi2_name As Long
    lgGrpi2_comment As Long
    lgGrpi2_group_id As Long
    lgGrpi2_attributes As Long
End Type
```

continues

```
Type TGroup1002
    lgGrpi1002_comment As Long
End Type

Type SERVER_INFO_100
    lgSvi100_platform_id As Long
    lgSvi100_servername As Long
End Type

Type SERVER_INFO_101
    lgSvi101_platform_id As Long
    lgSvi101_servername As Long
    lgSvi101_langroup As Long
    lgSvi101_ver_major As Long
    lgSvi101_ver_minor As Long
    lgSvi101_lanroot As Long
End Type

Type WKSTA_INFO_101
    lgWki101_platform_id As Long
    lgWki101_computername As Long
    lgWki101_langroup As Long
    lgWki101_ver_major As Long
    lgWki101_ver_minor As Long
    lgWki101_lanroot As Long
End Type

Type WKSTA_USER_INFO_1
    lgWkui1_username As Long
    lgWkui1_logon_domain As Long
    lgWkui1_logon_server As Long
    lgWkui1_oth_domains As Long
End Type

Type MungeLong
    lgX As Long
    inDummy As Integer
End Type

Type MungeInt
    inXLo As Integer
    inXHi As Integer
    inDummy As Integer
End Type

'******************************************************************************
'* Constant Declarations for User Priv
'******************************************************************************
Const USER_PRIV_MASK = &H3
Const USER_PRIV_GUEST = &H0
Const USER_PRIV_USER = &H1
Const USER_PRIV_ADMIN = &H2
```

```
'******************************************************************************
'* Constant Declarations for User Flags
'******************************************************************************
Const UF_SCRIPT = &H1                        ' Needs to be ORed with the other flags
Const UF_ACCOUNTDISABLE = &H2
Const UF_HOMEDIR_REQUIRED = &H8
Const UF_LOCKOUT = &H10
Const UF_PASSWD_NOTREQD = &H20
Const UF_PASSWD_CANT_CHANGE = &H40
Const UF_DONT_EXPIRE_PASSWD = &H10000
Const UF_MNS_LOGON_ACCOUNT = &H20000

Const UF_TEMP_DUPLICATE_ACCOUNT = &H100
Const UF_NORMAL_ACCOUNT = &H200
Const UF_INTERDOMAIN_TRUST_ACCOUNT = &H800
Const UF_WORKSTATION_TRUST_ACCOUNT = &H1000
Const UF_SERVER_TRUST_ACCOUNT = &H2000

'******************************************************************************
'* Constant Declarations for Filter
'******************************************************************************
Const FILTER_NORMAL_ACCOUNT = &H2

'******************************************************************************
'* Auth Flag Values
'******************************************************************************
Const AF_OP_PRINT = &H1
Const AF_OP_COMM = &H2
Const AF_OP_SERVER = &H4
Const AF_OP_ACCOUNTS = &H8

'******************************************************************************
'* Group Attributes
'******************************************************************************
Const SE_GROUP_MANDATORY = &H1
Const SE_GROUP_ENABLED_BY_DEFAULT = &H2
Const SE_GROUP_ENABLED = &H4
Const SE_GROUP_OWNER = &H8
Const SE_GROUP_LOGON_ID = &HC0000000

'******************************************************************************
'* Other Constant Declarations
'******************************************************************************
Const TIMEQ_FOREVER = -1
Const USER_MAXSTORAGE_UNLIMITED = -1
Const UNITS_PER_WEEK = 168
Const LG_INCLUDE_INDIRECT = &H1
Const UNKNOWN_VALUE = &HFFFFFFFF

'******************************************************************************
'* Universal well-known SIDs
'*      Null SID              S-1-0-0
'*      World                 S-1-1-0
```

continues

```
'*       Local                   S-1-2-0
'*       Creator Owner ID        S-1-3-0
'*       Creator Group ID        S-1-3-1
'*       (Non-unique IDs)        S-1-4
'*************************************************************************
Public Const SECURITY_NULL_RID = &H0
Public Const SECURITY_WORLD_RID = &H0
Public Const SECURITY_LOCAL_RID = &H0
Public Const SECURITY_CREATOR_OWNER_RID = &H0
Public Const SECURITY_CREATOR_GROUP_RID = &H1
'*************************************************************************
'* NT well-known SIDs
'*       NT Authority            S-1-5
'*       Dialup                  S-1-5-1
'*       Network                 S-1-5-2
'*       Batch                   S-1-5-3
'*       Interactive             S-1-5-4
'*       Service                 S-1-5-6
'*       AnonymousLogon          S-1-5-7         (aka null logon session)
'*       (Logon IDs)             S-1-5-5-X-Y
'*       (NT non-unique IDs)     S-1-5-0x15-...
'*       (Built-in domain)       s-1-5-0x20
'*************************************************************************
Public Const SECURITY_DIALUP_RID = &H1
Public Const SECURITY_NETWORK_RID = &H2
Public Const SECURITY_BATCH_RID = &H3
Public Const SECURITY_INTERACTIVE_RID = &H4
Public Const SECURITY_SERVICE_RID = &H6
Public Const SECURITY_ANONYMOUS_LOGON_RID = &H7
Public Const SECURITY_LOGON_IDS_RID = &H5
Public Const SECURITY_LOCAL_SYSTEM_RID = &H12
Public Const SECURITY_NT_NON_UNIQUE = &H15
Public Const SECURITY_BUILTIN_DOMAIN_RID = &H20


Public Const DOMAIN_USER_RID_ADMIN = &H1F4
Public Const DOMAIN_USER_RID_GUEST = &H1F5
Public Const DOMAIN_GROUP_RID_ADMINS = &H200
Public Const DOMAIN_GROUP_RID_USERS = &H201
Public Const DOMAIN_GROUP_RID_GUESTS = &H202
Public Const DOMAIN_ALIAS_RID_ADMINS = &H220
Public Const DOMAIN_ALIAS_RID_USERS = &H221
Public Const DOMAIN_ALIAS_RID_GUESTS = &H222
Public Const DOMAIN_ALIAS_RID_POWER_USERS = &H223
Public Const DOMAIN_ALIAS_RID_ACCOUNT_OPS = &H224
Public Const DOMAIN_ALIAS_RID_SYSTEM_OPS = &H225
Public Const DOMAIN_ALIAS_RID_PRINT_OPS = &H226
Public Const DOMAIN_ALIAS_RID_BACKUP_OPS = &H227
Public Const DOMAIN_ALIAS_RID_REPLICATOR = &H228


'*************************************************************************
'* ParmError Number Definitions
'*************************************************************************
```

```
Const USER_NAME_PARMNUM = 1
Const USER_PASSWORD_PARMNUM = 3
Const USER_PASSWORD_AGE_PARMNUM = 4
Const USER_PRIV_PARMNUM = 5
Const USER_HOME_DIR_PARMNUM = 6
Const USER_COMMENT_PARMNUM = 7
Const USER_FLAGS_PARMNUM = 8
Const USER_SCRIPT_PATH_PARMNUM = 9
Const USER_AUTH_FLAGS_PARMNUM = 10
Const USER_FULL_NAME_PARMNUM = 11
Const USER_USR_COMMENT_PARMNUM = 12
Const USER_PARMS_PARMNUM = 13
Const USER_WORKSTATIONS_PARMNUM = 14
Const USER_LAST_LOGON_PARMNUM = 15
Const USER_LAST_LOGOFF_PARMNUM = 16
Const USER_ACCT_EXPIRES_PARMNUM = 17
Const USER_MAX_STORAGE_PARMNUM = 18
Const USER_UNITS_PER_WEEK_PARMNUM = 19
Const USER_LOGON_HOURS_PARMNUM = 20
Const USER_PAD_PW_COUNT_PARMNUM = 21
Const USER_NUM_LOGONS_PARMNUM = 22
Const USER_LOGON_SERVER_PARMNUM = 23
Const USER_COUNTRY_CODE_PARMNUM = 24
Const USER_CODE_PAGE_PARMNUM = 25
Const USER_PRIMARY_GROUP_PARMNUM = 51
Const USER_PROFILE_PARMNUM = 52
Const USER_HOME_DIR_DRIVE_PARMNUM = 53


'*************************************************************************
'* Server Type Definitions
'*************************************************************************
Const SV_TYPE_WORKSTATION = &H1
Const SV_TYPE_SERVER = &H2
Const SV_TYPE_SQLSERVER = &H4
Const SV_TYPE_DOMAIN_CTRL = &H8
Const SV_TYPE_DOMAIN_BAKCTRL = &H10
Const SV_TYPE_TIMESOURCE = &H20
Const SV_TYPE_AFP = &H40
Const SV_TYPE_NOVELL = &H80
Const SV_TYPE_DOMAIN_MEMBER = &H100
Const SV_TYPE_PRINT = &H200
Const SV_TYPE_DIALIN = &H400
Const SV_TYPE_XENIX_SERVER = &H800
Const SV_TYPE_NT = &H1000
Const SV_TYPE_WFW = &H2000
Const SV_TYPE_MFPN = &H4000
Const SV_TYPE_SERVER_NT = &H8000
Const SV_TYPE_POTENTIAL_BROWSER = &H10000
Const SV_TYPE_BACKUP_BROWSER = &H20000
Const SV_TYPE_MASTER_BROWSER = &H40000
Const SV_TYPE_DOMAIN_MASTER = &H80000
Const SV_TYPE_WINDOWS = &H400000
```

continues

```
Const SV_TYPE_LOCAL_LIST_ONLY = &H40000000
Const SV_TYPE_DOMAIN_ENUM = &H80000000
Const SV_TYPE_ALL = &HFFFFFFFF

'************************************************************************
'* NetAPI32 Library; Memory Functions
'************************************************************************

Declare Function NetAPIBufferFree Lib "NetAPI32.DLL" Alias _
"NetApiBufferFree" (ByVal lgPtr As Long) As Long

Declare Function NetAPIBufferAllocate Lib "NetAPI32.DLL" Alias _
"NetApiBufferAllocate" (ByVal lgByteCount As Long, lgPtr As Long) As Long

'************************************************************************
'* Kernel32 Library; Memory & Pointer Functions
'************************************************************************

Declare Function PtrToStr Lib "Kernel32" Alias "lstrcpyW" _
(btRetVal As Byte, ByVal lgPtr As Long) As Long

Declare Function StrToPtr Lib "Kernel32" Alias "lstrcpyW" _
(ByVal lgPtr As Long, btSource As Byte) As Long

Declare Function PtrToInt Lib "Kernel32" Alias "lstrcpynW" _
(inRetVal As Integer, ByVal lgPtr As Long, ByVal lgCharCount As Long) As Long

Declare Function StrLen Lib "Kernel32" Alias "lstrlenW" _
(ByVal lgPtr As Long) As Long

Declare Sub CopyMemory Lib "Kernel32" Alias "RtlMoveMemory" _
(anDest As Any, ByVal lgSrc As Long, ByVal lgSize As Long)

'************************************************************************
'* Wrapper functions for PtrToStr and StrToPtr
'************************************************************************

Function Ptr2Str(lgPtrVal As Long) As String
    '* Takes a pointer value and gets the string value
    Dim btStrArray() As Byte, stStringVal As String, lgRetVal As Long

    lgRetVal = PtrToStr(btStrArray(0), lgPtrVal)
    stStringVal = btStrArray
    Ptr2Str = stStringVal

End Function

Function Str2Ptr(stStringVal As String) As Long
    '* Takes a string value and returns a pointer
    Dim btStrArray() As Byte, lgRetVal As Long, lgPtrVal As Long

    btStrArray = stStringVal
```

```
        lgRetVal = StrToPtr(lgPtrVal, btStrArray(0))
        Str2Ptr = lgPtrVal

End Function
```

Analysis

First, let's go through the functions listed earlier, then we'll get to the data types.

`NetAPIBufferAllocate` and `NetAPIBufferFree` are the functions used to allocate and free memory space for the data that the functions use. The `PtrToStr` function dereferences a pointer back to the string data to which it points.

The `StrToPtr` creates a pointer to string data.

Note

For `PtrToStr` and `StrToPtr` you might notice the use of byte data instead of string data. This is done to avoid the implicit conversion in VB from Unicode to ANSI and ANSI to Unicode. Those conversions can cause errors in interpreting the data that could be hard to troubleshoot, so I stuck to byte data for all the API calls used.

If you decide to stick to this method, simply convert your strings before sending them to the function by using

`btByteData = stStringData & vbNullChar`

You can also create a simple wrapper function for `StrToPtr` and `PtrToStr` that will do the conversions for you. I have included the functions `Str2Ptr` and `Ptr2Str` that accomplish this if you choose to use the wrapper method instead.

The `PtrToInt` function dereferences a pointer back to the integer data to which it points.

The `StrLen` function returns the length of the string data that is referenced by the pointer.

The `CopyMemory` function copies the contents of a buffer to another location.

These functions are used by the NetAPI32 to manipulate the data in memory and ensure that the buffers and C pointers are handled correctly.

Data Types

Several data types are available to the NetAPI32 code. Many of these data types are grouped by function or information contained in the structure. I present a selection of these structures here, and this should give you enough information to use many of the other data types. As previously stated, MSDN contains detailed information on all the data types available to the NetAPI32.

`MungeInt` and `MungeLong` are functions that do conversions of VB data types to and from C data types.

WKSTA_USER_INFO_1

- Username—Points to a Unicode string containing the username of the currently logged-on user.
- Logon_Domain—Points to a Unicode string containing the authenticating domain of the current logged-on user.
- Logon_Server—Points to a Unicode string containing the name of the computer that authenticated the logged-on user.
- Oth_Domains—Points to a Unicode string containing a list of other Windows NT or 95 domains browsed by this machine. The domain names are separated by blanks if more then one name is present.

WKSTA_INFO_101

- Platform_ID—Contains the information level that should be used to obtain platform-specific information.
- ComputerName—Points to a Unicode string containing the computer's machine name.
- LANGroup—Points to a Unicode string containing the name of the domain to which the machine belongs.
- Ver_Major—Contains the major version number of the Windows NT or 95 operating system running.
- Ver_Minor—Contains the minor version number of the Windows NT or 95 operating system running.
- LANRoot—Points to a Unicode string containing the path to the LANMAN directory.

SERVER_INFO_101

- Platform_ID—Contains the information levels to use to obtain platform-specific information.
- Name—Points to a Unicode string that holds the server name.
- Version_Major—The least significant four bits contain the major release version number for Windows NT or 95. The most significant bits specify the server type.
- Version_Minor—Contains the minor release version number for Windows NT or 95.
- Type—Contains the bit mask for the type of software the server is running. This value is directly related to the SV_TYPE_* variables shown in the preceding code.
- Comment—Points to a Unicode string that holds the comment for this server. This value may be NULL.

TGroup2

- Name—Points to a Unicode string that holds the group name. This parameter is ignored by NetGroupSetInfo calls.
- Comment—Points to a Unicode string that holds the group comment. This can be NULL.
- Group_ID—Contains the relative identifier of this account, which should be set to DOMAIN_GROUP_RID_USERS for normal accounts.
- Attributes—Contains the attributes bit mask for this group. This value is not configurable in Windows NT 4.0, and is set permanently to SE_GROUP_MANDATORY, SE_GROUP_ENABLED, SE_GROUP_ENABLED_BY_DEFAULT. You should set these same values on Windows NT 3.51.

TUser3

- Name—Points to a Unicode string that holds the username of this account.
- Password—Points to a Unicode string that holds the password for the account. For security reasons, NetUserEnum and NetUserGetInfo return NULL pointers for this member.
- Password_Age—Contains the number of seconds that have passed since the password has been changed. NetUserAdd and NetUserSetInfo ignore this value.
- Priv—Contains the bit mask value of the account privilege level. NetUserAdd and NetUserSetInfo ignore this value.
- Home_Dir—Points to a Unicode string that holds the path to the user's home directory. This value can be NULL.
- Comment—Points to a Unicode string that holds the account comment. This is a NULL-terminated string or a NULL string.
- Flags—Contains the flag's bit mask found in the UF_* values listed earlier. These values can be used to set various attributes on the account. NetUserSetInfo cannot be used to set the account type or to lock a previously unlocked account.
- Script_Path—Points to a Unicode string that holds the path to the user's logon script. This value can be NULL.
- Auth_Flags—Contains the bit mask value for the account privileges. NetUserAdd and NetUserSetInfo ignore this value. NetUserGetInfo and NetUserEnum return the AF_* values shown earlier.
- Full_Name—Points to a Unicode string that holds the full name of the user. This value can be NULL.
- Usr_Comment—Points to a Unicode string that holds a user comment, or it can be NULL.
- Parms—Points to a Unicode string that holds application-specific information. This data should not be changed. Microsoft products use this member to store user configuration information.
- Workstations—Points to a Unicode, comma-separated string of up to eight workstations to which the user can log on. A NULL value indicates no logon restrictions.
- Last_Logon—Contains the data for when the last logon occurred. It is stored as the number of seconds since 00:00:00 1Jan70. This data is maintained separately on each domain controller (DC), so to get an accurate result you must check each DC and use the largest result. NetUserAdd and NetUserSetInfo ignore this value.
- Last_Logoff—Contains the data for when the last logoff occurred. It is stored as the number of seconds since 00:00:00 1Jan70. This data is maintained separately on each domain controller (DC), so to get an accurate result you must check each DC and use the largest result. NetUserAdd and NetUserSetInfo ignore this value.
- Account_Expires—Contains the data for when the account will expire. Stored as the number of seconds passed since 00:00:00 1Jan70. A value of TIMEQ_FOREVER will indicate that the account never expires.
- Max_Storage—Contains the value for the maximum amount of storage that a user can use. A value of USER_MAXSTORAGE_UNLIMITED indicates the user can use all the available drive space.

- Units_Per_Week—Contains the number of equal-length time slices that the week is broken up into for use in the Logon_Hours parameter. For Windows NT services, the units must be one of the following: SAM_DAYS_PER_WEEK, SAM_HOURS_PER_WEEK, or SAM_MINUTES_PER_WEEK. A value of UNITS_PER_WEEK is suggested for normal operations. NetUserAdd and NetUserSetInfo ignore this value.

- Logon_Hours—Points to a 21-byte (168 bit) string that specifies the times when the user can log on. The first bit (Word 0 Bit 0) represents Sunday 0:00 to 0:59 (GMT). The second bit represents the next hour Sunday 1:00 to 1:59 (GMT) and so on. You will have to adjust the bits according to your local time zone as required. If this value is NULL for NetUserAdd, there are no restrictions. If this value is NULL for NetUserSetInfo, there are no changes to the restrictions.

- Bad_PW_Count—Contains the value of the number of bad logon attempts made on this account. A value of 0xFFFFFFFF indicates the value is unknown. This value is maintained separately by each DC. To get an accurate count, check each DC and use the largest result. NetUserAdd and NetUserSetInfo ignore this value.

- Num_Logons—Contains the number of successful logons by this user. A value of 0xFFFFFFFF indicates that the value is unknown. This value is maintained separately by each DC. To get an accurate count, check each DC and use the largest result. NetUserAdd and NetUserSetInfo ignore this value.

- Logon_Server—Points to a Unicode string that holds the server name to which the logon requests are sent. This string should contain the leading \\ on any server names. A value of * indicates the requests can be handled by any logon server. A NULL value indicates that the requests are sent to the DC. NetUserGetInfo and NetUserEnum return * for Windows NT machines. NetUserAdd and NetUserSetInfo ignore this value.

- Country_Code—Contains the user's country code.

- Code_Page—Contains the user's code page selection.

- User_ID—Contains the relative ID (RID) of the user. The SAM determines the RID when the user is created. It uniquely defines this user account to SAMs within the domain. NetUserAdd and NetUserSetInfo ignore this value.

- Primary_Group_ID—Contains the RID of the primary global group for this user. For NetUserAdd, this value should be set to DOMAIN_GROUP_RID_USERS, and for NetUserSetInfo, it must be the RID of a global group of which the user is a member.

- Profile—Points to a Unicode string that holds the path to the user's profile. This value can be NULL, a local absolute path (DRV:\Directory), or a UNC path (\\Machine\Directory).

- Home_Dir_Drv—Points to a Unicode string that holds the drive letter of the user's home directory for logon purposes.

- Password_Expired—Contains the value that determines whether the password has expired. NetUserGetInfo and NetUserEnum return 0 if not expired, nonzero if the password is expired. If you use NetUserAdd or NetUserSetInfo to change this value to nonzero, the User Must Change Password At Next Logon will be enabled. You can use NetUserSetInfo to set this value to 0 and remove the User Must Change Password At Next Logon message. You cannot specify 0 to negate the expiration of an already expired password.

13.2   ADD A GLOBAL GROUP

by Brian Shea

Description

This function adds a global group to the Windows NT Accounts database of a PDC or BDC. The application calling this function must be running under an Administrator or Account Operator level account on the target system to be able to use **AddGroup**. This example is using a Group Structure Level 2, but the function will work on a Level 0 or Level 1 structure as well. See section 13.1, "Supporting Functions" for more information on the data structures available.

Because member servers and workstations do not have global groups in their Accounts database, this function will not operate on those systems.

Syntax

```
lgReturn = AddGroup(stGrpName, stServer, stComment)
```

Part	Description
lgReturn	Required. The return value for the function. **0** indicates success, nonzero indicates an error state. The values for **lgReturn** can be from **2102** to **2690** if it is a NetAPI error, or it can be a WinAPI system error. MSDN has a complete listing of the NetAPI errors, and the Win32 API error handlers in sections 4.1 and 4.2 can help with the system errors.
stGrpName	Required. The string value for the group to add.
stServer	Optional. The string expression or **NULL** string that indicates where the function should execute. The server name should be preceded by \\. A **NULL** value indicates execution on the local machine, which must be a BDC or PDC for the function to operate.
stComment	Optional. The string value or **NULL** string for the comment that will appear for this group. This parameter can be removed if using a Level 0 structure.

Code Listing

```
'* Place these declarations in the global declaration section
'* The Group Data Structures used by this function
Type TGroup2
    lgGrpi2_name As Long
    lgGrpi2_comment As Long
    lgGrpi2_group_id As Long
    lgGrpi2_attributes As Long
End Type
```

continues

```
'* Declare the RID Used for normal groups
Public Const DOMAIN_GROUP_RID_USERS = &H201

'* These flags are ignored on Windows NT 4.0, but used by NT 3.x systems
'* Declare the Group Attribute Flags
Const SE_GROUP_MANDATORY = &H1
Const SE_GROUP_ENABLED_BY_DEFAULT = &H2
Const SE_GROUP_ENABLED = &H4

'* Declare the NetAPI32.dll Function
Declare Function NetGroupAdd Lib "NetAPI32.DLL" _
(btServerName As Byte, ByVal lgLevel As Long, anBuffer As Any, _
lgParmError As Long) As Long

'* Declare the buffer allocation and deallocation functions
Declare Function NetAPIBufferFree Lib "NetAPI32.DLL" Alias _
"NetApiBufferFree" (ByVal lgPtr As Long) As Long

Declare Function NetAPIBufferAllocate Lib "NetAPI32.DLL" Alias _
"NetApiBufferAllocate" (ByVal lgByteCount As Long, lgPtr As Long) As Long

'* Declare the String to Pointer Function
Declare Function StrToPtr Lib "Kernel32" Alias "lstrcpyW" _
(ByVal lgPtr As Long, btSource As Byte) As Long

'* This is the main function
Public Function AddGroup(stGrp As String, Optional stSrv As String,
        ➥ Optional stComment As String) As Long

    '****************************************************************
    '* Adds a new group to the PDC, using a level 2 structure
    '****************************************************************
    Dim lgResult As Long, lgCommtPtr As Long, lgGrpIDPtr As Long
    Dim btSNArray() As Byte, btGNArray() As Byte, btCommtArray() As Byte
    Dim lgGrpPtr As Long, lgParmError As Long
    Dim UserStruct As TGroup2 '* Change this value if using a different level

    '* Create Unicode Null Terminated Strings
    btSNArray = stSrv & vbNullChar
    btGNArray = stGrp & vbNullChar
    btCommtArray = stComment & vbNullChar

    '****************************************************************
    '* Allocate buffer space
    '****************************************************************
    lgResult = NetAPIBufferAllocate(UBound(btGNArray) + 1, lgGrpPtr)
    lgResult = NetAPIBufferAllocate(UBound(btCommtArray) + 1, lgCommtPtr)

    '****************************************************************
    '* Copy arrays to the buffer
    '****************************************************************
    lgResult = StrToPtr(lgGrpPtr, btGNArray(0))
```

```
lgResult = StrToPtr(lgCommtPtr, btCommtArray(0))

'**************************************************************
'* Fill the structure for the level used
'**************************************************************
With UserStruct
    .lgGrpi2_name = lgGrpPtr
    .lgGrpi2_comment = lgCommtPtr
    .lgGrpi2_group_id = DOMAIN_GROUP_RID_USERS
    .lgGrpi2_attributes = SE_GROUP_MANDATORY Or _
        SE_GROUP_ENABLED_BY_DEFAULT Or SE_GROUP_ENABLED
End With

'**************************************************************
'* Add the group
'**************************************************************
lgResult = NetGroupAdd(btSNArray(0), 2, UserStruct, lgParmError)
AddGroup = lgResult

'* Commented out the MsgBox Error handler, re enable if you want the program
'* flow halted by the errors.
'If lgResult <> 0 Then
    'MsgBox "Error Result = " & lgResult
'End If

'**************************************************************
'* Release buffers from memory
'**************************************************************
lgResult = NetAPIBufferFree(lgGrpPtr)
lgResult = NetAPIBufferFree(lgCommtPtr)

End Function
```

Analysis

This routine appears to be more complex on the surface, but it really is a simple function. I have used a Level 2 data structure for this function, which enables you to see the operation of the function entirely. You might want to use a Level 0 or 1 structure to cut down on the memory space allocated during operation of this function.

The function starts by accepting Group Name, Server Name, and Comment parameters. The Group Name and Comment are converted to Unicode strings, and then pointers are allocated. The byte arrays are moved into the buffer, and the data structure is built using the pointers.

The group_id parameter seen defines the relative ID used for this group. The value DOMAIN_GROUP_RID_USERS is used to define normal user groups. For most purposes, this should not be changed.

The attributes parameter defines a bit mask value for the attributes of a group. In this case, the attributes are set to the Windows NT 4.0 default values of MANDATORY, ENABLED, and ENABLED BY DEFAULT. These values are actually ignored by Windows NT 4.0 systems, but they are set here so the function will operate on Windows NT 3.x systems as well. Normally, these values should not be changed.

After these values are set, the NetGroupAdd function is called and the return value is checked for errors. The error state is trapped if it is other than 0. After the function is completed, the buffers that were allocated are freed to avoid leaking memory.

The return value of this function is the error code, so error handling can occur in the calling function as well as in this function. The lgParmError parameter of the NetGroupAdd function will hold the value of the first parameter that caused an error, if there is an error. The Supporting Functions section describes the values for each parameter.

13.3   ADD A USER

by Brian Shea

Description

The AddUser function listed here is one of the more complex NetAPI32 functions. The purpose is simply to add a user to the Windows NT User Accounts database. By using the Level 3 data structure here I show the function at its most complex, and using the Level 0, 1, or 2 structures in its place should be easier. You can find more information about the data structures in section 13.1, "Supporting Functions," in Microsoft Developer's Network (MSDN), or Microsoft TechNet. The function accepts several parameters that can be applied to a user account, but some are optional to keep things as simple as possible. You must still use a comma to hold the place of a parameter that isn't used.

This function also uses a helper function called MaskToByte that converts an 8-bit mask into a byte value. See section 13.1, "Supporting Functions," for more information on how to use this function.

Note

Because this function manipulates data directly on the primary domain controller (PDC), you should never use it without thoroughly testing your implementation. This function can cause errors on the PDC. In addition to this, the password data from this function is passed in clear text (by default) from the system using this function to the PDC. This means that a network sniffer could detect password data being passed to the server from an application using this function. It is up to you to evaluate the risks of these actions and protect your data accordingly.

Syntax

```
lgReturn = AddUser(stUserName, stPassword, stFullName, stComment, stHomePath, _
    stProfile, stScript, stServer)
```

Part	Description
lgReturn	Required. The return value of the function. 0 indicates success, nonzero indicates an error state.
stUserName	Required. The string value for the username to add to the User Accounts database.
stPassword	Required. The string value for the password to be assigned to the account. The value can be a NULL string, but it is subject to any account policies in place on the PDC.
stFullName	Optional. The string value for the user's full name. This value can be a NULL string.
stComment	Optional. The string value of the comment for this user account. It should be a maximum of 254 characters long.
stHomePath	Optional. The string value of the home path for the user. If not included, the home path is %systemroot%\system32. Otherwise the path should be a local drive and directory that already exists.
stProfile	Optional. The string value for the profile name to be used for this user.
stScript	Optional. The string value for the logon script to be used by the user.
stServer	Optional. The string value or NULL pointer or string that indicates where the function should be executed. The string value should contain the leading \\ characters. A NULL string indicates the function will run on the local machine.

Code Listing

```
'* Place these in the global declarations section

'*************************************************************************
'* Constant Declarations for User Priv
'*************************************************************************
Const USER_PRIV_MASK = &H3
Const USER_PRIV_GUEST = &H0
Const USER_PRIV_USER = &H1
Const USER_PRIV_ADMIN = &H2


'*************************************************************************
'* Constant Declarations for User Flags
'*************************************************************************
Const UF_SCRIPT = &H1                    '* Needs to be ORed with the other flags
Const UF_ACCOUNTDISABLE = &H2
Const UF_HOMEDIR_REQUIRED = &H8
```

continues

```
Const UF_LOCKOUT = &H10
Const UF_PASSWD_NOTREQD = &H20
Const UF_PASSWD_CANT_CHANGE = &H40
Const UF_DONT_EXPIRE_PASSWD = &H10000
Const UF_MNS_LOGON_ACCOUNT = &H20000

Const UF_TEMP_DUPLICATE_ACCOUNT = &H100
Const UF_NORMAL_ACCOUNT = &H200
Const UF_INTERDOMAIN_TRUST_ACCOUNT = &H800
Const UF_WORKSTATION_TRUST_ACCOUNT = &H1000
Const UF_SERVER_TRUST_ACCOUNT = &H2000

'***************************************************************************
'* Constant Declarations for Filter
'***************************************************************************
Const FILTER_NORMAL_ACCOUNT = &H2


'***************************************************************************
'* Auth Flag Values
'***************************************************************************
Const AF_OP_PRINT = &H1
Const AF_OP_COMM = &H2
Const AF_OP_SERVER = &H4
Const AF_OP_ACCOUNTS = &H8


'***************************************************************************
'* Other Constant Declarations
'***************************************************************************
Const TIMEQ_FOREVER = -1
Const USER_MAXSTORAGE_UNLIMITED = -1
Const UNITS_PER_WEEK = 168
Const LG_INCLUDE_INDIRECT = &H1
Const UNKNOWN_VALUE = &HFFFFFFFF


'***************************************************************************
'* RID Constants
'***************************************************************************
Const DOMAIN_USER_RID_ADMIN = &H1F4
Const DOMAIN_USER_RID_GUEST = &H1F5
Const DOMAIN_GROUP_RID_ADMINS = &H200
Const DOMAIN_GROUP_RID_USERS = &H201
Const DOMAIN_GROUP_RID_GUESTS = &H202
Const DOMAIN_ALIAS_RID_ADMINS = &H220
Const DOMAIN_ALIAS_RID_USERS = &H221
Const DOMAIN_ALIAS_RID_GUESTS = &H222
Const DOMAIN_ALIAS_RID_POWER_USERS = &H223
Const DOMAIN_ALIAS_RID_ACCOUNT_OPS = &H224
Const DOMAIN_ALIAS_RID_SYSTEM_OPS = &H225
Const DOMAIN_ALIAS_RID_PRINT_OPS = &H226
Const DOMAIN_ALIAS_RID_BACKUP_OPS = &H227
Const DOMAIN_ALIAS_RID_REPLICATOR = &H228
```

```
'* The Level 3 User Data Structure
Type TUser3                        '* Level 3 User Structure
    lgUsri3_name As Long
    lgUsri3_password As Long
    lgUsri3_password_age As Long
    lgUsri3_priv As Long
    lgUsri3_home_dir As Long
    lgUsri3_comment As Long
    lgUsri3_flags As Long
    lgUsri3_script_path As Long
    lgUsri3_auth_flags As Long
    lgUsri3_full_name As Long
    lgUsri3_usr_comment As Long
    lgUsri3_parms As Long
    lgUsri3_workstations As Long
    lgUsri3_last_logon As Long
    lgUsri3_last_logoff As Long
    lgUsri3_acct_expires As Long
    lgUsri3_max_storage As Long
    lgUsri3_units_per_week As Long
    lgUsri3_logon_hours As Long
    lgUsri3_bad_pw_count As Long
    lgUsri3_num_logons As Long
    lgUsri3_logon_server As Long
    lgUsri3_country_code As Long
    lgUsri3_code_page As Long
    lgUsri3_user_id As Long
    lgUsri3_primary_group_id As Long
    lgUsri3_profile As Long
    lgUsri3_home_dir_drive As Long
    lgUsri3_password_expired As Long
End Type

'* Declare the NetAPI function
Declare Function NetUserAdd Lib "NetAPI32.DLL" _
(btServerName As Byte, ByVal lgLevel As Long, anBuffer As Any, lgParmError _
As Long) As Long

'* Declare the memory and buffer functions
Declare Function NetAPIBufferFree Lib "NetAPI32.DLL" Alias _
"NetApiBufferFree" (ByVal lgPtr As Long) As Long

Declare Function NetAPIBufferAllocate Lib "NetAPI32.DLL" Alias _
"NetApiBufferAllocate" (ByVal lgByteCount As Long, lgPtr As Long) As Long

Declare Function StrToPtr Lib "Kernel32" Alias "lstrcpyW" _
(ByVal lgPtr As Long, btSource As Byte) As Long

'* This is the main function
Public Function AddUser(stUName As String, _
stPWD As String, Optional stFName As String, Optional stComment As String, _
Optional stHPath As String, Optional stProf As String, _
Optional stScr As String, Optional stSName As String) As Long
```

continues

```
'*******************************************************************
'* Adds the user using a level 3 structure
'*******************************************************************
Dim lgResult As Long, lgParmError As Long, lgPWDPtr As Long, lgUNPtr As Long
Dim lgFNPtr As Long, lgHPPtr As Long, lgPrfPtr As Long, lgScPtr As Long
Dim btSNArray() As Byte, btUNArray() As Byte, btPWDArray() As Byte
Dim btFNArray() As Byte, btHPArray() As Byte, btPrfArray() As Byte
Dim UserStruct As TUser3, btScArray() As Byte
Dim btNSArray() As Byte, lgNSPtr As Long, lgNullPtr As Long
Dim btLSArray() As Byte, lgLSPtr As Long, btNullArray() As Byte
Dim btHourArray() As Byte, lgHourPtr As Long
Dim I As Integer, btCommentArray() As Byte, lgCommentPtr As Long

 '*******************************************************************
 '* Create Null Terminated Strings and Move Data to byte arrays
 '*******************************************************************
 btSNArray = stSName & vbNullChar
 btUNArray = stUName & vbNullChar
 btPWDArray = stPWD & vbNullChar
 btFNArray = stFName & vbNullChar
 btNSArray = "" & vbNullChar
 btNullArray = vbNullChar
 btLSArray = "\\*" & vbNullChar

 '* Handle Optional Parameters
 If stComment = Null Or IsNull(stComment) Then
     btCommentArray = "" & vbNullChar
 Else
     btCommentArray = stComment & vbNullChar
 End If
 If stHPath = Null Or IsNull(stHPath) Then
     btHPArray = "" & vbNullChar
 Else
     btHPArray = stHPath & vbNullChar
 End If
 If stProf = Null Or IsNull(stProf) Then
     btPrfArray = "" & vbNullChar
 Else
     btPrfArray = stProf & vbNullChar
 End If
 If stScr = Null Or IsNull(stScr) Then
     btScArray = "" & vbNullChar
 Else
     btScArray = stScr & vbNullChar
 End If

 '* Logon Hours (handle conversion to byte array)
 ReDim stHourArray(22) As String
 ReDim btHourArray(22) As Byte
 For I = 0 To 20
     stHourArray(I) = "11111111"
     btHourArray(I) = MaskToByte(stHourArray(I))
```

```
Next I
lgResult = NetAPIBufferAllocate(UBound(btHourArray) + 1, lgHourPtr)
lgResult = StrToPtr(lgHourPtr, btHourArray(0))



'*************************************************
'* Allocate buffer space for data
'*************************************************
lgResult = NetAPIBufferAllocate(UBound(btUNArray) + 1, lgUNPtr)
lgResult = NetAPIBufferAllocate(UBound(btPWDArray) + 1, lgPWDPtr)
lgResult = NetAPIBufferAllocate(UBound(btFNArray) + 1, lgFNPtr)
lgResult = NetAPIBufferAllocate(UBound(btHPArray) + 1, lgHPPtr)
lgResult = NetAPIBufferAllocate(UBound(btPrfArray) + 1, lgPrfPtr)
lgResult = NetAPIBufferAllocate(UBound(btScArray) + 1, lgScPtr)
lgResult = NetAPIBufferAllocate(UBound(btNSArray) + 1, lgNSPtr)
lgResult = NetAPIBufferAllocate(UBound(btNullArray) + 1, lgNullPtr)
lgResult = NetAPIBufferAllocate(UBound(btLSArray) + 1, lgLSPtr)
lgResult = NetAPIBufferAllocate(UBound(btCommentArray) + 1, lgCommentPtr)



'*************************************************
'* Copy data arrays to the buffer
'*************************************************
lgResult = StrToPtr(lgUNPtr, btUNArray(0))
lgResult = StrToPtr(lgPWDPtr, btPWDArray(0))
lgResult = StrToPtr(lgFNPtr, btFNArray(0))
lgResult = StrToPtr(lgHPPtr, btHPArray(0))
lgResult = StrToPtr(lgPrfPtr, btPrfArray(0))
lgResult = StrToPtr(lgScPtr, btScArray(0))
lgResult = StrToPtr(lgNSPtr, btNSArray(0))
lgResult = StrToPtr(lgNullPtr, btNullArray(0))
lgResult = StrToPtr(lgLSPtr, btLSArray(0))
lgResult = StrToPtr(lgCommentPtr, btCommentArray(0))



'*************************************************
'* Fill the data structure
'*************************************************
With UserStruct
    .lgUsri3_name = lgUNPtr
    .lgUsri3_password = lgPWDPtr
    .lgUsri3_password_age = 3
    .lgUsri3_priv = USER_PRIV_USER
    .lgUsri3_home_dir = lgHPPtr
    .lgUsri3_comment = lgCommentPtr
    .lgUsri3_flags = UF_NORMAL_ACCOUNT Or UF_SCRIPT        '* Do Not Change!
    .lgUsri3_script_path = lgScPtr
    .lgUsri3_auth_flags = 0
    .lgUsri3_full_name = lgFNPtr
    .lgUsri3_usr_comment = lgNSPtr
    .lgUsri3_parms = lgNSPtr                               '* Do Not Change!
```

continues

```
            .lgUsri3_workstations = lgNSPtr
            .lgUsri3_last_logon = 0
            .lgUsri3_last_logoff = 0
            .lgUsri3_acct_expires = TIMEQ_FOREVER
            .lgUsri3_max_storage = USER_MAXSTORAGE_UNLIMITED        '* Do Not Change!
            .lgUsri3_units_per_week = UNITS_PER_WEEK
            .lgUsri3_logon_hours = lgHourPtr
            .lgUsri3_bad_pw_count = 0
            .lgUsri3_num_logons = 0
            .lgUsri3_logon_server = lgLSPtr
            .lgUsri3_country_code = 1
            .lgUsri3_code_page = 1252
            .lgUsri3_user_id = -1
            .lgUsri3_primary_group_id = DOMAIN_GROUP_RID_USERS        '* Do Not Change!
            .lgUsri3_profile = lgPrfPtr
            .lgUsri3_home_dir_drive = lgNSPtr
            .lgUsri3_password_expired = 1    '* Sets the "User Must Change Password"
        End With

    '************************************************
    '* Add the user
    '************************************************
    lgResult = NetUserAdd(btSNArray(0), 3, UserStruct, lgParmError)
    AddUser = lgResult

    '* Add More API Return Value Error Handling Here
    If lgResult <> 0 Then
        MsgBox "Add User Error " & lgResult & " in parameter " & _
            ➥ lgParmError _
        & " when adding User " & stUName
    End If
    If lgResult = 2224 Then
        MsgBox "User Already Exists Error", vbOKOnly, "AddUser Error"
    End If

    '************************************************
    '* Release buffers from memory
    '************************************************
    lgResult = NetAPIBufferFree(lgUNPtr)
    lgResult = NetAPIBufferFree(lgPWDPtr)
    lgResult = NetAPIBufferFree(lgFNPtr)
    lgResult = NetAPIBufferFree(lgHPPtr)
    lgResult = NetAPIBufferFree(lgPrfPtr)
    lgResult = NetAPIBufferFree(lgScPtr)
    lgResult = NetAPIBufferFree(lgNSPtr)
    lgResult = NetAPIBufferFree(lgNullPtr)
    lgResult = NetAPIBufferFree(lgLSPtr)
    lgResult = NetAPIBufferFree(lgCommentPtr)
    lgResult = NetAPIBufferFree(lgHourPtr)

End Function
```

```
Public Function MaskToByte(stIntStr As String) As Byte
    '* Converts Binary Mask String to a Byte value
    Dim btArrayVal() As Byte, inValue As Integer, I As Integer

    inValue = 0
    btArrayVal = stIntStr
    '* Get every other byte listed and convert to a value
    If Chr(btArrayVal(0)) = 1 Then inValue = inValue + 1
    If Chr(btArrayVal(2)) = 1 Then inValue = inValue + 2
    If Chr(btArrayVal(4)) = 1 Then inValue = inValue + 4
    If Chr(btArrayVal(6)) = 1 Then inValue = inValue + 8
    If Chr(btArrayVal(8)) = 1 Then inValue = inValue + 16
    If Chr(btArrayVal(10)) = 1 Then inValue = inValue + 32
    If Chr(btArrayVal(12)) = 1 Then inValue = inValue + 64
    If Chr(btArrayVal(14)) = 1 Then inValue = inValue + 128

    MaskToByte = CByte(inValue)

End Function
```

Analysis

This function is used to add a user to the User Accounts database, which appears simple. The complexity of this function lies in the number of variables that can be set on a user account. Much of this complexity is covered by the use of the Level 3 user data structure, which is explained in more detail in the "Supporting Functions" section. This section also covers the declaration of the header information in more detail.

First, the function declares the variables and functions used throughout the main function. Most of these declarations simply provide the bit mask values for the flags that can be set on the account. The full Level-3 user data structure is then defined for later use. Finally, the NetAPI and buffer functions are declared so the function can call them later.

Now you get into the function itself. After you're past the declaration of the necessary variables, you get to the preparation of the string data. The strings are null-terminated, and then moved to byte arrays. The optional parameters are tested first, then treated the same as the other parameters.

The next section of code shows the `btHourArray` being filled with a series of 8-bit bytes. This is because the logon hours are represented by a 21-byte (168 bit) array. Each bit represents an hour period, and 1 means that the user can logon during this period; 0 means no logon. By default this function enables the user to log on at any hour of the day. You may alter this behavior if you need to. More information about how the bit array for logon hours is evaluated can be found in the "Supporting Functions" section. Also, this is a bare minimum treatment of the logon hours parameter because it only sets the values to "all on" (all logon hours allowed by default). You can look at the `SetUserInfo` function for a more complete handling of this parameter.

Warning

Improper settings on the logon hours parameter can cause system instability on the PDC and the local system. Test this parameter carefully if you plan to change the settings.

Next you prepare the buffer space for the variables and copy the data into these buffers. Pointers are created for each buffer. The data is then assigned to the data structure. The User Info 3 data structure is covered in more detail in the "Supporting Functions" section, but here are a few things to look for:

■ The four parameters that are commented with Do Not Change are set to the values that the system expects and should not be changed. You can change these values in some cases but you likely will get unexpected behavior.

■ The last parameter is set to 1, which sets the User Must Change Password At Next Logon value on the account. This is the default behavior of User Manager For Domains and is a good thing to enforce. If you do not want this behavior to occur, change the value of this parameter to 0.

■ Some of the parameters listed are actually ignored by the NetUserAdd function, but are listed for consistency and so you can get a feel for the Level 3 data structure. The "Supporting Functions" section lists the data members that will be ignored by the various functions that call this data structure.

When the data structure is filled, you immediately call the NetUserAdd function from the NetAPI32 and set the return value to the function return value. There is a small bit of error handling that traps nonzero return codes and sends them to a message box for handling.

The last thing you do is free the buffers you had allocated earlier to prevent memory leaks.

Note

If you are testing this function and it fails before clearing the buffers, you might experience some unusual behavior in the subsequent runs of the program, at least until one runs correctly and clears the buffers. Saving your work frequently and shutting down VB after a particularly ugly run can help eliminate some of this strange behavior.

13.4   ADD A USER TO A GROUP

by Brian Shea

Description

The AddUserToGroup function adds an existing user to a global group in the Accounts database of the primary domain controller (PDC). The application that uses this function must be running with Administrator or Account Operator authority (on the PDC) to successfully call this function.

If you are calling this function from a Windows NT Workstation, the `stServer` value should be set to `\\<PDC_SERVER_NAME>`, where the `PDC_SERVER_NAME` is the NetBIOS name of your PDC.

Syntax

```
lgReturn = AddUserToGroup(stGrpName, stUserName, stServer)
```

Part	Description
lgReturn	Required. The return value for the function. 0 indicates success, nonzero indicates an error state. The values for `lgReturn` can be from 2102 to 2690 if it is a NetAPI error, or it can be a WinAPI system error. MSDN has a complete list of the NetAPI errors, and the Win32 API error handlers in sections 4.1 and 4.2 can help with the system errors.
stGrpName	Required. The string value of the group name to which the user will be added.
stUserName	Required. The string value for the user name that will be added to the group.
stServer	Optional. The string value or NULL pointer or string for the server name to run the function on. The server name should have a leading \\. If a NULL value is used, the function runs on the local machine. This value should be the name of the PDC, or the function should be run on the PDC using a NULL value.

Code Listing

```
'* Place this declaration in the global declarations section.
Declare Function NetGroupAddUser Lib "NetAPI32.DLL" (btServerName As Byte, _
btGroupName As Byte, btUserName As Byte) As Long

'* The main function
Public Function AddUserToGroup(ByVal stGName As String, _
ByVal stUName As String, Optional ByVal stSName As String) As Long

    '********************************************************************
    '* This only adds users to global groups - not to local groups
    '********************************************************************

    Dim btSNArray() As Byte, btGNArray() As Byte, btUNArray() As Byte
    Dim lgResult As Long

    '* Build the null terminated strings
    btSNArray = stSName & vbNullChar
    btGNArray = stGName & vbNullChar
    btUNArray = stUName & vbNullChar

    '* Call the NetAPI function
    lgResult = NetGroupAddUser(btSNArray(0), btGNArray(0), btUNArray(0))
    If lgResult = 2220 Then
        MsgBox "There is no GLOBAL group " & stGName
    ElseIf lgResult <> 0 Then
        MsgBox "Error Code = " & CStr(lgResult)
    End If
```

continues

```
        AddUserToGroup = lgResult

End Function
```

Analysis

The `AddUserToGroup` function is easy to follow. It accepts the string value parameters and converts the `UserName` and `GroupName` to NULL-terminated byte arrays. The `NetAPI` function is then called, and errors are trapped and sent to a message box. The 2220 error is specifically trapped here to help avoid the easy mistake of using this function on a local group.

This function will not operate correctly against the Accounts database of a Windows NT Workstation because Workstation systems don't recognize global group accounts. The `stServer` should be the name of the PDC or the function can be called on the PDC itself, using a `NULL` for `stServer`.

13.5   DELETE A USER

by Brian Shea

Description

The `DelUser` function deletes a user from the Windows NT User Accounts database. The application using this function must be logged on as an Administrator or Account Operator to use this function. An Account Operator-level user can't delete an Administrator-level account. Also, an account cannot be deleted while the account or application logged in as that account is using a server resource.

Syntax

```
lgReturn = DelUser(stUserName, stServer)
```

Part	Description
lgReturn	Required. The return value from the Delete User function. 0 indicates success, nonzero indicates error.
stUserName	Required. The string value for the name of the user account to delete.
stServer	Optional. The string value or NULL pointer or string for the server name on which the function should run. A NULL value indicates the function will run locally.

Code Listing

```
'* Declare the NetAPI Function
Declare Function NetUserDel Lib "NetAPI32.DLL" (btServerName As Byte, _
btUserName As Byte) As Long
```

```
Public Function DelUser(ByVal stUName As String, Optional ByVal stSName As
        ➥ String) As Long

    '****************************************************************
    '* This function deletes the user's account from the PDC
    '****************************************************************

    Dim btUNArray() As Byte, btSNArray() As Byte
    Dim lgResult As Long

    '*Convert to Unicode Null Terminated Strings
    btUNArray = stUName & vbNullChar
    btSNArray = stSName & vbNullChar

    lgResult = NetUserDel(btSNArray(0), btUNArray(0))
    If lgResult <> 0 Then
        MsgBox "Error Result = " & lgResult
    End If
    DelUser = lgResult

End Function
```

Analysis

The DelUser function is an easy way to delete a user account from the NT Accounts database. The normal restrictions apply to removing an account from the NT database. This function accepts the server name and username parameters, prepares the Unicode strings, and then calls the NetUserDel function from the NetAPI32.dll. Errors are trapped and sent to a message box for handling.

13.6   DELETE A USER FROM A GROUP

by Brian Shea

Description

This function removes a username from a global group in the Accounts database. The application using this function must be using Administrator or Account Operator authority to properly execute the DelUserFromGroup function.

Syntax

```
lgReturn = DelUserFromGroup(stGrpName, stUserName, stServer)
```

Part	Description
lgReturn	Required. The return value for this function. 0 indicates success, nonzero indicates an error state.
stGrpName	Required. The string value for the group name from which the user will be removed.
stUserName	Required. The string value for the username to be removed from the group.
stServer	Optional. The string value or NULL pointer or string that indicates where the function should be executed. The string value should begin with \\. A NULL value indicates that the function should run on the local machine.

Code Listing

```
'* Place this in the global declarations section
Declare Function NetGroupDelUser Lib "NetAPI32.DLL" (btServerName As _
Byte, btGroupName As Byte, btUserName As Byte) As Long

'* This is the main function
Public Function DelUserFromGroup(ByVal stGName As String, _
ByVal stUName As String, Optional ByVal stSName As String) As Long

    '*************************************************************************
    '* This only deletes users from global groups - not local groups
    '*    stSName = servername
    '*    stGName = groupname
    '*    stUName = username
    '*************************************************************************

    Dim btSNArray() As Byte, btGNArray() As Byte, btUNArray() As Byte
    Dim lgResult As Long

    '* Build Null Terminated Strings
    btSNArray = stSName & vbNullChar
    btGNArray = stGName & vbNullChar
    btUNArray = stUName & vbNullChar

    '* Call the NetAPI function
    lgResult = NetGroupDelUser(btSNArray(0), btGNArray(0), btUNArray(0))
    If lgResult = 2220 Then
        MsgBox "There is no GLOBAL group " & stGName
    ElseIf lgResult <> 0 Then
        MsgBox "Error Code = " & CStr(lgResult)
    End If

    DelUserFromGroup = lgResult

End Function
```

Analysis

The `DelUserFromGroup` function is easy to follow. It accepts the string value parameters and converts the `UserName` and `GroupName` to NULL-terminated byte arrays. The `NetAPI` function is then called to remove the user from the global group named, and errors are trapped and sent to a message box. The 2220 error is specifically trapped here to help avoid the easy mistake of using this function on a local group.

This function will not operate correctly against the Accounts database of a Windows NT Workstation because Workstation systems don't recognize global group accounts in their local Accounts database. The server name parameter should always point to a Windows NT server (usually the primary domain controller or backup domain controller), or the function can be run on a server using NULL for the server name parameter.

13.7   DISABLE A USER

by Brian Shea

Description

This function disables a user's account in the NT User Account database. The application using this function must be logged in as an Administrator or Account Operator–level user to use this function.

This function can be used to disable a user's account before choosing to delete it, to revoke user access while the user is on vacation, or as a trigger for an intrusion detection routine on a privileged account. The disabled account will not be able to log on, and but access can be restored simply by enabling the account.

Note

This implementation of this function will remove other flags that might be set on the user account when the account is disabled. This means that if the account had the properties of User Cannot Change Password or Password Never Expires before this function is executed, they will be removed. This function will also unlock an account when it is disabled.

Syntax

```
lgReturn = DisableUser(stServer, stUserName)
```

Part	Description
lgReturn	Required. The long integer value of the return code. This value will indicate **0** for success or nonzero for error states. The values for lgReturn can be from **2102** to **2690** if it is a NetAPI error, or it can be a WinAPI system error. MSDN has a complete listing of the NetAPI errors, and the Win32 API error handlers in sections 4.1 and 4.2 can help with the system errors.
stUserName	Required. The string value for the user account to disable.
stServer	Optional. The string value or NULL pointer or string that specifies the server on which to run the function. The server name should be preceded by the leading \\, or use a NULL to run the function on the local machine.

Code Listing

```
'* Place these declarations in the global declarations section
'* Declare value for the flag
Const UF_SCRIPT = &H1
Const UF_ACCOUNTDISABLE = &H2

'* The User Data Structure used to set user flags
Type TUser1008
    lgUsri1008_flags As Long
End Type

'* Declare the SetUserInfo Function
Declare Function NetSetUserInfo Lib "NetAPI32.DLL" Alias "NetUserSetInfo" _
(btServerName As Byte, btUserName As Byte, ByVal lgLevel As Long, anBuffer As
➥ Any, _
lgParmError As Long) As Long

'* This is the main function
Public Function DisableUser(ByVal stUserName As String, Optional ByVal stServer
➥ As String) As Long

    '**********************************************************
    '* Calls the NetSetUserInfo to disable the account
    '**********************************************************

    Dim lgResult As Long, UserStruct As TUser1008
    Dim btSNArray() As Byte, btUNArray() As Byte
    Dim lgParmError As Long

    '* Create null terminated strings
    btSNArray = stServer & vbNullChar
    btUNArray = stUserName & vbNullChar

    '************************************************
    '* Fill the structure
    '************************************************
    '* Removes the other flags, disables user.
    With UserStruct
```

```
        .lgUsri1008_flags = UF_ACCOUNTDISABLE Or UF_SCRIPT
    End With

    '**********************************************
    '* Disable the account
    '**********************************************

    lgResult = NetSetUserInfo(btSNArray(0), btUNArray(0), 1008, UserStruct,
    ➥ lgParmError)
    DisableUser = lgResult

    If lgResult <> 0 Then
        MsgBox "Error Result = " & lgResult
    End If

End Function
```

Analysis

The DisableUser function disables a user account in the Windows NT User Account database. The function accepts a value for the server to execute the function on, and the user account to disable. The string values are converted to Unicode style strings (NULL-terminated) and placed in byte arrays for the API call. The NetSetUserInfo function is called from the NetAPI32.dll, and the user account has the disabled flag set. Any returned error codes are trapped and sent to a message box for handling.

The Account Disabled flag is one of many account flags that can be set using the NetSetUserInfo call. The values are actually stored as bit mask values. This is why the function presented here resets the other flags to off when it is executed. The bit mask values are reset to zero. In a production environment this function can be used, but the values of the other flags might be lost. The other account flag values are listed here.

```
Hexadecimal Value of Variable                         Binary Value
Const UF_SCRIPT = &H1                          000000000000000001
Const UF_ACCOUNTDISABLE = &H2                   00000000000000010
Const UF_HOMEDIR_REQUIRED = &H8                 00000000000001000
Const UF_LOCKOUT = &H10                        000000000000010000
Const UF_PASSWD_NOTREQD = &H20                  00000000000100000
Const UF_PASSWD_CANT_CHANGE = &H40              000000000001000000
Const UF_DONT_EXPIRE_PASSWD = &H10000           010000000000000000
Const UF_MNS_LOGON_ACCOUNT = &H20000            100000000000000000

Const UF_TEMP_DUPLICATE_ACCOUNT = &H100         000000000100000000
Const UF_NORMAL_ACCOUNT = &H200                000000001000000000
Const UF_INTERDOMAIN_TRUST_ACCOUNT = &H800      000000100000000000
Const UF_WORKSTATION_TRUST_ACCOUNT = &H1000     000001000000000000
Const UF_SERVER_TRUST_ACCOUNT = &H2000         000010000000000000
```

These values must be ORed with other values, and the NetSetUserInfo can't change the account type (the second group of values). Windows NT and LanManager systems must have the UF_SCRIPT flag set.

You can find more information about user flags in section 13.1, "Supporting Functions," or through Microsoft Developer's Network (MSDN).

13.8   ENUMERATE GROUPS

by Brian Shea

Description

The EnumerateGroups function provides a list of global groups, but it can be a list for the entire server or a list showing the groups that a user is a member of. The best results will be achieved when the application that calls this function is running under Administrator or Account Operator authority. The NetUserEnum function should run fine for any user because it is only using the level 0 structure. Only Administrators or Account Operators can run the NetUserGetGroups function, or a user can query his own account. Information about the various data structures and levels used for the NetAPI functions can be found in section 13.1, "Supporting Functions," on MSDN, or in TechNet.

If this function is called with the ServerName and UserName parameters, it will return the list of global groups of which the user is a member. If the UserName parameter is set to a NULL string, it will return the list of global groups on the server.

Because this function attempts to get lists of global groups, it must be run against a Primary or Backup Domain Controller (PDC or BDC). Member servers and NT Workstations should not be used for the stServer parameter of this function.

Syntax

```
lgReturn = EnumerateGroups(stUserName, stServer)
```

Part	Description
lgReturn	Required. The return value of the function. 0 indicates success, nonzero indicates an error state. The values for lgReturn can be from 2102 to 2690 if it is a NetAPI error, or it can be a WinAPI system error. MSDN has a complete listing of the NetAPI errors, and the Win32 API error handlers in sections 4.1 and 4.2 can help with the system errors.
stUserName	Optional. The string value of the username for which you want to get the group list. It can be a valid user account in the Accounts database or a NULL string. If the UserName parameter is left off or NULL, the function returns a list of global groups on the server specified in stServer.
stServer	Optional. The string value for the server name where the function should be executed. This target server should be a PDC or BDC. This value can be NULL if the calling application is running on a PDC or BDC.

Code Listing

```
'* Declare the data types used
Type MungeLong
    lgX As Long
    inDummy As Integer
End Type

Type MungeInt
    inXLo As Integer
    inXHi As Integer
    inDummy As Integer
End Type

'* Declare the memory and pointer functions used
Declare Function NetAPIBufferFree Lib "NetAPI32.DLL" Alias _
"NetApiBufferFree" (ByVal lgPtr As Long) As Long

Declare Function PtrToInt Lib "Kernel32" Alias "lstrcpynW" _
(inRetVal As Integer, ByVal lgPtr As Long, ByVal lgCharCount As Long) As Long

Declare Function PtrToStr Lib "Kernel32" Alias "lstrcpyW" _
(btRetVal As Byte, ByVal lgPtr As Long) As Long

Declare Function StrLen Lib "Kernel32" Alias "lstrlenW" _
(ByVal lgPtr As Long) As Long

'* Declare the NetAPI Functions Used
Declare Function NetGroupEnum Lib "NetAPI32.DLL" _
(btServerName As Byte, ByVal lgLevel As Long, lgBuffer As Long, ByVal _
lgPrefMaxLen As Long, lgEntriesRead As Long, lgTotalEntries As Long, _
lgResumeHandle As Long) As Long

Declare Function NetUserGetGroups Lib "NetAPI32.DLL" _
(btServerName As Byte, btUserName As Byte, _
ByVal lgLevel As Long, anBuffer As Any, ByVal lgPrefMaxLen As Long, _
lgEntriesRead As Long, lgTotalEntries As Long) As Long

Public stGroupArray() As String

Public Function EnumerateGroups(Optional stUName As String,
        ➥ Optional stSName As String) As Long

    '******************************************************************************
    '* Enumerates Global Groups Only
    '* Enumerates Local system if servername = ""
    '******************************************************************************
    '* The buffer is filled from the left with pointers to user names that
    '* are filled from the right side. For example:
    '*      ptr1¦ptr2¦...¦ptrn¦<garbage>¦strn¦...¦str2¦str1
    '*      ^------------ lgBufPtr buffer --------------^
    '* lgBufPtr gets the address of the buffer (or ptr1 - add 4 to lgBufPtr for
    '* each additional pointer)
```

continues

```
'********************************************************************

Dim lgResult As Long, lgBufPtr As Long, lgEntriesRead As Long
Dim lgTotalEntries As Long, lgResumeHandle As Long, lgBufLen As Long
Dim btSNArray() As Byte, btGNArray(99) As Byte, btUNArray() As Byte
Dim stGName As String, I As Integer, lgUNPtr As Long
Dim TempPtr As MungeLong, TempStr As MungeInt, stText As String


btSNArray = stSName & vbNullChar          '* Move to byte array
btUNArray = stUName & vbNullChar          '* Move to Byte array
lgBufLen = 255                             '* Buffer size
lgResumeHandle = 0                          '* Start with the first entry
ReDim stGroupArray(0) As String


Do
If stUName = "" Then
    lgResult = NetGroupEnum(btSNArray(0), 0, lgBufPtr, lgBufLen, _
        lgEntriesRead, lgTotalEntries, lgResumeHandle)
Else
    lgResult = NetUserGetGroups(btSNArray(0), btUNArray(0), 0, lgBufPtr, _
        lgBufLen, lgEntriesRead, lgTotalEntries)
End If

EnumerateGroups = lgResult
'* Sizes the storage array for the number of elements
ReDim stGroupArray(lgTotalEntries) As String

If lgResult <> 0 And lgResult <> 234 Then
'* 234 means multiple reads required
    If lgResult = 2221 Then
        stText = "User Name Not Found"
    ElseIf lgResult = 2351 Then
        stText = "ServerName not found." & Chr$(13)
        stText = stText & "Be sure you used the leading \\ on the
      ➥ servername."
    Else
        stText = "Error " & lgResult & " enumerating group " & _
            lgEntriesRead & " of " & lgTotalEntries
    End If
    MsgBox stText
    Exit Function
End If

For I = 1 To lgEntriesRead
    '* Get pointer to string from beginning of buffer
    '* Copy 4 byte block of memory in 2 steps
    lgResult = PtrToInt(TempStr.inXLo, lgBufPtr + (I - 1) * 4, 2)
    lgResult = PtrToInt(TempStr.inXHi, lgBufPtr + (I - 1) * 4 + 2, 2)
    LSet TempPtr = TempStr ' munge 2 Integers to a Long
    '* Copy string to array and convert to a string
    lgResult = PtrToStr(btGNArray(0), TempPtr.lgX)
    stGName = Left(btGNArray, StrLen(TempPtr.lgX))
```

```
        '* Sets group name into the stGroupArray
        stGroupArray(I) = stGName
    Next I

    Loop Until lgEntriesRead = lgTotalEntries

    '* Free the buffer allocated
    lgResult = NetAPIBufferFree(lgBufPtr)

End Function
```

Analysis

This function returns a list of global groups. You get a user's groups or a list of all the global groups on the server from this function. It uses the `NetUserEnum` and `NetUserGetGroups` NetAPI functions to accomplish this.

The initial part of the listing shows the necessary declarations, which are described in the "Supporting Functions" section. The variables and `GroupArray` are initialized next, and the `NULL`-terminated byte arrays are created from the string values.

From here, the NetAPI functions are called and the return values are set. A limited amount of error trapping will indicate some of the common errors, and then the function starts to loop through the returned data. Each iteration of the loop dereferences one of the group name values from the buffer and places it into the `GroupArray` for later use. You can alter this behavior and have the function populate a control directly. After all the entries are read, the function frees the buffer and finishes.

13.9   ENUMERATE LOCAL GROUPS

by Brian Shea

Description

The `EnumerateLocalGroups` function returns a list of the local groups that are on the specified server or that contain the specified user. The application that is calling this function must be running with Administrator or Account Operator authority.

If this function is called with the `ServerName` and `UserName` parameters, it will return the local groups of which the specified user is a member. If the `UserName` parameter is set to a `NULL` string, the function will return the list of local groups on the server.

Syntax

```
lgReturn = EnumerateLocalGroups(stServer, stUserName)
```

Part	Description
lgReturn	Required. The return value of the function. **0** indicates success, nonzero indicates an error state. The values for lgReturn can be from **2102** to **2690** if it is a NetAPI error, or it can be a WinAPI system error. MSDN has a complete listing of the NetAPI errors, and the Win32 API error handlers in sections 4.1 and 4.2 can help with the system errors.
stServer	Optional. The string expression for the server name on which to run the function. The server name should contain the leading \\ for the machine name. The value can also be NULL, which indicates that the function will run locally.
stUserName	Optional. The string value of the username for which you want to get the local group list. This can be a valid user account in the domain or a NULL string. If the value is NULL, the function returns a list of local groups on the server specified in stServer.

Code Listing

```
'* Declare the data types used
Type MungeLong
    lgX As Long
    inDummy As Integer
End Type

Type MungeInt
    inXLo As Integer
    inXHi As Integer
    inDummy As Integer
End Type

'* Declare the constant values used
Const LG_INCLUDE_INDIRECT = &H1

'* Declare the memory and pointer functions used
Declare Function NetAPIBufferFree Lib "NetAPI32.DLL" Alias _
"NetApiBufferFree" (ByVal lgPtr As Long) As Long

Declare Function PtrToInt Lib "Kernel32" Alias "lstrcpynW" _
(inRetVal As Integer, ByVal lgPtr As Long, ByVal lgCharCount As Long) As Long

Declare Function PtrToStr Lib "Kernel32" Alias "lstrcpyW" _
(btRetVal As Byte, ByVal lgPtr As Long) As Long

Declare Function StrLen Lib "Kernel32" Alias "lstrlenW" _
(ByVal lgPtr As Long) As Long

'* Declare NetAPI Functions Used
Declare Function NetLocalGroupEnum Lib "NetAPI32.DLL" _
(btServerName As Byte, ByVal lgLevel As Long, lgBuffer As Long, ByVal _
lgPrefMaxLen As Long, lgEntriesRead As Long, lgTotalEntries As Long, _
lgResumeHandle As Long) As Long
```

```
Declare Function NetUserGetLocalGroups Lib "NetAPI32" (btServerName As Byte, _
btUserName As Byte, ByVal lgLevel As Long, ByVal lgFlags As Long, lgBuffer As
➥ Long, _
lgPreferedMaxLen As Long, lgEntriesRead As Long, lgTotalEntries As Long)
➥As Long

Public stLocalGrpArray() As String

Public Function EnumerateLocalGroups(Optional stSName As String,
➥ Optional stUName As String) As Long

    '****************************************************************************
    '* Enumerates Local Groups Only
    '* Enumerates Local system if servername = ""
    '****************************************************************************
    '* The buffer is filled from the left with pointers to user names that
    '* are filled from the right side. For example:
    '*      ptr1¦ptr2¦...¦ptrn¦<garbage>¦strn¦...¦str2¦str1
    '*      ^------------ lgBufPtr buffer --------------^
    '* lgBufPtr gets the address of the buffer (or ptr1 - add 4 to lgBufPtr for
    '* each additional pointer)
    '****************************************************************************

    Dim lgResult As Long, lgBufPtr As Long, lgEntriesRead As Long
    Dim lgTotalEntries As Long, lgResumeHandle As Long, lgBufLen As Long
    Dim btSNArray() As Byte, btLGNArray(99) As Byte, btUNArray() As Byte
    Dim stLGName As String, I As Integer, lgUNPtr As Long
    Dim TempPtr As MungeLong, TempStr As MungeInt, stText As String

    btSNArray = stSName & vbNullChar         '* Move to byte array
    btUNArray = stUName & vbNullChar         '* Move to Byte array
    lgBufLen = 255                            '* Buffer size
    lgResumeHandle = 0                        '* Start with the first entry
    ReDim stLocalGrpArray(0) As String

    Do
    If stUName = "" Then
        lgResult = NetLocalGroupEnum(btSNArray(0), 0, lgBufPtr, lgBufLen, _
            lgEntriesRead, lgTotalEntries, lgResumeHandle)
    Else
        lgResult = NetUserGetLocalGroups(btSNArray(0), btUNArray(0), 0, _
            LG_INCLUDE_INDIRECT, lgBufPtr, lgBufLen, lgEntriesRead,
            ➥ lgTotalEntries)
    End If

    EnumerateLocalGroups = lgResult
    '* Sizes the storage array for the number of elements
    ReDim stLocalGrpArray(lgTotalEntries) As String

    If lgResult <> 0 And lgResult <> 234 Then
```

continues

```
     '* 234 means multiple reads required
     If lgResult = 2221 Then
         stText = "User Name Not Found"
     ElseIf lgResult = 2351 Then
         stText = "Server Name not found." & Chr$(13)
         stText = stText & "Be sure you used the leading \\ on the
         ➥ servername."
     Else
         stText = "Error " & lgResult & " enumerating local group " _
             & lgEntriesRead & " of " & lgTotalEntries
     End If
     MsgBox stText
     Exit Function
 End If

 For I = 1 To lgEntriesRead
     '* Get pointer to string from beginning of buffer
     '* Copy 4 byte block of memory in 2 steps
     lgResult = PtrToInt(TempStr.inXLo, lgBufPtr + (I - 1) * 4, 2)
     lgResult = PtrToInt(TempStr.inXHi, lgBufPtr + (I - 1) * 4 + 2, 2)
     LSet TempPtr = TempStr ' munge 2 Integers to a Long
     '* Copy string to array and convert to a string
     lgResult = PtrToStr(btLGNArray(0), TempPtr.lgX)
     stLGName = Left(btLGNArray, StrLen(TempPtr.lgX))
     '* Sets local group name in the array
     stLocalGrpArray(I) = stLGName
 Next I

 '* Continue until all entries are read
 Loop Until lgEntriesRead = lgTotalEntries

 '* Free allocated buffer space
 lgResult = NetAPIBufferFree(lgBufPtr)

End Function
```

Analysis

The EnumerateLocalGroups function can be called to list the local groups on a server or a group that a specific user is a member of. This is accomplished by using either NetUserGetLocalGroups or NetLocalGroupEnum.

The function begins by declaring the necessary functions, data types, and variables. Additional details on these values can be found in section 13.1, "Supporting Functions." Then the variables are initialized and string values are NULL-terminated and converted to byte arrays.

After this is completed, the NetAPI functions are called. Each function uses the appropriate level 0 data structure, although as you will see later it is not handled directly. Also of interest here is that the call to NetUserGetLocalGroups uses the flag LG_INCLUDE_INDIRECT. As a result, the local group list includes any local groups that the user has indirect membership to by being a member of a global group that is in a local group. To disable this behavior, set this parameter to 0&.

The return value is trapped and the function return value is set, then a small amount of error handling is done. After this, the function loops through the entries read until all are completed.

Within that loop, the function gets the pointers to the string and dereferences the string data. This string data is then placed in the `Public stLocalGrpArray` for later use. This is where you would change the code to place the data in a control directly or add more data handling if your application must do so.

The function ends by releasing the buffer space allocated by the function to prevent memory leaks.

13.10 ENUMERATE SERVERS

by Brian Shea

Description

The `EnumerateServers` function gets a list of servers from the primary domain. This list can be filtered by the `ServerType` parameter to reflect a wide variety of types of machines that will appear on the list. The values for the server type can be combined to filter more specifically for a desired type. Be careful when filtering to make sure that there is a valid result for the filter. For example, if you filter for all Novell and Windows NT servers, the results will be blank. (No Novell server is also a Windows NT server.) The filter should be a Novell server or Windows NT server. The function places the returned list into a public string array for later use.

The function as written here uses a `NULL` string for the `CompName` and `Domain` parameters. As a result, the function executes on the local machine and gets the list from the default domain. You can add these values to the parameter list, and then you can specify different machines on which to execute the function, or different domains from which to get the lists.

Syntax

```
lgReturn = EnumerateServers(stType)
```

Part	Description
lgReturn	Required. The return value of the function. **0** indicates success, nonzero indicates an error state. The values for `lgReturn` can be from **2102** to **2690** if it is a NetAPI error, or it can be a WinAPI system error. MSDN has a complete listing of the NetAPI errors, and the Win32 API error handlers in sections 4.1 and 4.2 can help with the system errors.
stType	Required. The string value for the type of servers to retrieve. The possible values for this are described in the commented code example.

Code Listing

```
'* Place these in the general declarations section

'**************************************************************************
'* Server Type Definitions
'**************************************************************************
Const SV_TYPE_WORKSTATION = &H1   '* All Net Workstations
Const SV_TYPE_SERVER = &H2   '*All Net Servers
Const SV_TYPE_SQLSERVER = &H4   '* Any Server Running MS SQL Server
Const SV_TYPE_DOMAIN_CTRL = &H8   '* PDCs
Const SV_TYPE_DOMAIN_BAKCTRL = &H10   '* BDCs
Const SV_TYPE_TIMESOURCE = &H20   '* Servers running the TimeSource Service
Const SV_TYPE_AFP = &H40   '* Apple File Protocol Servers
Const SV_TYPE_NOVELL = &H80   '*  Novell Servers
Const SV_TYPE_DOMAIN_MEMBER = &H100   '* LAN Manager 2.x Domain Member
Const SV_TYPE_PRINT = &H200   '* Server sharing print queue
Const SV_TYPE_DIALIN = &H400   '* Server running dial-in service
Const SV_TYPE_XENIX_SERVER = &H800   '* Xenix server
Const SV_TYPE_NT = &H1000   '* Windows NT (either Workstation or Server)
Const SV_TYPE_WFW = &H2000   '* Server running Windows for Workgroups
Const SV_TYPE_MFPN = &H4000   '* Microsoft File and Print for Netware
Const SV_TYPE_SERVER_NT = &H8000   '* Windows NT Non-DC server
Const SV_TYPE_POTENTIAL_BROWSER = &H10000   '* Server that can run the Browser
 ➥ service
Const SV_TYPE_BACKUP_BROWSER = &H20000   '* Server running a Browser service as
 ➥ backup
Const SV_TYPE_MASTER_BROWSER = &H40000   '* Server running the master Browser
 ➥ service
Const SV_TYPE_DOMAIN_MASTER = &H80000   '* Server running the domain master
 ➥ Browser
Const SV_TYPE_WINDOWS = &H400000   '* Windows 95 or later
Const SV_TYPE_LOCAL_LIST_ONLY = &H40000000   '* Servers maintained
➥by the browser
Const SV_TYPE_DOMAIN_ENUM = &H80000000   '* Primary Domain
Const SV_TYPE_ALL = &HFFFFFFFF   '* All servers


'* Server Data Structure used for this function
Type SERVER_INFO_100
    lgSvi100_platform_id As Long
    lgSvi100_servername As Long
End Type


'* Declare the NetAPI function
Declare Function NetServerEnum Lib "NetAPI32.DLL" (btComputerName As Byte, _
ByVal lgLevel As Long, anBuffer As Any, lgPreferedMaxLen As Long, _
lgEntriesRead As Long, lgTotalEntries As Long, anServerType As Any, _
btDomain As Byte, lgResumeHandle As Long) As Long


'* Declare the function to free the buffer
Declare Function NetAPIBufferFree Lib "NetAPI32.DLL" Alias _
"NetApiBufferFree" (ByVal lgPtr As Long) As Long
```

```
'* Declare the CopyMemory function
Declare Sub CopyMemory Lib "Kernel32" Alias "RtlMoveMemory" _
(anDest As Any, ByVal lgSrc As Long, ByVal lgSize As Long)

'* Declare the Array used to store the servernames
Public stServerArray() As String

'* This is the main function
Public Function EnumerateServers(stType As String) As Long
    '* Enumerates Servers by Type Passed into function

    Dim lgResult As Long, lgTotalEntries As Long
    Dim lgPrefMaxLen As Long, lgEntriesRead As Long
    Dim lgResumeHandle As Long, stDomain As String
    Dim lgBufPtr As Long, lgServerType As Long
    Dim btSrvArray(32) As Byte, btDomain() As Byte, btCompName() As Byte
    Dim I As Integer, stCompName As String
    Dim stServerName As String, stText As String
    Dim ServerStruct As SERVER_INFO_100

    '* Clear values and initialize all of the variables
    lgResumeHandle = 0
    ReDim stServerArray(0) As String
    '* Set the domain to the default, primary domain
    stDomain = ""
    '* Set the computer name to the default, local system
    stCompName = ""

    '* Create Null Terminated Strings
    btDomain = stDomain & vbNullChar
    btCompName = stCompName & vbNullChar

    '* Determine stType Values and set servertype value
    '* You may add or remove these types as needed for your application
    stType = Ucase(stType)
    If stType = "DCS" Then
        '* Enumerate Domain Controllers
        lgServerType = Abs(SV_TYPE_DOMAIN_CTRL) + Abs(SV_TYPE_DOMAIN_BAKCTRL)
    ElseIf stType = "SVS" Then
        '* Enumerate Servers
        lgServerType = Abs(SV_TYPE_SERVER)
    ElseIf stType = "WKS" Then
        '* Enumerate Workstations
        lgServerType = Abs(SV_TYPE_WORKSTATION)
    ElseIf stType = "ALL" Then
        '* Enumerate All Machines
        lgServerType = Abs(SV_TYPE_ALL)
    ElseIf stType = "WFW" Then
        '* Windows for Workgroups Servers
        lgServerType = Abs(SV_TYPE_WFW)
    ElseIf stType = "SQL" Then
        '* Servers running SQL Server
        lgServerType = Abs(SV_TYPE_SQLSERVER)
```

continues

```
ElseIf stType = "NOV" Then
    '* Novell Servers
    lgServerType = Abs(SV_TYPE_NOVELL)
Else
    '* Select Default as all NT Servers
    lgServerType = Abs(SV_TYPE_SERVER) + Abs(SV_TYPE_NT)
End If

'* Call NetServerEnum to get a list of Servers
lgResult = NetServerEnum(btCompName(0), 100, lgBufPtr, lgPrefMaxLen, _
lgEntriesRead, lgTotalEntries, ByVal lgServerType, ByVal btDomain(0), _
lgResumeHandle)

EnumerateServers = lgResult

'* Now that we know how many entries were read, size the array
If lgTotalEntries <= 0 Then
    MsgBox "No Entries Read. Error Code = " & CStr(lgResult)
    Exit Function
End If
ReDim stServerArray(lgTotalEntries - 1) As String

'* Check for errors
If lgResult <> 0 And lgResult <> 234 Then    '* 234 means multiple reads
➥ required
    If lgResult = 2351 Then
        stText = "ServerName not found." & Chr$(13)
        StText = stText & "Be sure you used the leading \\ on the
        ➥ servername."
    Else
        stText = "Error " & lgResult & " enumerating server " &
        ➥ lgEntriesRead
        stText = stText & " of " & lgTotalEntries
    End If
    MsgBox stText
    Exit Function
End If

For I = 1 To lgTotalEntries
    '* Dereference the ServerStruct Data Structure
    CopyMemory ServerStruct, lgBufPtr, Len(ServerStruct)
    '* Dereference the server name variable
    CopyMemory btSrvArray(0), ServerStruct.lgSvi100_servername, 33
    stServerName = btSrvArray
    Trim (stServerName)
    '* send the servername to the array
    '* Change the code here to send the servername to a control, etc.
    stServerArray(I - 1) = stServerName
    '* Clear the servername variable here
    stServerName = ""
    '* Move to the next part of the buffer
    lgBufPtr = lgBufPtr + Len(ServerStruct)
Next I
```

```
'* Release the memory used for the ServerStruct buffer
lgResult = NetAPIBufferFree(lgBufPtr)

End Function
```

Analysis

This function depends on several declarations to operate, and those declarations are listed first. The `ServerType` variables are declared to enable the function to filter the output for a specified characteristic. The function as presented doesn't use all these filters, but they are listed for you to see and use as you see fit.

Next, the `ServerInfo` 100 data structure is declared so the `NetServerEnum` has a place to store the names it retrieves. Then the NetAPI functions used to get the names and memory function are declared. The final declaration is the `Public` string array used to store the returned values for later processing. This can be removed if you have the function fill a control directly, or otherwise handle the output of the function.

The main function accepts one parameter for the type of server being asked for. The function as written here sets the domain and computer name to `NULL` strings. As a result the function is run on the local machine and the list is returned from the default domain. You may change this behavior by making the `stCompName` and `stDomain` parameters for the function that can be specified when calling the function. This would allow you to get lists of servers from other domains.

After creating the `NULL`-terminated strings, the function determines the value for the server type based on the `stType` parameter. The function written here only accepts the values `DCs`, `SVs`, `WKs`, `ALL`, `WFW`, `SQL`, and `NOV`. Other values can be added, or these values can be removed as your needs dictate. As you can see in the `DCs` option, the values can be combined to provide additional filtering.

After the type is set, the `NetServerEnum` function is called. Now that you know how many entries were read, you can redimension the `ServerArray` to the correct length. If no entries have been read, the condition is trapped and sent to a message box for handling. There is a small amount of error handling after the array is sized.

The function now walks through the `EntriesRead` and gets the server name from the data structure and places it in the `ServerArray`. After the server name has been stored, the `stServerName` variable is cleared, and the pointer is moved to the next position.

Finally, the buffer used to hold the data structure is freed before the function ends.

Note

If you plan to do additional processing on the server name before displaying it in a control, you might need to use an `InStr(stServerName, vbNull)` to get the correct end of the string. This is because the 32-byte space provided in the data structure might not be filled completely by the server name. If it is not, extra data might be in the buffer space, and will not be trimmed automatically by the function. You can view this extra data if present by using `Debug.Print stServerName` before the variable is cleared.

13.11 ENUMERATE USERS

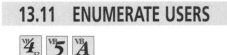

by Brian Shea

Description

The EnumerateUsers function has one purpose that can be used in two ways. The purpose is to list users from the Windows NT User Accounts database. If the ServerName and GroupName are passed to the function, it will return the users in the global group. If the GroupName is left as a NULL string, the function returns the user list for the ServerName. The GroupName parameter must be for a global group, and the ServerName parameter must contain the leading \\ for the machine name. Because the GroupName parameter must be a global group, the function will not operate completely on member servers or NT Workstation systems. This function will retrieve user lists from those machines, but it cannot get the group list for users because that list is maintained on the PDC or BDC.

This function contains two NetAPI functions, NetUserEnum and NetGroupGetUsers. To ensure full functionality of this function, the application calling it should be executing with Administrator or Account Operator level authority. The NetUserEnum can be called for a Level 0 or Level 10 call without any special group membership, and this function uses a Level 0 structure. This is because the Level 0 and Level 10 structures use information available to any user regardless of group membership. More information about the levels and data structures can be found in section 13.1, "Supporting Functions" or in MSDN or TechNet. The NetGroupGetUsers function is restricted to the Administrator or Account Operator group, but a member of the group being enumerated can also call it without restriction.

Syntax

```
lgReturn = EnumerateUsers(stServer, stGrpName)
```

Part	Description
lgReturn	Required. The return value for this function. 0 indicates success, nonzero indicates an error state. The values for lgReturn can be from 2102 to 2690 if it is a NetAPI error, or it can be a WinAPI system error. MSDN has a complete listing of the NetAPI errors, and the Win32 API error handlers in sections 4.1 and 4.2 can help with the system errors.
stServer	Optional. The string value for the server to run the function on. If this value is NULL and stGrpName is NULL, the function lists the users on the local machine. If the stGrpName is present and this is NULL, the function must be running on a PDC or BDC and it will then return the list of users in that global group.
stGrpName	Optional. The string value for the name of the global group to get the user list from. A NULL string here will return the user list for the entire server.

Code Listing

```
'* Declare the data types used
Type MungeLong
     lgX As Long
     inDummy As Integer
End Type

Type MungeInt
     inXLo As Integer
     inXHi As Integer
     inDummy As Integer
End Type

'* Declare the constant values used
Const FILTER_NORMAL_ACCOUNT = &H2

'* Declare the memory and pointer functions Used
Declare Function NetAPIBufferFree Lib "NetAPI32.DLL" Alias _
"NetApiBufferFree" (ByVal lgPtr As Long) As Long

Declare Function PtrToInt Lib "Kernel32" Alias "lstrcpynW" _
(inRetVal As Integer, ByVal lgPtr As Long, ByVal lgCharCount As Long) As Long

Declare Function PtrToStr Lib "Kernel32" Alias "lstrcpyW" _
(btRetVal As Byte, ByVal lgPtr As Long) As Long

Declare Function StrLen Lib "Kernel32" Alias "lstrlenW" _
(ByVal lgPtr As Long) As Long

'* Declare the NetAPI Functions used
Declare Function NetUserEnum Lib "NetAPI32.DLL" _
(btServerName As Byte, ByVal lgLevel As Long, ByVal lgFilter As Long, _
lgBuffer As Long, ByVal lgPrefMaxLen As Long, lgEntriesRead As Long, _
lgTotalEntries As Long, lgResumeHandle As Long) As Long

Declare Function NetGroupEnumUsers Lib "NetAPI32.DLL" Alias _
"NetGroupGetUsers" (btServerName As Byte, btGroupName As Byte, _
ByVal lgLevel As Long, lgBuffer As Long, ByVal lgPrefMaxLen As Long, _
lgEntriesRead As Long, lgTotalEntries As Long, lgResumeHandle As Long) As Long

'* Declare the Public Array to hold the users names
Public stUserArray() As String

Public Function EnumerateUsers(Optional stSName As String, Optional stGName As
          ➡ String) As Long

     '**********************************************************************
     '* Enumerates User Lists
     '* Enumerates Local system if servername = ""
     '**********************************************************************
     '* The buffer is filled from the left with pointers to user names
     '* that are filled from the right side. For example:
```

continues

```
'*      ptr1¦ptr2¦...¦ptrn¦<garbage>¦strn¦...¦str2¦str1
'*      ^------------- BufPtr buffer ---------------^
'* BufPtr gets the address of the buffer (or ptr1 - add 4 to BufPtr for
'* each additional pointer)
'**********************************************************************

Dim lgResult As Long, lgBufPtr As Long, lgEntriesRead As Long
Dim lgTotalEntries As Long, lgResumeHandle As Long, lgBufLen As Long
Dim btSNArray() As Byte, btGNArray() As Byte, btUNArray(99) As Byte
Dim stUName As String, I As Integer, lgUNPtr As Long, TempPtr As MungeLong
Dim TempStr As MungeInt, stText As String

btSNArray = stSName & vbNullChar          '* Move to byte array
btGNArray = stGName & vbNullChar          '* Move to Byte array
lgBufLen = 255                             '* Buffer size
lgResumeHandle = 0                         '* Start with the first entry
ReDim stUserArray(0) As String             '* Empty the array

Do
If stGName = "" Then
    lgResult = NetUserEnum(btSNArray(0), 0, FILTER_NORMAL_ACCOUNT,
        ➥ lgBufPtr, _
        lgBufLen, lgEntriesRead, lgTotalEntries, lgResumeHandle)
Else
    lgResult = NetGroupEnumUsers(btSNArray(0), btGNArray(0), 0, lgBufPtr, _
        lgBufLen, lgEntriesRead, lgTotalEntries, lgResumeHandle)
    '* Trap 2220 result here and handle EnumerateLocalGroups
End If

EnumerateUsers = lgResult
'* Sizes the storage array for the number of elements
ReDim stUserArray(lgTotalEntries) As String

If lgResult <> 0 And lgResult <> 234 Then
'* 234 means multiple reads required
    If lgResult = 2220 Then
        stText = "There is no GLOBAL Group with the name: " & stGName
    ElseIf lgResult = 2351 Then
        stText = "ServerName not found." & Chr$(13)
        stText = stText & "Be sure you used the leading \\ on the
        ➥ servername."
    Else
        stText = "Error " & lgResult & " enumerating group " &
        ➥ lgEntriesRead _
            & " of " & lgTotalEntries
    End If
    MsgBox stText
    Exit Function
End If

For I = 1 To (lgEntriesRead)
    '* Get pointer to string from beginning of buffer
```

```
            '* Copy 4-byte block of memory in 2 steps
            lgResult = PtrToInt(TempStr.inXLo, lgBufPtr + (I - 1) * 4, 2)
            lgResult = PtrToInt(TempStr.inXHi, lgBufPtr + (I - 1) * 4 + 2, 2)
            LSet TempPtr = TempStr '* munge 2 integers into a Long
            '* Copy string to array
            lgResult = PtrToStr(btUNArray(0), TempPtr.lgX)
            stUName = Left(btUNArray, StrLen(TempPtr.lgX))
            '* Sets the UserArray element to the name retreived
            stUserArray(I) = stUName
        Next I

        '* Continue until all entries are read
        Loop Until lgEntriesRead = lgTotalEntries

        '* Free the buffer
        lgResult = NetAPIBufferFree(lgBufPtr)

End Function
```

Analysis

The `EnumerateUsers` function will get a list of users from the server specified. If a global group is specified, the function returns the member users. If the group name is set to a `NULL` string, the function lists all the users on the specified server.

This is done by calling either `NetUserEnum` using a Level 0 data structure or by calling `NetGroupGetUsers` with a Level 0 data structure. Both functions return a buffer that contains a series of pointers followed by a series of buffers in the reverse order of the pointers. Each pointer is 4 bytes long and points to a string value in one of the buffers at the other end.

This can be shown in the following way:

```
ptr1¦ptr2¦...¦ptrn¦<garbage>¦strn¦...¦str2¦str1
^------------- BufPtr buffer ---------------^
```

The function starts by making the necessary declarations of the data types and functions used. Notice that the `Tgroup0` and `Tuser0` structures are not used, even though they are called by the functions used. You can do this because you do not work directly on the structure, but retrieve the data through the other memory and buffer functions available.

After the declarations, the function initializes the `stUserArray` to (`0`) to empty its contents, and prepares the other data for handling. String values are converted to `NULL`-terminated byte arrays, which can be handled as strings but do not get converted from Unicode to ANSI and back by VB and Windows NT.

Next, the NetAPI functions are called depending on the contents of the group name variable. The function's return value is set, and then the `UserArray` is adjusted to the correct size. You then move into a loop, running through it once for each username returned.

The pointer data is collected and dereferenced, then the pointer to the string is used to get the data. The `StrLen` function is then used to find the length of the string that will be returned. Finally, the string data is stored in the UserArray for later handling. This is where you could alter the code to fill a control directly or do additional manipulation of the data. The last step after all entries are handled is to free the buffer used.

13.12   GET THE PRIMARY DOMAIN CONTROLLER NAME

by Brian Shea

Description

The GetPrimaryDCName function retrieves the name of the primary domain controller (DC) for the specified domain. The function accepts a machine name and a domain name as parameters and returns the string value for the domain controller. The machine name and domain controller name must be preceded by \\.

Syntax

```
stDCName = GetPrimaryDCName(stComputer, stDomain)
```

Part	Description
stDCName	Required. The returned string value for the domain controller name.
stComputer	Optional. The string value of the computer name where the function should execute. This can be a string value with leading \\ or a NULL pointer or string.
stDomain	Optional. The string value for the domain name. This can be a string value or a NULL pointer or string.

Code Listing

```
'* Place these function declarations in the general declarations section

'* Get the Primary Domain Controller Name
Declare Function NetGetDCName Lib "NetAPI32.DLL" (btServerName As Byte, _
btDomainName As Byte, lgDCNPtr As Long) As Long

'* Declaration for the Buffer Free Function
Declare Function NetAPIBufferFree Lib "NetAPI32.DLL" Alias _
"NetApiBufferFree" (ByVal lgPtr As Long) As Long

'* Declaration for the dereference function
Declare Function PtrToStr Lib "Kernel32" Alias "lstrcpyW" _
(btRetVal As Byte, ByVal lgPtr As Long) As Long
```

```
'* This is the main function
Public Function GetPrimaryDCName(Optional ByVal stMName As String,
➡ Optional ByVal _
stDName As String) As String

    '****************************************************************
    '* Gets the primary Domain Controller's Name
    '****************************************************************
    '* MName = machine name of the system to run the function on
    '*    A NULL Pointer or string operates on the local system
    '* DName = domain name from which to get the DC Name
    '*    A NULL Pointer or String gets the DC of the primary domain
    '****************************************************************

    Dim lgResult As Long, stDCName As String, lgDCNPtr As Long
    Dim btDNArray() As Byte, btMNArray() As Byte, btDCNArray(100) As Byte

    '* Prepare the Null Terminated Strings and put into Byte Arrays
    btMNArray = stMName & vbNullChar
    btDNArray = stDName & vbNullChar

    lgResult = NetGetDCName(btMNArray(0), btDNArray(0), lgDCNPtr)

    If lgResult <> 0 Then
        MsgBox "Error: " & lgResult
        Exit Function
    End If

    '* Dereference the pointer
    lgResult = PtrToStr(btDCNArray(0), lgDCNPtr)
    '* Free the buffer in memory
    lgResult = NetAPIBufferFree(lgDCNPtr)
    stDCName = btDCNArray()
    GetPrimaryDCName = stDCName

End Function
```

Analysis

This function is fairly straightforward. It gets the machine name of the domain controller for the domain specified. Because NT deals in NetBIOS names, the machine and domain controller names should contain the leading \\. If the machine and domain names are not specified, the function runs on the local machine name and the default domain of the local machine. The function takes the parameters and converts them to NULL-terminated byte arrays. It then calls the NetGetDCName function from NetAPI32.dll. The return value of the DLL function is the error level, and the function also returns a pointer to the domain controller name. The pointer is then dereferenced and the buffer used to store the data is freed to avoid any memory leaks. The byte array is then converted to a string and returned.

This function is very useful to avoid having to hard-code domain controller names into code. Simply use the GetPrimaryDCName function, and you don't have to recompile if the NT domain is restructured or changed in the future. In addition, you can combine this function with the `SYSGetComputerName` function to ensure that the function runs on the local machine.

13.13   GET USER INFORMATION

by Brian Shea

Description

This function returns the available information about a specified user account. The information returned depends on which level of the user info data structure you use. MSDN and TechNet contain all the information you will need to understand all the available levels and structures.

This function also contains some supporting code functions used by the `GetUserInfo` function to retrieve meaningful data from the Level 3 data structure. These functions are `ByteToMask`, `SecsToYears`, and `TrimUniStr`. Each of these functions is discussed in greater detail in the "Analysis" section. You can also find information about each function and the data types used in section 13.1, "Supporting Functions."

Syntax

```
lgReturn = GetUserInfo(stUserName, stServer)
```

Part	*Description*
`lgReturn`	Required. The return value for the API function. **0** indicates success and nonzero indicates an error state. The values for `lgReturn` can be from **2102** to **2690** if it is a NetAPI error, or it can be a WinAPI system error. MSDN has a complete listing of the NetAPI errors, and the Win32 API error handlers in sections 4.1 and 4.2 can help with the system errors.
`stUserName`	Required. The string value for the username about which you want to get information.
`stServer`	Optional. The string value for the server on which you want the function to run. It can be a `NULL`-terminated string or a `NULL` string. A `NULL` string indicates that the function will run locally.

```
stMaskString = ByteToMask(inByteVal)
```

Part	*Description*
`stMaskString`	Required. The string value returned by the function. It will have an 8-bit mask for the specified integer value.
`inByteVal`	Required. An integer value from **0** to **255** representing an 8-bit mask.

```
stReturnStr = SecsToYears(lgTotalSeconds, stTimeSpan)
```

Part	Description
stReturnStr	Required. The string value that holds the returned time span. The format varies depending on the value of stTimeSpan or the total number of seconds entered into the function.
lgTotalSeconds	Required. The long integer value for the total number of seconds to convert to larger time periods.
stTimeSpan	Optional. The string value that specifies the target time span. The possible values are Years, Weeks, Days, Hours, or Minutes.

```
stReturnStr = TrimUniStr(stWideString)
```

Part	Description
stReturnStr	Required. The returned string value for the function.
stWideString	Required. The string value that might not be correctly NULL terminated. This value will be trimmed to contain the leftmost characters in the string, ending in the first vbNullChar found.

Code Listing

```
'* Place these in the global declaration section
'* Declare the level 3 data structure
Type TUser3
    lgUsri3_name As Long
    lgUsri3_password As Long
    lgUsri3_password_age As Long
    lgUsri3_priv As Long
    lgUsri3_home_dir As Long
    lgUsri3_comment As Long
    lgUsri3_flags As Long
    lgUsri3_script_path As Long
    lgUsri3_auth_flags As Long
    lgUsri3_full_name As Long
    lgUsri3_usr_comment As Long
    lgUsri3_parms As Long
    lgUsri3_workstations As Long
    lgUsri3_last_logon As Long
    lgUsri3_last_logoff As Long
    lgUsri3_acct_expires As Long
    lgUsri3_max_storage As Long
    lgUsri3_units_per_week As Long
    lgUsri3_logon_hours As Long
    lgUsri3_bad_pw_count As Long
    lgUsri3_num_logons As Long
    lgUsri3_logon_server As Long
    lgUsri3_country_code As Long
    lgUsri3_code_page As Long
```

continues

```
    lgUsri3_user_id As Long
    lgUsri3_primary_group_id As Long
    lgUsri3_profile As Long
    lgUsri3_home_dir_drive As Long
    lgUsri3_password_expired As Long
End Type

'* Declare values for Array Identifiers
Const name = 0
Const password = 1
Const password_age = 2
Const priv = 3
Const home_dir = 4
Const comment = 5
Const flags = 6
Const script_path = 7
Const auth_flags = 8
Const full_name = 9
Const usr_comment = 10
Const parms = 11
Const workstations = 12
Const last_logon = 13
Const last_logoff = 14
Const acct_expires = 15
Const max_storage = 16
Const unit_per_week = 17
Const logon_hours = 18
Const bad_pw_count = 19
Const num_logons = 20
Const logon_server = 21
Const country_code = 22
Const code_page = 23
Const user_id = 24
Const primary_group_id = 25
Const profile = 26
Const home_dir_drive = 27
Const password_expired = 28


'*******************************************************************************
'* Constant Declarations for User Priv
'*******************************************************************************
Const USER_PRIV_GUEST = &H0
Const USER_PRIV_USER = &H1
Const USER_PRIV_ADMIN = &H2
Const USER_PRIV_MASK = &H3


'*******************************************************************************
'* Constant Declarations for User Flags
'*******************************************************************************
Const UF_SCRIPT = &H1                 ' Needs to be ORed with the other flags
Const UF_ACCOUNTDISABLE = &H2
Const UF_HOMEDIR_REQUIRED = &H8
```

```
Const UF_LOCKOUT = &H10
Const UF_PASSWD_NOTREQD = &H20
Const UF_PASSWD_CANT_CHANGE = &H40
Const UF_DONT_EXPIRE_PASSWD = &H10000
Const UF_MNS_LOGON_ACCOUNT = &H20000

Const UF_TEMP_DUPLICATE_ACCOUNT = &H100
Const UF_NORMAL_ACCOUNT = &H200
Const UF_INTERDOMAIN_TRUST_ACCOUNT = &H800
Const UF_WORKSTATION_TRUST_ACCOUNT = &H1000
Const UF_SERVER_TRUST_ACCOUNT = &H2000

'*****************************************************************************
'* Constant Declarations for Filter
'*****************************************************************************
Const FILTER_NORMAL_ACCOUNT = &H2

'*****************************************************************************
'* Auth Flag Values
'*****************************************************************************
Const AF_OP_PRINT = &H1
Const AF_OP_COMM = &H2
Const AF_OP_SERVER = &H4
Const AF_OP_ACCOUNTS = &H8

'*****************************************************************************
'* Other Constant Declarations
'*****************************************************************************
Const TIMEQ_FOREVER = -1
Const USER_MAXSTORAGE_UNLIMITED = -1
Const UNITS_PER_WEEK = 168
Const LG_INCLUDE_INDIRECT = &H1
Const UNKNOWN_VALUE = &HFFFFFFFF

'*****************************************************************************
'* Universal well-known SIDs
'*       Null SID              S-1-0-0
'*       World                 S-1-1-0
'*       Local                 S-1-2-0
'*       Creator Owner ID      S-1-3-0
'*       Creator Group ID      S-1-3-1
'*       (Non-unique IDs)      S-1-4
'*****************************************************************************
Public Const SECURITY_NULL_RID = &H0
Public Const SECURITY_WORLD_RID = &H0
Public Const SECURITY_LOCAL_RID = &H0
Public Const SECURITY_CREATOR_OWNER_RID = &H0
Public Const SECURITY_CREATOR_GROUP_RID = &H1
'*****************************************************************************
'* NT well-known SIDs
'*       NT Authority          S-1-5
'*       Dialup                S-1-5-1
```

continues

```
'*      Network              S-1-5-2
'*      Batch                S-1-5-3
'*      Interactive          S-1-5-4
'*      Service              S-1-5-6
'*      AnonymousLogon       S-1-5-7        (aka null logon session)
'*      (Logon IDs)          S-1-5-5-X-Y
'*      (NT non-unique IDs)  S-1-5-0x15-...
'*      (Built-in domain)    s-1-5-0x20
'****************************************************************************
Public Const SECURITY_DIALUP_RID = &H1
Public Const SECURITY_NETWORK_RID = &H2
Public Const SECURITY_BATCH_RID = &H3
Public Const SECURITY_INTERACTIVE_RID = &H4
Public Const SECURITY_SERVICE_RID = &H6
Public Const SECURITY_ANONYMOUS_LOGON_RID = &H7
Public Const SECURITY_LOGON_IDS_RID = &H5
Public Const SECURITY_LOCAL_SYSTEM_RID = &H12
Public Const SECURITY_NT_NON_UNIQUE = &H15
Public Const SECURITY_BUILTIN_DOMAIN_RID = &H20


Public Const DOMAIN_USER_RID_ADMIN = &H1F4
Public Const DOMAIN_USER_RID_GUEST = &H1F5
Public Const DOMAIN_GROUP_RID_ADMINS = &H200
Public Const DOMAIN_GROUP_RID_USERS = &H201
Public Const DOMAIN_GROUP_RID_GUESTS = &H202
Public Const DOMAIN_ALIAS_RID_ADMINS = &H220
Public Const DOMAIN_ALIAS_RID_USERS = &H221
Public Const DOMAIN_ALIAS_RID_GUESTS = &H222
Public Const DOMAIN_ALIAS_RID_POWER_USERS = &H223
Public Const DOMAIN_ALIAS_RID_ACCOUNT_OPS = &H224
Public Const DOMAIN_ALIAS_RID_SYSTEM_OPS = &H225
Public Const DOMAIN_ALIAS_RID_PRINT_OPS = &H226
Public Const DOMAIN_ALIAS_RID_BACKUP_OPS = &H227
Public Const DOMAIN_ALIAS_RID_REPLICATOR = &H228


'* Declare the memory function used
Declare Sub CopyMemory Lib "Kernel32" Alias "RtlMoveMemory" _
(anDest As Any, ByVal lgSrc As Long, ByVal lgSize As Long)

Declare Function NetAPIBufferFree Lib "NetAPI32.DLL" Alias _
"NetApiBufferFree" (ByVal lgPtr As Long) As Long

'* Declare the NetAPI function used
Declare Function NetUserGetInfo Lib "NetAPI32.DLL" _
(btServerName As Byte, btUserName As Byte, ByVal lgLevel As Long, _
lgBufferPtr As Long) As Long

'* Declare the array to hold the returned data
Public stUserInfo() As String

Public Function GetUserInfo(stUserName As String, Optional stServerName
➥ As String) As Long
```

```
'* Gets Detailed User Account Info from a TUser3 Structure

Dim btSNArray() As Byte, btUNArray() As Byte, btHPArray() As Byte
Dim btCommentArray() As Byte, btScArray() As Byte, btFNArray() As Byte
Dim btUCommentArray() As Byte, btParmsArray() As Byte, btWkstaArray()
➥ As Byte
Dim btProfArray() As Byte, btLogonServerArray() As Byte
Dim btHoursArray() As Byte, btHomeDirDrvArray() As Byte
Dim btUsrComment() As Byte, btParms() As Byte, btLogonServer() As Byte

Dim UserStruct As TUser3, stHoursList As String
Dim lgBufferPtr As Long, lgResult As Long
Dim J As Integer, K As Integer, stMaskArray() As String
Dim stProbNote As String, lgFlags As Long, lgAuthFlags As Long

Dim stHP As String, stComment As String, stSc As String
Dim stFN As String, stUComment As String, stParms As String
Dim stWksta As String, stLogonServer As String, stLastLogoff As String
Dim stProf As String, stHomeDirDrv As String, stPWExpires As String
Dim stLastLogon As String, stAcctExpires As String, stPWAge As String
Dim stFlags As String, stUsrComment As String, stAuthFlags As String

'* String to byte conversion
btSNArray = stServerName & vbNullChar
btUNArray = stUserName & vbNullChar
ReDim stUserInfo(29) As String

'* Call NetAPI Function
lgResult = NetUserGetInfo(btSNArray(0), btUNArray(0), 3, lgBufferPtr)
GetUserInfo = lgResult

'* Handle any errors that might occur here
If lgResult = 2221 Then
    MsgBox "UserName Not Found", vbExclamation + vbOKOnly, "Get Info Error"
    Exit Function
ElseIf lgResult = 2351 Then
    MsgBox "ServerName Not Found: Invalid ComputerName", vbExclamation +
    ➥ vbOKOnly, "Get Info Error"
    Exit Function
ElseIf lgResult <> 0 Then
    MsgBox "Error " & lgResult & " when querying User " & stUserName
End If

'* Dereference the Pointer to the data Structure
CopyMemory UserStruct, lgBufferPtr, LenB(UserStruct)

stUserInfo(name) = "User Name = " & stUserName
stUserInfo(password) = "Password = ***************"

ReDim btFNArray(128) As Byte
CopyMemory btFNArray(0), UserStruct.lgUsri3_full_name, 129
stFN = btFNArray
```

continues

```
stFN = TrimUniStr(stFN)
If stFN = "" Then
    stFN = "None"
End If
stUserInfo(full_name) = "Full Name  = " & stFN

ReDim btCommentArray(255) As Byte
CopyMemory btCommentArray(0), UserStruct.lgUsri3_comment, 256
stComment = btCommentArray
stComment = TrimUniStr(stComment)
If stComment = "" Then
    stComment = "None"
End If
stUserInfo(comment) = "Comment = " & stComment

ReDim btProfArray(64) As Byte
CopyMemory btProfArray(0), UserStruct.lgUsri3_profile, 65
stProf = btProfArray
stProf = TrimUniStr(stProf)
If stProf = "" Then
    stProf = "None"
End If
stUserInfo(profile) = "Profile = " & stProf

ReDim btScArray(64) As Byte
CopyMemory btScArray(0), UserStruct.lgUsri3_script_path, 65
stSc = btScArray
stSc = TrimUniStr(stSc)
If stSc = "" Then
    stSc = "None"
End If
stUserInfo(script_path) = "Script = " & stSc

ReDim btHomeDirDrvArray(64) As Byte
CopyMemory btHomeDirDrvArray(0), UserStruct.lgUsri3_home_dir_drive, 65
stHomeDirDrv = btHomeDirDrvArray
stHomeDirDrv = TrimUniStr(stHomeDirDrv)
stUserInfo(home_dir_drive) = stHomeDirDrv

ReDim btHPArray(64) As Byte
CopyMemory btHPArray(0), UserStruct.lgUsri3_home_dir, 65
stHP = btHPArray
stHP = TrimUniStr(stHP)
If stHP = "" Then
    stHP = "Local System"
    stHomeDirDrv = "No Drive Mapped"
    stUserInfo(home_dir) = stHP
    stUserInfo(home_dir_drive) = stHomeDirDrv
Else
    stUserInfo(home_dir) = stHP
    stUserInfo(home_dir_drive) = stHomeDirDrv
End If
```

```
ReDim btWkstaArray(128) As Byte
CopyMemory btWkstaArray(0), UserStruct.lgUsri3_workstations, 129
stWksta = btWkstaArray
stWksta = TrimUniStr(stWksta)
If stWksta = "" Then
    stWksta = "Not Restricted"
End If
stUserInfo(workstations) = "Workstations Allowed " & stWksta

ReDim btUsrComment(255) As Byte
CopyMemory btUsrComment(0), UserStruct.lgUsri3_usr_comment, 256
stUsrComment = btUsrComment
stUsrComment = TrimUniStr(stUsrComment)
If stUsrComment = "" Then
    stUsrComment = "None"
End If
stUserInfo(usr_comment) = "Usr Comment = " & stUsrComment

ReDim btParms(128) As Byte
CopyMemory btParms(0), UserStruct.lgUsri3_parms, 129
stParms = btParms
stParms = TrimUniStr(stParms)
If stParms = "" Then
    stParms = "None"
End If
stUserInfo(parms) = "Parms = " & stParms

ReDim btLogonServer(32) As Byte
CopyMemory btLogonServer(0), UserStruct.lgUsri3_logon_server, 33
stLogonServer = btLogonServer
stLogonServer = TrimUniStr(stLogonServer)
If stLogonServer = "" Then
    stLogonServer = "Domain Controller"
ElseIf stLogonServer = "\\*" Then
    stLogonServer = "Any Logon Server"
End If
stUserInfo(logon_server) = "Logon Server = " & stLogonServer

'*************************************************************************
'* LastLogon Value set to Days and Hours
'*    This function only queries the PDC for info
'*    For accurate data, add queries to each of the BDCs and take
'*    the largest value
'*************************************************************************
stLastLogon = SecsToYears(UserStruct.lgUsri3_last_logon, "Days")
stLastLogon = stLastLogon & " Ago. Only PDC Queried."
stUserInfo(last_logon) = "Last Logon = " & stLastLogon

'*************************************************************************
'* LastLogoff Value set to Days and Hours
'*    This function only queries the PDC for info
'*    For accurate data, add queries to each of the BDCs and take
```

continues

```
'*   the largest value
'*******************************************************************
stLastLogoff = SecsToYears(UserStruct.lgUsri3_last_logoff, "Days")
stLastLogoff = stLastLogoff & " Ago. Only PDC Queried."
stUserInfo(last_logoff) = "Last Logoff = " & stLastLogoff


'*******************************************************************
'* Handle the ByteArray for the logon hours
'* The bytes go from 0 - 20, the 22nd byte is a null
'* The first 8 bits are for Sunday 12a to 8a, GMT Time.
'* Your application should adjust for the local offset.
'* For Example: Pacific time is -8 GMT, so the first byte would be
'* Saturday 4p to 12a, the second byte would be Sunday 12a to 8a.
'*******************************************************************
ReDim btHours(21) As Byte
CopyMemory btHours(0), UserStruct.lgUsri3_logon_hours, 22

ReDim stMaskArray(21) As String
K = 0
For J = 0 To 20
    If btHours(J) = 255 Then
        K = K + 1
    End If
    stMaskArray(J) = ByteToMask(CInt(btHours(J)))
Next J
If K = 21 Then
    stUserInfo(logon_hours) = "Workstation Hours = No Restrictions."
ElseIf K < 21 And K >= 0 Then
    stHoursList = "Restrictions As Listed: (Bit Mask Values) "
    J = 0
    For J = 0 To 20
        stHoursList = stHoursList & vbCrLf & stMaskArray(J)
    Next J
    stUserInfo(logon_hours) = stHoursList
Else
    stUserInfo(logon_hours) = "No Restrictions."
    stProbNote = "Unable to determine value for Logon Hour Restrictions"
    stProbNote = stProbNote & Chr$(13) & "Default value will be used."
    stProbNote = stProbNote & Chr$(13) & "If you wanted the account
    ➡ restricted to no logon hours"
    stProbNote = stProbNote & Chr$(13) & "you should disable the account."
    MsgBox stProbNote, vbOKOnly + vbExclamation, "Logon Hours Invalid"
End If

'* Flags Values
stFlags = "The Flags Set are: "
lgFlags = UserStruct.lgUsri3_flags
If lgFlags >= UF_MNS_LOGON_ACCOUNT Then
    '* Not used in NT at this time
    lgFlags = lgFlags - &H20000
End If
```

```
If lgFlags >= UF_DONT_EXPIRE_PASSWD Then
    '* PW Never Expires
    stFlags = stFlags & vbCrLf & "Password Never Expires."
    lgFlags = lgFlags - &H10000
ElseIf lgFlags < UF_DONT_EXPIRE_PASSWD Then
    '* PW can expire
    stFlags = stFlags & vbCrLf & "Password Can Expire."
    lgFlags = lgFlags - &H10000
End If
If lgFlags >= UF_SERVER_TRUST_ACCOUNT Then
    '* Server Trust Acct
    stFlags = stFlags & vbCrLf & "Acct Type: BDC Machine Account."
    lgFlags = lgFlags - &H2000
End If
If lgFlags >= UF_WORKSTATION_TRUST_ACCOUNT Then
    '* Machine Acct
    stFlags = stFlags & vbCrLf & "Acct Type: Machine Account."
    lgFlags = lgFlags - &H1000
End If
If lgFlags >= UF_INTERDOMAIN_TRUST_ACCOUNT Then
    '* Domain Trust
    stFlags = stFlags & vbCrLf & "Acct Type: Permit To Trust."
    lgFlags = lgFlags = &H800
End If
If lgFlags >= UF_NORMAL_ACCOUNT Then
    '* Global Acct
    stFlags = stFlags & vbCrLf & "Acct Type: Domain Member, Global."
    lgFlags = lgFlags - &H200
End If
If lgFlags >= UF_TEMP_DUPLICATE_ACCOUNT Then
    '* Local Acct
    stFlags = stFlags & vbCrLf & "Acct Type: Domain Member, Local."
    lgFlags = lgFlags - &H100
End If
If lgFlags >= UF_PASSWD_CANT_CHANGE Then
    '* Cant change PW
    stFlags = stFlags & vbCrLf & "User Can't Change Password."
    lgFlags = lgFlags - &H40
ElseIf lgFlags < UF_PASSWD_CANT_CHANGE Then
    stFlags = stFlags & vbCrLf & "User Permitted To Change Password."
    lgFlags = lgFlags - &H40
End If
If lgFlags >= UF_PASSWD_NOTREQD Then
    '* PW Not Required
    stFlags = stFlags & vbCrLf & "Password Not Required."
    lgFlags = lgFlags - &H20
End If
If lgFlags >= UF_LOCKOUT Then
    '* Acct Locked Out
    stFlags = stFlags & vbCrLf & "Account Locked Out."
    lgFlags = lgFlags - &H10
ElseIf lgFlags < UF_LOCKOUT Then
```

continues

```
        stFlags = stFlags & vbCrLf & "Account Not Locked Out."
End If
If lgFlags >= UF_HOMEDIR_REQUIRED Then
    '* Not Used in NT
    lgFlags = lgFlags - &H8
End If
If lgFlags >= UF_ACCOUNTDISABLE Then
    '* Acct Disabled
    stFlags = stFlags & vbCrLf & "Account Disabled."
    lgFlags = lgFlags - &H2
ElseIf lgFlags < UF_ACCOUNTDISABLE Then
    stFlags = stFlags & vbCrLf & "Account Not Disabled."
End If
If lgFlags >= UF_SCRIPT Then
    '* Logon Script Executed
    stFlags = stFlags & vbCrLf & "Logon Script Executed."
    lgFlags = lgFlags - &H1
End If
If lgFlags > 0 Then
    MsgBox "Flag Values Remaining: " & CStr(lgFlags)
End If
stUserInfo(flags) = stFlags

'* Sets the Label for password last set to Days and Hours
stPWAge = SecsToYears(UserStruct.lgUsri3_password_age) ', "Days")
stUserInfo(password_age) = "Password Age = " & stPWAge

'* AcctExpires Set to Weeks and Days, or Never
If UserStruct.lgUsri3_acct_expires = TIMEQ_FOREVER Then
    stUserInfo(acct_expires) = "Acct Expires = Never."
Else
    stUserInfo(acct_expires) = "Acct Expires In " & SecsToYears _
        (UserStruct.lgUsri3_acct_expires, "Weeks")
End If

'* PrimGrpID Values
If UserStruct.lgUsri3_primary_group_id = DOMAIN_GROUP_RID_ADMINS Then
    stUserInfo(primary_group_id) = "Primary Group = Domain Admins."
ElseIf UserStruct.lgUsri3_primary_group_id = DOMAIN_GROUP_RID_USERS Then
    stUserInfo(primary_group_id) = "Primary Group = Domain Users."
ElseIf UserStruct.lgUsri3_primary_group_id = DOMAIN_GROUP_RID_GUESTS Then
    stUserInfo(primary_group_id) = "Primary Group = Domain Guests."
Else
    stUserInfo(primary_group_id) = "Primary Group = Non-Standard Group."
End If

'* PWExpired (0 = OK, non-zero = expired)
If UserStruct.lgUsri3_password_expired <> 0 Then
    stUserInfo(password_expired) = "Password Has Expired, Must Change
    ➥ Password At Next Logon."
Else
    stUserInfo(password_expired) = "Password Has Not Expired."
```

```
End If

'* Priv Values
If UserStruct.lgUsri3_priv = USER_PRIV_GUEST Then
    stUserInfo(priv) = "Priv = Guest."
ElseIf UserStruct.lgUsri3_priv = USER_PRIV_USER Then
    stUserInfo(priv) = "Priv = User."
ElseIf UserStruct.lgUsri3_priv = USER_PRIV_ADMIN Then
    stUserInfo(priv) = "Priv = Admin."
End If

'Auth Flags
lgAuthFlags = UserStruct.lgUsri3_auth_flags
If lgAuthFlags = 0 Or IsNull(lgAuthFlags) Then stAuthFlags = "AuthFlags =
➥ None"
If lgAuthFlags >= AF_OP_ACCOUNTS Then
    stAuthFlags = "AuthFlags = Account Ops."
    lgAuthFlags = lgAuthFlags - AF_OP_ACCOUNTS
End If
If lgAuthFlags >= AF_OP_SERVER Then
    stAuthFlags = stAuthFlags & vbCrLf & "AuthFlags = Server Ops."
    lgAuthFlags = lgAuthFlags - AF_OP_SERVER
End If
If lgAuthFlags >= AF_OP_COMM Then
    stAuthFlags = stAuthFlags & vbCrLf & "AuthFlags = Communications Ops."
    lgAuthFlags = lgAuthFlags - AF_OP_COMM
End If
If lgAuthFlags >= AF_OP_PRINT Then
    stAuthFlags = stAuthFlags & vbCrLf & "AuthFlags = Print Ops."
    lgAuthFlags = lgAuthFlags - AF_OP_PRINT
End If
stUserInfo(auth_flags) = stAuthFlags

'* Max Storage Values
If UserStruct.lgUsri3_max_storage = USER_MAXSTORAGE_UNLIMITED Then
    stUserInfo(max_storage) = "Storage = No Limit."
Else
    stUserInfo(max_storage) = CStr(UserStruct.lgUsri3_max_storage)
End If

'* unit_per_week Values
stUserInfo(unit_per_week) = "Units per week = " &
➥ CStr(UserStruct.lgUsri3_units_per_week)

'* bad_pw_count Values
stUserInfo(bad_pw_count) = "Bad PW Count = " &
➥ CStr(UserStruct.lgUsri3_bad_pw_count)

'* num_logons Values
stUserInfo(num_logons) = "Num Logons = " &
➥ CStr(UserStruct.lgUsri3_num_logons)
```

continues

```
    '* country_code Values
    stUserInfo(country_code) = "Country Code = " &
➥ CStr(UserStruct.lgUsri3_country_code)

    '* code_page Values
    stUserInfo(code_page) = "Code Page = " &
➥ CStr(UserStruct.lgUsri3_code_page)

    '* user_id Values
    stUserInfo(user_id) = "User ID = " & CStr(UserStruct.lgUsri3_user_id)

    NetAPIBufferFree (lgBufferPtr)

End Function

Public Function ByteToMask(inByteVal As Integer) As String
    '* Converts the byte value to Binary Mask String
    Dim btArrayVal() As Byte, stMaskVal As String

    stMaskVal = ""
    ReDim btByteVal(8) As Byte
    If inByteVal >= 128 Then
        btByteVal(0) = 1
        inByteVal = inByteVal - 128
    Else
        btByteVal(0) = 0
    End If
    If inByteVal >= 64 Then
        btByteVal(1) = 1
        inByteVal = inByteVal - 64
    Else
        btByteVal(1) = 0
    End If
    If inByteVal >= 32 Then
        btByteVal(2) = 1
        inByteVal = inByteVal - 32
    Else
        btByteVal(2) = 0
    End If
    If inByteVal >= 16 Then
        btByteVal(3) = 1
        inByteVal = inByteVal - 16
    Else
        btByteVal(3) = 0
    End If
    If inByteVal >= 8 Then
        btByteVal(4) = 1
        inByteVal = inByteVal - 8
    Else
        btByteVal(4) = 0
    End If
    If inByteVal >= 4 Then
```

```
        btByteVal(5) = "1"
        inByteVal = inByteVal - 4
    Else
        btByteVal(5) = 0
    End If
    If inByteVal >= 2 Then
        btByteVal(6) = 1
        inByteVal = inByteVal - 2
    Else
        btByteVal(6) = 0
    End If
    If inByteVal >= 1 Then
        btByteVal(7) = 1
        inByteVal = inByteVal - 1
    Else
        btByteVal(7) = 0
    End If

    '* Reverse the bit order
    stMaskVal = CStr(btByteVal(7)) & CStr(btByteVal(6))
    stMaskVal = stMaskVal & CStr(btByteVal(5)) & CStr(btByteVal(4))
    stMaskVal = stMaskVal & CStr(btByteVal(3)) & CStr(btByteVal(2))
    stMaskVal = stMaskVal & CStr(btByteVal(1)) & CStr(btByteVal(0))
    ByteToMask = stMaskVal

End Function

Public Function SecsToYears(lgSecTotal As Long, Optional stSpan As String)
➥ As String
    '* Converts a Long Int Value of Seconds into a String of Days, Weeks, etc

    Dim lgSec As Long, lgMin As Long, lgHrs As Long, lgDays As Long
    Dim lgWeeks As Long, lgYears As Long
    Dim stNewValue As String, inFlag As Integer

    lgMin = lgSecTotal \ 60
    lgSec = lgSecTotal - (lgMin * 60)
    lgHrs = lgMin \ 60
    lgMin = lgMin - (lgHrs * 60)
    lgDays = lgHrs \ 24
    lgHrs = lgHrs - (lgDays * 24)
    lgWeeks = lgDays \ 7
    lgDays = lgDays - (lgWeeks * 7)
    lgYears = lgWeeks \ 52
    lgWeeks = lgWeeks - (lgYears * 52)

    stNewValue = ""
    If stSpan = "Years" Then
        '* Set stNewValue to Years and Weeks
        stNewValue = stNewValue & CStr(lgYears) & " Yrs "
        stNewValue = stNewValue & CStr(lgWeeks) & " Wks "
```

continues

```
ElseIf stSpan = "Weeks" Then
    '* Set stNewValue to Weeks and Days
    lgWeeks = (lgYears * 52) + lgWeeks
    stNewValue = stNewValue & CStr(lgWeeks) & " Wks "
    stNewValue = stNewValue & CStr(lgDays) & " Dys "

ElseIf stSpan = "Days" Then
    '* Set stNew Value to Days and Hours
    lgDays = (((lgYears * 52) + lgWeeks) * 7) + lgDays
    stNewValue = stNewValue & CStr(lgDays) & " Dys "
    stNewValue = stNewValue & CStr(lgHrs) & " Hrs "

ElseIf stSpan = "Hours" Then
    '* Set stNewValue to Hours and Minutes
    lgHrs = (((((lgYears * 52) + lgWeeks) * 7) + lgDays) * 24) + lgHrs
    stNewValue = stNewValue & CStr(lgHrs) & " Hrs "
    stNewValue = stNewValue & CStr(lgMin) & " Min "

ElseIf stSpan = "Minutes" Then
    '* Set stNewValue to Minutes and Seconds
    lgMin = (((((((lgYears * 52) + lgWeeks) * 7) + lgDays) * 24) + lgHrs)
    ➡ * 60) + lgMin
    stNewValue = stNewValue & CStr(lgMin) & " Min "
    stNewValue = stNewValue & CStr(lgSec) & " Sec "

ElseIf stSpan = "" Or IsNull(stSpan) Then
    '* Try to determine the best display
    inFlag = 0
    If lgYears >= 1 And inFlag < 2 Then
        stNewValue = stNewValue & CStr(lgYears) & " Yrs "
        inFlag = inFlag + 1
    End If
    If lgWeeks >= 1 And inFlag < 2 Then
        stNewValue = stNewValue & CStr(lgWeeks) & " Wks "
        inFlag = inFlag + 1
    End If
    If lgDays >= 1 And inFlag < 2 Then
        stNewValue = stNewValue & CStr(lgDays) & " Dys "
        inFlag = inFlag + 1
    End If
    If lgHrs >= 1 And inFlag < 2 Then
        stNewValue = stNewValue & CStr(lgHrs) & " Hrs "
        inFlag = inFlag + 1
    End If
    If inFlag < 2 Then
        stNewValue = stNewValue & CStr(lgMin) & " Min "
        inFlag = inFlag + 1
    End If
    If inFlag < 2 Then
        stNewValue = stNewValue & CStr(lgSec) & " Sec "
        inFlag = inFlag + 1
    End If
```

```
        End If

        SecsToYears = stNewValue

End Function

Public Function TrimUniStr(stWideValue As String) As String
        '* Remove extra spaces and trims string at the first null character
        Dim inStrLen As Integer, stStrValue As String

        Trim (stWideValue)
        inStrLen = InStr(stWideValue, vbNullChar)
        stStrValue = Left(stWideValue, inStrLen - 1)
        TrimUniStr = stStrValue

End Function
```

Analysis

The `GetUserInfo` function appears to be a somewhat more complex function than many of the NetAPI functions, but on closer inspection you can see that most of the complexity really turns out to be repetition of the dereferencing functions for the returned data type. Let's take it apart and see what's going on.

First, of course, you declare the data type for a Level 3 structure to be used. This structure is explored more in the section titled "Supporting Functions." Next I chose to declare some more friendly names for the index values used in the array that holds the returned values. I figured that a name like `stUserInfo(full_name)` was easier to read than `stUserInfo(9)` through a large function like this one. You can delete these values and replace the indexes in the function with integer values if you prefer.

The next few sections declare the constant values used or potentially returned by the function. I tried to get all the values listed that commonly are returned or used. Additional values can be found in Microsoft Developer's Network. The function declarations and array declaration finish this section. The array is used to hold string versions of the returned data, though you can easily have this function push the data into a control or other functions for continued processing.

After the variable declarations (which are plentiful due to the large amount of data returned in a Level 3 structure), you convert the string data to NULL-terminated byte arrays and then size the `UserInfo` array to hold 29 elements. You can do this because you already know that you will get 29 elements out of a Level 3 structure. You can change this value if you are using a smaller data type. You then call the API function and do a small amount of error handling.

Pretty simple huh? But now you must get to the data that was returned from the function. That's what the rest of the function accomplishes. Because several return values are treated in a similar fashion, I explain a few of each type and then mention the elements that are handled differently. That should give you enough to see what's going on without boring you with too many pages of repeated explanations.

The first thing you must do is copy the data from the returned pointer to the buffer you have ready for it (dereference the pointer to the data). The `CopyMemory` function does this. The Level 3 data type returns a collection of pointers to strings or long integer data. In this example, I have handled the string data first for no particular reason other than I had to start somewhere.

Because we passed the username to the function as a parameter, I chose not to dig for that data, but just to return it back from the initially passed value. Also here you see that the password value is filled out with a dummy value of 14 * characters. The password value will always be returned as a NULL string by GetUserInfo, so this just gives the user something to look at to show a password is present (even if it is blank).

The full name is the first string data to get out of the returned data, so first we size the full_name byte array. I selected the value of 128 characters on the assumption that a full name probably wouldn't be that long. If you have trouble with the full name value cutting off characters, increase this size to whatever works for you. Once again we use CopyMemory to get the data out of the full_name parameter of the data structure, and then assign it to a string value. The next thing we do is call the TrimUniStr function to ensure that we only get the full_name. The reason for this is that we selected to get a buffer of 128 characters, and if the full name is less than that, we might end up getting data that we do not want. The TrimUniStr function simply returns the first characters of a string up to the first NULL character. You can use Debug.Print to view the returned data if you are curious about what it contains. The string is then checked to be sure that a value is returned, or None is assigned. Finally, the returned value is placed in the full_name index of the stUserInfo array.

All the remaining string values are handled in a similar fashion. The home drive and home path values have some interdependencies, so I handled the blank home path to result in a blank home drive as well. The path listing for a blank home path is Local System.

The next section of interest is the LastLogon and LastLogoff data. Because these values are returned as long integer values instead of pointers, we can handle the data directly out of the data structure. Both values are stored as the number of seconds that have passed since 1 Jan, 1970. The value is passed directly into the SecsToYears function. The return value is a time span in days and hours since the last logon or last logoff. Please note that this value is stored separately on each domain controller (DC), so to get a true value you would have to query every DC and take the largest value.

Let's pause the discussion of the GetUserInfo function for a moment and talk about SecsToYears. This function has been designed to convert seconds to a specified span of time. It returns the time span as a string like "54 Dys 12 Hrs". As you can see from the function, it will return the specified time unit and the next lower unit as the remainder. You might also guess that this can lead to some inaccuracy when rounding. If you want to be completely accurate, this function should be modified to handle all the data down to the second. If the span isn't specified in the function call, the function will attempt to display the data in the most appropriate manner. It will select the largest time unit that has a nonzero value and the next lower time unit as a remainder.

The Logon hours are handled next, and they are a strange case all the way around. The data is stored as an array of 21 bytes, each with 8 bits. This structure is used to represent the hours available in a week (24 hours × 7 days = 168). A bit set to 1 means that access is allowed, and a bit set to 0 means access is denied for that hour. It is up to you as the programmer to handle any time offsets from GMT for your local time zone because the first byte in this structure represents 4 p.m. to 12 a.m. GMT. The function checks to see whether all the bits are on, returns `"No Restrictions"` if they are, and builds an array of bit mask values. If the function had trouble reading the array or the array index is not correct, `"No Restrictions"` is also returned. The user is sent a message box warning if the values are not read correctly. If the logon hours are restricted, the function then builds a string of all the bit masks and returns that string. Each 8-bit mask is listed on its own line for ease of reading.

For each of the remaining values, the data is pulled out of the data structure and the bit values are decoded or the value is handled directly. The handling of each is slightly different, but it should be clear in each case what is going on. Many integer values are converted to strings simply for storage in the `UserInfo` array. Normally, this would not be necessary for proper handling of the data.

The last thing for this function is to free the buffer used, which is done using the `NetAPIBufferFree` function.

The only thing left now is to briefly cover the `ByteToMask` function. `ByteToMask` simply takes a byte value (representing an 8-bit byte) and converts it to the binary value. The binary value is returned as a string that shows the bit mask. Using this function on a byte value of 255 would result in a bit mask of `11111111`. The complimentary `MaskToByte` function can be found in the `SetUserInfo` listing. You might notice that the byte order is reversed during this process, which corrects for a conversion that occurs internally. The `ByteToMask` and `MaskToByte` functions both take this conversion into account so you shouldn't have difficulty using either of them. If you plan to use either of these functions in other applications, be sure to correct the byte order.

The functions that support the `GetUserInfo` function are not limited to NT only (like `GetUserInfo` is) and can be used in other situations as required.

13.14   REMOVE A GROUP

by Brian Shea

Description

The `RemoveGroup` function is very straightforward. It removes a global group from the Windows NT Accounts database. If you try to remove a local group using this function, it will generate an error. The application calling this function must be operating with at least Administrator or Account Operator rights to execute this function.

Because this function works on global groups, you should use it only on the domain controllers. Member servers and workstations do not have global groups against which to run this function. NT will also not enable you to remove the built-in groups that are found on the system when it is initially built.

Syntax

```
lgReturn = RemoveGroup(stGrpName, stServer)
```

Part	Description
lgReturn	Required. The return value of the function. **0** indicates success, nonzero indicates an error state. The values for `lgReturn` can be from **2102** to **2690** if it is a NetAPI error, or it can be a WinAPI system error. MSDN has a complete listing of the NetAPI errors, and the Win32 API error handlers in sections 4.1 and 4.2 can help with the system errors.
stGrpName	Required. The string value of the group name that should be removed.
stServer	Optional. The string value or NULL pointer or string that indicates where the function should be run. The server name should have the leading \\. A NULL value indicates the function should be run on the local system.

Code Listing

```
'* Place this declaration in the global declarations section
Declare Function NetGroupDel Lib "NetAPI32.DLL" _
(btServerName As Byte, btGroupName As Byte) As Long

'* This is the main function
Public Function RemoveGroup(stGrp As String, Optional stSrv As String) As Long

    '**************************************************
    '* Removes a group from the PDC
    '**************************************************

    Dim lgResult As Long
    Dim btSNArray() As Byte, btGNArray() As Byte

    '* Create the null terminated strings
    btSNArray = stSrv & vbNullChar
    btGNArray = stGrp & vbNullChar

    '**********************************************
    '* Remove the group
    '**********************************************
    lgResult = NetGroupDel(btSNArray(0), btGNArray(0))
    RemoveGroup = lgResult

    If lgResult = 2234 Then
        MsgBox "Can Not Remove Special Group " & stGrp
    ElseIf lgResult <> 0 Then
        MsgBox "Error Code = " & CStr(lgResult)
    End If

End Function
```

Analysis

The `RemoveGroup` function is one of the easiest NetAPI functions. It simply accepts the group and server names, prepares the `NULL`-terminated strings, and then removes the group. Any error is trapped and displayed in a message box.

This function will not prompt for any confirmation of the removal, so if you want any confirmation messages for the user, you must have your application handle that itself. In addition, after a group is removed Access control entries on files, directories, or shares might still be out there. Re-creating a group of the same name will not restore this access, so be sure that the removal is a desired result before using this routine.

13.15 SET USER INFORMATION

by Brian Shea

Description

The `SetUserInfo` function is the complementary function to the `GetUserInfo` function. It enables you to set various pieces of information about the user account in the Windows NT user database. This function must be run from an application or account that has Administrator or Account Operator–level authority. The example shown here uses the Level 3 data structure, which is the most complex variation.

After you understand this function you should easily be able to use any of the other data types with this function. The data structures used by the user info function (Levels 0, 1, 2, and 3) are essentially the levels of detail about the account. The Level 3 structure is the most complex and detailed data structure for users, and more information about it can be found in section 13.1, "Supporting Functions." I also have attempted to include all the required variable and constant declarations, but if you find something that isn't here, you should be able to find all the required information in MSDN, TechNet, or the Win32 SDK.

Note

This function directly manipulates data on the primary domain controller (PDC) and local machines. Be sure to thoroughly test your implementation of this function before running it on a production machine. This function can cause errors on the local machine and on the PDC. In addition, the password parameter is passed (by default) in clear text from the local machine to the PDC. This might expose your network to security risks. It is up to you to evaluate this risk and handle it accordingly.

> **Note**
>
> The Logon Hours parameter can be a real pain to work with. There is no other way to say that. If you do not need to adjust the logon hours, I would suggest leaving the Logon Hours parameter set to " " (which evaluates to no change). You can then adjust the hours using User Manager or other management tools. If you plan to adjust them programmatically, save your work often.

Syntax

```
lgReturn = SetUserInfo(stUserName, stPassword, stHomePath, stComment, lgFlags,
 stScript, stFullName, stUsrComment, stParms, stWksta, lgAcctExpires, stHours,
lgCountryCode, lgCodePage, lgPrimGrpID, stProfile, stHomeDrv,
➥lgPasswordExpired, stServer)
```

Part	Description
lgReturn	Required. The return value of the function. A value of 0 indicates success, nonzero indicates an error state. The values for lgReturn can be from 2102 to 2690 if it is a NetAPI error, or it can be a WinAPI system error. MSDN has a complete listing of the NetAPI errors, and the Win32 API error handlers in sections 4.1 and 4.2 can help with the system errors.
stUserName	Required. The username for which you want to set the info.
stPassword	Optional. The string value for the new password for this account. Can be a NULL string.
stHomePath	Optional. The string value for the home path for this account. The home path must exist before setting this parameter, or it can be a NULL string.
stComment	Optional. The string value for the comment on this account. This can be a NULL string.
lgFlags	Optional. The integer value for the flags set for this account. If you pass 0& as the parameter, the account will be set to UF_SCRIPT and UF_NORMAL_ACCOUNT.
stScript	Optional. The string value for the script to set for this account. This may be a NULL string.
stFullName	Optional. The string for the full name to set for this account. This may be a NULL string.
stUsrComment	Optional. The string value for the UsrComment for the account. It can be set to a NULL string.
stParms	Optional. The string value for the account parms, which should not be changed.
stWksta	Optional. Either a NULL string or a comma-separated list of workstations to which this account will be restricted. The list can contain eight machine names (listed without the leading \\).
lgAcctExpires	Optional. The integer value for the account expires date, expressed as the number of seconds since 1 Jan, 1970 or set to TIMEQ_FOREVER, which means the account never expires.

Part	Description
stHours	Optional. The 168-character string representing the bit mask value for the logon hours. This can be set to "" for no change in the logon hours or None to set no restrictions. Otherwise, the value must contain 168 characters (1s or 0s).
lgCountryCode	Optional. The integer value for the country code. This function is set up to accept 0&, and it will set US English as the default.
lgCodePage	Optional. The integer value for the code page. This function is set up to accept 0& and is set to US English as the default.
lgPrimGrpID	Optional. The integer value that represents the primary group for this user. The user must already be a member of the group specified. A value of &H201 sets the primary group to Domain Users.
stProfile	Optional. The string value for the profile to use for this account. This can be set to a NULL string.
stHomeDrv	Optional. The string value that represents the drive letter to be mapped in conjunction with the HomePath parameter. This can be a NULL string.
lgPasswordExpired	Optional. The integer value for password expiration. 0 indicates not expired, nonzero indicates expired.
stServer	Optional. The string value for the server on which to execute the code. This can be a string value or NULL string. A NULL string runs the code on the local machine.

btByteValue = MaskToByte(stMaskString)

Part	Description
btByteValue	Required. The returned byte value for the bit mask passed into the function. The value should range from 0 to 255.
stMaskString	Required. The string value accepted by the function. It should contain an 8-bit mask.

Code Listing

```
'* Place these in the global declaration section
Type TUser3                        '* Level 3 User Structure
    lgUsri3_name As Long
    lgUsri3_password As Long
    lgUsri3_password_age As Long
    lgUsri3_priv As Long
    lgUsri3_home_dir As Long
    lgUsri3_comment As Long
    lgUsri3_flags As Long
    lgUsri3_script_path As Long
    lgUsri3_auth_flags As Long
    lgUsri3_full_name As Long
    lgUsri3_usr_comment As Long
    lgUsri3_parms As Long
    lgUsri3_workstations As Long
```

continues

```
      lgUsri3_last_logon As Long
      lgUsri3_last_logoff As Long
      lgUsri3_acct_expires As Long
      lgUsri3_max_storage As Long
      lgUsri3_units_per_week As Long
      lgUsri3_logon_hours As Long
      lgUsri3_bad_pw_count As Long
      lgUsri3_num_logons As Long
      lgUsri3_logon_server As Long
      lgUsri3_country_code As Long
      lgUsri3_code_page As Long
      lgUsri3_user_id As Long
      lgUsri3_primary_group_id As Long
      lgUsri3_profile As Long
      lgUsri3_home_dir_drive As Long
      lgUsri3_password_expired As Long
End Type

'**************************************************************************
'* Constant Declarations for User Flags
'**************************************************************************
Const UF_SCRIPT = &H1                ' Needs to be ORed with the other flags
Const UF_ACCOUNTDISABLE = &H2
Const UF_HOMEDIR_REQUIRED = &H8
Const UF_LOCKOUT = &H10
Const UF_PASSWD_NOTREQD = &H20
Const UF_PASSWD_CANT_CHANGE = &H40
Const UF_DONT_EXPIRE_PASSWD = &H10000
Const UF_MNS_LOGON_ACCOUNT = &H20000

Const UF_TEMP_DUPLICATE_ACCOUNT = &H100
Const UF_NORMAL_ACCOUNT = &H200
Const UF_INTERDOMAIN_TRUST_ACCOUNT = &H800
Const UF_WORKSTATION_TRUST_ACCOUNT = &H1000
Const UF_SERVER_TRUST_ACCOUNT = &H2000

'**************************************************************************
'* Constant Declarations for Filter
'**************************************************************************
Const FILTER_NORMAL_ACCOUNT = &H2

'**************************************************************************
'* Auth Flag Values
'**************************************************************************
Const AF_OP_PRINT = &H1
Const AF_OP_COMM = &H2
Const AF_OP_SERVER = &H4
Const AF_OP_ACCOUNTS = &H8

'**************************************************************************
'* Other Constant Declarations
'**************************************************************************
```

```
Const TIMEQ_FOREVER = -1
Const USER_MAXSTORAGE_UNLIMITED = -1
Const UNITS_PER_WEEK = 168
Const LG_INCLUDE_INDIRECT = &H1
Const UNKNOWN_VALUE = &HFFFFFFFF


'***************************************************************************
'* Universal well-known SIDs
'*      Null SID              S-1-0-0
'*      World                 S-1-1-0
'*      Local                 S-1-2-0
'*      Creator Owner ID      S-1-3-0
'*      Creator Group ID      S-1-3-1
'*      (Non-unique IDs)      S-1-4
'***************************************************************************
Public Const SECURITY_NULL_RID = &H0
Public Const SECURITY_WORLD_RID = &H0
Public Const SECURITY_LOCAL_RID = &H0
Public Const SECURITY_CREATOR_OWNER_RID = &H0
Public Const SECURITY_CREATOR_GROUP_RID = &H1
'***************************************************************************
'* NT well-known SIDs
'*      NT Authority          S-1-5
'*      Dialup                S-1-5-1
'*      Network               S-1-5-2
'*      Batch                 S-1-5-3
'*      Interactive           S-1-5-4
'*      Service               S-1-5-6
'*      AnonymousLogon        S-1-5-7         (aka null logon session)
'*      (Logon IDs)           S-1-5-5-X-Y
'*      (NT non-unique IDs)   S-1-5-0x15-...
'*      (Built-in domain)     s-1-5-0x20
'***************************************************************************
Public Const SECURITY_DIALUP_RID = &H1
Public Const SECURITY_NETWORK_RID = &H2
Public Const SECURITY_BATCH_RID = &H3
Public Const SECURITY_INTERACTIVE_RID = &H4
Public Const SECURITY_SERVICE_RID = &H6
Public Const SECURITY_ANONYMOUS_LOGON_RID = &H7
Public Const SECURITY_LOGON_IDS_RID = &H5
Public Const SECURITY_LOCAL_SYSTEM_RID = &H12
Public Const SECURITY_NT_NON_UNIQUE = &H15
Public Const SECURITY_BUILTIN_DOMAIN_RID = &H20

Public Const DOMAIN_USER_RID_ADMIN = &H1F4
Public Const DOMAIN_USER_RID_GUEST = &H1F5
Public Const DOMAIN_GROUP_RID_ADMINS = &H200
Public Const DOMAIN_GROUP_RID_USERS = &H201
Public Const DOMAIN_GROUP_RID_GUESTS = &H202
Public Const DOMAIN_ALIAS_RID_ADMINS = &H220
Public Const DOMAIN_ALIAS_RID_USERS = &H221
Public Const DOMAIN_ALIAS_RID_GUESTS = &H222
```

continues

```
Public Const DOMAIN_ALIAS_RID_POWER_USERS = &H223
Public Const DOMAIN_ALIAS_RID_ACCOUNT_OPS = &H224
Public Const DOMAIN_ALIAS_RID_SYSTEM_OPS = &H225
Public Const DOMAIN_ALIAS_RID_PRINT_OPS = &H226
Public Const DOMAIN_ALIAS_RID_BACKUP_OPS = &H227
Public Const DOMAIN_ALIAS_RID_REPLICATOR = &H228

Declare Function NetSetUserInfo Lib "NetAPI32.DLL" Alias "NetUserSetInfo" _
(btServerName As Byte, btUserName As Byte, ByVal lgLevel As Long, anBuffer As
➥ Any, _
lgParmError As Long) As Long

Declare Function NetAPIBufferFree Lib "NetAPI32.DLL" Alias _
"NetApiBufferFree" (ByVal lgPtr As Long) As Long

Declare Function NetAPIBufferAllocate Lib "NetAPI32.DLL" Alias _
"NetApiBufferAllocate" (ByVal lgByteCount As Long, lgPtr As Long) As Long

Declare Function StrToPtr Lib "Kernel32" Alias "lstrcpyW" _
(ByVal lgPtr As Long, btSource As Byte) As Long

'* This is the main function
Public Function SetUserInfo(stUserName As String, _
Optional stPassword As String, Optional stHomePath As String, _
Optional stComment As String, Optional lgFlags As Long, _
Optional stScript As String, Optional stFullName As String, _
Optional stUsrComment As String, Optional stParms As String, _
Optional stWorkstations As String, _Optional lgAcctExpires As Long,
➥ Optional stHours As String, _
Optional lgCountryCode As Long, Optional lgCodePage As Long, _
Optional lgPrimGrpID As Long, Optional stProfile As String, _
Optional stHomeDirDrv As String, Optional lgPWExpired As Long,
➥ Optional stServer As String) As Long

    '**********************************************************
    '* Calls the NetUserSetInfo to set the information
    '**********************************************************

    Dim lgResult As Long, UserStruct As TUser3, lgParmError As Long,
    ➥ I As Integer
    Dim inHourStringLen As Integer, stText As String, stHoursArray() As String
    Dim lgStart As Long

    Dim btSNArray() As Byte, btUNArray() As Byte, btPrfArray() As Byte
    Dim btPWArray() As Byte, btHPArray() As Byte, btCommentArray() As Byte
    Dim btScrArray() As Byte, btFNArray() As Byte, btUsrCommentArray() As Byte
    Dim btParmsArray() As Byte, btWkstaArray() As Byte,
    ➥btHomeDrvArray() As Byte
    Dim btHoursArray() As Byte

    Dim lgPrfPtr As Long, lgPWPtr As Long, lgHPPtr As Long,
    ➥lgCommentPtr As Long
```

```
Dim lgScrPtr As Long, lgFNPtr As Long, lgUsrCommentPtr As Long
Dim lgParmsPtr As Long, lgWkstaPtr As Long, lgHomeDrvPtr As Long
Dim lgHoursPtr As Long

'* Convert to Null Terminated Byte Arrays
btSNArray = stServer & vbNullChar
btUNArray = stUserName & vbNullChar
btPWArray = stPassword & vbNullChar
btHPArray = stHomePath & vbNullChar
btCommentArray = stComment & vbNullChar
btScrArray = stScript & vbNullChar
btFNArray = stFullName & vbNullChar
btUsrCommentArray = stUsrComment & vbNullChar
btParmsArray = stParms & vbNullChar
btWkstaArray = stWorkstations & vbNullChar
btPrfArray = stProfile & vbNullChar
btHomeDrvArray = stHomeDirDrv & vbNullChar

'* Logon Hours (handle conversion to byte array)
ReDim stHoursArray(22) As String
ReDim btHoursArray(22) As Byte
If stHours = "" Then
    stHours = vbNullChar
    btHoursArray = stHours & vbNullChar
    lgResult = StrToPtr(lgHoursPtr, btHoursArray(0))
ElseIf stHours = "None" Then
    For I = 0 To 20
        stHoursArray(I) = "11111111"
        btHoursArray(I) = MaskToByte(stHoursArray(I))
    Next I
    lgResult = NetAPIBufferAllocate(UBound(btHoursArray) + 1, lgHoursPtr)
    lgResult = StrToPtr(lgHoursPtr, btHoursArray(0))
Else
    inHourStringLen = Len(stHours)
    If inHourStringLen <> 168 Then
        stText = "The string passed for Logon Hours doesn't contain the
        ➥ correct" & _
            "amount of data."
        stText = stText & Chr$(13) & "Please ensure that it contains 168
        ➥ characters."
        stText = stText & Chr$(13) & "The allowed characters are 1 or 0."
        stText = stText & Chr$(13) & "No hours changes will be made."
        MsgBox stText, vbOKOnly + vbInformation, "Data Length Error"
        stHours = vbNullChar
        btHoursArray = stHours & vbNullChar
        lgResult = StrToPtr(lgHoursPtr, btHoursArray(0))
    Else
        '* Break string into 8 bit bytes
        For I = 0 To 20
            lgStart = (I * 8) + 1
            stHoursArray(I) = Mid(stHours, lgStart, 8)
            btHoursArray(I) = MaskToByte(stHoursArray(I))
```

continues

```
          Next I
          btHoursArray(21) = vbNull
          lgResult = NetAPIBufferAllocate(UBound(btHoursArray) + 1,
          ➥ lgHoursPtr)
          lgResult = StrToPtr(lgHoursPtr, btHoursArray(0))
     End If
End If

'* Fill in Default values here for integer parameters
If lgFlags = 0 Or IsNull(lgFlags) Then
     lgFlags = UF_NORMAL_ACCOUNT Or UF_SCRIPT
End If
If lgAcctExpires = 0 Or IsNull(lgAcctExpires) Then
     lgAcctExpires = TIMEQ_FOREVER
End If
If lgCountryCode = 0 Or IsNull(lgCountryCode) Then
     '* Default to US English, change this value to default to other
     ➥ languages
     lgCountryCode = 1
End If
If lgCodePage = 0 Or IsNull(lgCodePage) Then
     '* Default to US English, change this to default to other
     ➥default values
     lgCodePage = 1252
End If
If lgPrimGrpID = 0 Or IsNull(lgPrimGrpID) Then
     lgPrimGrpID = DOMAIN_GROUP_RID_USERS
End If

'*************************************************
'* Allocate buffer space
'*************************************************

lgResult = NetAPIBufferAllocate(UBound(btPWArray) + 1, lgPWPtr)
lgResult = NetAPIBufferAllocate(UBound(btHPArray) + 1, lgHPPtr)
lgResult = NetAPIBufferAllocate(UBound(btCommentArray) + 1, lgCommentPtr)
lgResult = NetAPIBufferAllocate(UBound(btScrArray) + 1, lgScrPtr)
lgResult = NetAPIBufferAllocate(UBound(btFNArray) + 1, lgFNPtr)
lgResult = NetAPIBufferAllocate(UBound(btUsrCommentArray) + 1,
➥ lgUsrCommentPtr)
lgResult = NetAPIBufferAllocate(UBound(btParmsArray) + 1, lgParmsPtr)
lgResult = NetAPIBufferAllocate(UBound(btWkstaArray) + 1, lgWkstaPtr)
lgResult = NetAPIBufferAllocate(UBound(btPrfArray) + 1, lgPrfPtr)
lgResult = NetAPIBufferAllocate(UBound(btHomeDrvArray) + 1, lgHomeDrvPtr)

'*************************************************
'* Copy arrays to the buffer
'*************************************************

lgResult = StrToPtr(lgPWPtr, btPWArray(0))
lgResult = StrToPtr(lgHPPtr, btHPArray(0))
lgResult = StrToPtr(lgCommentPtr, btCommentArray(0))
```

```
lgResult = StrToPtr(lgScrPtr, btScrArray(0))
lgResult = StrToPtr(lgFNPtr, btFNArray(0))
lgResult = StrToPtr(lgUsrCommentPtr, btUsrCommentArray(0))
lgResult = StrToPtr(lgParmsPtr, btParmsArray(0))
lgResult = StrToPtr(lgWkstaPtr, btWkstaArray(0))
lgResult = StrToPtr(lgPrfPtr, btPrfArray(0))
lgResult = StrToPtr(lgHomeDrvPtr, btHomeDrvArray(0))

'************************************************
'* Fill the structure
'************************************************

With UserStruct
    '.lgUsri3_name                                          '* Ignored
    '* Comment this value for no password change
    .lgUsri3_password = lgPWPtr
    '.lgUsri3_password_age = 0                              '* Ignored
    '.lgUsri3_priv = USER_PRIV_USER                        '* Ignored
    .lgUsri3_home_dir = lgHPPtr
    .lgUsri3_comment = lgCommentPtr
    .lgUsri3_flags = lgFlags
    ➡'* NT Requires UF_SCRIPT
    .lgUsri3_script_path = lgScrPtr
    '.lgUsri3_auth_flags                                    '* Ignored
    .lgUsri3_full_name = lgFNPtr
    .lgUsri3_usr_comment = lgUsrCommentPtr
    .lgUsri3_parms = lgParmsPtr
      ➡'* Do Not Change!
    .lgUsri3_workstations = lgWkstaPtr
    '.lgUsri3_last_logon                                    '* Ignored
    .lgUsri3_last_logoff = 0
    .lgUsri3_acct_expires = lgAcctExpires
    .lgUsri3_max_storage = USER_MAXSTORAGE_UNLIMITED
      ➡'* Should Not Change!
    .lgUsri3_units_per_week = 168
    .lgUsri3_logon_hours = lgHoursPtr
    '.lgUsri3_bad_pw_count = 0                              '* Ignored
    '.lgUsri3_num_logons = 0                                '* Ignored
    '.lgUsri3_logon_server                                  '* Ignored
    .lgUsri3_country_code = lgCountryCode
    .lgUsri3_code_page = lgCodePage
    '.lgUsri3_user_id                                       '* Ignored
    '* Primary Group must be group that this user is already a member of
    .lgUsri3_primary_group_id = lgPrimGrpID
    .lgUsri3_profile = lgPrfPtr
    .lgUsri3_home_dir_drive = lgHomeDrvPtr
    .lgUsri3_password_expired = lgPWExpired
End With

'************************************************
'* Set the information
'************************************************
```

continues

```
        lgResult = NetSetUserInfo(btSNArray(0), btUNArray(0), 3, UserStruct,
        ➥ lgParmError)
        SetUserInfo = lgResult

        If lgResult <> 0 Then
            MsgBox "Error Result = " & lgResult & " In Parmeter: " &
            ➥ CStr(lgParmError)
        End If

        '************************************************
        '* Release buffers from memory
        '************************************************

        lgResult = NetAPIBufferFree(lgPWPtr)
        lgResult = NetAPIBufferFree(lgHPPtr)
        lgResult = NetAPIBufferFree(lgCommentPtr)
        lgResult = NetAPIBufferFree(lgScrPtr)
        lgResult = NetAPIBufferFree(lgFNPtr)
        lgResult = NetAPIBufferFree(lgUsrCommentPtr)
        lgResult = NetAPIBufferFree(lgParmsPtr)
        lgResult = NetAPIBufferFree(lgWkstaPtr)
        lgResult = NetAPIBufferFree(lgPrfPtr)
        lgResult = NetAPIBufferFree(lgHomeDrvPtr)
        lgResult = NetAPIBufferFree(lgHoursPtr)

End Function

Public Function MaskToByte(stIntStr As String) As Byte
        '* Converts Binary Mask String to a Byte value
        Dim btArrayVal() As Byte, inValue As Integer, I As Integer

        inValue = 0
        btArrayVal = stIntStr
        '* Get every other byte listed and convert to a value
        If Chr(btArrayVal(0)) = 1 Then inValue = inValue + 1
        If Chr(btArrayVal(2)) = 1 Then inValue = inValue + 2
        If Chr(btArrayVal(4)) = 1 Then inValue = inValue + 4
        If Chr(btArrayVal(6)) = 1 Then inValue = inValue + 8
        If Chr(btArrayVal(8)) = 1 Then inValue = inValue + 16
        If Chr(btArrayVal(10)) = 1 Then inValue = inValue + 32
        If Chr(btArrayVal(12)) = 1 Then inValue = inValue + 64
        If Chr(btArrayVal(14)) = 1 Then inValue = inValue + 128

        MaskToByte = CByte(inValue)

End Function
```

Analysis

As with the other routines that use the Level 3 structure, this one appears more imposing than it really is. The majority of this function builds the data structure and handles and prepares the data for use by the API function. The actual call to the NetAPI is quite simple by comparison.

As noted earlier, this function can be dangerous to work with, and it manipulates data directly on the PDC. You should always test in a noncritical environment to be sure that you don't cause any trouble. Additionally, high-security environments should not use this function without using additional security to encrypt traffic between the local machine and the PDC.

Jump in and take a look at what is going on in this function. First, you declare the data types, the constants, and the API functions that you will be using. Most of the required data should be listed in this function, but if you need or want to learn more, check Microsoft Developer's Network (MSDN) or the Software Developer's Kits (SDKs).

The next thing you see is that this function accepts an awful lot of parameters, many of which are optional. This should allow the maximum flexibility when using this function. You should always use the commas to separate the parameter places, even if you pass empty values (for strings) or NULL values (for integer values). The variable declaration section looks a bit overblown at first glance, but you'll see through the function that you need them all.

Next you convert the string data to byte arrays that are terminated by NULLs. Then you jump right into the Logon Hours parameter. The function checks for values of stHours that are " " or None, and sets the array to a NULL or to an array full of ones (byte values of 255). Next it checks to see whether the passed data is 168 characters long. If not, it alerts the user and makes no changes to the logon hours. This is because the function would not be able to determine the correct hour settings without 168 characters to work with.

If the stHour data is correct, you then convert the bit mask values to 8-byte values and set up a pointer to the data for later use. This is the area where I have experienced the most trouble with this function. Typically if you are having difficulty with the SetUserInfo function, you can find the error in this section.

The next section checks the values for certain integer values and sets required minimum values if NULLs are passed. This section is where you can change the default country code or code page if you are not using US English. This is also where the default primary group is set to Domain Users, but that also can be changed. It is safest to leave the default group as Domain Users because normally all users are members of at least this group.

Next you find the function allocating all the buffers for the variables and then placing the data into each of the buffers. It then places all the data into the Level 3 data structure. Now that you have the data ready, you can call the NetAPI function and do minimal error handling.

Finally, the function frees the buffers that were allocated earlier so the application doesn't leak memory.

13.16 SET USER HOUR RESTRICTIONS

by Brian Shea

Description

This routine is designed to set hour restrictions on user accounts or remove restrictions from a user account. It uses the `NetUserSetInfo` API function and can be fairly straightforward. The application that calls this function should be running under Administrator or Account Operator–level authority for the function to execute properly.

This function can be used to set logon hours by passing it a string of 168 characters that represents a bit mask for the hours available in a week (24 hours × 7 days = 168). You can also remove all restrictions by passing the function a string that contains the word `None`. Unlike the `SetUserInfo` function, there is no option to make no changes using this function.

This function also contains the `MaskToByte` function that converts bit-mask values to byte values. This function is explained in the "`SetUserInfo`" section.

Four constants are declared in this function that represent the logon hour bit masks for some sample situations. They all are set up for GMT, so you will have to adjust for your specific time zone if you want to use them. The four examples are Work Hours Only (9 to 5 Monday through Friday), Non-Work Hours Only (everything except 9 to 5 Monday through Friday), Weekdays Only (no Saturday or Sunday Logon Permitted), and Weekends Only (only Saturday and Sunday logon permitted). You might want to declare some of the common logon hour restrictions you use as constants like this to avoid having to build them each time.

Syntax

```
lgReturn = SetUserHours(stServer, stUserName, stHours)
```

Part	Description
lgReturn	Required. The return value for the function. `0` indicates success and nonzero indicates an error state. The valid values for `lgReturn` range from `2102` to `2690` for NetAPI-specific errors and can also be WinAPI error codes. MSDN has a complete list of the meaning of the NetAPI error codes, and the WinAPI error handlers in sections 4.1 and 4.2 can help with the system errors.
stServer	Required. The string value for the server on which to run the code. A `NULL` string indicates the code should be run against the local machine. If you pass a server name, you should include the leading \\ on the machine name.

Part	Description
stUserName	Required. The string for the user account on which you want to alter the logon hour restrictions.
stHours	Required. The string value for the hour bit mask. This value must contain a 168-character bit mask or the value None.

Code Listing

```
'* Place these in the global declaration section
Type TUser1020
     lgUsri1020_units_per_week As Long
     lgUsri1020_logon_hours As Long
End Type

Const UNITS_PER_WEEK = 168


'*********************************************************************
'* Declare Logon Hours Constants
'* These are example stNewHourMask Strings
'* You may include, delete, or add to this list as needed
'*********************************************************************
Public Const LH_GMT_WORKHOURS_ONLY = "000000000000000000000000" & _
                                     "000000000111111111000000" & _
                                     "000000000111111111000000" & _
                                     "000000000111111111000000" & _
                                     "000000000111111111000000" & _
                                     "000000000111111111000000" & _
                                     "000000000000000000000000"
Public Const LH_GMT_NONWORK_ONLY = "111111111111111111111111" & _
                                   "111111111000000000111111" & _
                                   "111111111000000000111111" & _
                                   "111111111000000000111111" & _
                                   "111111111000000000111111" & _
                                   "111111111000000000111111" & _
                                   "111111111111111111111111"
Public Const LH_GMT_WEEKDAYS_ONLY = "000000000000000000000000" & _
                                    "111111111111111111111111" & _
                                    "111111111111111111111111" & _
                                    "111111111111111111111111" & _
                                    "111111111111111111111111" & _
                                    "111111111111111111111111" & _
                                    "000000000000000000000000"
Public Const LH_GMT_WEEKENDS_ONLY = "111111111111111111111111" & _
                                    "000000000000000000000000" & _
                                    "000000000000000000000000" & _
                                    "000000000000000000000000" & _
                                    "000000000000000000000000" & _
                                    "000000000000000000000000" & _
                                    "111111111111111111111111"
'*********************************************************************
```

continues

```
'* End of Optional Section
'*************************************************************************

Declare Function NetSetUserInfo Lib "NetAPI32.DLL" Alias "NetUserSetInfo" _
(btServerName As Byte, btUserName As Byte, ByVal lgLevel As Long, anBuffer As
➡ Any, _
lgParmError As Long) As Long

Declare Function StrToPtr Lib "Kernel32" Alias "lstrcpyW" _
(ByVal lgPtr As Long, btSource As Byte) As Long

Declare Function NetAPIBufferFree Lib "NetAPI32.DLL" Alias _
"NetApiBufferFree" (ByVal lgPtr As Long) As Long

Declare Function NetAPIBufferAllocate Lib "NetAPI32.DLL" Alias _
"NetApiBufferAllocate" (ByVal lgByteCount As Long, lgPtr As Long) As Long

'* This is the main function
Public Function SetUserHours(stServer As String, stUser As String, _
stNewHourMask As String) As Long

    '*************************************************************************
    '* Calls NetUserSetInfo with a 1020 Type to set the hour restrictions
    '*************************************************************************
    '* stNewHourMask should be a string of 168 characters (1s or 0s)
    '*************************************************************************

    Dim lgResult As Long, lgParmError As Long, lgHoursPtr As Long
    Dim btSNArray() As Byte, btUNArray() As Byte
    Dim UserStruct As TUser1020, I As Integer, inHourStringLen As Integer
    Dim stHoursArray() As String, btHoursArray() As Byte
    Dim stText As String, lgStart As Long

    btSNArray = stServer & vbNullChar
    btUNArray = stUser & vbNullChar

    ReDim stHoursArray(22) As String
    ReDim btHoursArray(22) As Byte
    If InStr(1, stNewHourMask, "N", vbTextCompare) <> 0 Then
        '* Change the Word none to uppercase
        stNewHourMask = UCase(stNewHourMask)
    End If
    If stNewHourMask = "NONE" Then
        For I = 0 To 20
            stHoursArray(I) = "11111111"
            btHoursArray(I) = MaskToByte(stHoursArray(I))
        Next I
        lgResult = NetAPIBufferAllocate(UBound(btHoursArray) + 1, lgHoursPtr)
        lgResult = StrToPtr(lgHoursPtr, btHoursArray(0))
    Else
        inHourStringLen = Len(stNewHourMask)
        If inHourStringLen <> 168 Then
```

```
            stText = "The string passed for Logon Hours doesn't contain the
            ➡ correct" & _
                "amount of data."
            stText = stText & Chr$(13) & "Please ensure that it contains 168
            ➡ characters."
            stText = stText & Chr$(13) & "The allowed characters are 1 or 0."
            stText = stText & Chr$(13) & "No hours changes will be made."
            MsgBox stText, vbOKOnly + vbInformation, "Data Length Error"
            Exit Function
        Else
            '* Break string into 8 bit bytes
            For I = 0 To 20
                lgStart = (I * 8) + 1
                stHoursArray(I) = Mid(stNewHourMask, lgStart, 8)
                btHoursArray(I) = MaskToByte(stHoursArray(I))
            Next I
            btHoursArray(21) = vbNull
            lgResult = NetAPIBufferAllocate(UBound(btHoursArray) + 1,
            ➡ lgHoursPtr)
            lgResult = StrToPtr(lgHoursPtr, btHoursArray(0))
        End If
    End If

    '************************************************
    '* Fill the structure
    '************************************************
    With UserStruct
        .lgUsri1020_units_per_week = UNITS_PER_WEEK
        .lgUsri1020_logon_hours = lgHoursPtr
    End With

    '************************************************
    '* Set the Hours
    '************************************************
    lgResult = NetSetUserInfo(btSNArray(0), btUNArray(0), 1020, UserStruct,
    ➡ lgParmError)

    If lgResult <> 0 Then
        MsgBox "Error Result = " & lgResult & " in Parameter: " &
        ➡ CStr(lgParmError)
    End If

    '************************************************
    '* Release buffers from memory
    '************************************************
    lgResult = NetAPIBufferFree(lgHoursPtr)

End Function

Public Function MaskToByte(stIntStr As String) As Byte
    '* Converts Binary Mask String to a Byte value
    Dim btArrayVal() As Byte, inValue As Integer, I As Integer
```

continues

```
    inValue = 0
    btArrayVal = stIntStr
    '* Get every other byte listed and convert to a value
    If Chr(btArrayVal(0)) = 1 Then inValue = inValue + 1
    If Chr(btArrayVal(2)) = 1 Then inValue = inValue + 2
    If Chr(btArrayVal(4)) = 1 Then inValue = inValue + 4
    If Chr(btArrayVal(6)) = 1 Then inValue = inValue + 8
    If Chr(btArrayVal(8)) = 1 Then inValue = inValue + 16
    If Chr(btArrayVal(10)) = 1 Then inValue = inValue + 32
    If Chr(btArrayVal(12)) = 1 Then inValue = inValue + 64
    If Chr(btArrayVal(14)) = 1 Then inValue = inValue + 128

    MaskToByte = CByte(inValue)

End Function
```

Analysis

The SetUserHours function sets or removes restrictions on the logon hours parameter of a user account. You can either set specific hours by passing the bit mask to the function or pass None and the restrictions will be removed. SetUserHours also uses the MaskToByte function, which is explained in more detail in the "SetUserInfo" section.

First you declare the necessary constants and function for use later, and then move into the function itself. You must convert the string data to NULL-terminated byte arrays, then you move into handling the bit mask values. For a value of None there is no bit mask, so you go through the process of building an "all on" bit mask. That is just a bit mask that contains all ones so the function will enable all the logon hours for the account.

Otherwise, you check the length of the bit mask and error out of the function if it is not correct. If it is correct, you break the bit mask into 8-bit chunks and convert the resulting bit masks to byte values. These byte values are stored in a byte array. You then allocate the buffer and create the pointer to the buffer and data. This enables you to fill the data structure and call the API function. After a minimal amount of error handling, the buffer is freed and the function ends.

Note

The API function is written to handle the bit mask that is passed to it as if the first eight bits are the first eight hours on Sunday in Greenwich Mean Time (GMT). If you are not in GMT, you will have to adjust the mask according to your local time offset. For example, Pacific Standard Time is GMT –800. That means that the bit mask values passed to this function would have to be "shifted" by –8 hours for the function to apply them correctly. That means that the first eight bits passed to the function in PST would represent the last eight hours of Saturday, and the second group of eight bits would be for the first eight hours of Sunday.

This might sound confusing, but with a little experimentation with the function you'll get the idea quickly.

13.17   SET A USER PROFILE PATH

by Brian Shea

Description

The `SetUserProfilePath` function can be used to set a profile for a user account in the Windows NT user database. It is very straightforward in its use and analysis. The application that uses this function should be running under the Administrator or Account Operator authority for best results.

Syntax

```
lgReturn = SetUserProfilePath(stUserName, stProfile, stServer)
```

Part	Description
lgReturn	Required. The return value for the function. `0` indicates success and nonzero indicates an error state. The values for `lgReturn` can be from `2102` to `2690` if it is a NetAPI error, or it can be a WinAPI system error. MSDN has a complete list of the NetAPI errors, and the Win32 API error handlers in sections 4.1 and 4.2 can help with the system errors.
stUserName	Required. The string expression for the target user account.
stProfile	Required. The string for the profile that you want to set on the account. Typically, these would look like \\netlogon\profilename.man and represent the name and path to the user's profile.
stServer	Optional. A string expression for the name of the server on which the code should run. If a NULL string is used, the code runs locally, and if a string is used, it should begin with the leading \\ for a machine name.

Code Listing

```
'* Place this in the global declarations section
Type TUser1052
    lgUsri1052_profile As Long
End Type

Declare Function NetSetUserInfo Lib "NetAPI32.DLL" Alias "NetUserSetInfo" _
(btServerName As Byte, btUserName As Byte, ByVal lgLevel As Long, anBuffer As
➥ Any, _
lgParmError As Long) As Long

Declare Function StrToPtr Lib "Kernel32" Alias "lstrcpyW" _
(ByVal lgPtr As Long, btSource As Byte) As Long

Declare Function NetAPIBufferFree Lib "NetAPI32.DLL" Alias _
```

continues

```
"NetApiBufferFree" (ByVal lgPtr As Long) As Long

Declare Function NetAPIBufferAllocate Lib "NetAPI32.DLL" Alias _
"NetApiBufferAllocate" (ByVal lgByteCount As Long, lgPtr As Long) As Long

'* this is the main function
Public Function SetUserProfilePath(ByVal stUserName As String, _
ByVal stPPath As String, Optional ByVal stServer As String) As Long

    '**********************************************************
    '* Calls the NetUserSetInfo to set the profile
    '**********************************************************

    Dim lgResult As Long, UserStruct As TUser1052
    Dim btSNArray() As Byte, btUNArray() As Byte, btPrfArray() As Byte
    Dim lgPrfPtr As Long, lgParmError As Long

    btSNArray = stServer & vbNullChar
    btUNArray = stUserName & vbNullChar
    If stPPath <> "" Or stPPath <> "None" Or IsNull(stPPath) Then
        btPrfArray = stPPath & vbNullChar
    Else
        btPrfArray = vbNullChar
    End If

    '*********************************************
    '* Allocate buffer space
    '*********************************************
    lgResult = NetAPIBufferAllocate(UBound(btPrfArray) + 1, lgPrfPtr)

    '*********************************************
    '* Copy arrays to the buffer
    '*********************************************
    lgResult = StrToPtr(lgPrfPtr, btPrfArray(0))

    '*********************************************
    '* Fill the structure
    '*********************************************

    With UserStruct
        .lgUsri1052_profile = lgPrfPtr
    End With

    '*********************************************
    '* Add the profile
    '*********************************************

    lgResult = NetSetUserInfo(btSNArray(0), btUNArray(0), 1052, UserStruct,
    ➥ lgParmError)
    SetUserProfilePath = lgResult
```

```
    If lgResult <> 0 Then
        MsgBox "Error Result = " & lgResult
    End If

    '************************************************
    '* Release buffers from memory
    '************************************************

    lgResult = NetAPIBufferFree(lgPrfPtr)

End Function
```

Analysis

This routine is very easy to understand. It simply accepts the string values for the server name, username, and profile (including the path), then prepares the data for use by the API call. After that is complete, the API call is made and a minimum amount of error handling is done. As always, the buffers are freed at the end to ensure memory leaks are not introduced into the application.

13.18   SET A USER PASSWORD

by Brian Shea

Description

This function is an easy-to-understand function that sets the password on a user account in the Windows NT Accounts database. It must be run under the authority of an Administrator or Account Operator. The function will check the password for at least one character and also checks to see whether the password is 14 asterisk (*) characters. Neither of these passwords is allowed, though both are legal in Windows NT. Otherwise, the password on the account is set to the password listed.

Note

The password is set on the account, and any password expiration is removed by using this function. The User Must Change Password At Next Logon message is removed if it was present, and not set if it wasn't present. This password function also passes the password data from the local machine to the primary domain controller (PDC) in clear text. This means that a network sniffer could be used to capture password changes using this function. You should evaluate the risks involved for your situation before using this function on a project.

Syntax

```
lgReturn = SetUserPassword(stServer, stUserName, stPassword)
```

Part	Description
lgReturn	Required. The return value for the function. 0 indicates success and nonzero indicates an error state. The values for lgReturn can be from 2102 to 2690 if it is a NetAPI error, or it can be a WinAPI system error. MSDN has a complete list of the NetAPI errors, and the Win32 API error handlers in sections 4.1 and 4.2 can help with the system errors.
stServer	Required. The string value for the server name on which the code should be run. A NULL string here will run the code on the local machine, and any other string should contain the leading \\ for the server name.
stUserName	Required. The account name that will be the recipient of the password change.
stPassword	Required. The password value to be set on the account.

Code Listing

```
'* Place these in the global declarations section
Type TUser1003
    lgUsri1003_password As Long
End Type

Declare Function NetSetUserInfo Lib "NetAPI32.DLL" Alias "NetUserSetInfo" _
(btServerName As Byte, btUserName As Byte, ByVal lgLevel As Long, anBuffer As
➡ Any, _
lgParmError As Long) As Long

Declare Function StrToPtr Lib "Kernel32" Alias "lstrcpyW" _
(ByVal lgPtr As Long, btSource As Byte) As Long

Declare Function NetAPIBufferFree Lib "NetAPI32.DLL" Alias _
"NetApiBufferFree" (ByVal lgPtr As Long) As Long

Declare Function NetAPIBufferAllocate Lib "NetAPI32.DLL" Alias _
"NetApiBufferAllocate" (ByVal lgByteCount As Long, lgPtr As Long) As Long

'* This is the main function
Public Function SetUserPassword(stServer As String, stUserName As String, _
stPWord As String) As Long

    '*********************************************************
    '* Calls the NetUserSetInfo to set the password
    '*********************************************************
    Dim lgResult As Long, UserStruct As TUser1003
    Dim btSNArray() As Byte, btUNArray() As Byte, btPWArray() As Byte
    Dim lgPWPtr As Long, lgParmError As Long, Note As String

    btSNArray = stServer & vbNullChar
    btUNArray = stUserName & vbNullChar
```

```
If stPWord <> "" Or stPWord <> "**************" Then
    btPWArray = stPWord & vbNullChar
Else
    Note = "You must type a password of 1-14 characters."
    MsgBox Note, vbCritical + vbOKOnly, "Blank Password Not Allowed"
    Exit Function
End If

'************************************************
'* Allocate buffer space
'************************************************
lgResult = NetAPIBufferAllocate(UBound(btPWArray) + 1, lgPWPtr)

'************************************************
'* Copy arrays to the buffer
'************************************************
lgResult = StrToPtr(lgPWPtr, btPWArray(0))

'************************************************
'* Fill the structure
'************************************************
With UserStruct
    .lgUsri1003_password = lgPWPtr
End With

'************************************************
'* Change The Password
'************************************************
lgResult = NetSetUserInfo(btSNArray(0), btUNArray(0), 1003, UserStruct,
➥ lgParmError)
SetUserPassword = lgResult

'* Handle password error return codes here
If lgResult <> 0 Then
    MsgBox "Error Result = " & lgResult
End If

'************************************************
'* Release buffers from memory
'************************************************
lgResult = NetAPIBufferFree(lgPWPtr)

End Function
```

Analysis

This function is one of the easiest NetAPI functions. It simply takes the parameters, prepares the data, and calls the NetAPI function to set the user's password. But you can also see that the function doesn't set the User Must Change Password At Next Logon message and can pass the password to the PDC in clear text. So why use it?

Frankly, in a business environment, I wouldn't. At least not without some significant modifications like a client/server application that performed encryption on the data or something like that. But this function can be enhanced to enforce stronger password selection by users before they set their password, and then run on the PDC to prevent passing clear text passwords across the network. Other solutions like that might make this a more useful function. Until then, it is merely a learning tool for the NetAPI functions.

13.19   SET A USER SCRIPT

by Brian Shea

Description

This function sets the logon script for a user account in the Windows NT user accounts database. The logon script value can be any string or a NULL string. You must run this function under Administrator or Account Operator authority to function properly.

Syntax

```
lgReturn = SetUserScript(stServer, stUserName, stScript)
```

Part	Description
lgReturn	Required. The return value for this function. A 0 indicates success and nonzero indicates an error state. The values for lgReturn can be from 2102 to 2690 if it is a NetAPI error, or it can be a WinAPI system error. MSDN has a complete list of the NetAPI errors, and the Win32 API error handlers in sections 4.1 and 4.2 can help with the system errors.
stServer	Required. The string value for the server name on which the code should run. This value should be a NULL string that runs on the local machine, or a string value that begins with the leading \\.
stUserName	Required. The string that contains the username for which you want to change the script.
stScript	Required. The string that contains the script that you want to set on the specified user account.

Code Listing

```
'* Place these in the global declaration section
Type TUser1009
     lgUsri1009_script_path As Long
End Type

Declare Function NetSetUserInfo Lib "NetAPI32.DLL" Alias "NetUserSetInfo" _
(btServerName As Byte, btUserName As Byte, ByVal lgLevel As Long, anBuffer
➡ As Any, _
```

```
lgParmError As Long) As Long

Declare Function StrToPtr Lib "Kernel32" Alias "lstrcpyW" _
(ByVal lgPtr As Long, btSource As Byte) As Long

Declare Function NetAPIBufferFree Lib "NetAPI32.DLL" Alias _
"NetApiBufferFree" (ByVal lgPtr As Long) As Long

Declare Function NetAPIBufferAllocate Lib "NetAPI32.DLL" Alias _
"NetApiBufferAllocate" (ByVal lgByteCount As Long, lgPtr As Long) As Long

'* This is the main function
Public Function SetUserScript(stServer As String, stUserName As String, _
stScrpt As String) As Long

    '**********************************************************
    '* Calls the NetUserSetInfo to set the script
    '**********************************************************

    Dim lgResult As Long, UserStruct As TUser1009
    Dim btSNArray() As Byte, btUNArray() As Byte, btScpArray() As Byte
    Dim lgScpPtr As Long, lgParmError As Long

    btSNArray = stServer & vbNullChar
    btUNArray = stUserName & vbNullChar
    If stScrpt <> "" Or stScrpt <> "None" Or IsNull(stScrpt) Then
        btScpArray = stScrpt & vbNullChar
    Else
        btScpArray = vbNullChar
    End If

    '***********************************************
    '* Allocate buffer space
    '***********************************************
    lgResult = NetAPIBufferAllocate(UBound(btScpArray) + 1, lgScpPtr)

    '***********************************************
    '* Copy arrays to the buffer
    '***********************************************
    lgResult = StrToPtr(lgScpPtr, btScpArray(0))

    '***********************************************
    '* Fill the structure
    '***********************************************
    With UserStruct
        .lgUsri1009_script_path = lgScpPtr
    End With

    '***********************************************
    '* Add the scipt
    '***********************************************
```

continues

```
    lgResult = NetSetUserInfo(btSNArray(0), btUNArray(0), 1009, UserStruct,
    ➥ lgParmError)
    SetUserScript = lgResult

    If lgResult <> 0 Then
        MsgBox "Error Result = " & lgResult
    End If

    '************************************************
    '* Release buffers from memory
    '************************************************

    lgResult = NetAPIBufferFree(lgScpPtr)

End Function
```

Analysis

This function is a simple case of using the `NetUserSetInfo` functionality to perform a simple task, in this case changing or setting a user's script. The function accepts the needed parameters, then converts them to `NULL`-terminated byte arrays. You then see the function allocating the buffer to store the data, placing the data into the buffer and getting a pointer to the data, and finally placing the pointer into the data structure for later use.

After your data structure is filled you can call the API function and do a minimal amount of error handling. The last thing you do is free the buffer you allocated to prevent memory problems.

13.20   SET A USER WORKSTATION RESTRICTION

by Brian Shea

Description

This function can be used to set or remove workstation restrictions to an account in Windows NT. You can specify up to eight workstations onto which an account can log, or you can clear any existing restrictions. You must run this function under Administrator or Account Operator authority for this function to operate properly.

The `stWksta` string should contain a `NULL` string for no restrictions or a comma-separated list for restricting the logons to the machines listed. The list should not contain spaces after the commas. Additionally, the machine names should not contain the leading \\ that are normally listed with machine names while using NetAPI32 functions.

Syntax

```
lgReturn = SetUserWksta(stServer, stUserName, stWksta)
```

Part	Description
lgReturn	Required. The return value for this function, which can be 0 for success or nonzero for an error state. The values for lgReturn can be from 2102 to 2690 if it is a NetAPI error, or it can be a WinAPI system error. MSDN has a complete list of the NetAPI errors, and the Win32 API error handlers in sections 4.1 and 4.2 can help with the system errors.
stServer	Required. The string value for the server name on which to run the code. It can be a NULL string (which runs the code locally) or a string value for a machine name (including the leading \\).
stUserName	Required. The string value for the user account for which you want to add or remove logon restrictions.
stWksta	Required. The string value for the workstation names to which the user account will be restricted. A NULL string here will clear any existing restrictions.

Code Listing

```
'* Place this in the global declarations section
Type TUser1014
    lgUsri1014_workstations As Long
End Type

Declare Function NetSetUserInfo Lib "NetAPI32.DLL" Alias "NetUserSetInfo" _
(btServerName As Byte, btUserName As Byte, ByVal lgLevel As Long,
➡ anBuffer As Any, _
lgParmError As Long) As Long

Declare Function StrToPtr Lib "Kernel32" Alias "lstrcpyW" _
(ByVal lgPtr As Long, btSource As Byte) As Long

Declare Function NetAPIBufferFree Lib "NetAPI32.DLL" Alias _
"NetApiBufferFree" (ByVal lgPtr As Long) As Long

Declare Function NetAPIBufferAllocate Lib "NetAPI32.DLL" Alias _
"NetApiBufferAllocate" (ByVal lgByteCount As Long, lgPtr As Long) As Long

'* This is the main function
Public Function SetUserWksta(ByVal stServer As String, _
➡ ByVal stUserName As String, _
ByVal stWkstaNames As String) As Long

    '*****************************************************************
    '* Calls the NetUserSetInfo to set the Workstation restrictions
    '*****************************************************************

    Dim lgResult As Long, UserStruct As TUser1014
```

continues

```
        Dim btSNArray() As Byte, btUNArray() As Byte, btWNameArray() As Byte
        Dim lgWNamePtr As Long, lgParmError As Long

        btSNArray = stServer & vbNullChar
        btUNArray = stUserName & vbNullChar
        If stWkstaNames <> "" Or stWkstaNames <> "None" Or
        ➡IsNull(stWkstaNames) Then
            btWNameArray = stWkstaNames & vbNullChar
        Else
            btWNameArray = vbNullChar
        End If

        '*************************************************
        '* Allocate buffer space
        '*************************************************
        lgResult = NetAPIBufferAllocate(UBound(btWNameArray) + 1, lgWNamePtr)

        '*************************************************
        '* Copy arrays to the buffer
        '*************************************************
        lgResult = StrToPtr(lgWNamePtr, btWNameArray(0))

        '*************************************************
        '* Fill the structure
        '*************************************************
        With UserStruct
            .lgUsri1014_workstations = lgWNamePtr
        End With

        '*************************************************
        '* Add the workstation names
        '*************************************************
        lgResult = NetSetUserInfo(btSNArray(0), btUNArray(0), 1014, UserStruct,
        ➡ lgParmError)
        SetUserWksta = lgResult

        If lgResult <> 0 Then
            MsgBox "Error Result = " & lgResult
        End If

        '*************************************************
        '* Release buffers from memory
        '*************************************************
        lgResult = NetAPIBufferFree(lgWNamePtr)

    End Function
```

Analysis

This function is fairly easy to analyze. The function accepts the string values for the server name, username, and workstation list. These values are converted to NULL-terminated byte arrays. The function then prepares the data for use by the API function and calls the API. A small amount of error handling occurs, then the function frees the buffer and it ends.

Remember that the list of workstations should be a comma-separated list that contains no spaces. The machine names also should not contain the leading \\ that you usually use while dealing with the NetAPI32 functions.

Index

SYMBOLS

A

Visual Basic 6 How-To

—Eric Brierley, Anthony Prince, and David Rinaldi

Visual Basic 6 How-To is a programmer-oriented, problem-solving guide that teaches you how to enhance your Visual Basic skills. Chapters are organized by topic and divided into How-To's. Each How-To describes a problem, develops a technique for solving the problem, presents a step-by-step solution, furnishes relevant tips, comments, and warnings, and presents alternative solutions where applicable. *Visual Basic 6 How-To* offers illustrated solutions and complete working code. Whenever possible, the code is modularized and fully encapsulated for easy transplant into other applications. *Visual Basic 6 How-To* demonstrates how to take advantage of new interface options and Windows APIs, and contains all-new How-To's on building multitier Web-based applications, Advanced Data Objects (ADO), and much more.

Price: $39.99 US/$57.95 CAN
ISBN: 1-57169-153-7

The Waite Group's Visual Basic 6 Database How-To

—Eric Winemiller, Jason T. Roff, Bill Heyman, and Ryan Groom

With the release of Visual Basic 6, database development in Visual Basic moves to a new level of sophistication. With *The Waite Group's Visual Basic 6 Database How-To*, you can keep abreast of the new developments. It contains more than 120 step-by-step solutions to challenging, real-world problems, presented in the Waite Group's award-winning How-To format, tackling even the most complex issues with easily understood solutions.

You will discover how to use the power of SQL Server in your own apps and learn how to use open database connectivity to create powerful, high-end programs quickly. For Visual Basic developers, this complete, easy-to-use guide provides the information and resources needed to write high-quality database applications, no matter the database management system.

Price: $39.99 US/$57.95 CAN
ISBN: 1-57169-152-9

The Waite Group's Visual Basic 6 Client/Server How-To

—Noel Jerke, George Szabo, David Jung, and Don Kiely

The Waite Group's Visual Basic 6 Client/Server How-To is a practical step-by-step guide to implementing three-tiered distributed client/server solutions using the tools provided in Microsoft's Visual Basic 6. It addresses the needs of programmers looking for answers to real-world questions and assures them that what they create really works. It also helps to simplify the client/server development process by providing a framework for solution development.

Price: $49.99 US/$71.95 CAN.
ISBN: 1-57169-154-5

Sams Teach Yourself Visual Basic 6 in 21 Days

—Greg Perry

In this book, Visual Basic programming techniques are presented in a logical and easy-to-follow sequence that helps you really understand the principles involved in developing programs. You begin by learning the basics to write a first program and then move on to adding voice, music, sound, and graphics. After reading this book, you will be able to write your own DLLs, create ActiveX controls, use object linking and embedding (OLE), write Visual Basic programs that support multiple document interfaces, and much more.

Price: $29.99 US/$42.95 CAN
ISBN: 0-672-31310-3

Sams Teach Yourself More Visual Basic 6 in 21 Days

—Lowell Mauer

Sams Teach Yourself More Visual Basic 6 in 21 Days provides comprehensive, self-taught coverage of the most sought after topics in Visual Basic programming. This book uses the step-by-step approach of the best-selling *Sams Teach Yourself* series to continue more detailed coverage of the latest version of Visual Basic. Not only does this book cover a wide array of topics, it also goes into each topic at a level that you will be able to apply to your own programs. In addition, this book includes various tips and tricks of Visual Basic programming that will help the more inexperience programmer.

Price: $29.99 US/$42.95 CAN
ISBN: 0-672-31307-3

Sams Teach Yourself Internet Programming with Visual Basic 6 in 21 Days

—Peter Aitken

In this book you learn how various capabilities and features of Visual Basic 6 can be used to solve real-world problems. You learn how to leverage your skills in developing desktop Visual Basic applications to multitier client/server applications across the Internet. By the end of the book, not only will you be able to develop sophisticated Visual Basic applications, you also will be able to leverage your VB skills for developing Active Server Pages using VBScript. Instead of learning how to create the usual FTP, email, and newsgroup applications, you learn how to integrate these technologies into your applications.

Price: $29.99 US/$42.95 CAN
ISBN: 0-672-31459-2

Sams Teach Yourself OOP with Visual Basic in 21 Days

—John D. Conley III

With *Sams Teach Yourself OOP with Visual Basic in 21 Days*, you learn object-oriented programming techniques in a logical and easy-to-follow sequence that helps you learn how to apply OOP methods within the Visual Basic programming environment. You will be able to use these OOP techniques in your personal to corporate-level programming endeavors. All lessons conclude with a series of questions and exercises to test you and reinforce the information presented in the chapter; answers and solutions are provided in an appendix.

Price: $39.99 US/$57.95 CAN
ISBN: 0-672-31299-9

Sams Teach Yourself Database Programming with Visual Basic 6 in 21 Days

—Curtis Smith and Mike Amundsen

Sams Teach Yourself Database Programming with Visual Basic 6 in 21 Days is a tutorial that teaches you how to work with databases in a set amount of time. The book presents a step-by-step approach to learning what can be a critical topic for developing applications. Each week focuses on a different aspect of database programming with Visual Basic.

Price: $45.00 US/$64.95 CAN
ISBN: 0-672-313081

Visual Basic 6 Unleashed

—Rob Thayer

Visual Basic 6 Unleashed provides comprehensive coverage of the most sought-after topics in Visual Basic programming. It enables a casual-level Visual Basic programmer to quickly become productive with the new release of Visual Basic. This book provides a comprehensive reference to virtually all the topics used in today's leading-edge Visual Basic applications.

Price: $39.99 US/$57.95 CAN
ISBN: 0-672-31309-X

Roger Jennings' Database Developer's Guide with Visual Basic 6, Third Edition

—Roger Jennings

Roger Jennings' Database Developer's Guide with Visual Basic 6, Third Edition, provides in-depth coverage of all new database-related features of Visual Basic 6.0: OLE DB 1.0; Active Data Objects (ADO) 2.0; Remote Data Services (RDS) 2.0; DataEnvironment and DataReport objects; hierarchical recordsets and SHAPE commands; and the new ADO Data, DataGrid, Hierarchical FlexGrid, DataCombo, and DataList ActiveX controls. Client/server chapters describe how to create high-performance decision support and OLTP applications with SQL Server 6.5 and 7.0. Advanced topics include executing parameterized stored procedures with ADO command objects, designing and deploying Microsoft Transaction Server 2.0 components, and writing Multidimensional Expressions (MDX) to extract summarized data from PivotTable and SQL Server OLAP Services (formerly Plato) DataCubes with ADOMD, ADO 2.0's implementation of MDX.

ISBN: 0-672-31063-5
Price: $59.99 US/$85.95 CAN

WHAT'S ON THE CD-ROM

WHAT'S ON THE CD-ROM

The companion CD-ROM contains all the authors' source code and samples from the book and some third-party software products.

WINDOWS NT 3.5.1 INSTALLATION INSTRUCTIONS

1. Insert the CD-ROM disc into your CD-ROM drive.
2. From File Manager or Program Manager, choose Run from the File menu.
3. Type `<drive>\START.EXE` and press Enter, where `<drive>` corresponds to the drive letter of your CD-ROM. For example, if your CD-ROM is drive D:, type `D:\START.EXE` and press Enter.
4. Follow the onscreen instructions to finish the installation.

WINDOWS 95, WINDOWS 98, AND WINDOWS NT 4 INSTALLATION INSTRUCTIONS

1. Insert the CD-ROM disc into your CD-ROM drive.
2. From the desktop, double-click the My Computer icon.
3. Double-click the icon representing your CD-ROM drive.
4. Double-click the icon titled START.EXE to run the installation program.
5. Follow the onscreen instructions to finish the installation.

Note

If Windows 95, Windows 98, or Windows NT 4 is installed on your computer and you have the AutoPlay feature enabled, the START.EXE program starts automatically whenever you insert the disc into your CD-ROM drive.